Glencoe Spanish 1

¡Buen viaje!

Conrad J. Schmitt

Protase E. Woodford

Teacher's Manual

New York, New York Columbus, Ohio Woodland Hills, California Peoria, Illinois

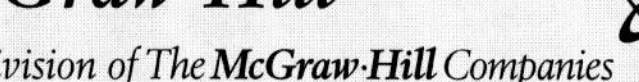

Glencoe/McGraw-Hill

A Division of The McGraw-Hill Companies

Send all inquiries to:
Glencoe/McGraw-Hill
8787 Orion Place
Columbus, OH 43240

ISBN: 0-02-641221-7 (Teacher's Wraparound Edition)
ISBN: 0-02-641257-8 (Teacher's Wraparound Edition Part A)
ISBN: 0-02-641259-4 (Teacher's Wraparound Edition Part B)

Printed in the United States of America.

3 4 5 6 7 8 9 003 08 07 06 05 04 03 02 01 00

National Standards Glencoe Correlation ¡*Buen viaje!* Spanish 1

NATIONAL STANDARDS FOR FOREIGN LANGUAGE LEARNING

OBJECTIVES	STUDENT EDITION PAGE REFERENCES
COMMUNICATION	
Communicate in Languages Other Than English	
Standard 1.1: Students engage in conversations, provide and obtain information, express feelings and emotions, and exchange opinions.	16, 40, 96, 132, 158, 188, 226, 256, 286, 350, 70, 314, 378, 79, 111, 245, 367
Standard 1.2: Students understand and interpret written and spoken language on a variety of topics.	23, 75, 161, 209, 417
Standard 1.3: Students present information, concepts, and ideas to an audience of listeners or readers on a variety of topics.	21, 67, 93, 387, 429
CULTURES	
Gain Knowledge and Understanding of Other Cultures	
Standard 2.1: Students demonstrate an understanding of the relationship between the practices and perspectives of the culture studied.	22, 54, 101, 143, 283, 178, 246, 248, 278, 116, 148, 150, 304, 368, 86, 88, 396
Standard 2.2: Students demonstrate an understanding of the relationship between the products and perspectives of the culture studied.	87, 151, 269, 291, 375, 30, 208, 210, 249, 276, 293, 306, 307, 370, 89, 332, 335, 60, 398, 422, 424, 425,
CONNECTIONS	
Connect with Other Disciplines and Acquire Information	
Standard 3.1: Students reinforce and further their knowledge of other disciplines through the foreign language.	34, 64, 90, 120, 152, 250, 182, 212, 280, 308, 372, 336, 400, 426
Standard 3.2: Students acquire information and recognize the distinctive viewpoints that are only available through the foreign language and its cultures.	36, 66, 91, 123, 154, 252

NATIONAL STANDARDS FOR FOREIGN LANGUAGE LEARNING

OBJECTIVES	STUDENT EDITION PAGE REFERENCES
COMPARISONS	
Develop Insight into the Nature of Language and Culture	
Standard 4.1: Students demonstrate understanding of the nature of language through comparisons of the language studied and their own.	22, 171, 203, 236, 266, 152, 33, 180
Standard 4.2: Students demonstrate understanding of the concept of culture through comparisons of the cultures studied and their own.	61, 92, 119, 149, 248, 246, 278, 116, 150, 295, 304, 77, 86, 88, 334, 400
COMMUNITIES	
Participate in Multilingual Communities at Home and Around the World	
Standard 5.1: Students use the language both within and beyond the school setting.	36, 95, 311, 383, 141, 155, 303, 309, 93, 338
Standard 5.2: Students show evidence of becoming life-long learners by using the language for personal enjoyment and enrichment.	69, 125, 187, 285, 303, 341, 377

ACTFL Proficiency Guidelines

The ***Glencoe Spanish*** series, Levels 1, 2, and 3, follow a logical progression through the ACTFL Proficiency Levels from Novice through Advanced. The initial chapters of ***¡Buen viaje!*** Level 1, for example, present and practice the formulaic language typical of the Novice level: greetings, expressions of courtesy, numbers, days, and dates. Later chapters of ***¡Buen viaje!*** Level 1 have students describing in some detail, expressing likes and dislikes, narrating in present and past, which are language behaviors representative of the Intermediate-Mid and -High levels.

It should be noted that it would be extremely rare for a student to perform at the same ACTFL level across all four language skills. What is usually to be expected is that the student will demonstrate a higher level of performance in receptive skills than in production skills. An Intermediate level speaker may be a fairly competent Advanced level listener. An Advanced level reader might be an intermediate level writer.

It is also the case that in the ***¡Buen viaje!*** materials, as in real life, the language level varies within any given situation. Superior level writers may leave notes written at an Advanced or even at an Intermediate level. Advanced level speakers may respond to a question with a single word, a response usually associated with the Novice level. Nevertheless, the steady, overall progression of complexity from Novice to Advanced holds true throughout the series.

Generic Descriptions

GENERIC DESCRIPTIONS—SPEAKING

Novice — The Novice level is characterized by the ability to communicate minimally with learned material.

Novice-Low — Oral production consists of isolated words and perhaps a few high-frequency phrases. Essentially no functional communicative ability.

Novice-Mid — Oral production continues to consist of isolated words and learned phrases within very predictable areas of need, although quality is increased. Vocabulary is sufficient only for handling simple, elementary needs and expressing basic courtesies. Utterances rarely consist of more than two or three words and show frequent long pauses and repetitions of interlocutor's words. Speaker may have some difficulty producing even the simplest utterances. Some Novice-Mid speakers will be understood only with great difficulty.

Intermediate — The Intermediate level is characterized by the speaker's ability to:

- create with the language by combining and recombining learned elements, though primarily in a reactive mode;
- initiate, minimally sustain, and close in a simple way basic communicative tasks; and
- ask and answer questions.

Intermediate-Low — Able to handle successfully a limited number of interactive task-oriented and social situations. Can ask and answer questions, initiate and respond to simple statements and maintain face-to-face conversation, although in a highly restricted manner and with much linguistic inaccuracy. Within these limitations, can perform such tasks as introducing self, ordering a meal, asking questions, and making purchases. Vocabulary is adequate to express only the most elementary needs. Strong interference from native language may occur. Misunderstandings frequently arise, but with repetition, the Intermediate-Low speaker can generally be understood by sympathetic interlocutors.

Intermediate-Mid

Able to handle successfully a variety of uncomplicated, basic and communicative tasks and social situations. Can talk simply about self and family members. Can ask and answer questions and participate in simple conversations on topics beyond the most immediate needs, e.g., personal history and leisure time activities. Utterance length increases slightly, but speech may continue to be characterized by frequent long pauses, since the smooth incorporation of even basic conversational strategies is often hindered as the speaker struggles to create appropriate language forms. Pronunciation may continue to be strongly influenced by first language and fluency may still be strained. Although misunderstandings still arise, the Intermediate-Mid speaker can generally be understood by sympathetic interlocutors.

Intermediate-High

Able to handle successfully most uncomplicated communicative tasks and social situations. Can initiate, sustain, and close a general conversation with a number of strategies appropriate to a range of circumstances and topics, but errors are evident. Limited vocabulary still necessitates hesitation and may bring about slightly unexpected circumlocution. There is emerging evidence of connected discourse, particularly for simple narration and description. The Intermediate-High speaker can generally be understood even by interlocutors not accustomed to dealing with speakers at this level but repetition may still be required.

Advanced

The Advanced level is characterized by the speaker's ability to:

- converse in a clearly participatory fashion;
- initiate, sustain, and bring to closure a wide variety of communicative tasks, including those that require an increased ability to convey meaning with diverse language strategies due to a complication or an unforeseen turn of events;
- satisfy the requirements of school and work situations; and
- narrate and describe with paragraph-length connected discourse.

Advanced Plus

Able to satisfy the requirements of a broad variety of everyday, school, and work situations. Can discuss concrete topics relating to particular interests and special fields of competence. There is emerging evidence of ability to support opinions, explain in detail, and hypothesize. The Advanced-Plus speaker often shows a well-developed ability to compensate for an imperfect grasp of some forms with confident use of communicative strategies, such as paraphrasing and circumlocution. Differentiated vocabulary and intonation are effectively used to communicate fine shades of meaning. The Advanced-Plus speaker often shows remarkable fluency and ease of speech but under the demands of Superior-level, complex tasks, language may break down or prove inadequate.

Superior

The Superior level is characterized by the speaker's ability to:

- participate effectively in most formal and informal conversations on practical, social, professional and abstract topics; and
- support opinions and hypothesize using native-like discourse strategies.

Able to speak the language with sufficient accuracy to participate effectively in most formal and informal conversations on practical, social, professional, and abstract topics. Can discuss special fields of competence and interest with ease. Can support opinions and hypothesize, but may not be able to tailor language to audience or discuss in depth highly abstract or unfamiliar topics. Usually the Superior level speaker is only partially familiar with regional or other dialectical variants. The Superior level speaker commands a wide variety of interactive strategies and shows good awareness of discourse strategies. The latter involves the ability to distinguish main ideas from supporting information through syntactic, lexical and suprasegmental features (pitch, stress, and intonation). Sporadic errors may occur, particularly in low-frequency structures and some complex high-frequency structures more common to formal writing, but no patterns of error are evident. Errors do not disturb the native speaker or interfere with communication.

GENERIC DESCRIPTIONS—LISTENING

These guidelines assume that all listening tasks take place in an authentic environment at a normal rate of speech using standard or near-standard norms.

Novice-Low	Understanding is limited to occasional isolated words, such as cognates, borrowed words, and high-frequency social conventions. Essentially no ability to comprehend even short utterances.
Novice-Mid	Able to understand some short, learned utterances, particularly where context strongly supports understanding and speech is clearly audible. Comprehends some words and phrases from simple questions, statements, high-frequency commands and courtesy formulae about topics that refer to basic personal information or the immediate physical setting. The listener requires long pauses for assimilation and periodically requests repetition and/or a slower rate of speech.
Novice-High	Able to understand short, learned utterances and some sentence-length utterances, particularly where context strongly supports understanding and speech is clearly audible. Comprehends words and phrases from simple questions, statements, high-frequency commands and courtesy formulae. May require repetition, rephrasing and/or slowed rate of speech for comprehension.
Intermediate-Low	Able to understand sentence-length utterances that consist of recombinations of learned elements in a limited number of content areas, particularly if strongly supported by the situational context. Content refers to basic personal background and needs, social conventions and routine tasks, such as getting meals and receiving simple instructions and directions. Listening tasks pertain primarily to spontaneous face-to-face- conversations. Understanding is often uneven; repetition and rewording may be necessary. Misunderstandings in both main ideas and details arise frequently.
Intermediate-Mid	Able to understand sentence-length utterances that consist of recombinations of learned utterances on a variety of topics. Context continues to refer primarily to basic personal background and needs, social conventions and somewhat more complex tasks, such as lodging, transportation, and shopping. Additional content areas include some personal interests and activities, and a greater diversity of instructions and directions. Listening tasks not only pertain to spontaneous face-to-face conversations but also to short routine telephone conversations and some deliberate speech, such as simple announcements and reports over the media. Understanding continues to be uneven.
Intermediate-High	Able to sustain understanding over longer stretches of connected discourse on a number of topics pertaining to different times and places; however, understanding is consistent due to failure to grasp main ideas and/or details. Thus, while topics do not differ significantly from those of an Advanced level listener, comprehension is less in quality and poorer in quality.
Advanced	Able to understand the main ideas and most details of connected discourse on a variety of topics beyond the immediacy of situation. Comprehension may be uneven due to a variety of linguistic and extralinguistic factors, among which topic familiarity is very prominent. These texts frequently involve description and narration in different time frames or aspects, such as present, nonpast, habitual, or imperfective. Texts may include interviews, short lectures on familiar topics, and news items and reports primarily dealing with factual information. Listener is aware of cohesive devices but may not be able to use them to follow the sequence of thought in an oral text.

Advanced Plus — Able to understand the main ideas of most speech in a standard dialect; however, the listener may not be able to sustain comprehension in extended discourse which is propositionally and linguistically complex. Listener shows an emerging awareness of culturally implied meanings beyond the surface meanings of the text but may fail to grasp sociocultural nuances of the message.

Superior — Able to understand the main ideas of all speech in a standard dialect, including technical discussion in a field of specialization. Can follow the essentials of extended discourse that is propositionally and linguistically complex, as in academic/professional settings, in lectures, speeches, and reports. Listener shows some appreciation of aesthetic norms of target language, of idioms, colloquialisms, and register shifting. Able to make inferences within the cultural framework of the target language. Understanding is aided by an awareness of the underlying organizational structure of the oral text and includes sensitivity for its social and cultural references and its affective overtones. Rarely misunderstands but may not understand excessively, rapid, highly colloquial speech or speech that has strong cultural references.

GENERIC DESCRIPTIONS—READING

These guidelines assume all reading texts to be authentic and legible.

Novice-Low — Able occasionally to identify isolated words and/or major phrases when strongly supported by context.

Novice-Mid — Able to recognize the symbols of an alphabetic and/or syllabic writing system and/or a limited number of characters in a system that uses characters. The reader can identify an increasing number of highly contextualized words and/or phrases including cognates and borrowed words, where appropriate. Material understood rarely exceeds a single phrase at a time, and rereading may be required.

Novice-High — Has sufficient control of the writing system to interpret written language in areas of practical need. Where vocabulary has been learned, can read for instructional and directional purpose standardized messages, phrases or expressions, such as some items on menus, schedules, timetables, maps, and signs. At times, but not on a consistent basis, the Novice-High level reader may be able to derive meaning from material at a slightly higher level where context and/or extralinguistic background knowledge are supportive.

Intermediate-Low — Able to understand main ideas and/or some facts from the simplest connected texts dealing with basic personal and social need. Such texts are linguistically noncomplex and have a clear underlying internal structure, for example chronological sequencing. They impart basic information about which the reader has to make only minimal suppositions or to which the reader brings personal interest and/or knowledge. Examples include messages with social purposes or information for the widest possible audience, such as public announcements and short, straightforward instructions dealing with public life. Some misunderstanding will occur.

Intermediate-Mid — Able to read consistently with increased understanding simple connected texts dealing with a variety of basic and social needs. Such texts are still linguistically noncomplex and have a clear underlying internal structure. They impart basic information about which the reader has to make minimal suppositions and to which the reader brings personal interest and/or knowledge. Examples may include short, straightforward descriptions of persons, places, and things written for a wide audience.

Intermediate-High — Able to read consistently with full understanding simple connected texts dealing with basic personal and social needs about which the reader has personal interest and/or knowledge. Can get some main ideas and information from texts at the next higher level featuring description and narration. Structural complexity may interfere with comprehension; for example, basic grammatical relations may be misinterpreted and temporal references may rely primarily on lexical items. Has some difficulty with the cohesive factors in discourse, such as matching pronouns with referents. While texts do not differ significantly from those at the Advanced level, comprehension is less consistent. May have to read material several times for understanding.

Advanced	Able to read somewhat longer prose of several paragraphs in length, particularly if presented with a clear underlying structure. The prose is predominantly in familiar sentence patterns. Reader gets the main ideas and facts and misses some details. Comprehension derives not only from situational and subject matter knowledge but also from increasing control of the language. Texts at this level include descriptions and narration such as simple short stories, news items, bibliographical information, social notices, personal correspondence, routinized business letters and simple technical material written for the general reader.
Advanced Plus	Able to follow essential points of written discourse at the Superior level in areas of special interest or knowledge. Able to understand parts of texts that are conceptually abstract and linguistically complex, and/or texts that treat unfamiliar topics and situations, as well as some texts that involve aspects of target-language culture. Able to comprehend the facts to make appropriate inferences. An emerging awareness of the aesthetic properties of language and of its literary styles permits comprehension of a wider variety of texts, including literary. Misunderstandings may occur.
Superior	Able to read with almost complete comprehension and at a normal speed expository prose on unfamiliar subjects and a variety of literary texts. Reading ability is not dependent on subject matter knowledge, although the reader is not expected to comprehend thoroughly texts which are highly dependent on knowledge of the target culture. Reads easily for pleasure. Superior-level texts feature hypotheses, argumentation and supported opinions and include grammatical patterns and vocabulary ordinarily encountered in academic/professional reading. At this level, due to the control of general vocabulary and structure, the reader is almost always able to match the meanings derived from extra-linguistic knowledge with meanings derived from knowledge of the language, allowing for smooth and efficient reading of diverse texts. Occasional misunderstandings may still occur; for example, the reader may experience some difficulty with unusually complex structures and low-frequency idioms. At the Superior level the reader can match strategies, top-down or bottom-up, which are most appropriate to the text. (Top-down strategies rely on real-world knowledge and prediction based on genre and organizational scheme of the text. Bottom-up strategies rely on actual linguistic knowledge.) Material at this level will include a variety of literary texts, editorials, correspondence, general reports and technical material in professional fields. Rereading is rarely necessary, and misreading is rare.

GENERIC DESCRIPTIONS—WRITING

Novice-Low	Able to form some letters in alphabetic system. In languages whose writing systems use syllabaries or characters, writer is able to both copy and produce the basic strokes. Can produce romanization of isolated characters, where applicable
Novice-Mid	Able to copy or transcribe familiar words or phrases and reproduce some from memory. No practical communicative writing skills.
Novice-High	Able to write simple fixed expressions and limited memorized material and some recombinations thereof. Can supply information on simple forms and documents. Can write names, numbers, dates, own nationality, and other simple autobiographical information as well as some short phrases and simple lists. Can write all the symbols in an alphabetic or syllabic system or 50–100 characters or compounds in a character writing system. Spelling and representation of symbols (letters, syllables, and characters) may be partially correct.

Intermediate-Low	Able to meet limited practical writing needs. Can write short messages, postcards, and take down simple notes, such as telephone messages. Can create statements or questions within the scope of limited language experience. Material produced consists of recombination of learned vocabulary and structures into simple sentences on very familiar topics. Language is inadequate to express in writing anything but elementary needs. Frequent errors in grammar, vocabulary, punctuation, spelling and information of nonalphabetic symbols, but writing can be understood by natives used to the writing of nonnatives.
Intermediate-Mid	Able to meet a number of practical writing needs. Can write short, simple letters. Content involves personal preferences, daily routine, everyday events, and other topics grounded in personal experience. Can express present time and at least one other time frame or aspect consistently, e.g., nonpast, habitual, imperfective. Evidence of control of the syntax of noncomplex sentences and basic inflectional morphology, such as declensions and conjugation. Writing tends to be loose collection of sentences or sentence fragments on a given topic and provides little evidence of conscious organization. Can be understood by natives used to the writing of nonnatives.
Intermediate-High	Able to meet most practical writing needs and limited social demands. Can take notes in some detail on familiar topics and respond in writing to personal questions. Can write simple letters, brief synopses and paraphrases, summaries of biographical data, work and school experiences. In those languages relying primarily on content words and time expressions to express time, tense, or aspect, some precision is displayed; where tense and/or aspect is expressed through verbal inflection, forms are produced rather consistently, but not always accurately. An ability to describe and narrate in paragraphs is emerging. Rarely uses basic cohesive elements, such as pronominal substitutions or synonyms in written discourse. Writing, though faulty, is generally comprehensible to natives used to the writing of nonnatives.
Advanced	Able to write social correspondence and join sentences in simple discourse of at least several paragraphs in length on familiar topics. Can write simple social correspondence, take notes, write cohesive summaries and resumes, as well as narratives and descriptions of a factual nature. Has sufficient writing vocabulary to express self simply with some circumlocution. May still make errors in punctuation, spelling, or the formation of nonalphabetic symbols. Good control of the morphology and the most frequently used syntactic structures, e.g., common word order patterns, coordination, subordination, but makes frequent errors in producing complex sentences. Uses a limited number of cohesive devices, such as pronouns, accurately. Writing may resemble literal translations from the native language, but a sense of organization (Rhetorical structure) is emerging. Writing is understandable to natives not used to the writing of nonnatives.
Advanced Plus	Able to write about a variety of topics with significant precision and in detail. Can write most types of social and informal business correspondence. Can describe and narrate experiences fully but has difficulty supporting points of view in written discourse. Can write about the concrete aspects of topics relating to particular interests and special fields of competence. Often shows remarkable fluency and ease of expression, but under time constraints and pressure writing may be inaccurate. Generally strong in either grammar or vocabulary, but not in both. Weakness and unevenness in one of the foregoing or in spelling or character writing formation may result in occasional miscommunication. Some misuse of vocabulary may still be evident. Style may still be obviously foreign.

About the Authors

CONRAD J. SCHMITT

Conrad J. Schmitt received his B.A. degree magna cum laude from Montclair State College, Upper Montclair, NJ. He received his M.A. from Middlebury College, Middlebury, VT. He did additional graduate work at Seton Hall University and New York University. Mr. Schmitt has taught Spanish and French at the elementary, junior, and senior high school levels. He was Coordinator of Foreign Languages for Hackensack, New Jersey, Public Schools. He also taught Spanish at Upsala College, East Orange, NJ; Spanish at Montclair State College; and Methods of Teaching a Foreign Language at the Graduate School of Education, Rutgers University, New Brunswick, NJ. He was editor-in-chief of Foreign Languages and Bilingual Education for McGraw-Hill Book Company and Director of English language Materials for McGraw-Hill International Book Company. Mr. Schmitt has authored or co-authored more than eighty books, all published by Glencoe, or other divisions of the McGraw-Hill Companies. He has addressed teacher groups and given workshops in all states of the U.S. and has lectured and presented seminars throughout the Far East, Europe, Latin America, and Canada. In addition, Mr. Schmitt has travelled extensively throughout Spain, Central and South America, and the Caribbean.

PROTASE E. WOODFORD

Protase "Woody" Woodford has taught Spanish at all levels from elementary through graduate school. At the Educational Testing Service in Princeton, NJ, he was Director of Test Development, Director of Language Programs, Director of International Testing Programs and Director of the Puerto Rico Office. He was appointed "Distinguished Linguist" at the U.S. Naval Academy in 1988. He is the author of over two dozen Spanish and English language textbooks for schools and colleges. He has served as a consultant to the American Council on the Teaching of Foreign Languages (ACTFL), the National Assessment of Educational Progress, the College Board, the United Nations Secretariat, UNESCO, the Organization of American States, the U.S. Office of Education, the United States Agency for International Development (AID), the World Bank, the Japanese Ministry of International Trade and Industry, and many ministries of education in Asia, Latin America, and the Middle East. In 1994 he was invited to chair the National Advisory Council on Standards in Foreign Language Education. Mr. Woodford served on the Board of Directors of the Northeast Conference during the period 1982–85. He received the 1993 NYSFLT National Distinguished Leadership Award, and the 1994 Central States Paul Simon Award for Support of Language and International Studies. From 1996–2000 he served as Chairman of the Board of Trustees, Center for Applied Linguistics.

Contents

Introduction

Welcome to ***Glencoe Spanish*** Levels 1, 2, and 3, the junior high and high school Spanish series from Glencoe/McGraw-Hill, a Division of the McGraw-Hill Companies. Every element in this series has been designed to help you create an atmosphere of challenge, variety, cooperation and enjoyment for your students. From the moment you begin to use ***Glencoe Spanish,*** you will notice that not only is it packed with exciting, practical materials and features designed to stimulate young people to work together towards language proficiency, but that it goes beyond by urging students to use their new skills in other areas of the curriculum.

Glencoe Spanish uses an integrated approach to language learning. The introduction and presentation of new material, reinforcement of previously learned material, evaluation, review, exercises and activities in ***Glencoe Spanish*** are designed to span all four language skills. Another characteristic of this series is that students use and reinforce these new skills while developing a realistic, up-to-date awareness of the Hispanic culture.

The Teacher's Edition you are reading has been developed based on the advice of experienced foreign language educators throughout the United States in order to meet your needs as a teacher both in and out of the foreign language classroom. Here are some of the features and benefits which make ***Glencoe Spanish*** a powerful set of teaching tools:

- flexible format
- student-centered instruction
- balance among all four language skills
- contextualized vocabulary
- thorough, contextual presentation of grammar
- an integrated approach to culture

Features and Benefits

FLEXIBLE FORMAT While we have taken every opportunity to use the latest in pedagogical developments in order to create a learning atmosphere of variety, vitality, communication and challenge, we have also made every effort to make the ***Glencoe Spanish*** series "teacher-friendly."

Although the Student Textbook and the Teacher's Edition provide an instructional method, every minute of every class period is not laid out. Plenty of room for flexibility has been built in to allow you to draw on your own education, experience and personality in order to tailor a language program that is suitable and rewarding for each individual class.

A closer look at the most basic component, the Student Textbook, serves as an example of this flexibility. Each chapter opens with two sections of vocabulary **(Vocabulario: Palabras 1** and **Palabras 2)** each with its own set of exercises. **Vocabulario** is followed by **Estructura,** consisting of a series of grammar points, each with accompanying exercises. But there is nothing which says that the material must be presented in this order. The items of vocabulary and grammar are so well integrated that you will find it easy, and perhaps preferable, to move back and forth between them. You may also wish to select from the third and fourth sections of each chapter (the **Conversación** and **Lecturas culturales** sections) at an earlier point than that in which they are presented, as a means of challenging students to identify or use the chapter vocabulary and grammar to which they have already been introduced.

These options are left to you. The only requirement for moving successfully through the Student Textbook is that the vocabulary and grammar of each chapter be presented in their entirety, since each succeeding chapter builds on what has come before.

In the Student Textbook, there is a marked difference between learning exercises **(Práctica)** and communication-based activities **(Actividades comunicativas),** both of which are provided in each chapter. The former serve as their name implies, as exercises for the acquisition and practice of new vocabulary and structures; while the latter are designed to get students communicating in open-ended contexts using the Spanish they have learned. You can be selective among these, depending on the needs of your students. The abundance of suggestions for techniques, strategies, additional practice, chapter projects, independent (homework) assignments, informal assessment, and more, which are provided in this Teacher's Edition—as well as the veritable banquet of resources available in the wide array of ancillary materials provided in the series—are what make ***Glencoe Spanish*** truly flexible and "teacher-friendly." They provide ideas and teaching tools from which to pick and choose in order to create an outstanding course.

STUDENT-CENTERED INSTRUCTION Today's classroom is comprised of students who have different learning styles, special needs, and represent different cultural backgrounds. The emphasis on student-centered instruction provided by ***Glencoe Spanish*** allows the teacher to capitalize on and deal positively with such diversity and encourages students to become involved in their own learning.

Glencoe Spanish anticipates the requirements of today's classroom by offering ideas for setting up a cooperative learning environment for students. Useful suggestions to this end accompany each chapter, under the heading COOPERATIVE LEARNING, in this Teacher's Edition. Additional paired and group activities occur in the Student Textbook **(Actividades comunicativas),** and in other headings such as Additional Practice in the Teacher's Edition. Besides cooperative learning strategies, ***Glencoe Spanish*** contains many other student-centered elements that allow students to expand their learning experiences.

Here are some examples: suggestions are offered in the Teacher's Edition for out-of-class chapter projects on topics related to the chapter theme and "For the Younger Student," activities aimed primarily at the middle school/junior-high student.

In the Student Textbook, new grammatical material is divided into "bite-sized" lessons, so as not to be intimidating. The Writing Activities Workbook provides a self-test after every unit of chapters, so that students can prepare alone or in study groups for teacher-administered quizzes and tests. The Audio Program allows students to work at their own pace, stopping the cassette (or compact disc) whenever necessary to make directed changes in the language, or to refer to their activity sheets in the Student Tape Manual. The Computer Testmaker component consists of pre-made tests, along with the option of tailoring these ready-made tests, or creating all-new tests.

These and other features discussed elsewhere in this Teacher's Manual have been designed with the student in mind. They assure that each individual, regardless of learning style, special need, background, or age, will have the necessary resources for becoming proficient in Spanish.

Balance Among All Four Language Skills

Glencoe Spanish provides a balanced focus on the listening, speaking, reading, and writing skills throughout all phases of instruction. It gives you leeway if you wish to adjust the integration of these skills to the needs of a particular individual, group or class. Several features of the series lend themselves to this: the overall flexibility of format, the abundance of suggested optional and additional activities and the design of the individual activities themselves. Let's look at some sections of a typical chapter as examples of the other two characteristics mentioned.

If the suggested presentation is followed, students are introduced to new words and phrases in **Vocabulario** by the teacher, and/or by the audiocassette or compact disc presentation. The focus is on listening and speaking through modeling and repetition. The **Práctica** which accompany the **Vocabulario** section can be done with books either closed (accentuating listening and speaking) or open (accentuating reading, listening and speaking). However, these **Práctica** can just as well be assigned or reassigned as written work if the teacher wishes to have the whole class or individuals begin to concentrate on reading and writing. Throughout the **Vocabulario** section, optional and additional reinforcement activities are suggested in the Teacher's Edition. These suggestions address all four language skills. Later in each chapter, students are asked to combine the material learned in **Vocabulario** with material from the grammar section **(Estructura)** using a combination of listening, reading, writing and speaking skills in the process.

Reading and writing activities are brought into play early in the ***Glencoe Spanish*** series. The authors realize that communication in Spanish includes the use of reading and writing skills and that these skills are indispensable for the assimilation and retention of new language and the organization of thought. Students are launched into writing, for example, as early as Chapter 1, through the use of brief assignments such as lists, labeled diagrams, note taking or short answers. Longer writing activities are added in later chapters. These textbook activities are further reinforced in the Writing Activities Workbook.

Let's take a closer look at how each of the four skills is woven into the Student Textbook, the Teacher's Edition and the ancillary materials.

LISTENING You the teacher are the primary source for listening, as you model new vocabulary, dialogs, structure and pronunciation, share your knowledge of Spanish culture, history and geography, talk to students about their lives and your own, or engage in culturally oriented activities and projects. As always, it is your ability to use Spanish as much as possible with your students, both in and outside of the classroom, which determines how relevant and dynamic their learning experience will be.

Glencoe Spanish offers numerous ways in which to develop the listening skill. There are teacher-focused activities, which provide the consistent modeling that students need. Teachers who use the Audio Program will find that these recordings help students become accustomed to a variety of voices, as well as rates of speed. Activities in which students interact with each other develop listening spontaneity and acuity.

In the Student Textbook, new vocabulary will be modeled by the teacher. Students' attention to the sounds of the new words can be maximized by presenting this material with books closed and using the Vocabulary Transparencies to convey meaning. Following each **Palabras** segment are several **Práctica** exercises for rehearsing the new vocabulary. These can also be done with books closed. With each vocabulary presentation there are **Actividades comunicativas,** in which students may work in pairs or groups and must listen to each other in order to find information, take notes or report to others on what was said in their group. In **Estructura,** students listen as the teacher models new grammatical material and then are given a chance to practice each structure in several **Práctica** and **Actividades comunicativas** situations. Once again, closing the book will provide increased focus on the listening skill. The next section of each chapter is **Conversación,** in which a real-life dialog is modeled either by the teacher or by playing the recorded version from the Audio Program. In Level 1, **Conversación** also contains a **Pronunciación** segment, covering an aspect of pronunciation related to the chapter material. Here again, students will be listening either to teacher or recorded models. The last section of each chapter, **Culminación,** offers more listening-intensive activities **(Actividades orales)** where students must be able to understand what their partners say in order to play out their role.

In addition to the Student Textbook, the Teacher's Edition offers several other listening-based activities correlated to the chapters. Some of these listening activities are "Total Physical Response" (Level 1) and "Pantomime" (Level 2). Here students must perform an action after listening to a spoken command. There are other listening-based activities suggested under the heading "Cooperative Learning" and often under "Additional Practice," both of which appear in the Teacher's Edition.

The Audio Program has two main listening components. The first is practice-oriented, wherein students further reinforce vocabulary and grammar, following directions and making changes in speech. They can self-check their work by listening to the correctly modeled utterances, which are supplied after a pause.

The second part of the program places more attention on the receptive listening skills. Students listen to language in the form of dialogs, announcements, or advertisements—language delivered at a faster pace and in greater volume—and then are asked to demonstrate their understanding of the main ideas and important details in what they have heard. The Student Tape Manual contains activity sheets for doing this work. The Teacher's Edition contains the complete transcript of all audio materials to assist you in preparing listening tasks for your class.

More listening practice is offered through the Video Program. This material corresponds to and enriches that in the Student Textbook, and gives students a chance to hear variations of the language elements they have been practicing, as spoken by a variety of native speakers. Students' listening comprehension can be checked and augmented by using the corresponding print activities in the Video Activities Booklet.

SPEAKING Most of the areas of the Student Textbook and the Teacher's Edition mentioned above simultaneously develop the speaking skill. After hearing a model in the **Vocabulario** or **Estructura** sections, students will repeat it, either as a whole class, in small groups, or individually. From these models, they will progress to visual ones, supplied by the Vocabulary Transparencies or the photos and graphics in the textbook. The real thrust in the **Práctica** accompanying these two sections is to get students to produce this new material actively. In the **Actividades comunicativas,** students have the opportunity to apply what they have learned by asking for and giving information to their classmates on a given topic. Here, and in the **Conversación** sections, students are engaged in meaningful, interesting sessions of sharing information, all designed to make them want to speak and experiment with the language. The suggestions in the "About the Language" section in the Teacher's Edition enrich speaking skills by offering variants of expressions and speech mannerisms currently popular in Hispanic culture, especially among teenagers, so that from the start your students will be accustomed to speaking in a way that is accurate and reflective of contemporary Spanish. In Chapter 1, for example, this feature discusses the variations of **muchacho(a) / chico(a),** the difference between **bolígrafo** and **pluma,** and provides information on the use and formation of nicknames, among other things. In the Student Textbook, previously presented material is constantly recycled in the communication based activities, so that students' speaking vocabularies and knowledge of structure are always increasing. The length of utterances is increased over time, so that when students complete ***Glencoe Spanish*** Level 1 they will have acquired an appreciation of the intonation and inflection of longer streams of language. To assist you in fine-tuning your students' speech patterns, the **Pronunciación** section is presented in each chapter of Level 1.

The speaking skill is stressed in the first part of each recorded chapter of the Audio Program, where pauses are provided for the student to produce directed, spoken changes in the language. This is an excellent opportunity for those students who are self-conscious about speaking out in class to practice speaking. The Audio Program gives these students a chance to work in isolation. The format of making a change in the language, uttering the change and then listening for the correct model improves the speaking skill. The Audio Program can serve as a confidence-builder for self-conscious students, allowing them to work their way gradually into more spontaneous speech with their classmates.

The packet of Situation Cards provides students with yet another opportunity to produce spoken Spanish. They place the student into a contextualized, real-world situation. Students must ask and/or answer questions in order to perform successfully.

READING Each chapter of the Student Textbook has readings based on the chapter theme under the heading **Lecturas culturales.** Each of these readings is accompanied by a series of comprehension exercises called **Después de leer,** which focus on useful strategies for vocabulary-building and recognizing word relationships, which students can carry over into other readings. The optional readings in each chapter **(Lecturas opcionales),** are shorter, and are intended to be read with less attention to detail. In the next section of each chapter, **Conexiones,** students again use their reading skills albeit to a lesser degree. Here students have a chance to stretch their reading abilities in Spanish by reading basic information they may have already learned in other academic subjects. The material has been carefully written to include themes (as well as words and structures) which students have learned in previous chapters. The **Conexiones** sections are optional. You can choose to use them for independent reading, as a home-work assignment with in-class followup, or as an intensive in-class activity.

After every unit of chapters of the Student Textbook, ***Glencoe Spanish*** provides a unique section called **Vistas.** This presentation was prepared by the National Geographic Society. Each **Vista** focuses on one Spanish-speaking country via a dazzling display of photos representative of both that country's past as well as its present. Students have the opportunity to read the photo captions accompanying these **Vista** pages.

The Writing Activities Workbook offers additional readings under the heading **Un poco más**. These selections and the accompanying exercises focus on reading strategies such as cognate recognition, related word forms and the use of context clues. In addition to the reading development above, students are constantly presented with authentic Spanish texts such as announcements from periodicals, telephone listings, transportation schedules, labeled diagrams, floor plans, travel brochures, school progress reports and many others, as sources of information. Sometimes these documents serve as the bases for language activities, and other times they appear in order to round out a cultural presentation, but, in varying degrees, they all require students to apply their reading skills.

WRITING Written work is interwoven throughout the language learning process in ***Glencoe Spanish.*** The exercises, which occur throughout the **Vocabulario** and **Estructura** sections of each chapter in the Student Textbook, are designed in such a way that they can be completed in written form as well as orally. Frequently, you may wish to reassign exercises which you have gone through orally in class as written homework. The Teacher's Edition makes special note of this under the topic "Independent Practice." At the end of each chapter of the Student Textbook, direct focus is placed on writing in the **Culminación** section, under the heading **Actividades escritas.** Here there are one or more activities that encourage students to use the new vocabulary and structure they have learned in the chapter to create their own writing samples. These are short and may be descriptive, narrative, argumentative, analytical or in the form of dialogs or interviews. Often a context is set up and then students are asked to develop an appropriate written response.

The Writing Activities Workbook is the component in which writing skills receive the most overt attention. All of the exercises in it require writing. They vary in length from one word answers to short compositions. They are designed to focus on the same vocabulary and grammar presented in the corresponding chapter of the Student Textbook, but they are all new and all contextualized around fresh visual material or situational vignettes. Since they often have students making lists, adding to charts and labeling, they provide an excellent means for students to organize the chapter material in their minds and make associations which will help them retain it. As students' knowledge of Spanish increases, longer written pieces are required of them. One workbook section entitled **Mi autobiografía** has students write installments of their own autobiographies. This is an effective way of stretching student writing skills. It also challenges students to personalize the Spanish they have been studying.

Students are also asked to make implicit use of writing almost everywhere in the series. They are constantly taking notes, listing, categorizing, labeling, summarizing, comparing or contrasting on paper. Even the Audio Program and the Video Program involve students in writing through the use of activity sheets. By choosing among these options, you can be sure that your students will receive the practice they need to develop their writing skills successfully.

Contextualized Vocabulary

From the moment students see new words at the beginning of each chapter in ***Glencoe Spanish,*** they see them within an identifiable context. From the start, students learn to group words by association, thereby enhancing their ability to assimilate and store vocabulary for long-term retention. This contextualization remains consistent throughout the practice, testing and recycling phases of learning.

In the **Vocabulario** section, each of the **Palabras** segments contains a short exchange or a few lead-in sentences or phrases which, together with colorful visuals, establish the context of the topic. Other vocabulary items which occur naturally within this topic are laid out among additional visuals, often as labels. The result is that students see at a glance the new language set into a real-life situation which provides "something to talk about"—a reason for using the language. The accompanying exercises enrich the context of the language. The items to each **Historieta** exercise are related so that when taken together they form a meaningful vignette or story. In other sections of the chapter, these words and phrases are reintroduced frequently.

Moreover, future chapters build on vocabulary and grammar from previous ones. Chapter themes introduced in Level 1 are reintroduced in Level 2 along with additional related vocabulary. Special attention has been given to vocabulary in the reading sections of the series as well. For example, in the **Lecturas culturales,** students are encouraged to stretch their vocabularies in order to get as much meaning as possible from the selections. In addition to glossed words and frequent use of cognate recognition, the corresponding **Después de leer** exercises are there to help them with this.

Thorough, Contextual Presentation of Grammar

A quick look through the chapters of ***Glencoe Spanish*** Levels 1 and 2 will show the role grammar plays in the overall approach of the series. Although grammar is by no means the driving force behind the series, it is indeed an important aspect. Grammar is presented as one of seven sections in each chapter. What makes this series particularly effective is that, as well as being thorough, the presentation of grammar runs concurrent with, and is embedded in, the chapter-long situational themes. Students are presented with Spanish structure both directly, as grammar, and also as a set of useful functions. These will aid in communicating, expanding and improving their Spanish across the four skills, and learning about Hispanic culture as well as other areas of the school curriculum. Another important series characteristic is that the presentation of grammar has been divided into short, coherent "doses," which prevent grammar from becoming overwhelming to the student.

Throughout this series you will see that as you teach the various grammar topics, student interest remains high because each exercise relates to a communicative topic and the format always varies. As is the case with many of the vocabulary exercises, the individual practice items in the grammar exercises are often related to each other contextually, in order to heighten student interest. All such exercises are labeled **Historieta.**

You will find that it is easy to move in and out of the teaching of grammar, dipping into the other sections of a chapter or other components as you see fit. The grammar segments are short and intelligently divided. Each one provides a good sense of closure; they are taught in one section, are included as much as possible in the others; and have a coherent contextual theme.

Aside from the Student Textbook and Teacher's Edition, with their focus on grammar in the **Estructura** section of each chapter and in the **Repasos** after every unit, ***Glencoe Spanish*** offers students opportunities to practice grammar in other components as well. Chapter by chapter, the Writing Activities Workbook provides ample tasks in which students must put to writing the new structures on which they have been working in class. The Audio Program includes recorded sections in every chapter of the Student Tape Manual which correspond directly to **Estructura** in the Student Textbook. Students' knowledge of grammar is evaluated in the Chapter Quizzes and in the Testing Program. Each grammatical structure is practiced in other components, such as the Expansion Activities, Situation Cards, and Video Program.

An Integrated Approach to Culture

True competence in a foreign language cannot be attained without simultaneous development of an awareness of the culture in which the language is spoken. That is why ***Glencoe Spanish*** places such great importance on culture. Accurate, up-to-date information on Hispanic culture is presented either implicitly or explicitly throughout every phase of language learning and in every component of the series.

The presentation of Spanish in each chapter of the Student Textbook is embedded in running contextual themes. These themes richly reflect the varied cultures of Latin America, Spain and Hispanic communities in the U.S. Even in chapter sections which focus primarily on vocabulary or grammar, the presence of culture comes through in the language used as examples or items in exercises, as well as in the content of the accompanying illustrations, photographs, charts, diagrams, maps or other reproductions of authentic documents in Spanish. This constant, implicit inclusion of cultural information creates a format which not only aids in the learning of new words and structures, but piques student interest, invites questions and stimulates discussion of the people behind the language.

Many culturally oriented questions raised by students may be answered in the sections devoted to culture: **Lecturas culturales,** and **Conexiones.** Through readings, captioned visuals and guided activities, these sections provide fundamental knowledge about such topics as family life, school, restaurants, markets, sports, transportation, food, hotels, offices and hospitals, among many others. This information is presented with the idea that culture is a product of people-their attitudes, desires, preferences, differences, similarities, strengths and weaknesses-and that it is ever changing. Students are always encouraged to compare or contrast what they learn about Hispanic culture with their own, thereby learning to think critically and progress towards a more mature vision of the world.

Throughout the Teacher's Edition, there are sections entitled About the Language. In each of these sections, teachers are given regional differences for lexical items such as **el carril, la pista, la vía, la banda, el canal**—all of which can refer to the lane of a highway, or **el autobús, la guagua, el camión, el micro**—all of which can refer to a bus. In addition to lexical regionalisms, explanations are given for structural variations: **contestar** versus **contestar a; jugar** versus **jugar a.**

Series Components

In order to take full advantage of the student-centered, "teacher-friendly" curriculum offered by ***Glencoe Spanish***, you may want to refer to this section to familiarize yourself with the various resources the series has to offer. Both Levels 1 and 2 of ***Glencoe Spanish*** contain the following components:

- Student Edition
- Teacher's Edition
- Writing Activities Workbook
- Writing Activities Workbook, Teacher's Edition
- Audio Program (Cassette or Compact Disc)
- Student Tape Manual
- Student Tape Manual, Teacher's Edition (tapescript)
- Transparency Binder
- Video Program (Videocassette or Videodisc)
- Video Activities Booklet
- Computer Testmaker Software (Windows/Macintosh)
- Expansion Activities
- Situation Cards
- Lesson Plans
- Block Scheduling Lesson Plans
- Electronic Teacher's Classroom Resources
- Online Internet Activities
- Mindjogger Videoquiz (Videocassette or Videodisc)
- Chapter Quizzes with Answer Key
- Testing Program with Answer Key
- Performance Assessment
- CD-ROM Interactive Textbook
- Spanish for Spanish Speakers: ***Nosotros y nuestro mundo***

Level 1 in Two Volumes

At the junior high and intermediate school levels, where the material in Level 1 is normally presented in two years, a two-volume edition is available consisting of Part A and Part B. This two-volume edition may also be more suitable for other types of language programs, where students are studying Spanish for limited periods of time, where student aptitude varies from the norm, or for those programs where the teacher chooses to modify the pacing for other reasons. In addition to the two-volume Student Edition, the components which are also available in two volumes are the Teacher's Edition, the Writing Activities Workbook, and the Student Tape Manual. All other Level 1 components are completely compatible with this "split" edition of the Student Textbook.

Level 1 Part A consists of Chapters 1 through 7. Level 1 Part B opens with 33 pages of **Repaso,** a review section containing new activities designed to reenter the material in Part A. Part B then continues with Chapters 8 through 14.

Organization of the Student Textbook

¡*Buen viaje!* Preliminary Lessons Chapter 1 of the Level 1 textbook is preceded by four preliminary lessons entitled **Bienvenidos**. These short lessons A, B, C, and D, will help orient your students to some of the routines of the foreign language classroom at the beginning of the term. They prime students with a few essential question words and get them using high-frequency Spanish phrases for greetings and leave-takings, expressions of courtesy, and telling the days of the week. Each preliminary lesson contains exercises and activities to help students retain this introductory material. If you guide them through these preliminary lessons, your students will be able to make a smooth transition into the regular chapter material, and you will be able to conduct more of the classroom activities, including giving directions, in Spanish.

Following the four preliminary lessons, each chapter of Level 1 is divided into the following sections:

- **Vocabulario (Palabras 1 & Palabras 2)**
- **Estructura**
- **Conversación**
- **Lecturas culturales**
- **Conexiones**
- **Culminación**

VOCABULARIO The new vocabulary is laid out in two segments, **Palabras 1** and **Palabras 2.** Each of these presents new words in a cultural context in keeping with the theme of the chapter. Ample use is made of labeled illustrations to convey meaning and to provide an interesting introduction to the new vocabulary. The contextual vignettes into which the vocabulary items are embedded make use of the same grammatical structures which will be formally addressed in the chapter, and recycle words and structures from previous chapters. Accompanying each **Palabras** segment is a series of **Práctica** and **Actividades comunicativas** that require students to use the new words in context. These practice exercises employ techniques such as short answer, matching, multiple choice and labeling. Many of the **Práctica** exercises are contextual, forming coherent vignettes. For this reason they bear the additonal label **Historieta.** Each time **Historieta** appears as part of the exercise title, it means that the answers form a short story.

The **Práctica** lend themselves well to any variations you might wish to apply to their delivery (books open, books closed, done as a class, in groups or pairs, written for homework). The activities labeled **Actividades comunicativas** are communicative-based. These are more open-ended activities, requiring students to personalize the new language by performing such tasks as gathering information from classmates, interviewing, taking notes, making charts or reporting to the class.

ESTRUCTURA This is the grammar section of each chapter. It is conveniently and logically divided into two to four segments to aid in student assimilation of the material. Each segment provides a step-by-step description in English of how the new grammatical structure is used in Spanish, accompanied by examples, tables and other visuals. Each segment's presentation is followed by a series of flexible **Práctica** and **Actividades comunicativas,** designed along the same lines as those which accompany the **Vocabulario** section, and focusing on the grammar point. As in **Vocabulario,** the presentation of the new structures and the subsequent exercises are contextualized. The **Práctica** exercises labeled **Historieta** always fit together in vignettes to enhance meaning. These vignettes are directly related to the overall chapter theme or a theme from a previous chapter. The

Estructura section makes regular use of the new vocabulary from **Palabras 1** and **Palabras 2,** allowing for free interplay between these two sections of the chapter. This thorough yet manageable layout allows you to adapt the teaching of grammar to your students' needs and to your own teaching style.

CONVERSACIÓN Now that students have had a chance to see and practice the new items of vocabulary and grammar for the chapter, this section provides a recombined version of the new language in the form of an authentic, culturally rich dialog. This can be handled in a variety of ways, depending on the teacher and the class and as suggested by accompanying notes in the Teacher's Edition. Teacher modeling, modeling from the recorded version, class or individual repetitions, reading aloud by students, role-playing or adaptation through substitution are some of the strategies suggested. The dialog is accompanied by one or more **Después de conversar** exercises which check comprehension and allow for some personalization of the material. Then students are invited once again to recombine and use all the new language in a variety of group and paired activities in the **Actividades comunicativas** that follow. New vocabulary and expressions are sometimes offered here, but only for the sake of richness and variation, and not for testing purposes

Every chapter in Level 1 also contains a **Pronunciación** segment which appears after the **Conversación.** It provides a guide to the pronunciation of one or more Spanish phonemes, a series of words and phrases containing the key sound(s), and an illustration which cues a key word or sentence containing the sound(s). These pronunciation illustrations are part of the Transparency Binder accompanying the series. **Pronunciación** can serve both as a tool for practice as students perform the chapter tasks, and as a handy speaking-skills reference to be used at any time.

LECTURAS CULTURALES These readings are about people and places from Latin America and Spain, offering further cultural input to the theme of the chapter and providing yet another recombination of the chapter vocabulary and grammar. As is always the case with ***Glencoe Spanish***, material from previous chapters is recycled. Following the **Lecturas culturales** reading are **Después de leer** comprehension exercises based on the reading, along with exercises that give students a chance to experiment with and expand their Spanish vocabularies by using strategies such as searching for synonyms, identifying cognates, completing cloze exercises, matching and others. Note that the second and third reading selections among the **Lecturas culturales** are optional, and they are clearly labeled as such.

CONEXIONES This section offers yet another type of reading by presenting topics from other areas of the curriculum, allowing students to reinforce and further their knowledge of these disciplines through the study of Spanish. The focus is on the interdisciplinary content rather than the language itself. By engaging your students in some or all of these readings, you will encourage them to stretch their Spanish reading skills in order to obtain useful, interesting information which will be of great service to them in their other academic courses. You will be giving students the opportunity to judge for themselves the added insight that the study of Spanish offers to their overall education. The **Conexiones** section in each chapter is optional.

CULMINACIÓN This wrap-up section requires students to consolidate material from the present as well as previous chapters in order to complete the tasks successfully. **Culminación** provides an opportunity for students to assess themselves on their own and to spend time on areas in which they are weak. You the teacher can pick and choose from these activities as you see fit. The first segment of **Culminación** consists of **Actividades orales,** where students must use the Spanish they have learned to talk about various aspects of themselves: likes, dislikes, favorite activities, hobbies or areas of expertise, among others. This is followed by **Actividades escritas** which encourages students to apply their knowledge of Spanish in written form. The **Vocabulario** page reviews the words and expressions that were taught in the current chapter, listing them by functional category. The **Vocabulario** serves as a handy reference resource for both the student and the teacher.

Finally, the **Tecnotur** page previews three key multi-media components of the ***Glencoe Spanish*** series, the Video Program, the CD-ROM Interactive Textbook (an electronic version of the Student Textbook), and the Online Internet Activities.

After each unit of chapters, the following special sections appear in ***Glencoe Spanish:***

- **Repasos**
- **Vistas**

REPASOS This review section, designed to coincide with the more comprehensive Unit Tests in the Testing Program, occurs after chapters 4, 7, 11, and 14 in the Student Textbook. In each **Repaso,** the main vocabulary and grammar points from the previous chapters are recycled through a variety of new exercises, activities and dialogs. While in the individual chapters new grammar was divided into smaller, "bite-sized" portions to aid in the planning of daily lessons and help students assimilate it, now it is reviewed in a more consolidated format. This allows students to see different grammatical points side by side for the first time, to make new connections between the different points, and to progress toward a generative, "whole grammar." For example, in the **Repaso** following Chapter 4 of Level 1, the salient nouns and adjectives from the first four chapters are reviewed together. All forms of **-ar** verbs and those of **ir, dar** and **estar** are reviewed together on one page for the first time, accompanied by exercises, so that students can make final associations between each subject pronoun and its correct verb form. This material was previously spread out among the first four chapters.

Every possible combination of vocabulary and grammar does not reappear in the **Repaso,** but by carefully going through these exercises and activities and referring to the preceding chapters, students will be encouraged to make necessary connections and extrapolations themselves and therefore develop a true, working knowledge of the Spanish they have studied. The **Repaso** is designed to be used by students studying alone, in study groups or as a whole class with teacher guidance.

VISTAS The **Vista**s were prepared by National Geographic Society. Their purpose is to give students greater insight, through colorful and inviting images, into the cultures and people of four different Spanish-speaking countries. In Level 1, these countries are Mexico, Spain, Puerto Rico, and Ecuador. The first two pages of each **Vista** focus on the traditional aspects of the country, while the final two pages portray the contemporary look and feel of that particular country. Students are encouraged to look at the photographs on the **Vista** pages for enjoyment. If they would like to talk about the photographs, let them say anything they can, using the vocabulary they have learned to this point.

LITERATURA At the back of the Level 1 Student Textbook, there is a special section entitled **Literatura** consisting of four brief literary selections:

Versos sencillos by José Martí
"Una moneda de oro" by Francisco Monterde
La camisa de Margarita by Ricardo Palma
El Quijote by Miguel de Cervantes Saavedra

The literary selections provide an additional opportunity to develop students' reading skills in an enjoyable and rewarding context. Each literary selection can be read following the completion of the corresponding unit of chapters. For example, after completing Chapter 4, students will be prepared to read ***Versos sencillos*** by José Martí with relative ease. The exposure to literature early in one's study of a foreign language should be a pleasant experience. As students read these selections it is not necessary that they understand every word. Explain to them that they should try to enjoy the experience of reading literature in a new language. As they read they should look for the following:

- Who are the main characters
- What are they like
- What are they doing—what's the plot
- What happens to them—what's the outcome

These literary readings are totally optional. The point in time you choose to introduce your students to them is your decision.

Suggestions for Teaching the Student Textbook

Teaching the Four Preliminary Lessons in Level 1

The first day of class, teachers may wish to involve students in a discussion concerning the importance of the language they have chosen to study. Some suggestions are:

- Show students a map (the maps located in the back of the Student Textbook can be used) to remind them of the extent of the Spanish-speaking world.
- Have students discuss the areas within North America in which there are a high percentage of Spanish speakers. Ask them to name local Spanish-speaking sources including any individuals or groups they may know in their community.
- Make a list of place names such as San Francisco, Los Angeles, El Paso, Las Vegas, or names in your locality that are of Spanish origin.
- Explain to students the possibility of using Spanish in numerous careers such as: government, teaching, business, (banking, import/export), tourism, translating.
- The first day teachers will also want to give each student a Hispanic name. Teachers may want to give Hispanic nicknames to students with names like Kevin or Candy.

The short Preliminary Lessons in Level 1 are designed to give students useful, everyday expressions that they can use immediately. Each lesson is designed to take less than one day. The topics present students with easily learned expressions such as **Hola, Buenos días, ¿Qué tal?, Adiós,** etc., but do not confuse students by expecting them to make structural changes such as the manipulation of verb endings. Formal grammar begins with Chapter 1. No grammar is taught in the **Bienvenidos** Preliminary Lessons.

Teaching Various Sections of the Chapter

One of the major objectives of the ***Glencoe Spanish*** series is to enable teachers to adapt the material to their own philosophy, teaching style, and students' needs. As a result, a variety of suggestions are offered here for teaching each section of the chapter.

Vocabulario

The **Vocabulario** section always contains some words in isolation, accompanied by an illustration that depicts the meaning of the new word. In addition, new words are used in contextualized sentences. These contextualized sentences appear in the following formats: 1) one to three sentences accompanying an illustration, 2) a short conversation, 3) a short narrative or paragraph. In addition to teaching the new vocabulary, these contextualized sentences introduce, but do not teach, the new structure point of the chapter. A vocabulary list summarizing all of the words and expressions taught in the **Vocabulario** section appears at the end of each chapter in the Student Textbook.

General Techniques

- The Vocabulary Transparencies contain all illustrations necessary to teach the new words and phrases. With an overhead projector, they can easily be projected as large visuals in the classroom for those teachers who prefer to introduce the vocabulary with books closed. The Vocabulary Transparencies contain no printed words.

- All the vocabulary in each chapter **(Palabras 1** and **Palabras 2)** is recorded on the Audio Program. Students are asked to repeat the isolated words after the model.

Specific Techniques

OPTION 1 Option 1 for the presentation of vocabulary best meets the needs of those teachers who consider the development of oral skills a prime objective.

- While students have their books closed, project the Vocabulary Transparencies. Point to the item being taught and have students repeat the word after you or the audiocassette (or compact disc) several times. After you have presented several words in this manner, project the transparencies again and ask questions such as
  ¿Es una mesa?
  ¿Qué es?
  ¿Es el mesero?
  ¿Quién es? (Level 1, Chapter 5)
- To teach the contextualized segments on the **Palabras** pages, project the Vocabulary Transparency in the same way. Point to the part of the illustration that depicts the meaning of any new word in the sentence, be it an isolated sentence or a sentence from a conversation or narrative. Immediately ask questions about the sentence. For example, the following sentence appears in Level 1, Chapter 6: **Los García tienen un apartamento en el quinto piso.**
  Questions to ask are:
  ¿Los García tienen una casa o un apartamento?
  ¿Quiénes tienen un apartamento?
  ¿Los García tienen un apartamento en el quinto piso o en el cuarto piso?
- Dramatizations by the teacher, in addition to the illustrations, can also help convey the meaning of many words such as **cantar, bailar,** etc.
- After this basic presentation of the **Palabras** vocabulary, have students open their books and read the **Palabras** section for additional reinforcement.
- Go over the exercises in the **Palabras** section orally.
- Assign the exercises in the **Palabras** section for homework. Also assign the corresponding vocabulary exercises in the Writing Activities Workbook. If the **Palabras** section should take more than one day, assign only those exercises that correspond to the material you have presented.
- The following day, go over the exercises that were assigned for homework.

OPTION 2 Option 2 will meet the needs of those teachers who wish to teach the oral skills but consider reading and writing equally important.

- Project the Vocabulary Transparencies and have students repeat each word once or twice after you or the audiocassette (compact disc).
- Have students repeat the contextualized sentences after you or the audiocassette as they look at the illustration.
- Ask students to open their books. Have them read the **Palabras** section. Correct pronunciation errors as they are made.
- Go over the exercises in each **Palabras** section.
- Assign the exercises in the **Palabras** section for homework. Also assign the vocabulary exercises in the Writing Activities Workbook.
- The following day, go over the exercises that were assigned for homework.

OPTION 3 Option 3 will meet the needs of those teachers who consider the reading and writing skills of utmost importance.

- Have students open their books and read the **Palabras** items as they look at the illustrations.
- Give students several minutes to look at the **Palabras** words and vocabulary exercises. Then go over the exercises.
- Go over the exercises the following day.

Additional Activities

Teachers may use any of the following activities occasionally. These can be done in conjunction with the options previously outlined.

- After the vocabulary has been presented, project the Vocabulary Transparencies or have students open their books and make up as many original sentences as they can, using the new words. This can be done orally or in writing.
- Have students work in pairs or small groups. As they look at the illustrations in the textbook, have them make up as many questions as they can. They can direct their questions to their peers. It is often fun to make this a competitive activity. Individuals or teams can compete to make up the most questions in three minutes. This activity provides the students with an excellent opportunity to use interrogative words.
- Call on one student to read to the class one of the vocabulary exercises that tells a story. Then call on a more able student to retell the story in his or her own words.
- With slow groups you can have one student go to the front of the room. Have him or her think of one of the new words. Let classmates give the student the new words from the **Palabras** until they guess the word the student in the front of the room has in mind. This is a very easy way to have the students recall the words they have just learned.

Estructura

The **Estructura** section of the chapter opens with a grammatical explanation in English. Each grammatical explanation is accompanied by many examples. Verbs are given with complete paradigms. In the case of other grammar concepts such as the object pronouns, many examples are given with noun versus pronoun objects. Irregular patterns are grouped together to make them appear more regular. For example, **ir, dar,** and **estar** are taught together in Chapter 4, as are **hacer, poner, traer, salir** and **venir** in Chapter 11. Whenever the contrast between English and Spanish poses problems for students in the learning process, a contrasting analysis between the two languages is made. Two examples of this are the reflexive construction in Level 1 and the subjunctive in Level 2. Certain structure points are taught more effectively in their entirety and others are more easily acquired if they are taught in segments. An example of the latter is the presentation of the preterite of irregular verbs in Chapters 13 and 14. In Level 1, Chapter 8, the object pronouns **me, te, nos** are presented immediately followed by **lo, la, los, las** in Chapter 9, and **le, les** in Chapter 10.

Learning Exercises

The exercises that follow the grammatical explanation are presented from simple to more complex. In the case of verbs with an irregular form, for example, emphasis is placed on the irregular form, since it is the one students will most often confuse or forget. In all cases, students are given one or more exercises that force them to use all forms at random. The first few exercises that follow the grammatical explanation are considered learning exercises because they assist the students in grasping and internalizing the new grammar concept. These learning exercises are immediately followed by test exercises—exercises that make students use all aspects of the grammatical point they have just learned. This format greatly assists teachers in meeting the needs of the various ability levels of students in their classes. Every effort has been made to make the grammatical explanations as succinct and as complete as possible. We have purposely avoided extremely technical grammatical or linguistic terminology that most students would not understand. Nevertheless, it is necessary to use certain basic grammatical terms.

Certain grammar exercises from the Student Textbook are recorded on the Audio Program. Whenever an exercise is recorded, it is noted with an appropriate icon in the Teacher's Edition.

The exercises in the Writing Activities Workbook also parallel the order of presentation in the Student Textbook. The Resource boxes and the Independent Practice topics in the Teacher's Edition indicate when certain exercises from the Writing Activities Workbook can be assigned.

Specific Techniques for Presenting Grammar

OPTION 1 Some teachers prefer the deductive approach to the teaching of grammar. When this is the preferred method, teachers can begin the **Estructura** section of the chapter by presenting the grammatical rule to students or by having them read the rule in their textbooks. After they have gone over the rule, have them read the examples in their textbooks or write the examples on the chalkboard. Then proceed with the exercises that follow the grammatical explanation.

OPTION 2 Other teachers prefer the inductive approach to the teaching of grammar. If this is the case, begin the **Estructura** section by writing the examples that accompany the rule on the chalkboard or by having students read them in their textbooks. Let us take, for example, the direct object pronouns **lo, la, los** and **las.** The examples the students have in their books are:

Ella compró el bañador.	**Ella lo compró.**
Compró los anteojos de sol.	**Los compró en la misma tienda.**
¿Compró loción bronceadora?	**Sí, la compró.**
¿Compró las toallas en la misma tienda?	**No, no las compró en la misma tienda.**
¿Invitaste a Juan a la fiesta?	**Sí, lo invité.**
¿Invitaste a Elena?	**Sí, la invité.**

Ella compró el regalo.	**Ella lo compró.**
Invitó a Juan.	**Lo invitó.**
No miré la fotografía.	**No la miré.**
No miré a Julia.	**No la miré.**

In order to teach this concept inductively, teachers can ask students to do or answer the following:

- Have students find the object of each sentence in the first column. Say it or underline the object if it is written on the board.
- Have students notice that the nouns disappeared in the sentences in the second column.
- Have students give (or underline) the word that represents the noun.
- Ask students what word replaced **el bañador, los anteojos de sol, loción bronceadora, etc.**
- Ask: What do we call a word that replaces a noun?
- Ask: What direct object replaces a masculine noun? A feminine noun?, etc.
- Have students look again. Ask: What word replaces **el bañador? ¿A Juan? ¿A Julia?**
- Ask: Can **lo** and **la** be used to replace either a person or a thing?
- Ask: Where do the direct object pronouns **lo, la, los, las** go, before or after the verb?

By answering these questions, students have induced, on their own, the rule from the examples. To further reinforce the rule, have students read the grammatical explanation and then continue with the grammar exercises that follow. Further suggestions for the inductive presentation of the grammar topics are given on the relevant page of this Teacher's Edition, at the point of use.

Specific Techniques for Teaching Structure Exercises

In the development of the ***Glencoe Spanish*** series, we have purposely provided a wide variety of exercises in the **Estructura** section so that students can proceed from one exercise to another without becoming bored. The types of exercises they will encounter are: short conversations, answering questions, conducting or taking part in an interview, making up questions, describing an illustration, filling in the blanks, multiple choice, completing a conversation, completing a narrative, etc. In going over the exercises with students, teachers may want to conduct the exercises themselves or they may want students to work in pairs. The **Estructura** exercises can be done in class before they are assigned for homework or they may be assigned before they are done. Many teachers may want to vary their approach.

All the **Práctica** and **Actividades comunicativas** in the Student Textbook can be done with books open. Many of the exercises such as question-answer, interview, and transformation can also be done with books closed.

Types of Exercises

HISTORIETA EXERCISES The answers to many question exercises build to tell a complete story. For this reason, these exercises are labeled **Historieta.** Once you have gone over the exercise by calling on several students (Student 1 answers items numbered 1, 2, 3; Student 2 answers items numbered 4, 5, 6 etc.), you can call on one student to give the answers to the entire exercise. Now the entire class has heard an uninterrupted story. Students can ask one another questions about the story, give an oral synopsis of the story in their own words, or write a short paragraph about the story.

ACTIVIDADES COMUNICATIVAS These activities assist students in working with the language on their own. All **Actividades comunicativas** are optional. In some cases, teachers may want the whole class to do the activities. In other cases, teachers can decide which activities the whole class will do. Another possibility is to break the class into groups and have each group work on a different activity.

PERSONAL QUESTIONS OR INTERVIEW EXERCISES Students can easily work in pairs or teachers can call a student moderator to the front of the room to ask questions of various class members. Two students can come to the front of the room and the exercise can be performed as follows—one student takes the role of the interviewer and the other takes the role of the interviewee.

COMPLETION OF A CONVERSATION See Chapter 11, **Práctica B,** page 329 as an example. After students complete the exercise, they can be given time either in class or as an outside assignment to prepare a skit for the class based on the conversation.

Conversación

Specific Techniques Teachers may wish to vary the presentation of the **Conversación** section from one chapter to another. In some chapters, the dialog can be presented thoroughly and in others it may be presented quickly as a reading exercise. Some possible options are:

- Have the class repeat the dialog after you twice. Then have students work in pairs and present the dialog to the class. The dialog does not have to be memorized. If students change it a bit, all the better.
- Have students read the dialog several times on their own. Then have them work in pairs and read the dialog as a skit. Try to encourage them to be animated and to use proper intonation. This is a very important aspect of the **Conversación** section of the chapter.
- Rather than read the dialog, students can work in pairs, having one make up as many questions as possible related to the topic of the dialog. The other students can answer his/her questions.
- Once students can complete the **Después de conversar** exercise(s) that accompany the dialog with relative ease, they know the dialog sufficiently well without having to memorize it.
- Students can tell or write a synopsis of the dialog.

Pronunciación (Level 1)

SPECIFIC TECHNIQUES Have students read on their own or go over with them the short explanation in the book concerning the particular sound that is being presented. For the more difficult sounds such as **ñ, ll, j, g, d, t,** etc., teachers may wish to demonstrate the tongue and lip positions. Have students repeat the words after you or the model speaker on the audio recording.

Lecturas culturales

SPECIFIC TECHNIQUES:

OPTION 1 Just as the presentation of the dialog can vary from one chapter to the next, the same is true of the **Lecturas culturales** readings. In some chapters, teachers may want students to go over the reading selection very thoroughly. In this case all or any combination of the following techniques can be used.

- Give students a brief synopsis of the reading selection in Spanish.
- Ask questions about the brief synopsis.

- Have students open their books and repeat several sentences after you or call on individuals to read.
- Ask questions about what was just read.
- Have students read the story at home and write the answers to the exercises that accompany the reading selection.
- Go over the **Después de leer** in class the next day.
- Call on a student to give a review of the reading in his/her own words. Guide students to make up an oral review. Ask five or six questions to review the salient points of the reading selection.
- After the oral review, the more able students can write a synopsis of the reading selection in their own words.

It should take less than one class period to present a given **Lecturas culturales** reading in the early chapters. Later, you may wish to spend two days on those selections you want students to know thoroughly.

OPTION 2 When teachers wish to present a reading selection less thoroughly, the following techniques may be used:

- Call on an individual to read a paragraph.
- Ask questions about the paragraph read.
- Assign the reading selection to be read at home. Have students write the answers to the **Después de leer** exercises that accompany the reading.
- Go over the **Después de leer** exercises the following day.

OPTION 3 With some reading selections, teachers may wish merely to assign them to be read at home and then go over the exercises the following day. This is possible since the only new material in the readings consists of a few new vocabulary items that are always footnoted.

Lecturas opcionales

The reading selections that are labeled **Lectura opcional** provide additional reading topics that are based on the general cultural theme of the chapter. You can omit any or all of these selections, or you may choose certain selections that you would like the whole class to read. The same suggestions given earlier can be followed. Teachers may also assign the optional reading selections to different groups. Students can read the selection outside of class and prepare a report for those students who did not read that particular selection. This activity is very beneficial for slower students. Although they may not read the selection, they learn the material by listening to what their peers say about it. The **Lecturas opcionales** can also be done by students on a voluntary basis for extra credit.

Conexiones

The purpose of the **Conexiones** is to offer readings from other areas of the school curriculum. These readings are optional. You may choose any of the following approaches:

OPTION 1: INDEPENDENT READING Have students read the selection and do the post-reading activities as homework, which you collect. This option is least intrusive on class time and requires a minimum of teacher involvement.

OPTION 2: HOMEWORK WITH IN-CLASS FOLLOWUP Assign the reading and post-reading activities as homework. Review and discuss the material in class the next day.

OPTION 3: INTENSIVE IN-CLASS ACTIVITY This option includes a pre-reading vocabulary presentation, in-class reading and discussion, assignment of the activities for homework, and a discussion of the assignment in class the following day.

Organization of the Teacher's Edition

One important component which adds to the series' flexible, "teacher-friendly" nature, is the Teacher's (Wraparound) Edition, of which this Teacher's Manual is a part. A complete method for the presentation of all the material in the Student Textbook is provided—basically, a complete set of lesson plans—as well as techniques for background-building, additional reinforcement of new language skills, creative and communicative recycling of material from previous chapters and a host of other alternatives from which to choose. This banquet of ideas has been developed and conveniently laid out in order to save valuable teacher preparation time and to aid you in designing the richest, most varied language experience possible for you and your students. A closer look at the kinds of support in the Teacher's Edition will help you decide which ones are right for your pace and style of teaching and for each of your classes.

The topics in the Teacher's Edition can be divided into two general categories:

1. **Core topics,** appearing in the left- and right-hand margins, are those which most directly correspond to the material in the accompanying two-page spread of the Student Textbook. Core topics consist of suggestions for presenting the corresponding material on the student page, as well as general notes (**¡OJO!**) to the teacher about the material being presented on the student page. In addition to core topics, enrichment topics are included in the side margins when space permits.
2. **Answers and enrichment topics** are found in the bottom margin of the Teacher's Edition. The enrichment topics offer a wide range of options aimed at getting students to practice and use the Spanish they are learning in diverse ways, individually and with their classmates, in the classroom and for homework. The enrichment topics also include tips to the teacher on clarifying and interconnecting elements in the Spanish language, Hispanic culture, geography and history—ideas that have proved useful to other teachers and which are offered for your consideration.

Description of Major Topics in the Teacher's Edition

CHAPTER OVERVIEW At the beginning of each chapter a brief description is given of the language functions which students will be able to perform by chapter's end. Mention is made of any closely associated functions presented in other chapters. This allows for effective articulation between chapters and serves as a guide for more successful teaching.

NATIONAL STANDARDS Due to the importance of standards in second language learning, we have signaled student pages where the National Standards apply most obviously. Of the five National Standards, the Communication standard is consistently identified early in each chapter, since communication in Spanish is the most fundamental objective throughout the ***Glencoe Spanish*** series. Examples of the other four National Standards—Cultures, Connections, Comparisons, and Communities—are cited as they are manifested on specific pages in the Student Textbook.

TEACHING VOCABULARY (STRUCTURE, CONVERSATION, PRONUNCIATION, READING)
Step-by-step suggestions for the presentation of the material in all of the major sections in each chapter—**Vocabulario, Estructura, Conversación, Lecturas culturales**—are presented in the left- and right-hand margins. These are suggestions on what to say, whether to have books open or closed, whether to perform tasks

individually, in pairs or in small groups, expand the material, reteach, and assign homework. These are indeed suggestions. You may wish to follow them as written or choose a more eclectic approach to suit time constraints, personal teaching style and class "chemistry." Please note, however, that the central vocabulary and grammar included in each chapter's **Vocabulario** and **Estructura** sections are intended to be taught in their entirety, since this material will appear in succeeding chapters.

Answers for all the **Práctica** and **Actividades comunicativas** in each chapter section are consistently located at the bottom of the page. Because individual student answers to the **Actividades comunicativas** will vary, they are usually not provided. However, whenever practical, model answers to the **Actividades comunicativas** are given, along with key words, expressions and structures that will likely be used in the answers.

BELL RINGER REVIEWS These short activities recycle vocabulary and structures from previous chapters and sections. They serve as effective warm-ups, urging students to begin thinking in Spanish, and helping them make the transition from their previous class to Spanish. Minimal direction is required to get the Bell Ringer Review activity started, so students can begin meaningful, independent work in Spanish as soon as the class hour begins, rather than wait for the teacher to finish administrative tasks, such as attendance, etc. Bell Ringer Reviews occur consistently throughout each chapter of Levels 1 and 2.

ABOUT THE SPANISH LANGUAGE Since Spanish is such a growing, living language, spoken in so many different places of the world by people of different cultures and classes, the usage and connotation of words can vary greatly. Under this topic, information is offered on the many differences that exist. The most important aspect of this topic is the presentation of regionalisms. In the student text itself, we present those words that are most universally understood. The many regional variants are then given under the "About the Spanish Language" topic.

VOCABULARY EXPANSION These notes provide the teacher handy access to vocabulary items which are thematically related to those presented in the Student Textbook. They are offered to enrich classroom conversations, allowing students more varied and meaningful responses when talking about themselves, their classmates or the topic in question. Note that none of these items, or for that matter any information in the Teacher's Edition, is included in the Chapter Quizzes, or in the Testing Program accompanying ***Glencoe Spanish***.

COGNATE RECOGNITION Since the lexical relationship between Spanish and English is so rich, these notes have been provided to help you take full advantage of the vocabulary building strategy of isolating them. The suggestions occur in the **Vocabulario** section of each chapter and are particularly frequent in Level I in order to train students from the very beginning in the valuable strategy of recognizing cognates. Various methods of pointing out cognates are used, involving all four language skills, and the activities frequently encourage students to personalize the new words by using them to talk about things and people they know. Pronunciation differences are stressed between the two languages. The teacher notes also call attention to false cognates when they occur in other chapter sections.

INFORMAL ASSESSMENT Ideas are offered for making quick checks on how well students are assimilating new material. These checks are done in a variety of ways and provide a means whereby both teacher and students can monitor daily progress. By using the "Informal Assessment" topic, you will be able to ascertain as you go along the areas in which students are having trouble, and adjust your pace accordingly or provide extra help for individuals, either by making use of other activities offered in the Teacher's Edition or devising your own. The assessment strategies are simple and designed to help you elicit from students the vocabulary word, grammatical structure, or other information you wish to check. Because they occur on the same page as the material to which they correspond you may want to come back to them again when it is time to prepare students for tests or quizzes.

RETEACHING These suggestions provide yet another approach to teaching a specific topic in the chapter. In the event some students were not successful in the initial presentation of the material, a reteaching activity offers an alternate strategy. At the same time, it provides successful students another chance to further consolidate their learning.

HISTORY CONNECTION Following these suggestions can be seen as a very effective springboard from the Spanish classroom into the history and social studies areas of the curriculum. Students are asked to focus their attention on the current world map, or historical ones, then they are invited to discuss the cultural, economic and political forces which shape the world with an eye on Hispanic influence. The notes will assist you in providing this type of information yourself or in creating projects in which students do their own research, perhaps with the aid of a history teacher. By making the history connection, students are encouraged to either import or export learning between the Spanish classroom and the history or social studies realms.

GEOGRAPHY CONNECTION These suggestions encourage students to use the maps provided in the Student Textbook as well as refer them to outside sources in order to familiarize them with the geography of Hispanic America and Spain. These optional activities are another way in which ***Glencoe Spanish*** crosses boundaries into other areas of the curriculum. Their use will instill in students the awareness that Spanish class is not just a study of language but an investigation into a powerful culture that has directly or indirectly affected the lives of millions of people all over the globe. By studying geography, students will be urged to trace the presence of Hispanic culture throughout Europe and the Americas. The notes also supply you the teacher with diverse bits of geographical and historical information which you may decide to pass on to your students.

Additional Topics in the Teacher's Edition

CHAPTER PROJECTS Specific suggestions are given at the start of each chapter for launching individual students or groups into a research project related to the chapter theme. Students are encouraged to gather information by using resources in school and public libraries, visiting local Hispanic institutions or interviewing Spanish-speaking people or other persons knowledgeable in the area of Hispanic culture whom they may know. In Chapter 3, for example, they are asked to compare their own educational system with one from a Spanish-speaking country. These projects may serve as another excellent means for students to make connections between their learning in the Spanish classroom and other areas of the curriculum.

LEARNING FROM PHOTOS AND REALIA Each chapter of ***Glencoe Spanish*** contains many colorful photographs and reproductions of authentic Spanish documents, filled with valuable cultural information. In order to help you take advantage of this rich source of learning, notes have been provided in the way of additional, interesting information to assist you in highlighting the special features of these up-to-date photos and realia. The questions that appear under this topic have been designed to enhance learners' reading and critical thinking skills.

TOTAL PHYSICAL RESPONSE (LEVEL 1) At least one Total Physical Response (TPR) activity is provided with each **Palabras** segment that makes up the **Vocabulario** section of the chapter. Students must focus their attention on commands spoken by the teacher (or classmates) and demonstrate their comprehension by performing the task as requested. This strategy has proven highly successful for concentrating on the listening skill and assimilating new vocabulary. Students are relieved momentarily of the need to speak—by which some may be intimidated—and yet challenged to show that they understand spoken Spanish. The physical nature of these activities is another of their benefits, providing a favorable change of pace for students, who must move about the room and perhaps handle some props in order to perform the tasks. In addition, Total Physical Response is in keeping with cooperative learning principles, since many of the commands require students to interact and assist each other in accomplishing them.

COOPERATIVE LEARNING Several cooperative learning activities are included in each chapter. These activities include guidelines both on the size of groups to be organized and on the tasks the groups will perform. They reflect two basic principles of cooperative learning: (a) that students work together, being responsible for their own learning, and (b) that they do so in an atmosphere of mutual respect and support, where the contributions of each peer are valued. For more information on this topic, please see the section in this Teacher's Manual entitled COOPERATIVE LEARNING.

ADDITIONAL PRACTICE There are a variety of additional practice activities to complement and follow up the presentation of material in the Student Textbook. Frequently the additional practice focuses on personalization of the new material and employs more than one language skill. Examples of "Additional Practice" activities include having students give oral or written descriptions of themselves or their classmates; asking students to conduct interviews around a topic and then report their findings to the class. The additional practice will equip you with an ample, organized repertoire from which to pick and choose should you need extra practice beyond that in the Student Textbook.

INDEPENDENT PRACTICE Many of the exercises in each chapter lend themselves well to assignment or reassignment as homework. In addition to providing extra practice, reassigning on paper exercises that were performed orally in class makes use of additional language skills and aids in informal assessment. The suggestions under the "Independent Practice" heading in the bottom margin of the Teacher's Edition will call your attention to exercises that are particularly suited to this. In addition to reassigning exercises in the Student Textbook as independent practice, additional sources are suggested from the various ancillary components, especially the Writing Activities Workbook.

CRITICAL THINKING ACTIVITY To broaden the scope of the foreign language classroom, suggestions are given that will encourage students to make inferences and organize their learning into a coherent "big picture" of today's world. These and other topics offered in the enrichment notes provide dynamic content areas to language skills and their growing knowledge of Hispanic culture. The guided discussions suggested, derived from the chapter themes, invite students to make connections between what they learn in the Spanish class and other areas of the curriculum.

DID YOU KNOW? This is a teacher resource topic where you will find additional details relevant to the chapter theme. You might wish to add the information given under this topic to your own knowledge and share it with your students to spur their interest in research projects, enliven class discussions and round out their awareness of Hispanic culture, history or geography.

FOR THE YOUNGER STUDENT Because Level 1 is designed for use at the junior high and intermediate level as well as the high school level, this topic pays special attention to the needs of younger students. Each chapter contains suggestions for meaningful language activities and tips to the teacher that cater to the physical and emotional needs of these youngsters. There are ideas for hands-on student projects, such as creating booklets or bringing and using their own props, as well as suggestions for devising games based on speed, using pantomime, show and tell, performing skits and more.

FOR THE NATIVE SPEAKER This feature has been provided with the realization that the modern Spanish-as-a-second-language class in the U.S. often includes students whose first language is Spanish. These students can provide the class, including the teacher, with valuable information about Hispanic culture as well as the living Spanish language they use in their everyday lives. "For the Native Speaker" invites them to share this information in an atmosphere of respect and trust. There are often lexical and structural variations in the parlance of native speakers from different areas of the Spanish-speaking world. "For the Native Speaker" points out, or asks the native speakers to point out, many of these variations. When such variations are caused by the interference of English—for example, the inclusion of the indefinite article with professions and nationalities **(Juan es un médico)**—the interference is pointed out, and native speakers are guided in practicing the corrected structure. Such correction is handled with sensitivity. The idea is more to inform native speakers that borrowed words and structures are not used in all situations, rather than to make value judgments as to which usage is right and which is wrong.

Additional Ancillary Components

All ancillary components are supplementary to the Student Textbook. Any or all parts of the following ancillaries can be used at the discretion of the teacher.

Writing Activities Workbook

The workbook offers additional writing practice to reinforce the vocabulary and grammatical structures in each chapter of the Student Textbook. The workbook exercises are presented in the same order as the material in the Student Textbook. The exercises are contextualized, often centering around line art illustrations. Workbook activities employ a variety of elicitation techniques, ranging from short answers, matching and answering personalized questions, to writing paragraphs and brief compositions. To encourage personalized writing, there is a special section in each chapter entitled **Mi autobiografía.** The workbook provides further reading skills development with the **Un poco más** section, where students are introduced to a number of authentic readings for the purpose of improving their reading comprehension and expanding their vocabulary. The **Un poco más** section also extends the cultural themes presented in the corresponding Student Textbook chapter. The Writing Activities Workbook includes a Self-Test after Chapters 4, 7, 11 and 14. The Writing Activities Workbook, Teacher's Edition provides the teacher with all the material in the student edition of the Writing Activities Workbook, plus the answers—whenever possible—to the activities.

Audio Program (Cassette or Compact Disc)

The recorded material for each chapter of ***Glencoe Spanish***, Levels 1 and 2, is divided into two parts—**Primera parte** and **Segunda parte.** The **Primera parte** consists of listening and speaking practice for the **Vocabulario (Palabras 1** and **Palabras 2)** and the **Estructura** sections of each chapter. There is also a dramatization of the **Conversación** dialog from the Student Textbook, and a pronunciation section. The **Segunda parte** contains a series of activities designed to further stretch students' receptive listening skills in more open-ended, real-life situations. Students indicate their understanding of brief conversations, advertisements, announcements, etc., by making the appropriate response on their activity sheets located in the Student Tape Manual.

Student Tape Manual

The Student Tape Manual contains the activity sheets which students will use when listening to the audio recordings. The Teacher's Edition of the Student Tape Manual contains the answers to the recorded activities, plus the complete tapescript of all recorded material.

Transparency Binder

There are six categories of overhead transparencies in the Transparency Binder accompanying ***Glencoe Spanish***, Level 1. Each category of transparencies has its special purpose. Following is a description:

- **VOCABULARY TRANSPARENCIES** These are full-color transparencies reproduced from each of the **Palabras** presentations in the Student Textbook. In converting the **Palabras** vocabulary pages to transparency format, all accompanying words and phrases on the **Palabras** pages have been deleted to allow for greater flexibility in their use. The Vocabulary Transparencies can be used for the initial presentation of new words and phrases in each chapter. They can also be used to review or reteach vocabulary during the course of teaching the chapter, or as a tool for giving quick vocabulary quizzes. With more able groups, teachers can show the Vocabulary Transparencies from previous chapters and have students make up original sentences using a particular word. These sentences can be given orally or in writing.

- **BELL RINGER REVIEW TRANSPARENCIES** These are identical to the Bell Ringer Reviews found in each chapter of the Teacher's Edition. For the teacher's convenience, they have been converted to transparency format.

- **PRONUNCIATION TRANSPARENCIES** In the **Pronunciación** section of each chapter of Level 1, an illustration has been included to visually cue the key phrase or sentence containing the sound(s) being taught, e.g., Chapter 3, page 85. Each of these illustrations has been converted to transparency format. These Pronunciation Transparencies may be used to present the key sound(s) for a given chapter, or for periodic pronunciation reviews where several transparencies can be shown to the class in rapid order. Some teachers may wish to convert these Pronunciation Transparencies to black and white paper visuals by making a photocopy of each one.

- **COMMUNICATION TRANSPARENCIES** For each chapter in Levels 1 and 2 of the series there is one original composite illustration which visually summarizes and reviews the vocabulary and grammar presented in that chapter. These transparencies may be used as cues for additional communicative practice in both oral and written formats. There are 14 Communication Transparencies for Level 1, and 14 for Level 2.

- **MAP TRANSPARENCIES** The full-color maps located at the back of the Student Textbook have been converted to transparency format for the teacher's convenience. These transparencies can be used when there is a reference to them in the Student Textbook, or when there is a history or geography map reference in the Teacher's Edition. The Map Transparencies can also be used for quiz purposes, or they may be photocopied in order to provide individual students with a black and white version for use with special projects.

- **FINE ART TRANSPARENCIES** These are full-color reproductions of works by well known Spanish-speaking artists including Velázquez, Goya, and others. Teachers may use these transparencies to reinforce specific culture topics in both the **Lecturas culturales** sections, as well as the **Conexiones** sections of the Student Textbook.

Video Program (Videocassette or Videodisc)

The Video Program for Level 1 consists of two 45-minute videos and an accompanying Video Activities Booklet. Together, they are designed to reinforce the vocabulary, structures, and cultural themes presented in the corresponding chapter of the Student Textbook. The ***Glencoe Spanish*** Video Program encourages students to be active listeners and viewers by asking them to respond to each video episode through a variety of previewing, viewing and post-viewing activities. Students are asked to view the video episode multiple times as they are led, via the activities in their Video Activities Booklet, to look and listen for more detailed information in the video episode they are viewing.

Video Activities Booklet

The Video Activities Booklet is the companion piece to the video episodes. For each chapter there are a series of pre-viewing, viewing, and post-viewing activities on Blackline Masters. These activities include specific instructions to students on what to watch and listen for as they view a given video episode. The Video Activities Booklet also contains Teacher Guidelines for using the video medium, culture notes, a chapter-by-chapter synopsis of each video episode, and a complete video script.

Expansion Activities

For each chapter of the Student Textbook, there are several activities on Blackline Masters which provide further opportunities for students to practice their communication skills in motivating, game-like formats. Some activities are designed for paired work, while others are whole class activities, and still others, such as the crossword puzzles, can be done individually. Any or all of these activities can be used in block scheduling configurations, or as independent practice.

Situation Cards

This is another component of ***Glencoe Spanish*** aimed at developing listening and speaking skills through guided conversation. For each chapter of the Student Textbook, there is a corresponding set of guided conversational situations printed on hand-held cards. Working in pairs, students use appropriate vocabulary and grammar from the chapter to converse on the suggested topics. Although they are designed primarily for use in paired activities, the Situation Cards may also be used in preparation for "the speaking portion of the Testing Program or for informal assessment." Additional uses for the Situation Cards are described in the Situation Cards package, along with specific instructions and tips for their duplication and incorporation into your teaching plans. The cards are in Blackline Master form for easy duplication.

Lesson Plans

Flexible lesson plans have been developed to meet a variety of class schedules. The various support materials are incorporated into these lesson plans at their most logical point of use, depending on the nature of the presentation material on a given day. For example, the Vocabulary Transparencies and the Audio (Cassette or Compact Disc) Program can be used most effectively when presenting the chapter vocabulary. On the other hand, the Chapter Quizzes are recommended for use one or two days after the initial presentation of vocabulary, or following the presentation of a specific grammar topic. Because student needs and teacher preferences vary, space has been provided on each lesson plan page for the teacher to write additional notes and comments in order to adjust the day's activities as required.

Block Scheduling Lesson Plans

The Block Scheduling Lesson Plans have been developed to show how the material may be distributed over the Level 1 Spanish course in a typical 90-day block scheduling framework. The plans may be used as presented or, they are flexible enough to allow for the teacher's own creative adaptation. There are no specific time limits placed on any teaching activity. Space has been provided on each day's lesson plan for the teacher to write additional and/or alternate teaching activities to those suggested. The plans include use of the numerous support materials comprising the Level 1 teaching package.

Internet Activities

The On-line Internet Activities serve as a dynamic, real-world connection between cultural themes introduced in ***Glencoe Spanish,*** and related topics available via the Internet. In addition to serving as an innovative avenue for cultural reinforcement, the activities encourage both students and teachers to view the Internet as an engaging and valuable tool for learning the Spanish language. Through this medium, students are able to further their knowledge of the Spanish language, as well as increase their opportunities for participating in Spanish-speaking communities around the world.

The Internet Activities include directions for the activities and instructions for downloading and printing the student response sheets and accompanying background teacher information, all on a chapter-by-chapter basis. Students will find the information required to complete each Internet activity by going to one or more of the Web sites whose addresses are provided on the Glencoe Foreign Language Home Page.

Chapter Quizzes with Answer Key

This component consists of short (5 to 10 minute) quizzes, designed to help both students and teachers evaluate quickly how well a specific vocabulary section or grammar topic has been mastered. For both Levels 1 and 2, there is a quiz for each **Palabras** section (vocabulary) and one quiz for each grammar topic in the **Estructura** section. The quizzes are on Blackline Masters. All answers are provided in an Answer Key at the end of the Chapter Quizzes booklet.

Maratón Mental Mindjogger Videoquiz

This multimedia program, available on either videocassette or videodisc, offers hours of informal assessment opportunities within a game show format. The videoquizzes combine oral questioning, written questions that appear on the screen, and engaging visuals. By incorporating these modes of communication, the shows are geared to both auditory and visual learners. This multi-faceted approach is helpful in facilitating group learning.

For each chapter of ***Glencoe Spanish,*** Levels 1 and 2, there is a videoquiz. There are three rounds to each videoquiz, with each round slightly more difficult than the previous one. Students can be organized into cooperative groups or teams. Each team should be supplied with a set of answer cards provided in the Mindjogger package. During each round, questions are asked by the game show hostess, and a time limit in which to answer each question is announced.

Assessment

TESTING PROGRAM WITH ANSWER KEY The Testing Program booklet consists of two types of Chapter Tests, both on Blackline Masters.

The first Chapter Test is discrete-point in nature, and uses evaluation techniques such as fill-in-the-blank, completion, short answers, true/false, matching, and multiple choice. Illustrations are frequently used as visual cues. The tests measure vocabulary, grammar and culture concepts via listening, speaking, reading, and writing formats. (As an option to the teacher, the Listening section of each Chapter Test has been recorded by native Spanish speakers.) For the teacher's convenience, the Chapter Tests have been designed so that different sections of the test can be measured on different days. For example, the Listening Test can be administered separately from the Reading, Writing and Speaking Tests. Likewise, the Speaking Test can be administered on a different day than the Reading and Writing Test, etc., All Chapter Tests can be administered upon the completion of each chapter of the Student Textbook. The Unit Tests can be administered upon the completion of each **Repaso** section of the Student Textbook, following Chapters 4, 7, 11, and 14.

The Blackline Master Testing Program booklet also contains Chapter Proficiency Tests. These measure students' mastery of each chapter's vocabulary and grammar on a more global, whole-language level.

COMPUTER TESTMAKER SOFTWARE The Computer Testmaker Software, available for Windows PC and Macintosh platforms, offers teachers the option of simply printing out ready-made chapter tests, or customizing a ready-made test by selecting certain items, and/or adding original test items. For more information, see the User's Guide accompanying the Testmaker Software.

PERFORMANCE ASSESSMENT In addition to the tests described earlier, the Performance Assessment tasks provide an alternate approach to measuring student learning, compared to the more traditional paper and pencil tests. The performance assessment tasks include teacher-student interviews, individual and small-group research tasks with follow-up presentations, and skits that students perform for the class. The Performance Assessment tasks can be administered after every unit of chapters in the textbook. They appear in conjunction with the **Repaso** following Chapters 4, 7, 11, and 14.

Spanish for Spanish Speakers: *Nosotros y nuestro mundo*

Each of the fourteen chapters takes into account the diversified background of these students—many of whom have a very strong command of the Spanish language and others who have a somewhat limited knowledge of the Spanish language. The textbook also attempts to take into account the specific problems facing the teacher of classes with native Spanish speakers. In some cases, the native-speaking students are placed in separate courses an in other cases, they are in classes with English-speaking students learning Spanish as a foreign language. For these reasons ***Nosotros y nuestro mundo*** can be used as a basal textbook in courses for native speakers, or it can be used as an adjunct to the ***Glencoe Spanish*** series in classes that have both native speakers of Spanish and English. In the latter case, it is presumed that the teacher will have less time with their students and a fair amount of the material will need to be acquired by students through independent study or cooperative group work.

Organization of *Nosotros y nuestro mundo*

Each chapter of the Spanish for Spanish speakers textbook is divided into the following sections:

Nuestro conocimiento académico
Nuestro idioma
Nuestra cultura
Nuestra literatura
Nuestra creatividad
Nuestras diversiones

Cooperative Learning

Cooperative learning provides a structured, natural environment for student communication that is both motivating and meaningful. When students develop friendly relationships in their cooperative groups and become accustomed to the multiple opportunities to hear and rehearse new communicative tasks, the filter that prevents many students from daring to risk a wrong answer when called upon to speak in front of a whole class can be minimzed. The goal of cooperative learning is to provide opportunities for learning in an environment where students contribute freely and responsibly to the success of the group. The key is to strike a balance between group goals and individual accountability. Group (team) members plan how to divide the activity among themselves, then each member of the group carries out his or her part of the assignment. Cooperative learning provides each student with a "safe," low-risk environment rather than a whole-class atmosphere. As you implement cooperative learning in your classroom, we urge you to take time to explain to students what will be expected of every group member—listening, participating, and respecting other opinions.

In the Teacher's Edition, cooperative learning activities have been written to accompany each chapter of the Student Textbook. These activities have been created to assist both the teacher who wants to include cooperative learning for the first time, and the experienced practitioner of cooperative learning.

Classroom Management: Implementing Cooperative Learning Activities

Many of the suggested cooperative learning activities are based on a four-member team structure in the classroom. Teams of four are recommended because there is a wide variety of possible interactions. At the same time the group is small enough that students can take turns quickly within the group. Pairs of students as teams may be too limited in terms of possible interactions, and trios frequently work out to be a pair with the third student left out. Teams of five may be unwieldy in that students begin to feel that no one will notice if they don't really participate.

If students sit in rows on a daily basis, desks can be pushed together to form teams of four. Teams of students who work together need to be balanced according to as many variables as possible: academic achievement in the course, personality, ethnicity, gender, attitude, etc. Teams that are as heterogeneous as possible will ensure that the class progresses quickly through the curriculum.

Following are descriptions of some of the most important cooperative learning structures, adapted from Spencer Kagan's Structural Approach to Cooperative Learning, as they apply to the content of ***Glencoe Spanish.***

ROUND-ROBIN Each member of the team answers in turn a question, or shares an idea with teammates. Responses should be brief so that students do not have to wait long for their turn.

Example from Level 1, Preliminary Lesson D, Days of the week:

> Teams recite the days of the week in a round-robin fashion. Different students begin additional rounds so that everyone ends up needing to know the names of all the days. Variations include starting the list with a different day or using a race format, i.e., teams recite the list three times in a row and raise their hands when they have finished.

ROUNDTABLE Each student in turn writes his or her contribution to the group activity on a piece of paper that is passed around the team. If the individual student responses are longer than one or two words, there can be four pieces of paper with each student contributing to each paper as it is passed around the team.

A TO Z ROUNDTABLE Using vocabulary from Level 1, Chapters 11 and 13, students take turns adding one word at a time to a list of words associated with plane or train travel in A to Z order. Students may help each other with what to write, and correct spelling. Encourage creativity when it comes to the few letters of the alphabet that don't begin a specific travel word from their chapter lists. Teams can compete in several ways: first to finish all 28 letters; longest word; shortest word; most creative response.

NUMBERED HEADS TOGETHER Numbered Heads Together is a structure for review and practice of high consensus information. There are four steps:

Step 1: Students number off in their teams from 1 to 4.

Step 2: The teacher asks a question and gives the teams some time to make sure that everyone on the team knows the answer.

Step 3: The teacher calls a number.

Step 4: The appropriate student from each team is responsible to report the group response.

Answers can be reported simultaneously, i.e., all students with the approrpiate number either stand by their seats and recite the answer together, or they go to the chalkboard and write the answer at the same time. Answers can also be reported sequentially. Call on the first student to raise his or her hand or have all the students with the appropriate number stand. Select one student to give the answer. If the other students agree, they sit down, if not they remain standing and offer a different response.

Example from Level 1, Chapter 2, Telling Time:

Step 1: Using a blank clockface on the overhead transparency, or the chalkboard, the teacher adjusts the hand on the clock.

Step 2: Students put their heads together and answer the question: **¿Qué hora es?**

Step 3: The teacher calls a number.

Step 4: The appropriate student from each team is responsible to report the group response.

Pantomimes

Give each team one card. Have each team decide together how to pantomime for the class the action identified on the card. Each team presents the pantomime for ten seconds while the rest of the teams watch without talking. Then each of the other teams tries to guess the phrase and writes down their choice on a piece of paper. (This is a good way to accommodate kinesthetic learning styles as well as vary classroom activities.)

Example from Level 1, Chapter 4 vocabulary. The teacher writes the following sentences on slips of paper and places them in an envelope:

1. **Hablan.**
2. **Hablan por teléfono.**
3. **Estudian en la biblioteca.**
4. **Escuchan discos.**
5. **Miran la televisión.**
6. **Preparan una merienda.**
7. **Toman un refresco.**
8. **Bailan.**
9. **Cantan.**
10. **Llegan a una fiesta.**

Each team will draw one slip of paper from the envelope and decide together how to pantomime the action for the class. As one team pantomimes their action for 30 seconds, the other teams are silent. Then the students within each team discuss among themselves what sentence was acted out for them. When they have decided on the sentence, each team sends one person to write it on the chalkboard.

INSIDE/OUTSIDE CIRCLE Students form two concentric circles of equal number by counting off 1-2, 1-2 in their teams. The ones form a circle shoulder to shoulder and facing out. The twos form a circle outside the ones to make pairs. With an odd number of students, there can be one threesome. Students take turns sharing information, quizzing each other, or taking parts of a dialog. After students finish with their first partners, rotate the inside circle to the left so that the students repeat the process with new partners. For following rounds alternate rotating inside and outside circles so that students get to repeat the identified tasks, but with new partners. This is an excellent way to structure 100% student participation combined with extensive practice of communication tasks.

Other suggested activities are similarly easy to follow and to implement in the classroom. Student enthusiasm for cooperative learning activities will reward the enterprising teacher. Teachers who are new to these concepts may want to refer to Dr. Spencer Kagan's book Cooperative Learning, published by Resources for Teachers, Inc., Paseo Espada, Suite 622, San Juan Capistrano, CA 92675

Student Portfolios

The use of student portfolios to represent long-term individual accomplishments in learning Spanish offers several benefits. With portfolios, students can keep written records of their best work and thereby document their own progress as learners. For teachers, portfolios enable us to include our students in our evaluation and measurement process. For example, the content of any student's portfolio may offer an alternative to the standardized test as a way of measuring student writing achievement. Assessing the contents of a student's portfolio can be an option to testing the writing skill via the traditional writing section on the chapter or unit test.

There are as many kinds of portfolios as there are teachers working with them. Perhaps the most convenient as well as permanent portfolio consists of a three-ring binder which each student will add to over the school year and in which the student will place his or her best written work. In the ***Glencoe Spanish*** series, selections for the portfolio may come from the Writing Activities Workbook; the more open-ended activities in the Student Tape Manual and the Video Activities Booklet, as well as from written assignments in the Student Textbook, including the **Actividades escritas** section. The teacher is encouraged to refer actively to student's portfolios so that they are regarded as more than just a storage device. For example, over the course of the school year, the student may be asked to go back to earlier entries in his or her portfolio in order to revise certain assignments, or to develop an assignment further by writing in a new tense, e.g., the preterit. In this way the student can appreciate the amount of learning that has occurred over several months time.

Portfolios offer students a multidimensional look at themselves. A "best" paper might be the one with the least errors or one in which the student reached and synthesized a new idea, or went beyond the teacher's assignment. The Student Portfolio topic is included in each chapter of the Teacher's Edition as a reminder that this is yet another approach the teacher may wish to use in the Spanish classroom.

Glencoe Spanish 1 CD-ROM Interactive Textbook

The *Glencoe Spanish* 1 CD-ROM Interactive Textbook is a complete curriculum and instructional system for Spanish students. The four-disc CD-ROM program contains all elements of the Student Textbook with enhancements that include video, animation, audio, interactive exercises, and games. Although especially suited for individual or small-group use, the Interactive Textbook can be connected to a large monitor or LCD panel for whole class instruction. With this flexible, interactive system, you can introduce, reinforce, or remediate any part of the *Glencoe Spanish* Level 1 curriculum at any time.

The CD-ROM program has four major components—Contents, Games, References and Portfolio.

The Contents Menu

The following selections can be found in the Contents menu.

INTRODUCCIÓN Video footage introduces the cultural theme of the chapter. Chapter objectives are then viewed on-screen.

VOCABULARIO Vocabulary is introduced in thematic contexts. New words are introduced and communication activities based on real-life situations are presented.

ESTRUCTURA Students are given explanations of Spanish structures. They then practice through contextualized exercises.

CONVERSACIÓN Interactive video enhances this feature comprised of real-life dialogs. Students may listen to and watch a conversation and then choose to participate as a character as they record their part of the dialog.

LECTURAS CULTURALES These readings give students insight into Hispanic culture. They are also able to listen to these readings. The similarities and differences between Hispanic and U.S. cultures are emphasized.

CONEXIONES These readings address other areas of the school curriculum, thereby reinforcing knowledge of other disciplines through the study of Spanish.

CULMINACIÓN End-of-chapter activities require students to integrate the concepts they have learned. Special **Actividades interactivas,** located here as well as in earlier sections of the chapter, allow students to practice listening and speaking skills in simulated conversations. An on-screen character asks a series of questions and the user responds by recording his or her answers.

The **Culminación** section includes a **Vocabulario** review that is linked to the glossary (Reference Menu). By clicking on the **Expansión cultural** photo, students can listen to an expanded version of the photo caption. The **Culminación** section also provides a link to the Glencoe Foreign Language Web site.

REPASO In this section, students participate in a variety of review activities.

LITERATURA These short selections from Spanish literature provide rewarding reading opportunities.

VISTAS The photos featured in this section were prepared by the National Geographic Society. The Vistas in Level 1 focus on Mexico, Spain, Puerto Rico, and Ecuador. Those in Level 2 showcase Peru, Chile, Costa Rica, and Guatemala.

The Games Menu: *Juegos de repaso*

There are two game formats: *¿Cuánto sabes?* and *¡El tucán pregunta!*. The games are designed as Self-Tests. The content lets the user review vocabulary and structure concepts for a particular chapter in a motivating and enjoyable format.

The References Menu

The References menu contains the following selections:

MAPS Students can access the maps of the Spanish-speaking world: Spain, Mexico and Central America, and South America.

VERBS The verb charts reproduce all of the verbs highlighted at the back of the Student Textbook.

GLOSSARY Students can search this interactive Spanish/English glossary and hear the words pronounced in Spanish.

The Portfolio Menu

The Portfolio menu reinforces the writing skill. There are a variety of writing templates from which to choose, in order to create dialogs, write postcards and letters, and short essays. The writing samples can be saved to the hard drive. These writings tasks can also be recorded and played back.

For more information, see the User's Guide accompanying the ***Glencoe Spanish*** 1 CD-ROM Interactive Textbook.

Suggestions for Correcting Homework

Correcting homework, or any tasks students have done on an independent basis, should be a positive learning experience rather than mechanical busywork. Following are some suggestions for correcting homework. These ideas may be adapted as the teacher sees fit.

1. Put the answers on an overhead transparency. Have students correct their own answers.
2. Ask one or more of your better students to write their homework answers on the chalkboard at the beginning of the class hour. While the answers are being put on the chalkboard, the teacher involves the rest of the class in a non-related activity. At some point in the class hour, take a few minutes to go over the homework answers that have been written on the board, asking student to check their own work. You may then wish to have students hand in their homework so that they know this independent work is important.
3. Go over the homework assignment quickly in class. Write the key word(s) for each answer on the chalkboard so students can see the correct answer.
4. When there is no correct answer, i.e., "Answers will vary," give one or two of the most likely answers. Don't allow students to inquire about all other possibilities however.
5. Have all students hand in their homework. After class, correct every other (every third, fourth, fifth, etc.) homework paper. Over several days, you will have checked every student's homework at least once.
6. Compile a list of the most common student errors. Then create a worksheet that explains the underlying problem areas, providing additional practice in those areas.

Pacing

¡BUEN VIAJE! **Level 1** has been developed so that it may be completed in one school year. However, it is up to the individual teacher to decide how many chapters will be covered. Although completion of the textbook by the end of the year is recommended, it is not necessary. The final two chapters of ***¡Buen viaje!*** **Level 1** (Chapters 13 and 14) are replicated as the first two chapters of ***¡Buen viaje!*** Level 2. In addition, the important structures of Level 1 Chapters 1 through 12 are reviewed in a new context at the beginning of Level 2 .

The establishment of lesson plans helps the teacher visualize how a chapter can be presented. By emphasizing certain aspects of the program and de-emphasizing others, the teacher can change the focus and the approach of a chapter to meet students' needs and to suit his or her own teaching style and techniques. They include some of the suggestions and techniques that have been described earlier in this Teacher's Manual. For detailed, day by day lesson plans, see either the Lesson Plans booklet, or the Block Scheduling Lesson Plans booklet.

Glencoe Spanish 1

¡Buen viaje!

About the Front Cover
Plaza Mayor, Madrid This is one of the largest squares in Europe. It was designed by the architect of Felipe II, but construction on it was completed in 1620, during the reign of Fernando III. The Plaza Mayor is closed to traffic, making it a pleasant spot to enjoy food and beverages at one of the many cafés.

About the Back Cover
(top) Montefrío (Andalucía), España; *(middle)* Ruinas de Tulúm, Yucatán, México; *(bottom)* Ballet Folklórico de México

The colorful and inviting **Vistas** featured in this textbook were designed and developed by the National Geographic Society's Educational Division. Their purpose is to give greater insight into the people and places found in the Spanish-speaking countries listed below.

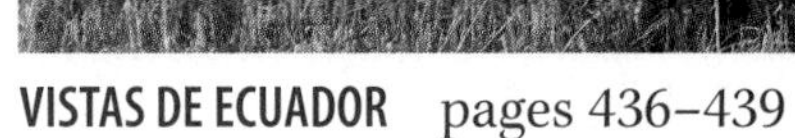

Glencoe Spanish 1

¡Buen viaje!

CONRAD J. SCHMITT

PROTASE E. WOODFORD

New York, New York Columbus, Ohio Woodland Hills, California Peoria, Illinois

The National Geographic Society

The **National Geographic Society**, founded in 1888 for the increase and diffusion of geographic knowledge, is the world's largest nonprofit scientific and educational organization. Since its earliest days, the Society has used sophisticated communication technologies and rich historical and archival resources to convey knowledge to a worldwide membership. The Education Division supports the Society's mission by developing innovative educational programs—ranging from traditional print materials to multimedia programs including CD-ROMs, videodiscs, and software.

Meet our Authors

Conrad J. Schmitt

Conrad J. Schmitt received his B.A. degree magna cum laude from Montclair State College, Upper Montclair, NJ. He received his M.A. from Middlebury College, Middlebury VT. He did additional graduate work at Seton Hall University and New York University. Mr. Schmitt has taught Spanish and French at the elementary, junior, and senior high school levels. In addition, he has travelled extensively throughout Spain, Central and South America, and the Caribbean.

Protase E Woodford

Protase "Woody" Woodford has taught Spanish at all levels from elementary through graduate school. At Educational Testing Service in Princeton, NJ, he was Director of Test Development, Director of Language Programs, Director of International Testing Programs and Director of the Puerto Rico Office. He has served as a consultant to the United Nations Secretariat, UNESCO, the Organization of American States, the U.S. Office of Education, and many ministries of education in Asia, Latin America, and the Middle East.

Glencoe/McGraw-Hill

A Division of The ***McGraw·Hill*** *Companies*

Send all inquiries to:
Glencoe/McGraw-Hill
21600 Oxnard Street, Suite 500
Woodland Hills, CA 91367

ISBN: 0-02-641219-5 (Student Edition)
ISBN: 0-02-641221-7 (Teacher's Wraparound Edition)

Printed in the United States of America.

2 3 4 5 6 7 8 9 10 003 08 07 06 05 04 03 02 01 00 99

Contenido

Bienvenidos

CAPÍTULO 1
Un amigo o una amiga

CAPÍTULO 2
Alumnos y cursos

CAPÍTULO 3
Las compras para la escuela

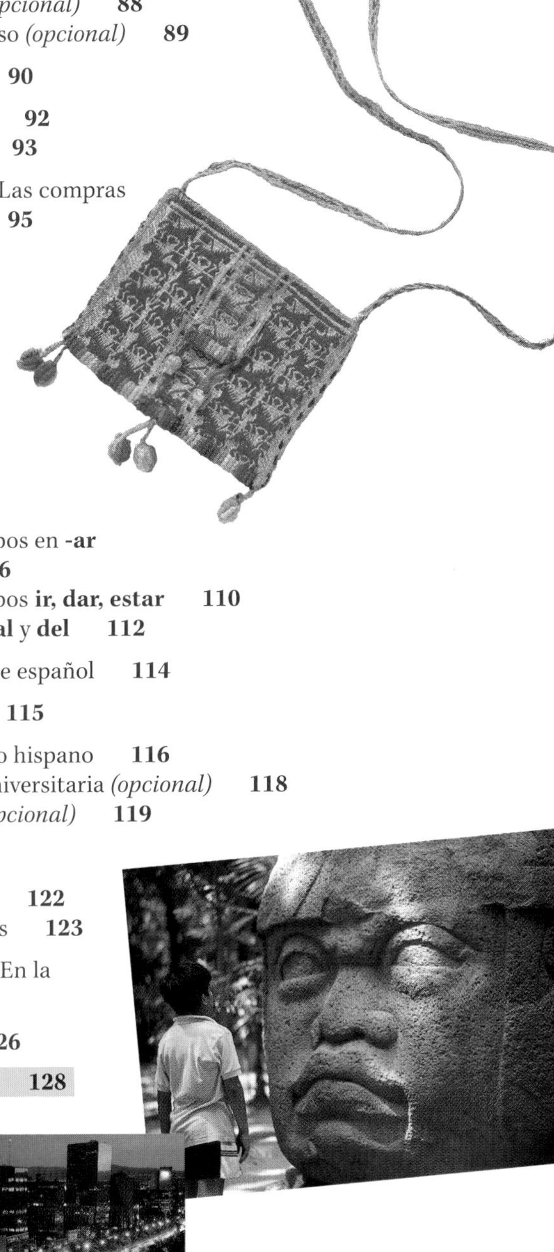

CAPÍTULO 4

En la escuela

CAPÍTULO 5
En el café

CAPÍTULO 6
La familia y su casa

CAPÍTULO 7
Deportes de equipo

CAPÍTULO 8
La salud y el médico

CAPÍTULO 9
El verano y el invierno

CAPÍTULO 10
Diversiones culturales

CAPÍTULO 11
Un viaje en avión

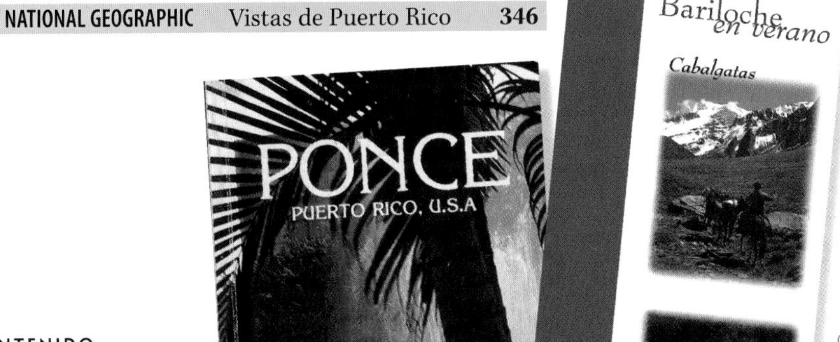

CAPÍTULO 12
Una gira

CAPÍTULO 13
Un viaje en tren

CAPÍTULO *14*

En el restaurante

Literatura

Apéndices

RESOURCES

- Vocabulary Transparencies BV-1, BV-2
- CD-ROM, Disc 1, pages 1–11

OVERVIEW

In the **Bienvenidos** section, students will begin their study by communicating immediately in Spanish. In this preliminary section they will learn to greet one another, take leave of one another, use some expressions of courtesy, and give the date and season.

National Standards

Communication

In this preliminary section students will communicate in spoken Spanish on the following topics:

- saying hello
- saying good-bye
- being polite
- dates and seasons

Students will obtain and provide information and engage in short conversations dealing with these introductory topics and situations.

¡OJO! In the short lessons in this preliminary section, students only learn expressions that do not require any grammatical or structural manipulation. For example, **¿Qué tal?** is presented rather than **¿Cómo estás?** and **¿Cómo está Ud.?**

Bienvenidos

BIENVENIDOS

Spotlight On Culture

Artefacto The handmade ceramic jar is from Nicaragua.
Fotografía The students in this photo are arriving at a house in Cádiz, Spain.

OVERVIEW

In this short lesson, which should take less than one class period, students will learn to greet their peers and older people.

Greeting people

A. Have students repeat **¡Hola!**
B. Use a gesture to convey **¿Qué tal?** (Rubbing the stomach will do.)
C. Smile as you say and have class repeat **Bien, gracias.**
D. Point directly to a student as you say and have them repeat **¿Y tú?**
E. Have students repeat the entire mini-conversation after you with books closed. You may also wish to use Structure Transparency BV-1 for this activity.
F. Then have students open their books and read the conversation aloud in pairs.

Actividades comunicativas

A and **B** Students can move around the room or stay at their desks as they do these activities.

B When doing **Actividad B,** have students change partners after each conversation so that each practices three or four conversations.

PRELIMINAR A

Saludos

Greeting people

Actividades comunicativas

A **¡Hola!** Get up from your desk. Walk around the classroom. Say hello to each classmate you meet.

B **¿Qué tal?** Work with a classmate. Greet one another and find out how things are going.

Puerto Vallarta, México

ANSWERS

Actividades comunicativas

A Students will either say **¡Hola!**, or **¡Hola! ¿Qué tal?**

B Students will use the greetings presented in the speech bubbles on this page.

Greeting people throughout the day

1. Some greetings are more formal than **Hola.** When you greet an older person, you may use one of the following expressions.

Buenos días, señora. **Buenas tardes, señorita.** **Buenas noches, señor.**

2. The titles **señor, señora,** and **señorita** are often used without the last name of the person.

Buenos días, señor.
Buenas tardes, señora.

Actividades comunicativas

A **Buenos días** Draw some figures on the board. Some will represent friends your own age and others will represent older people. Greet each of the figures on the board properly.

B **Saludos** Look at these photographs of young people in Spain and Mexico. As they greet one another, they do some things that are different from what we do when we greet each other. What do you notice in the photographs?

ANSWERS

Actividades comunicativas

A Students will use the appropriate greetings taught on page 3.

B Women typically give each other a light kiss on the cheek when greeting one another. Men frequently shake hands, then give each other **un abrazo,** *a bearhug.*

Greeting people throughout the day

A. Have students repeat each greeting. You may also wish to write an appropriate time of day on the board. Students do not have to give the time.

B. Explain that the use of the title without a name is common when we don't know the name of the person. We can use the title with a last name when we know the person: **Buenos días, Señora Romero.**

National Standards

Comparisons
Indicate to students how the information above concerning titles is not the same when speaking English. In English, *Hello, Mr.* or *Hello, Mrs.* would not be said. The title would not be used without the person's name.

Learning From Photos

El besito Have students look at the people in the photo giving each other the **besito,** which is exchanged both when greeting and taking leave of someone. Note that the **besito** is merely touching cheek to cheek.

Dar la mano Also have students look at the people shaking hands in these photos. The handshake is much more common in the Spanish-speaking countries, even among young people, than it is in the U.S.

El abrazo Have students look at the lower right-hand photo. Two men who know one another will tend to give one another a "bear hug" with a slap on the back.

¡OJO! It is suggested that you present these preliminary lessons for oral work only. Writing begins in Chapter 1.

BIENVENIDOS
Preliminar B

OVERVIEW

In this lesson students will learn farewell expressions. **Preliminar A** and **B** together should take about one classroom period.

Saying good-bye

A. Have students look at the photo as they repeat the expressions for leave-taking.

B. Have them read Steps 1, 2, 3 aloud or read them to the students. Have the class repeat each word or expression in unison.

C. You may wish to use Structure Transparency BV-1 to review the expressions.

Students can circulate around the room as they do these activities.

PRELIMINAR B

Saying good-bye

1. The usual expression to use when saying good-bye to someone is **Adiós.**
2. If you plan to see the person again soon, you can say **¡Hasta pronto!** or **¡Hasta luego!** If you plan to see the person the next day, you can say **¡Hasta mañana!**
3. An informal expression you often hear, particularly in Spain and in Argentina is **¡Chao!**

Actividades comunicativas

A **¡Chao!** Go over to a classmate and say good-bye to him or her.

B **¡Hasta luego!** Work with a classmate. Say **Chao** to one another and let each other know that you will be getting together again soon.

C **¡Adiós!** Say good-bye to your Spanish teacher. Then say good-bye to a friend. Use a different expression with each person.

ANSWERS

Actividades comunicativas

A Students will either say **Adiós** or **Chao** (followed by the person's name) or **¡Hasta luego!**

B Students will say **Chao,** followed by either **¡Hasta luego!**, **¡Hasta pronto!**, or **¡Hasta mañana!**

C Students will use two of the expressions taught on page 4—one for the Spanish teacher, another for their friend.

Conversando más

—¡Hola, Julio!
—¡Hola, Verónica! ¿Qué tal?
—Bien. ¿Y tú?
—Muy bien, gracias.

—Chao, Julio.
—Chao, Verónica. ¡Hasta luego!

Actividad comunicativa

A **¡Hola, amigo(a)!** Work with a classmate. Have a conversation in Spanish. Say as much as you can to one another.

Salamanca, España

Conversando más

A. This conversation recombines the greetings and farewells.

B. Have pairs of students present the conversation to the class. They can read it, if necessary, but many will probably be able to do it on their own. If they make any changes that make sense, that's fine.

C. Encourage students to use as much expression and as many gestures as possible when presenting the conversation.

GEOGRAPHY CONNECTION

Salamanca, España This city is situated on the banks of the río Tormes about 205 kilometers northwest of Madrid. The Plaza Mayor, shown here, is one of the most elegant squares in Spain. Salamanca remains one of the richest Spanish cities architecturally and is especially known for its buildings dating from the Spanish Renaissance.

HISTORY CONNECTION

Salamanca, España Salamanca was an important settlement even in Iberian times. The later importance of the town was due mainly to its famous university, which grew out of a college founded by Alfonso IV in about 1220. Isabel la Católica was a great supporter of the university and she had it rebuilt during her reign. The university today is once again one of the most prestigious in Europe.

ANSWERS

Actividad comunicativa

A Encourage students to use as many of the expressions for saying hello and goodbye as they have learned to date.

OVERVIEW

In this lesson students will learn to order a few simple food items. They will also learn the polite expressions one needs to know when dealing with people.

Ordering food politely

A. The expressions in this conversation should be very easy to present since most students are probably already familiar with them, with the exception of **No hay de qué**.

B. Have students read the information about *You're welcome* and repeat the expressions aloud several times.

C. Now have students do the **Actividades comunicativas.**

PRELIMINAR C

La cortesía

Ordering food politely

¡Hola!
Una Coca-Cola, por favor.

No hay de qué.
Gracias.

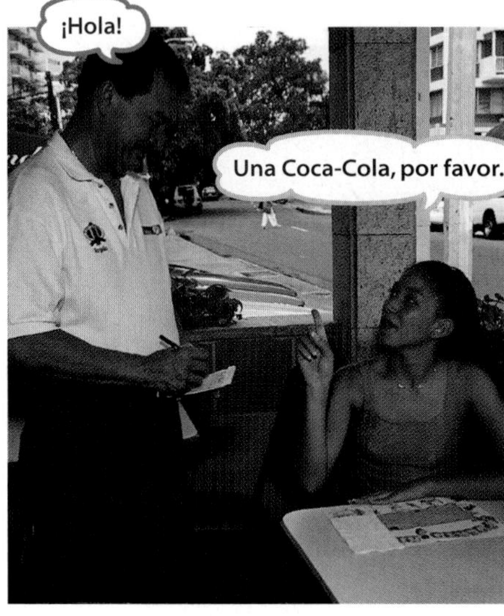

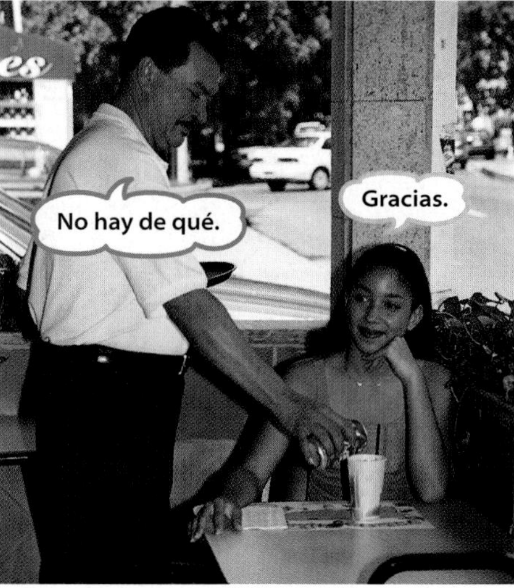

There are several ways to express "you're welcome":

No hay de qué.
De nada.
Por nada.

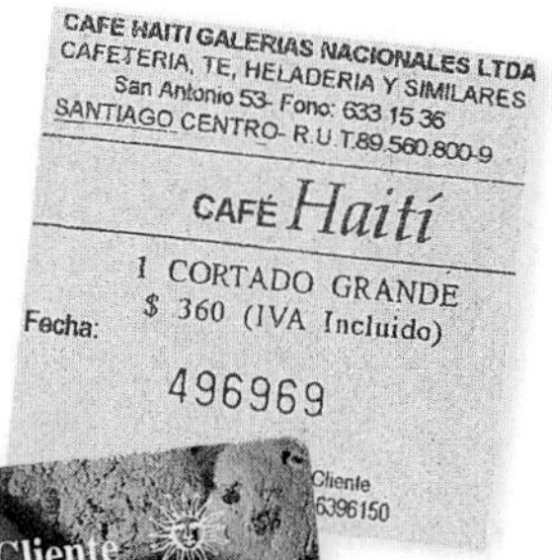

CAFE HAITI GALERIAS NACIONALES LTDA
CAFETERIA, TE, HELADERIA Y SIMILARES
San Antonio 53- Fono: 633 15 36
SANTIAGO CENTRO- R.U.T.89.560.800-9
CAFÉ Haití
1 CORTADO GRANDE
$ 360 (IVA Incluido)
Fecha:
496969
Cliente
6396150

Actividades comunicativas

A **La cortesía** With a classmate, practice reading the conversation. Be as animated and polite as you can.

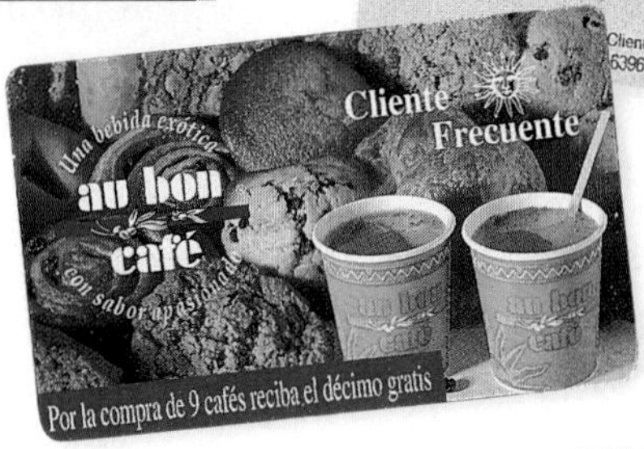

Una bebida exótica
au bon café
con sabor apasionado
Cliente Frecuente
Por la compra de 9 cafés reciba el décimo gratis

B **Una Coca-Cola, por favor.** You are at a café in Manzanillo, Mexico. Order the following things from the waiter or waitress (your partner). Be polite when you order.

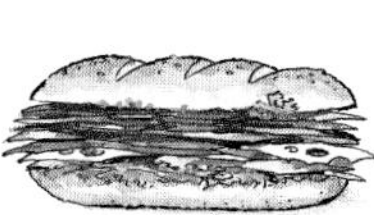

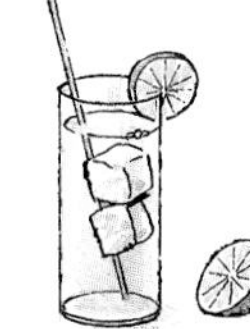

1. un sándwich **2.** una Coca-Cola **3.** una limonada

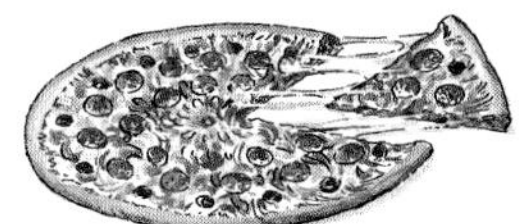

4. un café **5.** una pizza

C **Tacos, enchiladas, tamales** You are in a Mexican restaurant. Order the following foods from the waiter or waitress (your partner). Be polite to each other.

1. un taco **2.** una enchilada **3.** un tamal

Guanajuato, México

BIENVENIDOS
Preliminar C

Did You Know?

La cocina mexicana **Un taco** is a hard or soft tortilla that has been fried, folded, and stuffed with chicken, shredded beef, beans and/or cheese. **Una enchilada** is a soft tortilla that is rolled and stuffed with the same ingredients as a taco, and then baked. **Un tamal** is a tortilla made of corn meal. It is stuffed with some type of meat, wrapped in a leaf, and steamed.

Geography Connection

Guanajuato, México
Guanajuato was once an important silver mining city. It is a stunning city with beautiful colonial architecture and lovely, narrow cobblestoned streets. Guanajuato also has a very good university.

ANSWERS

Actividades comunicativas

B and C Answers will vary, but students should follow the model conversation on page 6 when doing these activities.

BIENVENIDOS

Preliminar D

OVERVIEW

In this lesson students learn the days of the week, the months, the seasons, and the numbers from 1 to 30. These topics will be reinforced and recycled in later chapters.

Telling the days of the week and the months

A. Have students repeat the days of the week and months of the year.

B. Have them give different days of the week and months at random rather than in a fixed order. Many students know the days of the week when they recite them in a row, but don't know the difference between **martes** and **jueves**, for example. Having them give the days of the week in other than a set order helps avoid this problem.

C. Although we will concern ourselves with writing starting in Chapter 1, you may want to point out to students that days and months are not capitalized in Spanish.

PRELIMINAR **D**

La fecha

Telling the days of the week

lunes	martes	miércoles	jueves	viernes	sábado	domingo
1	2	3	4	5	6	7
8	9	10	11	12	13	14

To find out and give the day of the week, you say:

—¿Qué día es hoy?
—Hoy es lunes.

Actividad comunicativa

A **¿Qué día es?** Answer the following questions in Spanish.

1. ¿Qué día es hoy?
2. ¿Qué día es mañana?
3. ¿Cuáles son los días del fin de semana o *weekend?*

Telling the months

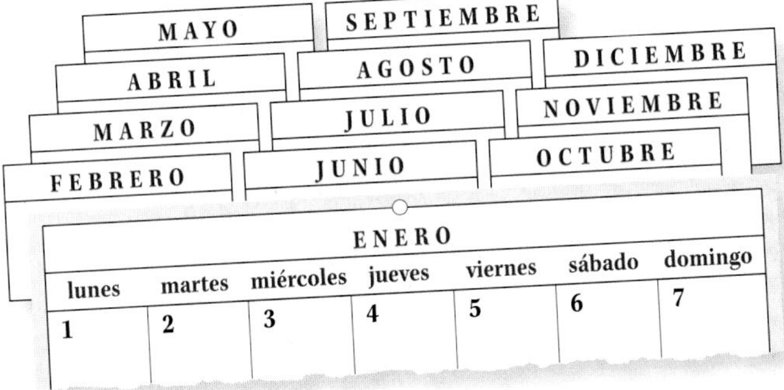

ANSWERS

Actividad comunicativa

A 1. Hoy es ___.
2. Mañana es ___.
3. Sábado y domingo son los días del fin de semana.

Finding out and giving the date

NOTA

1	uno	11	once	21	veintiuno
2	dos	12	doce	22	veintidós
3	tres	13	trece	23	veintitrés
4	cuatro	14	catorce	24	veinticuatro
5	cinco	15	quince	25	veinticinco
6	seis	16	dieciséis	26	veintiséis
7	siete	17	diecisiete	27	veintisiete
8	ocho	18	dieciocho	28	veintiocho
9	nueve	19	diecinueve	29	veintinueve
10	diez	20	veinte	30	treinta

Primero is used for the first day of the month. For other days you use: **dos, tres, cuatro,** etc.

Avenida 9 de Julio, Argentina

Celebración del Cinco de Mayo

BIENVENIDOS
Preliminar D

Finding out and giving the date

In this lesson we have presented the numbers from 1 to 30 so students can say the date. At this point, students should not be expected to know these numbers perfectly. They will be reintroduced in Chapters 1, 2, and 3. It is suggested that you not make students write the numbers.

Geography Connection

Avenida 9 de Julio, Argentina
This avenue in Buenos Aires is 425 feet across. **Los porteños,** residents of Buenos Aires, claim it is the world's widest street. It is also 26 blocks long. It is an ideal street for strolling and people-watching from one of the many **confiterías**—Argentine tearooms or cafés. The obelisk reminds some of the Washington Monument. It marks the intersection of **Avenida 9 de Julio** and **Corrientes**, a main thoroughfare in Buenos Aires.

History Connection

Celebración del Cinco de Mayo
Many people erroneously think that **el Cinco de Mayo** is Mexican Independence Day but it is not. **El Cinco de Mayo** marks the anniversary of a French defeat by Mexican troops in Puebla in 1862. **El día de la Independencia** is September 15–16.

Telling the seasons

A. Have students look at Transparency BV-2 as they repeat the name of each season.

B. Then have them open their books and read for additional reinforcement.

Telling the seasons

Actividades comunicativas

A ¿Cuántos? Answer the following questions in Spanish.

1. ¿Cuántos días hay en una semana, siete o cuatro?
2. ¿Cuántos meses hay en un año, siete o doce?
3. ¿Cuántas estaciones hay en un año, cuatro o doce?

B ¿En qué mes? Each of you will stand up in class and give your birthday **(cumpleaños)** in Spanish. Listen carefully and keep a record of how many classmates were born in the same month. Then tell in Spanish in which month the greatest number of students in the class were born. In which month were the fewest born?

C La estación, por favor Tell in which season the following months are. Answer in Spanish.

1. ¿En qué estación es mayo?
2. ¿En qué estación es enero?
3. ¿En qué estación es julio?
4. ¿En qué estación es octubre?

ANSWERS

Actividades comunicativas

A **1. Hay siete días en una semana.**
2. Hay doce meses en un año.
3. Hay cuatro estaciones en un año.

B Answers will vary. Students will answer with the day and the month. For example: **el 4 de noviembre.**

C **1. Mayo es en la primavera.**
2. Enero es en el invierno
3. Julio es en el verano.
4. Octubre es en el otoño.

Vocabulario

GREETING PEOPLE

¡Hola!	Buenas noches.
Buenos días.	¿Qué tal?
Buenas tardes.	Muy bien.

IDENTIFYING TITLES

señor
señora
señorita

SAYING GOOD-BYE

¡Adiós!	¡Hasta pronto!
¡Chao!	¡Hasta mañana!
¡Hasta luego!	

BEING COURTEOUS

Por favor.	De (Por) nada.
Gracias.	No hay de qué.

IDENTIFYING THE DAYS OF THE WEEK

lunes	sábado
martes	domingo
miércoles	hoy
jueves	mañana
viernes	el fin de semana

IDENTIFYING THE MONTHS OF THE YEAR

enero	julio
febrero	agosto
marzo	septiembre
abril	octubre
mayo	noviembre
junio	diciembre

IDENTIFYING THE SEASONS

la primavera	el otoño
el verano	el invierno

OTHER USEFUL EXPRESSIONS

¿Qué día es hoy?
¿Cuál es la fecha?

VOCABULARY REVIEW

This vocabulary list provides both teacher and students with a reference list of the words and expressions presented in these preliminary lessons.

Chapter 1 Overview

SCOPE AND SEQUENCE pages 12–39

TOPICS	FUNCTIONS	STRUCTURE	CULTURE
◆ Describing people and places ◆ Nationalities ◆ Numbers: 0–30	◆ How to ask who someone is ◆ How to state where someone is from ◆ How to describe a person or thing ◆ How to identify people or things ◆ How to count from 0 to 30	◆ Singular forms of definite and indefinite articles—**el, la, un, una** ◆ Singular forms of adjectives ◆ Singular forms of **ser**	◆ ***El Quijote,*** the novel ◆ Miguel de Cervantes Saavedra ◆ Map of Spain **(La Mancha)** ◆ Alicia Bustelo, a student from Venezuela ◆ Plaza Simón Bolívar, Caracas ◆ Two Latin American heroes: Simón Bolívar and San Martín ◆ Geographical terms in Spanish

CHAPTER 1 RESOURCES

PRINT	MULTIMEDIA
Planning Resources	
Lesson Plans	Interactive Lesson Planner
Block Scheduling Lesson Plans	
Reinforcement Resources	
Writing Activities Workbook	Transparencies Binder
Student Tape Manual	Audiocassette/Compact Disc Program
Video Activities Booklet	Videocassette/Videodisc Program
Web Site User's Guide	Online Internet Activities
	Electronic Teacher's Classroom Resources
Assessment Resources	
Situation Cards	**Maratón mental** Mindjogger Videoquiz
Chapter Quizzes	Testmaker Computer Software (Macintosh/Windows)
Testing Program	Listening Comprehension Audiocassette/Compact Disc
Performance Assessment	Communication Transparency: C-1
Motivational Resources	
Expansion Activities	Café Glencoe: www.cafe.glencoe.com
	Keypal Internet Activities
Enrichment	
Spanish for Spanish Speakers	Fine Art Transparency: F-1

Chapter 1 Planning Guide

SECTION	PAGES	SECTION RESOURCES
Vocabulario Palabras 1 ¿Quién es? ¿Qué es? ¿Cómo es el muchacho? ¿Cómo es la muchacha?	14–17	Vocabulary Transparencies 1.1 Audiocassette 2A/ Compact Disc 1 Student Tape Manual, TE, pages 1–2 Workbook, pages 1–2 Chapter Quizzes, page 1 CD-ROM, Disc 1, pages 14–17
Vocabulario Palabras 2 ¿Quién soy yo y de dónde soy? ¿Quién es y cómo es? Los números	18–21	Vocabulary Transparencies 1.2 Audiocassette 2A/ Compact Disc 1 Student Tape Manual, TE, pages 2–4 Workbook, pages 3–4 Chapter Quizzes, page 2 CD-ROM, Disc 1, pages 18–21
Estructura Artículos—el, la, un, una Adjetivos en el singular Presente del verbo ser en el singular	22–27	Workbook, pages 5–8 Audiocassette 2A/Compact Disc 1 Student Tape Manual, TE, pages 5–6 Structure Transparency S-1 Chapter Quizzes, pages 3–5 Computer Testmaker CD-ROM, Disc 1, pages 22–27
Conversación ¿De dónde eres? Pronunciación: Las vocales a, o, u	28–29	Audiocassette 2A/Compact Disc 1 Student Tape Manual, TE, pages 7–8 CD-ROM, Disc 1, pages 28–29
Lecturas culturales *El Quijote* Una alumna *(opcional)* Simón Bolívar y José de San Martín *(opcional)*	30–33	Testing Program, page 4 CD-ROM, Disc 1, pages 30–33
Conexiones La geografía *(opcional)*	34–35	Testing Program, page 4 CD-ROM, Disc 1, pages 34–35
Culminación Actividades orales Actividades escritas Vocabulario Tecnotur	36–39	**¡Buen viaje!** Video, Episode 1 Video Activities, pages 65–68 Internet Activities www.glencoe.com/sec/fl Testing Program, pages 1–4; 101; 133; 155–156 CD-ROM, Disc 1, pages 36–39

CAPÍTULO 1

OVERVIEW

In this chapter students will learn to describe themselves as well as a friend, using the singular forms of the verb **ser** and high-frequency descriptive adjectives. The plural forms of the verb **ser** will be presented in Chapter 2, to avoid introducing an overwhelming number of forms in this initial chapter.

National Standards

Communication

In Chapter 1, students will communicate in spoken and written Spanish to:

- identify and describe themselves and others
- find out where people are from and say their nationality

Students will engage in conversations, provide and obtain information, and exchange opinions as they fulfill the chapter objectives listed on this page.

Spotlight On Culture

Artefacto The handwoven fabrics shown on this page are from Guatemala.

Fotografía The students in the photo on pages 12–13 are standing in the Plaza de Armas, the oldest plaza in Santiago, the capital of Chile.

CAPÍTULO 1

Un amigo o una amiga

Objetivos

In this chapter you will learn to do the following:

- ask or tell who someone is
- ask or tell what something is
- ask or tell where someone is from
- ask or tell what someone is like
- describe yourself or someone else
- talk about a famous Spanish novel and some Latin American heroes

interNET CONNECTION

The **Glencoe Foreign Language Web site (http://www.glencoe.com/sec/fl)** offers three options that enable you and your students to experience the Spanish-speaking world via the Internet:

- The online **Actividades** are correlated to the chapters and utilize Hispanic Web sites around the world. For the Chapter 1 activity, see student page 39.
- The **Correspondencia electrónica** section provides information on how to set up a keypal (pen pal) exchange between your class and a class in the Spanish-speaking world.
- At **Café Glencoe,** the interactive "after-school" section of the site, you and your students can access a variety of additional online resources, including interactive games. The Chapter 1 click-and-drag game practices singular, masculine and feminine adjectives and nouns.

CAPÍTULO 1

¡OJO! Note on Interrogatives It is extremely important that students be able to use and respond correctly to interrogative expressions in the very early stages of language acquisition. In this chapter, the interrogative words **¿quién?**, **¿qué?**, **¿cómo?**, and **¿de dónde?** are introduced.

The most common interrogative wording throughout **¡Buen viaje!** is inverted order. **¿Es Juan americano? ¿De dónde es el muchacho?** However, students will sometimes encounter the upward intonation pattern: **¿Juan es americano? ¿Él es de qué nacionalidad?** since it is so frequently used in many areas of the Spanish-speaking world, particularly when speaking.

Pacing

Chapter 1 will require approximately eight to ten days. Pacing will vary according to the length of the class, the age of your students, and student aptitude.

Block Scheduling

The extended timeframe provided by block scheduling affords you the opportunity to implement a greater number of activities and projects to motivate and involve your students. See the Block Scheduling Lesson Plans Booklet for suggestions on how to present the chapter material within a block scheduling framework.

Chapter Projects

Héroes hispanos Have one or more students do a research project on an important hero from Spain, Mexico, or Latin America, and prepare a brief biography of the person. Some possibilities include: Simón Bolívar, José de San Martín, and Benito Juárez.

RESOURCES

- Vocabulary Transparencies 1.1 (A & B)
- Student Tape Manual, TE, pages 1–2
- Audiocassette 2A/CD1
- Workbook, pages 1–2
- Quiz 1, page 1
- CD-ROM, Disc 1, pages 14–17

Bell Ringer Review

Use BRR Transparency 1-1, or write the following on the board: Make a list in Spanish of the months for fall and winter.

TEACHING VOCABULARY

A. Present the vocabulary first with books closed using Vocabulary Transparencies 1.1 (A & B). You may also wish to use students as "models" as you present many of the descriptive adjectives.

B. Present one word or phrase at a time and build to a complete sentence. For example, point to Guadalupe (lower righthand photo) as the class says **Guadalupe.** Point to the map of Mexico as you and the class say **mexicana.** Then have the class say the entire sentence: **Guadalupe es mexicana.**

C. After the initial presentation with the overhead transparencies, have students open their books and look at the new vocabulary words as they repeat either after you or Cassette 2A/Compact Disc 1.

D. You may ask the following types of questions during the oral presentation of the vocabulary or as the students are reading from

(continued on page 15)

Vocabulario

PALABRAS 1

¿Qué es un colegio?
Un colegio es una escuela secundaria.
Es una escuela secundaria en Latinoamérica.

Guadalupe es mexicana.
Guadalupe es de San Miguel de Allende.
Ella es alumna en un colegio.
Es alumna en el Colegio Juárez.
Guadalupe es una amiga de José Antonio.

Total Physical Response

Getting ready
The expressions **levántate, anda, párate,** and **señala** are new to the students. You can convey their meanings by doing the activity yourself the first time and having a student imitate you while the others look on.

Begin
___, levántate.
Anda por la sala de clase. Párate.
Señala o indica a un muchacho.
Señala a un muchacho alto.
Señala a un muchacho moreno.
Señala a un muchacho alto y rubio.
Señala a una muchacha.
Señala a una muchacha rubia.
Señala a una muchacha alta.
Señala a una muchacha alta y morena.

¿Cómo es el muchacho?

alto bajo

guapo

feo

rubio

moreno

gracioso, cómico

serio

ambicioso

perezoso

¿Cómo es la muchacha?

alta baja

bonita, linda

fea

rubia

morena

graciosa, cómica

seria

ambiciosa

perezosa

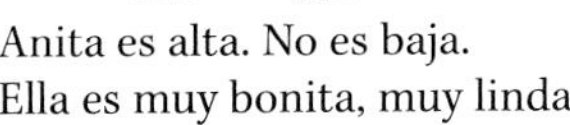

Anita es alta. No es baja.
Ella es muy bonita, muy linda.

José es rubio.
Él es guapo. No es feo.

NOTA There are many ways to express "good-looking," "handsome," or "pretty" in Spanish. The word **guapo(a)** can be used to describe a boy or a girl. The words **bonito, lindo, hermoso,** and **bello** all mean "pretty." They can describe a pretty girl or a pretty item. The word **feo** in Spanish is not as strong as the word "ugly" in English. To get a friend's attention, you could even say jokingly, **¡Oye, feo!**

The following words are used to express degrees:

Él es guapo. **Ella es bonita.**

CAPÍTULO 1
Vocabulario

their books: **¿Es Guadalupe? ¿Es Guadalupe o María? ¿Es mexicana Guadalupe? ¿Quién es mexicana? ¿De qué nacionalidad es Guadalupe?** These questions that build from very easy to more complex permit you to take into account the varying abilities of your students. Gear the questions to the skill level of each student.

E. Use the overhead transparencies to check comprehension. Ask **¿Cómo es el muchacho (la muchacha)?** as you point to the illustrations randomly.

TEACHING TIPS

A. Use gestures to help convey the meaning of words such as: **gracioso, cómico, serio, ambicioso, perezoso, alto, bajo,** or call on students who like to perform and have them pantomime the meaning of each word.

B. Use intonation and stress to convey the meaning of **Es bastante guapo** and **Es muy guapo.**

VOCABULARY EXPANSION

When students ask for additional related vocabulary in the early chapters, it is strongly recommended that they not be given words that will complicate or confuse the language concepts being presented. For example, in this chapter do not give irregular adjectives.

ABOUT THE SPANISH LANGUAGE

- In many areas of the Spanish-speaking world, the terms **el chico** and **la chica** are heard as frequently as **el muchacho** and **la muchacha.**
- The word **moreno** refers to hair coloring and complexion. A dark-haired person is **moreno.** In some areas of the Caribbean, **moreno** can refer to a person of color.
- **El alumno** and **la alumna** are used for both elementary and secondary school students. **El/la estudiante** usually refers to a university student but can sometimes be used to refer to a secondary school student.

¡OJO! **Práctica** When students are doing the **Práctica** activities, accept any answer that makes sense. The purpose of these activities is to have students use the new vocabulary. They are not factual recall activities. Thus, do not expect students to remember specific information from the vocabulary presentation when answering. If you wish, have students use the photos on this page as a stimulus, when possible.

Historieta Each time **Historieta** appears, it means that the answers to the activity form a short story. Encourage students to look at the title of the **Historieta** since it can help them do the activity.

A and **B** Have students close their books. Model the cognates that appear in **Práctica A** and **B** on page 16, and have students repeat them: **mexicano, colombiano, americana, secundaria, seria.**

Now ask the questions and call on a different student to answer each one. Then have students open their books and do the activities again.

PAIRED ACTIVITIES You may have students work in pairs when doing **Práctica A** and **B**. One reads the question and the other answers.

C and **D** These activities can be done first with books closed and then with books open.

REINFORCEMENT Note that **Práctica C** reinforces the interrogative word **quién**, and **Práctica D** reinforces **cómo.**

Writing Development
Have students write the answers to **Práctica C** in a paragraph to illustrate how all of the items tell a story.

A HISTORIETA **Un muchacho mexicano**

Contesten. *(Answer.)*

1. ¿Es Manolo mexicano o colombiano?
2. ¿Es de San Miguel de Allende o de Bogotá?
3. ¿Es alumno en el Colegio Juárez?
4. ¿Es el Colegio Juárez un colegio mexicano?
5. ¿Es Manolo un amigo de Alicia Gómez?

B HISTORIETA **Una muchacha americana**

Contesten. *(Answer.)*

1. ¿Es Debbi una muchacha americana?
2. ¿Es ella de Miami?
3. ¿Es ella alumna en una escuela secundaria de Miami?
4. ¿Es ella una alumna seria?
5. ¿Es Debbi una amiga de Bárbara Jones?

C **¿Quién? ¿Manolo o Debbi?** Contesten. *(Answer.)*

1. ¿Quién es de San Miguel de Allende?
2. ¿Quién es de Miami?
3. ¿Quién es alumno en el Colegio Juárez?
4. ¿Quién es alumna en una escuela secundaria de Miami?

San Miguel de Allende, México

Miami, La Florida

D HISTORIETA **¿Cómo es Fernando?**

Contesten según la foto. *(Answer according to the photo.)*

1. ¿Cómo es Fernando? ¿Es alto o bajo?
2. ¿Cómo es Fernando? ¿Es gracioso o serio?
3. ¿Cómo es Fernando? ¿Es guapo o feo?
4. ¿Cómo es Fernando? ¿Es rubio o moreno?

ANSWERS

Práctica

A
1. **Manolo es mexicano.**
2. **Es de San Miguel de Allende.**
3. **Sí, (No, no) es alumno en el Colegio Juárez.**
4. **Sí, es un colegio mexicano.**
5. **Sí, (No, no) es un amigo de Alicia Gómez.**

B
1. **Sí, Debbi es una muchacha americana.**
2. **Sí, ella es de Miami.**
3. **Sí, ella es alumna en una escuela secundaria de Miami.**
4. **Sí, (No) ella (no) es una alumna seria.**
5. **Sí, (No, no) es una amiga de Bárbara Jones.**

C
1. **Manolo es de San Miguel de Allende.**
2. **Debbi es de Miami.**
3. **Manolo es alumno en el Colegio Juárez.**
4. **Debbi es alumna en una escuela secundaria de Miami.**

D
1. **Es alto.**
2. **Es serio.**
3. **Es guapo.**
4. **Es moreno.**

E **Todo lo contrario** Contesten según el modelo. *(Answer according to the model.)*

1. ¿Es muy seria Teresa?
2. ¿Es morena Teresa?
3. ¿Es alta Teresa?

Málaga, España

Actividades comunicativas

A **¿Quién es?** Work with a classmate. Choose one of the illustrations below, but don't tell which one. Describe the student in the illustration. Your partner has to guess which one it is. Take turns.

JUEGO **¿Es un muchacho o una muchacha?** Work with a classmate. Describe someone in the class. First your partner will tell whether you're describing a boy or a girl and will guess who it is. Take turns.

Práctica

E **Práctica E** can be done as a mini-conversation. You may have students work in pairs.

Actividades comunicativas

¡OJO! **Práctica versus Actividades comunicativas** All activities which provide guided practice are labeled **Práctica.** The more open-ended communicative activities are labeled **Actividades comunicativas.**

Additional Practice

¿Como es? After completing the activities on pages 16 and 17, reinforce the lesson with the following:

Have students work in pairs to compare two other students. For example: **Roberto es moreno. Y Tadeo es moreno también. Roberto es de México. Es mexicano. Tadeo no es de México. Él es de Los Ángeles. Tadeo es americano.**

Learning From Photos

San Miguel de Allende, México (page 16) Manolo is from this lovely, small city in the mountains of central Mexico, home to many artists and writers.
Miami, La Florida (page 16) Debbi is from Miami, the American city considered the gateway to Latin America.

Independent Practice

Assign any of the following:
1. Workbook, pages 1–2.
2. Activities on student pages 16–17.

ANSWERS

Práctica

E 1. **No, de ninguna manera. Es bastante graciosa.**
2. **... Es bastante rubia.**
3. **... Es bastante baja.**

Actividades comunicativas

A Students could use the following:
1: **Es rubia, guapa, baja, bonita, linda.**
2: **Es alto, guapo, moreno, serio.**
3: **Es serio, rubio, guapo, ambicioso.**
4: **Es alta, graciosa, cómica, morena.**

RESOURCES

- Vocabulary Transparencies 1.2 (A & B)
- Student Tape Manual, TE, pages 2–4
- Audiocassette 2A/CD1
- Workbook, pages 3–4
- Quiz 2, page 2
- CD-ROM, Disc 1, pages 18–21

Bell Ringer Review

Use BRR Transparency 1-2, or write the following on the board: On a piece of paper write three words that describe a student seated near you. If possible, put these words into sentences.

TEACHING VOCABULARY

¡OJO! In this lesson we have students identify themselves and give their names using **soy.** This is done to avoid the perennial **me llamo (es)** problem. The verb **llamarse** is presented in the lesson on reflexive verbs. It is recommended that the students not be given this form at this point.

A. Have students close their books. Present the vocabulary, using Vocabulary Transparencies 1.2 (A & B) or student models.

B. If you have a male student whose pronunciation is quite good, call him to the front of the room. Say to the class: **Él es Roberto Davidson.** Tell the students in English that Roberto is going to tell them something about himself. Then have the student taking the role of Roberto read Roberto's lines on page 18 to the class.

Vocabulario

PALABRAS 2

¿Quién soy yo y de dónde soy?

Total Physical Response

Getting ready

Dramatize the meaning of **gestos.** You may also dramatize or give the meaning of **haz, compórtate,** and **indica.**

Begin

___, ven acá. Vas a hacer gestos.
Compórtate de una manera tímida.
Haz algo cómico.
Haz una expresión seria.
Indica que eres alto(a).
Compórtate de una manera perezosa.

¿Quién es y cómo es?

Los números

0	cero				
1	uno	11	once	21	veintiuno
2	dos	12	doce	22	veintidós
3	tres	13	trece	23	veintitrés
4	cuatro	14	catorce	24	veinticuatro
5	cinco	15	quince	25	veinticinco
6	seis	16	dieciséis	26	veintiséis
7	siete	17	diecisiete	27	veintisiete
8	ocho	18	dieciocho	28	veintiocho
9	nueve	19	diecinueve	29	veintinueve
10	diez	20	veinte	30	treinta

NOTA Words that look alike in Spanish and English are called "cognates." It is very easy to guess the meaning of cognates. But, **¡Cuidado!** *(Watch out)* because even though they look alike and mean the same thing, they are pronounced differently. Here are some cognates. Take care to pronounce them correctly.

fantástico **honesto**
tímido **generoso**

CAPÍTULO 1
Vocabulario

C. In addition to having students look at the illustrations, you can use gestures when describing Don Quijote and Sancho Panza.

D. Ask the following questions as you present the vocabulary on this page:

¿Quién es alto? ¿Don Quijote o Sancho Panza?
¿Quién es flaco? ¿Don Quijote o Sancho Panza?
¿Quién es gordo? ¿Don Quijote o Sancho Panza?
¿De dónde es don Quijote?
¿Es la Mancha una región de España?

Los números

A. Have students repeat the numbers after you.

B. Write some numbers in random order on the board and call on individuals to give the number in Spanish.

C. To avoid teaching too many numbers at once, they have been presented in two other chapters (Chapter 2, page 47; Chapter 3, page 77).

D. It is suggested that you not stress the spelling of the numbers since students will very seldom, if ever, have to spell them out in real-life situations.

INFORMAL ASSESSMENT

Check for comprehension by asking yes/no questions and either/or questions. Call on the entire class as well as individual students to respond. For example:

¿Es Roberto Davidson o Pablo González?
¿Es Roberto americano o colombiano?
¿Es él alumno en un colegio o en una escuela secundaria?

Ask the same type of questions about Carmen on page 18.

For the Native Speaker

Escuelas In the Hispanic world there are different names for different levels of schooling:

pre-primary	**kínder, jardín de infancia**
primary	**escuela primaria o elemental**
secondary	**liceo, instituto, escuela superior**

Actividad Have students talk about the different kinds of schools they know of and the schools they attended in the past. Ask questions such as:

¿A qué edad ingresan/entran los niños en el kínder/primer grado/liceo/la escuela superior?
¿Qué les enseñan a los niños en kínder?
¿Fuiste al kínder? ¿Te gustó? ¿Qué aprendiste?

Ask students who attended schools in other countries to compare them with American schools.

Práctica

A and **B** Go over the activities on page 20 once in class before assigning them as homework.

A **Práctica A** reinforces the interrogative word **¿dónde?** This activity can be done with books closed or open.

EXPANSION After students complete this activity, have a student summarize all the information about Jim in his or her own words.

B Have students look at the illustrations as they give the description of each girl.

Additional Practice

Una alumna Ask students the following questions about one of their female classmates:

¿Es ___ americana o colombiana?
¿Es alumna?
¿Es una alumna seria?
¿Es ___ alumna en una escuela secundaria americana o en un colegio colombiano?
¿Ella es alumna en qué escuela?

Práctica

A HISTORIETA Jim Collins, un muchacho americano

Contesten. *(Answer.)*

1. ¿Quién es americano, Jim Collins o Eduardo Dávila?
2. ¿De dónde es Jim? ¿Es de California o es de Guadalajara, México?
3. ¿De qué nacionalidad es Jim? ¿Es americano o mexicano?
4. ¿Dónde es alumno Jim? ¿En un colegio mexicano o en una escuela secundaria de California?
5. ¿Cómo es Jim? ¿Es serio o gracioso?

San Francisco, California

B **¿Cómo es la muchacha?** Describan a cada muchacha. *(Describe each girl.)*

1. Ana

2. Alicia

3. Isabel

4. Victoria

5. Beatriz

6. Juanita

ANSWERS

Práctica

A
1. **Jim Collins es americano.**
2. **Es de California.**
3. **Es americano.**
4. **Es alumno en una escuela secundaria de California.**
5. **Es serio (gracioso).**

B Answers will vary, but may include:
1. **Es cómica (graciosa).**
2. **Es bonita (linda, morena).**
3. **Es seria (morena).**
4. **Es generosa.**
5. **Es rubia (linda, bonita).**
6. **Es alta (ambiciosa).**

C **HISTORIETA** Gabriela Torres, la graciosa

Completen. *(Complete.)*

Una muchacha mexicana, San Miguel de Allende

Gabriela Torres es de México. Ella es ___1___. No es americana. Gabriela es alumna en un ___2___ mexicano. No es alumna en una ___3___ secundaria americana. Gabriela no es baja. Ella es bastante ___4___. ¿Es ella muy seria? No, de ninguna manera. Gabriela es muy ___5___. Ella es una amiga ___6___.

Actividades comunicativas

A **¿Quién es?** Think of a student in the class. A classmate will ask you questions about the person and try to guess who it is. Take turns.

B **Un(a) amigo(a) ideal** What are some of the qualities an ideal friend would have? With a classmate discuss what you think an ideal friend is like.

El Zócalo, Ciudad de México

C Have students do **Práctica C** with books open.

Actividades comunicativas

¡OJO! These activities encourage students to use the chapter vocabulary and structures in open-ended situations. It is not necessary to have them do all the activities. Let students choose the ones they wish to take part in.

RETEACHING

Bring to class a magazine photo of a well-known personality all the students will recognize. Have them describe the person using vocabulary they know.

Learning From Photos

El Zócalo, Ciudad de México The formal name of **el Zócalo** is **la Plaza de la Constitución**. It is the main square of Mexico City and was built by the Spaniards on the site of the main temple of Tenochtitlán, the capital of the Aztecs. **La Catedral metropolitana**, seen in this photo, is the oldest and largest cathedral in Latin America. Construction began in 1573. Over the centuries the cathedral has been sinking in the subsoil.

ANSWERS

Práctica

C **1. mexicana** **4. alta**
2. colegio **5. cómica (graciosa)**
3. escuela **6. buena (sincera)**

Actividades comunicativas

A Students should use the vocabulary from **Palabras 1** and **2.**

B Answers will vary, but may include: **Un(a) amigo(a) ideal es simpático(a), sincero(a), generoso(a), cómico(a), etc.**

RESOURCES

- Workbook, pages 5–8
- Student Tape Manual, TE, pages 5–6
- Audiocassette 2A/CD1
- Structure Transparency S-1
- Quizzes 3–5, pages 3–5
- Computer Testmaker
- CD-ROM, Disc 1, pages 22–27

Bell Ringer Review

Use BRR Transparency 1-3, or write the following on the board: Using the verb **soy,** write your name and where you are from.

TEACHING STRUCTURE

Describing one person or thing

A. Read Steps 1–3 aloud.

B. Have students repeat the examples in Step 3 as you write them on the board. Underline the article and the **o** or **a** ending.

C. Contrast the use of a definite article to refer to a specific person with the indefinite article to refer to any person. Say **el muchacho** and have students point to a specific boy in the class. Say **un muchacho** and have students look around the class and say **¿Quién? ¿Roberto o José?**

A You can do **Práctica A** with books closed and then with books open.

Estructura

Describing one person or thing
Artículos—el, la, un, una

1. The name of a person, place, or thing is a noun. In Spanish, every noun has a gender, either masculine or feminine. Many Spanish nouns end in either **o** or **a.** Almost all nouns that end in **o** are masculine, and almost all nouns that end in **a** are feminine.

2. There are two types of articles. The English word *the* is called a definite article because it is used to refer to a definite or specific person or thing—*the* girl, *the* school. The word *a (an)* is called an indefinite article because it refers to any person or thing, not a specific one—*a* girl, *a* school.

3. The definite articles in Spanish are **el** and **la. El** is used with a masculine noun and **la** is used with a feminine noun. The indefinite articles are **un** and **una. Un** is used with a masculine noun and **una** is used with a feminine noun.

el muchacho	**la muchacha**	**un muchacho**	**una muchacha**
el colegio	**la escuela**	**un colegio**	**una escuela**

A HISTORIETA El muchacho y la muchacha

Contesten con **sí.** *(Answer with* sí.*)*

1. ¿Es americano el muchacho?
2. ¿Y la muchacha? ¿Es ella americana?
3. ¿Es bastante guapo el muchacho?
4. ¿Es muy bonita la muchacha?

ANSWERS

Práctica

A 1. **Sí, el muchacho es americano.**
2. **Sí, es americana.**
3. **Sí, es bastante guapo.**
4. **Sí, es muy bonita.**

B **HISTORIETA El muchacho mexicano y la muchacha americana**

Completen con **el** o **la.** *(Complete with* el *or* la.*)*

____ (1) muchacho es mexicano. ____ (2) muchacha es americana. ____ (3) muchacho mexicano es Paco y ____ (4) muchacha americana es Linda. ____ (5) muchacha es morena y ____ (6) muchacho es moreno. ____ (7) muchacha es alumna en ____ (8) Escuela Belair en Houston. ____ (9) muchacho es alumno en ____ (10) Colegio Hidalgo en Guadalajara.

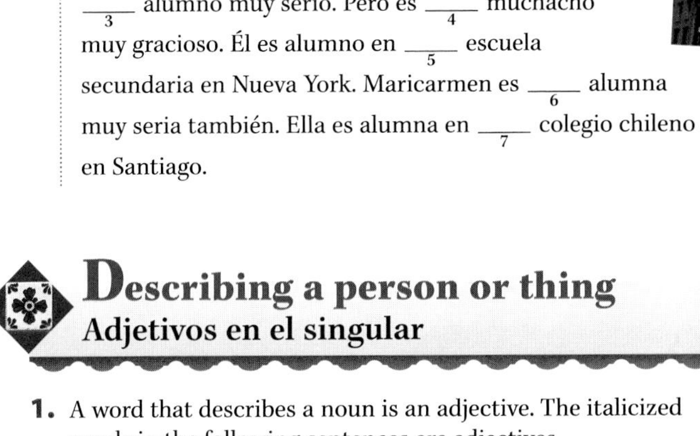

Nueva York

C **HISTORIETA Un muchacho y una muchacha**

Completen con **un** o **una.** *(Complete with* un *or* una.*)*

Roberto es ____ (1) muchacho americano y Maricarmen es ____ (2) muchacha chilena. Roberto es ____ (3) alumno muy serio. Pero es ____ (4) muchacho muy gracioso. Él es alumno en ____ (5) escuela secundaria en Nueva York. Maricarmen es ____ (6) alumna muy seria también. Ella es alumna en ____ (7) colegio chileno en Santiago.

Santiago de Chile

Describing a person or thing
Adjetivos en el singular

1. A word that describes a noun is an adjective. The italicized words in the following sentences are adjectives.

   El muchacho *rubio* es muy *guapo.*
   La muchacha *morena* es una alumna muy *buena.*

2. In Spanish, an adjective must agree with the noun it describes or modifies. If the noun is masculine, then the adjective must be in the masculine form. If the noun is feminine, the adjective must be in the feminine form. Many singular masculine adjectives end in **o,** and many singular feminine adjectives end in **a.**

un muchacho gracioso	**una muchacha graciosa**
un alumno serio	**una alumna seria**

B and **C** These activities must be done with books open. Have one student complete two or three sentences before calling on the next student.

If a student makes an error, call on another to get the correct response. Return to the student who made the error and see if he or she can now give the correct response.

EXPANSION After calling on several individuals to answer **Práctica B** and **C,** have one student do each of the activities in its entirety. Call on other students in the class to ask questions about the information in the activities. This allows them to use the interrogative words on their own. You can answer the questions, or have students answer them.

Bell Ringer Review

Use BRR Transparency 1-4, or write the following on the board: Write a list of words that can be used to describe people.

TEACHING STRUCTURE

Describing a person or thing

A. Draw two stick figures on the board. Name them Paco and Elena. Point to Paco as you say **alto, cómico, cubano, etc.** Point to Elena as you say **alta, cómica, cubana, etc.** Ask students what sound they hear repeated when describing a boy. Ask what sound they hear when describing a girl.

B. Model the sentences given in Steps 1 and 2 and have the students repeat them after you.

ANSWERS

Práctica

B	C
1. El	**1. un**
2. La	**2. una**
3. El	**3. un**
4. la	**4. un**
5. La	**5. una**
6. el	**6. una**
7. La	**7. un**
8. la	
9. El	
10. el	

Práctica

A You can do **Práctica A** with books closed and then with books open.

EXPANSION Have students give a description of Elena and another description of Eduardo in their own words.

B Encourage students to use both affirmative and negative sentences in their answers.

EXPANSION You can also make a game out of **Práctica B.** Students can work in pairs or groups and guess who is being described.

Actividades comunicativas

Allow students to choose the activities they would like to take part in.

Did You Know?

Guanajuato, México The photo of Pablo (bottom, left) was taken in Guanajuato, the home of the prestigious Universidad de Guanajuato. It is a colonial city in the central part of Mexico that played an important role during the Mexican Revolution.

Práctica

A HISTORIETA Elena y Eduardo

Contesten. *(Answer.)*

1. ¿Es Elena americana o venezolana?
2. Y Eduardo, ¿es él americano o venezolano?
3. ¿Es moreno o rubio el muchacho?
4. Y la muchacha, ¿es ella rubia o morena?
5. ¿Es Elena una alumna seria?
6. ¿Es ella alumna en una escuela americana?
7. Y Eduardo, ¿es él un alumno serio también?
8. ¿Es él alumno en un colegio venezolano?

San Francisco, California

Caracas, Venezuela

B **¿Quién es gracioso?** Describan. *(Here are some adjectives that describe people. Choose a classmate and an adjective that describes that person. Then make up a sentence about him or her.)*

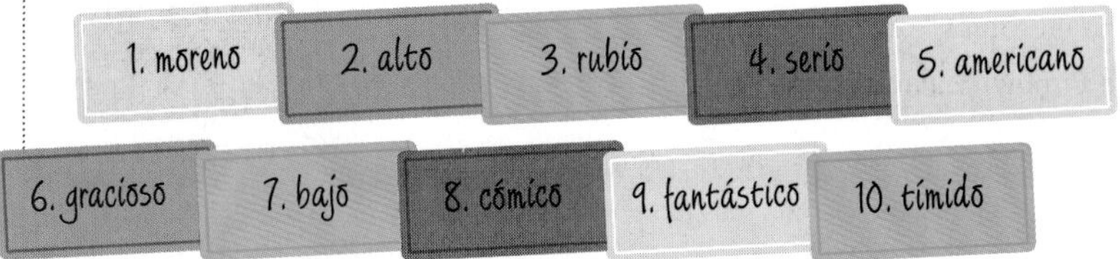

Actividades comunicativas

A **¿Quién es y cómo es?** Show a classmate this photo of Isabel García, a new friend you made in San Miguel de Allende, Mexico. One of your classmates wants to know all about Isabel. Answer his or her questions.

B **¿Quién es y cómo es?** Here's a photo of Pablo Gómez, another friend you met on your trip. He's from Guanajuato. Answer your classmate's questions about him.

Guanajuato, México

San Miguel de Allende, México

ANSWERS

Práctica

A
1. **Es americana.**
2. **Es venezelano.**
3. **Es moreno.**
4. **Es rubia.**
5. **Sí, es una alumna seria.**
6. **Sí, es una alumna en una escuela americana.**
7. **Sí, es un alumno serio también. (No, no es un alumno serio.)**
8. **Sí, es un alumno en un colegio venezolano.**

B Answers will vary, but students will use the adjectives in the colored boxes in the appropriate masculine or feminine form.

Actividades comunicativas

A Answers will vary, but may include: **Es de San Miguel de Allende. Es mexicana. Es morena y muy simpática, etc.**

B Answers will vary, but may include: **Es de Guanajuato. Es mexicano. Es moreno, bajo y serio, etc.**

Identifying a person or thing

Presente del verbo ser en el singular

1. The verb *to be* in Spanish is **ser.** Study the following forms of this verb.

SER	
yo	soy
tú	eres
él	es
ella	es

2.

You use **yo** to talk about yourself.	You use **tú** to address a friend.	You use **él** or the person's name to talk about a boy or man.	You use **ella** or the person's name to talk about a girl or woman.

Note that the form of the verb changes with each person.

3. Since the form of the verb changes with each person, the subjects **yo, tú, él,** and **ella** can be omitted.

Soy Paco.
Eres mexicano, ¿no?
Es alumna.

4. To make a sentence negative, you simply put **no** in front of the verb.

Él es mexicano. No es colombiano.
Yo soy de Bogotá. No soy de Cali.

Bell Ringer Review

Use BRR Transparency 1-5, or write the following on the board: Write the name of a friend. Then write two or three things about him or her.

TEACHING STRUCTURE

Identifying a person or thing

A. Before presenting the verb **ser,** go over the meaning of the personal pronouns **yo, tú, él, ella.**
Have students do the following:
- point to themselves as they say **yo**
- look at a neighbor as they say **tú**
- point to a boy as they say **él**
- point to a girl as they say **ella**

B. Have students look at the illustrations as they read the sentences in Step 2 aloud.

C. Read the explanatory material in Step 3 to the students and have them read the sentences in unison.

D. Write the affirmative and negative examples on the board and have students read them aloud.

E. Have students close their books. Use Structure Transparency S-1 to review the verb **ser.** Ask students to supply the appropriate subject and verb for each illustration.

INFORMAL ASSESSMENT

Ask students questions that require naming appropriate male and female students. For example: **¿Quién es rubio? ¿Quién es rubia?**

For the Native Speaker

Profesiones Because of interference from English, students may use the indefinite article incorrectly with nationalities and professions. Provide them with a list of professions such as:

abogado(a)	**médico(a)**
dentista	**agricultor(a)**
policía	**enfermero(a)**
ingeniero(a)	**vendedor(a)**

Ask: **¿A quién conoces que es abogado(a)/médico(a), etc.?** If they use the article, correct them, but first provide examples such as: **Tom Cruise es actor.** Do the same with a list of adjectives of nationality such as **alemán(a), español(a), mexicano(a), argentino(a), americano(a), ruso(a), etc.** For this activity, you can use pictures of famous people like Napoleon Bonaparte: **¿Es mexicano?**

Práctica

A Have students work in pairs and read the conversation in **Práctica A** aloud. Insist that they use the best intonation and expression possible. Call on a pair of students to present the conversation to the class.

B Before having students do **Práctica B,** you may wish to ask questions such as:
¿Es Julia de California?
¿De dónde es Julia?
¿De qué nacionalidad es?, etc.
Ask similar questions about Emilio, then have students do the activity.

C Do this activity first with books closed and then with books open.

EXPANSION Once you have elicited all the answers to this activity from various students, have one student give the same information about him- or herself.

PAIRED ACTIVITY You may have students work in pairs and interview one another using **Práctica C** as their guide.

D and **E** You may do **Práctica D** and **E** on page 27 a second time as paired activities. One student asks the questions and another answers.

Práctica

A **¡Qué coincidencia!** Practiquen la conversación. *(Practice the conversation.)*

B **Julia Rivera y Emilio Ortega** Hablen de Julia y Emilio. *(Tell what you know about Julia and Emilio.)*

C **Yo soy...** Contesten personalmente. *(Answer these questions about yourself.)*

1. ¿Eres americano(a) o cubano(a)?
2. ¿Eres alumno(a)?
3. ¿Eres alumno(a) en una escuela secundaria?
4. ¿De dónde eres?
5. ¿Cómo eres? ¿Eres alto(a) o bajo(a)?
6. ¿Eres muy serio(a) o bastante gracioso(a)?

ANSWERS

Práctica

B Answers will vary, but may include:
Julia es simpática. Es morena. Es mexicana.
Emilio es de México también. Es simpático y moreno también.

C Answers will vary, but may include:
1. **Soy americano(a). (Soy cubano[a].)**
2. **Sí, soy alumno(a).**
3. **Sí, soy alumno(a) en una escuela secundaria.**
4. **Soy de ___.**
5. **Soy alto(a). (Soy bajo[a].)**
6. **Soy muy serio(a). (Soy bastante gracioso[a].)**

D **Historieta** José, ¿eres... ?

Pregúntenle a José Fuentes si es...
(Ask José Fuentes if he is . . .)

1. puertorriqueño
2. de Ponce
3. alumno en un colegio de Ponce
4. un amigo de Inés García

Ponce, Puerto Rico

Santiago de Chile

E **Historieta** Inés, ¿eres... ?

Pregúntenle a Inés García si es...
(Ask Inés García if she is . . .)

1. de Chile
2. de Santiago
3. alumna en un colegio
4. una amiga de José Fuentes

Actividades comunicativas

A **En un café** You've just met a student your own age at a café in San Miguel de Allende, Mexico. Have a conversation to get to know one another better.

B **Un(a) amigo(a) nuevo(a)**
A classmate will think of someone in class you both know and pretend that that person is his or her new boyfriend or girlfriend. Ask as many questions as you can to try and find out who the new boyfriend or girlfriend is.

San Miguel de Allende, México

Juego **¡Soy una persona fantástica!** Have a contest with a classmate to see which one of you can boast the most. Say something good about yourself and then your partner will "one-up" you.

ALUMNA 1: **Yo soy simpática.**
ALUMNA 2: **Yo soy simpática. Y soy generosa también.**

ANSWERS

Práctica

D 1. **¿Eres puertorriqueño?**
2. **¿Eres de Ponce?**
3. **¿Eres alumno en un colegio de Ponce?**
4. **¿Eres un amigo de Inés García?**

E 1. **¿Eres de Chile?**
2. **¿Eres de Santiago?**
3. **¿Eres alumna en un colegio?**
4. **¿Eres una amiga de José Fuentes?**

Actividades comunicativas

A The conversations will encourage students to be as creative as possible and say as much as they can.

B Questions will vary, but may include:
¿Es rubio(a)?
¿Es alto(a)?
¿Es serio(a) o gracioso(a)?

Additional Practice

Soy yo Ask students to bring photos of themselves to class and have them describe the photos to their classmates.

¿De dónde eres? To reinforce the singular forms of the verb **ser,** ask individual students the following questions:
¿Eres ___? ¿Eres de ___?
¿Eres un(a) amigo(a) de ___?
¿Es simpático(a)?
¿De dónde es él/ella?
¿Dónde es alumno(a)?

¡OJO! All new material in the chapter has been presented. The sections that follow recombine and reintroduce the vocabulary and structures that have already been introduced.

Learning From Photos

Ponce, Puerto Rico The cathedral and square are located in Ponce, the second largest city in Puerto Rico after the capital San Juan. Ponce is in the southern part of the island on the Caribbean Sea. The firehouse in the photo, **el Parque de bomberos,** is very colorful and it attracts thousands of visitors annually.

Santiago de Chile The capital of Chile, located at the foot of the Andes, stretches 40 miles north to south, and 20 miles east to west. Santiago is situated in a valley with some of the most productive farmland in the nation. The city is about a one-hour drive from the thriving port of Valparaíso and the beautiful resort of Viña del Mar.

San Miguel de Allende, México These teenagers are seated at a café called La Terraza.

CAPÍTULO 1
Conversación

RESOURCES

- Audiocassette 2A/CD1
- CD-ROM, Disc 1, page 28

Bell Ringer Review

Use BRR Transparency 1-6, or write the following on the board: Write three sentences about yourself. Read them to a classmate. Then convert each of your sentences into a question and ask a classmate the questions.

TEACHING THE CONVERSATION

A. Tell students that they are going to hear a conversation among three boys, Rafael, José, and Felipe. Rafael wants to know who someone is. It turns out they have something in common.

B. Ask students to open their books to page 28. Have them follow along as you read the conversation or play the recorded version on Cassette 2A/Compact Disc 1.

C. Have students work in groups of three to practice the conversation. Then have several groups present it to the class.

D. After presenting the conversation, go over the **Después de conversar** activity. If students can answer the questions with relative ease, move on. Students should not be expected to memorize the conversation.

TECHNOLOGY OPTION

On the CD-ROM (Disc 1, page 28), students can watch a dramatization of this conversation. They can then play the role of either one of the characters, and record themselves in the conversation.

Conversación

¿De dónde eres?

RAFAEL: ¡Hola, José! ¿Qué tal, amigo?
JOSÉ: Bien, Rafael.
RAFAEL: Oye, José. ¿Quién es el muchacho alto allí?
JOSÉ: ¿Quién? ¿El rubio?
RAFAEL: Sí, él.
JOSÉ: Pues, es Felipe García. Él es un alumno nuevo. Soy un amigo de Felipe. ¡FELIPE!
FELIPE: Hola, José.
JOSÉ: Felipe, Rafael.
FELIPE: Hola, Rafael. Mucho gusto.
RAFAEL: Mucho gusto. ¿De dónde eres, Felipe?
FELIPE: Soy de Puerto Rico.
RAFAEL: ¿Sí? Hombre, yo también soy puertorriqueño.

Después de conversar

Contesten. *(Answer.)*

1. ¿Es José un amigo de Rafael?
2. ¿Quién es el muchacho alto?
3. ¿Es rubio el muchacho alto?
4. ¿Quién es un alumno nuevo en la escuela?
5. ¿Es José un amigo de Felipe?
6. ¿Es Rafael un amigo de Felipe?
7. ¿De dónde es Felipe?
8. Y Rafael, ¿de qué nacionalidad es?

ANSWERS

Después de conversar

1. **Sí, José es un amigo de Rafael.**
2. **Es Felipe García.**
3. **Sí, es rubio.**
4. **Felipe García es un alumno nuevo en la escuela.**
5. **Sí, José es un amigo de Felipe.**
6. **No, Rafael no es un amigo de Felipe.**
7. **Felipe es de Puerto Rico.**
8. **Rafael es puertorriqueño también.**

Actividades comunicativas

A **¿Quién es?** Think of someone in the class, but don't tell who it is. Say just one thing about the person and let your partner take a guess. If he or she guesses incorrectly, give another hint. Continue until your partner guesses correctly. Take turns.

JUEGO **¿Quién soy yo?** Play a guessing game. Think of someone in the class. Pretend you're that person and describe yourself. A classmate has to guess who you are.

Pronunciación

Las vocales a, o, u

When you speak Spanish, it is important to pronounce the vowels carefully. The vowel sounds in Spanish are very short, clear, and concise. The vowels in English have several different pronunciations, but in Spanish they have only one sound. Imitate carefully the pronunciation of the vowels **a, o,** and **u.** Note that the pronunciation of **a** is similar to the *a* in *father,* **o** is similar to the *o* in *most,* and **u** is similar to the *u* in *flu.*

a	o	u
Ana	**o**	**uno**
baja	**no**	**mucha**
amiga	**Paco**	**mucho**
alumna	**amigo**	**muchacho**

Repeat the following sentences.

Ana es alumna.
Adán es alumno.
Ana es amiga de Adán.

Actividades comunicativas

A **TECHNOLOGY OPTION**

In the CD-ROM version of this activity (Disc 1, page 29), students can interact with an on-screen, native speaker and record their voice.

TEACHING PRONUNCIATION

A. Have students repeat the vowels after you or the recording on Cassette 2A/Compact Disc 1. Have them imitate very carefully.

B. Now have students repeat the words after you or the recording on Cassette 2A/Compact Disc 1.

C. Have students open their books to page 29. Call on individuals to read the sentences carefully.

D. All model sentences on page 29 can be used for dictation.

TECHNOLOGY OPTION

In the CD-ROM version of the Pronunciation section (Disc 1, page 29), students will see an animation of the cartoon on this page. They can also listen to, record, and play back the vowels, words, and sentences presented here.

ANSWERS

Actividades comunicativas

A Students should use descriptive adjectives taught in this chapter.

National Standards

Cultures
The short, simple reading exposes students to the two main characters of the famous Spanish novel, ***El Quijote.***

TEACHING THE READING

Pre-reading

A. Point out the location of La Mancha on the map of Spain, page 463, or use the Map Transparency.

B. Ask students the names of the two characters from a famous Spanish novel that they learned about in the Vocabulary section of this chapter (see page 19).

Reading

A. Lead students through the **Lectura** on page 30 by reading it aloud. Have students repeat each sentence after you.

B. After every two or three sentences, ask questions such as: **¿Es *El Quijote* una novela famosa? ¿Es una novela mexicana o española? ¿Quién es el autor de la novela?**

C. Call on some students to read aloud individually. After a student has read about three sentences, ask questions of other students to check comprehension.

Post-reading

Have students do the **Después de leer** activities on page 31.

TECHNOLOGY OPTION

Students may listen to a recorded version of the **Lectura** on the CD-ROM, Disc 1, page 30.

Lecturas CULTURALES

Reading Strategy

Cognates

Words that look alike and have similar meanings in Spanish and English (**famoso,** *famous*) are called "cognates." Look for cognates whenever you read in Spanish. Recognizing cognates can help you figure out the meaning of many words in Spanish and will thus help you understand what you read.

EL QUIJOTE

El Quijote es una novela famosa de la literatura española. El autor de *El Quijote* es Miguel de Cervantes Saavedra.

El Quijote es la historia del famoso caballero andante[1], don Quijote de la Mancha. La Mancha es una región de España.

Don Quijote es alto y flaco. Sancho Panza es el compañero o escudero[2] de don Quijote. ¿Es alto y flaco como don Quijote? No, de ninguna manera. Sancho es bajo y gordo. Sancho Panza es una persona muy graciosa. Es muy cómico. ¿Y don Quijote? De ninguna manera. No es cómico. Él es muy serio y es muy honesto y generoso. Pero según[3] Sancho Panza, don Quijote es muy tonto[4]. Y según don Quijote, Sancho es perezoso.

[1]caballero andante *knight errant*
[2]escudero *knight's attendant*
[3]según *according to*
[4]tonto *foolish*

Miguel de Cervantes Saavedra

ESPAÑA
Madrid ★
La Mancha

Sancho Panza y Don Quijote

Did You Know?

El Quijote With the exception of the Bible, it is claimed that this novel is the most widely-read book in the world. Ask how many students have seen the Broadway musical, *Man of La Mancha.* Show a videocassette clip of the movie version to the class and encourage them to see the play or the movie on their own.

Independent Practice

Assign any of the following:

1. Después de leer activities, page 31
2. Workbook, **Un poco más,** page 9
3. CD-ROM, Disc 1, pages 30–31

La Mancha, España

Después de leer

A **¿Es don Quijote o Sancho Panza?** Decidan. *(Decide whether each sentence describes Don Quijote or Sancho Panza.)*

1. Es bajo.
2. Es alto.
3. Es muy gracioso.
4. Es gordo.
5. Es flaco.
6. Es muy serio.
7. Es un caballero andante.
8. Es honesto y generoso.
9. Es un escudero.

B **Palabras afines** Busquen cinco palabras afines en la lectura. *(Find five cognates in the reading.)*

«Don Quijote» de Pablo Picasso

National Standards

Communication Have students say as much as they can in their own words about don Quijote and Sancho Panza.

Geography Connection

La Mancha La Mancha is located in Central Spain. This area is very arid and has very few trees. The delicious, well-known **queso manchego** comes from this area. See the map of Spain on page 30.

ANSWERS

Después de leer

A
1. **Sancho Panza**
2. **Don Quijote**
3. **Sancho Panza**
4. **Sancho Panza**
5. **Don Quijote**
6. **Don Quijote**
7. **Don Quijote**
8. **Don Quijote**
9. **Sancho Panza**

B Answers will vary, but may include: **novela, famosa, literatura, autor, región, compañero, persona, cómico, serio, honesto, generoso**

LECTURA OPCIONAL 1

TEACHING TIPS

¡OJO! This reading is optional. You may skip it completely, have the entire class read it, have only several students read it, or assign it for extra credit.

HISTORY CONNECTION

Simón Bolívar Bolívar was born in Venezuela in 1783. Although he came from a wealthy family he was always interested in the welfare of the less fortunate. He spent time in France, Spain, and the United States. In 1810, he returned to Venezuela to take part in the rebellion against the Spaniards.

Después de leer

A Have students scan the reading for the answers to this activity.

INFORMAL ASSESSMENT

You may want to give the following quiz to those students who read this selection:

Ask.

1. **¿De dónde es Alicia Bustelo?**
2. **¿Cuál es la capital de Venezuela?**
3. **¿Cómo es Alicia?**
4. **¿Dónde es ella alumna?**
5. **¿Quién es un héroe latinoamericano?**

LECTURA OPCIONAL 1

UNA ALUMNA VENEZOLANA

Alicia Bustelo es una muchacha venezolana. Ella es de Caracas, la capital de Venezuela. Alicia es alta y es una muchacha bastante bonita. Es muy graciosa. Pero es también una alumna muy seria. Es alumna en el Colegio Simón Bolívar. En Latinoamérica un colegio es una escuela secundaria. El Colegio Simón Bolívar es una escuela muy buena.

Plaza Simón Bolívar, Caracas

Después de leer

A Latinoamérica Busquen la información en la lectura. *(Find the information in the reading.)*

1. the name of a Latin American country
2. the name of a Latin American capital
3. the name of a Latin American hero
4. the term for the Spanish-speaking countries of the Americas

ANSWERS

Después de leer

A 1. Venezuela
2. Caracas
3. Simón Bolívar
4. Latinoamérica

Did You Know?

Venezuela The land that is today called Venezuela was discovered by Columbus during his third voyage to the New World in 1498. One year later Alonso de Ojeda and Amerigo Vespucci mapped the coastal area where the Orinoco River empties into the Atlantic and the area where one finds Lake Maracaibo. The many waterways reminded the explorers of the canals of Venice and they thus named the area **Venezuela,** or *little Venice.*

LECTURA OPCIONAL 2

SIMÓN BOLÍVAR Y JOSÉ DE SAN MARTÍN

María Iglesias es una muchacha venezolana. Ella es de Caracas, la capital. El colegio de María Iglesias es el Colegio Simón Bolívar. Y la plaza principal de Caracas es la Plaza Simón Bolívar. Simón Bolívar es un héroe famoso de la América del Sur.

José Ayerbe no es venezolano. Él es peruano. Es de Lima, la capital del Perú. El colegio de José Ayerbe es el Colegio San Martín. Y la plaza principal de Lima es la Plaza San Martín. San Martín es otro héroe famoso de la América del Sur.

Simón Bolívar y José de San Martín luchan contra[1] España por la independencia de los países[2] de la América del Sur. Simón Bolívar es el gran[3] «libertador» de los países del norte del continente sudamericano y San Martín es el libertador de los países del sur.

[1]luchan contra *fight against*
[2]países *countries*
[3]gran *great*

Simón Bolívar

José de San Martín

Después de leer

A Héroes Den ejemplos. *(Give examples.)*
Many schools in Spain and in Latin America are named after heroes. Is the same true in the United States? Give some examples.

B El libertador Expliquen. *(Explain.)*
What is the meaning of the word **libertador** or *liberator* in English? What does a liberator do?

C Historia de los Estados Unidos Contesten. *(Answer.)*
Who is considered the liberator of the United States? What did he fight for?

LECTURA OPCIONAL 2

HISTORY CONNECTION

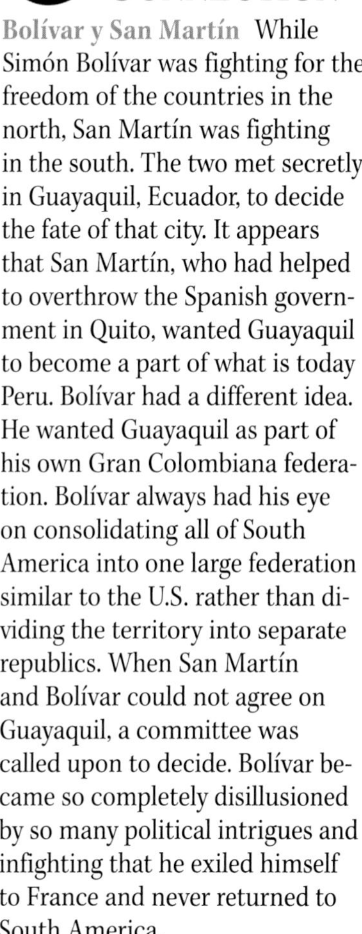

Bolívar y San Martín While Simón Bolívar was fighting for the freedom of the countries in the north, San Martín was fighting in the south. The two met secretly in Guayaquil, Ecuador, to decide the fate of that city. It appears that San Martín, who had helped to overthrow the Spanish government in Quito, wanted Guayaquil to become a part of what is today Peru. Bolívar had a different idea. He wanted Guayaquil as part of his own Gran Colombiana federation. Bolívar always had his eye on consolidating all of South America into one large federation similar to the U.S. rather than dividing the territory into separate republics. When San Martín and Bolívar could not agree on Guayaquil, a committee was called upon to decide. Bolívar became so completely disillusioned by so many political intrigues and infighting that he exiled himself to France and never returned to South America.

A monument in downtown Guayaquil commemorates the spot where their secret meeting took place.

National Standards

Comparisons
In the **Después de leer** activities students are encouraged to compare Spanish and English and to make comparisons between Hispanic and American cultures.

GEOGRAPHY CONNECTION

América del Sur Have students locate Caracas and Lima on the map of South America on page 464, or use the Map Transparency. Point out that both cities are close to the sea. This is the case with most of the major cities in South America.

ANSWERS

Después de leer

A Many American schools are named after presidents or other famous political and historical figures such as John F. Kennedy, Martin Luther King, George Washington.

B A *liberator* is a person who frees a country from a foreign power.

C George Washington fought to free the colonies from British rule in order to gain religious and political freedom, and freedom from unfair taxation.

CAPÍTULO 1
Conexiones

National Standards

Connections

This reading establishes a connection with another discipline—geography. Knowledge students already have from previous study will enable them to read this selection with ease as they increase their vocabulary in Spanish and learn more about the geography of Spain and Latin America.

¡OJO! The readings in the **Conexiones** section are optional. They focus on some of the major disciplines taught in schools and universities. The vocabulary is useful for discussing such topics as history, literature, art, economics, business, science, etc.

You may choose any of the following ways to do the readings in the **Conexiones** sections.

Independent reading Have students read the selections and do the post-reading activities as homework, which you collect. This option is least intrusive on class time and requires a minimum of teacher involvement.

Homework with in-class follow-up Assign the readings and post-reading activities as homework. Review and discuss the material in class the next day.

Intensive in-class activity This option includes a pre-reading vocabulary presentation, in-class reading and discussion, assignment of the activities for homework, and a discussion of the assignment in class the following day.

Conexiones

Las ciencias sociales

La geografía

Geography is the study of the Earth; it deals with all of Earth's features, particularly the natural forces that create these features and cause them to change. It is also the study of where people, animals, and plants live and how rivers, deserts, and other of Earth's features affect their lives. It is a subject that has interested human beings since earliest times.

Look at the map of South America. Notice how many geographical terms you will be able to recognize in Spanish. Now find out how easy it is to read about geography in Spanish.

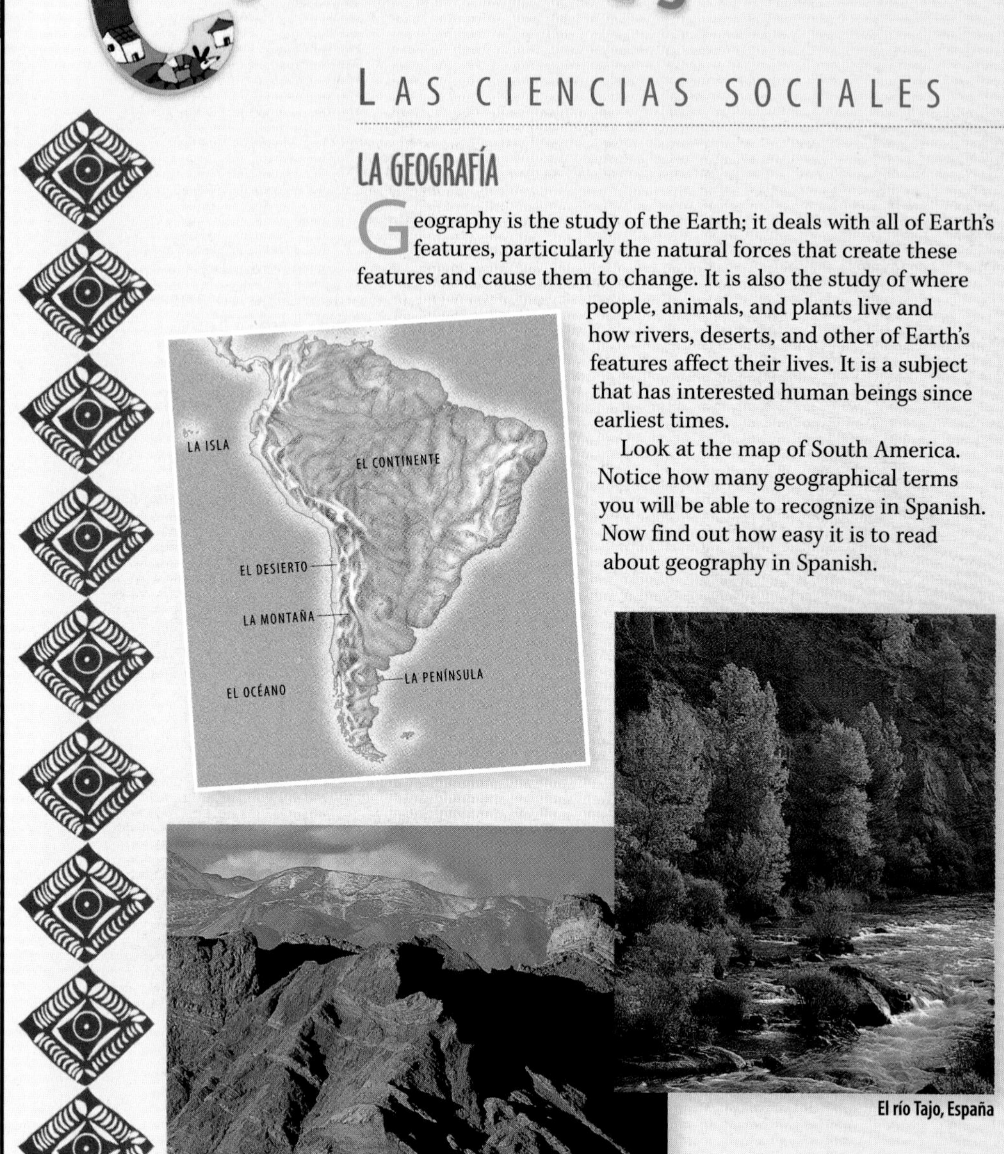

El río Tajo, España

El desierto Atacama, Chile

Class Motivator

¿Sí o no? Have students play the following **sí o no** game after they complete the reading:

1. **Puerto Rico es una península.**
2. **El norte es uno de los cuatro puntos cardinales.**
3. **Hay cinco puntos cardinales.**
4. **La América del Norte es un continente.**
5. **Australia es una isla.**
6. **Puerto Rico es una isla.**
7. **España es parte de una isla.**
8. **El Atlántico es un océano.**
9. **El Pacífico es un río.**

La geografía

Hay cuatro puntos cardinales: el norte, el sur, el este y el oeste.

Hay siete continentes: la América del Norte, la América del Sur, Europa, África, Asia, Australia y la Antártida.

El océano Atlántico es muy grande. Es inmenso. El océano Pacífico es muy grande también.

España es parte de una península. Puerto Rico es una isla. El español es la lengua[1] de España. Es la lengua de Puerto Rico también. El español es una lengua muy importante. Es la lengua de 21 (veintiún) países[2] en la América del Sur, en la América Central, en la América del Norte y en Europa.

Tossa de Mar, Costa Brava, España

Los Andes, Argentina

[1]lengua *language*
[2]países *countries*

Después de leer

A Un poco de geografía Escojan la palabra. *(Choose the correct word to complete each sentence. You may use a word more than once.)*

1. Europa es un ____.
2. España no es una isla. España es parte de una ____.
3. Puerto Rico es una ____.
4. Cuba es otra ____.
5. El Sahara es un ____ de África y el Atacama es un ____ de la América del Sur.

continente | isla | océano | desierto | península

B Estrategias Adivinen. *(Guess the meaning of the following words.)*

Often you can guess the meaning of words because of other knowledge you have. You may not know the meaning of **el río** but when you see **el río Misisipí** or **el río Hudson,** you can probably figure out what **río** means.

1. el **río** Hudson
2. la **bahía** Chesapeake
3. el **lago** Superior, el **lago** Erie
4. el **golfo** de México
5. el **mar** Mediterráneo

CAPÍTULO 1
Conexiones

LAS CIENCIAS SOCIALES
LA GEOGRAFÍA

A. Have students read the introduction in English on page 34.
B. Have them quickly skim the terms on the map of South America. You may also have them repeat the terms after you.
C. Have students read the selection quickly or have them skim it.
D. You may wish to have them find and repeat all the cognates in the reading selection. Explain to them that there are two important strategies to use when reading unfamiliar material—they should learn to recognize cognates and derive meaning from context.

Después de leer

A Have students do this activity. Call on one student to read all the answers as the others listen.

B Explain to students that the strategy outlined in this activity is very important. Quite often previous knowledge will help their comprehension.

INFORMAL ASSESSMENT

You may wish to give the following quiz to students who have done the **Conexiones** section.

Find the following information:
1. **los cuatro puntos cardinales**
2. **los nombres de cuatro continentes**
3. **un país que forma parte de una península**
4. **la lengua de Puerto Rico**
5. **el número de países donde el español es la lengua oficial**

interNET CONNECTION

The Internet activity for Chapter 1 is a map activity that reinforces the material presented in this reading. Students are asked to identify the countries of the Spanish-speaking world, their major cities, and geographical features. Maps and worksheets for this activity are available at the **Glencoe Foreign Language Web site** (**http://www.glencoe.com/sec/fl**).

ANSWERS

Después de leer

A
1. **continente**
2. **península**
3. **isla**
4. **isla**
5. **desierto, desierto**

B
1. **river**
2. **bay**
3. **lake**
4. **gulf**
5. **sea**

CAPÍTULO 1
Culminación

RECYCLING

The **Actividades orales** and the **Actividad escrita** allow students to use the vocabulary and structure from this chapter in open-ended, real-life settings.

Actividades orales

Encourage students to say as much as possible when they do these activities. Tell them not to be afraid of making mistakes since the goal of the activities is real-life communication. If someone in the group makes an error, allow the others to politely correct him or her.

Let students choose the activities they would like to do.

Student Portfolio

Have students keep a notebook containing their best written work from each chapter. These selected writings can be based on assignments from the Student Textbook and the Writing Activities Workbook. The two activities on page 37 are examples of writing assignments that may be included in each student's portfolio.

In the Workbook, students will develop an organized autobiography **(Mi autobiografía).** These workbook pages may also become a part of their portfolio. See the Teacher's Manual for more information on the Student Portfolio.

Culminación

Actividades orales

A Un amigo nuevo Work with a classmate. Here's a picture of your new friend, Carlos Álvarez. He's from Barcelona, Spain. Say as much as you can about him and answer any questions your partner may have about Carlos.

Barcelona, España

B Una alumna nueva Inés Figueroa (a classmate) is a new girl in your school. You want to get to know her better and help her feel at home. Find out as much as you can about her. Tell Inés about yourself, too.

C Oye, ¿quién es? You and a friend (a classmate) are in a café in San Juan, Puerto Rico. You see an attractive girl or boy across the room. It just so happens your friend knows the person. Ask your friend as many questions as you can to find out more about the boy or girl you're interested in.

San Juan, Puerto Rico

ANSWERS

Actividades orales

A Answers will vary, but may include: **Es Carlos Álvarez. Es bajo y moreno. Carlos es de Barcelona, España. Es alumno en una escuela secundaria de Barcelona.**

B Answers will vary.

C Answers will vary. Students can use the conversation on page 28 as a model.

Independent Practice

Assign any of the following:

1. Activities, pages 36–37
2. Workbook, **Mi autobiografía,** page 10
3. Situation Cards
4. CD-ROM, Disc 1, Chapter 1, **Juego de repaso**

Actividad escrita

A **Un amigo español** The following is a letter you just received from a new pen pal. First read the letter. Then answer it. Give Jorge similar information about yourself.

¡Hola!
Soy Jorge Pérez Navarro. Soy de Madrid, la capital de España. Soy español. Soy alumno en el Colegio Sorolla. Soy rubio y bastante alto. Soy bastante gracioso. No soy muy serio. Y no soy tímido. De ninguna manera.
Hasta pronto,
Jorge

Plaza de Cibeles, Madrid, España

Writing Strategy

Freewriting

One of the easiest ways to begin any kind of personal writing is simply to begin—to let your thoughts flow and write the first thing that comes to mind. Sometimes as you think of one word, another word will come to mind. If you get stuck, take several minutes to think of another word or phrase. Such brainstorming and freewriting are sometimes the best sources when doing any type of writing about yourself.

¿Quién soy yo?

On a piece of paper write down as much as you can about yourself in Spanish. Your teacher will collect the descriptions and choose students to read them to the class. You'll all try to guess who's being described.

CAPÍTULO 1
Culminación

Actividad escrita

A Students can write this letter on a sheet of paper or you may have them use the technology options listed below.

TECHNOLOGY OPTIONS

Go to the **Correspondencia electrónica** section at the **Glencoe Foreign Language Web site** to find out how to set up a key-pal (pen pal) exchange between your class and a class in a Spanish-speaking country.

Students can use the Portfolio feature on the CD-ROM to write this letter.

Writing Strategy

Freewriting

A. Have students read the Writing Strategy on page 37.

B. If students have difficulty thinking of words to describe themselves, have them use the vocabulary list on page 38.

Learning From Photos

Plaza de Cibeles, Madrid, España This beautiful building in Madrid is the Palacio de Telecomunicaciones, the main post office of the capital, on the Plaza de Cibeles. In this photo we also see the Fuente de Cibeles. This famous fountain depicts Sybil, wife of Saturn, driving a chariot drawn by lions. The fountain is lit at night and it has come to symbolize Madrid. The **madrileños** love the fountain to such a degree that during the Civil War (1936–1939) many citizens risked their lives sandbagging the fountain as Nationalist aircraft bombed the city.

ANSWERS

Actividad escrita

A Letters will vary in content, but may include: **Soy *(nombre)*. Soy de *(ciudad)*. Soy *(nacionalidad)*. Soy alumno en *(nombre de la escuela)*. Soy alto(a), moreno(a), etc.**

Writing Strategy

Answers will vary. Students should describe themselves, using as many adjectives and words as possible from the chapter vocabulary.

ASSESSMENT RESOURCES

- Chapter Quizzes
- Testing Program
- Computer Testmaker
- Situation Cards
- Communication Transparency C-1
- Performance Assessment
- **Maratón mental** Videoquiz

VOCABULARY REVIEW

The words and phrases in the **Vocabulario** have been taught for productive use in this chapter. They are summarized here as a resource for both students and teacher. This list also serves as a convenient resource for the **Culminación** activities on pages 36 and 37. There are approximately eighteen cognates in this vocabulary list. Have students find them.

Vocabulario

IDENTIFYING A PERSON OR THING

el muchacho
la muchacha
el amigo
la amiga
el alumno
la alumna
la persona
el colegio
la escuela

DESCRIBING A PERSON

alto(a)
bajo(a)
guapo(a)
bonito(a)
lindo(a)
feo(a)
moreno(a)
rubio(a)
flaco(a)
gordo(a)
gracioso(a)
cómico(a)
serio(a)
ambicioso(a)
perezoso(a)
bueno(a)
fantástico(a)
tímido(a)
sincero(a)
honesto(a)
generoso(a)
simpático(a)
ser

STATING NATIONALITY

americano(a)
chileno(a)
colombiano(a)
cubano(a)
mexicano(a)
puertorriqueño(a)
venezolano(a)

FINDING OUT INFORMATION

¿quién?
¿qué?
¿cómo?
¿de dónde?
¿de qué nacionalidad?
¿no?

EXPRESSING DEGREES

bastante
muy
no, de ninguna manera

OTHER USEFUL EXPRESSIONS

secundario(a)

For the Younger Student

Características Have students draw a series of faces that illustrate the meaning of adjectives presented in this chapter. Have them label each drawing with the appropriate Spanish word. Select the most attractive ones and put them on a bulletin board entitled **Características.**

TECNOTUR

VIDEO

¡Buen viaje!

EPISODIO 1 ▸ Hola, yo soy...

Juan Ramón

Cristina

Teresa

Isabel

Luis

CD-ROM

Expansión cultural

El Instituto Malaca en Málaga, España, es un instituto internacional para clases de español.

interNET CONNECTION

In this video episode, we are introduced to five teenagers: Juan Ramón and Cristina are Hispanic Americans from Los Angeles. Juan Ramón's family is originally from Puerto Rico, and Cristina's is from Colombia. Their friends Isabel and Luis are from Mexico, and Teresa is from Spain. To find out where these countries are located and other countries where Spanish is spoken, go to the Capítulo 1 Internet activity at the Glencoe Foreign Language Web site:

http://www.glencoe.com/sec/fl

Video Synopsis

In this episode we meet the five main characters, Juan Ramón, Cristina, Isabel, Luis, and Teresa. They tell us about themselves—where they are from, what they're like, and what their interests are. We also discover that, after attending the technology institute in Los Angeles, the teens visited one another and created a Web site to promote international friendships. The video traces the adventures of the five teenagers in Spain and Mexico as they learn more about each other's cultures, film video clips, and gather material for use on their Web site.

CAPÍTULO 1
Tecnotur

OVERVIEW

This page previews three key multimedia components of the **Glencoe Spanish** series. Each reinforces the material taught in Chapter 1 in a unique manner.

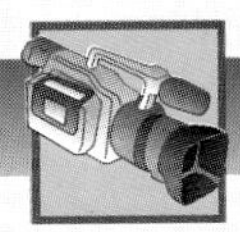

VIDEO

The Video Program allows students to see how the chapter vocabulary and structures are used by native speakers within an engaging story line. For maximum reinforcement, show the video episode as a final activity for Chapter 1.

A. Here are the photos of the five main characters from the Video Program. Before viewing the episode, you may want to present the teens to your students and have them describe each one using the adjectives from the chapter.

B. Now show the Chapter 1 video episode. See the Video Activities Booklet for detailed suggestions for using this resource.

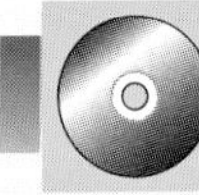

CD-ROM

A. The **Expansión cultural** photo shows a language institute in Málaga, Spain, similar to the one that the five main characters attended in Los Angeles. Have students read the caption on page 39.

B. In the CD-ROM version of **Expansión cultural** (Disc 1, page 39), students can listen to additional recorded information about **Instituto Malaca.**

INTERNET

Teacher Information and Student Worksheets for this activity can be accessed at the Web site.

Chapter 2 Overview ◆◆◆◆◆◆◆◆◆◆◆◆◆◆◆◆◆◆◆◆◆◆◆◆◆◆◆◆◆

SCOPE AND SEQUENCE pages 40–69

TOPICS	FUNCTIONS	STRUCTURE	CULTURE
◆ School subjects and courses ◆ Telling time ◆ Nationalities ◆ Numbers: 31–90	◆ How to describe people and things ◆ How to talk about more than one person or thing ◆ How to discuss classes in school ◆ How to express opinions about classes ◆ How to tell time ◆ How to tell at what time an event takes place ◆ How to count from 31 to 90	◆ Plural forms of nouns, articles, and adjectives ◆ Plural forms of **ser** ◆ Telling time	◆ Alejandro Chávez and Guadalupe Garza, two Mexican-Americans ◆ Raúl Ugarte and Marta Dávila, two Cuban-Americans ◆ San Antonio, a bilingual city ◆ The Alamo, San Antonio, Texas ◆ Coyoacán, a suburb of Mexico City ◆ The Frida Kahlo Museum

CHAPTER 2 RESOURCES

PRINT	MULTIMEDIA
Planning Resources	
Lesson Plans Block Scheduling Lesson Plans	Interactive Lesson Planner
Reinforcement Resources	
Writing Activities Workbook Student Tape Manual Video Activities Booklet Web Site User's Guide	Transparencies Binder Audiocassette/Compact Disc Program Videocassette/Videodisc Program Online Internet Activities Electronic Teacher's Classroom Resources
Assessment Resources	
Situation Cards Chapter Quizzes Testing Program Performance Assessment	**Maratón mental** Mindjogger Videoquiz Testmaker Computer Software (Macintosh/Windows) Listening Comprehension Audiocassette/Compact Disc Communication Transparency: C-2
Motivational Resources	
Expansion Activities	Café Glencoe: www.cafe.glencoe.com Keypal Internet Activities
Enrichment	
Spanish for Spanish Speakers	Fine Art Transparency: F-2

Chapter 2 Planning Guide

SECTION	PAGES	SECTION RESOURCES
Vocabulario Palabras 1 **¿Quiénes son?** **¿Cómo son las clases?**	42–45	Vocabulary Transparencies 2.1 Audiocassette 2B/ Compact Disc 2 Student Tape Manual, TE, pages 11–12 Workbook, pages 11–12 Chapter Quizzes, page 6 CD-ROM, Disc 1, pages 42–45
Vocabulario Palabras 2 **Los cursos escolares** **¿Qué son?**	46–49	Vocabulary Transparencies 2.2 Audiocassette 2B/ Compact Disc 2 Student Tape Manual, TE, pages 13–15 Workbook, page 13 Chapter Quizzes, page 7 CD-ROM, Disc 1, pages 46–49
Estructura **Sustantivos, artículos y adjetivos en el plural** **Presente de ser en el plural** **La hora**	50–57	Workbook, pages 14–16 Audiocassette 2B/Compact Disc 2 Student Tape Manual, TE, pages 15–19 Structure Transparency S-2A, S-2B Chapter Quizzes, pages 8–10 Computer Testmaker CD-ROM, Disc 1, pages 50–57
Conversación **¿De qué nacionalidad son Uds.?** **Pronunciación: Las vocales e, i**	58–59	Audiocassette 2B/Compact Disc 2 Student Tape Manual, TE, pages 19–20 CD-ROM, Disc 1, pages 58–59
Lecturas culturales **El español en los Estados Unidos** **San Antonio *(opcional)*** **Coyoacán *(opcional)***	60–63	Testing Program, page 8 CD-ROM, Disc 1, pages 60–63
Conexiones **La sociología *(opcional)***	64–65	Testing Program, page 8 CD-ROM, Disc 1, pages 64–65
Culminación **Actividades orales** **Actividades escritas** **Vocabulario** **Tecnotur**	66–69	**¡Buen viaje!** Video, Episode 2 Video Activities, pages 69–71 Internet Activities **www.glencoe.com/sec/fl** Testing Program, pages 5–8; 102; 134; 157 CD-ROM, Disc 1, pages 66–69

OVERVIEW

In this chapter students will learn to describe people and things, using the plural forms of articles, adjectives, and the verb **ser.** (The singular forms were taught in Chapter 1.) Active vocabulary from Chapter 1 is recycled in this chapter as new descriptive adjectives and school-related terms are presented.

National Standards

Communication
In Chapter 2, students will communicate in spoken and written Spanish on the following topics:

- obtaining and providing information about their friends and courses
- talking about themselves

Students will engage in conversations, provide and obtain information, and exchange opinions as they fulfill the chapter objectives listed on this page.

Pacing

Chapter 2 will require approximately eight to ten days. Pacing will vary according to the length of the class, the age of your students, and student aptitude.

Block Scheduling

The extended timeframe provided by block scheduling affords you the opportunity to implement a greater number of activities and projects to motivate and involve your students. See the Block Scheduling Lesson Plans Booklet for suggestions on how to present the chapter material within a block scheduling framework.

CAPÍTULO 2

Alumnos y cursos

Objetivos

In this chapter you will learn to do the following:

- describe people and things
- talk about more than one person or thing
- tell what subjects you take in school and express some opinions about them
- tell time
- tell at what time an event takes place
- talk about Spanish speakers in the United States

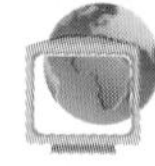

interNET CONNECTION

The **Glencoe Foreign Language Web site (http://www.glencoe.com/sec/fl)** offers three options that enable you and your students to experience the Spanish-speaking world via the Internet:

- The online **Actividades** are correlated to the chapters and utilize Hispanic Web sites around the world. For the Chapter 2 activity, see student page 69.
- The **Correspondencia electrónica** feature provides information on how to set up a keypal (pen pal) exchange between your class and a class in the Spanish-speaking world.
- At **Café Glencoe,** the interactive "after-school" section of the site, you and your students can access a variety of additional online resources, including interactive games. The Chapter 2 Concentration game practices telling time.

cuarenta y uno 41

CAPÍTULO 2

¡OJO! **Cognates** Since the vocabulary in this chapter has to do with school and school subjects, there are many cognates. The large number of cognates will help students learn the new words quickly. However, cognates often present a pronunciation problem. Since they are so similar to the English words, students will often anglicize the pronunciation. Take care to model the pronunciation of cognates very carefully. The cognates do, however, give students the feeling that they are progressing rapidly in their language acquisition.

Spotlight On Culture

Artefacto This typical Spanish pitcher or **jarro** is from Andalucía.

Fotografía This photo shows some friends who are students in Madrid. They are at one of the entrances to Retiro Park in Madrid.

Teacher Notes

Chapter Projects

Amigos hispanos Have students begin a correspondence with a Spanish or Latin American pen pal. By the end of this chapter they will be able to say something about themselves and about the courses they are taking in school.

TECHNOLOGY OPTION For information on e-mail correspondence, see the Internet Connection, page 40.

RESOURCES

- Vocabulary Transparencies 2.1 (A & B)
- Student Tape Manual, TE, pages 11–12
- Audiocassette 2B/CD2
- Workbook, pages 11–12
- Quiz 1, page 6
- CD-ROM, Disc 1, pages 42–45

Bell Ringer Review

Use BRR Transparency 2-1, or write the following on the board: Use the following words in a sentence: **serio, cómico, alto, mexicano, guapo**

TEACHING VOCABULARY

A. Have students close their books. Present the vocabulary, using Vocabulary Transparencies 2.1 (A & B). Point to the girls as you have students repeat **las alumnas** after you. Point to the girls and the books to help convey the meaning of **alumnas.** Then do the same with the boys. Now indicate that both girls are together, and then that both boys are together, as the class repeats: **las amigas, los amigos.**

B. Have the class repeat their names: **Marta, Adela, Juan, Ricardo.** Then ask questions:
¿Son alumnas Marta y Adela?
¿Quiénes son alumnas?
¿Son amigas también?
¿Son las dos muchachas amigas?
Then do the same with the boys.

C. Point to the map of Puerto Rico as students repeat **Puerto Rico. Los amigos son de Puerto Rico.**

(continued on page 43)

Vocabulario

¿Quiénes son?

¿Qué son?

Marta y Adela son puertorriqueñas.
Juan y Ricardo son puertorriqueños también.
Los cuatro amigos son de Ponce.
Ellos son alumnos en la misma escuela.
Son muy inteligentes.

Total Physical Response

Getting ready
Before doing this activity, make sure students understand each of the following verbs by acting them out: **levántate, ven acá, toma, señala, dame, siéntate.** You will need a ruler in order to do this activity.

Begin
___, levántate.
Ven acá.
Toma. (Hand him/her the ruler.)
Con la regla, señala a un muchacho moreno.
Señala a dos muchachos rubios.
Señala a una muchacha.
Señala a una muchacha rubia.
Señala a dos muchachas morenas.
Muy bien. Dame la regla.
Gracias, ___. Siéntate.

¿Cómo son las clases?

Es una clase pequeña.
¿Cuántos alumnos hay en la clase?
Hay pocos alumnos en la clase.
Es una clase aburrida.

Es una clase grande.
Hay muchos alumnos en la clase.
Es una clase interesante.

El curso de español no es difícil.
Es fácil.

El curso de matemáticas es bastante difícil (duro).

NOTA Once again you will see how many Spanish words you already know because they are cognates. You should have no trouble guessing the meaning of these words.

el curso
la clase
el profesor, la profesora

inteligente
interesante
popular

dominicano
ecuatoriano
panameño

ABOUT THE SPANISH LANGUAGE

- You may wish to give students the word **el/la maestro(a)** and explain to them that this is the term most frequently used when referring to an elementary school teacher.
- The most frequently heard term for an elementary school used to be **la escuela primaria.** However, it is very common these days to hear **la escuela elemental.**

Son puertorriqueños. Son inteligentes.
Ask questions such as:
¿De dónde son los alumnos?
¿Son amigos?
¿Son puertorriqueños los cuatro amigos?
¿De qué nacionalidad son los amigos?
¿Son alumnos en la misma escuela o en escuelas diferentes?

D. Have students repeat words in isolation first and build to complete sentences. For example: **la clase, pequeña, aburrida (no interesante). Es una clase pequeña. Es una clase aburrida. No es una clase interesante.** Then ask questions using the new words.

E. You can use a gesture to help convey the meaning of **difícil**—wipe your brow, make a hand motion. Then say **fácil, no difícil.**

F. After presenting the vocabulary orally, have students open their books and read the words and sentences, Intersperse questions throughout the reading to continue to elicit oral responses.

VOCABULARY EXPANSION

To have some fun you may wish to present the opposite of **fantástico** or **fabuloso—horrible.**
You may also present:
estupendo
sensacional
genial
Genial is a rather "in" expression in some areas. It is used for anything that is great or "awesome."

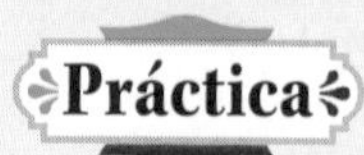

¡OJO! **Práctica** When students are doing the **Práctica** activities, accept any answer that makes sense. The purpose of these activities is to have students use the new vocabulary. They are not factual recall activities. Thus, do not expect students to remember specific information from the vocabulary presentation when answering. If you wish, have students use the photos on this page as a stimulus, when possible.

Historieta Each time **Historieta** appears, it means that the answers to the activity form a short story. Encourage students to look at the title of the **Historieta** since it can help them do the activity.

A Do **Práctica A** orally with books closed, then have students read it for additional reinforcement.

EXPANSION Call on one student to answer all the questions. Then have another student retell the **Historieta** in his or her own words.

B Go over **Práctica B** once orally, asking questions of individual students. Have them open their books and read it for additional reinforcement.

Now reverse the process. Have students close their books and give them the response. Have them ask you the question.

Writing Development

Have students write the answers to **Práctica B** in a paragraph. Answers will give them a unified story.

Práctica

A HISTORIETA Los cuatro amigos argentinos

Contesten. *(Answer.)*

1. ¿Son amigas Sara y Julia?
2. ¿Son amigos David y Alejandro?
3. ¿Son argentinos o mexicanos los cuatro amigos?
4. ¿Son de Buenos Aires o de Puebla?
5. ¿Son ellos alumnos muy buenos?

Plaza San Martín, Buenos Aires, Argentina

B HISTORIETA La clase de español

Contesten. *(Answer based on your own experience.)*

1. ¿Es grande o pequeña la clase de español?
2. ¿Hay muchos o pocos alumnos en la clase de español?
3. ¿Quién es el profesor o la profesora de español?
4. ¿De qué nacionalidad es él o ella?
5. ¿Cómo es el curso de español? ¿Es un curso interesante o aburrido?
6. ¿Es fácil o difícil el curso de español?
7. ¿Son muy inteligentes los alumnos en la clase de español?
8. ¿Son ellos alumnos serios?
9. ¿Cuántos alumnos hay en la clase de español?

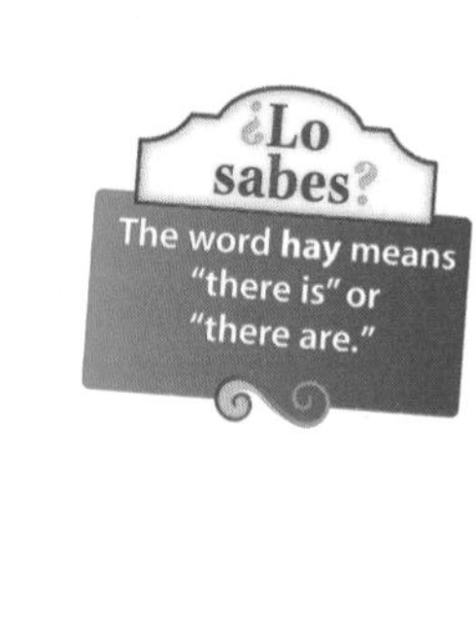

Una clase de español

ANSWERS

Práctica

A
1. **Sí, son amigas.**
2. **Sí, son amigos.**
3. **Los cuatro amigos son argentinos.**
4. **Son de Buenos Aires.**
5. **Sí, son alumnos muy buenos.**

B Answers will vary, but may include:
1. **La clase de español es grande (pequeña).**
2. **Hay muchos (pocos) alumnos en la clase de español.**
3. **El/La profesor(a) de español es ___.**
4. **Es ___.**
5. **El curso de español es interesante (aburrido).**
6. **El curso de español es fácil (difícil).**
7. **Sí, los alumnos en la clase de español son muy inteligentes.**
8. **Sí, (No, no) son alumno serios.**
9. **Hay ___ alumnos en la clase de español.**

C De ninguna manera Sigan el modelo. *(Follow the model.)*

1. Son pequeños, ¿no?
2. Son aburridos, ¿no?
3. Son fáciles, ¿no?
4. Son altos, ¿no?
5. Son bonitos, ¿no?

Actividades comunicativas

A ¿Cómo es la clase? With a classmate, look at the illustration. Take turns asking each other questions about it. Use the following question words: **¿qué? ¿quién? ¿cómo? ¿de dónde? ¿cuántos?**

B La escuela ideal Get together with a classmate. Describe what for each of you is an ideal school. Say as much as you can about the teachers, classes, and students. Determine whether you agree.

ANSWERS

Práctica

C Students will follow the model.

Actividades comunicativas

A Answers will vary, but may include:

¿Cómo son los alumnos?
¿Cómo es la profesora?
¿Quién es la profesora?
¿De dónde es la profesora?
¿Qué clase es?
¿Cuantos alumnos hay en la clase?

B Answers will vary, but may include:

—**En una escuela ideal, las clases son interesantes.**
—**En una escuela ideal, las clases son fáciles.**

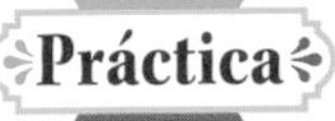

Práctica

C Have students do **Práctica C** as a mini-conversation. Encourage them to use as much expression as possible.

Actividades comunicativas

A Encourage students to make up as many questions as they possibly can. It is important to get the students actively using the question words on their own.

B You can help weaker students do **Actividad B** by asking: **¿Cómo son los alumnos de una escuela ideal? Y las clases, ¿cómo son? ¿grandes, pequeñas, interesantes, aburridas?, ¿y los profesores?**

Learning From Photos

Plaza San Martín, Buenos Aires, Argentina The students in the photo on page 44 are standing in front of the statue of San Martín, in the Plaza San Martín, a favorite downtown gathering place. Children play on the swings and people read newspapers on the benches under the many trees in the plaza.

Independent Practice

Assign any of the following:

1. Workbook, **Palabras 1,** pages 11–12
2. Activities, pages 44–45
3. CD-ROM, Disc 1, pages 42–45

RESOURCES

- Vocabulary Transparencies 2.2 (A & B)
- Student Tape Manual, TE, pages 13–15
- Audiocassette 2B/CD2
- Workbook, page 13
- Quiz 2, page 7
- CD-ROM, Disc 1, pages 46–49

Bell Ringer Review

Use BBR Transparency 2-2, or write the following on the board: Write some information about your Spanish class using the following words.

la clase de español
interesante/aburrida
grande/pequeña
el/la profesor(a)

TEACHING VOCABULARY

A. Have students imitate the pronunciation of these words as carefully as they can. Since they are almost all cognates students will have a tendency to mispronounce them.

B. Point to Germany on a map as students say **el alemán**—or say: **el alemán, una lengua germánica.**

Vocabulario

PALABRAS 2

Los cursos escolares

Las ciencias
la biología
la química
la física

Las matemáticas
la aritmética
el álgebra
la geometría
el cálculo

Las lenguas
el español
el inglés
el francés
el alemán
el latín

Las ciencias sociales
la historia
la geografía

Otras asignaturas o disciplinas
la educación física
la música
el arte
la economía doméstica
la informática

Total Physical Response

Getting ready
Before doing this activity, make sure students understand each of the following commands by acting them out: **levántate, levanta la mano.**

Begin
Hold up a book that represents the subject mentioned and point to a student as you say:

Si tomas un curso de historia, levanta la mano.
Si tomas un curso de música, levanta la mano.
Si tomas un curso de química, levanta la mano.
Si tomas un curso de educación física, levanta la mano.
Si tomas un curso de arte, levanta la mano.
Si tomas un curso de latín, levanta la mano, etc.

¿Qué son?

Más números

31	treinta y uno	36	treinta y seis	50	cincuenta
32	treinta y dos	37	treinta y siete	60	sesenta
33	treinta y tres	38	treinta y ocho	70	setenta
34	treinta y cuatro	39	treinta y nueve	80	ochenta
35	treinta y cinco	40	cuarenta	90	noventa

C. Call two students to the front of the room. Select two who have fairly good pronunciation. Have them open their books to page 47 and read the words in the speech bubble to the class, as if they were the people in the illustration. This procedure helps students grasp the meaning of **nosotros(as).**

D. Go around the room pointing to two students at a time and say **Uds**. Have someone point to him-self/herself and someone else and say **nosotros(as).**

E. Más números Have students repeat the numbers. Then write numbers on the board in random order and have students say them aloud.

VOCABULARY EXPANSION

You may want to give the following additional vocabulary if there are students in the class who are taking these subjects.

la trigonometría
el japonés
el ruso
la mecánica
la psicología
las artes manuales

Did You Know?

Los libros In the public schools of Spain and some Latin American countries students must buy their textbooks. Textbooks are selected and approved by the Ministry of Education and sold in bookstores and supermarkets.

Additional Practice

Los cursos Have students make a list of their courses and indicate whether they consider each one **fácil** or **difícil.** They can then tell about the class using **interesante** or **aburrida.**

CAPÍTULO 2
Vocabulario

A **Práctica A** can be done with books open. Note that it serves as an introduction to the plural since it contrasts **es/son** and singular and plural forms of nouns and adjectives.

B Ask questions from **Práctica B** and have students answer orally with books closed.

C Have students refer to the photograph as they answer the questions in **Práctica C.**

D Students should be able to recognize the cognates used in **Práctica D** but should not be expected to learn or produce this receptive vocabulary.

Learning From Photos

Córdoba, España (page 49) The **puente romano** which dates from the time of the Romans is still in use. It crosses the **río Guadalquivir.** From the bridge we see the **Mezquita** built between the 8th and 10th centuries. The **Mezquita de Córdoba** is one of the earliest and most beautiful examples of Muslim architecture in Spain.

Práctica

A **Ciencias, lenguas o matemáticas** Contesten con **sí** o **no.** *(Answer with* sí *or* no.)

1. La biología es una ciencia.
2. La historia y la geografía son matemáticas.
3. El cálculo es una lengua.
4. El latín y el francés son lenguas.
5. El arte y la música son cursos obligatorios.

B **Cursos fáciles y difíciles** Contesten personalmente. *(Answer based on your own experience.)*

1. ¿Es el español un curso difícil o fácil?
2. ¿Es grande o pequeña la clase de español?
3. ¿Qué cursos son fáciles?
4. ¿Cuántos cursos son fáciles?
5. ¿Qué cursos son difíciles?
6. ¿Cuántos cursos son difíciles?
7. ¿Qué cursos son interesantes?
8. ¿Qué cursos son aburridos?

C **HISTORIETA** **Alumnos americanos**

Completen. *(Complete.)*

1. ¿De qué nacionalidad son los alumnos?
2. ¿Son alumnos en una escuela secundaria?
3. ¿Son alumnos de química?
4. ¿Son alumnos buenos o malos en la química?

Una clase de ciencias

D **¿Qué curso o asignatura es?** Identifiquen el curso. *(Identify the course.)*

1. el problema, la ecuación, la solución, la multiplicación, la división
2. la literatura, la composición, la gramática
3. un microbio, un animal, una planta, el microscopio, el laboratorio
4. el círculo, el arco, el rectángulo, el triángulo
5. el piano, el violín, la guitarra, el concierto, la ópera, el coro
6. las montañas, los océanos, las capitales, los recursos naturales
7. la pintura, la estatua, la escultura
8. el fútbol, el básquetbol, el béisbol, el voleibol, el tenis

ANSWERS

Práctica

A
1. **Sí, la biología es una ciencia**
2. **No, la historia y la geografía no son matemáticas.**
3. **No, el cálculo no es una lengua.**
4. **Sí, el latín y el francés son lenguas.**
5. **No, el arte y la música no son cursos obligatorios.**

B Answers will vary, but may include:
1. **El español es un curso fácil (difícil).**
2. **La clase de español es grande (pequeña).**
3. **Las lenguas (Las ciencias, etc.) son fáciles.**
4. **Dos (Tres) cursos son fáciles. (Un curso es fácil.)**
5. **Las lenguas (Las ciencias, etc.) son difíciles.**
6. **Dos (Tres) cursos son difíciles. (Un curso es difícil.)**
7. **El español, el inglés, etc. son interesantes.**
8. **Las matemáticas, la biología, etc. son aburridas.**

Actividades comunicativas

A **¡Qué clase tan difícil!** Divide into groups of three or four. In each group rate your courses as **fácil, difícil, regular, interesante, aburrido, fantástico.** Tally the results and report the information to the class.

Córdoba, España

B **En España** You are spending the summer with a family in Córdoba in southern Spain. Tell your Spanish "brother" or "sister" (your partner) all you can about your Spanish class and your Spanish teacher. Answer any questions he or she may have.

JUEGO **Un número secreto** Think of a number between 1 and 99. Your partner will try to guess the number you have in mind. Use a hand gesture to indicate whether the number you are thinking of is higher or lower. Continue until your partner guesses the correct number. Take turns.

ANSWERS CONTINUED

C **1. Los alumnos son americanos.**
2. Sí, son alumnos en una escuela secundaria.
3. Sí, son alumnos de química.
4. Son alumnos buenos (malos) en la química.

D **1. el álgebra (las matemáticas)**
2. el inglés
3. la biología
4. la geometría
5. la música
6. la geografía
7. el arte
8. la educación física

Actividades comunicativas

A Answers will vary.

B Students should use adjectives that can describe a class: **interesante, aburrido, fácil, difícil, etc.**

Actividades comunicativas

¡OJO! Práctica versus Actividades comunicativas All activities which provide guided practice are labeled **Práctica.** The more open-ended communicative activities are labeled **Actividades comunicativas.**

You may have students do either of these activities. Allow them to select the activity or activities they wish to take part in.

RECYCLING

These activities recycle the singular forms of nouns, adjectives, and the verb *ser* from Chapter 1.

B **TECHNOLOGY OPTION** In the CD-ROM version of this activity, Disc 1, page 49, students can interact with an on-screen, native speaker and record their voice.

This is a good, end-of-class activity. **Hint:** You may want to change the number span if your time is limited.

HISTORY CONNECTION

La Mezquita de Córdoba The Great Mosque was built between the 8th and 10th centuries. The Arabs crossed the Straits of Gilbraltar in 711 and conquered most of Spain. They remained there until 1492 when Ferdinand and Isabel conquered Granada, the last Arab territory in Spain. Ask students if they know what a mosque is.

RESOURCES

- Workbook, pages 14–16
- Student Tape Manual, TE, pages 15–19
- Audiocassette 2B/CD2
- Structure Transparencies S-2A, S2-B
- Quizzes 3–5, pages 8–10
- Computer Testmaker
- CD-ROM, Disc 1, pages 50–57

Bell Ringer Review

Use BRR Transparency 2-3, or write the following on the board: Quickly write down in Spanish the names of the subjects you are taking this semester.

TEACHING STRUCTURE

Describing more than one

A. If you wish to present the grammar point deductively, have students close their books. On the board write the singular forms of the nouns from Step 1 on page 50. Now ask students to supply the plural forms. (They know the plural forms of the articles from the vocabulary presentation in **Palabras 1.**) Then have students open their books and read Steps 1 and 2.

B. Have students read the model sentences aloud in Steps 3 and 4.

Estructura

Describing more than one
Sustantivos, artículos y adjetivos en el plural

1. Plural means "more than one." In Spanish, the plural of most nouns is formed by adding an **s.**

SINGULAR	PLURAL
el muchacho	**los muchachos**
el colegio	**los colegios**
la amiga	**las amigas**
la escuela	**las escuelas**

2. The plural of the definite articles **el** and **la** are **los** and **las.** The plural forms of the indefinite articles **un** and **una** are **unos** and **unas.**

SINGULAR	PLURAL
el curso	**los cursos**
la alumna	**las alumnas**
un amigo	**unos amigos**
una amiga	**unas amigas**

3. To form the plural of adjectives that end in **o, a,** or **e,** you add **s** to the singular form.

El alumno es serio.	**Los alumnos son serios.**
La alumna es seria.	**Las alumnas son serias.**
La lengua es interesante.	**Las lenguas son interesantes.**

4. To form the plural of adjectives that end in a consonant, you add **es.**

El curso es fácil.	**Los cursos son fáciles.**
La lengua es fácil.	**Las lenguas son fáciles.**

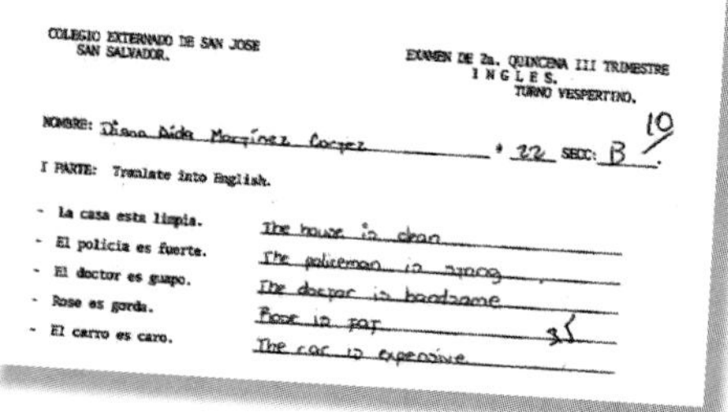

COLEGIO EXTERNADO DE SAN JOSE
SAN SALVADOR.

EXAMEN DE 2a. QUINCENA III TRIMESTRE
I N G L E S.
TURNO VESPERTINO.

NOMBRE: Diana Aida Martínez Cortez # 22 SECC: B 10

I PARTE: Translate into English.

- La casa esta limpia. The house is clean
- El policia es fuerte. The policeman is strong
- El doctor es guapo. The doctor is handsome
- Rose es gorda. Rose is fat
- El carro es caro. The car is expensive

Class Motivator

¿Singular o plural? Give students a word orally. Have them raise one hand if it is singular, two hands if it is plural. Example: **la clase, los libros.**

Práctica

Santiago de Chile

A HISTORIETA **Amigos nuevos**

Contesten con **sí.** *(Answer with* sí.)

1. ¿Son amigos nuevos los dos muchachos?
2. ¿Son chilenos los dos muchachos?
3. ¿Son ellos alumnos en un colegio en Santiago de Chile?
4. ¿Son alumnos serios?
5. ¿Son ellos muchachos populares?

B **¿Cómo son?** Describan a las personas. *(Describe the people.)*

1. David, Domingo

2. Inés, Susana

3. Paco, Eduardo

4. Isabel, Carmen

C HISTORIETA **La señora Ortiz**

Completen. *(Complete with any logical response.)*

La señora Ortiz es una profesora muy ___1___. Las clases de la señora Ortiz son ___2___. Las clases de la señora Ortiz no son ___3___. Los alumnos de la señora Ortiz son ___4___. No son ___5___.

Práctica

A This activity can be done with books closed or open.

B Have students look at the illustrations and make up any sentences that describe them accurately.

C Do **Práctica C** with books open. Note that it reinforces both the singular and plural forms.

EXPANSION After going over **Práctica C**, you can call on one student to read the entire activity as a story.

Additional Practice

Descripciones Have students make up original sentences about one or more persons.

ANSWERS

Práctica

A
1. **Sí, son amigos nuevos.**
2. **Sí, los dos muchachos son chilenos.**
3. **Sí, son alumnos en un colegio en Santiago de Chile.**
4. **Sí, son alumnos serios.**
5. **Sí, son muchachos populares.**

B Answers will vary, but may include:
David y Domingo son rubios.
Inés y Susana son graciosas.
Paco y Eduardo son cómicos.
Isabel y Carmen son bajas.

C Answers will vary, but may include:
1. **buena (interesante, aburrida)**
2. **interesantes (aburridas)**
3. **difíciles (interesantes, fáciles)**
4. **buenos (malos, americanos, serios)**
5. **malos (buenos, mexicanos, perezosos)**

CAPÍTULO 2
Estructura

TEACHING STRUCTURE

Talking about more than one

A. Have students keep their books closed as you write **yo, tú, él/ella** on the board with the appropriate forms of the verb **ser.** Use the standard conjugation format shown in the chart on page 52. Remind students that they learned the singular forms of the verb **ser** in Chapter 1.

B. Now write in **ellos/ellas** and ask students if they remember the corresponding verb form (from the **Palabras 1** section). Do the same with **nosotros,** and then introduce the **Uds.** form. (The difference between **tú** and **Ud.** will be presented in Chapter 3, page 83.)

C. Have students open their books and read the information in Step 3 aloud. It is important that students understand to whom they are referring when they use a verb form.

D. Have students read the sentences in the speech bubbles with correct intonation.

Additional Practice

Actividad Use Structure Transparency S-2A and ask students to make up their own sentences using **nosotros, ellos, ellas,** and **Uds.**

Talking about more than one
Presente de ser en el plural

1. You have already learned the singular forms of the verb **ser.** Review the following.

yo	soy
tú	eres
él	es
ella	es

2. Now study the plural forms of the verb **ser.**

nosotros(as)	somos
ellos	son
ellas	son
Uds.	son

3.

When you talk about yourself and another person or other people, you use the **nosotros(as)** form.

You use **ellos** when talking about two or more males or a mixed group of males and females.

You use **ellas** when talking about two or more females.

When talking to more than one person, you use **ustedes,** the plural form for **tú.** **Ustedes** is commonly abbreviated as **Uds.**

A **Somos alumnos americanos.** Practiquen la conversación. *(Practice the conversation.)*

¿Son Uds. americanos?
Sí, somos americanos.
¿Son Uds. alumnos?
Sí, somos alumnos. Y somos alumnos serios.
¿En qué escuela son Uds. alumnos?
Somos alumnos en la Escuela Jorge Wáshington. Y Uds., ¿son Uds. alumnas?
Sí, somos alumnas en la Escuela Martin Luther King.

Completen según la conversación. *(Complete according to the conversation.)*

Los muchachos ___1___ americanos. Ellos ___2___ alumnos. ___3___ alumnos muy serios. ___4___ alumnos buenos. ___5___ alumnos en la Escuela Jorge Wáshington. Las muchachas ___6___ americanas también. ___7___ alumnas en la Escuela Martin Luther King.

B **Él, ella y yo** Contesten. *(Answer with a classmate.)*

1. ¿Son Uds. amigos?
2. ¿Son Uds. alumnos serios?
3. ¿Son Uds. graciosos?
4. ¿En qué escuela son Uds. alumnos?
5. ¿Son Uds. alumnos en la misma clase de español o en clases diferentes?
6. ¿Son Uds. alumnos buenos en español?

Práctica

A Have students work in pairs and dramatize this conversation. Have them read with as much expression as possible. Note that the conversation acquaints students with the **somos** response to **son Uds.** questions. After a few pairs of students have read the conversation aloud, call on individuals to complete the narrative that follows.

B Have students close their books and ask them the questions yourself. This **Práctica** has students supply answers to questions with **Uds.** They hear **son** and must answer with **somos.**

ANSWERS

Práctica

A
1. **son**
2. **son**
3. **Son**
4. **Son**
5. **Son**
6. **son**
7. **Son**

B
1. **Sí, (No, no) somos amigos.**
2. **Sí, (No, no) somos alumnos serios.**
3. **Sí, (No, no) somos graciosos.**
4. **Somos alumnos en la Escuela ___.**
5. **Somos alumnos en la misma clase de español. (Somos alumnos en clases diferentes.)**
6. **Sí, (No, no) somos alumnos buenos en español.**

C Have students do **Práctica C** as a paired activity.

D Call on an individual to supply the responses to about three sentences in **Práctica D** before going on to another student. Note that this **Práctica** makes students use all forms of **ser.**

Writing Development

After going over **Práctica D**, have students read it silently. Then have them close their books and rewrite it in their own words.

Learning From Photos

Santo Domingo, República Dominicana This photo was taken on the outskirts of Santo Domingo, the capital of the Dominican Republic. The Dominican Republic occupies the eastern two thirds of the island of Hispaniola. The western section is Haiti.

C **¿Qué son Uds.?** Formen preguntas según el modelo. *(Ask classmates questions according to the model.)*

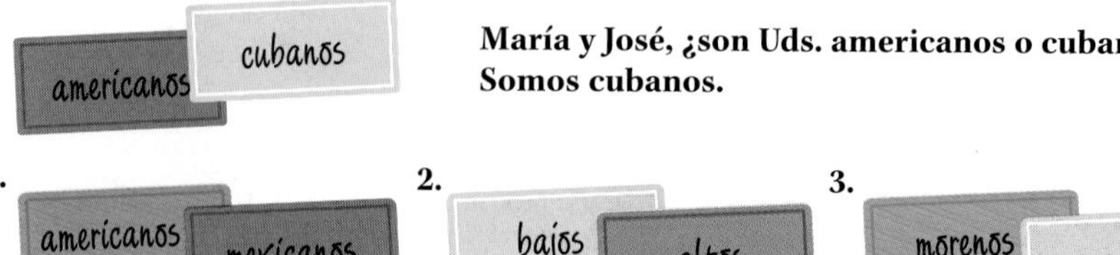

María y José, ¿son Uds. americanos o cubanos?
Somos cubanos.

D **HISTORIETA** El amigo de Carlos

Completen con **ser.** *(Complete with* ser.)

Yo ___1___ un amigo de Carlos. Carlos ___2___ muy simpático. Y él ___3___ gracioso. Carlos y yo ___4___ dominicanos. ___5___ de la República Dominicana.

La República Dominicana ___6___ parte de una isla en el mar Caribe. Nosotros ___7___ alumnos en un colegio en Santo Domingo. Santo Domingo ___8___ la capital de la República Dominicana. Nosotros ___9___ alumnos de inglés. La profesora de inglés ___10___ la señora Drake. Ella ___11___ americana.

La clase de inglés ___12___ bastante interesante. Nosotros ___13___ muy buenos en inglés. Nosotros ___14___ muy inteligentes. ¿Y Uds.? Uds. ___15___ americanos, ¿no? ¿De dónde ___16___ Uds.? ¿___17___ Uds. alumnos en una escuela secundaria? ¿___18___ Uds. alumnos de español?

Santo Domingo, República Dominicana

ANSWERS

Práctica

C Answers will vary, but may resemble the following:

1. **Sara y Ángel, ¿son Uds. americanos o mexicanos? Somos americanos.**
2. **María y Andrés, ¿son Uds. bajos o altos? Somos altos.**
3. **Juan y José, ¿son Uds. morenos o rubios? Somos rubios.**

D
1. **soy**
2. **es**
3. **es**
4. **somos**
5. **Somos**
6. **es**
7. **somos**
8. **es**
9. **somos**
10. **es**
11. **es**
12. **es**
13. **somos**
14. **somos**
15. **son**
16. **son**
17. **Son**
18. **Son**

Actividad comunicativa

A ¿De qué nacionalidad son? Work in groups of four. Two of you get together and choose a city below, but don't tell the other students in your group which one. The other two have to guess where you're from by asking you questions. Take turns. You may use the model as a guide.

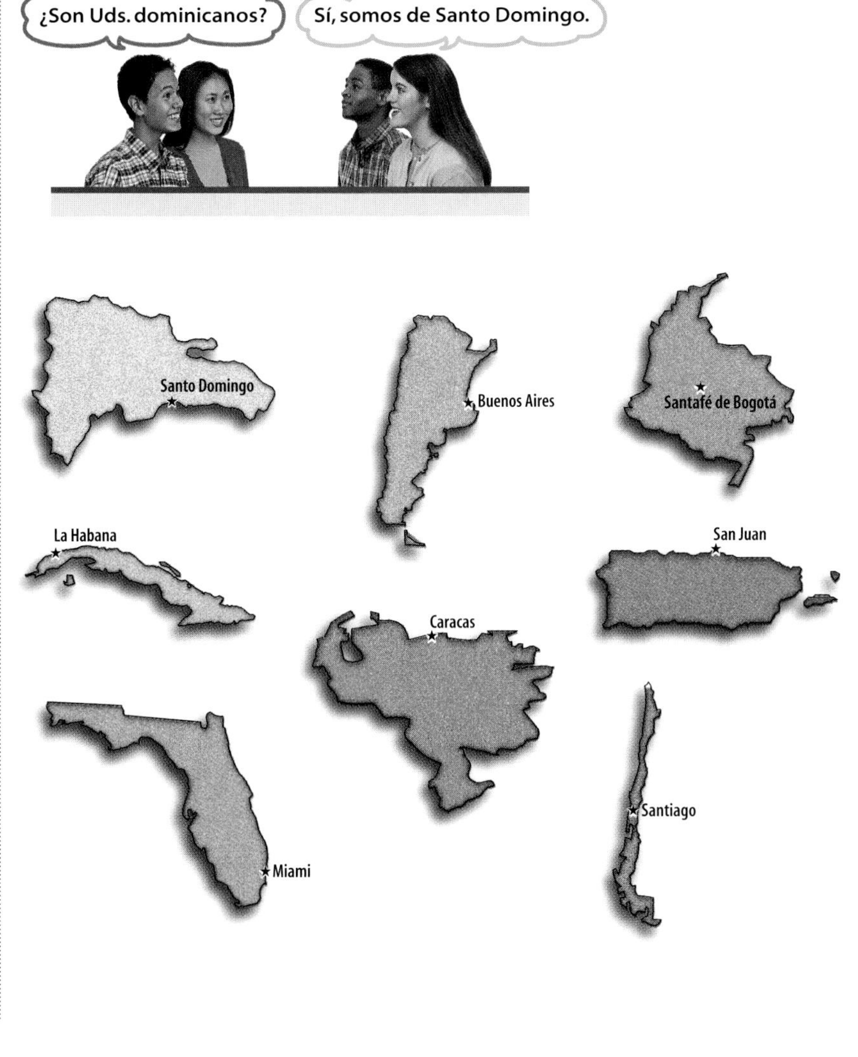

ANSWERS

Actividad comunicativa

A Answers will vary, but may include:

—¿Son Uds. argentinos?
—Sí, somos de Buenos Aires.

—¿Son Uds. colombianos?
—Sí, somos de Santafé de Bogotá.

—¿Son Uds. cubanos?
—Sí, somos de La Habana.

—¿Son Uds. venezolanos?
—Sí, somos de Caracas.

—¿Son Uds. puertorriqueños?
—Sí, somos de San Juan.

—¿Son Uds. americanos?
—Sí, somos de Miami.

—¿Son Uds. chilenos?
—Sí, somos de Santiago.

Actividades comunicativas

A Since students may not be very familiar with the geography of the Spanish-speaking world, it is suggested that you point out these cities and countries on a larger map, or have them open their books to the maps on pages 464–465. Another option is to use the Map Transparencies located in the **¡Buen viaje!** Transparency Binder as students do the activity.

CAPÍTULO 2
Estructura

TEACHING STRUCTURE

Telling time

¡OJO! It is recommended that you teach a few of these time expressions each day rather than present them all at once. A possible plan is:

Day 1: **Es la una. Son las dos, etc. (Hours)**

Day 2: **Es la una y cinco. Son las dos y diez, etc. (After the hour)**

Day 3: **Es la una menos cinco. Son las dos menos diez, etc. (Before the hour)**

Day 4: **Son las dos y media, y cuarto, etc.**

Day 5: **¿A qué hora es... ? Es a las...**

A. Have students open their books to page 56 or use Structure Transparency S-2B. Have them repeat the time shown on each clock after you.

B. Introduce the question, **¿Qué hora es?** Then ask the time for each clock.

C. Introduce the concept **¿A qué hora?** to indicate at what time an event takes place. Contrast this concept with simply asking what time it is.

Telling time
La hora

1. Observe the following examples of how to tell time.

¿Qué hora es?

Es la una.

Son las dos.

Son las diez.

Son las doce.

Es el mediodía.

Es la medianoche.

Es la una y diez.

Son las tres y cinco.

Son las cuatro y veinticinco.

Son las cinco menos veinte.

Son las seis menos diez.

Son las diez menos cinco.

Son las dos y cuarto.

Son las siete menos cuarto.

Son las seis y media.

For the Younger Student

Mi rutina Have students draw pictures of themselves doing their various daily activities. Have them label the drawings with the time of day that they do each activity.

2. To indicate A.M. and P.M. in Spanish, you use the following expressions.

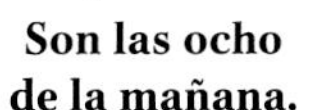

Son las ocho de la mañana. **Son las tres de la tarde.** **Son las once de la noche.**

3. Note how to ask and tell what time something (such as a party) takes place.

¿*A* qué hora es la fiesta? **La fiesta es *a* las nueve.**

Práctica

A **¿Qué hora es?** Digan la hora. *(Tell the time on each clock.)*

1. 2. 3. 4. 5. 6.

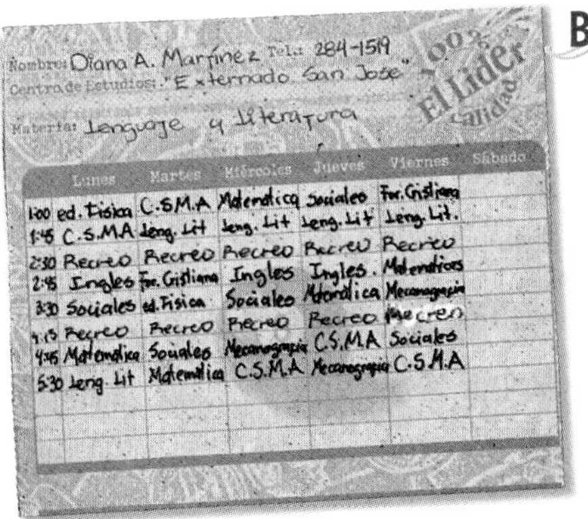

Nombre: Diana A. Martínez Tel.: 284-1519
Centro de Estudios: "Externado San José"
Materia: Lenguaje y literatura

	Lunes	Martes	Miércoles	Jueves	Viernes	Sábado
1:00	ed. Física	C.S.M.A	Matemática	Sociales	For. Cristiana	
1:45	C.S.M.A	Leng. Lit	Leng. Lit	Leng. Lit	Leng. Lit.	
2:30	Recreo	Recreo	Recreo	Recreo	Recreo	
2:45	Ingles	For. Cristiana	Ingles	Ingles.	Matemáticas	
3:30	Sociales	ed. Física	Sociales	Matemática	Mecanografía	
4:15	Recreo	Recreo	Recreo	Recreo	Recreo	
4:45	Matemática	Sociales	Mecanografía	C.S.M.A	Sociales	
5:30	Leng. Lit	Matemática	C.S.M.A	Mecanografía	C.S.M.A	

B **El horario escolar** Digan la hora de la clase. *(Tell the time of each class.)*

CAPÍTULO 2
Estructura

Práctica

TEACHING TIP

Use a toy clock or make your own cardboard clock with movable hands. Using the clock, ask **¿Qué hora es?** Repeat the question as many times as you can and monitor student responses. Then have a student ask the question and have another respond.

A and **B** Students can do these activities in pairs. In **Práctica A,** Student 1 will ask: **¿Qué hora es?** while pointing to each clock. In **Práctica B,** Student 1 will ask: **¿A qué hora es la clase de... ?** In both cases, Student 2 will respond accordingly. Have them reverse roles and repeat the activities.

¡OJO! There is no more new material to present in this chapter. The sections that follow recombine and reinforce the vocabulary and structures that have already been introduced.

ANSWERS

Práctica

A
1. **Son las ocho y cuarto.**
2. **Son las once.**
3. **Son las cinco y media.**
4. **Es la una menos cuarto.**
5. **Son las dos y veinticinco.**
6. **Son las cuatro menos diez.**

B Answers will vary according to the day students choose. One possibility could be the following:

La clase de educación física es a la una.
La clase de C.S.M.A. es a las dos menos cuarto.
El recreo es a las dos y media.
La clase de inglés es a las tres menos cuarto.
La clase de (ciencias) sociales es a las tres y media.
El recreo es a las cuatro y cuarto.
La clase de matemáticas es a las cinco menos cuarto.
La clase de lengua y literatura es a las cinco y media.
La clase de mecanografía es a las cinco menos cuarto.

Independent Practice

Assign any of the following:
1. Activities, pages 50–57
2. CD-ROM, Disc 1, pages 50–57
3. Workbook, pages 14–16

CAPÍTULO 2
Conversación

RESOURCES

- Audiocassette 2B/CD2
- CD-ROM, Disc 1, page 58

Bell Ringer Review

Use BRR Transparency 2-4, or write the following on the board: Write down the times of your classes. Follow the model:
La clase de ___ es a las ___.

TEACHING THE CONVERSATION

A. Tell students they are going to hear a conversation between Patricio and Manuel. Have students repeat the conversation after you once or twice, or have them listen to the recording on Cassette 2B/Compact Disc 2. Begin with the whole class and then have individual students repeat.

B. Call on pairs of students to present the conversation to the class.

TECHNOLOGY OPTION

In the CD-ROM version (Disc 1, page 58), students can watch a dramatization of this conversation. They can then play the role of either one of the characters, and record themselves in the conversation.

ABOUT THE SPANISH LANGUAGE

The word **colonia** is used in Mexico City to refer to a section of the city—Colonia de Chapultepec, Colonia de Coyoacán.

Conversación

¿De qué nacionalidad son Uds.?

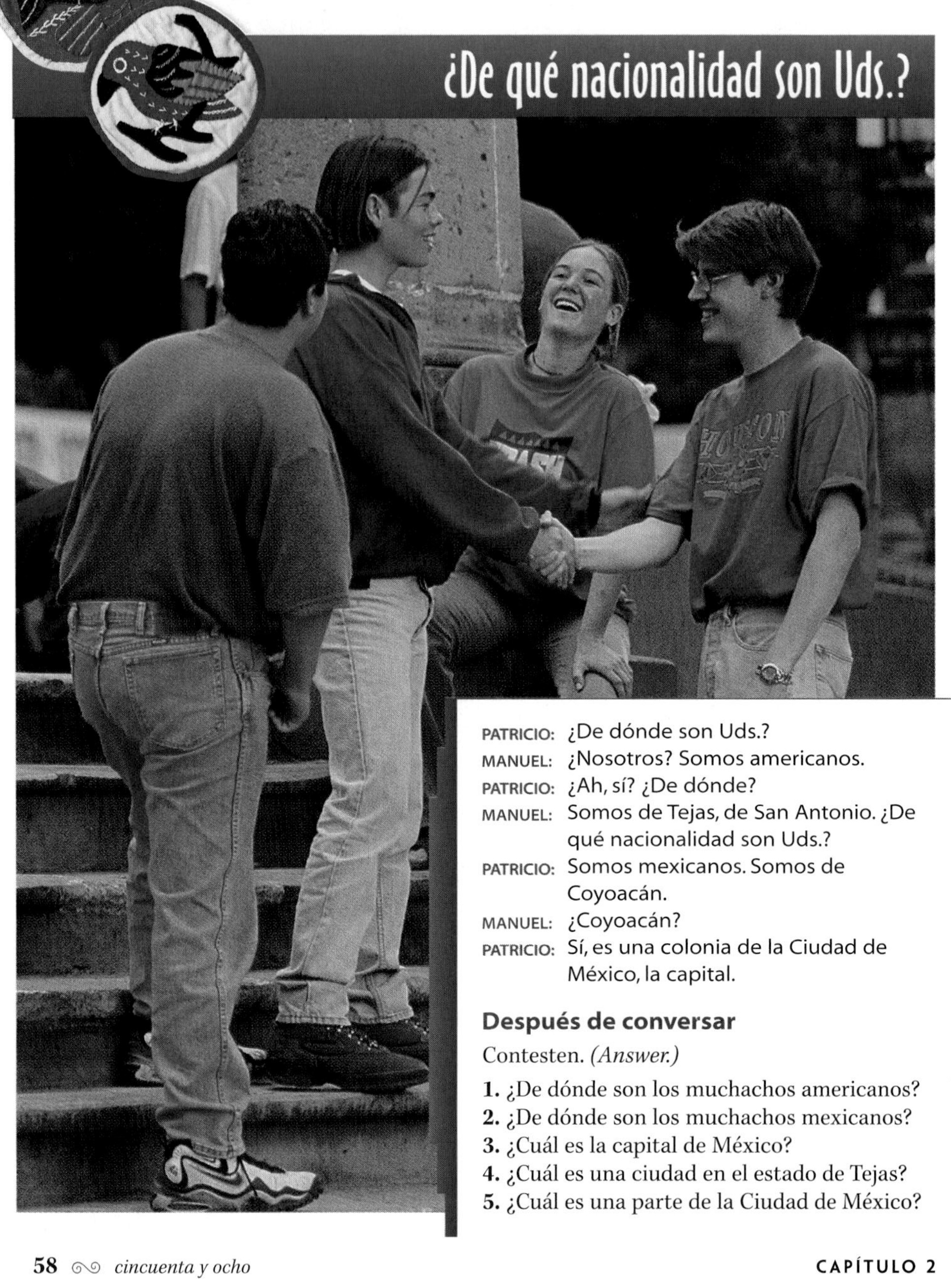

PATRICIO: ¿De dónde son Uds.?
MANUEL: ¿Nosotros? Somos americanos.
PATRICIO: ¿Ah, sí? ¿De dónde?
MANUEL: Somos de Tejas, de San Antonio. ¿De qué nacionalidad son Uds.?
PATRICIO: Somos mexicanos. Somos de Coyoacán.
MANUEL: ¿Coyoacán?
PATRICIO: Sí, es una colonia de la Ciudad de México, la capital.

Después de conversar

Contesten. *(Answer.)*

1. ¿De dónde son los muchachos americanos?
2. ¿De dónde son los muchachos mexicanos?
3. ¿Cuál es la capital de México?
4. ¿Cuál es una ciudad en el estado de Tejas?
5. ¿Cuál es una parte de la Ciudad de México?

ANSWERS

Después de conversar

1. **Los muchachos americanos son de Tejas (de San Antonio).**
2. **Los muchachos mexicanos son de Coyoacán.**
3. **La capital de México es la Ciudad de México.**
4. **San Antonio.**
5. **Coyoacán.**

Did You Know?

Coyoacán Once upon a time Coyoacán was a suburb of Mexico City. It has now been incorporated into the city proper.

Actividades comunicativas

A **En la Argentina** Work in groups of four. Two of you are visiting Buenos Aires and you meet two Argentine students in a café. Find out as much about each other and your schools as you can.

La Recoleta, Buenos Aires, Argentina

JUEGO **¿Qué clase es?** Work with a classmate. He or she gives you a one-sentence description of a class. Guess what class it is. If you're wrong, your partner will give you another hint. Continue until you guess the class being described. Take turns.

Pronunciación

Las vocales e, i

The sounds of the Spanish vowels **e** and **i** are short, clear, and concise. The pronunciation of **e** is similar to *a* in *mate*. The pronunciation of **i** is similar to the *ee* in *bee* or *see*. Imitate the pronunciation carefully.

e	i
Elena	**Isabel**
peso	**Inés**

Repeat the following sentences.

Elena es una amiga de Felipe.
Inés es tímida.
Sí, Isabel es italiana.

Actividades comunicativas

You may have students do one or both of these activities. Allow them to select the activity they wish to take part in.

TEACHING PRONUNCIATION

A. Have students repeat the vowels **e** and **i** very carefully. English speakers tend to make them into a diphthong or to produce the "shwa" sound.

B. Using Pronunciation Transparency P-2, model the word **Italia.** Have students say it in unison and individually.

C. Now lead students through the presentation on page 59, modeling the words and phrases.

D. For additional pronunciation practice, you may wish to play the Pronunciation section on Cassette 2B/Compact Disc 2.

E. The sentences on page 59 can also be used as a dictation exercise.

TECHNOLOGY OPTION

In the CD-ROM version of the Pronunciation section (Disc 1, page 59), students will see an animation of the cartoon on this page. They can also listen to, record, and play back the vowels, words, and sentences presented here.

Learning From Photos

La Recoleta, Buenos Aires, Argentina This café is in the Recoleta section of Buenos Aires, an upscale neighborhood with many cafés, boutiques, and beautiful apartment buildings.

ANSWERS

Actvidades comunicativas

A Answers will vary, but may include:

—¿De dónde son Uds.?
—Somos de Los Ángeles.
—¿De qué nacionalidad son Uds.?
—Nosotros somos argentinos. Somos de Buenos Aires.
—¿En qué escuela son Uds. alumnos?
—Somos alumnos en la Escuela ___, en Buenos Aires.

National Standards

Cultures This reading and the related activities on pages 60–61 about the Hispanic population in the United States give students an understanding of the importance of learning Spanish.

Did You Know?

Nombres hispanos Due to both Spanish and Mexican influences there are many places in the United States with Spanish names. This is particularly true in many parts of the Southwest, but it is not limited to this area. Some examples are: Arizona, Colorado, New Mexico, Albuquerque, Pueblo, El Paso, Laredo, Los Angeles, San Francisco, Nevada, Sierra Nevada, Florida, San Agustín.

TEACHING THE READING

Pre-reading

A. Have students locate Pueblo, Colorado on a map.

B. Show students a map of the U.S. Have them point out places with Spanish names.

Reading

A. Have students close their books as you read the selection for them. Then have them listen as they follow along in their books.

B. Ask questions from **Después de leer A,** page 61, as you read the selection. Call on a student to read several sentences. Ask questions after every three sentences.

Lecturas CULTURALES

Reading Strategy

Using titles and subtitles

Look at titles and subtitles before you begin to read. They will usually help you know what a reading selection will be about. Having an idea of what a reading will be about will help you understand better as you read.

EL ESPAÑOL EN LOS ESTADOS UNIDOS

Mexicanoamericanos

¡Hola! Somos Alejandro Chávez y Guadalupe Garza. Somos alumnos en una escuela secundaria de Pueblo, Colorado. Somos alumnos en una escuela secundaria americana. Pero para nosotros el español no es una lengua extranjera[1]. ¿Por qué[2]? Porque nosotros somos de ascendencia[3] mexicana. Somos mexicanoamericanos.

[1]extranjera *foreign*
[2]¿Por qué? *Why?*
[3]ascendencia *background, descent*

Jóvenes de ascendencia mexicana

Learning From Photos

Una descripción Have students look at this photo and describe the boy and girl in their own words.

Jóvenes de ascendencia cubana

Miami, La Florida

Cubanoamericanos

Nosotros somos Raúl Ugarte y Marta Dávila. Somos de Miami, en la Florida. Como muchas personas en Miami, somos de ascendencia cubana. Somos cubanoamericanos.

En los Estados Unidos hay unos veinte millones de hispanohablantes[4]. El español es una lengua muy importante en los Estados Unidos.

[4]hispanohablantes *Spanish speakers*

Después de leer

A Alejandro Chávez y Guadalupe Garza Contesten. *(Answer.)*

1. ¿Quiénes son Alejandro Chávez y Guadalupe Garza?
2. ¿Dónde son alumnos?
3. ¿De dónde son ellos?
4. Para Alejandro y Guadalupe, ¿es el español una lengua extranjera?
5. ¿Por qué no? ¿Qué son ellos?

B Raúl Ugarte y Marta Dávila Corrijan. *(Correct the false statements.)*

1. Raúl Ugarte y Marta Dávila son de ascendencia mexicana.
2. Ellos son mexicanoamericanos.
3. Ellos son de San Antonio, Tejas.
4. Hay unos veinte millones de hispanohablantes en Cuba.

Post-reading

A. Have students do the activities in the **Después de leer** section.

B. Call on several students to give, in their own words, some information about Spanish speakers in the U.S.

TECHNOLOGY OPTIONS

Students may listen to a recorded version of the **Lectura** on the CD-ROM, Disc 1, pages 60–61.

Students can find out more about American cities with large Spanish-speaking populations by doing the Chapter 2 Internet Activity. For more information, see the Internet Connection, page 69.

ANSWERS

Después de leer

A
1. **Alejandro Chávez y Guadalupe Garza son alumnos.**
2. **Son alumnos en una escuela secundaria americana.**
3. **Son de Pueblo, Colorado.**
4. **El español no es una lengua extranjera para ellos.**
5. **Porque son de ascendencia mexicana. Son mexicanoamericanos.**

B
1. **Raúl Ugarte y Marta Dávila son de ascendencia cubana.**
2. **Ellos no son mexicanoamericanos. Son cubanoamericanos.**
3. **Ellos son de Miami, en la Florida.**
4. **Hay unos veinte millones de hispanohablantes en los Estados Unidos.**

Independent Practice

Assign any of the following:
1. **Después de leer** activities, page 61
2. Workbook, **Un poco más,** page 17
3. CD-ROM, Disc 1, pages 60–61

LECTURA OPCIONAL 1

TEACHING TIPS

¡OJO! This reading on San Antonio is optional. You may skip it completely, have the entire class read it, have only several students read it, or assign it for extra credit.

A. Have students read the short selection quickly and then respond to the **sí/no** questions of **Después de leer A**.

HISTORY CONNECTION

Domingo Terán de los Ríos

Domingo Terán de los Ríos arrived in what is now San Antonio in 1691. He called it San Antonio because he arrived on Saint Anthony's Day. In 1718 a Franciscan priest established a mission called San Antonio de Valero. In order to boost the non-Indian population, Spain allowed 55 colonists from the Canary Islands to emigrate to San Antonio. San Antonio grew and became the capital of Spanish Texas. The Misión San Antonio became a military garrison. After the Mexican Revolution of 1821, San Antonio became a part of the Republic of Mexico. When López de Santa Ana seized the Mexican presidency and abolished the constitution, many Texans, both Anglo and Hispanic, refused to recognize his dictatorship. That led to the famous Battle of the Alamo and the declaration of Texas independence from Mexico.

LECTURA OPCIONAL 1

SAN ANTONIO

San Antonio es una ciudad[1] muy bonita de Tejas. Es una ciudad muy histórica. Es la ciudad favorita de muchos turistas. San Antonio es una ciudad bilingüe. Hay mucha gente[2] de ascendencia mexicana en San Antonio. Hay muchos mexicanoamericanos.

[1]ciudad *city*
[2]gente *people*

El río, San Antonio

El Álamo, San Antonio

Después de leer

A **¿Cómo es San Antonio?** Contesten con **sí** o **no.** *(Answer with* sí *or* no.*)*

1. San Antonio es una ciudad bastante fea.
2. Hay monumentos históricos en San Antonio.
3. San Antonio es una ciudad de México.
4. Hay muchos hispanohablantes en San Antonio.
5. Hay muchos mexicanoamericanos en San Antonio.

B **En español, por favor.** Busquen las palabras afines en la lectura. *(Find the following cognates in the reading.)*

1. favorite
2. historic
3. bilingual
4. tourists

ANSWERS

Después de leer

A
1. **No, San Antonio es una ciudad muy bonita.**
2. **Sí, hay monumentos históricos en San Antonio.**
3. **No, San Antonio es una ciudad de Tejas.**
4. **Sí, hay muchos hispanohablantes en San Antonio.**
5. **Sí, hay muchos mexicanoamericanos en San Antonio.**

B
1. **favorita**
2. **histórica**
3. **bilingüe**
4. **turistas**

LECTURA OPCIONAL 2

COYOACÁN

La Ciudad de México es hoy día[1] la ciudad más grande del mundo[2]. Coyoacán es una colonia en la zona sur de la ciudad. Es una colonia bonita y tranquila. Es elegante también. Muchos residentes o habitantes de Coyoacán son personas famosas.

[1]hoy día *these days*
[2]mundo *world*

El Museo de Frida Kahlo, Coyoacán

Coyoacán, México

Después de leer

A La Ciudad de México Completen. *(Complete.)*

1. ____ es la ciudad más grande del mundo.
2. ____ es una colonia de la Ciudad de México.
3. Coyoacán es una colonia en la zona ____ de la ciudad.
4. Hay muchas personas ____ en Coyoacán.

B En español, por favor. Busquen las palabras afines en la lectura. *(Find the following cognates in the reading.)*

1. zone
2. tranquil, calm
3. elegant
4. residents
5. inhabitants

LECTURA OPCIONAL 2

TEACHING TIPS

¡OJO! This reading on Coyoacán is optional. You may skip it completely, have the entire class read it, have only several students read it, or assign it for extra credit.

A. Have students read the short selection quickly and then have them do the **Después de leer** activities.

Did You Know?

Coyoacán Coyoacán is in the southern part of Mexico City. It was originally settled by the Toltecas in the 10th century. Bernal Díaz del Castillo said that at the time of the conquest there were 6,000 homes in Coyoacán. It was here that Cortes set up headquarters during his siege of Tenochtitlán.

Contemporary Coyoacán is a charming area with buildings of traditional colonial architecture and an animated street life. Some of its famous inhabitants have been:

Miguel de la Madrid, president of Mexico
José Clemente Orozco, muralist
Dolores del Río, film star
Frida Kahlo, artist
Elena Poniatowska, writer

ANSWERS

Después de leer

A
1. **La Ciudad de México**
2. **Coyoacán**
3. **sur**
4. **famosas**

B
1. **zona**
2. **tranquila**
3. **elegante**
4. **residentes**
5. **habitantes**

National Standards

Connections
This reading about the different ethnic groups in the Spanish-speaking world establishes a connection with another discipline—social sciences. It allows students to draw from material they have most probably learned in their social studies classes. At the same time it increases their knowledge by presenting the specific ethnicities of Latin America.

¡OJO! The readings in the **Conexiones** section are optional. They focus on the major disciplines taught in schools and universities. The vocabulary is useful for discussing such topics as history, literature, art, economics, business, science, etc.

See page 34 of this Teacher's Wraparound Edition for general suggestions on how to present these readings.

LAS CIENCIAS SOCIALES

LA SOCIOLOGÍA

A. Have students look at the photographs of the many types of people that make up the population of Latin America. You may wish to give the information in the introduction in Spanish. See if students can understand.
La sociología es el estudio de la sociedad en todos sus aspectos. En una sociedad hay muchos grupos. Todos somos miembros de varios grupos—un grupo familiar, un grupo lingüístico, un grupo étnico o racial. En España y Latinoamérica hay muchos grupos étnicos.

(continued on page 65)

Conexiones

LAS CIENCIAS SOCIALES

LA SOCIOLOGÍA

Sociology is the study of society in all its aspects. A society is composed of many groups. All of us belong to a number of groups. We belong to a family group, a language group, and an ethnic or racial group.

The large Spanish-speaking world is one of great diversity. There are many ethnic groups living in Spain and in Latin America. Let's take a look at some of these groups.

Caras de Latinoamérica

Grupos étnicos de Latinoamérica

En Latinoamérica hay muchos grupos étnicos. ¿Cuáles son los grupos étnicos de Latinoamérica?

Influencia africana
En la región del Caribe hay mucha influencia africana. En Puerto Rico, Cuba, la República Dominicana, Panamá y en la costa norte de la América del Sur, la influencia negra es notable. Hay mucha gente[1] de ascendencia africana. Hay también muchos mulatos. En Latinoamérica, un mulato es una persona de sangre[2] blanca y negra.

Influencia india o indígena
En México, Guatemala y la región andina—de los Andes—hay muchos indios. En Ecuador, Perú y Bolivia, hay muchos descendientes de los incas. En México y Guatemala hay muchos descendientes de los mayas. Hay también muchos mestizos. Un mestizo es una persona con una mezcla[3] de sangre india y blanca.

Criollos
¿Y quiénes son los criollos? Los criollos son los blancos nacidos[4] en las colonias—los españoles nacidos en América.

[1]gente *people*
[2]sangre *blood*
[3]mezcla *mixture*
[4]nacidos *born*

«La almendra del cacao» de Diego Rivera

Después de leer

A En español Busquen las palabras afines en la lectura. *(Find the cognates in the reading.)*

B La palabra, por favor Pareen. *(Match.)*

1. área de las Américas donde el español es la lengua oficial
2. una persona de África
3. la región de los Andes
4. los indios del Perú, Ecuador y Bolivia
5. los indios de México y Guatemala
6. una persona de sangre india y blanca
7. una persona de sangre blanca y negra

a. mestizo
b. Latinoamérica
c. mulato
d. africano
e. andina
f. descendientes de los incas
g. descendientes de los mayas

C ¿Cuáles son las palabras? Busquen las palabras equivalentes. *(Find the equivalent words.)*

In this reading, there are two important terms that are the same in Spanish and English. The words came to English from the Spanish language. Which words are they?

B. Have students read the selection silently on their own.

C. Then have them go over the **Después de leer** activities very quickly. Students should be able to recognize the cognates and easily understand the reading selection. They should not, however, be expected to learn the vocabulary or produce it, since it is receptive vocabulary only.

Teacher Notes

ANSWERS

Después de leer

A Answers will vary, but may include: **grupos, étnicos, región, influencia, africana, notable, mulatos, descendientes, colonias**

B **1. b** **2. d** **3. e** **4. f** **5. g** **6. a** **7. c**

C **mulato, mestizo**

RECYCLING

The **Actividades orales** and **Actividad escrita** allow students to use the vocabulary and structures from this chapter in open-ended, real-life settings. They also give students the opportunity to reuse the vocabulary and structure from Chapter 1.

Actividades orales

You may allow students to do as many of the **Actividades** as they wish.

Student Portfolio

Have students keep a notebook containing their best written work from each chapter. These selected writings can be based on assignments from the Student Textbook and the Writing Activities Workbook. The two activities on page 67 are examples of writing assignments that may be included in each student's portfolio.

In the Workbook, students will develop an organized autobiography **(Mi autobiografía).** These workbook pages may also become a part of their portfolio. See the Teacher's Manual for more information on the Student Portfolio.

Culminación

Actividades orales

A **Nosotros(as)** Work with a classmate. Together prepare a speech that you are going to present to the class. To help you organize your presentation, use the following as a guide:

- tell who you are
- tell where you're from
- give the name of your school
- describe one of your classes

B **Cursos obligatorios y opcionales** You are speaking with a student you met recently. He is from Chile and he doesn't know much about our schools. Tell him something about your school curriculum. Which courses are required and which ones are electives? Answer any questions he may have about your courses.

*** LICEO SALVADORENO ***

INFORME DE NOTAS

22 - MANUEL ERNESTO MARTINEZ CORTEZ

PROF. RODRIGO RAMIREZ SANTOS

TERCERA AREA

Nombre materia	1ra. Area	2da. Area	Act 10%	Activ. 40%	P.O. 50%	Nota	30%	3ra. Area	Nota Acum.	Obs.
EDUCACION EN LA FE	0.9	1.3	10	34	44	88	26.4	2.6	4.8	
LENGUAJE	1.2	1.3	9	31	46	86	25.8	2.6	5.1	
ESTUDIOS SOCIALES	1.0	1.2	8	33	46	87	26.1	2.6	4.8	
INGLES	1.4	1.2	10	38	49	97	29.1	2.9	5.5	
MATEMATICAS	1.2	1.4	10	37	40	87	26.1	2.6	5.2	
CIENCIA,SALUD Y MEDIO A	1.3	1.4	9	38	36	83	24.9	2.5	5.2	
EDUCACION ESTETICA	1.2	1.2	9	36	50	95	28.5	2.9	5.3	
EDUCACION FISICA	1.4	1.4	10	40	50	100	30.0	3.0	5.8	
MECANOGRAFIA	1.2	1.3	10	31	45	86	25.8	2.6	5.1	
COMPUTACION	1.3	1.3	9	36	50	95	28.5	2.9	5.5	

FIRMA ENCARGADO

ANSWERS

Actividades orales

A Answers will include the following:
Soy *(nombre).*
Soy de *(ciudad).*
Soy alumno en la Escuela ____.
La clase de ____ es ____.

B Answers will vary. Allow students to say as much as they can. They will use several forms of the verb **ser** and adjectives that describe their courses.

Independent Practice

Assign any of the following:

1. Activities, pages 66–67
2. Workbook, **Mi autobiografía,** page 18
3. Situation Cards
4. CD-ROM, Disc 1, Chapter 2, **Juego de repaso**

Actividad escrita

A **Una postal a una amiga** You're in Barcelona, Spain. Write a postcard to a friend at home, telling him or her about your new Spanish friends—José Luis, Nando, Alejandra, and Guadalupe.

BARCELONA

Writing Strategy

Keeping a journal

There are many kinds of journals you can keep, each having a different purpose. One type of journal is the kind in which you write about daily events and record your thoughts and impressions about these events. It's almost like "thinking out loud." By keeping such a journal, you may find that you discover something new that you were not aware of.

Clases y profesores

You've been in school for about a month. You've had a chance to get to know what your courses are like and to become familiar with your teachers. Create a journal entry in which you write about your classes and your teachers. Try to write about your classes—the days and times of each, whether there are many or few students, whether the class is big or small, what the class is like, who the teacher is, and what he or she is like. When you have finished, reread your journal entry. Did you discover anything about your courses or your teachers that you hadn't thought of before?

CAPÍTULO 2
Culminación

Actividad escrita

A TECHNOLOGY OPTION
Students can use the Portfolio feature on the CD-ROM to write this postcard.

Writing Strategy

Keeping a Journal

A. Have students read the Writing Strategy on page 67.

B. If they need help getting started, have them use the vocabulary list on page 68.

Learning From Photos

Barcelona Barcelona is in Cataluña in northeastern Spain. Barcelona is a very large city with a great deal of commerce and industry. It also enjoys an active cultural life.

Career Connection

Profesor(a) de español
Teaching is an excellent way to use one's knowledge of a foreign language and culture. Have your students interview you about the education and training that was necessary for you to obtain your position. Be sure to mention your travel and study abroad experiences or any specialized workshops that you attended. At this level, the interview will be in English.

Did You Know?

Personas famosas Many famous people are from the Barcelona area. The painter Joan Miró was born in Barcelona. Pablo Picasso spent his formative years there. The cellist Pablo Casals, the painter Salvador Dalí, and the opera singers Montserrat Caballé and José Carreras are all from Cataluña.

ANSWERS

Actividad escrita

A Answers will vary. Students will use the verb **ser** and adjectives they know to describe a person.

Writing Strategy

Answers will vary.

ASSESSMENT RESOURCES

- Chapter Quizzes
- Testing Program
- Computer Testmaker
- Situation Cards
- Communication Transparency C-2
- Performance Assessment
- **Maratón mental** Videoquiz

VOCABULARY REVIEW

The words and phrases in the **Vocabulario** have been taught for productive use in this chapter. They are summarized here as a resource for both students and teacher. This list also serves as a convenient resource for the **Culminación** activities on pages 66 and 67.

There are approximately 30 cognates in this vocabulary list. Have students find them.

Vocabulario

IDENTIFYING A PERSON OR THING

el profesor
la profesora
la clase
el curso

IDENTIFYING SCHOOL SUBJECTS

las ciencias
la biología
la química
la física
las matemáticas
la aritmética
el álgebra
la geometría
el cálculo
las ciencias sociales
la historia
la geografía
las lenguas
el inglés
el español
el francés
el alemán
el latín
otras asignaturas o disciplinas
la educación física
la música
el arte
la economía doméstica
la informática

DESCRIBING TEACHERS AND COURSES

inteligente
interesante
aburrido(a)
pequeño(a)
grande
fácil
difícil, duro(a)
popular
obligatorio(a)

IDENTIFYING OTHER NATIONALITIES

argentino(a)
dominicano(a)
ecuatoriano(a)
panameño(a)

FINDING OUT INFORMATION

¿quiénes?
¿cuántos(as)?

AGREEING AND DISAGREEING

sí, también
no, de ninguna manera

OTHER USEFUL EXPRESSIONS

hay
mucho
poco
mismo(a)
todos(as)

TECNOTUR

VIDEO ¡Buen viaje!

EPISODIO 2 ▸ Alumnos y cursos

En la escuela de Isabel y Luis

Isabel y Luis con Cristina

CD-ROM Expansión cultural

El inglés es una lengua muy importante y popular en el mundo hispano.

interNET CONNECTION

In this video episode Cristina attends Isabel's English class at her school in Mexico City. Like the students in the video, Cristina had to learn English when her family emigrated from Colombia to Los Angeles. To find out more about American cities like Los Angeles with large Spanish-speaking populations and Hispanic origins, go to the Capítulo 2 Internet activity at the Glencoe Foreign Language Web site:

http://www.glencoe.com/sec/fl

Video Synopsis

In this episode Cristina visits Isabel and Luis' school in Mexico City. She has the opportunity to film an English class and also finds out more about her friend Isabel's classes. The girls run into Luis, Isabel's brother, in the schoolyard. He is chatting with his music teacher, Señor Cervantes, one of the most popular teachers in the school. The episode ends with Cristina videotaping her favorite friends, Isabel and Luis.

OVERVIEW

This page previews three key multimedia components of the **Glencoe Spanish** series. Each reinforces the material taught in Chapter 2 in a unique manner.

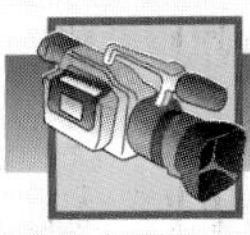

VIDEO

The Video Program allows students to see how the chapter vocabulary and structures are used by native speakers within an engaging story line. For maximum reinforcement, show the video episode as a final activity for Chapter 2.

A. Tell students that this episode takes place in a combination junior high/high school in Mexico City. Ask them to read the captions and then say as much as they can about the photos.

B. Now show the Chapter 2 video episode. See the Video Activities Booklet for detailed suggestions for using this resource.

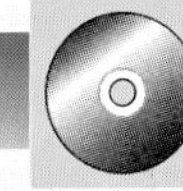

CD-ROM

A. The **Expansión cultural** photo shows an English class in a Spanish-speaking country. Have students read the caption on page 69. Ask them why so many Spanish speakers want to learn English.

B. In the CD-ROM version of **Expansión cultural** (Disc 1, page 69), students can listen to an expanded version of this caption.

INTERNET

Teacher Information and Student Worksheets for this activity can be accessed at the Web site.

Chapter 3 Overview ◆◆◆◆◆◆◆◆◆◆◆◆◆◆◆◆◆◆◆◆◆◆◆◆◆◆◆◆◆◆

SCOPE AND SEQUENCE pages 70–95

TOPICS	FUNCTIONS	STRUCTURE	CULTURE
◆ School supplies ◆ Clothing ◆ Colors, sizes ◆ Shopping ◆ Numbers: 100–1,000	◆ How to identify and describe school supplies ◆ How to describe articles of clothing ◆ How to state colors and sizes ◆ How to count from 100 to 1,000 ◆ How to talk formally and informally	◆ Singular forms of **-ar** verbs ◆ **Tú** versus **Usted**	◆ Julio Torres, a student from Madrid ◆ Discussing differences between school in the U.S. and in Spanish-speaking countries ◆ El Retiro, Madrid ◆ Indigenous clothing in Central and South America ◆ A famous clothing designer: Oscar de la Renta ◆ Computer vocabulary in Spanish

CHAPTER 3 RESOURCES

PRINT	MULTIMEDIA
Planning Resources	
Lesson Plans Block Scheduling Lesson Plans	Interactive Lesson Planner
Reinforcement Resources	
Writing Activities Workbook Student Tape Manual Video Activities Booklet Web Site User's Guide	Transparencies Binder Audiocassette/Compact Disc Program Videocassette/Videodisc Program Online Internet Activities Electronic Teacher's Classroom Resources
Assessment Resources	
Situation Cards Chapter Quizzes Testing Program Performance Assessment	**Maratón mental** Mindjogger Videoquiz Testmaker Computer Software (Macintosh/Windows) Listening Comprehension Audiocassette/Compact Disc Communication Transparency: C-3
Motivational Resources	
Expansion Activities	Café Glencoe: www.cafe.glencoe.com Keypal Internet Activities
Enrichment	
Spanish for Spanish Speakers	

Chapter 3 Planning Guide

SECTION	PAGES	SECTION RESOURCES
Vocabulario Palabras 1 **Los materiales escolares** **En la papelería**	72–75	Vocabulary Transparencies 3.1 Audiocassette 3A/ Compact Disc 2 Student Tape Manual, TE, pages 24–25 Workbook, pages 19–20 Chapter Quizzes, pages 11–12 CD-ROM, Disc 1, pages 72–75
Vocabulario Palabras 2 **La ropa** **Los colores** **Más números**	76–79	Vocabulary Transparencies 3.2 Audiocassette 3A/ Compact Disc 2 Student Tape Manual, TE, pages 26–27 Workbook, TE, pages 21–22 Chapter Quizzes, TE, pages 13–14 CD-ROM, Disc 1, pages 76–79
Estructura **Presente de los verbos en -ar en el singular** **Tú o Ud.**	80–83	Workbook, pages 23–24 Audiocassette 3A/Compact Disc 2 Student Tape Manual, TE, pages 28–31 Structure Transparency S-3 Chapter Quizzes, pages 15–16 Computer Testmaker CD-ROM, Disc 1, pages 80–83
Conversación **En la tienda de ropa** **Pronunciación: Las consonantes l, f, p, m, n**	84–85	Audiocassette 3A/Compact Disc 2 Student Tape Manual, TE, pages 31–32 CD-ROM, Disc 1, pages 84–85
Lecturas culturales **Un alumno madrileño** **La ropa indígena *(opcional)*** **Un diseñador famoso *(opcional)***	86–89	Testing Program, pages 12–13 CD-ROM, Disc 1, pages 86–89
Conexiones **La computadora *(opcional)***	90–91	Testing Program, page 13 CD-ROM, Disc 1, pages 90–91
Culminación **Actividades orales** **Actividades escritas** **Vocabulario** **Tecnotur**	92–95	**¡Buen viaje!** Video, Episode 3 Video Activities, pages 72–75 Internet Activities www.glencoe.com/sec/fl Testing Program, pages 9–12; 103; 135; 158 CD-ROM, Disc 1, pages 92–95

CAPÍTULO 3

OVERVIEW

In this chapter students will learn to identify, describe, and shop for school supplies and clothing. They will also learn to use singular forms of **-ar** verbs to communicate in various situations that arise when shopping. Plural forms will be presented in Chapter 4.

National Standards

Communication

In Chapter 3, students will communicate in spoken and written Spanish on the following topics:

- clothing
- school supplies and related subjects

Students will engage in conversations, provide and obtain information, and exchange opinions as they fulfill the chapter objectives listed on this page.

Pacing

Chapter 3 will require approximately six to eight days. Pacing will vary according to the length of the class, the age of your students, and student aptitude.

Block Scheduling

The extended timeframe provided by block scheduling affords you the opportunity to implement a greater number of activities and projects to motivate and involve your students. See the Block Scheduling Lesson Plans Booklet for suggestions on how to present the chapter material within a block scheduling framework.

CAPÍTULO 3

Las compras para la escuela

Objetivos

In this chapter you will learn to do the following:

- identify and describe school supplies
- identify and describe articles of clothing
- shop for school supplies and clothing
- state color and size preferences
- speak to people formally and informally
- discuss differences between schools in the United States and in Spanish-speaking countries

interNET CONNECTION

The **Glencoe Foreign Language Web site (http://www.glencoe.com/sec/fl)** offers three options that enable you and your students to experience the Spanish-speaking world via the Internet:

- The online **Actividades** are correlated to the chapters and utilize Hispanic Web sites around the world. For Chapter 3 activities, see student page 95.
- The **Correspondencia electrónica** section provides information on how to set up a keypal (pen pal) exchange between your class and a class in the Spanish-speaking world.
- At **Café Glencoe,** the interactive "after-school" section of the site, you and your students can access a variety of additional online resources, including interactive games. In Chapter 3, the Concentration game practices clothing vocabulary.

CAPÍTULO 3

Spotlight On Culture

Artefacto The hand-woven baskets on page 70 are from Colombia. The province of Boyacá is the leading area for Colombian crafts. Many of the baskets are woven from esparto grass.

Fotografía The photo on pages 70–71 is of the Galerías Pacífico shopping mall on Calle Florida in Buenos Aires, Argentina. It is the only mall in the central downtown area of the city.

Galerías Pacífico has an interesting architectural history. Construction began in 1889 on the building, which was supposed to house a department store in the style of the famous Galeries Lafayette in Paris. Economic difficulties, however, changed the course of events. Eventually the entire building had to be put up for sale. The new buyer, the now defunct Ferrocarril de Buenos Aires al Pacífico, gave the building its present name.

Two famous Argentine architects, Aslan and Ezcurra, completed construction of the building. A large central dome was added and five leading Argentine artists were commissioned to paint murals.

Galerías Pacífico opened as a retail outlet in 1946. It was refurbished in 1992 and reopened as the California-style mall we see today. In addition to the many shops and boutiques, Galerías Pacífico has an eating area that is famous for people-watching.

Chapter Projects

El catálogo Have students prepare a catalogue containing the articles of clothing taught in this chapter. Tell students to label each item of clothing in Spanish and make sure the clothing colors can be described by their classmates.

En la tienda de ropa Have pairs of students prepare a skit that takes place at a clothing store. One student is the customer, the other is the store clerk. Students should use some articles of clothing and price tags with prices in **pesos** as props.

Desfile de modas Organize a fashion show. Tell students on what day they should wear a special outfit. Encourage them to be creative. During the fashion show, have individual students model their clothes in front of the class while other students describe what the person in wearing. Have the class vote on their favorite outfit.

CAPÍTULO 3
Vocabulario

PALABRAS 1

RESOURCES

- Vocabulary Transparencies 3.1 (A & B)
- Student Tape Manual, TE, pages 24–25
- Audiocassette 3A/CD2
- Workbook, pages 19–20
- Quiz 1, pages 11–12
- CD-ROM, Disc 1, pages 72–75

Bell Ringer Review

Use BRR Transparency 3-1, or write the following on the board: Write as much as you can about one of the following topics:

- **Un(a) alumno(a)**
- **La clase de español**
- **Un colegio**

TEACHING VOCABULARY

A. Have students close their books. Model the new vocabulary on pages 72–73 using Vocabulary Transparencies 3.1 (A & B). Have them repeat each word or expression two or three times.

B. Identify the school supplies your students are actually using. Have the class repeat each item after you once or twice. Ask **¿Qué es?** and have a student respond.

Vocabulario

PALABRAS 1

Los materiales escolares

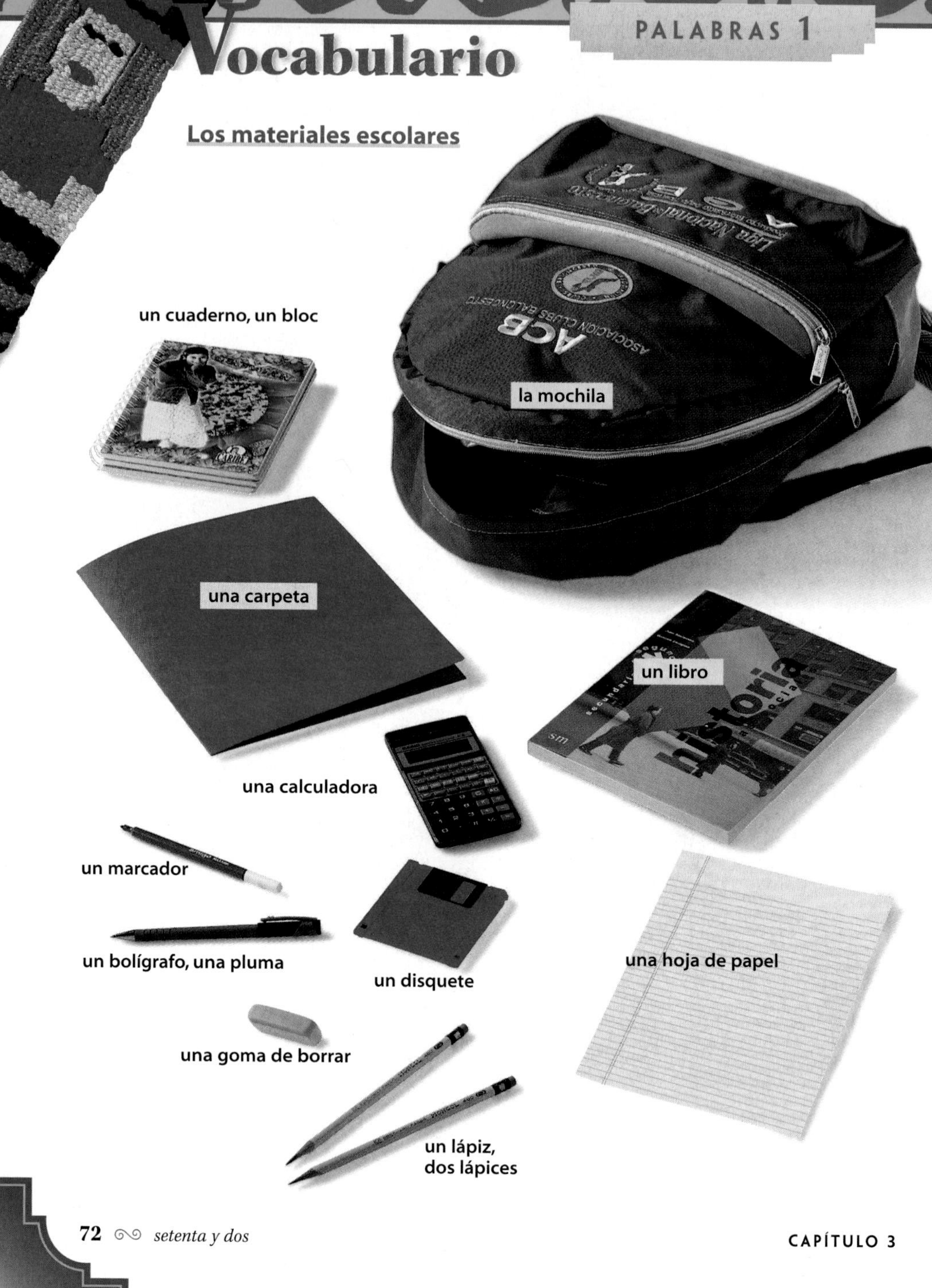

Total Physical Response

Getting ready

If students don't already know the meaning of **levántate**, **ven acá**, and **siéntate**, teach these expressions by using the appropriate gestures as you say each expression.

Begin

___, levántate y ven acá, por favor.
Busca un libro.
Mira el libro
Dame el libro. (Gesture to convey the meaning of **dame.**)
Ahora, busca una goma.
Dame la goma, por favor.
Busca una hoja de papel. Dame la hoja de papel.
Busca un lápiz. Dame el lápiz.
Gracias, ___. Siéntate.

Now call on another student to do the following:

___, levántate y ven acá, por favor.
Busca un cuaderno.
Mira el cuaderno.
Dame el cuaderno.
Gracias, ___. Siéntate.

En la papelería

Alejandro necesita materiales escolares.
Busca un cuaderno en la papelería.

Alejandro mira un cuaderno.
Mira un bolígrafo también.

Alejandro habla con la dependienta.

Alejandro compra el cuaderno.
El cuaderno cuesta noventa pesos.
Alejandro paga noventa pesos.
Paga en la caja.

Alejandro lleva los materiales escolares en una mochila.

C. Pantomime **busca** and **mira** to help convey their meaning.

D. Have students repeat the short conversation with the clerk in the photo on page 73.

E. Have students repeat the sentences under the two illustrations at the bottom of page 73. As they do, intersperse with questions such as the following, building from simple to more complex sentences:

¿Compra Alejandro el cuaderno?
¿Qué compra Alejandro?
¿Quién compra el cuaderno?
¿Compra el cuaderno en la papelería?
¿Dónde compra Alejandro el cuaderno?

Have students answer with the complete sentence or sometimes have them use just the specific word or expression that responds to the question word.

F. After presenting the vocabulary orally, have students open their books and read the new vocabulary aloud. You can have the class read in chorus, or call on individuals to read. Intersperse with questions such as those outlined above.

ABOUT THE SPANISH LANGUAGE

- The words **el cuaderno**, **la libreta**, and **el bloc** are all commonly used to refer to a notebook. **Una carpeta** is more like a folder.
- Some Spanish speakers use **el bolígrafo** when referring to a ball-point pen, others use **la pluma**, which also means a *fountain pen*. In some countries **la pluma** is used for both a ballpoint pen and a fountain pen.

Class Motivator

¿Qué hay en la mochila? Bring an empty backpack to class. Pass the backpack around the room As each person gets the backpack close, he or she puts a school supply in it, names it and tells what else is in the pack: **En la mochila hay un cuaderno, una goma, etc.** If someone has already put an item in the pack, the others can still put in the same item. However, the other students now have to say how many notebooks, pens, etc. are in the backpack. The last student has to name everything in the pack. (**Hint:** You may allow students to look in the pack if they need help remembering.)

CAPÍTULO 3
Vocabulario

Práctica

¡OJO! **Práctica** When students are doing the **Práctica** activities, accept any answer that makes sense. The purpose of these activities is to have students use the new vocabulary. They are not factual recall activities. Do not expect students to remember specific information from the vocabulary presentation when answering. If you wish, have students use the photos on this page as a stimulus, when possible.

Historieta Each time **Historieta** appears, the answers to the activity form a short story. Encourage students to look at the title of the **Historieta** since it can help them do the activity.

A Have a contest to see who has written the most words for **Práctica A.**

B Do **Práctica B** with books closed first. Then have a student retell it in his or her own words.

C Have individual students read the entire sentence, including the correct completion word.

EXPANSION Ask the more able students to make up original sentences using the word choices that do not fit in the blanks. In Item 1, for example, they could say: **Diego paga los materiales escolares en la caja. Diego habla con el dependiente.**

Writing Development

Have students write the answers to **Práctica C** in one paragraph to illustrate how all of the items tell a story.

Práctica

A **Los materiales escolares** Preparen una lista de materiales escolares importantes. *(Make a list of important school supplies.)*

B **HISTORIETA En la papelería**

Contesten. *(Answer.)*

1. ¿Necesita la muchacha materiales escolares?
2. ¿Busca los materiales escolares en la papelería?
3. ¿Mira ella un bolígrafo?
4. ¿Habla con el dependiente?
5. ¿Compra el bolígrafo?
6. ¿Paga en la caja?

Santiago de Chile

C **HISTORIETA De compras**

Escojan. *(Choose.)*

1. Diego ____ materiales escolares.
   a. paga **b.** habla **c.** necesita
2. Él ____ un bolígrafo y un cuaderno.
   a. mira **b.** cuesta **c.** habla
3. Diego ____ con el empleado.
   a. paga **b.** habla **c.** mira
4. Él necesita ____ para la computadora.
   a. un disquete **b.** un bloc **c.** un lápiz
5. Diego ____ en la caja.
   a. paga **b.** compra **c.** lleva
6. Él ____ los materiales escolares en una mochila.
   a. compra **b.** mira **c.** lleva

ANSWERS

Práctica

A Answers will vary but may include: **unos lápices, unos bolígrafos (unas plumas), unos marcadores, unos cuadernos (unos blocs), unas carpetas, unos libros, unas hojas de papel, una calculadora, unos disquetes, una(s) goma(s), una mochila.**

B **1. Sí, la muchacha necesita materiales escolares.**
2. Sí, busca los materiales escolares en la papelería.
3. Sí, ella mira un bolígrafo.
4. Sí, habla con el dependiente.
5. Sí, compra el bolígrafo.
6. Sí, paga en la caja

C **1. c** **2. a** **3. b** **4. a** **5. a** **6. c**

D HISTORIETA Una calculadora, por favor.

Contesten. *(Answer.)*

Málaga, España

1. ¿Con quién habla Casandra en la papelería?
2. ¿Qué necesita ella?
3. ¿Qué busca?
4. ¿Compra la calculadora?
5. ¿Cuánto cuesta la calculadora?
6. ¿Dónde paga Casandra?

Actividades comunicativas

A En la papelería Work with a classmate. You're buying the school supplies below. Take turns being the customer and the salesperson.

JUEGO ¿Qué es? Play a guessing game. Your partner will hide a school supply behind his or her back. Guess what he or she is hiding. Take turns.

CAPÍTULO 3
Vocabulario

D Do **Práctica D** with books closed first. Then have a student retell the information given in items 1–6 in his or her own words.

Actividades comunicativas

A Have students work in pairs. The first student will ask the price of the item, the second student will respond with the price given.

Make sure each student has the opportunity to role-play both the customer and the salesperson before ending this activity. Have students volunteer to role-play this activity for the class.

JUEGO This is a good activity to use at the beginning or the end of the class period.

Learning From Realia

Los materiales escolares Have students look at the ad on page 74. Ask them to figure out what's being advertised by using the vocabulary of the chapter and their knowledge of cognates.

Learning From Photos

Santiago de Chile Have students look at the photo on page 74 and say something about it in their own words. For example, they could say: **La muchacha busca materiales escolares. La muchacha habla con el dependiente. La muchacha mira un bolígrafo.**

Málaga, España Ask the following questions about the photo on page 75: **¿Es grande o pequeña la papelería? ¿Hay muchos materiales escolares en la papelería? ¿Quién es rubia, la muchacha o la empleada?**

ANSWERS

Práctica

D 1. **Casandra habla con la dependienta en la papelería.**
2. **Necesita una calculadora.**
3. **Busca una calculadora.**
4. **Sí, (No, no) compra la calculadora.**
5. **La calculadora cuesta ___ pesos.**
6. **Casandra paga en la caja.**

Actividades comunicativas

A Students can make up their own conversations. They may use words such as: **necesitar, buscar, ¿cuánto cuesta?, pagar.**

JUEGO Answers will vary. Students will use items taught in **Palabras 1**.

RESOURCES

-  Vocabulary Transparencies 3.2 (A & B)
- Student Tape Manual, TE, pages 26–27
- Audiocassette 3A/CD2
- Workbook, pages 21–22
- Quiz 2, pages 13–14
- CD-ROM, Disc 1, pages 76–79

Bell Ringer Review

Use BRR Transparency 3-2, or write the following on the board: Make a list of some school supplies you use almost every day.

TEACHING VOCABULARY

A. Have students close their books. Then model the new vocabulary on pages 76–77 using Vocabulary Transparencies 3.2 (A & B). Have students repeat each word or expression two or three times.

B. Identify articles of clothing students are actually wearing. Have the class repeat each item after you once or twice. Ask **¿Qué es?** and have a student respond.

C. Ask the following questions as you present the vocabulary: **¿Lleva la muchacha un blue jean? ¿Lleva una chaqueta también? ¿Qué lleva? ¿Lleva una falda? ¿Lleva zapatos o un par de tenis?**

D. Have students read the two conversations on page 77 aloud, with as much expression as possible. *(continued on page 77)*

PALABRAS 2

Vocabulario

La ropa

una gorra
una blusa
un pantalón corto
un traje
una chaqueta
un pantalón largo
un T-shirt, una camiseta
una camisa
38
la talla, el tamaño
una falda
36
el número
los zapatos
una corbata
un blue jean
los calcetines
un par de tenis

La muchacha lleva un T-shirt y un blue jean.
Lleva un par de tenis.
Lleva una chaqueta.
No lleva una falda.

Total Physical Response

Getting ready

Teach the words **anda** and **indica** by acting them out in front of the class. Point to individual students as you say the word **indica**.

Begin

___, ven acá. Anda por la sala de clase.
Indica una camisa blanca.
Contesta: ¿Quién lleva una camisa blanca?
Indica una falda azul.
¿Quién lleva una falda azul?
Indica un pantalón.
Contesta: ¿Es un pantalón largo o corto?
Gracias, ___.

Now repeat the above with another student. Change the articles of clothing.

Gloria habla con la dependienta.
La dependienta trabaja en la tienda de ropa.

Rubén compra un par de zapatos.
Él habla con el dependiente.

La camisa cuesta mucho.
Es muy cara.

35 pesos

La gorra no cuesta mucho.
Cuesta poco.
Es bastante barata.

¿Lo sabes?
Ciento is shortened to cien before any word that is not a number: cien pesos, ciento ochenta pesos.

Los colores

¿De qué color es?

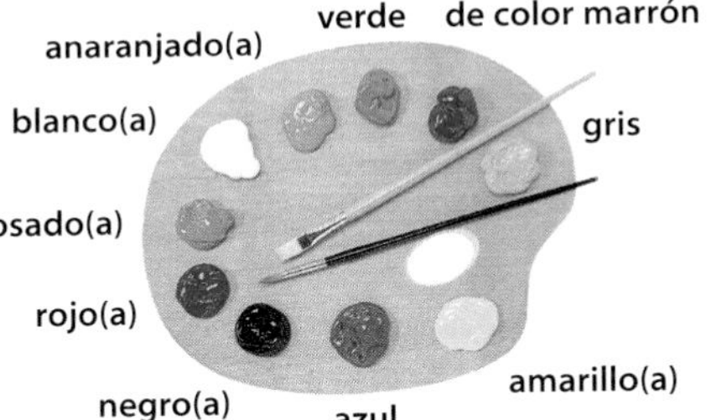

Más números

100	ciento, cien	600	seiscientos
200	doscientos	700	setecientos
300	trescientos	800	ochocientos
400	cuatrocientos	900	novecientos
500	quinientos	1000	mil

150	ciento cincuenta
790	setecientos noventa
1800	mil ochocientos

E. As you present the sentences on page 77, ask questions such as, **¿Con quién habla Gloria? ¿Habla con la dependienta en la tienda? ¿Dónde trabaja la dependienta? ¿En qué tipo de tienda trabaja?**

F. After you present the colors on page 77, have students identify the colors of the clothes on page 76.

G. **Más números** Model and have students repeat the numbers. Write random numbers on the board and call on students to say them.

VOCABULARY EXPANSION

You may wish to give students a few extra words that are useful when shopping for clothing:

a rayas	*striped*
a cuadros	*checked*
de lana	*wool*
de algodón	*cotton*
de nilón	*nylon*

National Standards

Comparisons
Students learn on page 77 that clothing sizes are not the same in Spain or in many areas of Latin America as the sizes used in the United States.

Did You Know?

¿Qué talla usas? In Spanish-speaking countries, clothing sizes are different from those in the United States. Many garments today have labels with both European and American sizes. Ask students what size shoe the young man in the illustration is trying on (38). Ask them to figure out what the equivalent U.S. size would be. Ask them what size shoe they would ask for in a Spanish shoe store. (See chart on page 81.)

ABOUT THE SPANISH LANGUAGE

- **El saco** is used for both a man's and a woman's jacket. In Spain, **la chaqueta** or **la americana** are common terms. In Mexico, the word **chamarra** is used. Other kinds of outer jackets are **la cazadora, el blusón, el chaquetón.** One will also hear **el gabán** used for jacket.
- In many areas of Latin America, **medias** is used for women's stockings and men's socks. In other areas **medias** are women's stockings only and socks are **calcetines.**
- **El pantalón** is often used in the plural: **los pantalones.** Blue jeans are called **blue jeans** or **blujins, vaqueros,** and **pantalones de mezclilla.** In Puerto Rico, the word **mahones** is used.
- **Zapatería** can mean a shoe store (department) or factory. Another term is **tienda (departamento) de calzado.**
- Other words for sweater are **la chompa,** and **el pulóver.**
- When counting and using 100 alone, **ciento** should be used. You will frequently hear **cien** but it is not considered correct.

CAPÍTULO 3
Vocabulario

Práctica

A Before doing this activity, review the colors on page 77. Now have students identify each item by saying what article of clothing it is, as well as the color(s) of the item.

B Students should answer in complete sentences. For example: **Eugenio habla con el dependiente.**

C This activity can be done first with books closed. Change your intonation slightly when giving students the cue.

Have individual students answer each of the items. Then have one student answers items 1–3 and a second student answer 4–6.

Learning From Photos

Miraflores, Lima, Perú Give students the following information about the photo on page 78: **Es una tienda de ropa para caballeros. La tienda está en Miraflores. Miraflores es una parte muy bonita de Lima, la capital del Perú. Hay muchas tiendas elegantes en Miraflores.**

Práctica

A **¿Qué es?** Identifiquen. *(Identify.)*

Miraflores, Lima, Perú

B **HISTORIETA En la tienda de ropa**

Contesten según se indica. *(Answer according to the cues.)*

1. ¿Con quién habla Eugenio? (con el dependiente)
2. ¿Dónde trabaja el dependiente? (en la tienda de ropa)
3. ¿Qué necesita Eugenio? (un T-shirt)
4. ¿Qué talla usa? (treinta y ocho)
5. ¿De qué color es el T-shirt? (blanco)
6. ¿Cuánto es? (cinco pesos)
7. ¿Cuesta mucho? (no, poco)
8. ¿Es caro? (no, barato)
9. ¿Compra Eugenio el T-shirt? (sí)
10. ¿Dónde paga? (en la caja)

C **¿De qué color es?** Completen con el color. *(Complete with the color.)*

1. Tomás compra un pantalón ____.
2. Ana compra una blusa ____.
3. Emilio compra una camisa ____.

4. Paco compra una gorra ____.
5. Adriana compra una falda ____.
6. César compra zapatos de color ____.

ANSWERS

Práctica

A
1. **Es una camisa.**
2. **Es una gorra.**
3. **Es una falda.**
4. **Es un blue jean.**
5. **Es una mochila.**
6. **Es un par de tenis.**

B
1. **Eugenio habla con el dependiente.**
2. **El dependiente trabaja en la tienda de ropa.**
3. **Eugenio necesita un T-shirt.**
4. **Usa la talla (el tamaño) treinta y ocho.**
5. **El T-shirt es blanco.**
6. **Es cinco pesos.**
7. **No, (cuesta) poco.**
8. **No, (es) barato.**
9. **Sí, Eugenio compra el T-shirt.**
10. **Paga en la caja.**

C
1. **negro**
2. **roja**
3. **blanca**
4. **azul y blanca (a rayas)**
5. **verde**
6. **marrón**

Actividades comunicativas

A **¿Qué es?** With a classmate, take turns asking each other what each of the following items is. Then ask questions about each one. Find out how much it costs and tell what you think about the price. Is it a real bargain—**¿una ganga?**

1. 2. 3. 4. 5.

B **¿Quién es?** Work in small groups. One person tells what someone in the class is wearing. The others have to guess who it is. If several people are wearing the same thing, you will have to give more details.

C **En la tienda de ropa** With a classmate, look at the photograph. Ask one another questions about it. Answer each other's questions. Then work together to make up sentences about the photograph. Put the sentences in logical order to form a paragraph.

JUEGO **¿Cuál es el número?** Give some numbers in a mathematical pattern but leave one out. Your partner will try to figure out what the missing number is. Take turns. You can use the model as a guide.

ANSWERS

Actividades comunicativas

A Answers will vary.

B Answers will vary, but students should use the verb **llevar**, articles of clothing, and colors.

C Answers will vary. Students can use any articles of clothing and verbs such as: **necesitar, buscar, mirar, hablar, comprar, pagar** or sentences such as: **¿Cuánto cuesta?**

Actividades comunicativas

¡OJO! The **Actividades comunicativas** allow the students to use the vocabulary and structures of the chapter in open-ended, real-life situations. They also give students another opportunity to use words and structures from previous chapters.

Have students work on as many activities as you wish. You may also allow them to select those activities they want to do. Different groups can work on different activities.

A Have students work in pairs. Student 1 begins by asking, **¿Qué es?** Student 2 then identifies the object. Student 1 then asks the price, **¿Cuánto cuesta?** Students can use **dólares** instead of **pesos**, since they will need to make up the price of each object.

B As students work in their groups, you may wish to circulate to make sure they are on task.

RECYCLING If students need to give additional details about the person they are describing, they can use words they learned in Chapter 1, such as **alto, bajo, rubio, etc.**

C Have students work in pairs to come up with at least six questions about the photo on page 79.

JUEGO This is a good activity to use when students need a "break" during the class period, or as an opening or closing activity.

Writing Development

Actividad C works well as a written activity. When students have finished their paragraphs, ask volunteers to read them to the class.

RESOURCES

- Workbook, pages 23–24
- Student Tape Manual, TE, pages 28–31
- Audiocassette 3A/CD2
- Structure Transparency S-3
- Quizzes 3–4, pages 15–16
- Computer Testmaker
- CD-ROM, Disc 1, pages 80–83

TEACHING STRUCTURE

Telling what people do

A. Draw two stick figures on the board. Give them the names **Paco** and **Julia**. Write the verbs **hablar, comprar,** and **mirar.** Have students make up sentences about either **Paco** or **Julia**. They can do this because they know the **él/ella** verb form from the vocabulary presentation.

B. Ask students what they say when they talk about themselves **(yo).** Write **yo** on the board and explain that the ending changes to **o** with **yo**. Write **yo hablo** on the board and have students give you the **yo** form of the other verbs.

C. Follow the same procedures outlined above for the **tú** form.

D. Write the verb forms on the board, underline the endings, and have students repeat once again. **Note:** Have students point to themselves as they say **yo**, or when they use the **-o** ending. Have them look directly at a friend as they say **tú** or use the **-as** ending. It is important that they always realize to whom they are referring when they use a specific verb ending.

Estructura

Telling what people do
Presente de los verbos en -ar en el singular

1. All verbs, or action words, in Spanish belong to a family, or conjugation. Verbs whose infinitive ends in **-ar** (**hablar:** *to speak,* **comprar:** *to buy)* are called first conjugation verbs.

necesitar	**comprar**
buscar	**hablar**
mirar	**pagar**

2. Spanish verbs change their endings according to the subject. Study the following forms.

INFINITIVE	hablar	comprar	mirar	
STEM	habl-	compr-	mir-	ENDINGS
yo	hablo	compro	miro	-o
tú	hablas	compras	miras	-as
él	habla	compra	mira	-a
ella	habla	compra	mira	-a

¿Te acuerdas?

To make a sentence negative, put **no** in front of the verb.
Hablo español.
No hablo francés.
Necesita una hoja de papel.
No necesita una pluma.

3. Since the ending of the verb in Spanish indicates who performs the action, the subjects **(yo, tú, él, ella)** are often omitted.

Use **-o** when you talk about yourself.
Use **-as** when you talk to a friend.
Use **-a** when you talk about someone.

Additional Practice

Have students make up questions using the following words:

1. **quién**
2. **cómo**
3. **qué**
4. **dónde**
5. **cuándo**

For the Native Speaker

¿Qué talla usas? Some Spanish-speaking countries use U.S. sizes; others use metric or European sizes. If there are students in the class from different Hispanic countries, ask them to tell what sizes they use in those countries: **¿Qué número (tamaño) usan para los zapatos (las blusas, las camisas, los pantalones, las medias, los sacos, los abrigos)?**

Práctica

Una papelería, Caracas, Venezuela

A HISTORIETA En la papelería

Contesten. *(Answer.)*

1. ¿Necesita Andrea materiales escolares?
2. ¿Busca ella un bolígrafo?
3. ¿Compra un bolígrafo en la papelería?
4. ¿Habla ella con la empleada?
5. ¿Paga ella en la caja?
6. ¿Lleva los materiales escolares en una mochila?

B HISTORIETA Llevo un blue jean.

Contesten personalmente. *(Answer these questions about yourself.)*

1. ¿Llevas un blue jean?
2. ¿Necesitas un nuevo blue jean?
3. ¿Compras el blue jean en una tienda de ropa?
4. ¿Con quién hablas en la tienda?
5. ¿Qué talla usas?
6. ¿Dónde pagas?
7. ¿Pagas mucho?
8. ¿Cuánto pagas?

CONVERSION DE TALLAS

Ropa de señora – Vestidos y abrigos						
Estados Unidos	6	8	10	12	14	16
España	36	38	40	42	44	46
Sudamérica	34	36	38	40	42	44
Ropa de señora – Blusas y jersey						
Estados Unidos	30	32	34	36	38	40
España	38	40	42	44	46	48
Sudamérica	38	40	42	44	46	48
Ropa de caballeros – Trajes						
Estados Unidos	34	36	38	40	42	44
España	44	46	48	50	52	54
Sudamérica	44	46	48	50	52	54
Calzado – señoras						
Estados Unidos	4	5	6	7	8	9
España	34/35	35/36	36/37	38/39	39/40	41/42
Sudamérica	2	3	4	5	6	7
Calzado – caballeros						
Estados Unidos	8	8½	9	9½	10	10½
España	41	42	43	43	44	45
Sudamérica	6	6½	7	7½	8	8½

C HISTORIETA Necesito un par de tenis, por favor.

Contesten según se indica. *(Answer according to the cues.)*

1. ¿Qué necesitas? (un par de tenis)
2. ¿Dónde buscas los tenis? (en la tienda González)
3. ¿Qué número usas? (treinta y seis)
4. ¿Miras un par de tenis? (sí)
5. ¿Compras los tenis? (sí)
6. ¿Cuánto pagas? (quinientos pesos)
7. ¿Dónde pagas? (en la caja)

D Perdón, ¿qué necesitas?

Sigan el modelo. *(Follow the model.)*

1. Necesito una hoja de papel.
2. Busco una goma de borrar.
3. Compro un disquete.
4. Llevo una mochila.

Práctica

¡OJO! The **Práctica** activities on pages 81–82 give students guided practice on **-ar** verb forms in the singular. These activities build from simple to more complex: **Práctica A** uses the **-a** ending only. **Práctica B** and **C** enable students to hear **-as** as they answer with **-o**. **Práctica D** makes students use both **-as** and **-o** endings. **Práctica E**, the most difficult activity, has them use all forms.

Práctica A, B, and **C** can be done first with books closed and then with books open.

A For visual learners, the photo on page 81 provides cues to the answers.

B Have students look at one another as they answer the questions.

PAIRED ACTIVITY This is a good activity for students to do in pairs because they are communicating information about themselves.

C This activity, like those above, tells a story. You can call on a student to retell the story in his or her own words.

D Have two students role-play the dialogue. Ask volunteers to come up with additional items. For example: **Necesito una camisa; Busco la tienda de ropa, etc.**

ANSWERS

Práctica

A
1. **Sí, Andrea necesita materiales escolares.**
2. **Si, (No), ella (no) busca un bolígrafo.**
3. **Sí, (No, no) compra un bolígrafo en la papelería.**
4. **Sí, (No, no) habla con la empleada.**
5. **Sí, paga en la caja.**
6. **Sí, lleva los materiales escolares en una mochila.**

B Answers will vary but may include:
1. **Sí, (No, no) llevo un blue jean.**
2. **Sí, (No, no) necesito un nuevo blue jean.**
3. **Sí, compro el blue jean en una tienda de ropa.**
4. **Hablo con el/la dependiente(a) (el/la empleado[a]) en la tienda.**
5. **Uso el tamaño (la talla) ___.**
6. **Pago en la caja.**
7. **Sí, (No, no) pago mucho.**
8. **Pago ___ dólares.**

C
1. **Necesito un par de tenis.**
2. **Busco los tenis en la tienda González.**
3. **Uso treinta y seis.**
4. **Sí, miro un par de tenis.**
5. **Sí, compro los tenis.**
6. **Pago quinientos pesos.**
7. **Pago en la caja.**

D All answers begin with: **Perdón, ¿qué... ?**
1. **... necesitas**
2. **... buscas**
3. **... compras**
4. **... llevas**

E This activity recombines all singular forms of **-ar** verbs.

Call on three students to read **Práctica E** aloud. One reads the narration, the other two role-play the conversation.

Actividades comunicativas

A Have students do the activity in pairs, according to the directions on page 82. This activity makes students use all singular forms of the verb on their own.

B Encourage students to say as much as they possibly can. Follow up by having students report to the class what their friend said he or she needs for the beginning of the school.

TECHNOLOGY OPTION In the CD-ROM version of this activity (Disc 1, page 82), students can interact with an on-screen native speaker and record their voices.

For the Native Speaker

Usted vs. tú (page 83) In some areas children still refer to their parents as **usted**. In other areas people use **tú** even with strangers. Ask students with whom they use **tú**, and with whom they use **usted**. Ask whether they think it is simpler to have only one form as in English. Encourage them to discuss the subtleties in usage of **tú** and **usted**.

Learning From Photos

Santiago, Chile Tell students the following about the photo on page 82: **Es una galería o centro comercial en Santiago, la capital de Chile.**
Now ask them: **¿Es grande o pequeña la galería? ¿Es bonita? ¿Hay muchas tiendas en la galería?**

E HISTORIETA En la tienda de ropa

Completen. *(Complete.)*

Casandra ___1___ (necesitar) una blusa. Ella ___2___ (buscar) una blusa verde. En la tienda de ropa Casandra ___3___ (hablar) con una amiga.

—Casandra, ¿qué ___4___ (buscar)?

—Yo ___5___ (buscar) una blusa.

—¿___6___ (Necesitar) un color especial?

—Sí, verde.

—¿Qué talla ___7___ (usar)?

—Treinta y seis.

—¿Por qué no ___8___ (hablar) con la dependienta?

—¡Buena idea!

Casandra ___9___ (hablar) con la dependienta. Ella ___10___ (mirar) varias blusas verdes. Casandra ___11___ (comprar) una blusa que es muy bonita. Ella ___12___ (pagar) en la caja.

Santiago, Chile

Actividades comunicativas

A **¿Trabajas o no?** Find out from a classmate whether he or she works. Try to find out where and when. Tell the class about your friend's work.

B **¿Qué necesitas?** You're talking on the phone with a good friend. The new school year **(la apertura de clases)** is about to begin. You need lots of things. Have a conversation with your friend. You may want to use some of the following words and expressions.

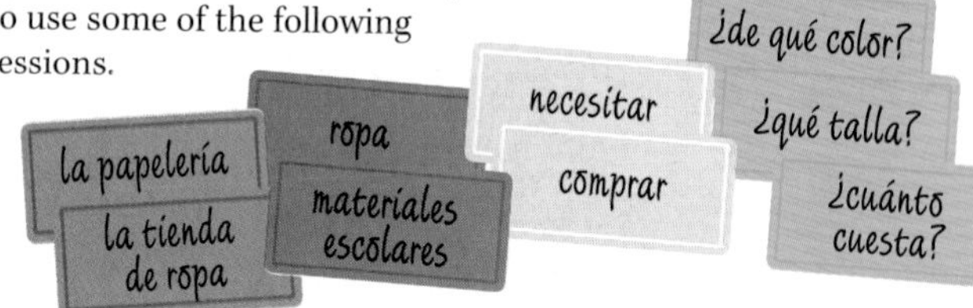

ANSWERS

Práctica

E
1. **necesita**
2. **busca**
3. **habla**
4. **buscas**
5. **busco**
6. **Necesitas**
7. **usas**
8. **hablas**
9. **habla**
10. **mira**
11. **compra**
12. **paga**

Actividades comunicativas

A Answers will vary; however, students should use the correct form of **trabajar,** as well as the question words **dónde** and **cuándo** (**¿a qué hora?**).

B Answers will vary; however, students should use the verb **necesitar** and the cues in the colored boxes on this page.

Talking formally and informally
Tú o Ud.

1. In Spanish, there are two ways to say "you." You can use **tú** when talking to a friend, to a person your own age, or to a family member. **Tú** is called the informal or familiar form of address.

   José, ¿hablas español?
   Carolina, ¿qué necesitas?

2. You use **usted** when talking to an older person, a person you do not know very well, or anyone to whom you wish to show respect. The **usted** form of address is polite, or formal. **Usted** is usually abbreviated **Ud. Ud.** takes the same verb ending as **él** or **ella.**

   Señor, ¿habla Ud. inglés?
   Señora, Ud. trabaja en la papelería, ¿no?

Práctica

A ¿Tú o Ud.? Pregunten. *(Ask the following people what they need and what they are looking for. Use* tú *or* Ud. *as appropriate.)*

1. 2. 3. 4. 5.

B Claudia y el señor Sigan el modelo. *(Follow the model.)*

Necesito una hoja de papel.
Y tú, Claudia, ¿qué necesitas?
¿Y qué necesita Ud., señor?

1. Necesito un cuaderno.
2. Busco una goma de borrar.
3. Compro una camisa.
4. Hablo español.

ANSWERS

Práctica

A
1. ¿Qué necesita Ud. y qué busca Ud.?
2. ¿Qué necesitas tú y qué buscas tú?
3. ¿Qué necesita Ud. y qué busca Ud.?
4. ¿Qué necesitas tú y qué buscas tú?
5. ¿Qué necesitas tú y qué buscas tú?

B
1. Y tú Claudia, ¿qué necesitas? ¿Y qué necesita Ud., señor?
2. Y tú Claudia, ¿qué buscas? ¿Y qué busca Ud., señor?
3. Y tú Claudia, ¿qué compras? ¿Y qué compra Ud., señor?
4. Y tú Claudia, ¿hablas español? ¿Y habla Ud. español, señor?

TEACHING STRUCTURE

Talking formally and informally

A. Have students open their books to page 83. Explain how the two forms of "you" are used, leading students through the examples on this page. Explain that **tú** is also used when talking to a pet.

B. You may present **usted** and **tú** using magazine photos. Show a photo of a child when using **tú** and a photo of an adult when using **usted.** Show both photos when teaching the plural form **ustedes.**

C. Use additional magazine photos of pets, young children, and adults, each labeled with a name, and ask students to respond in unison with either **usted** or **tú.**

D. Give the magazine pictures to various students. Each student takes the role of the person whose picture he/she is holding. Now ask the person questions. For example: **Señora Martínez, ¿es usted inteligente? Elena, ¿eres una alumna seria?**

Práctica

A Have students make up a name for each person on page 83. For example, item 1: **Sra. García, ¿qué necesita usted? Sra. García, ¿qué busca usted?**

B Ask students to make up original sentences using other vocabulary. For example: **Necesito una limonada; Busco zapatos negros, etc.**

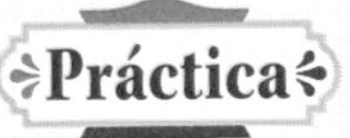

There is no more new material in this chapter. The sections that follow recombine and reinforce the vocabulary and structures that have already been introduced.

RESOURCES

- Audiocassette 3A/CD2
- CD-ROM, Disc 1, page 84

Bell Ringer Review

Use BRR Transparency 3-3, or write the following on the board: Make up a brief story entitled **En la tienda.** Use the following words: **necesitar, buscar, hablar, comprar, pagar.**

TEACHING THE CONVERSATION

A. Have students open their books to page 84. Before reading the conversation, have them look at the photo and guess what the conversation is about.

B. Now have students listen to the conversation on Cassette 3A/Compact Disc 2. Then have them repeat the conversation after you.

C. Call on two individuals to read the conversation in its entirety with as much expression as possible.

D. Do the comprehension activity that follows the conversation.

TECHNOLOGY OPTION

On the CD-ROM (Disc 1, page 84) students can watch a dramatization of this conversation. They can then play the role of either one of the characters, and record themselves in the conversation.

Conversación

En la tienda de ropa

EMPLEADA: Sí, señor. ¿Qué desea Ud.?
CLIENTE: Necesito una camisa.
EMPLEADA: Una camisa. ¿De qué color, señor?
CLIENTE: Una camisa blanca.
EMPLEADA: De acuerdo. ¿Qué talla usa Ud.?
CLIENTE: Treinta y seis.
(After looking at some shirts)
CLIENTE: ¿Cuánto es, por favor?
EMPLEADA: Ciento cincuenta pesos.
CLIENTE: Bien. ¿Pago aquí o en la caja?
EMPLEADA: En la caja, por favor.

Después de conversar

Contesten. *(Answer.)*

1. ¿Con quién habla el cliente?
2. ¿Qué necesita?
3. ¿Qué talla usa?
4. ¿Mira el señor una camisa?
5. ¿Cuánto es la camisa?
6. ¿Compra el señor la camisa?
7. ¿Dónde paga?

ANSWERS

Después de conversar

1. **El cliente habla con la dependienta (la empleada).**
2. **Necesita una camisa.**
3. **Usa la talla treinta y seis.**
4. **Sí, el señor mira una camisa.**
5. **La camisa es (cuesta) ciento cincuenta pesos.**
6. **Sí, el señor compra la camisa.**
7. **Paga en la caja.**

Did You Know?

Inglés, lengua extranjera English is the most popular foreign language in Spain and in many countries of Latin America, supplanting French in many of those countries. English is also the most commonly taught foreign language almost everywhere. You may wish to tell students: **El inglés es la lengua extranjera más popular de las escuelas de España y Latinoamérica.**

Actividades comunicativas

A Para la apertura de clases Ask a classmate what school supplies he or she needs at the beginning of the new school year and where he or she usually **(generalmente)** buys them. Then tell the class what you find out.

B En las tiendas Work with a classmate. Take turns playing the roles of the salesperson and the customer in the following situations.

- **En la papelería** You want to buy two pens—preferably red ones—, a notebook, and a calculator.
- **En la tienda de ropa** You want to buy a blue shirt for your friend. They have his size, but only in white.
- **En la zapatería** You need a pair of brown shoes. The ones the salesperson shows you are expensive.

JUEGO ¿Qué lleva? Have one student leave the room while the others choose a classmate to describe. The student who left comes back in and has to guess which classmate the others have chosen by asking questions about his or her clothes. Use the model as a guide.

PRONUNCIACIÓN

Las consonantes l, f, p, m, n

The pronunciation of the consonants **l, f, p, m,** and **n** is very similar in both Spanish and English. However, the **p** is not followed by a puff of breath as it often is in English. Repeat the following sentences.

Lolita es linda y elegante.
La falda de Felisa no es fea.
Paco es una persona popular.
La muchacha mexicana mira una goma.
Nando necesita un cuaderno nuevo.

ANSWERS

Actividades comunicativas

A Answers will vary; however, students should ask the following questions:
¿Qué materiales escolares necesitas?
Generalmente, ¿dónde compras...?
Student responses to these questions should begin with **Necesito...** and **Generalmente compro...**

B Students can use the **Conversación** dialogue, page 84, as a model for these activities.

Actividades comunicativas

A To enable students to report to the class, have them write down the school supplies their partners mention. Model the activity with one of your more able students.

B Have each pair of students choose one of the three situations in **Actividad B**. As a follow-up, have different pairs role-play each situation for the class.

TECHNOLOGY OPTION Students can use the Portfolio feature on the CD-ROM to record these conversations.

This is a good end-of-class activity.

TEACHING PRONUNCIATION

¡OJO! The consonant-vowel combinations presented in this chapter should not create problems for students. These sounds are rather easy for English speakers to pronounce properly.

A. Write the following on the board and have students pronounce each sound after you.
la le li lo lu
ma me mi mo mu
fa fe fi fo fu
pa pe pi po pu

B. You may wish also wish to have students repeat the following phrases and sentences:
La sala de Lolita
El amigo de Manolo Malo
Felipe es profesor de física.
El papá de Pepe Pinto

C. Now have students open their books and repeat the sentences on page 85 after you or the recording on Cassette 3A/Compact Disc 2.

D. These sentences can also be used as a dictation.

National Standards

Cultures
The reading on page 86 gives students some insights into some aspects of the school life of their counterparts in Spain.

Comparisons
The reading on this page makes some comparisons between schools in Latin America and Spain and those in the U.S.

TEACHING THE READING

Pre-reading

A. You may wish to present one paragraph of the story per day, or you may want to present the reading in its entirety.

B. Have students open their books to page 86. Tell them they are going to read a story about a student in Madrid.

C. Do the Reading Strategy activity on page 86. Then have students look at the photos on this page. Tell them that as they read, they are going to learn about a difference between the schools in Madrid and their own school. The photo may help them guess what this difference is.

D. Have students scan the reading quickly and silently.

E. Ask them to locate Madrid on the map on page 463.

Reading

A. Have students open their books and ask the entire class to repeat two or three sentences after you. Ask some of the **Después de leer** questions on page 87 to check for comprehension. Then continue reading.

B. Now go over the reading again, calling on individual students to read aloud.
(continued on page 87)

Lecturas CULTURALES

Reading Strategy

Using pictures and photographs
Before you begin to read, look at pictures, photographs, or any other visuals that accompany a reading. By doing this, you can often tell what the reading selection is about before you actually read it.

UN ALUMNO MADRILEÑO

Julio Torres es de Madrid. Él es alumno en el Liceo Joaquín Turina en Madrid. Un liceo o colegio es una escuela secundaria en España. En Madrid, la apertura de clases[1] es a fines de[2] septiembre. Julio necesita muchas cosas para la apertura de clases. Necesita materiales escolares. En una papelería compra un libro, un bolígrafo, tres lápices y varios cuadernos. Compra también un disquete para la computadora.

Pero Julio no necesita ropa nueva para la escuela. ¿Por qué? Porque Julio no lleva un blue jean o una camiseta a la escuela. Él lleva un uniforme. Es obligatorio llevar uniforme a la escuela. Un muchacho lleva un pantalón negro y una camisa blanca. En algunas[3] escuelas es necesario llevar chaqueta y corbata también. Una muchacha lleva una falda y una blusa. Y a veces[4] es necesario llevar una chaqueta. ¿Qué opinas? ¿Es una buena idea llevar uniforme a la escuela?

[1]apertura de clases *opening of school*
[2]a fines de *at the end of*
[3]algunas *some*
[4]a veces *sometimes*

Did You Know?

Uniformes escolares Explain to students that wearing a uniform to school is very common in Spain and throughout Latin America. In some elementary schools, the uniform is simply a smock. In some secondary schools the uniform can be quite formal.

Learning From Photos

Colegio de Nuestra Señora de la Consolación, Madrid Give students the following information about the top photo on page 87: **Muchas escuelas en España son religiosas. Hay muchas escuelas católicas en España.**

Después de leer

A Un alumno madrileño Contesten. *(Answer.)*

1. ¿De dónde es Julio Torres?
2. ¿En qué escuela es alumno?
3. ¿Cuándo es la apertura de clases en Madrid?
4. ¿Qué necesita Julio para la apertura de clases?
5. ¿Dónde compra las cosas que necesita?
6. ¿Necesita Julio ropa nueva para la escuela?
7. ¿Qué lleva él a la escuela?
8. ¿Qué lleva una muchacha a la escuela?

Colegio de Nuestra Señora de la Consolación, Madrid

B Julio Torres Busquen la información en la lectura. *(Find the information in the reading.)*

1. de dónde es Julio Torres
2. la escuela de Julio
3. cuándo es la apertura de clases en Madrid
4. las cosas que compra Julio
5. lo que es obligatorio llevar a la escuela
6. lo que Julio no lleva a la escuela
7. el uniforme típico de un muchacho
8. el uniforme típico de una muchacha

C Discusión ¿Qué opinas? *(What is your opinion?)*

¿Es una buena idea llevar uniforme a la escuela?

El Retiro, Madrid

Post-reading

Have students do the **Después de leer** activities on page 87 orally after reading the selection in class. Then assign these activities to be written at home. Go over them again the following day.

TECHNOLOGY OPTION

Students may listen to a recording of the **Lectura** on the CD-ROM, Disc 1, page 86.

Después de leer

A Allow students to refer to the story to look up the answers, or you may use this activity as a testing device for factual recall.

B Have individual students read the appropriate phrase or sentence aloud. Make sure all students find the information in the **Lectura.**

C The **Discusión** on page 87 can be done in English. Students should enjoy discussing this topic. To start the discussion, ask them how they would react if they were required to wear uniforms to school beginning the next semester. How would their lives be different?

ANSWERS

Después de leer

A
1. Es de Madrid.
2. Es alumno en el Liceo Joaquín Turina.
3. La apertura de clases es a fines de septiembre.
4. Necesita materiales escolares.
5. Compra las cosas que necesita en una papelería.
6. Julio no necesita ropa nueva para la escuela.
7. Julio lleva un uniforme (un pantalón negro y una camisa blanca).
8. Una muchacha lleva un uniforme también. Lleva una falda y una blusa.

B
1. de Madrid
2. Liceo Joaquín Turina
3. a fines de septiembre
4. un libro, un bolígrafo, tres lápices, varios cuadernos y un disquete
5. un uniforme
6. un blue jean o una camisa
7. un pantalón negro y una camisa blanca
8. una falda y una blusa

LECTURA OPCIONAL 1

National Standards

Cultures

This selection familiarizes students with the dress of several different indigenous groups that live in various regions of Latin America.

TEACHING TIPS

A. Have students read the passage quickly as they look at the photos that accompany it. The photos will increase comprehension because students can visualize what they are reading.

B. Have students discuss what information they find interesting.

C. Ask students to think of at least one article of clothing that they know with a Spanish name.

HISTORY CONNECTION

Guatemaltecos A very large percentage of Guatemalans are descendants of the famous Mayans. As in other areas of South and Central America, the Indians were severely oppressed by their Spanish conquerors. However, the native people of Guatemala remained defiantly apart from the culture of their conquerors. The highland Mayans of Guatemala retained their own cultural identity, which continues to be very strong.

LECTURA OPCIONAL 1

LA ROPA INDÍGENA

La ropa que lleva la población india o indígena de Latinoamérica es muy interesante y muy bonita. En Guatemala, por ejemplo, la ropa cambia o varía de un pueblo[1] a otro. El traje que lleva una señora de Santiago de Atitlán no es el mismo traje que lleva una señora de Chichicastenango.

La india de Guatemala no lleva sombrero. Pero la india del Perú, sí. Ella lleva sombrero.

La india del famoso pueblo de Otavalo en el Ecuador lleva dos faldas de lana[2] oscura con una blusa muy brillante. El señor otavaleño lleva un pantalón blanco, una camisa blanca y un poncho azul.

[1]pueblo *town* [2]lana *wool*

Después de leer

A La ropa indígena
Identifiquen. *(Identify.)*
There are some articles of clothing that retain their Spanish names in English. Look at the photographs to find out what they are.

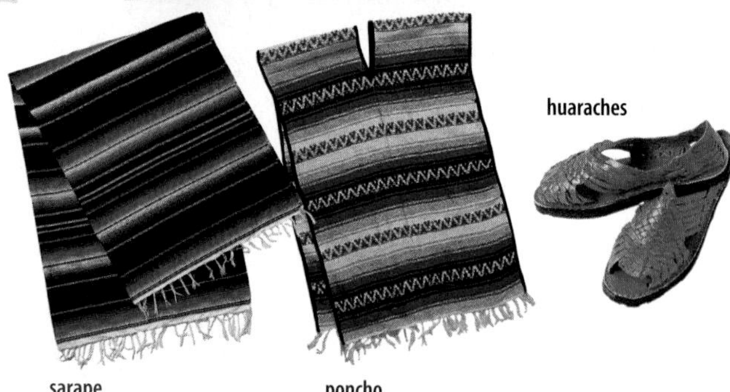

Learning From Photos

La ropa indígena The woman on the top left is from Chichicastenango, Guatemala. The woman in the center is from Santiago de Atitlán, one of the twelve villages on Lake Atitlán named after the apostles. The woman on the bottom left is from Ecuador. The hat she is wearing is the same as or very similar to those worn by women in Perú and Bolivia. The photos below the reading are of **otavaleños**, from the famous market town of Otavalo, north of Quito. They are famous around the world for their weavings.

Although it is not evident in these photos, the men of Otavalo wear their hair in a long braid.

LECTURA OPCIONAL 2

UN DISEÑADOR FAMOSO

El famoso diseñador de ropa Oscar de la Renta es de Santo Domingo, la capital de la República Dominicana. Los estilos de de la Renta son muy elegantes y lujosos. Los trajes de gala de de la Renta son muy caros. La fama de Oscar de la Renta es mundial[1].

Oscar de la Renta es también una persona muy buena y muy humana. En la República Dominicana, de la Renta funda un orfanato[2] y un tipo de «Boys' Town». El «Boys' Town» es para niños desamparados[3]. Funda también una escuela especial para sordos[4].

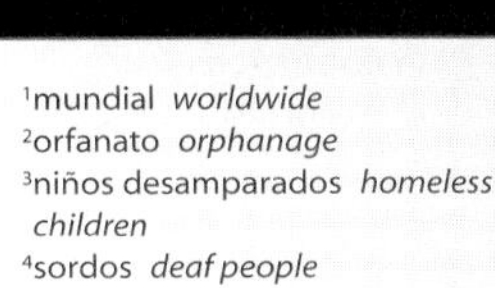

[1]mundial *worldwide*
[2]orfanato *orphanage*
[3]niños desamparados *homeless children*
[4]sordos *deaf people*

Después de leer

A En español, por favor. Busquen las palabras afines en la lectura. *(Look for the cognates in the reading.)*

B Oscar de la Renta Contesten. *(Answer.)*

1. ¿De dónde es Oscar de la Renta?
2. ¿Por qué es él un hombre (señor) muy famoso?

LECTURA OPCIONAL 2

TEACHING TIPS

A. Have students read the selection to themselves.

B. Now have students do the **Después de leer** activity on page 89.

C. You may wish to ask students to bring to class any articles of clothing they may have that were made in a Spanish-speaking country. These could be clothing items mentioned in the reading or other items.

INFORMAL ASSESSMENT

You may want to give the following quiz to those students who read this selection.

Answer

1. **¿De dónde es Oscar de la Renta?**
2. **¿Cuál es la capital de la República Dominicana?**
3. **¿Qué es Oscar de la Renta? ¿Cuál es la profesión de de la Renta?**
4. **¿Cómo son los estilos de de la Renta?**
5. **¿Qué tipo de persona es de la Renta?**
6. **¿Qué funda él?**
7. **¿Para quiénes es el «Boy's Town»?**

Critical Thinking Activity

Giving opinions Put the following on the board or on a transparency or read the information to the students: **En tu opinión, ¿necesitas pagar mucho dinero por la ropa o no?**

ANSWERS

Después de leer

A **famoso, la capital, elegantes, la fama, una persona, humana, un tipo, especial**

B
1. **Es de Santo Domingo en la República Dominicana.**
2. **Es un diseñador de ropa muy elegante y lujosa.**

CAPÍTULO 3
Conexiones

National Standards

Connections

This reading establishes a connection with Computer Science. Since most students today are very familiar with computers they should find it very easy to use computer terms in Spanish and thus increase their Spanish vocabulary.

This introduction to computer vocabulary in Spanish is very useful for reading advertisements or instructions concerning the use of computers.

¡OJO! These readings on computers are optional. You may choose any of the following ways to do them with your students.
Independent reading Have students read the selections and do the post-reading activities as homework, which you collect. This option is least intrusive on class time and requires a minimum of teacher involvement.
Homework with in-class follow-up Assign the readings and post-reading activity as homework. Review and discuss the material in class the next day.
Intensive in-class activity This option includes a pre-reading vocabulary presentation, in-class reading and discussion, assignment of the activities for homework, and a discussion of the assignment in class the following day.

LA TECNOLOGÍA

LA COMPUTADORA

A. Most students will be familiar with these computer terms in English. Model the terms in Spanish and have students repeat after you.

B. If there is a computer in your classroom, have students name the equipment in Spanish.

Conexiones

LA TECNOLOGÍA

LA COMPUTADORA

Some years ago computers began to revolutionize the way people conduct their lives. They have changed the way we view the world and, in reality, they've changed the world. Computers have a place in our homes, in our schools, and in our world of business. If you are interested in computers, you may want to familiarize yourself with some basic computer vocabulary in Spanish. Then read the information about computers on the next page.

ABOUT THE SPANISH LANGUAGE

In Spain, **el ordenador** is used instead of **la computadora**. The latter is used in all countries in Latin America.

Critical Thinking Activity

Drawing conclusion, making inferences Ask students why so many computer-related terms come from English. Point out that languages constantly borrow words from other languages. For example, on page 88 of this chapter, students were shown several articles of clothing that have retained their Spanish names in English.

¡Conecta la computadora y a trabajar!

Una computadora procesa datos. El hardware es la computadora y todo el equipo[1] conectado con la computadora. El software son los programas de la computadora. Un programa es un grupo o conjunto de instrucciones.

La computadora almacena[2] datos. Envía o transmite los datos a un disco. La computadora calcula, compara y copia datos. Pero la computadora no piensa[3]. El operador o la operadora de la computadora entra las instrucciones y la computadora procesa la información.

El módem adapta una terminal a una línea telefónica para transmitir información por todo el mundo[4].

El Internet—¡Conecta al mundo!

Con el Internet hay acceso al mundo entero. Hay información sobre la historia, la economía, el arte, la música y muchas otras áreas de interés. Cuando navegas por la red[5], es posible conectar con los centros de noticias. Es posible enviar correo[6] electrónico y conversar con amigos en otras partes del mundo. Y hay la posibilidad de crear una página Web. Sí, ¡el mundo entero en una pantalla!

[1]equipo *equipment*
[2]almacena *stores*
[3]piensa *think*
[4]mundo *world*
[5]red *Net*
[6]correo *mail*

Después de leer

A **En español, por favor.** Busquen las palabras en la lectura. *(Find the following words in the reading.)*

1. hardware
2. software
3. program
4. data
5. terminal
6. surf the Net
7. Web page
8. e-mail (electronic mail)
9. to process information
10. access
11. computer operator

B **Una página Web** Look at the monitor on page 90. If you have access to the Internet either at home or at school, go to www.glencoe.com/sec/fl
¡a practicar el español!

Una oficina, Caracas, Venezuela

C. Explain to students that there are some basic strategies to use when reading unfamiliar material. They should learn to (1) recognize cognates and (2) derive meaning from context.

D. Ask students to scan the reading on page 91 and make a list of words they do not know the meaning of.

E. As a whole-class activity, go over the words students have listed, asking other students to guess their meaning based on the context.

Después de leer

A This is a skimming activity designed to provide practice in reading for specific information. Do this activity orally.

B Tell students that the monitor on page 90 shows the Glencoe Foreign Language Home page. At the Web site there are Internet activities designed to accompany and reinforce the material presented in each chapter of the textbook. (See student page 95 for a description of the Internet activity for this chapter and page 70 of this Teacher's Wraparound Edition for more information about the content of the **Glencoe Foreign Language Web site.**)

Career Connection

Empresas internacionales Explain to students that a knowledge of computer vocabulary in Spanish could be a tremendous asset in careers in business and finance. Have them do some research to find out what U.S. companies have offices in Spanish-speaking countries.

ANSWERS

Después de leer

A
1. el hardware
2. el software
3. el programa
4. los datos
5. la terminal
6. navegar por la red
7. una página Web
8. el correo electrónico
9. procesar la información
10. el acceso
11. el/la operador(a) de computadora

Bell Ringer Review

Use BRR Transparency 3-4, or write the following on the board: Rewrite the following in the **tú** form:
1. Ud. habla francés.
2. ¿Llega Ud. a la escuela?

RECYCLING

The **Actividades orales** and the **Actividad escrita** allow students to use the vocabulary and structures from this chapter and earlier chapters in open-ended, real-life settings.

Actividades orales

¡OJO! Encourage students to say as much as possible when they do these activities. Tell them not to be afraid of making mistakes since the goal of the activities is real-life communication. If someone in the group makes an error, allow the others to politely correct him or her.

Let students choose the activities they would like to take part in.

Student Portfolio

Have students keep a notebook containing their best written work from each chapter. These selected writings can be based on assignments from the Student Textbook, the Writing Activities Workbook, and the Communication Activities Masters. The two activities on page 93 are examples of writing assignments that may be included in each student's portfolio.

In the Workbook, students will develop an organized autobiography **(Mi autobiografía).** These workbook pages may also become a part of their portfolio. See the Teacher's Manual for more information on the Student Portfolio.

Culminación

Actividades orales

A ¿Qué necesitas y cuánto es? With a classmate, take turns playing the parts of a student and a salesperson in a stationery store. Tell the salesperson what school supplies you need. The salesperson will tell you how much money you need.

B Regalos You have just spent a few weeks in Spain and want to buy some gifts for several friends. Make a list of what you want to buy. Go to the different stores to buy the items you want. With a classmate, take turns being the customer and salesperson at the stores where you are purchasing the items on your list.

C En la papelería With a classmate, look at the illustrations. Take turns asking and answering questions about each illustration.

ANSWERS

Actividades orales

A Answers will vary, but may follow this model:
—Necesito una goma. ¿Cuánto cuesta?
—Una goma cuesta 12 pesos.

B The conversations between the student and salesperson will vary depending on the gifts students choose. The following is a sample conversation:
—¿Qué desea Ud.?
—Necesito una mochila.
—¿De qué color?
— Una mochila roja. ¿Cuánto es, por favor?
—80 pesos.
—¿Pago aquí o en la caja?
—En la caja, por favor.

C Answers will vary but may include:
1. **¿Qué desea el muchacho?**
Desea una calculadora.
2. **¿Con quién habla el muchacho?**
Con la dependienta.
3. **¿Cuánto cuesta la calculadora?**
745 pesos.

Actividad escrita

A **La apertura de clases** You have received a letter from a pen pal in Salamanca, Spain. Write back to her in Spanish. She wants to know all about you. She also wants to know when school starts and what you wear to school. Give her as much information as you can.

Salamanca, España

Writing Strategy

Preparing for an interview

An interview is one way to gather information for a story or a report. A good interviewer should prepare questions ahead of time. In preparing the questions, think about what you hope to learn from the interview. The best interview questions are open ended. Open-ended questions cannot be answered with "yes" or "no." They give the person being interviewed more opportunity to "open up" and speak freely.

¿De dónde?
¿Cuánto? ¿Cómo?
¿Quién? ¿Dónde?
¿Qué?

Guadalupe Álvaro

It is the beginning of a new school year. Your first assignment for the school newspaper is to write an article about a new exchange student, Guadalupe Álvaro. Guadalupe is from Salamanca, Spain.

You decide to interview Guadalupe before writing your article. To prepare for the interview, write down as many questions as you can. Ask her about her personal life, school life in her country, her friends, etc.

After you have prepared your questions, conduct the interview with a partner who plays the role of Guadalupe. Write down your partner's answers to your questions. Then organize your notes and write your article.

Actividad escrita

A Have students edit each others' letters.

TECHNOLOGY OPTIONS

Go to the **Correspondencia electrónica** section at the **Glencoe Foreign Language Web site (http://www.glencoe.com/sec/fl)** to find out how to set up a keypal (penpal) exchange between your class and a class in a Spanish-speaking country.

Students can use the Portfolio feature on the CD-ROM to write this letter.

Writing Strategy

Preparing for an interview

Have students read the Writing Strategy on page 93. Now give students the following pairs of questions and have them decide which are open-ended.

¿Necesitas un bolígrafo?
¿Qué necesitas?
¿Es cara la camisa?
¿Cuánto cuesta la camisa?

National Standards

Communities

If possible, have students conduct the interview they have prepared on page 93 with a Spanish-speaking student in their school.

ANSWERS

Actividad escrita

A For this **Actividad** students should give a description of themselves using **ser** and appropriate adjectives. They may use the expression **la apertura de clases es en ___** and the verb **llevar** with articles of clothing.

Writing Strategy

Answers will vary, depending on the questions students prepare for the interview.

ASSESSMENT RESOURCES

- Chapter Quizzes
- Testing Program
- Computer Testmaker
- Situation Cards
- Communication Transparency C-3
- Performance Assessment
- **Maratón mental** Videoquiz

VOCABULARY REVIEW

The words and phrases in the **Vocabulario** have been taught for productive use in this chapter. They are summarized here as a resource for both student and teacher. This list also serves as a convenient resource for the **Culminación** activities on page 92 and 93. There are approximately six cognates in this vocabulary list. Have students find them.

Vocabulario

IDENTIFYING SCHOOL SUPPLIES

los materiales escolares	el cuaderno, el bloc
la mochila	la carpeta
el lápiz, los lápices	el libro
el bolígrafo, la pluma	la hoja de papel
el marcador	la calculadora
la goma de borrar	el disquete

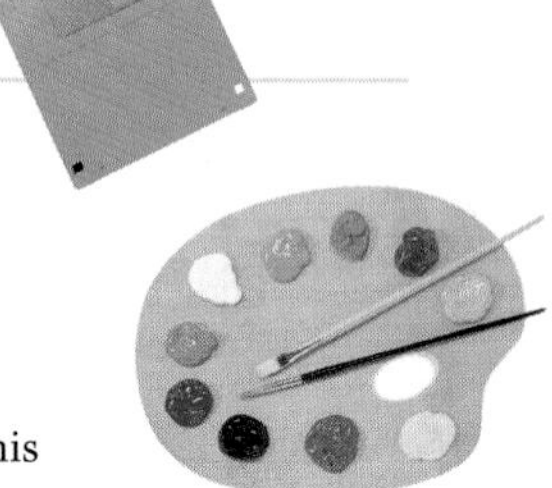

IDENTIFYING ARTICLES OF CLOTHING

la ropa	la blusa
el pantalón	la chaqueta
la camisa	el traje
la corbata	la gorra
el T-shirt, la camiseta	los calcetines
el blue jean, los blue jeans	los zapatos
la falda	los tenis, un par de tenis

DESCRIBING CLOTHES

largo(a)	corto(a)

IDENTIFYING COLORS

¿De qué color es?	anaranjado(a)
blanco(a)	rojo(a)
negro(a)	rosado(a)
gris	verde
azul	de color marrón
amarillo(a)	

IDENTIFYING SOME TYPES OF STORES

la papelería	la tienda de ropa

SHOPPING

el/la dependiente(a)	necesitar
el/la empleado(a)	buscar
la caja	mirar
la talla, el tamaño	comprar
el número	pagar
barato(a)	usar, calzar
caro(a)	llevar
mucho	hablar
poco	trabajar

OTHER USEFUL EXPRESSIONS

¿Qué desea Ud.?	¿Cuánto es?, ¿Cuánto cuesta?

For the Younger Student

Ropa Have students draw a picture with colored markers or crayons of a boy or a girl wearing an outfit they like. Ask students to label the clothes and their colors in Spanish.

Independent Practice

Assign any of the following:

1. Activities, pages 92–93
2. Workbook, **Mi autobiografía,** page 28
3. Situation Cards
4. CD-ROM, Disc 1, Chapter 3, **Juego de repaso**

TECNOTUR

VIDEO

¡Buen viaje!

EPISODIO 3 ▸ Las compras para la escuela

Teresa compra un cuaderno y un lápiz para Pilar.

En la tienda, Teresa busca ropa nueva.

CD-ROM

Expansión cultural

Hay muchas tiendas elegantes en la calle Serrano, Madrid.

In this video episode Teresa and Pilar go shopping for school clothes in Madrid. To find out what Hispanic teens are wearing this year, go to the Capítulo 3 Internet activity at the Glencoe Foreign Language Web site:

http://www.glencoe.com/sec/fl

Video Synopsis

Teresa and her little sister, Pilar, are shopping at a department store in Madrid. Pilar needs some school supplies, and Teresa is looking for new clothes. Although Pilar would love to have a new computer, she ends up buying some small items for school. Teresa tries on several different outfits as she and Pilar discuss sizes, colors, and prices. This episode ends when Pilar gives her sisterly approval to Teresa's clothing choices.

CAPÍTULO 3

Tecnotur

OVERVIEW

This page previews three key multimedia components of the **Glencoe Spanish** series. Each reinforces the material taught in Chapter 3 in a unique manner.

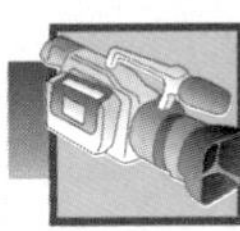

VIDEO

The Video Program allows students to see how the chapter vocabulary and structures are used by native speakers within an engaging storyline. For maximum reinforcement, show the video episode as a final activity for Chapter 3.

A. These two photos show highlights from the Chapter 3 video episode. Before watching it, remind students who Teresa is by asking **¿De dónde es Teresa? ¿Quién es la muchacha?**

B. Now show the episode. See the Video Activities Booklet for detailed suggestions for using this resource.

CD-ROM

A. In the video episode Teresa and Pilar go clothes shopping in Madrid. The **Expansión cultural** photo shows one of the famous shopping streets in Madrid. Have students read the caption on page 95.

B. In the CD-ROM version of **Expansión cultural** (Disc 1, page 95), students can listen to additional recorded information about **la calle Serrano.**

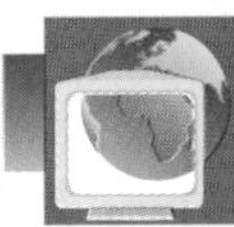

INTERNET

Teacher Information and Student Worksheets for this activity can be accessed at the Web site.

Chapter 4 Overview ◆◆◆◆◆◆◆◆◆◆◆◆◆◆◆◆◆◆◆◆◆◆◆◆◆◆◆◆◆◆◆◆◆◆

SCOPE AND SEQUENCE pages 96–125

TOPICS	FUNCTIONS	STRUCTURE	CULTURE
◆ Going to school ◆ School activities ◆ Afterschool activities ◆ Numbers: 1,000–2,000,000	◆ How to talk about going to school ◆ How to talk about classes and school events ◆ How to greet people and ask how they feel ◆ How to count from 1,000 to 2,000,000	◆ Plural forms of **-ar** verbs ◆ **Ir, dar,** and **estar** ◆ The contractions **al** and **del**	◆ Paula and Armando, two students from Peru ◆ Differences between schools in the U.S. and schools in Spanish-speaking countries ◆ Miraflores, a suburb of Lima, Peru ◆ A famous Chilean poet: Gabriela Mistral ◆ Punta Arenas, Chile ◆ Biology terms in Spanish ◆ Vistas de México

CHAPTER 4 RESOURCES

PRINT	MULTIMEDIA
Planning Resources	
Lesson Plans Block Scheduling Lesson Plans	Interactive Lesson Planner
Reinforcement Resources	
Writing Activities Workbook Student Tape Manual Video Activities Booklet Web Site User's Guide	Transparencies Binder Audiocassette/Compact Disc Program Videocassette/Videodisc Program Online Internet Activities Electronic Teacher's Classroom Resources
Assessment Resources	
Situation Cards Chapter Quizzes Testing Program Performance Assessment	**Maratón mental** Mindjogger Videoquiz Testmaker Computer Software (Macintosh/Windows) Listening Comprehension Audiocassette/Compact Disc Communication Transparency: C-4
Motivational Resources	
Expansion Activities	Café Glencoe: www.cafe.glencoe.com Keypal Internet Activities
Enrichment	
Spanish for Spanish Speakers	Fine Art Transparency: F-3

Chapter 4 Planning Guide

SECTION	PAGES	SECTION RESOURCES
Vocabulario Palabras 1 **Llegar a la escuela** **En la escuela**	98–101	Vocabulary Transparencies 4.1 Audiocassette 3B/ Compact Disc 3 Student Tape Manual, TE, pages 34–36 Workbook, page 29 Chapter Quizzes, page 17 CD-ROM, Disc 1, pages 98–101
Vocabulario Palabras 2 **En la clase** **La fiesta del Club de español** **Más números**	102–105	Vocabulary Transparencies 4.2 Audiocassette 3B/ Compact Disc 3 Student Tape Manual, TE, pages 37–38 Workbook, pages 30–31 Chapter Quizzes, page 18 CD-ROM, Disc 1, pages 102–105
Estructura **Presente de los verbos en -ar en el plural** **Presente de los verbos ir, dar, estar** **Las contracciones al y del**	106–113	Workbook, pages 32–37 Audiocassette 3B/Compact Disc 3 Student Tape Manual, TE, pages 39–41 Structure Transparency S-4 Chapter Quizzes, pages 19–21 Computer Testmaker CD-ROM, Disc 1, pages 106–113
Conversación **La fiesta del Club de español** **Pronunciación: La consonante t**	114–115	Audiocassette 3B/Compact Disc 3 Student Tape Manual, TE, pages 41–42 CD-ROM, Disc 1, pages 114–115
Lecturas culturales **Escuelas del mundo hispano** **Una conferencia universitaria *(opcional)*** **Gabriela Mistral *(opcional)***	116–119	Testing Program, pages 17–18 CD-ROM, Disc 1, pages 116–119
Conexiones **La biología *(opcional)***	120–121	Testing Program, page 18 CD-ROM, Disc 1, pages 120–121
Culminación **Actividades orales** **Actividades escritas** **Vocabulario** **Tecnotur**	122–125	**¡Buen viaje!** Video, Episode 4 Video Activities, pages 76–78 Internet Activities www.glencoe.com/sec/fl Testing Program, pages 14–17; 104; 136; 159–160 CD-ROM, Disc 1, pages 122–125

CAPÍTULO 4

OVERVIEW

In this chapter students will learn to discuss how they get to school and to describe many typical school activities. To do this they will learn to use the plural forms of **-ar** verbs to communicate in situations related to school. They will also learn the verbs **ir, dar,** and **estar**.

National Standards

Communication
In Chapter 4, students will communicate in spoken and written Spanish on the following topics:
- getting to school
- participating in classroom activities
- enjoying club activities

Students will obtain and provide information, engage in conversations and discuss schooling in the U.S. and Spanish-speaking countries as they fulfill the objectives listed on this page.

Spotlight On Culture

Artefacto The antique hand-woven purse pictured here is from Bolivia.
Fotografía The photo on pages 96–97 shows students on their way to school in a residential area of San Juan, Puerto Rico. Have students note that the teens are wearing uniforms. They are going to a coed school. Since the educational system in Puerto Rico is the same as the system in the continental United States there are more coed schools in Puerto Rico than in many other Spanish-speaking countries.

CAPÍTULO 4

En la escuela

Objetivos

In this chapter you will learn to do the following:
- talk about going to school
- talk about some school activities
- greet people and ask how they feel
- tell how you feel
- describe where you and others go
- describe where you and others are
- discuss some differences between schools in the United States and schools in Spanish-speaking countries

The **Glencoe Foreign Language Web site (http://www.glencoe.com/sec/fl)** offers three options that enable you and your students to experience the Spanish-speaking world via the Internet:
- The online **Actividades** are correlated to the chapters and utilize Hispanic Web sites around the world. For the Chapter 4 activity see student page 125.
- The **Correspondencia electrónica** section provides information on how to set up a keypal (pen pal) exchange between your class and a class in the Spanish-speaking world.
- At **Café Glencoe**, the interactive "after-school" section of the site, you and your students can access a variety of additional online resources, including interactive games.

CAPÍTULO 4

Learning From Photos

Los alumnos After you have presented the structure in this lesson, you may want to ask students the following questions about this photo: **¿Están en San Juan los alumnos? ¿Son puertorriqueños? ¿Es San Juan la capital de Puerto Rico? ¿Van los alumnos a la escuela? ¿Van a pie o toman el bus escolar? ¿Llevan los alumnos uniforme a la escuela? ¿Qué llevan los muchachos? ¿Qué llevan las muchachas? ¿Cuántos muchachos hay? ¿Y cuántas muchachas hay?**

Pacing

Chapter 4 will require approximately eight to ten days. Pacing will vary according to the length of the class, the age of your students, and student aptitude.

Block Scheduling

The extended timeframe provided by block scheduling affords you the opportunity to implement a greater number of activities and projects to motivate and involve your students. See the Block Scheduling Lesson Plans Booklet for suggestions on how to present the chapter material within a block scheduling framework.

Chapter Projects

Actividades escolares Have students prepare a list of things they do in school. Have them include only those activities they learned to discuss in Spanish. Use their lists for a bulletin board display.

Una invitación a una fiesta Have students prepare an invitation for a Spanish Club party.

RESOURCES

- Vocabulary Transparencies 4.1 (A & B)
- Student Tape Manual, TE, pages 34–36
- Audiocassette 3B/CD3
- Workbook, page 29
- Quiz 1, page 17
- CD-ROM, Disc 1, pages 98–101

Bell Ringer Review

Use BRR Transparency 4-1, or write the following on the board: Complete the following statements.

1. Yo soy alumno(a) en ___.
2. Yo llevo los materiales escolares en ___.
3. Yo llevo ___ a la escuela.

TEACHING VOCABULARY

A. Have students close their books. Model the new vocabulary using Vocabulary Transparencies 4.1 (A & B). Have students repeat each expression two or three times.

B. As you present the vocabulary in sentences, you may want to break the sentences in segments as follows:
Los alumnos llegan.
Llegan a la escuela.
Ask: **¿Llegan los alumnos?**
¿Llegan los alumnos a la escuela?
¿Llegan a la escuela o a la tienda?
¿Quiénes llegan a la escuela?
¿Adónde llegan los alumnos?
Interspersing these simple questions enables students to use the new words so that they become a part of their active vocabulary.
(continued on page 99)

Vocabulario

PALABRAS 1

Llegar a la escuela

a pie

en el bus escolar

en carro, en coche

Los alumnos llegan a la escuela.
¿Cuándo llegan a la escuela?
¿A qué hora llegan?
Llegan a eso de las ocho menos cuarto.
No llegan a las ocho menos cuarto en punto.
Algunos van a la escuela a pie.
Algunos van en carro.
Otros toman el bus escolar.

Total Physical Response

Getting ready
Do the TPR activities after presenting the vocabulary. Tell students they are going to act out what you say.

Begin

___, ven acá. Tú vas a la escuela. Vas a la escuela a pie.

___, tú no vas a la escuela a pie. Tomas el bus. Toma tu asiento en el bus. (Use a classroom chair.)

___, tú entras en la sala de clase.
___, tú hablas con la profesora.
___, tú miras la pizarra.
___, tú miras al (a la) profesor(a).
___, tú hablas.
___, tú no hablas. Tú escuchas al (a la) profesor(a).

En la escuela

Los alumnos entran en la escuela.

Los alumnos están en la sala de clase.
Los alumnos estudian.
La profesora enseña.

la sala de clase, el salón de clase

The natural progression when providing questions from easy to more complex is: yes/no questions, either/or questions, questions with interrogative words.

C. Hint When presenting **en punto** write 8:00 on the board. Say: **a las ocho en punto—precisamente o exactamente a las ocho.**

D. After presenting the vocabulary with books closed using the overhead transparencies, have students open their books and call on individuals to read aloud.

TEACHING TIP

The type of questioning described in Step B on page 98 allows students to hear and use the words so they become an active part of their vocabulary in a natural way. It also lets you take into account individual differences when presenting new material. Ask the easy yes/no questions of the less able students and the more difficult questions with the interrogative words of the more able students.

ABOUT THE SPANISH LANGUAGE

- **Ir a pie** literally means to *go on foot* or *to walk* and it is understood wherever Spanish is spoken. **Andar** can also mean *to go on foot* or *to walk*. It is commonly used in Spain but would not be understood in all areas of Latin America in this context. **Caminar** is more frequently used in Latin America.
- There are many ways to express *bus*. The most commonly heard terms are **el autobús; el camión** in Mexico and some areas of Central America; **la guagua** in the Caribbean and the Canary Islands. Other words for *bus* will be presented in later chapters.
- In Latin America the word for *car* is **el carro.** In Spain it is **el coche.** In many areas of Latin America, however, **el coche** sounds archaic.
- **El/La profesor(a)** refers to a secondary school teacher or a college professor. **El/La catedrático(a)** is also used for a college professor. **El/La maestro(a)** refers to an elementary school teacher.

CAPÍTULO 4
Vocabulario

¡OJO! **Práctica** When students are doing the **Práctica** activities, accept any answer that makes sense. The purpose of these activities is to have students use the new vocabulary. They are not factual recall activities. Thus, do not expect students to remember specific information from the vocabulary presentation when answering. If you wish, have students use the photos on this page as a stimulus, when possible.
Historieta Each time **Historieta** appears, it means that the answers to the activity form a short story. Encourage students to look at the title of the **Historieta** since it can help them do the activity.

A and **B** Do these activities orally, and then have students open their books and read them for reinforcement. For **Práctica A,** have students answer first with complete sentences, and then with just the word or phrase that responds to the interrogative word.

Writing Development

Have students write the answers to **Práctica B** in a paragraph to illustrate how all items are connected in meaning.

Práctica

A HISTORIETA ¡A la escuela!

Contesten. *(Answer.)*

1. ¿Llegan los alumnos a la escuela?
   ¿Adónde llegan los alumnos?
   ¿Quiénes llegan a la escuela?
2. ¿Llegan a la escuela a eso de las ocho menos cuarto?
   ¿Cuándo llegan a la escuela?
   ¿A qué hora llegan a la escuela?
3. ¿Van algunos alumnos a la escuela a pie?
   ¿Cómo van a la escuela?
   ¿Adónde van a pie?
4. ¿Toman otros alumnos el bus escolar?
   ¿Qué toman?
   ¿Adónde toman el bus escolar?
   ¿Cómo llegan ellos a la escuela?

Colegio San José, Estepona, España

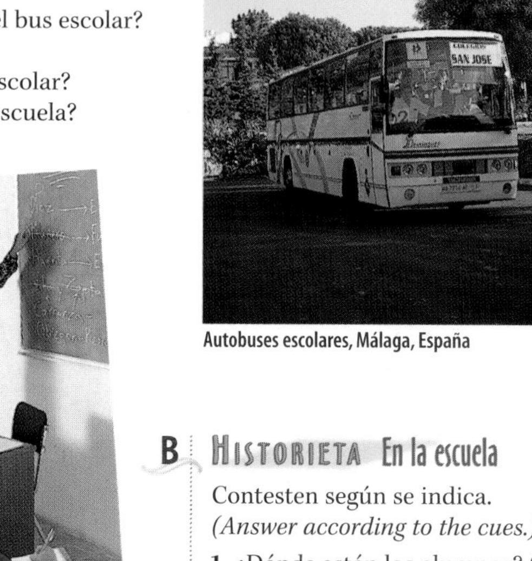

Autobuses escolares, Málaga, España

Una clase, San Miguel de Allende, México

B HISTORIETA En la escuela

Contesten según se indica.
(Answer according to the cues.)

1. ¿Dónde están los alumnos? (en clase)
2. ¿Quiénes estudian? (los alumnos)
3. ¿Estudian mucho? (sí)
4. ¿Quién no estudia? (la profesora)
5. ¿Quién enseña? (la profesora)

GEOGRAPHY CONNECTION

¿Dónde está... ? Have students locate Málaga and Estepona, west of Málaga, on the map of Spain, page 463, and San Miguel de Allende on the map of Mexico, page 465. (You may also use the Map Transparencies for this activity.)

ANSWERS

Práctica

A
1. **Sí, los alumnos llegan a la escuela.**
   A la escuela.
   Los alumnos.
2. **Sí, llegan a la escuela a eso de las ocho menos cuarto.**
   A las ocho menos cuarto.
   A las ocho menos cuarto.
3. **Sí, algunos alumnos van a la escuela a pie.**
   A pie.
   A la escuela.
4. **Sí, otros alumnos toman el bus escolar.**
   Toman el bus escolar.
   A la escuela.
   En el bus.

B
1. **Los alumnos están en clase.**
2. **Los alumnos estudian.**
3. **Sí, estudian mucho.**
4. **La profesora no estudia.**
5. **La profesora enseña.**

C HISTORIETA ¡A la escuela, todos!

Completen. *(Complete.)*

Una clase, Santurce, Puerto Rico

Los alumnos ___1___ a la escuela. Llegan a eso de las ___2___ menos cuarto—a las ocho menos veinte o a las ocho menos trece. No ___3___ a las ocho menos cuarto en punto. Algunos van a la escuela a ___4___. Algunos ___5___ en carro. Y otros ___6___ el bus escolar.

Los alumnos entran en la ___7___ de clase a eso de las ocho. Cuando entran en la clase, hablan con el ___8___. Los alumnos ___9___ mucho en la escuela. Pero el profesor no ___10___; él ___11___.

Actividad comunicativa

A **Entrevista** Work with a classmate. Pretend you are on the staff of your school newspaper and have been assigned to interview a Mexican exchange student about a school day in his or her hometown. Interview him or her.

Salón de clase, San Miguel de Allende, México

CAPÍTULO 4 Vocabulario

C Have a student retell the information in **Práctica C** in his or her own words.

Note Go over all the **Práctica** activities in class before assigning them for homework.

Learning From Photos

Colegio San José, Estepona, España (page 100) Ask the following questions: **¿Es el Colegio San José una escuela moderna? ¿Qué llevan los alumnos a la escuela? ¿Es una escuela mixta para muchachos y muchachas?**

Autobuses escolares, Málaga, España Ask: **Los autobuses escolares, ¿cómo son? ¿Son grandes o pequeños? ¿Son modernos?**

Une clase, San Miguel de Allende, México (page 100) Ask: **¿Llevan los alumnos uniforme a la escuela en San Miguel de Allende? ¿Es una escuela mixta? ¿Toman apuntes los alumnos? ¿Quién habla?**

Santurce, Puerto Rico (page 101) Explain to students that Santurce is the name of a large section of San Juan. Santurce has both residential and commercial areas.

ANSWERS

Práctica

C
1. **llegan**
2. **ocho**
3. **llegan**
4. **pie**
5. **van**
6. **toman**
7. **sala**
8. **profesor**
9. **estudian**
10. **estudia**
11. **enseña**

Actividad comunicativa

A Answers can vary greatly but may include:

—¿A qué hora llegas a la escuela?
—A eso de las siete y treinta.
—¿Cómo vas a la escuela? ¿Tomas el bus?
—No, voy a pie a la escuela.
—¿A qué hora entran los alumnos en la sala de clase?
—A eso de las ocho menos diez.

RESOURCES

- Vocabulary Transparencies 4.2 (A & B)
- Student Tape Manual, TE, pages 37–38
- Audiocassette 3B/CD3
- Workbook, pages 30–31
- Quiz 2, page 18
- CD-ROM, Disc 1, pages 102–105

Bell Ringer Review

Use BRR Transparency 4-2, or write the following on the board:
Find the opposite.

1. alto	**a. hablar**
2. fácil	**b. serio**
3. escuchar	**c. bajo**
4. primario	**d. interesante**
5. aburrido	**e. difícil**
6. cómico	**f. secundario**

TEACHING VOCABULARY

A. You may wish to refer to suggestions on page 98.

B. Use gestures to help convey meaning and to assist in eliciting responses.
mirar *(point to eyes)*
hablar *(point to mouth)*
escuchar *(point to ears)*
tomar apuntes *(make a writing motion with hand)*

C. Note that vocabulary is presented in the third person so students can immediately use the new words and respond to questions without having to make ending changes. Students will learn how to manipulate these verbs in the **Estructura** section of this chapter.

Vocabulario

PALABRAS 2

En la clase

la pizarra, el pizarrón

un examen

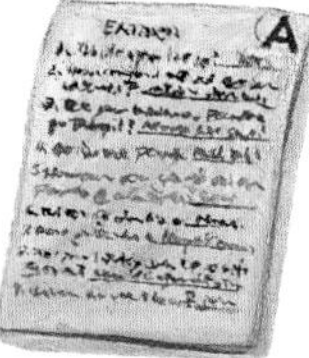

una nota buena, una nota alta

una nota mala, una nota baja

Los alumnos miran la pizarra.
Miran al profesor también.

El profesor habla.
El profesor explica la lección.
Los alumnos escuchan al profesor.
Prestan atención.
Cuando el profesor habla,
los alumnos escuchan.

Los alumnos toman apuntes.

Ahora la profesora da un examen.
Los alumnos toman el examen.

Elena saca una nota buena.

Total Physical Response

Getting ready
Before doing these activities, make sure students understand the meaning of **levántate, ven acá,** and **anda por la sala de clase.** Now call on individual students to do the following.

Begin
___, levántate.
Ven acá.
Anda por la sala de clase.
Indica a un muchacho alto.
Indica a una muchacha alta.
Mira al (a la) profesor(a).
Habla con el (la) profesor(a).
Toma una hoja de papel.
Toma un lápiz.
Pon unos apuntes en el papel.
Escucha al (a la) profesor(a).
Gracias, ___.

La fiesta del Club de español

un casete

un disco compacto

El Club de español da una fiesta.
Muchos alumnos van a la fiesta.
Escuchan discos compactos y casetes.
Los miembros del club bailan y cantan.
Toman una merienda también.

Más números

1000	mil
2000	dos mil
2002	dos mil dos
2500	dos mil quinientos
3000	tres mil
3015	tres mil quince
3650	tres mil seiscientos cincuenta
1200	mil doscientos
1492	mil cuatrocientos noventa y dos
1814	mil ochocientos catorce
1898	mil ochocientos noventa y ocho
1,000,000	un millón
2,000,000	dos millones

D. Más números Write additional numbers on the board and have students say them. It is suggested that you not make students spell the numbers. If you wish to check comprehension of numbers on paper, give a number orally and have students write the number using numerals.

National Standards

Communication
After learning the vocabulary presented on pages 102–103, students will be able to communicate with others about their school activities.

VOCABULARY EXPANSION

You may wish to present these additional useful terms:

la tarea para mañana
la tiza
el borrador
la prueba

Note Many teachers use **la prueba** for a quiz and **el examen** for a bigger test.

ABOUT THE SPANISH LANGUAGE

- The word **pizarrón** is used in many areas of Latin America. **Pizarra** is used in Spain and some areas of Latin America.
- The expression **sacar una nota buena** is more commonly heard in Spain. **Recibir una nota buena** will be presented when students learn **-er** and **-ir** verbs.
- Another commonly-used word for a student's grade in school is **calificación.**
- **Tomar un curso** is the most commonly used term, but in Spain you will hear **seguir un curso.**

CAPÍTULO 4
Vocabulario

Práctica

A B and C After completing **Práctica A, B,** and **C** with the class, call on individual students to retell the story in each activity in their own words.

PAIRED ACTIVITIES Students can work in pairs and ask one another their own questions about the stories in the **Práctica** activities.

Writing Development

Have students write the answers to **Práctica A, B,** and **C** in paragraph form. Have students close their books and rewrite the information from **Práctica B** in their own words.

Learning From Photos

Colegio San José, Estepona, España Have students compare this photo of El Colegio San José to the photo of the classroom on page 102. For each photo, ask them: **¿Qué clase es?** Point out to students that this is the same room in both photos and that the teachers, not the students, have changed rooms. (This point is also discussed in the **Lectura,** page 116.)

Práctica

A HISTORIETA En clase

Contesten. *(Answer.)*

1. ¿Miran los alumnos la pizarra?
2. ¿Habla la profesora?
3. ¿Escuchan los alumnos?
4. ¿Prestan atención cuando la profesora habla?
5. ¿Toman los alumnos apuntes en un cuaderno?
6. ¿Estudian mucho los alumnos?
7. ¿Trabajan ellos mucho?
8. ¿Da la profesora un examen?
9. ¿Toman los alumnos el examen?
10. ¿Sacan notas buenas o malas en el examen?

Colegio San José, Estepona, España

B HISTORIETA La escuela

Completen. *(Complete.)*

Los alumnos llegan a la escuela y luego van a ____(1). Los alumnos ____(2) mucho en la escuela y los profesores ____(3). Los alumnos toman ____(4) en un cuaderno. Cuando el profesor habla, los alumnos ____(5) atención. El profesor da un ____(6) y los alumnos toman el ____(7). Algunos alumnos sacan notas ____(8) y otros sacan notas ____(9). Una nota buena es una nota ____(10) y una nota mala es una nota ____(11).

C HISTORIETA El Club de español

Contesten según la foto. *(Answer according to the photo.)*

1. ¿Da una fiesta el Club de español?
2. ¿Van muchos alumnos a la fiesta?
3. ¿Bailan en la fiesta?
4. ¿Cantan también?
5. ¿Preparan los miembros del club una merienda?
6. ¿Toman una merienda?

ANSWERS

Práctica

A
1. **No, los alumnos no miran la pizarra.**
2. **Sí, la profesora habla.**
3. **Sí, los alumnos escuchan.**
4. **Sí, prestan atención cuando la profesora habla.**
5. **Sí, los alumnos toman apuntes en un cuaderno. (No, los alumnos no toman apuntes en un cuaderno.)**
6. **Sí (No), los alumnos (no) estudian mucho.**
7. **Sí (No), ellos (no) trabajan mucho.**
8. **Sí (No), la profesora (no) da un examen.**
9. **Sí (No), los alumnos (no) toman el examen.**
10. **Sacan notas buenas (malas) en el examen.**

B
1. **la sala de clase**
2. **estudian**
3. **enseñan**
4. **apuntes**
5. **prestan**
6. **examen**
7. **examen**
8. **buenas (malas)**
9. **malas (buenas)**
10. **alta**
11. **baja**

Actividades comunicativas

A **En clase** With a classmate, look at the illustration. Take turns saying as much as you can about it.

B **¿Es importante el año?** Think of a year that has some significance. Say the year in Spanish for your partner, who will write it down. Tell him or her whether the number is correct. Have your partner tell you (in English, if necessary) why that year is important. Take turns.

«Tres músicos» de Pablo Picasso

ANSWERS CONTINUED

C 1. **Sí, el Club de español da una fiesta.**
2. **Sí, muchos alumnos van a la fiesta.**
3. **Sí, bailan en la fiesta.**
4. **Sí, cantan también.**
5. **Sí, los miembros del club preparan una merienda.**
6. **Sí, toman una merienda.**

Acividades comunicativas

A Students can say many things about the illustration. They will most probably use the verbs **escuchar, prestar, hablar, mirar** and the classroom vocabulary presented in this chapter.

B Answers will vary but may include:
Mil novecientos ochenta y cuatro.
(I was born in 1984.)
Mil quatrocientos noventa y dos.
(Columbus discovered America.)

Actividades comunicativas

¡OJO! It is suggested that you let students select the activity they want to participate in. Let students say as much as they can. When doing these open-ended activities, as per the ACTFL Guidelines, it is recommended that you not correct all errors.

A This is a very worthwhile activity because it enables students to use question (interrogative) words.

VARIATION Students love to ask the teacher questions. Have students look at the illustration and ask you questions about it.

FINE ART CONNECTION

Un pintor famoso Picasso is one of the most famous of modern Spanish painters. He was born on October 25, 1881 in Málaga. Both his parents were Andalusian. His father was an artist and taught in La Coruña. He did not like the cold, damp weather of Galicia and shortly after their arrival, Picasso's sister Concepción died of diphtheria. His father decided to leave La Coruña immediately to return to Málaga. On the way they stopped in Madrid and the young Picasso was enthralled by the works of the Spanish painters he saw in the Prado. Shortly thereafter his father was appointed to teach at the famous Escuela de Bellas Artes in Barcelona. The young Picasso passed the entrance exam immediately and the jury was stupefied by the talent of this young boy.

RESOURCES

- Workbook, pages 32–37
- Student Tape Manual, TE, pages 39–41
- Audiocassette 3B/CD3
- Structure Transparency S-4
- Quizzes 3–5, pages 19–21
- Computer Testmaker
- CD-ROM, Disc 1, pages 106–113

Bell Ringer Review

Use BRR Transparency 4-3, or write the following on the board:
Answer the following questions.

1. **¿Estudias español en la escuela?**
2. **¿Hablas mucho con el profesor de español?**
3. **¿Escuchas al profesor?**
4. **¿Tomas apuntes?**
5. **¿Miras al profesor cuando él habla?**

TEACHING STRUCTURE

Talking about things people do

A. Write the verbs **hablar, estudiar,** and **tomar** on the board. Ask students what endings they use with **los alumnos** or **los amigos.** They can respond because they know the ending from the vocabulary presentation. Write **hablan, estudian,** and **toman** on the board.

B. Tell students they have a new form to learn when talking about themselves and someone else. Then have them repeat **nosotros** and write **hablamos** on the board. If it is **hablamos** with the verb **hablar**, ask students what they think the verb form is with **estudiar**. Have them volunteer **estudiamos** and **tomamos.**

(continued on page 107)

Estructura

Talking about things people do
Presente de los verbos en -ar en el plural

1. You have already learned the singular forms of regular **-ar** verbs. Now study the plural forms.

INFINITIVE	hablar	estudiar	tomar	
STEM	habl-	estudi-	tom-	ENDINGS
nosotros(as)	hablamos	estudiamos	tomamos	-amos
ellos, ellas, Uds.	hablan	estudian	toman	-an

2.

When you talk about yourself and someone else, you say **-amos.**

When you talk about two or more people, you say **-an.**

3. In most parts of the Spanish-speaking world, except for some regions of Spain, there is no difference between formal and informal address in the plural.

When speaking to more than one person, you use the **ustedes** form of the verb. Note that **Uds.** is an abbreviation of **ustedes.**

¿Lo sabes?
Vosotros(as) is a familiar form used in much of Spain. ¿Cantáis y bailáis en la fiesta?

ABOUT THE SPANISH LANGUAGE

Students learned the difference between the **tú** and **usted** forms in Chapter 3. Explain to students that **ustedes (Uds.)** is the plural form of both **tú** and **usted** throughout Latin America. **Ustedes** is used for both formal and familiar address in all countries of Latin America. In many parts of Spain, however, **vosotros** is the plural of **tú.** When speaking to two or more friends or family members you would use the **vosotros** form: **habláis, estudiáis, tomáis.** Throughout **Glencoe Spanish** the **vosotros** form is included in all explanations but students are not required to use the **vosotros** form actively.

5. Now review all the forms of the present tense of the regular **-ar** verbs.

INFINITIVE	hablar	estudiar	tomar	
STEM	habl-	estudi-	tom-	ENDINGS
yo	hablo	estudio	tomo	-o
tú	hablas	estudias	tomas	-as
él, ella, Ud.	habla	estudia	toma	-a
nosotros(as)	hablamos	estudiamos	tomamos	-amos
vosotros(as)	*habláis*	*estudiáis*	*tomáis*	*-áis*
ellos, ellas, Uds.	hablan	estudian	toman	-an

Práctica

A Historieta En la escuela

Sigan el modelo.
(Follow the model.)

llegar
Los alumnos llegan.

1. llegar a la escuela a las ocho
2. llevar los materiales escolares en una mochila
3. entrar en la sala de clase
4. hablar con el profesor
5. prestar atención
6. tomar apuntes
7. estudiar mucho
8. sacar notas buenas

El Viejo San Juan, Puerto Rico

B Historieta ¿Y Uds.?

Contesten personalmente. *(Answer about yourself and a friend.)*

1. ¿A qué hora llegan Uds. a la escuela?
2. ¿Toman Uds. el bus escolar a la escuela?
3. ¿Estudian Uds. mucho?
4. ¿Toman Uds. un curso de español?
5. ¿Hablan Uds. mucho en la clase de español?
6. ¿Escuchan Uds. al profesor cuando habla?
7. ¿Miran Uds. un video?
8. ¿Escuchan Uds. casetes?

ANSWERS

Práctica

A
1. **Los alumnos llegan a la escuela a las ocho.**
2. **Los alumnos llevan los materiales escolares en una mochila.**
3. **Los alumnos entran en la sala de clase.**
4. **Los alumnos hablan con el profesor.**
5. **Los alumnos prestan atención.**
6. **Los alumnos toman apuntes.**
7. **Los alumnos estudian mucho.**
8. **Los alumnos sacan notas buenas.**

B Answers will vary, but may include:
1. **Llegamos a la escuela a las ocho menos cuarto.**
2. **Sí, (No, no) tomamos el bus escolar a la escuela.**
3. **Sí, (No, no) estudiamos mucho.**
4. **Sí, tomamos un curso de español.**
5. **Sí, hablamos mucho en la clase de español.**
6. **Sí, escuchamos al profesor (a la profesora) cuando habla.**
7. **Sí, miramos un video.**
8. **Sí, escuchamos casetes.**

C. Go over Step 3 to explain **Uds.** Then have students give the **Uds.** form of some other verbs.

D. Use Structure Transparency S-4 to review the plural forms.

Práctica

¡OJO! Note that the **Práctica** exercises build from simple to more complex. In **Práctica A, B,** and **C,** students concentrate on only one subject and verb form in each activity. In **Práctica D** students use all forms.

A and B Do **Práctica A** and **B** first with books closed for strictly oral practice. Then have students read the material for additional reinforcement. You may ask the questions from **Práctica B** or students can do it as a paired activity.

ABOUT THE SPANISH LANGUAGE

El voseo The pronoun **vos** is used in many areas of Latin America instead of **tú.** This phenomenon is referred to as **el voseo.** In some areas **el voseo** is used by speakers from all social and educational levels in both oral and written form. In other areas it is considered popular. The ending for **vos** is **-ás: hablás, estudiás, tomás. Vos** is widely used throughout the Southern Cone—Argentina, Uruguay, Paraguay, and Chile. It is also used in varying degrees in the following areas: Bolivia, parts of Peru, Ecuador, Colombia (excluding northern coast), parts of Venezuela and Panama, Costa Rica, Nicaragua, El Salvador, Honduras, Guatemala, the state of Chiapas in Mexico, and in a very small area of Cuba.
(**Note** You may wish to explain **el voseo** to students at a later time.)

Práctica

C You may wish to have students do this activity in small groups.

D After going over **Práctica D,** have students work in groups. Ask each group to think of as many questions as possible about the story in **Práctica D.** Now have the groups ask other groups their questions. They can then tell the story in their own words.

C **Sí, estudiamos.** Sigan el modelo. *(Follow the model.)*

1. Uds. necesitan estudiar mucho.
2. Uds. necesitan mirar el video.
3. Uds. necesitan escuchar los casetes.
4. Uds. necesitan trabajar.
5. Uds. necesitan prestar atención.
6. Uds. necesitan escuchar al profesor cuando habla.

D **HISTORIETA** **En un colegio del Perú**

Completen. *(Complete.)*

Emilio ___1___ (ser) un muchacho peruano. Él ___2___ (estudiar) en un colegio en Lima. Los amigos de Emilio ___3___ (llevar) uniforme a la escuela. Uno de los amigos de Emilio ___4___ (hablar):

—Sí, todos nosotros ___5___ (llevar) uniforme a la escuela. ___6___ (Llevar) un pantalón negro, una camisa blanca y una corbata negra. ¿___7___ (Llevar) Uds. uniforme a la escuela en los Estados Unidos?

Los amigos de Emilio ___8___ (tomar) muchos cursos. Y Emilio también ___9___ (tomar) muchos cursos. Algunos cursos ___10___ (ser) fáciles y otros ___11___ (ser) difíciles. Los amigos de Emilio ___12___ (hablar):

—Nosotros ___13___ (tomar) nueve cursos. En algunos cursos nosotros ___14___ (sacar) notas muy buenas y en otros ___15___ (sacar) notas bajas—. Un amigo ___16___ (preguntar):

—¡Oye, Emilio! ¿En qué cursos ___17___ (sacar) tú notas buenas y en qué cursos ___18___ (sacar) tú notas malas?

Emilio ___19___ (contestar):

—Cuando yo ___20___ (trabajar) y ___21___ (estudiar) yo ___22___ (sacar) notas buenas en todos los cursos.

Plaza de Armas, Lima, Perú

ANSWERS

Práctica

C
1. **Pero, estudiamos mucho.**
2. **Pero, miramos el video.**
3. **Pero, escuchamos los casetes.**
4. **Pero, trabajamos.**
5. **Pero, prestamos atención.**
6. **Pero, escuchamos al profesor cuando habla.**

D
1. **es**
2. **estudia**
3. **llevan**
4. **habla**
5. **llevamos**
6. **Llevamos**
7. **Llevan**
8. **toman**
9. **toma**
10. **son**
11. **son**
12. **hablan**
13. **tomamos**
14. **sacamos**
15. **sacamos**
16. **pregunta**
17. **sacas**
18. **sacas**
19. **contesta**
20. **trabajo**
21. **estudio**
22. **saco**

Actividades comunicativas

A **Una clase** Ask a classmate about one of his or her classes. Then he or she will ask you about one of your classes. The following are some words or expressions you may want to use.

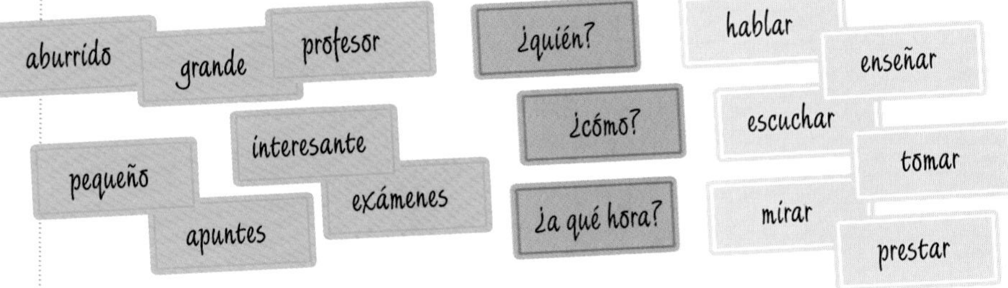

B **Un día típico** With a classmate look at the illustrations. Take turns talking about them.

C **¿Cuándo? ¿En clase, después de las clases o en una fiesta?** Work with a classmate. He or she will suggest an activity. You will tell where or when you and your friends typically take part in the activity. Take turns.

Actividades comunicativas

¡OJO! Allow students to select the activity or activities they want to take part in. Different groups can be doing different activities at the same time. Circulate from group to group to ensure that students are focusing on the task at hand.

A The call-out words in **Actividad A** deter students from becoming frustrated by trying to use words and structures they do not know.

B You may wish to assign only one or two illustrations to each group or pair to work on.

RECYCLING Have students say what time the activity in each illustration is taking place (Chapter 2, pages 56–57).

C Encourage students to think of as many activities as possible and see who comes up with the longest list.

ANSWERS

Actividades comunicativas

A Answers will vary, but may include:

—¿A qué hora es la clase de español?
—A las ocho.
—¿Es aburrida o interesante la clase de español?
—La clase de español es interesante y es fácil.
—¿Cómo es el profesor?
—El profesor es interesante.
—¿Sacas notas buenas o malas en los exámenes?
—Yo saco notas buenas.
—¿Tomas apuntes cuando el profesor habla?
—No, no tomo apuntes cuando el profesor habla. Yo escucho al profesor.
—¿Es grande tu clase?
—No, no es grande, es pequeña.

B Answers may include:

Illustration 1
—Los alumnos llegan a la escuela por la mañana.
—Algunos alumnos van a la escuela a pie.

Illustration 2
—Los alumnos van a clase.
—Los alumnos no llevan uniforme.

Illustration 3
—La profesora enseña.
—Los alumnos escuchan.

Illustration 4
—El profesor habla.
—Es una clase de geografía.

C Answers will vary. Students should use the **nosotros** form of the verbs they have learned up to now.

CAPÍTULO 4
Estructura

TEACHING STRUCTURE

Describing people's activities

¡OJO! These verbs are presented together since students only need to learn one new form. All the other forms are a review of the **-ar** verb endings they just learned.

A. Have students point to themselves as they repeat **voy, doy, estoy** after you. Write the forms on the board and have the class repeat again.

B. Explain to students that for these verbs these are the only different or irregular forms they will have to learn. The endings for all other forms are the same as those of an **-ar** verb.

C. Now read Steps 1 and 2 with the students. Use the verbs you have written on the board to emphasize the similarities between regular **-ar** verbs and these irregular verbs.

Práctica

A **Práctica A** is a very good example of communicative practice. Students must realize that when they hear a question with the **tú** form, they must answer with the **yo** form. This practice is extremely important since beginners so often tend to answer using the same form they hear in the question.

Learning From Photos

San Juan, Puerto Rico Explain to students that many school buses in Puerto Rico are the same as our yellow school buses because they are imported from the States.

This photo was taken on a street that parallels the Atlantic Ocean between Ocean Park and Punta Las Marías in San Juan.

Describing people's activities
Presente de los verbos ir, dar, estar

1. The verbs **ir** *(to go)*, **dar** *(to give)*, and **estar** *(to be)* are irregular. An irregular verb does not conform to the regular pattern. Note the similarity in the irregular **yo** form of these verbs.

   yo voy doy estoy

2. The other forms of these verbs are the same as those you have learned for regular **-ar** verbs.

INFINITIVE	ir	dar	estar
yo	voy	doy	estoy
tú	vas	das	estás
él, ella, Ud.	va	da	está
nosotros(as)	vamos	damos	estamos
vosotros(as)	*vais*	*dais*	*estáis*
ellos, ellas, Uds.	van	dan	están

Práctica

A **HISTORIETA** Voy a la escuela.

Contesten. *(Answer.)*

1. ¿Vas a la escuela?
2. ¿A qué hora vas a la escuela?
3. ¿Vas a la escuela a pie?
4. ¿Vas en el bus escolar?
5. ¿Vas en carro?
6. ¿Cómo vas?
7. ¿Estás en la escuela ahora?
8. ¿En qué clase estás ahora?

San Juan, Puerto Rico

ANSWERS

Práctica

A Answers will vary, but may include:
1. **Sí, (No, no) voy a la escuela.**
2. **Voy a la escuela a las ocho menos cuarto.**
3. **Sí, (No, no) voy a la escuela a pie.**
4. **Sí, (No, no) voy en el bus escolar.**
5. **Sí (No, no) voy en carro.**
6. **Voy a pie (en carro, etc.)**
7. **Sí, (No, no) estoy en la escuela ahora.**
8. **Estoy en la clase de ___ ahora. (No estoy en clase.)**

(PAGE 111)

B All answers will be:
Perdón, ¿adónde vas?

C All answers will begin:
¿Dónde están Uds.?
1. **—... ¿En la cafetería?**
   —Sí, estamos en la cafetería.
2. **—... ¿En la clase de español?**
   —Sí, estamos en la clase de español.

B Perdón, ¿adónde vas?

Sigan el modelo. *(Follow the model.)*

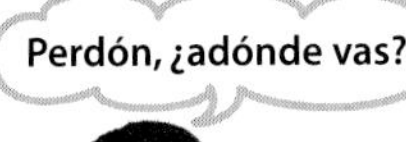

1. Voy a la clase de español.
2. Voy a la clase de biología.
3. Voy a la cafetería.
4. Voy al laboratorio.
5. Voy al gimnasio.
6. Voy a la papelería.

Santurce, Puerto Rico

C ¿Dónde están Uds.?

Preparen una conversación.
(Prepare a conversation.)

Tomamos una merienda. (en la cafetería)
—¿Dónde están Uds.? ¿En la cafetería?
—Sí, estamos en la cafetería.

1. Tomamos un sándwich. (en la cafetería)
2. Miramos un video. (en la clase de español)
3. Compramos un cuaderno. (en la papelería)
4. Estudiamos biología. (en el laboratorio)
5. Damos una fiesta. (en el Club de español)

D HISTORIETA La escuela

Contesten. *(Answer.)*

1. ¿A qué hora van Uds. a la escuela?
2. ¿Cómo van?
3. ¿Están Uds. en la escuela ahora?
4. ¿En qué clase están?
5. ¿Está el/la profesor(a)?
6. ¿Da él/ella muchos exámenes?
7. ¿Da él/ella exámenes difíciles?
8. ¿Qué profesores dan muchos exámenes?

La Torre del Oro, Sevilla, España

B and **C** These activities can be done as paired activities.

D After going over **Práctica D**, have one student retell all the information in his or her own words.

HISTORY CONNECTION

La Torre del Oro, Sevilla, España This famous monument is on the banks of the Guadalquivir in Seville. A twelve-sided tower, it was built by the Moors in 1220. In times of attack they closed off the harbor by attaching a chain from this tower to another tower (no longer in existence) on the opposite bank of the river. In 1248, however, an admiral named Ramón de Bonifaz was able to break through the barrier, allowing Fernando III to capture the city. The Torre del Oro today houses a naval museum.

There is controversy as to how the tower got its name. Some say it got its name from the golden color of its tiles, **azulejos.** Other claim that is was once a warehouse for gold from the New World.

ANSWERS CONTINUED

3. **—... ¿En la papelería?**
   —Sí, estamos en la papelería.
4. **—... ¿En el laboratorio?**
   —Sí, estamos en el laboratorio.
5. **—... ¿En el Club de español?**
   —Sí, estamos en el Club de español.

D Answers will vary, but may include:

1. **Vamos a la escuela a las ocho (a las ocho menos cuarto, etc.).**
2. **Vamos en carro (a pie, etc.).**
3. **Sí, (No, no) estamos en la escuela ahora.**
4. **Estamos en la clase de __. (No estamos en clase.)**
5. **Sí, el/la profesor(a) está. (No, el/la profesor[a] no está.)**
6. **Sí, él/ella da muchos exámenes. (No, él/ella no da muchos exámenes.)**
7. **Sí, él/ella da exámenes difíciles. (No, él/ella no da exámenes difíciles.)**
8. **El profesor de ___ y la profesora de ___ dan muchos exámenes.**

CAPÍTULO 4
Estructura

TEACHING STRUCTURE

Expressing direction and possession

A. Ask students to open their books to page 112. Have students follow along as you read Steps 1–4 aloud to the class.

B. Have students repeat all the model sentences after you in unison.

C. You may wish to explain to students that these contractions are very logical. Indicate to them how difficult it would be, when speaking, to separate the sounds of **a el** and **de el**, particularly in rapid speech.

Bell Ringer Review

Use BRR Transparency 4-4, or write the following on the board: Put a check next to the words for places.

el alumno	**la cafetería**
el colegio	**el café**
la escuela	**la mochila**
la ropa	**la sala de clase**
la tienda	**el laboratorio**

Expressing direction and possession
Las contracciones **al** y **del**

1. The preposition **a** means "to" or "toward." **A** contracts with the article **el** to form one word: **al.** The preposition **a** does not change when used with the other articles **la, las,** and **los.**

a + el = al

En la escuela voy al laboratorio.
Después voy a la cafetería.
Y después voy a las tiendas.

2. The preposition **a** is also used before a direct object that refers to a specific person or persons. It is called the "personal **a**" and has no equivalent in English.

Miro la televisión.	**Miro al profesor.**
Escucho el disco compacto.	**Escucho a los amigos.**

3. The preposition **de** can mean "of," "from," or "about." Like **a,** the preposition **de** contracts with the article **el** to form one word: **del.** The preposition **de** does not change when used with the other articles **la, las,** and **los.**

de + el = del

Él habla del profesor de español.
Es de la ciudad de Nueva York.
Él es de los Estados Unidos.

4. You also use the preposition **de** to indicate possession.

Es la calculadora del profesor.
Son los bolígrafos de Teresa y Sofía.
Son los cuadernos de Juan y Fernando.

Práctica

A **¿Qué o a quién?** Contesten con **sí.** *(Answer with* sí.)

1. ¿Miras el video?
2. ¿Miras la pizarra?
3. ¿Miras al muchacho?
4. ¿Miras a la muchacha?
5. ¿Escuchas el disco compacto?
6. ¿Escuchas la música?
7. ¿Escuchas al profesor?
8. ¿Escuchas a las profesoras?

B **¿Adónde vas?** Preparen una conversación. *(Prepare a conversation based on each illustration.)*

—¿Adónde vas?
—¿Quién? ¿Yo?
—Sí, tú.
—Pues, voy a la escuela.

1.

2.

3.

4.

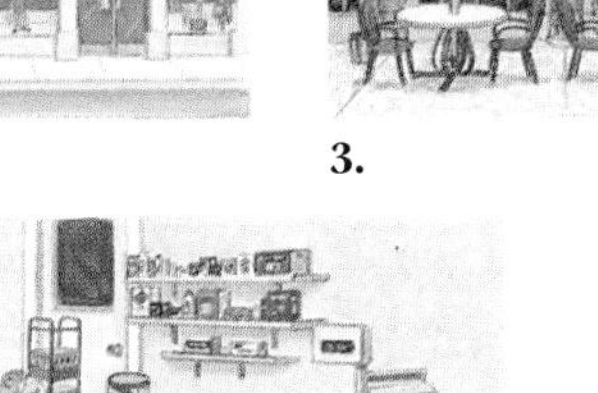

5.

C **HISTORIETA Roberta Smith**

Contesten. *(Answer.)*

1. ¿Es Roberta de la ciudad de Nueva York?
2. ¿Es Roberta de los Estados Unidos?
3. ¿Habla Roberta del curso de biología?
4. ¿Habla del profesor de biología?
5. Y después de las clases, ¿habla Roberta con los amigos?
6. ¿Hablan de la escuela?
7. ¿Hablan de los cursos que toman?
8. ¿Hablan de la fiesta del Club de español?

Práctica

A Before doing **Práctica A**, give students the following words orally. Tell them to raise their hands when the word they hear refers to a person.

el bolígrafo **la alumna** **el muchacho** **la caja** **el dependiente** **el disco** **el profesor** **la clase** **la amiga**

B You may have students work in pairs as they do **Práctica B**. Have each pair present their mini-conversation to the class.

Learning From Photos

En el laboratorio Ask the following questions about the photo:

¿Dónde están los alumnos?
¿Son americanos?
¿Cuántos alumnos hay?
¿En qué clase están los alumnos?
¿Están en el laboratorio?
¿Qué estudian?

¡OJO! All new material has been presented. The remaining sections of the chapter recombine and reintroduce the vocabulary and structures that have already been introduced.

ANSWERS

Práctica

A
1. **Sí, miro el video.**
2. **Sí, miro la pizarra.**
3. **Sí, miro al muchacho.**
4. **Sí, miro a la muchacha.**
5. **Sí, escucho el disco compacto.**
6. **Sí, escucho la música.**
7. **Sí, escucho al profesor.**
8. **Sí, escucho a las profesoras.**

B
1. **—¿Adónde vas?**
   —¿Quién? ¿Yo?
   —Sí, tú.
   —Pues, voy a la escuela.
2. **—... Pues, voy a las tiendas.**
3. **—... Pues, voy al café Sol.**
4. **—... Pues, voy a la sala de clase.**
5. **—... Pues, voy a la caja.**

C
1. **Sí, Roberta es de la ciudad de Nueva York.**
2. **Sí, Roberta es de los Estados Unidos.**
3. **Sí, Roberta habla del curso de biología.**
4. **Sí, habla del profesor de biología.**
5. **Sí, después de las clases Roberta habla con los amigos.**
6. **Sí, hablan de la escuela.**
7. **Sí, hablan de los cursos que toman.**
8. **Sí, hablan de la fiesta del Club de español.**

RESOURCES

- Audiocassette 3B/CD3
- CD-ROM, Disc 1, page 114

Bell Ringer Review

Use BRR Transparency 4-5, or write the following on the board:
Answer the following:
1. ¿Quién eres?
2. ¿Cómo estás?
3. ¿Adónde vas?
4. ¿Quién da una fiesta?
5. ¿Vas a la fiesta?

TEACHING THE CONVERSATION

A. Tell the students they are going to hear a conversation between two friends, Rubén and Héctor. They are discussing an upcoming event. You may want to have students listen to the recording of the conversation on Cassette 3B/Compact Disc 3.
B. Have students open their books to page 114 and repeat the conversation after you, sentence by sentence.
C. Call on two students to read the conversation aloud with as much expression as possible. Repeat this two or three times with different students.
D. Now do the **Después de conversar** activity on page 114. Students should be able to do this with relative ease.

TECHNOLOGY OPTION

On the CD-ROM (Disc 1, page 114), students can watch a dramatization of this conversation. They can then play the role of either one of the characters, and record themselves in the conversation.

Conversación

La fiesta del Club de español

RUBÉN: Hola, amigo. ¿Qué tal? ¿Cómo estás?
HÉCTOR: Bien. ¿Y tú?
RUBÉN: Muy bien. Oye, ¿adónde vas el viernes?
HÉCTOR: ¿El viernes? Pues, voy a la fiesta del Club de español. ¿Tú no vas, hombre?
RUBÉN: Sí, voy. ¿Por qué no vamos juntos?
HÉCTOR: ¿Por qué no? ¡Buena idea!
RUBÉN: En la fiesta bailamos, cantamos.
HÉCTOR: Sí, y tomamos una merienda—¡con tacos y enchiladas!

Después de conversar

Contesten. *(Answer.)*

1. ¿Con quién habla Rubén?
2. ¿Cómo están los dos muchachos?
3. ¿Adónde va Héctor el viernes?
4. ¿Va Rubén también?
5. ¿Quién da la fiesta?
6. ¿Van juntos los dos muchachos?
7. ¿Bailan en la fiesta?
8. ¿Cantan?
9. ¿Toman una merienda?
10. ¿Qué toman?

ANSWERS

Después de conversar

1. **Rubén habla con Héctor.**
2. **Los dos muchachos están bien.**
3. **Va a la fiesta del Club de español.**
4. **Sí, Rubén va tambien.**
5. **El Club de español da la fiesta.**
6. **Sí, los dos muchachos van juntos.**
7. **Sí, bailan en la fiesta.**
8. **Sí, cantan.**
9. **Sí, toman una merienda.**
10. **Toman una merienda con tacos y enchiladas.**

Did You Know?

Tacos y enchiladas Ask students if they know what tacos and enchiladas are. If they don't, give them the following information.

A taco can be either a hard or soft tortilla with chicken, beef or beans and usually some shredded lettuce and tomato. An enchilada is a soft, rolled tortilla stuffed with beef, chicken, pork or cheese. It is baked in the oven.

Actividades comunicativas

A **Para ser un(a) alumno(a) bueno(a)** Work with a classmate. Prepare a list of things one has to do to be a good student. Take turns telling each other what you have to do. Each will respond to the other's advice. Use the models as a guide.

ALUMNO 1: **Necesitas estudiar.**	ALUMNO 1: **Es necesario estudiar.**
ALUMNO 2: **Pues, estudio.**	ALUMNO 2: **Sí, y yo no estudio.**

B **¿Bailan o qué?** With a classmate, look at the places below. Choose one and tell several things students usually do in that place. Take turns.

1.

2.

3.

4.

C **Un día típico** Work with a classmate. Each of you will tell about your typical school-day activities. When you finish, identify those things that both of you do.

Pronunciación

La consonante t

The **t** in Spanish is pronounced with the tip of the tongue pressed against the upper teeth. It is not followed by a puff of air.

ta	te	ti	to	tu
taco	**Teresa**	**tienda**	**toma**	**tú**
canta	**interesante**	**tiempo**	**tomate**	**estudia**
está	**casete**	**latín**	**Juanito**	**estupendo**

Repeat the following sentences.

Tito necesita siete disquetes de la tienda.
Tú tomas apuntes en latín.
Teresa invita a Tito a la fiesta.

ANSWERS

Actividades comunicativas

A Answers will follow the models provided.

B Answers will vary, but may include:

1. **En una sala de clase los alumnos estudian y escuchan el profesor.**
2. **En una tienda miran y compran ropa.**
3. **En una papelería compran materiales escolares. Pagan en la caja.**
4. **En una fiesta los alumnos bailan y cantan. Toman una merienda.**

C Answers will vary. Encourage students to say as much as they can reincorporating any language they have learned so far.

Actividades comunicativas

A Be sure students use the correct intonation when doing **Actividad A.**

B Have a contest to see who can come up with the most activities for each place.

C **TECHNOLOGY OPTION** In the CD-ROM version of this activity (Disc 1, page 115), students can interact with a native speaker and record their voice.

TEACHING PRONUNCIATION

A. The sound of **t** is difficult for English speakers to make. The **t** is breathy in English because the tongue hits the upper part of the mouth. In Spanish, the tongue must strike the back of the teeth to make the proper sound, not the upper part of the mouth.

B. You may use the Pronunciation section on Cassette 3B/Compact Disc 3 when presenting this topic.

C. All model sentences on page 115 can also be used for dictation.

¡OJO! It is recommended that you try to have students pronounce as perfectly as possible, but students should not be inhibited if they have a bit of an accent as long as what they say is comprehensible.

TECHNOLOGY OPTION

On the CD-ROM (Disc 1, page 115), students will see an animation of the cartoon on this page. They can also listen to, record, and play back the sentences presented here.

National Standards

Cultures

The reading about public and private schools in Latin America on page 116, and the related activities on page 117, give students insight into some aspects of Hispanic culture.

Comparisons

Students learn some differences between schools in the United States and those in Spain and Latin America.

Bell Ringer Review

Use BRR Transparency 4-6, or write the following on the board: Use the following words in a short sentence.

estudiar
tomar
escuchar
mirar

TEACHING THE READING

Pre-reading

A. Tell students they are going to read about a school in Peru.

B. Have them scan the selection quickly. Tell them to look for at least one difference between their school and this school in Peru.

Reading

A. Have students open their books. Ask the entire class to repeat two or three sentences.

B. Ask questions about the sentences they just read. For example:

¿Quiénes son dos amigos peruanos?
¿De dónde son?
¿Qué es Miraflores?

(continued on page 117)

Lecturas CULTURALES

Reading Strategy

Making comparisons while reading

If you read a passage that discusses a topic from different points of view, you can make comparisons while reading. Noting such similarities and differences will help make the ideas clearer and you will probably remember more of what you read. You can either make these comparisons in your head or write them down as you read.

ESCUELAS DEL MUNDO HISPANO

Paula y Armando son dos amigos peruanos. Son de Miraflores. Miraflores es un suburbio bonito de Lima.

Paula y Armando no van a la misma escuela. Paula va a una academia privada y Armando va a un colegio privado. Muchas escuelas privadas en España y Latinoamérica no son para muchachos y muchachas. No son mixtas. Pero la mayoría[1] de las escuelas públicas son mixtas.

Hay otra diferencia interesante entre una escuela norteamericana y una escuela hispana. Aquí los alumnos van de un salón a otro. El profesor o la profesora de álgebra enseña en un salón y el profesor o la profesora de español enseña en otro. En España y Latinoamérica, no. Los alumnos no van de un salón a otro. Pasan la mayor parte[2] del día en el mismo salón. Son los profesores que «viajan[3]» o van de una clase a otra.

[1]mayoría *majority*
[2]mayor parte *greater part*
[3]viajan *travel*

Colegio de Nuestra Señora del Carmen, Miraflores, Perú

Una vista de Miraflores

Learning From Photos

Colegio del Nuestra Señora del Carmen, Miraflores, Perú You may wish to ask the following questions about the photo:

¿Es el colegio de Nuestra Señora del Carmen una escuela moderna? ¿Es una escuela mixta o no?
¿Llevan uniforme a la escuela los alumnos? ¿Son de Miraflores los dos amigos?¿Son guapos? ¿Son simpáticos? ¿Son rubios o morenos?
¿Lleva el muchacho una mochila?

Después de leer

A **¿En Latinoamérica o en los Estados Unidos?** Decidan. *(Decide whether each statement describes more accurately a school in Latin America or one in the United States.)*

1. Los muchachos y las muchachas van a la misma escuela.
2. Los alumnos van de un salón a otro.
3. Los profesores van de un salón a otro.

B **Las escuelas de Paula y Armando** Contesten. *(Answer.)*

1. ¿De dónde son Paula y Armando?
2. ¿Van a la misma escuela?
3. ¿Va Paula a una escuela pública o privada?
4. ¿Y Armando? ¿Va él a una escuela pública o privada?
5. ¿Son mixtas la mayoría de las escuelas privadas en Latinoamérica?
6. ¿Dónde pasan la mayor parte del día los alumnos hispanos?
7. ¿Quiénes «viajan» de una clase a otra?

C **En español, por favor.** Busquen las palabras afines. *(Find the cognates in the reading.)*

Miraflores, Perú

C. Vary the procedure in Step A and call on a student to read several sentences aloud. Then ask questions about what the student read.

Post-reading

Assign the reading selection, as well as the **Después de leer** activities that follow, for homework.

TECHNOLOGY OPTION

Students may listen to a recording of the **Lectura** on the CD-ROM, Disc 1, page 116.

GEOGRAPHY CONNECTION

Miraflores, Lima, Perú
Miraflores is a lovely section of Lima. It is a small and elegant suburb along the Pacific. The beachfront road is called **el malecón.** It is lined with expensive apartment buildings and grand, colonial mansions. Many of the mansions, however, have been torn down to make room for the more profitable high-rises. There are many pretty little parks in Miraflores. San Isidro is the most elegant residential area in greater Lima. San Isidro is between downtown central Lima and Miraflores.

ANSWERS

Después de leer

A
1. **en los Estados Unidos**
2. **en los Estados Unidos**
3. **en Latinoamérica**

B
1. **Paula y Armando son de Miraflores.**
2. **No, no van a la misma escuela.**
3. **Paula va a una escuela privada.**
4. **Armando va a una escuela privada.**
5. **La mayoría de las escuelas privadas en Latinoamérica no son mixtas.**
6. **Los alumnos hispanos pasan la mayor parte del día en el mismo salón.**
7. **Los profesores «viajan» de una clase a otra.**

C Answers will vary but may include the following: **suburbio, academia, privada, Latinoamérica, mixtas, públicas, diferencia, interesante, norteamericana, hispana, otro, profesor(a), álgebra, parte, clase**

LECTURA OPCIONAL 1

TEACHING TIPS

¡OJO! You may skip these reading selections entirely, have the entire class read them or assign them as extra credit.

For suggestions on presenting these optional readings and the **Conexiones** readings, see page 34 of this Teacher's Wraparound Edition.

GEOGRAPHY CONNECTION

La República Dominicana
Have students locate the Dominican Republic on the map on page 465, or use the Map Transparency. The Dominican Republic occupies the eastern two-thirds of the island of Hispaniola, in the West Indies. Haiti occupies the western third. The Mona Passage separates the Dominican Republic from Puerto Rico. Hispaniola was discovered and explored by Columbus during his first voyage in 1492.

LECTURA OPCIONAL 1

Harvard University, Massachussetts

UNA CONFERENCIA UNIVERSITARIA

En la universidad los profesores dan conferencias a los estudiantes. Hay una conferencia universitaria muy histórica y famosa. Es famosa porque es la primera[1] conferencia universitaria de las Américas. Y la primera conferencia que da un profesor en una universidad de América es una conferencia en español.

¿Por qué en español? Es en español porque el profesor da la conferencia en la Universidad de Santo Domingo. La universidad más antigua[2] de las Américas es la Universidad de Santo Domingo (1538). La universidad más antigua de los Estados Unidos es Harvard (1636).

[1]primera *first*
[2]más antigua *oldest*

Antigua Universidad de Santo Domingo

¿Lo sabes?
The Spanish word **conferencia** is a false cognate. It looks like the English word *conference* but it actually means *lecture.*

Después de leer

A En inglés, por favor. Expliquen. *(Explain the significance of the information presented in the reading.)*

ANSWERS

Después de leer

A Answers will vary, but may include: The first lecture given by a professor in the Americas was in Spanish at the University of Santo Domingo, the oldest university in the Americas (1538).

Punta Arenas, Chile

GABRIELA MISTRAL (1889–1957)

Gabriela Mistral es una poeta famosa. Es de Vicuña. Vicuña es un pequeño pueblo rural de Chile. De joven[1], Gabriela Mistral enseña en varias escuelas primarias en áreas rurales de Chile. Ella pasa unos años[2] como directora de una escuela en Punta Arenas, en el extremo sur de la Patagonia chilena. Hoy la escuela lleva el nombre[3] de la maestra y poeta—el Liceo Gabriela Mistral. Es una maestra excelente y es también una poeta excelente. Como poeta, Gabriela Mistral recibe un gran honor. Gana[4] el Premio Nóbel de Literatura.

[1]De joven *As a young woman*
[2]años *years*
[3]nombre *name*
[4]Gana *She wins*

Liceo Gabriela Mistral, Punta Arenas

Después de leer

A Gabriela Mistral Digan que sí o que no. *(Tell whether the statements are true or false.)*

1. Gabriela Mistral es novelista.
2. Gabriela Mistral es venezolana.
3. Ella es de Santiago de Chile.
4. Ella enseña en muchas áreas urbanas de Chile.
5. Ella enseña en varias escuelas secundarias.

B No es así. Corrijan. *(Correct the statements in Activity A that are not correct.)*

C Un poco de geografía Busquen en el mapa. *(On the map of South America in the back of your book, locate* Punta Arenas *and* la Patagonia. Patagonia *is in two countries. What countries are they?)*

LECTURA OPCIONAL 2

TEACHING TIPS

For suggestions on presenting these optional readings and the **Conexiones** readings, see page 34 of this Teacher's Wraparound Edition.

GEOGRAPHY CONNECTION

Punta Arenas Have students locate Punta Arenas on the map of South America on page 464, or use the Map Transparency. The only city of the Americas that is farther south than Punta Arenas is Ushuaia in Argentina.

Punta Arenas is a stark little port on the Straits of Magellan in Patagonia. This is a gray land where the sun seldom shines. Most days are drizzly and hazy. Even in the summer, cold biting winds howl between 70 and 85 miles an hour. In winter, the daylight hours are from 9 a.m. to 4 p.m., in summer from 4 a.m. to 11 p.m.

ANSWERS

Después de leer

A 1. No. 2. No. 3. No. 4. No. 5. No.

B
1. Gabriela Mistral es poeta.
2. Es chilena.
3. Es de Vicuña.
4. Enseña en áreas rurales de Chile.
5. Enseña en varias escuelas primarias.

C Patagonia está en la Argentina y Chile.

National Standards

Connections

This reading on biology establishes a connection with another discipline. It enables students to draw from previous knowledge and to talk about a scientific topic in Spanish.

¡OJO! The readings in the **Conexiones** section are optional. They focus on some of the major disciplines taught in schools and universities. The vocabulary is useful for discussing such topics as history, literature, art, economics, business, science, etc.

See page 34 of this Teacher's Wraparound Edition for general suggestions on how to present these readings and the other optional readings.

LAS CIENCIAS NATURALES

LA BIOLOGÍA

A. Most students will be familiar with the biological terms in this selection from their study of science.

B. You may wish to have only those students who are interested in science read this selection.

(continued on page 121)

Conexiones

LAS CIENCIAS NATURALES

LA BIOLOGÍA

Sciences are an important part of the school curriculum. If you like science, it would be fun to be able to read some scientific material in Spanish. You will see how easy it is. It's easy because you already have some scientific background and knowledge. The knowledge you already have helps you understand what you are reading. In addition, many scientific terms are cognates. The following is a short selection in Spanish about biology.

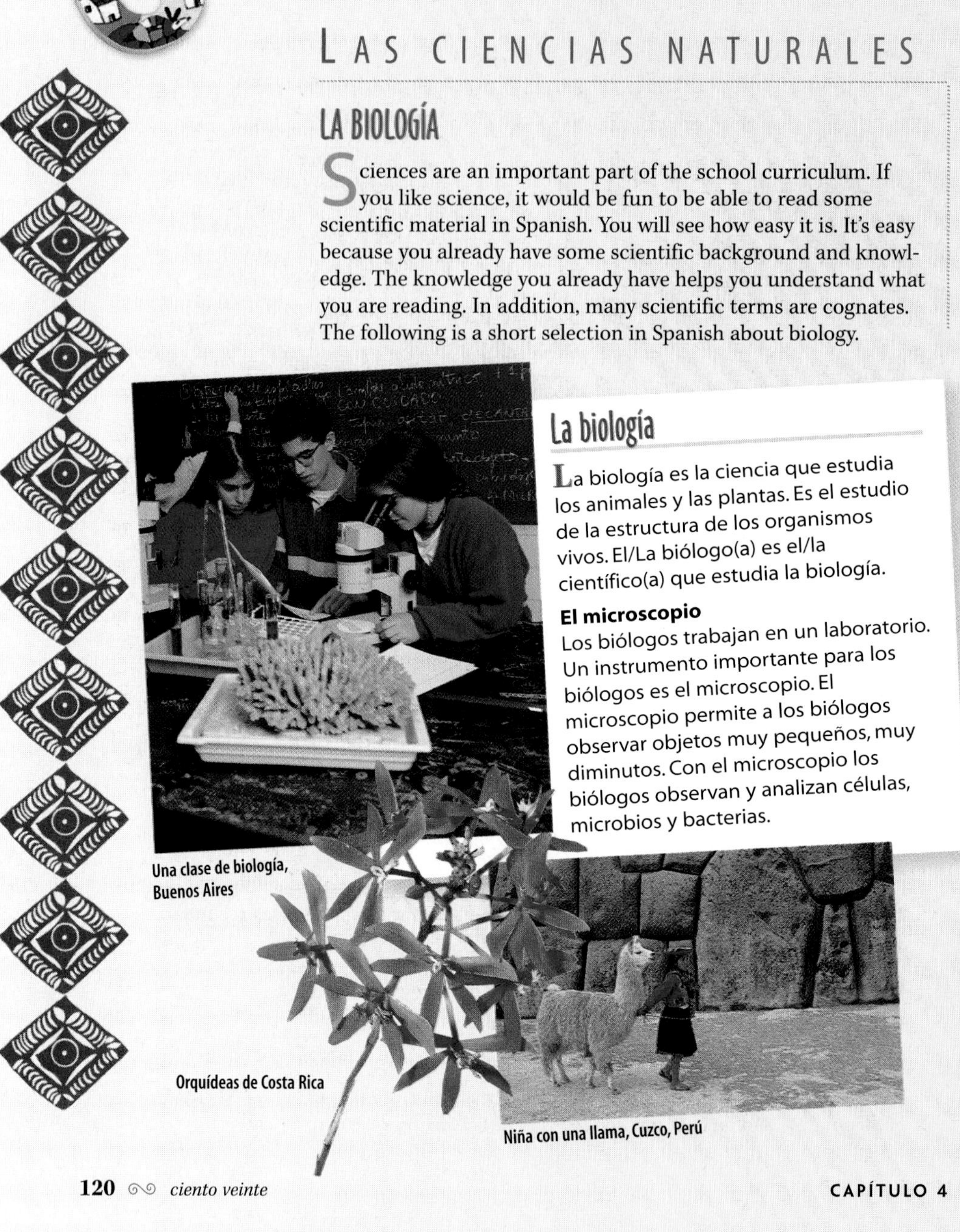

La biología

La biología es la ciencia que estudia los animales y las plantas. Es el estudio de la estructura de los organismos vivos. El/La biólogo(a) es el/la científico(a) que estudia la biología.

El microscopio

Los biólogos trabajan en un laboratorio. Un instrumento importante para los biólogos es el microscopio. El microscopio permite a los biólogos observar objetos muy pequeños, muy diminutos. Con el microscopio los biólogos observan y analizan células, microbios y bacterias.

Una clase de biología, Buenos Aires

Orquídeas de Costa Rica

Niña con una llama, Cuzco, Perú

La célula

¿Qué es una célula? La célula es el elemento básico y más importante de los seres vivientes[1]. Generalmente una célula es microscópica. Consiste en una masa llamada[2] «protoplasma» envuelta[3] en una membrana. Un microbio es un ser monocelular vegetal o animal. El microbio es solamente visible con el microscopio.

LA CÉLULA **2**

2-1. LA CÉLULA PROCARIOTA Y EUCARIOTA

En el objetivo anterior hemos esbozado una breve reseña histórica del descubrimiento de la célula y del desarrollo de la **teoría celular.**

Hemos llegado a la conclusión de que todos los seres vivos están constituidos por células.

La célula se define como:

> La unidad vital, estructural, funcional y reproductora de los seres vivos, capaz de generar otras semejantes.

2.1. A) Célula eucariota y B) Célula procariota.

• La célula es la **unidad vital**, porque todos los seres vivos, desde los protozoarios hasta los organismos pluricelulares más complejos, están constituidos por células.

• La célula es la **unidad funcional**, porque realiza todas las funciones propias de los seres vivos.

• La célula es la **unidad reproductora**, por que da origen a otras células semejantes y transmite los caracteres hereditarios.

De acuerdo con el grado de complejidad y estructura, las células se dividen en dos tipos: **células procariotas** y **células eucariotas**.

[1]seres vivientes *living creatures*
[2]llamada *called*
[3]envuelta *wrapped, encased*

Una clase de biología, Buenos Aires

Después de leer

A Palabras científicas Hagan una lista. *(Make a list of science terms you recognize.)*

B La biología Digan que sí o que no. *(Tell whether the statements are true or false.)*

1. La biología es la ciencia que estudia los elementos químicos.
2. Los biólogos estudian los animales y las plantas.
3. Un vegetal es un animal.
4. Los biólogos trabajan en un laboratorio.
5. Los biólogos usan un telescopio.
6. Hay muchas cosas que son visibles solamente con el microscopio.
7. Una célula es bastante grande.
8. Un microbio es un ser de una sola célula—es monocelular.

C Estudio de palabras Adivinen. *(Note that the following words are all related to one another. If you know the meaning of one of them, you can guess the meaning of the others.)*

1. la biología, el biólogo, biológico
2. observar, la observación, el observador
3. analizar, el análisis, analítico
4. la célula, celular
5. el microscopio, microscópico

C. You may ask the following comprehension questions:
¿Qué estudia la biología?
¿Dónde trabajan los biólogos?
¿Cuál es un instrumento que usan?
¿Qué observan los biólogos con el microscopio?
¿Qué es una célula?
¿Es grande o pequeña una célula?
¿Qué es un microbio?

ANSWERS

Después de leer

A Answers will vary, but may include: **animales, plantas, estructura, organismos, microscopio, laboratorio, instrumento, observar, objetos, analizan, células, bacteria, elemento, básico, microscópica, masa, protoplasma, membrana, monocelular, vegetal, visible**

B
1. **No.**
2. **Sí.**
3. **No.**
4. **Sí.**
5. **No.**
6. **Sí.**
7. **No.**
8. **Sí.**

CAPÍTULO 4
Culminación

Bell Ringer Review

Use BRR Transparency 4-7, or write the following on the board: Write four things you do in Spanish class.

RECYCLING

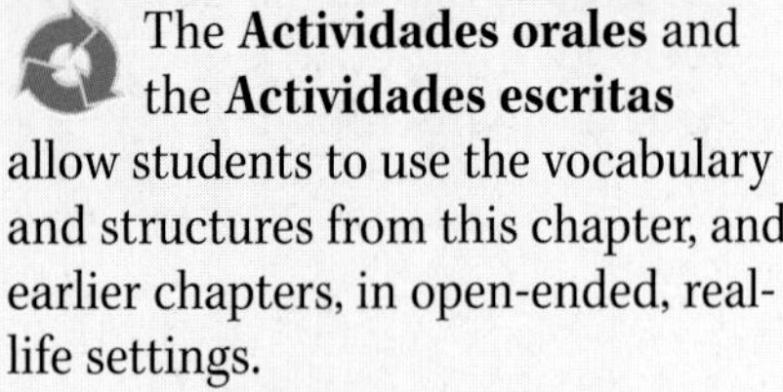

The **Actividades orales** and the **Actividades escritas** allow students to use the vocabulary and structures from this chapter, and earlier chapters, in open-ended, real-life settings.

Actividades orales

¡OJO! Encourage students to say as much as possible when they do these activities. Tell them not to be afraid to make mistakes since the goal of the activities is real-life communication. If someone in the group makes an error, allow the others to politely correct him or her.

Let students choose the activities they would like to do.

Student Portfolio

Have students keep a notebook containing their best written work from each chapter. These selected writings can be based on assignments from the Student Textbook, the Writing Activities Workbook, and the Communication Activities Masters. The two activities on page 123 are examples of writing assignments that may be included in each student's portfolio.

In the Workbook, students will develop an organized autobiography **(Mi autobiografía).** These workbook pages may also become a part of their portfolio. See the Teacher's Manual for more information on the Student Portfolio.

Culminación

Actividades orales

A **Diferencias** Your school is going to have an exchange student from Spain. Based on what you have learned about schools in the Spanish-speaking world, tell some things the exchange student will find that are different. Tell also what he or she will find that is similar.

B **Las mismas cosas** With a classmate, look at the illustrations. Then compare your own daily school habits with those of the students in the illustrations. Use **nosotros.**

ANSWERS

Actividades orales

A Answers will vary. Let students say whatever they want about the topic. Some may give just one or two bits of information and others may talk a lot.

B Answers will vary, but may include:

Illustration 1: **Los alumnos entran en la sala de clase a las nueve.**
Nosotros entramos en la sala de clase a las ___.

Illustration 2: **Los alumnos hablan cuando el profesor habla.**
Nosotros no hablamos cuando el profesor habla. Prestamos atención y escuchamos al profesor.

Illustration 3: **Los alumnos no estudian en clase. Nosotros estudiamos en clase.**

Illustration 4: **Los alumnos sacan notas malas en los exámenes.**
Nosotros sacamos notas buenas.

Actividades escritas

A La vida escolar Your Spanish pen pal wants to know what a typical school day is like. In a short letter, tell him or her all you can about a typical day in school. Don't forget to mention grades.

B El horario escolar Write out your daily school schedule in Spanish.

Writing Strategy

Ordering ideas

You can order ideas in a variety of ways when writing. Therefore, you must be aware of the purpose of your writing in order to choose the best way to organize your material. When describing an event, it is logical to put the events in the order in which they happen. Using a sensible and logical approach helps readers develop a picture in their minds.

Una fiesta

In the most recent letter from your Spanish pen pal, Gloria Velázquez, she described a party she had for her best friend. She also sent you this photograph. She told you what she had to do to prepare for the party and what her friends did at the party. She wants to know whether the types of parties she has are similar to the ones teenagers give here in the United States. Write her a letter explaining what you do to prepare for a party and what the parties are like. Include as many details as you can. These words may be helpful to you: **dar, invitar, necesitar, preparar, llegar, estar, hablar, tomar, escuchar, bailar, cantar.**

Puerto Sol, España

CAPÍTULO 4
Culminación

Actividades escritas

A Have students edit each others' letters.

TECHNOLOGY OPTIONS

Go to the **Correspondencia electrónica** section at the **Glencoe Foreign Language Web site (http://www.glencoe.com/sec/fl)** to find out how to set up a keypal (pen pal) exchange between your class and a class in a Spanish-speaking country.

Students can use the Portfolio feature on the CD-ROM to write this letter.

B Students could use the school schedule on page 57 as a model.

National Standards

Communities

If possible, have students speak with a student in your school who came from a Spanish-speaking country. Have them find out as much as they can about schools and schooling in that person's country.

ANSWERS

Actividades escritas

A Answers will vary. Please note that these "answers" should be used only as a guide as to what students may and can say. Give students free rein to say whatever they want.

B Answers will vary, but may include:

A las ocho:	**clase de español**
A las nueve:	**clase de arte**
A las diez:	**clase de matemáticas**
A las diez y cincuenta:	**descanso**
A las once:	**clase de biología**
A las doce:	**almuerzo**
A la una:	**clase de inglés**
A las dos:	**clase de educación física**
A las tres:	**clase de historia**

Writing Strategy

Answers will vary, but students will use vocabulary associated with parties.

Vocabulario

ASSESSMENT RESOURCES

- Chapter Quizzes
- Testing Program
- Computer Testmaker
- Situation Cards
- Communication Transparency C-4
- Performance Assessment
- **Maratón mental** Videoquiz

VOCABULARY REVIEW

The words and expressions in the **Vocabulario** have been presented for productive use in this chapter. They are summarized as a resource for both students and teacher. Have the students look at the list. If there are any words they don't know, tell them to find them in the **Vocabulario** sections on pages 98–99 and 102–103. If absolutely necessary, students can look up an unknown word in the end vocabulary. There are approximately ten cognates in this chapter. Have students find them.

Vocabulario

GETTING TO SCHOOL

llegar
ir a pie
en el bus escolar
en carro, en coche
entrar en la escuela

IDENTIFYING CLASSROOM OBJECTS

la sala (el salón) de clase
la pizarra, el pizarrón

DISCUSSING CLASSROOM ACTIVITIES

estar en clase
estudiar
enseñar
mirar
escuchar
prestar atención
tomar apuntes
dar un examen
sacar notas buenas (altas)
sacar notas malas (bajas)

DISCUSSING THE SPANISH CLUB

el Club de español
el miembro
la fiesta
la música
el disco compacto
el casete
la merienda
bailar
cantar
preparar
dar una fiesta

FINDING OUT INFORMATION

¿a qué hora?
¿cuándo?
¿adónde?

OTHER USEFUL EXPRESSIONS

a eso de
en punto
otros(as)
algunos(as)
ahora
también

For the Younger Student

Una fiesta Have students draw a picture of a party. Have them write several sentences to describe their picture.

El Club de español Have students prepare an invitation for the next meeting of the Spanish Club.

Independent Practice

Assign any of the following:

1. Activities, pages 122–123
2. Workbook, **Mi autobiografía,** page 40
3. Situation Cards
4. CD-ROM, Disc 1, Chapter 4, **Juego de repaso**

TECNOTUR

VIDEO

¡Buen viaje!

EPISODIO 4 ▸ En la escuela

Cristina visita a Isabel en la escuela.

¿Estudia Luis para el examen de biología?

CD-ROM

Expansión cultural

El Paseo de la Reforma es una avenida muy famosa en la Ciudad de México.

In this video episode Cristina experiences campus life in a Mexican school with her friends Isabel and Luis. To find out more about Spanish-speaking schools worldwide, go to the **Capítulo 4 Internet** activity at the **Glencoe Foreign Language Web site:**

http://www.glencoe.com/sec/fl

Video Synopsis

In this episode Cristina visits Isabel and Luis' school for the second time. It's not quite time for the first bell as we see students arriving on campus. Cristina talks to one of Isabel's classmates about the daily schedule. Isabel and Cristina then join Luis who is in his car, supposedly studying for his biology exam. As the three of them talk, Isabel comments about her brother's poor study habits. Cristina changes the subject by asking Luis about the grading system in Mexico. The scene ends when Isabel invites Cristina to join her later that day at the party sponsored by the English Club.

OVERVIEW

This page previews three key multimedia components of the **Glencoe Spanish** series. Each reinforces the material taught in Chapter 4 in a unique manner.

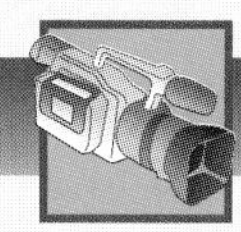

VIDEO

The Video Program allows students to see how the chapter vocabulary and structures are used by native speakers within an engaging story line. For maximum reinforcement, show the video episode as a final activity for Chapter 4.

A. Have students read the captions. Ask students where Luis and Isabel are from. and what they think Luis is really doing.

B. Now show the Chapter 4 video episode. See the Video Activities Booklet for detailed suggestions for using this resource.

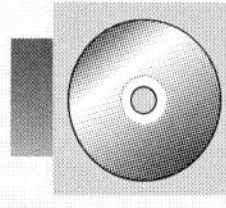

CD-ROM

A. The **Expansión cultural** photo shows **el Paseo de la Reforma** in Mexico City, Luis and Cristina's hometown.

B. In the CD-ROM version of **Expansión cultural** (Disc 1, page 125), students can listen to additional recorded information about Mexico City.

INTERNET

Teacher Information and Student Worksheets for this activity can be accessed at the Web site.

CAPÍTULOS 1–4
Repaso

RESOURCES

- Workbook: Self-Test 1, pp. 41–44
- CD-ROM, Disc 1, pp. 126–127
- Tests: Unit 1, pp. 19; 105; 137

OVERVIEW

This section reviews the salient points from Chapters 1–4. In the **Conversación** students will review school vocabulary, regular **-ar** verbs, and the irregular verbs **ser, ir,** and **estar** in context. In the **Estructura** section, they will study the conjugations of these verbs and review articles, nouns, and adjective agreement. They will practice these structures as they talk about some Spanish friends.

TEACHING THE CONVERSATION

A. Have students open their books to page 126. Call on two students to read this short conversation aloud.

B. Go over the activities in the **Después de conversar** section.

Repaso CAPÍTULOS 1–4

Conversación

La apertura de clases

JULIO: Anamari, ¿cómo estás?
ANAMARI: Muy bien, Julio. ¿Y tú?
JULIO: Bien. ¿Adónde vas?
ANAMARI: Voy a la papelería. Necesito comprar algunas cosas para la apertura de clases.
JULIO: ¡Ay, septiembre, una vez más y la apertura de clases! ¡Es increíble!

Estepona, España

Después de conversar

A **Anamari y Julio** Contesten. *(Answer.)*

1. ¿Con quién habla Anamari?
2. ¿Cómo está Julio?
3. ¿Son amigos Julio y Anamari?
4. ¿Son alumnos?
5. ¿Adónde va Anamari? ¿Qué necesita?
6. ¿De qué hablan los dos amigos?

B **¿Qué compra Anamari?** Preparen una lista de los materiales escolares que Anamari compra para la apertura de clases. *(Prepare a list of school supplies that Anamari buys for the beginning of school.)*

ANSWERS

Después de conversar

A
1. **Anamari habla con Julio.**
2. **Julio está bien.**
3. **Sí, son amigos.**
4. **Sí, son alumnos.**
5. **Anamari va a la papelería. Necesita comprar algunas cosas para la apertura de clases.**
6. **Hablan de la apertura de clases.**

B Answers will vary; however, the list should include the school supplies that students learned in Chapter 3.

Estructura

Verbos, sustantivos, artículos y adjetivos

1. Review the forms of regular **-ar** verbs.

HABLAR	**hablo**	**hablas**	**habla**	**hablamos**	***habláis***	**hablan**
LLEVAR	**llevo**	**llevas**	**lleva**	**llevamos**	***lleváis***	**llevan**

2. Review the irregular verbs you have learned so far.

SER	**soy**	**eres**	**es**	**somos**	***sois***	**son**
IR	**voy**	**vas**	**va**	**vamos**	***vais***	**van**
ESTAR	**estoy**	**estás**	**está**	**estamos**	***estáis***	**están**
DAR	**doy**	**das**	**da**	**damos**	***dais***	**dan**

3. An adjective must agree with the noun it describes. Remember that adjectives that end in **o** have four forms.

el amigo sincero	**los amigos sinceros**	**la amiga sincera**	**las amigas sinceras**
el curso difícil	**los cursos difíciles**	**la clase difícil**	**las clases difíciles**

Práctica

A **Entrevista** Contesten personalmente. *(Answer.)*

1. ¿Vas a una escuela secundaria?
2. ¿Estás en la escuela ahora?
3. ¿Cuántos cursos tomas?
4. ¿Habla mucho la profesora?
5. ¿Son buenos los alumnos de español?
6. ¿Escuchan Uds. cuando la profesora habla?
7. ¿Sacan Uds. notas buenas?
8. ¿Dan los profesores muchos exámenes?

Actividades comunicativas

A **Julio y Anamari** Work with a classmate. Look at the photo of Julio and Anamari. They are from Málaga, Spain. Say as much as you can about Julio. Then say as much as you can about Anamari. Take turns.

B **Los amigos** Look at the photo of a group of friends from Estepona, Spain on page 126. With a classmate, talk about the group. Ask one another questions about some of the people in the photo.

TEACHING STRUCTURE

Verbos, sustantivos, artículos y adjetivos

A. Quickly go over the verb paradigms that appear here.

B. You may also write the verbs on the board and underline the endings.

C. Point out to students that, except for the verb **ser,** all forms of these verbs are the same as those of an **-ar** verb with the exception of the **yo** form.

D. When going over Step 3, draw some stick figures on the board and have students make up sentences.

Actividades comunicativas

A Have students refer to the top photo on page 126 as they do **Actividad A.**

Note: You may wish to do the first literary selection (pages 440–441) with students at this time.

ANSWERS

Práctica

A 1. **Sí, voy a una escuela secundaria.**
2. **Sí, (No, no) estoy en la escuela ahora.**
3. **Tomo ___ cursos.**
4. **Sí (No), la profesora (no) habla mucho.**
5. **Sí (No), los alumnos de español (no) son buenos.**
6. **Sí, (No, no) escuchamos cuando la profesora habla.**
7. **Sí, (No, no) sacamos notas buenas.**
8. **Sí, (No,) los profesores (no) dan muchos exámenes.**

Actividades comunicativas

A and B Answers will vary. Remind students that they should try to use as much of the vocabulary and as many of the structures as they can from **Capítulos 1–4.**

Independent Practice

Assign any of the following:

1. Activities, pages 126–127
2. Workbook, pages 41–44
3. CD-ROM, Disc 1, pages 126–127
4. CD-ROM, Disc 1, Chapters 1–4, **Juegos de repaso**

VISTAS DE MÉXICO

OVERVIEW

The **Vistas de México** were prepared by National Geographic Society. Their purpose is to give students greater insight, through these visual images, into the culture and people of Mexico. Have students look at the photographs on pages 128–131 for enjoyment. If they would like to talk about them, let them say anything they can, using the vocabulary they have learned to this point.

National Standards

Cultures
The **Vistas de México** photos, and the accompanying captions, allow students to gain insights into the people and culture of Mexico.

Learning From Photos

1. Ruinas de Uxmal Uxmal is located south of Mérida on the Yucatán Peninsula. The ruins at Uxmal, although mostly unrestored, are considered the most beautiful and the purest strictly Mayan ruins in the area.

2. Estatua olmeca, parque La Venta, Veracruz The Olmecs have long been considered the mother culture of Mesoamerica. Recent research, however, suggests that the Olmecs may have been influenced by the Mayans rather than the other way around. The giant stone heads carved by the Olmecs were salvaged from the oil fields of La Venta on the western edge of Tabasco near the state of Veracruz. The heads are now on display in **el parque La Venta** just west of Villahermosa. These Olmec heads have triggered endless debate. They are Negroid heads, six feet tall and weigh up to 20 tons. *(continued)*

1. Ruinas de Uxmal
2. Estatua olmeca, parque La Venta, Veracruz
3. Mercado indio Tzotzil, Chiapas
4. Guanajuato
5. Tuna con vestimenta del siglo XVI, Guanajuato
6. Tejedor de caña, Querétaro
7. Pescadores, lago Pátzcuaro, Michoacán

Learning From Photos

3. Mercado indio Tzotzil, Chiapas Indian markets such as this one in the small village of Tzotzil exist in many areas of Latin America. Each village usually has a special day or days for its market. The market place is frequently the town square and the Church is almost always on the square.

4. Guanajuato This is a beautiful colonial city tucked into the mountains at an altitude of some 7,000 feet. As one can see in this photograph, many of Guanajuato's houses are painted pastel colors. Guanajuato is the home of the Universidad de Guanajuato. The university was originally a seminary founded by the Jesuits in 1732. In 1945 it became a state university. One of its famous alumni is Diego Rivera, one of Mexico's great muralists. Rivera was born in Guanajuato and his home is now a museum. *(continued)*

VISTAS DE MÉXICO

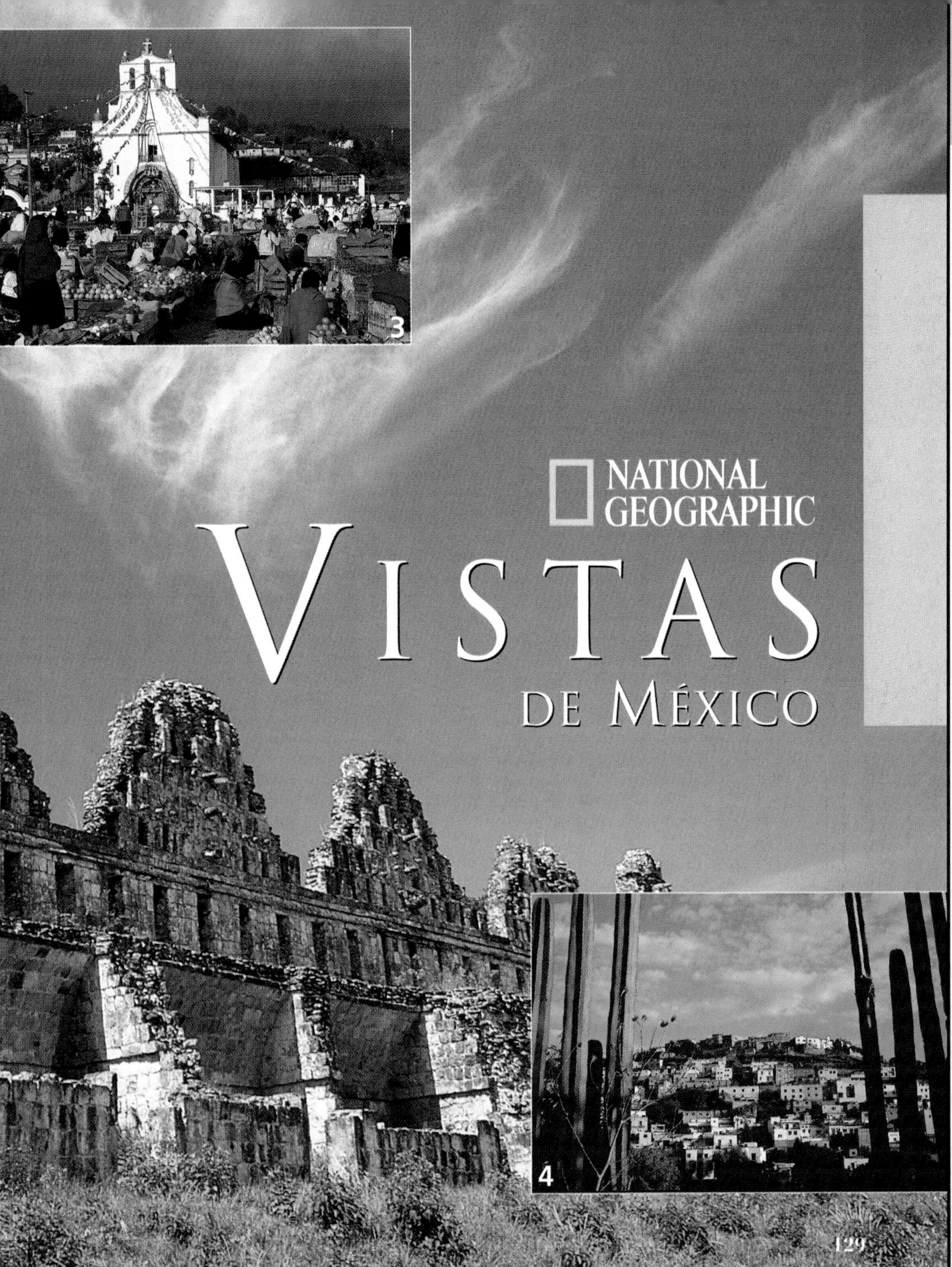

Learning From Photos

(continued)
6. Tejedor de caña, Querétaro Querétaro has played a significant role in Mexican history. The first plans for independence were made here. The Mexican-American War ended with the signing of the Treaty of Guadalupe Hidalgo in Querétaro. In 1867 the emperor Maximilian was executed just north of town and the present day Mexican Constitution was signed here in 1917. Today, Querétaro is an industrial center of some 800,000 people.

7. Pescadores, lago Pátzcuaro, Michoacán Pátzcuaro was the 16th-century capital of the state of Michoacán. It is a beautiful lakeside community situated at 7,200 feet in the Sierra Madre. Pátzcuaro is the home of the Tarascan Indians. The men wear a traditional straw hat (see photo) and one of their means of livelihood is fishing on Lake Pátzcuaro with these graceful butterfly nets.

Learning From Photos

(continued from page 128)
5. Tuna con vestimenta del siglo XVI, Guanajuato **Una tuna** is a group of meandering singers dressed as medieval troubadours. The members of the group are called **tunos**. They are very popular in Spain. **Los tunos** are traditionally university students but today many are older and they make a career or part-time living being **tunos**. The only place outside of Spain where some type of group entertains with its singing is in the university town of Guanajuato. They are more commonly referred to as **estudiantinas** and on weekend nights they serenade the public in city squares. In the small city of Guanajuato there are fifteen plazas.

(continued)

VISTAS DE MÉXICO

Learning From Photos

1. Alhóndiga, museo, Guanajuato This musuem is located in the center of Guanajuato. It was the site of the first battle in Mexico's War of Independence from Spain. Today the Alhóndiga de Granaditas is a state museum. There are exhibits on local history, crafts, and archeology.

2. Niña maya delante de la catedral de San Cristóbal de las Casas, Chiapas Chiapas is a state in southern Mexico. Most of its eastern part borders on Guatemala. Because of its isolation, it is one of the poorest states in Mexico and tensions are high among various indigenous groups who live there. San Cristóbal de las Casas is a small colonial town. Its cathedral, which was was built in 1528, was demolished and rebuilt in 1693.

3. Bolsa de valores, Ciudad de México The Stock Exchange in Mexico City is one of the world's most important exchanges. Since Mexico has one of the world's largest economies, economic shifts in Mexico impact all world economies.

4. Cosecha de toronjas, Oaxaca Oaxaca is in the southermost part of Mexico. Along with Chiapas, Oaxaca has one of the largest indigenous populations in the country. Most inhabitants are descendants of the Mixtec or Zapotec Indians. Two of Mexico's most important leaders and political figures, presidents Benito Juárez and Porfirio Díaz, were from Oaxaca. Today the city of Oaxaca is a major tourist attraction. *(continued)*

1. *Alhóndiga, museo, Guanajuato*
2. *Niña maya delante de la catedral de San Cristóbal de las Casas, Chiapas*
3. *Bolsa de valores, Ciudad de México*
4. *Cosecha de toronjas, Oaxaca*
5. *Maquiladora de televisores, Tijuana*
6. *Plataforma petrolera, Campeche*
7. *Monumento de la Independencia, Paseo de la Reforma, Ciudad de México*

130

NATIONAL GEOGRAPHIC SOCIETY TEACHER'S CORNER

Index to NATIONAL GEOGRAPHIC MAGAZINE

The following articles may be used for research relating to this chapter:

- "Popocatépetl: Mexico's Smoking Mountains," by A. R. Williams, January 1999.
- "The Royal Crypts of Copán," by George E. Stuart, December 1997.
- "Emerging Mexico: Bright with Promise, Tangled in the Past," by Michael Parfit, August 1996.
- "Heartland and the Pacific: Eternal Mexico," by Michael Parfit, August 1996.
- "Mexico City: Pushing the Limits," by Michael Parfit, August 1996.
- "Monterrey: Confronting the Future," by Michael Parfit, August 1996.
- "Veracruz: Gateway to the World," by Cassandra Franklin-Barbajosa, August 1996.
- "Mexico's Desert Aquarium," by George Grall, October 1995.
- "Cave Quest: Trial and Tragedy a Mile Beneath Mexico," by William C. Stone, September 1995.
- "Maya Masterpiece Revealed at Bonampak," by Mary Miller, February 1995.

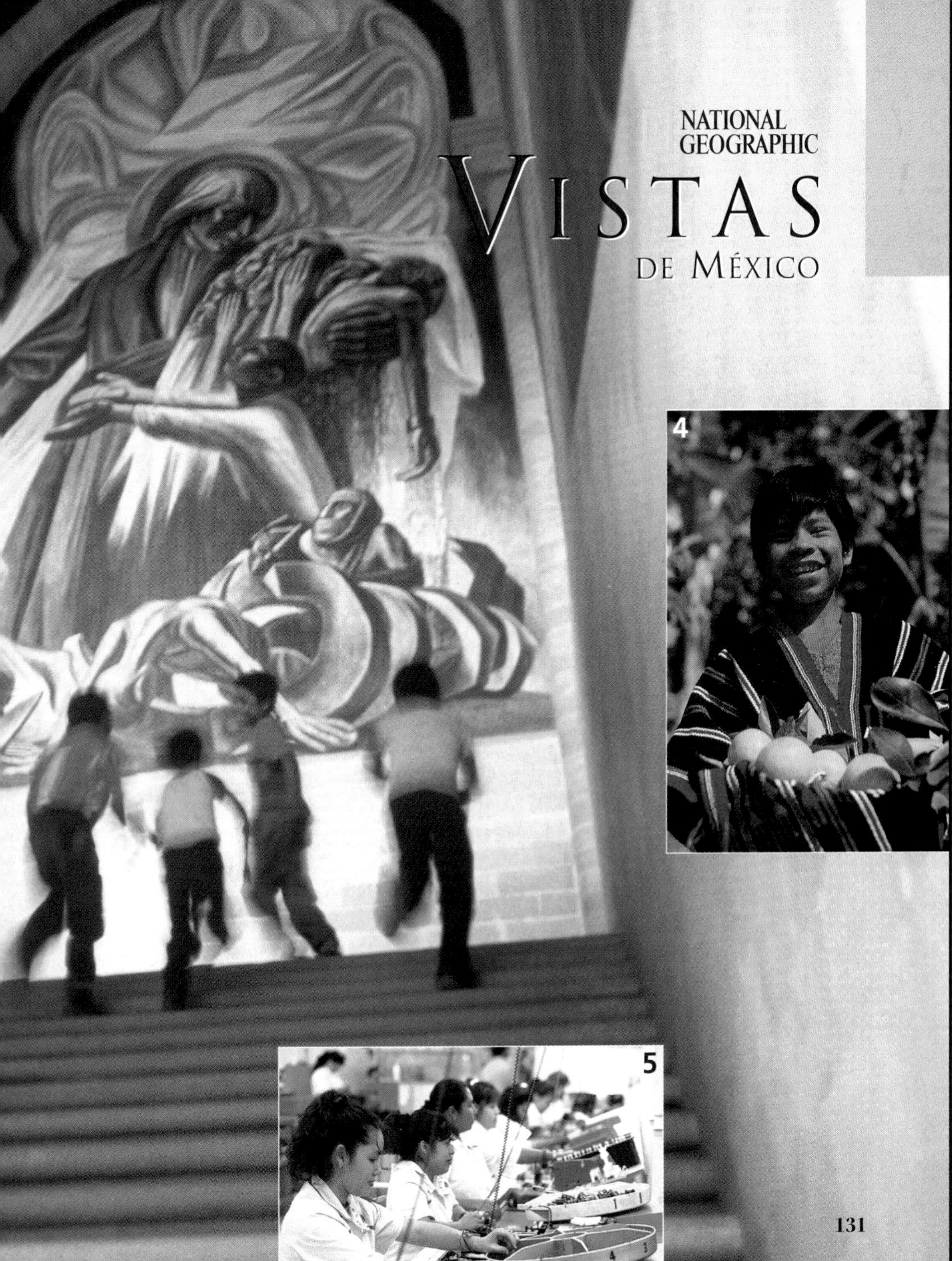

VISTAS DE MÉXICO

Learning From Photos

(continued from page 130)

5. Maquiladora de televisores, Tijuana **Maquiladora** is a regional term used in Mexico, particularly in the North near the U.S. border. It means **planta de ensamblaje de una empresa estadounidense.** There are many such assembly plants along the border.

6. Plataforma petrolera, Campeche Campeche is a state in the western part of the Yucatán Peninsula facing the Bahía de Campeche, a part of the Gulf of Mexico. There is a great deal of oil drilling in this area.

7. Monumento de la Independencia, Paseo de la Reforma, Ciudad de México The type of traffic circle we see here surrounding the Monumento de la Independencia is called **una glorieta** in Mexico City. The Monumento de la Independencia is a Corinthian column with a golden angel on the top. For this reason the monument is commonly called **el Ángel.**

Products available from GLENCOE/MCGRAW-HILL

To order the following products, call Glencoe/McGraw-Hill at 1-800-334-7344.

CD-ROMs
- Picture Atlas of the World
- The Complete National Geographic: 109 Years of National Geographic Magazine

Software
- ZingoLingo: Spanish Diskettes

Transparency Set
- NGS PicturePack: Geography of North America

Products available from NATIONAL GEOGRAPHIC SOCIETY

NATIONAL GEOGRAPHIC SOCIETY

To order the following products, call National Geographic Society at 1-800-368-2728.

Books
- Exploring Your World: The Adventure of Geography
- National Geographic Satellite Atlas of the World

Videos
- Mexicans: Through Their Eyes
- Mexico ("Nations of the World" Series)

Chapter 5 Overview

SCOPE AND SEQUENCE pages 132–157

TOPICS	FUNCTIONS	STRUCTURE	CULTURE
◆ Foods and beverages ◆ Eating at a café ◆ Shopping for food	◆ How to find a table at a café ◆ How to order in a café ◆ How to pay the bill in a café ◆ How to identify food ◆ How to shop for food ◆ How to describe breakfast, lunch, and dinner	◆ **-er** and **-ir** verbs in the present	◆ Differences between eating habits in the U.S. and in the Spanish-speaking world ◆ Eating times in the Spanish-speaking world compared to the U.S. ◆ Paseo de la Castellana, Madrid ◆ Buenos Aires, Argentina ◆ Open-air markets and supermarkets in Spain and Latin America ◆ Math terms in Spanish

CHAPTER 5 RESOURCES

PRINT	MULTIMEDIA
Planning Resources	
Lesson Plans Block Scheduling Lesson Plans	Interactive Lesson Planner
Reinforcement Resources	
Writing Activities Workbook Student Tape Manual Video Activities Booklet Web Site User's Guide	Transparencies Binder Audiocassette/Compact Disc Program Videocassette/Videodisc Program Online Internet Activities Electronic Teacher's Classroom Resources
Assessment Resources	
Situation Cards Chapter Quizzes Testing Program Performance Assessment	**Maratón mental** Mindjogger Videoquiz Testmaker Computer Software (Macintosh/Windows) Listening Comprehension Audiocassette/Compact Disc Communication Transparency: C-5
Motivational Resources	
Expansion Activities	Café Glencoe: www.cafe.glencoe.com Keypal Internet Activities
Enrichment	
Spanish for Spanish Speakers	

Chapter 5 Planning Guide

SECTION	PAGES	SECTION RESOURCES
Vocabulario Palabras 1 **En el café** **Para beber / Para comer** **Antes de comer / Después de comer**	134–137	Vocabulary Transparencies 5.1 Audiocassette 4A/ Compact Disc 3 Student Tape Manual, TE, pages 47–50 Workbook, pages 45–46 Chapter Quizzes, pages 22–23 CD-ROM, Disc 2, pages 134–137
Vocabulario Palabras 2 **En el mercado** **En el supermercado** **Las comidas**	138–141	Vocabulary Transparencies 5.2 Audiocassette 4A/ Compact Disc 3 Student Tape Manual, TE, pages 50–52 Workbook, pages 47–48 Chapter Quizzes, page 24 CD-ROM, Disc 2, pages 138–141
Estructura **Presente de los verbos en -er e -ir**	142–145	Workbook, pages 49–52 Audiocassette 4A/Compact Disc 3 Student Tape Manual, TE, pages 53–54 Chapter Quizzes, page 25 Computer Testmaker CD-ROM, Disc 2, pages 142–145
Conversación **En la terraza de un café** **Pronunciación: La consonante d**	146–147	Audiocassette 4A/Compact Disc 3 Student Tape Manual, TE, pages 55–56 CD-ROM, Disc 2, pages 146–147
Lecturas culturales **En un café en Madrid** **Las horas para comer *(opcional)*** **¿Mercado o supermercado? *(opcional)***	148–151	Testing Program, pages 26–27 CD-ROM, Disc 2, pages 148–151
Conexiones **La aritmética *(opcional)***	152–153	Testing Program, page 27 CD-ROM, Disc 2, pages 152–153
Culminación **Actividades orales** **Actividades escritas** **Vocabulario** **Tecnotur**	154–157	**¡Buen viaje!** Video, Episode 5 Video Activities, pages 79–84 Internet Activities www.glencoe.com/sec/fl Testing Program, pages 23–26; 106; 138; 161 CD-ROM, Disc 2, pages 154–157

CAPÍTULO 5

OVERVIEW

In this chapter students will learn how to order food at a café and shop for food at a store or market. To do this they will learn to identify some food items, to use expressions needed for ordering food, and the **-er** and **-ir** verbs. They will also learn some differences between eating customs in the U.S. and the Spanish-speaking countries.

National Standards

Communication In Chapter 5, students will communicate in spoken and written Spanish on the following topics:

- ordering food at a café
- shopping for food at a market or supermarket
- eating habits

Students will obtain and provide information and engage in conversations in a café or market setting as they fulfill the objectives listed on this page.

Pacing

Chapter 5 will require approximately six to eight days. Pacing will vary according to the length of the class, the age of your students, and student aptitude.

Block Scheduling

See the Block Scheduling Lesson Plans Booklet for suggestions on how to present the chapter material within a block scheduling framework.

CAPÍTULO 5

En el café

Objetivos

In this chapter you will learn to do the following:

- order food or a beverage at a café
- identify some food
- shop for food
- talk about activities
- talk about differences between eating habits in the United States and in the Spanish-speaking world

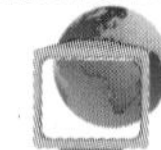

interNET CONNECTION

The **Glencoe Foreign Language Web site (http://www.glencoe.com/sec/fl)** offers three options that enable you and your students to experience the Spanish-speaking world via the Internet:

- The online **Actividades** are correlated to the chapters and utilize Hispanic Web sites around the world. For the Chapter 5 activity, see student page 157.
- The **Correspondencia electrónica** section provides information on how to set up a keypal (pen pal) exchange between your class and a class in the Spanish-speaking world.
- At **Café Glencoe,** the interactive "after-school" section of the site, you and your students can access a variety of additional online resources, including interactive games.

Spotlight On Culture

Artefacto The decorative cloth is a traditional design from Guatemala. Colorful designs such as this one are commonly seen in many parts of Central America, especially in Guatemala and Honduras.

Fotografía This photo was taken on the Plaza Mayor in Madrid. This historic 17th-century plaza has been superbly restored. The square is closed to traffic and is a pleasant spot to have a coffee or refreshment at one of the many cafés. The Plaza Mayor is one of the largest squares in Europe. It was designed by the architect of Felipe II, but construction on it was completed in 1620 during the reign of Fernando III.

Teacher Notes

Chapter Projects

Una fiesta Have students plan a menu for a Spanish Club party. They should plan who will bring the beverages and various food items.

La cocina hispana Prepare a dish from a Spanish-speaking country or have students bring some Spanish or Latin American foods to class. Students should be prepared to say something about the food they bring, such as where it comes from and what the main ingredients are.

Al supermercado Have students check their local supermarket to find out what kinds of Hispanic foods they sell. Have them report back to the class about their findings.

RESOURCES

- Vocabulary Transparencies 5.1 (A & B)
- Student Tape Manual, TE, pages 47–50
- Audiocassette 4A/CD3
- Workbook, pages 45–46
- Quiz 1, pages 22–23
- CD-ROM, Disc 2, pages 134–137

Bell Ringer Review

Use BRR Transparency 5-1, or write the following on the board:
Complete the following:

1. **Compro una camisa en una tienda de ___.**
2. **¿Qué ___ necesitas? ¿Blanca o roja?**
3. **¿Buscas una camisa de ___ largas o cortas?**
4. **¿Qué ___ usas? ¿Pequeña, mediana o grande?**
5. **Pagas en la ___.**

TEACHING VOCABULARY

A. Have students close their books. Point to each new vocabulary item using Vocabulary Transparencies 5.1 (A & B). Have students repeat each word several times. Intersperse questions such as: **¿Qué es?, ¿Quién es?**

B. When you present sentences ask questions, building from simple to more complex. For example:
¿Va Rafael al café?
¿Quién va al café?
¿Adónde va Rafael?
¿Va al café con Catalina?
¿Con quién va?

Vocabulario

PALABRAS 1

En el café

Rafael va al café.
Él va al café con Catalina.
Ellos van juntos.
Buscan una mesa.
Ven una mesa libre.

Catalina lee el menú.

Total Physical Response

Getting ready
If students don't already know the meaning of **levántate, ven acá,** and **siéntate,** teach these expressions by using the appropriate gestures as you say each expression. Call on individual students to do the following.

Begin
___, levántate. Ven acá.
Es el café.
Busca una mesa libre.
Siéntate en el café.
___, ven acá. Tú vas a ser el/la mesero(a).
Ve a la mesa donde está ___.
Habla con ___.
___, habla con el/la mesero(a).
___, dale el menú a ___.
___, lee el menú.
Da la orden al/a la mesero(a).
___, toma el lápiz.
___, escribe la orden.
Gracias, ___. Siéntate.

Para beber

Para comer

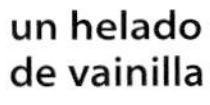

Antes de comer

Los clientes hablan con el mesero.
El mesero escribe la orden.

Después de comer

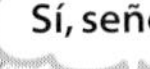

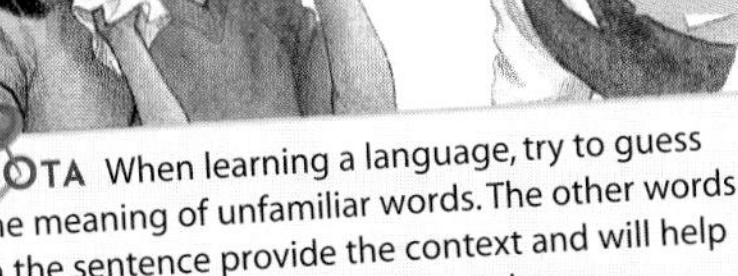

NOTA When learning a language, try to guess the meaning of unfamiliar words. The other words in the sentence provide the context and will help you understand words you do not know.

Elena estudia español en la escuela. *Aprende* el español en la escuela. Elena lee un menú en español. Ella *comprende* el menú. *Comprende* porque *aprende* el español en la escuela. Elena *comprende*, habla, lee y escribe el español. Es una alumna buena. *Recibe* notas muy buenas.

CAPÍTULO 5
Vocabulario

C. Have students dramatize the mini-conversations using as much expression as possible.

D. After the initial presentation of the vocabulary with the overhead transparencies, have students open their books and read the new material for additional reinforcement.

E. Read the **Nota** aloud to the class. Emphasize the new words they are learning from context. You may add the following to give further clarification.
Elena aprende porque es una alumna buena y estudia.
Point to your ears as you say:
Ella comprende el español. El mesero habla español y Elena comprende al mesero.

ABOUT THE SPANISH LANGUAGE

- The word **el mesero** is used throughout Latin America. **El camarero** is used in Spain.
- The **tortilla** shown here is a Spanish **tortilla** which is similar to an omelette. **Una tortilla a la española** is an omelette with potatoes and onions.
- The two most common words for sandwich are **el sándwich** and **el bocadillo**. **Bocadillo** is more common in Spain. In Spain you will also hear **la bocata**. **El emparedado** is also used in Spain and in some areas of Latin America.
- **Papas** is used throughout Latin America. **Patatas** is used in Spain.
- **Helado** is the most commonly used word for ice cream. **Mantecado**, however, is often used for vanilla ice cream.
- Among friends **la cuenta** is sometimes referred to as **la dolorosa**.

¡OJO! Práctica When students are doing the **Práctica** activities, accept any answer that makes sense. The purpose of these activities is to have students use the new vocabulary. They are not factual recall activities. Thus, do not expect students to remember specific information from the vocabulary presentation when answering. If you wish, have students use the photos on this page as a stimulus, when possible.

Historieta Each time **Historieta** appears, it means that the answers to these activities form a short story. Encourage students to look at the title of the **Historieta** since it will sometimes help them do the activity.

A thru D Have students close their books. Do all the activities orally first, then reinforce by calling on individuals to read. It is suggested that you go over all the activities in class before assigning them for homework.

PAIRED ACTIVITIES These **Práctica** can also be done as paired activites.

EXPANSION

Have students retell the stories in **Práctica A, B,** and **D** in their own words.

A HISTORIETA Al café

Contesten. *(Answer.)*

1. ¿Adónde van los amigos?
2. ¿Qué buscan?
3. ¿Están ocupadas todas las mesas?
4. ¿Ven una mesa libre?
5. ¿Toman la mesa?
6. ¿Lee Gabriela el menú?
7. ¿Con quién hablan los amigos?
8. ¿Quién escribe la orden?
9. ¿Qué bebe Gabriela?
10. ¿Qué bebe Tomás?
11. ¿Toman un refresco los amigos?

Caracas, Venezuela

B HISTORIETA En el café

Contesten. *(Answer.)*

1. Los amigos van ____.
   a. al café **b.** a la cafetería de la escuela
2. Buscan ____.
   a. una mesa ocupada **b.** una mesa libre
3. Los amigos leen ____.
   a. el menú **b.** la orden
4. El mesero ____ la orden.
   a. lee **b.** escribe
5. Para ____ hay café, té y soda.
   a. comer **b.** beber
6. El cliente paga ____.
   a. el menú **b.** la cuenta

C ¿Qué toma José? Sigan el modelo. *(Follow the model.)*

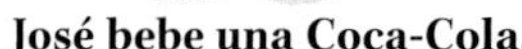

José bebe una Coca-Cola.

José come un bocadillo de jamón y queso.

1.

2.

3.

4.

5.

6.

Writing Development

Have students write the answers to **Práctica A, B,** and **D** in one paragraph to illustrate how all of the items tell a story.

ANSWERS

Práctica

A
1. **Los amigos van al café.**
2. **Buscan una mesa.**
3. **No, todas las mesas no están ocupadas.**
4. **Sí, (No, no) ven una mesa libre.**
5. **Sí, (No, no) toman la mesa.**
6. **Sí (No), Gabriela (no) lee el menú.**
7. **Los amigos hablan con el/la mesero(a) (camarero[a]).**
8. **El/La mesero(a) (camarero[a]) escribe la orden.**
9. **Gabriela bebe ___.**
10. **Tomás bebe ___.**
11. **Sí, los amigos toman un refresco.**

B
1. **a**
2. **b**
3. **a**
4. **b**
5. **b**
6. **b**

C
1. **José come papas fritas.**
2. **José come una hamburguesa.**
3. **José bebe una limonada.**
4. **José come un helado**
5. **José bebe un café solo.**
6. **José come una ensalada.**

D HISTORIETA **Una experiencia buena**

Contesten. *(Answer.)*

1. ¿Va Linda a un café?
2. ¿Va a un café en Madrid?
3. ¿Va con un grupo de alumnos americanos?
4. ¿Habla Linda con el camarero?
5. ¿Lee Linda el menú?
6. ¿Es en español el menú?
7. ¿Comprende Linda el menú?
8. ¿Y comprende Linda al camarero cuando él habla?
9. ¿Por qué comprende Linda? ¿Aprende ella el español en la escuela?
10. ¿Habla, lee y comprende Linda el español?

Madrid, España

Actividades comunicativas

A **Al café** Work in small groups. You're in a café in Mexico City. One of you will be the server. Have a conversation from the time you enter the café until you leave. You will get a table, order, get the check, and pay.

B **¿Qué toman los amigos?** Look at the illustrations below. With a classmate, take turns telling one another what's happening in each one.

CAPÍTULO 5
Vocabulario

Actividades comunicativas

¡OJO! Práctica versus Actividades comunicativas All activities which provide guided practice are labeled **Práctica.** The more open-ended communicative activities are labeled **Actividades comunicativas.** Allow students to select the activity they wish to take part in.

A Students can present their conversations from **Actividad A** to the class.

B Have students ask you questions about the illustrations that accompany **Actividad B.** This encourages students to use the interrogative words.

Learning From Photos

Caracas, Venezuela Ask the following questions about the photo on page 136:
¿Están en Caracas los amigos?
¿Van a un café?
¿Entran en el café?
¿Quién indica dónde hay una mesa libre, Tomás o Gabriela?

Madrid, España Have students tell a story by describing the photo on page 137. They can use **Práctica D** as a guide.

For review, have students tell what each person is wearing. They know all the necessary vocabulary with the exception of *apron,* **el delantal.**

ANSWERS

Práctica

D
1. **Sí, Linda va a un café.**
2. **Sí, va a un café en Madrid.**
3. **Sí, va con un grupo de alumnos americanos.**
4. **Sí, Linda habla con el camarero.**
5. **Sí, Linda lee el menú.**
6. **Sí, el menú es en español.**
7. **Sí, Linda comprende el menú.**
8. **Sí, Linda comprende al camarero cuando él habla.**
9. **Linda comprende porque aprende el español en la escuela.**
10. **Sí, Linda habla, lee y comprende el español.**

Actividades comunicativas

A Answers will vary. Students may use the mini-conversations on page 135 as a guide.

B Answers will vary, but may include:
1. **Los amigos buscan una mesa.**
2. **Leen el menú.**
3. **El mesero escribe la orden.**
4. **Los amigos pagan la cuenta.**

CAPÍTULO 5

Vocabulario

PALABRAS 2

RESOURCES

- Vocabulary Transparencies 5.2 (A & B)
- Student Tape Manual, TE, pages 50–52
- Audiocassette 4A/CD3
- Workbook, pages 47–48
- Quiz 2, page 24
- CD-ROM, Disc 2, pages 138–141

Bell Ringer Review

Use BRR Transparency 5-2, or write the following on the board:
Answer:

1. **¿Dónde compras los materiales escolares?**
2. **¿En qué llevas los materiales escolares?**
3. **¿Cuáles son algunos materiales escolares?**

TEACHING VOCABULARY

A. Have students close their books. Present the vocabulary, using Vocabulary Transparencies 5.2 (A & B). Have students repeat each word several times.

B. Have students dramatize the mini-conversations on page 139, using as much expression as possible.

C. When you present the sentences on page 139, ask questions building from simple to more complex. For example: **¿Va de compras la señora? ¿Quién va de compras? ¿Va de compras en México? ¿Adónde va la señora? ¿Dónde vive la señora?**

D. After presenting the vocabulary with the transparencies, have students open their books and read the new material.

Vocabulario

PALABRAS 2

En el mercado

las manzanas
la lechuga
las naranjas
los plátanos
las papas
los tomates
las judías verdes
las frutas
las zanahorias
las habichuelas, los frijoles
los guisantes
los vegetales
los mariscos
la carne

los huevos

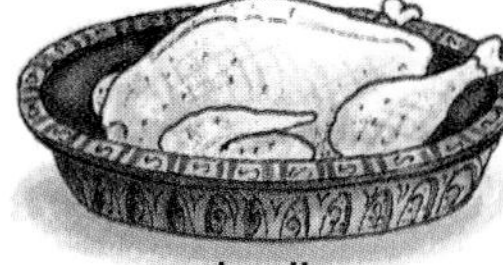
el pollo

el pescado

Total Physical Response

Getting ready
If students don't already know the meaning of **levántate, ven acá, siéntate,** and **hacer unos gestos,** teach these expressions by using the appropriate gestures as you say each expression. Call on individual students to pantomime the following.

Begin
___, ven acá, por favor.
Vas a hacer unos gestos.
Come la manzana.
Come el tomate.
Bebe la Coca-Cola.
Bebe el café.
Toma el paquete.
Abre el paquete.
Come las papas fritas.
Toma la lata.
Mira la lata.
Abre la lata.
Prepara una ensalada de atún.
Gracias, ___. Siéntate.

La señora va de compras.
Va de compras en México,
La señora vive en México.

En el supermercado

Venden:

Las comidas

el desayuno

el almuerzo

la cena

CAPÍTULO 5
Vocabulario

ABOUT THE SPANISH LANGUAGE

- There are many different words for *beans:* **las habichuelas, los frijoles, los frejoles, las judías,** and **los porotos**. The most commonly used term for *green beans* is **las judías verdes** but you will also hear **los ejotes, las vainitas, las chauchas, los porotos verdes,** and **las verduras.**
- **El tomate** in Mexico is **el jitomate.**
- In areas of the Caribbean, **la naranja** is **la china.**
- The words for vegetables can be **los vegetales, las legumbres** or **las verduras.**
- Another common expression for **¿A cuánto están?** is **¿A cómo son?** (It is recommended that you do not confuse students by introducing this expression.)
- The word **la bolsa** can be problematic. A bag is sometimes **el bolso** but **la bolsa** is quite universal for a paper bag or a bag or package of potato chips, for example. **La bolsa** can also be a lady's purse.
- In almost all countries **huevos** can have a vulgar meaning. It is safe to use the word, however, in the proper context. In Mexico and Guatemala people will sometimes avoid it and use **blanquillos,** which is literally *egg whites.*
- The official names for the meals are: **el desayuno, el almuerzo, la cena. La comida** is the general term for *meal* but it is often associated with the main meal of the day. In some countries **la comida** is the mid-day meal or **el almuerzo,** and in others, it is the evening meal or **la cena.**

Práctica

A Have students close their books, then ask them the questions from **Práctica A** orally. Call on individuals to respond. Then ask a student to retell all the information in his or her own words.

Writing Development

Have students write out **Práctica B** as a paragraph.

Learning From Photos

Miraflores, Perú Have students identify the products they recognize in the market.
San Miguel de Allende, México Ask the following questions about the photo:
¿Qué vende la señora?
¿A cuánto están los huevos ahora?
¿Compra la señora los huevos?
¿Paga ella?
¿Da el dinero a la empleada?

Práctica

A HISTORIETA Al mercado

Contesten. *(Answer.)*

1. ¿Van Uds. al mercado?
2. ¿Compran Uds. comida en el mercado?
3. En el mercado, ¿venden vegetales y frutas?
4. ¿Venden carne y pescado también?
5. ¿Quiénes venden, los clientes o los empleados?
6. ¿Van Uds. al supermercado también?
7. En el supermercado, ¿venden productos en botes, paquetes y bolsas?
8. ¿Venden también muchos productos congelados?

Miraflores, Perú

San Miguel de Allende, México

B HISTORIETA De compras

Completen según la foto.
(Complete according to the photo.)

La señora está en el ___1___. La señora va a un mercado en México porque ella ___2___ en México. Habla con la empleada. Compra una docena de ___3___. Hoy los huevos están a ___4___ pesos la docena. La señora compra los huevos pero no necesita ___5___ más.

ANSWERS

Práctica

A
1. **Sí, vamos al mercado.**
2. **Sí, compramos comida en el mercado.**
3. **Sí, en el mercado venden vegetales y frutas.**
4. **Sí, venden carne y pescado también.**
5. **Los empleados venden.**
6. **Sí, vamos al supermercado también.**
7. **Sí, en el supermercado venden productos en botes, paquetes y bolsas.**
8. **Sí, venden también muchos productos congelados.**

B
1. **mercado**
2. **vive**
3. **huevos**
4. **diez**
5. **nada**

C **¿El desayuno, el almuerzo o la cena?** Contesten con **sí** o **no.** *(Answer with* sí *or* no.)

1. En el desayuno comemos cereales, huevos, pan dulce, yogur y pan tostado con mermelada.
2. En la cena comemos un biftec.
3. En el desayuno comemos un bocadillo de pollo con papas fritas y una ensalada de lechuga y tomate.
4. En la cena comemos carne o pescado, papas o arroz, un vegetal y un postre.

D **Lo contrario** Escojan lo contrario. *(Choose the opposite.)*

1. algo	**a.** escribir
2. ocupado	**b.** aprender
3. para beber	**c.** nada
4. leer	**d.** libre
5. comprar	**e.** vender
6. enseñar	**f.** para comer

Actividades comunicativas

A **Al mercado** Visit a Hispanic market in your community with your classmates. If you don't know the names of some foods that appeal to you, ask the vendor. Choose a few items and find out how much you owe. Be sure to speak Spanish. If there isn't a Latin American market in your community, set one up in your classroom. Bring in photos of food items. Take turns pretending to be the vendor and the customers.

B **¿Qué compras en el mercado?** You're at an open-air food market in Peru. Make a list of the items you want to buy. With a classmate, take turns being the vendor and the customer as you shop for the items on your lists.

C **Las comidas para mañana** Work with a classmate. Prepare a menu for tomorrow's meals—**el desayuno, el almuerzo y la cena.** Based on your menus, prepare a shopping list.

Lima, Perú

ANSWERS

Práctica

C 1. Sí. **3. No.**
2. Sí. **4. Sí.**

D 1. c **4. a**
2. d **5. e**
3. f **6. b**

Actividades comunicativas

A and **B** Answers will vary. Students should use the vocabulary from **Palabras 2.** Their conversations should be similar to those on page 139.

C Answers will vary. Students should use the vocabulary from **Palabras 1** and **2.**

C Have students open their books and do **Práctica C.** In more able groups you may have students correct the false statements in **Práctica C.**

D You may wish to have more able students use the words in **Práctica D** in an original sentence.

Actividades comunicativas

¡OJO! These **Actividades comunicativas** enable students to use the language creatively on their own as if they were communicating in real-life, survival situations. They are an excellent follow-up to the more controlled communicative activities in the **Práctica** section.

Let students choose the activities they wish to participate in. It is to be expected that students will make some errors as they communicate on their own.

A **TECHNOLOGY OPTION**
Students can use the Portfolio feature on the CD-ROM to record their conversation in **Actividad A.**

National Standards

Communities
You may wish to organize your students' visit to a Hispanic market in your community (**Actividad A,** page 141) as a class field trip. This would give students an opportunity to practice the vocabulary and structures of the chapter in a real-life setting.

RESOURCES

- Workbook, pages 49–52
- Student Tape Manual, TE, pages 53–54
- Audiocassette 4A/CD3
- Quiz 3, page 25
- Computer Testmaker
- CD-ROM, Disc 2, pages 142–145

Bell Ringer Review

Use BRR Transparency 5-3, or write the following on the board: Complete each verb with the correct ending.

1. **Yo estudi__ mucho.**
2. **Yo prest__ atención cuando la profesora habl__.**
3. **Nosotros tom__ apuntes en clase.**
4. **Tú escuch__ a la profesora cuando ella habl__, ¿no?**
5. **Durante la fiesta yo bail__ y ellos cant__.**

TEACHING STRUCTURE

Describing people's activities

A. Read the introductory paragraph on page 142 to the class.

B. Now have them take a look at the verb paradigms.

C. Put the verbs **comer** and **vivir** on the board. Ask students what to say when:

- talking about someone or talking to a stranger: **Juan/Ud.**
- talking about two people, or to two or more people: **Juan y Sandra/Uds.**
- talking about yourself: **yo**
- talking to a friend: **tú**

(continued on page 143)

Estructura

Describing people's activities
Presente de los verbos en -er e -ir

You have already learned that many Spanish verbs end in **-ar.** These verbs are referred to as first conjugation verbs. Most regular Spanish verbs belong to the **-ar** group. The other two groups of regular verbs in Spanish end in **-er** and **-ir.** Verbs whose infinitive ends in **-er (comer, beber, leer, vender, aprender, comprender)** are second conjugation verbs. Verbs whose infinitive ends in **-ir (vivir, escribir, recibir)** are third conjugation verbs. Study the following forms. Note that the endings of **-er** and **-ir** verbs are the same except for the **nosotros** and **vosotros** forms.

-ER VERBS			
INFINITIVE	comer	leer	
STEM	com-	le-	ENDINGS
yo	como	leo	-o
tú	comes	lees	-es
él, ella, Ud.	come	lee	-e
nosotros(as)	comemos	leemos	-emos
vosotros(as)	*coméis*	*leéis*	*-éis*
ellos, ellas, Uds.	comen	leen	-en

-IR VERBS			
INFINITIVE	vivir	escribir	
STEM	viv-	escrib-	ENDINGS
yo	vivo	escribo	-o
tú	vives	escribes	-es
él, ella, Ud.	vive	escribe	-e
nosotros(as)	vivimos	escribimos	-imos
vosotros(as)	*vivís*	*escribís*	*-ís*
ellos, ellas, Uds.	viven	escriben	-en

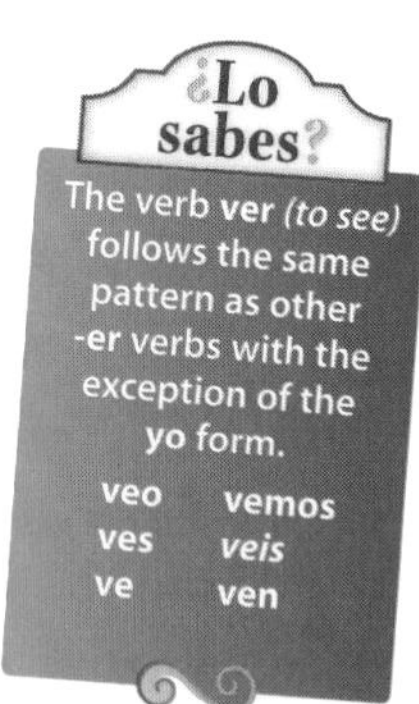

For the Younger Student

Tirar la pelota Have students stand in a circle. Give one student a ball. This student asks a question using an **-er** or **-ir** verb. He or she then throws the ball to another student. The student who catches the ball answers, asks his or her question, and then throws the ball to another student.

Learning From Realia

Mesón Restaurante El Tablón (page 143) Ask the following questions about the restaurant's business card: **¿Cuál es el nombre del restaurante? ¿Dónde está? ¿Cuál es el número de teléfono?** Now find the following expressions on the card: *air conditioning, fine cuisine.*
El menú Ask the following about the menu: **¿Es caro o barato un menú económico? ¿Lleva un plato combinado varias cosas?**

Práctica

A Historieta Un menú español

Lean y contesten. *(Read and answer.)*

PABLO: Linda, ¿lees el menú en español?
LINDA: ¡Sí, claro!
PABLO: Pero, ¿comprendes un menú en español?
LINDA: Sí, comprendo. ¿Por qué preguntas?
PABLO: Pero no eres española. Y no vives aquí en Madrid. ¿Lees el español? ¿Cómo es posible?
LINDA: Pues, aprendo el español en la escuela en Nueva York. En clase hablamos mucho. Leemos y escribimos también.
PABLO: Pues, yo aprendo el inglés aquí en Madrid. Hablo un poco, pero cuando leo no comprendo casi nada. Comprendo muy poco.

1. ¿Qué lee Linda?
2. ¿En qué lengua lee el menú?
3. ¿Comprende el menú?
4. ¿Es de España Linda?
5. ¿Vive ella en Madrid?
6. ¿Por qué comprende? ¿Donde aprende ella el español?
7. En la clase de español, ¿hablan mucho los alumnos?
8. ¿Leen y escriben también?
9. ¿Qué lengua aprende Pablo en Madrid?
10. ¿Comprende él cuando lee algo en inglés?

Madrid, España

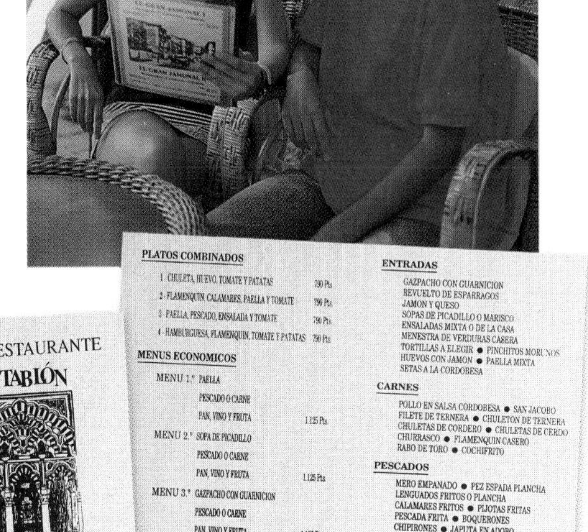

MESON RESTAURANTE
EL TABLÓN
PATIO ANDALUZ
AIRE ACONDICIONADO
AMPLIOS SALONES
COMIDA SELECTA
Y GARANTIZADA
Cardenal González, 69
Teléfono 47 60 61 - Fax 48 62 40
14003 CORDOBA

PLATOS COMBINADOS
MENUS ECONOMICOS
ENTRADAS
CARNES
PESCADOS

ANSWERS

Práctica

A
1. **Linda lee el menú.**
2. **Lee el menú en español.**
3. **Sí, comprende el menú.**
4. **No, Linda no es de España.**
5. **No, no vive en Madrid.**
6. **Comprende porque aprende el español en la escuela en Nueva York.**
7. **Sí, los alumnos hablan mucho.**
8. **Sí, leen y escriben también.**
9. **Pablo aprende el inglés en Madrid.**
10. **No, no comprende nada cuando lee algo en inglés.**

Write the forms on board as you elicit the responses from the class. Point out that the endings for these forms are the same for both **–er** and **–ir** verbs.

D. Teach the **nosotros** form separately from the others since it has a different ending depending on whether it is an **-er** or **-ir** verb. Put more verbs on board and have students repeat the **nosotros** forms: **comemos, leemos, aprendemos, comprendemos, vivimos, escribimos, recibimos.**

Práctica

A Have students open their books to page 143 and repeat the conversation in **Práctica A** after you. Call on two individuals with good pronunciation to read the conversation aloud with as much expression as possible.

Ask the class in English why Pablo is so surprised. Then ask the questions that follow the conversation.

EXPANSION Have a student retell the information in the conversation in his or her own words in narrative form.

RECYCLING

Have students give a complete description of the couple seated at the café in the photo. Have them describe their clothes, as well as their phsical characteristics, and personalities. This activity recycles vocabulary and structures from Chapters 1, 2, and 3.

Práctica

¡OJO! All of the **Práctica** activities can be done with books closed or open. It is recommended that you go over the **Práctica** in class before assigning them for homework.

Writing Development

Students can write **Práctica B, C** and **E** in paragraph form.

Learning From Photos

Cádiz, España Ask the following questions about the photo:
¿Qué lleva el muchacho?
Y la muchacha, ¿qué lleva ella?
¿Cómo es el muchacho?
¿Cómo es la muchacha?
¿Lee el muchacho el periódico?
¿Toman ellos un refresco?
¿Es un café al aire libre?
¿Es el verano o el invierno?

B **Historieta** En un café

Completen. *(Complete.)*

En el café los clientes ___1___ (ver) al mesero. Ellos ___2___ (hablar) con el mesero. Los clientes ___3___ (leer) el menú y ___4___ (decidir) lo que van a comer o beber. Los meseros ___5___ (tomar) la orden y ___6___ (escribir) la orden en una hoja de papel o en un bloc pequeño. Los meseros no ___7___ (leer) el menú. Los clientes ___8___ (leer) el menú. Y los clientes no ___9___ (escribir) la orden. Los meseros ___10___ (escribir) la orden.

C **Yo** Contesten personalmente. *(Answer about yourself.)*

1. ¿Dónde vives?
2. En casa, ¿hablas inglés o español?
3. ¿Aprendes el español en la escuela?
4. En la clase de español, ¿hablas mucho?
5. ¿Lees mucho?
6. ¿Escribes mucho?
7. ¿Comprendes al profesor o a la profesora cuando él o ella habla?
8. ¿Comprendes cuando lees?

D **¿Qué comen todos?** Sigan el modelo. *(Follow the model.)*

carne
Teresa come carne.
—Yo como carne también. / Yo no como carne.
—Y tú, ¿comes carne o no?

1. vegetales
2. pescado
3. mariscos
4. ensalada
5. postre
6. pollo
7. huevos

Cádiz, España

ANSWERS

Práctica

B
1. ven
2. hablan
3. leen
4. deciden
5. toman
6. escriben
7. leen
8. leen
9. escriben
10. escriben

C
1. Vivo en ___.
2. Hablo inglés (español) en casa.
3. Sí, aprendo el español en la escuela.
4. Sí, (No, no) hablo mucho en la clase de español.
5. Sí, (No, no) leo mucho.
6. Sí, (No, no) escribo mucho.
7. Sí, (No, no) comprendo al profesor (a la profesora) cuando él (ella) habla.
8. Sí, (No, no) comprendo cuando leo.

D Answers will follow the model.

E Nosotros Contesten personalmente. *(Answer about yourself and a friend.)*

1. ¿Dónde viven Uds.?
2. ¿A qué escuela asisten Uds. (van Uds.)?
3. ¿Escriben Uds. mucho en la clase de español?
4. ¿Escriben Uds. mucho en la clase de inglés?
5. ¿Leen Uds. mucho en la clase de español?
6. ¿En qué clase leen Uds. novelas y poemas?
7. ¿Aprenden Uds. mucho en la clase de español?
8. ¿Comprenden Uds. cuando el profesor o la profesora habla?
9. ¿Ven Uds. un video en la clase de español?
10. Recibimos notas buenas en español. ¿Reciben Uds. notas buenas también?

¿Lo sabes? The verb asistir is a false cognate. It means "to attend."

F ¿Toman Uds. un refresco? Sigan el modelo. *(Follow the model.)*

Coca-Cola
Nosotros bebemos Coca-Cola. / No bebemos Coca-Cola.
¿Y Uds.? ¿Beben Coca-Cola o no?

1. café solo
2. café con leche
3. leche
4. limonada
5. té

Actividades comunicativas

A ¿Qué comes? With a classmate, take turns finding out what each of you eats for breakfast, lunch, and dinner.

B ¿Cuánto es, por favor? You are at a little café in South America. Your classmate is the waiter or waitress. Order something you want to eat and drink. Then find out how much it is. The waiter or waitress can refer to the menu to tell you how much you owe.

Café Luna

sándwich	14 pesos
tamal	10 pesos
enchilada	11 pesos
café	2 pesos
limonada	3 pesos
Coca-Cola	3 pesos

C El curso de inglés Have a discussion with a classmate about your English class. Tell as much as you can about what you do and learn in class. You may want to use some of the following words.

CAPÍTULO 5
Estructura

E and **F** You may wish to have students do these activities in small groups.

Actividades comunicativas

A TECHNOLOGY OPTION In the CD-ROM version of this activity (Disc 2, page 145), students can interact with an on-screen, native speaker and record their voice.

B Groups doing **Actividad B** can also present their skit to the class.

TECHNOLOGY OPTION Students can also use the Portfolio feature on the CD-ROM to record this conversation.

C Students doing **Actividad C** can put their information together as a report and present it to the class.

¡OJO! All new material in this chapter has been presented. The sections that follow recombine and reintroduce the vocabulary and structures that have already been introduced.

ANSWERS

Práctica

E
1. **Vivimos en ___.**
2. **Asistimos a la Escuela ___.**
3. **Sí, (No, no) escribimos mucho en la clase de español.**
4. **Sí, (No, no) escribimos mucho en la clase de inglés.**
5. **Sí, (No, no) leemos mucho en la clase de español.**
6. **Leemos novelas y poemas en la clase de inglés (en la clase de español).**
7. **Sí, (No, no) aprendemos mucho en la clase de español.**
8. **Sí, (No, no) comprendemos mucho cuando el/la profesor(a) habla.**
9. **Sí, (No, no) vemos un video en la clase de español.**
10. **Sí, (No, no) recibimos notas buenas en español.**

F Answers will follow the model.

Actividades comunicativas

A and B Answers will vary. Students should use the vocabulary from **Palabras 1** and **2**.

C Answers will vary, however, students should use the appropriate forms of the verbs in the colored boxes.

RESOURCES

- Audiocassette 4A/CD3
- CD-ROM, Disc 2, page 146

Bell Ringer Review

Use BRR Transparency 5-4, or write the following on the board: Read the following conversation and write down where it takes place.

—Necesito un cuaderno.
—Hay muchos cuadernos allí en la mesa.
—¿Cuánto es?
—Doscientas pesetas.
—¿Pago aquí o en la caja?
—Ud. paga en la caja.

TEACHING THE CONVERSATION

A. To vary the presentation, tell students nothing at all about the conversation. Have them listen to it as you play Cassette 4A/Compact Disc 3.
B. Play the recording once again and have students look at the photo as they listen.
C. Have three students take the roles of Julia, Carlos, and the **mesero** and read the conversation aloud using as much expression as possible.
D. Ask the questions that follow in the **Después de conversar** section.
E. Have students make up a similar conversation on their own.
F. After presenting the conversation, go over the **Después de conversar** activity. If students can answer the questions with relative ease, move on. Students should not be expected to memorize the conversation.

Conversación

En la terraza de un café

JULIA: Carlos, hay mucha gente en el café.
CARLOS: Sí, veo que no hay muchas mesas libres.
JULIA: Verdad, pero allí hay una. ¿Ves? ¡Vamos!
CARLOS: ¡Vale!
(Llegan a la mesa y Julia lee el menú.)
MESERO: Señores, ¿desean Uds. tomar algo?
JULIA: Sí, para mí una limonada, por favor.
CARLOS: Y para mí un café con leche.
MESERO: Sí, señores. Enseguida.
(Julia y Carlos hablan mientras toman el refresco.)
CARLOS: ¿Qué lees, Julia?
JULIA: Leo una novela de Isabel Allende. Es excelente.
(Unos momentos después)
CARLOS: Mesero, la cuenta, por favor.
MESERO: Sí, señor.

Después de conversar

Contesten. *(Answer.)*

1. ¿Dónde están Julia y Carlos?
2. ¿Hay mucha gente en el café?
3. ¿Qué ve Julia?
4. ¿Qué lee Julia?
5. ¿Con quién hablan Carlos y Julia?
6. ¿Qué desea Julia?
7. ¿Y Carlos?
8. ¿Qué novela lee Julia?
9. ¿Cómo es la novela?

ANSWERS

Después de conversar

1. **Julia y Carlos están en (la terraza de) un café.**
2. **Sí, hay mucha gente en el café.**
3. **Julia ve una mesa libre.**
4. **Lee el menú.**
5. **Carlos y Julia hablan con el mesero.**
6. **Julia desea una limonada.**
7. **Carlos desea un café con leche.**
8. **Julia lee una novela de Isabel Allende.**
9. **La novela es excelente.**

ABOUT THE SPANISH LANGUAGE

The expression **¡Vale!** is used a great deal in Spain. It's similar to the English expression *OK.*

Actividades comunicativas

A **En el café** Work in groups of three or four. You're all friends from Madrid. After school you go to a café where you talk about lots of things—school, teachers, friends, etc. One of you will play the role of the waiter or waitress at the café. You have to interrupt the conversation once in a while to take the orders and serve.

B **¿Qué preparamos?** Work in groups of three or four. The Spanish Club is having a party and you're planning the menu. You want to have one dish with meat and one without meat, since there are quite a few students who are vegetarians **(vegetarianos)**. Look at the menu the club members have prepared and decide what you have to buy at the supermarket.

para comer:
sándwiches
hamburguesas
ensaladas
fruta
para beber:
refrescos
café

PRONUNCIACIÓN

La consonante d

The pronunciation of **d** in Spanish varies according to its position in the word. When a word begins with **d** (initial position) or follows the consonants **l** or **n,** the tongue gently strikes the back of the upper front teeth.

da	de	di	do	du
da	**dependiente**	**difícil**	**domingo**	**dulce**
merienda	**vende**	**andino**	**condominio**	

When **d** appears within the word between vowels (medial position), **d** is extremely soft. Your tongue should strike the lower part of your upper teeth, almost between the upper and lower teeth.

da	de	di	do	du
privada	**modelo**	**estudio**	**helado**	**educación**
ensalada	**cuaderno**	**medio**	**congelado**	

When a word ends in **d** (final position), **d** is either extremely soft or omitted completely—not pronounced.

nacionalidad **ciudad**

Repeat the following sentences.

Diego da el disco compacto a Donato en la ciudad.
El dependiente vende helado y limonada.
Adela compra la merienda en la tienda.

ANSWERS

Actividades comunicativas

A Answers will vary. Students may wish to use the conversation on page 146 as a model.

B Answers will vary, but should include the food items from **Palabras 1** and **2.**

TECHNOLOGY OPTION

In the CD-ROM version (Disc 2, page 146), students can watch a dramatization of the conversation on page 146. They can then play the role of either one of the characters, and record themselves in the conversation.

Actividades comunicativas

Allow students to choose the activities they would like to participate in.

TEACHING PRONUNCIATION

A. This is a very difficult sound for most English speakers to produce correctly. Have students imitate the sounds carefully, paying particular attention to the position of the tongue, as explained in the presentation. You may also wish to use Cassette 4A/Compact Disc 3 to present this material.

B. The model words and sentences on page 147 can also be used for dictation to determine the accuracy of students' spelling.

TECHNOLOGY OPTION

In the CD-ROM version of the Pronunciation section (Disc 2, page 147), students will see an animation of the cartoon on this page. They can also listen to, record, and play back the sounds, words, and sentences presented here.

CAPÍTULO 5
Lecturas

Bell Ringer Review

Use BRR Transparency 5-5, or write the following on the board: Complete with the correct nationality.

1. **Tomás es de San Juan. Él es ___.**
2. **Teresa es de Santiago de Cuba. Ella es ___.**
3. **Los amigos de José son de Santiago de Chile. Ellos son ___.**
4. **Las dos profesoras son de Guanajuato, México. Ellas son ___.**

National Standards

Cultures

The reading about cafés in Madrid and meal times in Spain on page 148, and the related activities on page 149, give students insight into daily life in Spain.

TEACHING THE READING

Pre-reading

A. Give students about two minutes to scan the first paragraph on page 148. In English, have them tell in one sentence what it's about.

B. Do the same with the second paragraph on page 149.

Reading

A. Call on individual students to read aloud.

B. Intersperse comprehension questions such as:

¿Dónde vive José Luis?
¿Adónde van los amigos de José Luis?
¿Cuándo van?
¿Cómo van al café?

(continued on page 149)

Lecturas CULTURALES

Reading Strategy

Guessing meaning from context

It's easy to understand words you have already studied. There are also ways to understand words you are not familiar with. One way is to use the context—the way these words are used in the sentence or reading—to help you guess the meaning of those words you do not know.

EN UN CAFÉ EN MADRID

José Luis vive en Madrid. Después de las clases, los amigos de José Luis van juntos, en grupo, a un café. En el otoño y en la primavera, ellos van a un café al aire libre[1]. Pasan una hora o más en el café. Toman un refresco y a veces comen un bocadillo o un pan dulce. En el café, hablan y hablan. Hablan de la escuela, de los amigos, de la familia. Y a veces miran a la gente que pasa.

[1]al aire libre *outdoor*

Paseo de la Castellana, Madrid

Madrid, España

Learning From Photos

Paseo de la Castellana, Madrid The café in the top photo is on Paseo de la Castellana, a lovely, wide boulevard that runs for several kilometers. It is lined with beautiful old mansions and elegant apartment buildings.
Madrid, España This photo was taken just off the Puerta del Sol. Located right in the city center, the Puerta del Sol is Madrid's traffic nerve center. The bronze statue in the background of **el oso y el madroño** is Madrid's official symbol—a bear sniffing a strawberry tree.

Independent Practice

Assign any of the following:

1. **Después de leer** activities, page 149
2. Workbook, **Un poco más,** pages 153–155
3. CD-ROM, Disc 2, pages 148–149

Después de una hora o más, van a casa. Cuando llegan a casa, ¿comen o cenan enseguida, inmediatamente? No, no comen inmediatamente. En España, no cenan hasta las diez o las diez y media de la noche. Pero en España y en algunos países latinoamericanos la comida principal es la comida del mediodía.

Estepona, España

Después de leer

A **José Luis** Contesten con **sí** o **no.** *(Answer with* sí *or* no.)

1. José Luis es un muchacho de la Ciudad de México.
2. José Luis va solo al café.
3. En el invierno, José Luis y un grupo de amigos van a un café al aire libre.
4. En el café, toman un refresco.
5. Hablan de muchas cosas diferentes.
6. Pasan solamente unos minutos en el café.
7. Cuando llegan a casa, los muchachos comen enseguida con la familia.
8. La comida principal es la cena.

B **La verdad, por favor.** Corrijan las oraciones falsas de la Actividad A. *(Correct the false statements from Activity A.)*

These questions have a dual objective. They check comprehension and they also allow students to use the language so that, upon completion of the reading, they can discuss the information on their own.

Post-reading

A. Go over the **Después de leer** activities on this page.

B. Call on a student to summarize the **Lectura** in his or her own words.

TECHNOLOGY OPTION

Students may listen to a recorded version of the **Lectura** on the CD-ROM, Disc 2, pages 148–149.

Writing Development

You may wish to have some students write a summary of the **Lectura.**

ANSWERS

Después de leer

A
1. **No, José Luis no es un muchacho de la Ciudad de México.**
2. **No, José Luis no va solo al café.**
3. **No, José Luis y un grupo de amigos no van a un café al aire libre en el invierno.**
4. **Sí, toman un refresco en el café.**
5. **Sí, hablan de muchas cosas diferentes.**
6. **No, no pasan solamente unos minutos en el café.**
7. **No, cuando llegan a casa, los muchachos no comen enseguida.**
8. **No la comida principal no es la cena.**

B
1. **José Luis es un muchacho de Madrid.**
2. **José Luis y un grupo de amigos van juntos al café.**
3. **En el otoño y en la primavera, José Luis y un grupo de amigos van a un café al aire libre.**
4. **Pasan una hora o más en el café.**
5. **Cuando llegan a casa, los muchachos no comen hasta las diez o las diez y media de la noche.**
6. **La comida principal es la comida del mediodía.**

LECTURA OPCIONAL 1

National Standards

Cultures
The reading about dining hours and meals in the Spanish-speaking world, and the related activities on page 150, give students an understanding of daily life in Spain and Latin America.

Comparisons
This reading selection compares dining hours and eating habits in the Spanish-speaking world with those of the United States.

TEACHING TIPS

¡OJO! This reading is optional. You may skip it completely, have the entire class read it, have only several students read it, or assign it for extra credit.

Learning From Photos

Buenos Aires, Argentina Have students take a look at the colorful buses in Buenos Aires. There are many different terms for *bus* and in Argentina a municipal bus is usually called **un colectivo.**

LECTURA OPCIONAL 1

LAS HORAS PARA COMER

El desayuno

En España y en los países de Latinoamérica, la gente suele[1] comer más tarde que aquí en los Estados Unidos. Como nosotros, toman el desayuno a eso de las siete o las ocho de la mañana. A eso de las diez van a un café o a una cafetería donde toman otro café con leche y un churro o pan dulce.

Buenos Aires, Argentina

El almuerzo

El almuerzo es a la una o, en el caso de España, a eso de las dos de la tarde. Hoy día la mayoría[2] de la gente no va a casa a tomar el almuerzo. Toman el almuerzo en la cafetería de la escuela o en la cafetería donde trabajan. Si no, comen en un café o en un restaurante. Muchos no van a casa a tomar el almuerzo porque hay mucho tráfico. Tarda (toma) demasiado tiempo[3].

La cena

En la mayoría de los países latinoamericanos la gente suele cenar a las ocho y media o a las nueve. Pero, en España, no. En España la cena es a las diez o a las diez y media.

[1]suele *tend to*
[2]mayoría *majority*
[3]demasiado tiempo *too much time*

Después de leer

A ¡A comer en el mundo hispano! Contesten. *(Answer.)*

1. ¿Dónde suele comer la gente más tarde, en los Estados Unidos o en los países hispanos?
2. ¿A qué hora toman el desayuno en los países hispanos?
3. ¿A qué hora toman Uds. el desayuno?
4. ¿A qué hora es el almuerzo?
5. ¿Dónde toma la gente el almuerzo?
6. ¿Van muchos a casa?
7. ¿Por qué no van a casa?
8. ¿A qué hora cenan en Latinoamérica?
9. Y en España, ¿a qué hora cenan?
10. ¿A qué hora cenan Uds.?

ANSWERS

Después de leer

A
1. **La gente suele comer más tarde en los países hispanos.**
2. **Toman el desayuno a eso de las siete o las ocho de la mañana en los países hispanos.**
3. **Tomamos el desayuno a eso de las ___.**
4. **El almuerzo es a la una o, en el caso de España, a eso de las dos de la tarde.**
5. **La gente toma el almuerzo en la cafetería de la escuela o en la cafetería donde trabajan.**
6. **No, muchos no van a casa.**
7. **No van a casa porque hay mucho tráfico. Tarda demasiado tiempo.**
8. **Cenan a las ocho y media o a las nueve.**
9. **En España cenan a las diez o a las diez y media.**
10. **Cenamos a eso de las ___.**

LECTURA OPCIONAL 2

¿MERCADO O SUPERMERCADO?

En los países hispanos hay muchos mercados. Algunos son mercados al aire libre. En el mercado la gente compra los alimentos o comestibles[1] que necesitan para las tres comidas. Los productos que venden en los mercados están muy frescos[2]. ¡Qué deliciosos!

Barcelona, España

Sevilla, España

Hay también supermercados—sobre todo (particularmente) en las grandes ciudades y en los alrededores[3] de las grandes ciudades. En los supermercados venden muchos productos en lata, en paquete o en bolsa. En los supermercados hay un gran surtido[4] de productos congelados.

[1]comestibles *foods*
[2]frescos *fresh*
[3]alrededores *outskirts*
[4]surtido *assortment*

Después de leer

A De compras para la comida Completen. *(Complete.)*

1. En los países hispanos hay ____.
2. En los mercados la gente compra ____.
3. Los productos del mercado están ____.
4. Hay supermercados en ____.
5. En los supermercados venden ____.

B Otra expresión Busquen una expresión equivalente en la lectura. *(Find an equivalent expression in the reading for the italicized words.)*

1. En *las naciones* hispanas hay muchos mercados al aire libre.
2. La gente compra *los alimentos* que necesitan.
3. Están muy frescos. ¡Y qué ricos y *sabrosos!*
4. Venden productos *enlatados.*
5. Hay *una gran selección.*

LECTURA OPCIONAL 2

National Standards

Cultures The reading and the related activities on this page introduce students to the types of food stores that exist in the Spanish-speaking world.

TEACHING TIPS

A. Have students read the two paragraphs quickly on their own.

B. Now do the **Despúes de leer** activities with them orally.

INFORMAL ASSESSMENT

You may want to give the following quiz to those students who read this selection:

Answer.

1. **¿Qué hay en los países hispanos?**
2. **¿Están al aire libre algunos de los mercados?**
3. **¿Qué compra la gente en el mercado?**
4. **¿Cómo están los productos que venden en el mercado?**
5. **¿Hay supermercados?**
6. **¿Dónde hay supermercados?**
7. **¿Qué venden en los supermercados?**

ANSWERS

Después de leer

A
1. **muchos mercados**
2. **los alimentos o comestibles que necesita para las tres comidas**
3. **muy frescos**
4. **las grandes ciudades y en los alrededores de las grandes ciudades**
5. **muchos productos en lata, en paquete o en bolsa y productos congelados**

B
1. **los países**
2. **los comestibles**
3. **deliciosos**
4. **en lata**
5. **un gran surtido**

Learning From Photos

Sevilla, España Small supermarkets like this one are often found in large cities. Supermarkets located on the outskirts of the city are much larger.

National Standards

Connections

This reading about arithmetic establishes a connection with another discipline, allowing students to reinforce and further their knowledge of mathematics through the study of Spanish.

Comparisons

Students are introduced to the different way some numbers are handwritten and the different use of the decimal point.

¡OJO! The readings in the **Conexiones** section are optional. They focus on the some of the major disciplines taught in schools and universities. The vocabulary is useful for discussing such topics as history, literature, art, economics, business, science, etc.

You may choose any of the following ways to do this reading on arithmetic with your students.

Independent reading Have students read the selections and do the post-reading activities as homework, which you collect. This option is least intrusive on class time and requires a minimum of teacher involvement.

Homework with in-class follow-up Assign the readings and post-reading activities as homework. Review and discuss the material in class the next day.

Intensive in-class activity This option includes a pre-reading vocabulary presentation, in-class reading and discussion, assignment of the activities for homework, and a discussion of the assignment in class the following day.

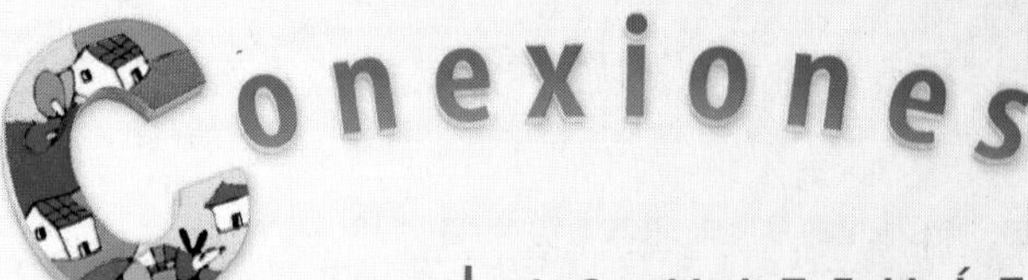

Las matemáticas

La aritmética

When we go shopping or out to eat, it is often necessary to do some arithmetic. We either have to add up the bill ourselves or check the figures someone else has done for us. In a café or restaurant we want to figure out how much tip we should leave. In order to do this we have to do some arithmetic.

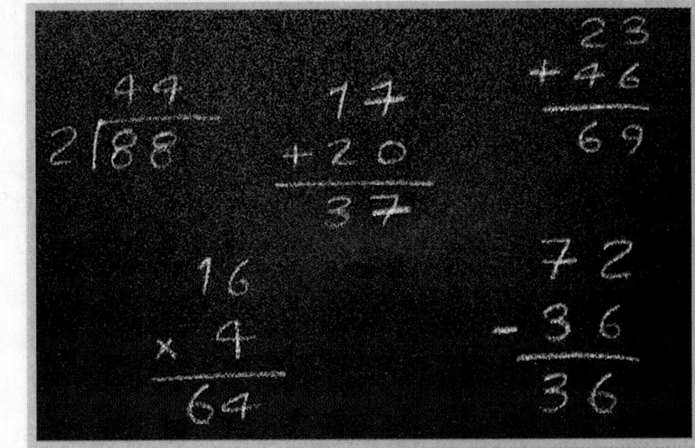

We seldom do a great deal of arithmetic in a foreign language. We normally do arithmetic in the language in which we learned it. It is fun, however, to know some basic arithmetical terms in case we have to discuss a bill or a problem with a Spanish-speaking person.

Before we learn some of these terms in Spanish, let's look at some differences in numbers. Note how the numbers 1 and 7 are written in some areas of the Spanish-speaking world.

1 7

Note too the difference in the use of the decimal point in some countries.

1,000 1.000 1,07 1.07

La aritmética

sumar	+
restar	−
multiplicar	×
dividir	÷

Para resolver un problema oralmente

Suma dos y dos.
Dos y dos son cuatro. $2 + 2 = 4$

Resta dos de cinco.
Cinco menos dos son tres. $5 - 2 = 3$

Multiplica dos por cinco.
Dos por cinco son diez. $2 \times 5 = 10$

Divide quince entre tres.
Quince entre tres son cinco. $15 \div 3 = 5$

El diez por ciento de ciento cincuenta pesos son quince pesos.

Después de leer

A **¿Cuánto es?** Resuelvan los problemas aritméticos en voz alta. *(Solve the following problems aloud.)*

1. $2 + 2 = 4$	**5.** $4 \times 4 = 16$
2. $14 + 6 = 20$	**6.** $8 \times 3 = 24$
3. $30 - 8 = 22$	**7.** $27 \div 9 = 3$
4. $20 - 4 = 16$	**8.** $80 \div 4 = 20$

B **La respuesta, por favor.** Contesten en español. *(Do the following problems in Spanish.)*

1. Suma 5 y 2.	**5.** Multiplica 5 por 3.
2. Suma 20 y 3.	**6.** Multiplica 9 por 4.
3. Resta 3 de 10.	**7.** Divide 9 entre 3.
4. Resta 8 de 25.	**8.** Divide 16 entre 2.

C **La cuenta, por favor.** Sumen. *(Add up the following bill in Spanish.)*

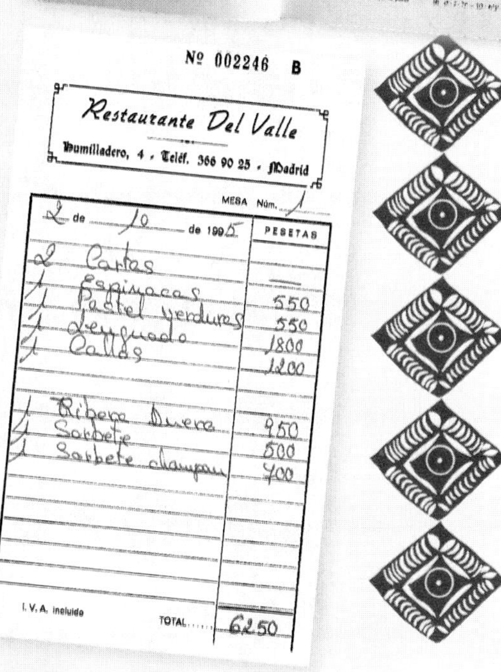
Nº 002246 B
Restaurante Del Valle
Humilladero, 4 · Teléf. 366 90 25 · Madrid
MESA Núm. 1
2 de 10 de 1995 — PESETAS

2	Cartas	
1	Espinacas	550
1	Pastel verduras	550
1	Lenguado	1800
1	Callos	1200
1	Ribera Duero	950
1	Sorbete	500
1	Sorbete champaña	700

I.V.A. incluido — TOTAL 6250

Las matemáticas

La aritmética

¡OJO! As the introduction states, one rarely does arithmetic in a foreign language. The purpose of this section is to introduce students to only the most basic and important arithmetical terms.

A. Go over the reading with the students. Before beginning the **Despúes de leer** activities, call on students to do the math problems orally from the blackboard on page 152.

Learning From Realia

La cuenta, por favor. Have students look at the way the numbers 1 and 7 are written on this bill.

ANSWERS

Después de leer

A
1. **Dos y dos son cuatro.**
2. **Catorce y seis son veinte.**
3. **Treinta menos ocho son veintidós.**
4. **Veinte menos cuatro son dieciséis.**
5. **Cuatro por cuatro son dieciséis.**
6. **Ocho por tres son veinticuatro.**
7. **Veintisiete entre nueve son tres.**
8. **Ochenta entre cuatro son veinte.**

B
1. **Cinco y dos son siete.**
2. **Veinte y tres son veintitrés.**
3. **Diez menos tres son siete.**
4. **Veinticinco menos ocho son diecisiete.**
5. **Cinco por tres son quince.**
6. **Nueve por cuatro son treinta y seis.**
7. **Nueve entre tres son tres.**
8. **Dieciséis entre dos son ocho.**

C Students should say all the amounts in Spanish and then give the total: **Seis mil doscientas cincuenta**

CAPÍTULO 5
Culminación

RECYCLING

The **Actividades orales** and the **Actividad escrita** allow students to use the vocabulary and structure from this chapter in open-ended, real-life settings. Students should feel free to use any Spanish they have learned up to this point.

Actividades orales

¡OJO! Encourage students to say as much as possible when they do these activities. Tell them not to be afraid of making mistakes since the goal of the activities is real-life communication. If someone in the group makes an error, allow the others to politely correct him or her. Let students choose the activities they would like to participate in.

B TECHNOLOGY OPTION
Students can use the Portfolio feature on the CD-ROM to record this conversation.

Student Portfolio

Have students keep a notebook containing their best written work from each chapter. These selected writings can be based on assignments from the Student Textbook and the Writing Activities Workbook. The two activities on page 155 are examples of writing assignments that may be included in each student's portfolio.

In the Workbook, students will develop an organized autobiography **(Mi autobiografía).** These workbook pages may also become a part of their portfolio. See the Teacher's Manual for more information on the Student Portfolio.

Culminación

Actividades orales

A En el mercado You are spending a semester studying in Spain. You are going to prepare a dinner for your "Spanish family." Decide what you need to buy at the market. Then have a conversation with a classmate who will be the clerk at the food store.

B En el café Work with a classmate. One of you is the customer and the other is a waiter or waitress in a café. Have a conversation. Say as much as you can to each other.

JUEGO Una competición Compete with a classmate. See which one of you can make up the most expressions using the following words.

un kilo | un paquete | una botella | una docena | una lata | una bolsa

Las Ramblas, Barcelona

Madrid, España

ANSWERS

Actividades orales

A Answers will vary. Students should write their grocery lists before beginning their conversations.

B Answers will vary.

Learning From Photos

Las Ramblas, Barcelona Las Ramblas is a series of boulevards, each with its own name—Rambla Santa Mónica, Ramblas de les Flors, in Catalan. People stroll them 24 hours a day. The market seen here is Barcelona's most spectacular food market, **la Boquería** or **Mercat de Sant Josep.**
Madrid, España The store in the bottom photo, **El Museo del jamón,** is one of a chain of stores specializing in all types of ham and sausage, such as **jamón serrano** and **chorizo.**

Actividad escrita

A El menú Write a menu in Spanish for your school cafeteria.

Estepona, España

Writing Strategy

Clustering

Most writers brainstorm ideas before they begin to write. The next logical step is to "cluster" these ideas. This is done by writing down your main ideas and drawing a box around each one. Then draw a line indicating which ideas are connected to each other. Once you do this, it is easy to add other details to each cluster of ideas. When beginning to write, sort out your clusters and present each in a logical and organized paragraph.

Un restaurante bueno

You have been asked to write a short article about a Spanish restaurant in your community. If there isn't one where you live, make one up. Be sure to include the name of the restaurant, whether it's big or small, expensive or inexpensive, what you usually eat and drink there, whether the meals are good, and what the restaurant's specialty **(la especialidad)** is, if any.

Actividad escrita

A You may ask students to write the school cafeteria menu in Spanish for a given day or for the whole week.

Writing Strategy

Clustering

Have students read the Writing Strategy on page 155 and identify the main ideas before they begin to write.

National Standards

Communities

To do the Writing Strategy activity, **Un restaurante bueno**, on page 155, students should go, if possible, to a Spanish restaurant in their community. You may wish to organize this as a field trip with your class so that the students can practice their Spanish in a real-life setting.

Learning From Photos

Estepona, España Tell students: **Es el Colegio San José en Estepona,** then ask them: **¿Están las muchachas en clase o en la cafetería?¿Toman el almuerzo en la escuela?¿Qué llevan los muchachos?** Students may want to know how to say *tray,* **la bandeja**.

El churrasco Have students look at the restaurant sign. Tell them that in Argentina, Uruguay and Chile, **el churrasco** is the word for *steak* or *filet of beef.*

ANSWERS

Actividad escrita

A Answers will vary, but should include the various food items taught in this chapter.

Writing Strategy

Answers will vary.

CAPÍTULO 5
Vocabulario

ASSESSMENT RESOURCES

- Chapter Quizzes
- Testing Program
- Computer Testmaker
- Situation Cards
- Communication Transparency C-5
- Performance Assessment
- **Maratón mental** Videoquiz

VOCABULARY REVIEW

The words and phrases in the **Vocabulario** have been taught for productive use in this chapter. They are summarized here as a resource for both students and teacher. This list also serves as a convenient resource for the **Culminación** activities on pages 154 and 155. More foods will be presented in Chapter 14. There are approximately twenty cognates in this vocabulary list. Have students find them.

Did You Know?

Churros Churros are fried in olive oil and coated with sugar. Ideally they are served hot. People dunk them in either **café con leche** or **chocolate.**

Vocabulario

GETTING ALONG IN A CAFÉ

el café
la mesa
el/la mesero(a),
  el/la camarero(a)
el menú
la orden
la cuenta
libre
ocupado(a)
ver
leer
comer
beber
¿Qué desean Uds.?
¿Está incluido el servicio?

IDENTIFYING SNACKS AND BEVERAGES

los refrescos
una Coca-Cola
un café solo, con leche
un té helado
una limonada
el cereal
el pan tostado
un yogur
una sopa
un bocadillo,
  un sándwich
el jamón
el queso
una hamburguesa
papas fritas
una tortilla
una ensalada
el postre
un helado de vainilla,
  de chocolate
un pan dulce

SHOPPING FOR FOOD

el mercado
el supermercado
un bote, una lata
un paquete
una bolsa
un kilo
congelado(a)
vender
¿A cuánto está(n)?
algo más
nada más

IDENTIFYING FOODS AND MEALS

los vegetales
  los guisantes
  las habichuelas,
    los frijoles
  las judías verdes
  las zanahorias
  las papas
  la lechuga
las frutas
  las naranjas
  las manzanas
  los plátanos
  los tomates
la carne
el biftec
los mariscos
el pescado
el pollo
el huevo
el atún
el arroz
las comidas
el desayuno
el almuerzo
la cena

OTHER USEFUL EXPRESSIONS

juntos(as)
antes de
después de
enseguida
comprender
aprender
escribir
recibir
vivir

For the Younger Student

El mercado Have students set up a little market place in class. You can use boxes or desks and chairs and plastic foods. Have them go to the "market" when they do the activities in the chapter that are market- or store-related.

Independent Practice

Assign any of the following:
1. Activities, pages 154–155
2. Workbook, **Mi autobiografía,** page 56
3. Situation Cards
4. CD-ROM, Disc 2, Chapter 5, **Juego de repaso**

VIDEO

¡Buen viaje!

EPISODIO 5 ▸ En el café

Después de llegar a Madrid, Juan Ramón y Teresa comen en un café.

Después, van de compras a un mercado.

CD-ROM

Expansión cultural

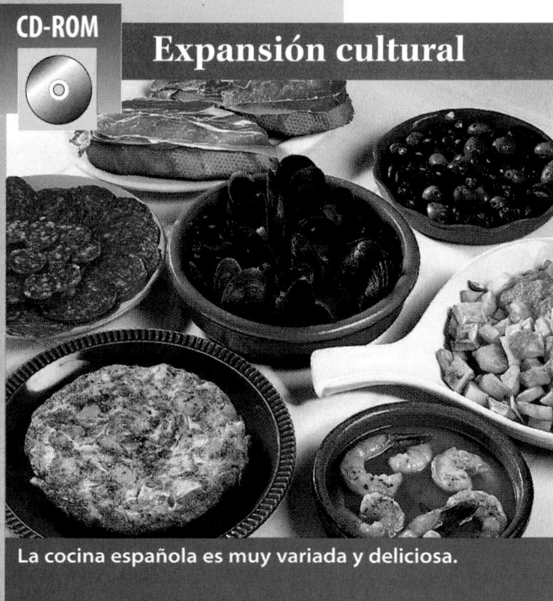

La cocina española es muy variada y deliciosa.

In this video episode, Juan Ramón and Teresa have lunch at a café in Madrid and stop at the market on the way home to pick up a few things. To find out more about foods in the Spanish-speaking world, go to the Capítulo 5 Internet activity at the Glencoe Foreign Language Web site:

http://www.glencoe.com/sec/fl

Video Synopsis

In this episode Juan Ramón arrives in Madrid to stay with Teresa and her family while they work on the Web site project. The teens exchange e-mail messages describing what they'll be wearing so that they will be sure to recognize each other when they meet for the first time at a café in Madrid. Their first "live" conversation is a little awkward as the teens get to know each other. During lunch Juan Rámon, who is from Los Angeles, discovers the difference between **una tortilla mexicana** and **una tortilla española.** He and Teresa make a grocery list before stopping by a local produce market on the way home to pick up a few items for Teresa's mother.

CAPÍTULO 5

Tecnotur

OVERVIEW

This page previews three key multimedia components of the **Glencoe Spanish** series. Each reinforces the material taught in Chapter 5 in a unique manner.

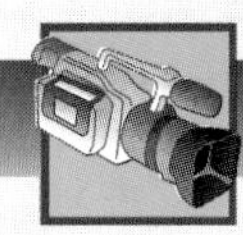

VIDEO

The Video Program allows students to see how the chapter vocabulary and structures are used by native speakers within an engaging story line. For maximum reinforcement, show the video episode as a final activity for Chapter 5.

A. These photos show highlights of the Chapter 5 video episode. Before watching it, have students imagine Teresa and Juan Ramon's conversation as they meet for the first time. Have them name as many items as they can from the market photo.

B. Now show the episode. See the Video Activities Booklet for detailed suggestions for using this resource.

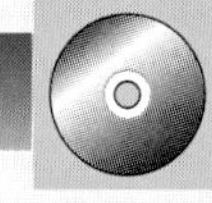

CD-ROM

A. The **Expansión cultural** photo shows some typical Spanish **tapas: jamón serrano, aceitunas, chorizo, mejillones, tortilla española,** and **gambas al ajillo.**

B. In the CD-ROM version of **Expansión cultural** (Disc 2, page 157), students can listen to additional recorded information about Spanish foods.

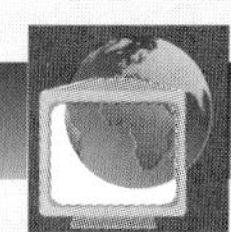

INTERNET

Teacher Information and Student Worksheets for this activity can be accessed at the Web site.

Chapter 6 Overview

SCOPE AND SEQUENCE pages 158–187

TOPICS	FUNCTIONS	STRUCTURE	CULTURE
◆ Family relationships ◆ Rooms in a house or apartment ◆ Telling your age	◆ How to talk about your family ◆ How to describe your home ◆ How to talk about birth-days ◆ How to tell what you have to do ◆ How to discuss what you are going to do ◆ How to talk about what belongs to you and others	◆ The verb **tener** ◆ **Tener que; Ir a** ◆ Possessive adjectives	◆ The importance of family ◆ Godparents ◆ An invitation to a baptism ◆ **La quinceañera** ◆ ***Las Meninas*** by Diego Velázquez ◆ Great artists from Spain and Latin America

CHAPTER 6 RESOURCES

PRINT	MULTIMEDIA
Planning Resources	
Lesson Plans Block Scheduling Lesson Plans	Interactive Lesson Planner
Reinforcement Resources	
Writing Activities Workbook Student Tape Manual Video Activities Booklet Web Site User's Guide	Transparencies Binder Audiocassette/Compact Disc Program Videocassette/Videodisc Program Online Internet Activities Electronic Teacher's Classroom Resources
Assessment Resources	
Situation Cards Chapter Quizzes Testing Program Performance Assessment	**Maratón mental** Mindjogger Videoquiz Testmaker Computer Software (Macintosh/Windows) Listening Comprehension Audiocassette/Compact Disc Communication Transparency: C-6
Motivational Resources	
Expansion Activities	Café Glencoe: www.cafe.glencoe.com Keypal Internet Activities
Enrichment	
Spanish for Spanish Speakers	Fine Art Transparencies: F-4, F-5, F-6, F-7, F-8, F-9

Chapter 6 Planning Guide

SECTION	PAGES	SECTION RESOURCES
Vocabulario Palabras 1 **La familia**	160–163	Vocabulary Transparencies 6.1 Audiocassette 4B/ Compact Disc 4 Student Tape Manual, TE, pages 60–63 Workbook, pages 57–58 Chapter Quizzes, pages 26–27 CD-ROM, Disc 2, pages 160–163
Vocabulario Palabras 2 **La casa** **Una casa de apartamentos (departamentos)**	164–167	Vocabulary Transparencies 6.2 Audiocassette 4B/ Compact Disc 4 Student Tape Manual, TE, pages 64–67 Workbook, pages 58–60 Chapter Quizzes, page 28 CD-ROM, Disc 2, pages 164–167
Estructura **Presente de tener** **Tener que; Ir a** **Adjetivos posesivos**	168–175	Workbook, pages 61–64 Audiocassette 4B/Compact Disc 4 Student Tape Manual, TE, pages 67–70 Chapter Quizzes, pages 29–31 Computer Testmaker CD-ROM, Disc 2, pages 168–175
Conversación **¿Tú tienes una hermana?** **Pronunciación: Las consonantes b, v**	176–177	Audiocassette 4B/Compact Disc 4 Student Tape Manual, TE, pages 71–72 CD-ROM, Disc 2, pages 176–177
Lecturas culturales **La familia hispana** **La quinceañera *(opcional)*** ***Las Meninas (opcional)***	178–181	Testing Program, pages 33–34 CD-ROM, Disc 2, pages 178–181
Conexiones **El arte *(opcional)***	182–183	Testing Program, page 34 CD-ROM, Disc 2, pages 182–183
Culminación **Actividades orales** **Actividades escritas** **Vocabulario** **Tecnotur**	184–187	**¡Buen viaje!** Video, Episode 6 Video Activities, pages 85–88 Internet Activities www.glencoe.com/sec/fl Testing Program, pages 28-33; 107; 139; 162–163 CD-ROM, Disc 2, pages 184–187

OVERVIEW

In this chapter students will learn to describe their family and home. To do this they will learn vocabulary associated with family members and housing. They will also learn to use the verb **tener** to describe what kind of family and house they have. They will also learn the possessive adjectives. The cultural focus of the chapter is the importance of the family in Hispanic cultures.

National Standards

Communication In Chapter 6, students will communicate in spoken and written Spanish on the following topics:
- describing their family
- describing some family functions
- describing their house

Students will obtain and provide information about these topics and engage in conversations concerning their own family and families throughout the Spanish-speaking world.

Spotlight On Culture

Artefacto The beautiful cloth is of a Peruvian **arpillera (tapiz).** **Fotografía** This photo shows a typical Spanish family walking through Retiro Park in Madrid. It is very common for families to get together to take a stroll, particularly on Sunday afternoon after the main mid-day meal. Families usually have this meal at a favorite restaurant rather than at their home.

CAPÍTULO 6

La familia y su casa

Objetivos

In this chapter you will learn to do the following:
- talk about your family
- describe your home
- tell your age and find out someone else's age
- tell what you have to do
- tell what you are going to do
- tell what belongs to you and to others
- talk about families in Spanish-speaking countries

The Glencoe Foreign Language Web site (**http://www.glencoe.com/sec/fl**) offers three options that enable you and your students to experience the Spanish-speaking world via the Internet:
- The online **Actividades** are correlated to the chapters and utilize Hispanic Web sites around the world. For the Chapter 6 activity, see student page 187.
- The **Correspondencia electrónica** section provides information on how to set up a keypal (pen pal) exchange between your class and a class in the Spanish-speaking world.
- At **Café Glencoe**, the interactive "after-school" section of the site, you and your students can access a variety of additional online resources, including interactive games. The Chapter 6 crossword puzzle practices the chapter vocabulary and structures.

El Parque del Retiro Ask the following questions about the photo after presenting the new vocabulary on pages 160–161.

¿Está la familia en el parque?
El parque está en Madrid.
¿Es la primavera o el otoño en Madrid?
¿Lleva la familia ropa de invierno o ropa de verano?
¿Anda la familia por el parque?
¿Dan un paseo?

VOCABULARY EXPANSION

Explain to students that in Spain the verb **andar** means *to walk;* **caminar** is used in Latin America. The expression **dar un paseo** means *to take a walk.*

Pacing

Chapter 6 will require approximately eight to ten days. Pacing will vary according to the length of the class, the age of your students, and student aptitude.

Block Scheduling

The extended timeframe provided by block scheduling affords you the opportunity to implement a greater number of activities and projects to motivate and involve your students. See the Block Scheduling Lesson Plans Booklet for suggestions on how to present the chapter material within a block scheduling framework.

ciento cincuenta y nueve 159

Chapter Projects

Dos personas famosas Have students think of at least two famous people. Students will pretend they are working for a magazine such as ***¡Hola!*** and describe the people, explain where they live, and tell something about their homes. Have them present the information as if it were an article for the magazine. Encourage them to include some photographs in the article.

Mi casa Have students make floor plans of their house or apartment and give a "tour" to other classmates.

Tarjetas Have students find out if the local card store, stationery store, or supermarket has greeting cards in Spanish. If they are not too expensive, have each student buy one and prepare a bulletin board of Spanish-language greeting cards. If your students can't buy cards in your town, have them draw their own greeting cards.

TECHNOLOGY OPTION Students can send electronic postcards and greeting cards from Café Glencoe **(www.cafe.glencoe.com)** at the **Glencoe Foreign Language Web site.**

CAPÍTULO 6
Vocabulario

PALABRAS 1

RESOURCES

- Vocabulary Transparencies 6.1 (A & B)
- Student Tape Manual, TE, pages 60–61
- Audiocassette 4B/CD4
- Workbook, pages 57–58
- Quiz 1, pages 26–27
- CD-ROM, Disc 2, pages 160–163

 Bell Ringer Review

Use BRR Transparency 6-1, or write the following on the board:
Complete.

1. **Yo ___ el menú. (leer)**
2. **Mis amigos ___ un libro interesante. (leer)**
3. **Nosotros ___ una composición en la clase de inglés. (escribir)**
4. **¿ ___ tú en la cafetería de la escuela? (comer)**
5. **¿Qué ___ Uds. con el almuerzo? (beber)**
6. **¿Dónde ___ Uds.? Nosotros ___ en ___ . (vivir)**

TEACHING VOCABULARY

A. Have students close their books. Present the vocabulary using Vocabulary Transparencies 6.1 (A & B). Have students repeat the names of the Moliner family after you or the recording on Cassette 4B/Compact Disc 4. Be sure that they pronounce the words as carefully as possible.

Vocabulario

PALABRAS 1

La familia

Total Physical Response

Getting ready
Dramatize the meaning of **escribe**.
Begin
Si tienen un hermano, levántense.
Y ahora siéntense.
Si tienen una hermana. Levanten la mano.
___, ¿tú tienes una hermana, no?
Levántate, por favor.
Ven acá.
Ve a la pizarra.
Toma la tiza.
Escribe el nombre de tu hermana en la pizarra.
¿Cuántos años tiene? Escribe su edad.
¿Ella va a qué escuela? Escribe el nombre de su escuela.
Gracias, ___ . Pon la tiza aquí, por favor.
Y ahora, regresa a tu asiento y siéntate.

Es la familia Moliner. Son de Quito.
El señor y la señora Moliner tienen dos hijos.
Tienen un hijo, Felipe, y una hija, Verónica.
Los Moliner tienen un gato, Tico.
La familia no tiene un perro.

¿Cuántos años tienen los hijos?
Felipe, el hijo, tiene dieciséis años.
Verónica, la hija, tiene catorce años.
Son jóvenes. No son viejos (ancianos).

Hoy es el 28 de noviembre.
Es el cumpleaños de Verónica.
Los Moliner van a dar una fiesta para Verónica.
Van a invitar a todos sus parientes (los tíos, los abuelos) a la fiesta.
Los amigos van a llevar regalos para Verónica.

Vocabulario

B. Ask the following questions as students look at the transparencies: **¿Es la familia Moliner? ¿Es la familia Moliner o Marechal? ¿Qué familia es? ¿Tienen el señor y la señora Moliner dos hijos? ¿Tienen un hijo? ¿Tienen una hija? ¿Tienen dos o tres hijos? ¿Cuántos hijos tienen los Moliner? ¿Tienen un perro? ¿Tienen un gato? ¿Qué animalito tienen?**

C. Now have students open their books to pages 160–161 and read the words and sentences for additional reinforcement.

VOCABULARY EXPANSION

You may wish to give students the following additional words:

una mascota *pet*
un cachorro *puppy*
hijo único *only child (m.)*
hija única *only child (f.)*
gemelos *twins*

ABOUT THE SPANISH LANGUAGE

- Explain to students that in Spanish when you want to refer to a whole family, you do not add a **s** to the family name like you do in English. Instead you use **los** before the family name: **los García, los Dávila, los Marechal, los Álvarez.**
- To express relationships such as stepfather, stepmother, etc., you use the suffix **-astro(a): el padrastro, la madrastra, el hijastro, la hijastra.** In many areas its meaning is almost pejorative and it is not used. Depending on the degree of intimacy, and whether or not the biological parent is deceased, one may say **mi madre** for a stepmother. If the biological mother is alive, one would say, **la esposa de mi padre**. Instead of **hermanastro(a)** one would say either **hermano(a)** or **el/la hijo(a) de la esposa de mi padre.**

¡OJO! **Práctica** When students are doing the **Práctica** activities, accept any answer that makes sense. The purpose of these activities is to have students use the new vocabulary. They are not factual recall activities. Do not expect students to remember specific information from the vocabulary presentation when answering. If you wish, have students use the photos on this page as a stimulus, when possible.

Historieta Each time **Historieta** appears, it means that the answers to the activity form a short story. Encourage students to look at the title of the **Historieta** since it can sometimes help them do the activity.

A You can have students refer to the photo as they respond to **Práctica A** or they can respond freely about any family named Rodríguez. You may want to point out to students that **Rodríguez** is one of the most common names in the Spanish language. It is like the name Smith in English.

B When doing **Práctica B,** you may wish to have younger students make their own dictionary page. For example, **Abuelo: el padre de mi padre.**

Práctica

A HISTORIETA La familia Rodríguez de España

Contesten. *(Answer.)*

1. ¿Vive la familia Rodríguez en España?
2. ¿Tienen dos hijos los señores Rodríguez?
3. ¿Es grande o pequeña la familia Rodríguez?
4. ¿Cuántos años tiene Antonio?
5. ¿Cuántos años tiene Maricarmen?
6. ¿Tienen los Rodríguez un gato o un perro?

Madrid, España

B Los parientes Completen. *(Complete.)*

1. El hermano de mi padre es mi ____.
2. La hermana de mi padre es mi ____.
3. El hermano de mi madre es mi ____.
4. La hermana de mi madre es mi ____.
5. El hijo de mi tío o de mi tía es mi ____.
6. La hija de mis tíos es mi ____.
7. Los hijos de mis tíos son mis ____.
8. Los padres de mis padres son mis ____.

Lima, Perú

C Y yo Escojan la respuesta correcta. *(Choose the correct completion.)*

1. Yo soy ____ de mis abuelos.
   a. el nieto **b.** la nieta
2. Yo soy ____ de mis padres.
   a. el hijo **b.** la hija
3. Yo soy ____ de mis tíos.
   a. el sobrino **b.** la sobrina
4. Yo soy ____ de mis primos.
   a. el primo **b.** la prima

Writing Development

Have students write the answers to **Práctica A** in a paragraph to illustrate how all of the items tell a story.

ANSWERS

Práctica

A
1. **Sí, la familia Rodríguez vive en España.**
2. **Sí, los señores Rodríguez tienen dos hijos.**
3. **La familia Rodríguez es pequeña.**
4. **Antonio tiene ___ años.**
5. **Maricarmen tiene ___ años.**
6. **Los Rodríguez tienen un gato (perro).**

B
1. **tío**
2. **tía**
3. **tío**
4. **tía**
5. **primo**
6. **prima**
7. **primos**
8. **abuelos**

C Answers will vary according to the gender of the student.

D HISTORIETA El cumpleaños de Luisa

Contesten según se indica. *(Answer according to the cues.)*

1. ¿Qué es hoy? (el cumpleaños de Luisa)
2. ¿Cuántos años tiene hoy? ¿Cuántos años cumple? (quince)
3. ¿Qué dan sus padres en su honor? (una fiesta)
4. ¿A quiénes invitan a la fiesta? (a sus amigos y a sus parientes)
5. ¿Qué va a recibir Luisa? (muchos regalos)

Actividades comunicativas

A La familia Guzmán With a classmate, look at the picture of the Guzmán family. Take turns saying as much as you can about each person in the photo.

JUEGO ¿Cúal de los parientes es? Give a definition in Spanish of a relative. Your partner will then tell which relative you're referring to. Take turns.

Actividades comunicativas

¡OJO! Práctica versus Actividades comunicativas All activities which provide guided practice are labeled **Práctica.** The more open-ended communicative activities are labeled **Actividades comunicativas.**

A Students can discuss each person in relationship to the other members of the **familia**. They can also give a description of each person and tell what they are wearing. The only word they don't know is *scarf,* **la bufanda,** which the grandmother is wearing.

TECHNOLOGY OPTION Students can use the Portfolio feature on the CD-ROM to record their responses or to write this activity.

ANSWERS

Práctica

D
1. **Hoy es el cumpleaños de Luisa.**
2. **Tiene (cumple) quince años hoy.**
3. **Sus padres dan una fiesta en su honor.**
4. **Invitan a sus amigos y a sus parientes a la fiesta.**
5. **Luisa va a recibir muchos regalos.**

Actividades comunicativas

A Answers will vary, but may include:
Es la familia Guzmán.
El señor y la señora Guzmán tienen dos hijos.
Tienen un hijo, Pedro, y una hija, Sarita.
La familia Guzmán tiene un perro.
Pedro tiene ___ años.
Sarita tiene ___ años.
La señora Peña es la abuela.

Independent Practice

Assign any of the following:
1. Workbook, pages 57–58
2. Activities on student pages 162–163

RESOURCES

- Vocabulary Transparencies 6.2 (A & B)
- Student Tape Manual, TE, pages 64–67
- Audiocassette 4B/CD4
- Workbook, pages 58–60
- Quiz 2, page 28
- CD-ROM, Disc 2, pages 164–167

Bell Ringer Review

Use BRR Transparency 6-2, or write the following on the board: Which of your relatives do you communicate with the most? Complete.

1. **Yo hablo mucho a ___ .**
2. **Yo escribo mucho a ___ .**
3. **Yo veo mucho a ___ .**

Vocabulario

PALABRAS 2

La casa

Es la casa de la familia Moliner.
Alrededor de la casa hay un jardín.
El garaje está cerca de la casa.
Los Moliner viven en una casa privada (particular).
Tienen un carro.
El carro está en el garaje.
La casa está en la calle Juan Elcano.

La casa de los Moliner tiene siete cuartos.

TEACHING VOCABULARY

A. Using Vocabulary Transparencies 6.2 (A & B), have students repeat each word after you two or three times.

B. Ask the question **¿Qué es?** as you point to various objects on the transparencies.

C. When presenting the sentences, intersperse them with questions to allow students to use the new words. For example: **¿Es la casa de la familia Moliner? ¿Tiene la casa un jardín? ¿Hay un jardín alrededor de la casa? ¿Dónde está el jardín?**

D. When teaching **alrededor de,** with your hand, make a circle around the house as you show the transparency.

(continued on page 165)

Total Physical Response

Begin
___, ven acá.
Aquí hay un libro. Toma el libro.
Abre el libro.
Lee el libro.
___, ven acá.
Toma el periódico.
Abre el periódico.
Lee el periódico.
___, ven acá.
Es la televisión. Pon la televisión.
(Pantomime turning on the T.V.)
¡Qué aburrido! Cambia el canal.
Gracias, ___. Siéntate.

las noticias

una película

Después de la cena, la familia va a la sala.
En la sala leen.
Y ven la televisión.

Una casa de apartamentos (departamentos)

Los García tienen un apartamento en el quinto piso.
Suben al apartamento en el ascensor.
No toman la escalera.
Toman el ascensor.

E. Stand close to the classroom door and say: **Estoy cerca de la puerta.** Go to the far corner away from the door and say: **No estoy cerca de la puerta; estoy lejos de la puerta**. Ask: **¿Está** *(name of your town)* **cerca de Nueva York? ¿___ está cerca de qué ciudad?**

ABOUT THE SPANISH LANGUAGE

- **El garaje** has two spellings: **el garaje, el garage.**
- The word **apartamento** is the most universally used word for *apartment.* It would be understood anywhere in the Spanish-speaking world. However, in many areas of the Caribbean the term used is **apartamiento.** In many countries of South America the word is **departamento. El piso** is used in Spain.
- The word for bedroom varies. **Habitación** usually means *bedroom,* however, it can sometimes mean *room.* In Mexico the words **recámara** and **dormitorio** are both used for *bedroom.* In the Río de la Plata (where is this?) area, **el cuarto** is the *bedroom* and **habitación** or **pieza** is *room.* In most areas **el cuarto** by itself means *room,* not specifically a *bedroom.*
- The term **el living** is often used to refer to a living room. **La sala** and **el salón** are also used.

Cooperative Learning

Mi casa Have students work in pairs. Each student draws and labels a floor plan of his or her own house or apartment. Then, without showing the drawing to their partner, students will describe their house or apartment. Each student draws the floor plan according to the description provided by the partner. When finished, they compare the two plans and discuss any differences.

History Connection

Juan Elcano Juan Elcano or Juan Sebastián de El Cano was a famous navigator and explorer who accompanied Magallanes on his voyage around the world. Magallanes died during the voyage and Elcano completed the circumnavigation in 1512.

Did You Know?

In Spain and most areas of Latin America, the ground floor of a building is called **la planta baja**. What is referred to as **el primer piso** is what we call the second floor.

A and **B** Do **Práctica A** and **B** orally first. Then have students open their books and do the activities again.

Writing Development

Students can write the information in **Práctica A** and **B** in paragraph form.

Learning From Photos

Málaga, España Have students describe the photograph in their own words.

ABOUT THE SPANISH LANGUAGE

- You will hear both **mirar la televisión** and **ver la televisión**. There is a tendency to shorten many words. **La televisión** is often referred to as **la tele**.
- In addition to **el ascensor** you will hear **el elevador** in many areas.
- You may wish to explain briefly to the students that **primero** and **tercero** are shortened to **primer** and **tercer** before a masculine singular noun.

Práctica

A HISTORIETA La casa de los Baeza

Contesten. *(Answer.)*

1. ¿Tienen los Baeza una casa bonita?
2. ¿En qué calle está la casa?
3. ¿Cuántos cuartos tiene la casa?
4. ¿Tiene dos pisos la casa?
5. ¿Qué cuartos están en la planta baja?
6. ¿Qué cuartos están en el primer piso?
7. ¿Tienen los Baeza un carro?
8. ¿Está en el garaje el carro?
9. ¿Está el garaje cerca de la casa?
10. ¿Hay un jardín alrededor de la casa?

Málaga, España

B HISTORIETA Actividades en casa

Completen. *(Complete.)*

1. La familia prepara la comida en la ____.
2. La familia come en ____ o ____. A veces comen en ____ y a veces comen en ____.
3. Después de la cena, la familia va o pasa a ____.
4. En la sala leen ____, ____ o ____. No escriben cartas.
5. En la sala ven ____.
6. Ven ____, ____ o ____ en la televisión.

Madrid, España

ANSWERS

Práctica

A
1. **Sí, (No, no) los Baeza (no) tienen una casa bonita.**
2. **La casa está en la calle ___.**
3. **La casa tiene ___ cuartos.**
4. **Sí, la casa tiene dos pisos.**
5. **___ están en la planta baja.**
6. **___ están en el primer piso.**
7. **Sí (No), los Baeza (no) tienen un carro.**
8. **Sí (No), el carro (no) está en el garaje.**
9. **Sí (No), el garaje (no) está cerca de la casa.**
10. **Sí, (No, no) hay un jardín alrededor de la casa.**

B
1. **cocina**
2. **el comedor, la cocina; el comedor, la cocina (la cocina, el comedor)**
3. **la sala**
4. **periódicos, revistas, libros**
5. **la televisión**
6. **una película, una emisión deportiva, las noticias**

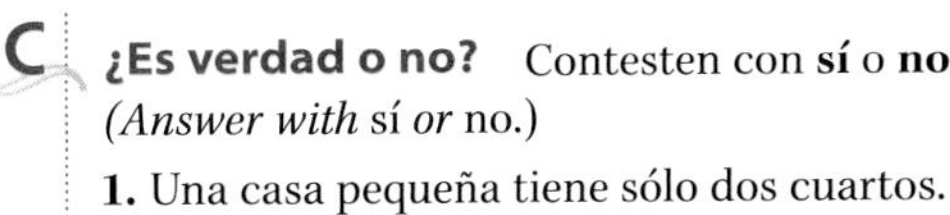

C **¿Es verdad o no?** Contesten con **sí** o **no.** *(Answer with* sí *or* no.)

1. Una casa pequeña tiene sólo dos cuartos.
2. Un apartamento grande tiene dos cuartos.
3. La casa de apartamentos es alta.
4. Una casa privada o particular tiene sólo uno o dos pisos y una casa de apartamentos tiene muchos pisos.
5. En una casa privada la familia sube de un piso a otro en el ascensor.
6. La familia toma la escalera para subir de un piso a otro en una casa particular.

Caraballeda, Venezuela

Santiago, Chile

Buenos Aires, Argentina

El Viejo San Juan, Puerto Rico

Actividades comunicativas

A **Mi casa** Work with a classmate. One of you lives in a private house and the other lives in an apartment building. Ask each other as many questions as you can about your homes. Answer each other's questions, too.

B **La rutina de mi familia** Get together with a classmate and discuss the routine your family follows after school or after work. You may want to use some of the following words.

escribir
mirar
tomar
ver
leer
comer
preparar

CAPÍTULO 6
Vocabulario

C Have students do **Práctica C** with books open. Students can also correct the false statements in **Práctica C.**

Actividades comunicativas

¡OJO! These activities encourage students to use the chapter vocabulary and structures in open-ended situations. It is not necessary to have them do all the activities. Choose the ones you consider most appropriate.

Learning From Photos

Actividad oral Have students listen to the following short descriptions of the dwellings in the photos on page 167 and ask them to tell you which one is being described by telling where it's located.

1. **La casa tiene sólo un piso. (Es la casa en Caraballeda.)**
2. **Hay un jardín alrededor de la casa. (Es la casa en Santiago.)**
3. **No hay carros en la calle. (Es la casa en el Viejo San Juan.)**
4. **Tiene muchos pisos. (Es la casa de apartamentos en Buenos Aires.)**
5. **Es una casa grande y blanca. (Es la casa en Santiago.)**

ANSWERS

Práctica

C **1. Sí.** **2. No.** **3. Sí.** **4. Sí.** **5. No.** **6. Sí.**

Actividades comunicativas

A Answers will vary, however students should use the vocabulary from **Palabras 1** and **2.**

B Answers will vary. Encourage students to use the vocabulary in the colored boxes.

RESOURCES

- Workbook, pages 61–64
- Student Tape Manual, TE, pages 67–70
- Audiocassette 4B/CD4
- Quizzes 3–5, pages 29–31
- Computer Testmaker
- CD-ROM, Disc 2, pages 168–175

Bell Ringer Review

Use BRR Transparency 6-3, or write the following on the board: Answer.

1. **¿Cuáles son los cuartos de una casa?**
2. **¿Tiene muchos o pocos cuartos una casa grande?**

TEACHING STRUCTURE

Telling what you and others have

A. Review the **tiene** and **tienen** forms which students already know from the **Vocabulario** section of this chapter.

B. Draw a stick figure on the board. Label it **Roberto.** Have students make up sentences with **Roberto tiene.** Do the same with **Carolina y Juana tienen.**

C. Have students repeat **yo tengo** after you as they point to themselves. Then have them tell some things they have.

D. Have students open their books to page 168 and read the verb paradigm. You may also want to write the verb forms on the board.

E. Go over the information about expressing age in Step 2.

Estructura

Telling what you and others have
Presente de tener

1. The verb **tener** *(to have)* is irregular. Study the following forms.

INFINITIVE	tener
yo	tengo
tú	tienes
él, ella, Ud.	tiene
nosotros(as)	tenemos
vosotros(as)	*tenéis*
ellos, ellas, Uds.	tienen

2. You also use the verb **tener** to express age in Spanish.

¿Cuántos años tienes?
Tengo dieciséis años.
¿Cuántos años tiene Ud.?

Práctica

A **¿Cómo es tu familia?** Contesten personalmente.
(Answer these questions about yourself.)

1. ¿Tienes un hermano?
2. ¿Cuántos hermanos tienes?
3. ¿Tienes una hermana?
4. ¿Cuántas hermanas tienes?
5. ¿Tienes un perro?
6. ¿Tienes un gato?
7. ¿Tienes muchos amigos?
8. ¿Tienes una familia grande o pequeña?

¡NO VAYAS A TANTOS LUGARES AQUI TENEMOS TODO!

PREGUNTA POR NUESTROS PAQUETES "TODO INCLUIDO"

VESTIDO
MAQUILLAJE
PEINADO
MANICURE

CHAMBELANES
CADETES
VESTUARIOS

FILMACION
VIDEO-CLIP
FOTOGRAFO
FOTO-ESTUDIO
INVITACIONES

AUTO DEL AÑO
CALABAZA
LIMOUSINE
CARCACHA
O AUTO ANTIGUO

SALON DE FIESTAS
GRUPO
SONIDO
SHOW EN LA CENA
ARREGLOS FLORALES

MESAS
SILLAS
MANTELES
MESEROS
BANQUETES

ANSWERS

Práctica

A
1. **Sí, (No, no) tengo un hermano.**
2. **Tengo ___ hermano(s). (No tengo hermanos.)**
3. **Sí, (No, no) tengo una hermana.**
4. **Tengo ___ hermana(s). (No tengo hermanas.)**
5. **Sí, (No, no) tengo un perro.**
6. **Sí, (No, no) tengo un gato.**
7. **Sí, (No, no) tengo muchos amigos.**
8. **Tengo una familia grande (pequeña).**

PAGE 169

B **Ernesto no tiene un hermano. Tiene una hermana. La hermana de Ernesto tiene 14 años. Ernesto tiene 16 años. La familia de Ernesto no tiene un perro, pero tiene una gata adorable.**

C
1. **¿Tienes un hermano?**
2. **¿Tienes una hermana?**
3. **¿Tienes primos?**
4. **¿Tienes un perro?**
5. **¿Tienes un gato?**
6. **¿Tienes muchos amigos?**

B **¿Tienes un hermano?** Practiquen la conversación.
(Practice the conversation.)

Ernesto y Teresa Hablen de Ernesto y Teresa.
(In your own words, tell all about Ernesto and Teresa.)

C **¿Qué tienes?** Formen preguntas con **tienes.**
(Form questions with tienes.)

1. un hermano
2. una hermana
3. primos
4. un perro
5. un gato
6. muchos amigos

D **¿Qué tienen Uds.?** Sigan el modelo.
(Follow the model.)

una casa o un apartamento
Marcos y Adela, ¿ Uds. tienen una casa o un apartamento?
Tenemos una casa. / Tenemos un apartamento.

1. un perro o un gato
2. un hermano o una hermana
3. un sobrino o una sobrina
4. una familia grande o pequeña
5. una bicicleta o un carro
6. discos compactos o casetes

Santiago, Chile

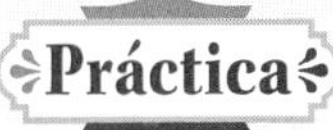

A Note that **Práctica A** on page 168 focuses attention on the **yo tengo** form. Students get practice hearing **tienes** and then responding with **tengo.**

B Have students present **Práctica B** as a real conversation. They can dramatize it in front of the class using as much expression as possible. Then have students retell it in narrative form. Note that the conversation reinforces the **tú** and **yo** forms and that the follow-up activity has students use the third person in their narration.

C You can also do **Práctica C** as a paired activity and have the second student provide the answer to each question.

D You may wish to do **Práctica D** as a small group activity since it practices the plural forms.

VOCABULARY EXPANSION

You may wish to teach the students the following:
¿De qué raza es el perro?
Es un dálmata.
Some other dog breeds are:

un perro cruzado	***mutt***
un pastor alemán	***German shepherd***
un labrador	***labrador***
un caniche	***poodle***
un dóberman	***doberman***
un rotweiler	***rotweiler***

ANSWERS CONTINUED

D 1. **Marcos y Adela, ¿Uds. tienen un perro o un gato?**
Tenemos un perro. / Tenemos un gato.
2. **Marcos y Adela, ¿Uds. tienen un hermano o una hermana?**
Tenemos un hermano. / Tenemos una hermana.
3. **Marcos y Adela, ¿Uds. tienen un sobrino o una sobrina?**
Tenemos un sobrino. / Tenemos una sobrina.
4. **Marcos y Adela, ¿Uds. tienen una familia grande o pequeña?**
Tenemos una familia grande. / Tenemos una familia pequeña.
5. **Marcos y Adela, ¿Uds. tienen una bicicleta o un carro?**
Tenemos una bicicleta. / Tenemos un carro.
6. **Marcos y Adela, ¿Uds. tienen discos compactos o casetes?**
Tenemos discos compactos. / Tenemos casetes.

E **Práctica E** makes students use all forms of the verb **tener.**

Writing Development

Have students write a paragraph about the Sánchez family based on their answers to **Práctica E.**

Actividad comunicativa

A This is a very natural, communicative situation since students usually enjoy talking about themselves and their families.

Learning From Photos

La Plaza, Chinchón, España
Chinchón is a lovely town just 54 kilometers southeast of Madrid. This photo is of its famous Plaza Mayor. The plaza is surrounded by ancient three and four story houses with wooden balconies. From time to time the plaza is still converted into a bullring.

E HISTORIETA La familia Sánchez

Completen con **tener.** *(Complete with* tener.)

Aquí ___(1) (nosotros) una foto de la familia Sánchez. La familia Sánchez ___(2) un piso (apartamento) muy bonito en Madrid. El piso ___(3) seis cuartos y está en Salamanca, una zona bastante elegante de Madrid. Los Sánchez ___(4) una casa de campo en Chinchón también. La casa de campo en Chinchón es un pequeño chalé donde los Sánchez pasan los fines de semana o los *weekend* y sus vacaciones. La casa de campo ___(5) cinco cuartos.

Hay cuatro personas en la familia Sánchez. Carolina ___(6) nueve años y su hermano Gerardo ___(7) once años. Gerardo y Carolina ___(8) un perrito encantador, Chispa. Adoran a su Chispa.

¿Tú ___(9) un perro? ¿Tú ___(10) un gato? ¿Tu familia ___(11) un apartamento o una casa? ¿Uds. también ___(12) una casa de campo donde pasan los fines de semana como los Sánchez?

La Plaza, Chinchón, España

Actividad comunicativa

A **Tengo tres hermanos.** With a classmate, take turns telling one another some things about your family. Tell whether you have a large or small family; tell the numbers of brothers and sisters you have and their ages, etc.

ANSWERS

Práctica

E
1. **tenemos**
2. **tiene**
3. **tiene**
4. **tienen**
5. **tiene**
6. **tiene**
7. **tiene**
8. **tienen**
9. **tienes**
10. **tienes**
11. **tiene**
12. **tienen**

Actividad comunicativa

A Answers will vary, however students should use the appropriate forms of the verb **tener** when describing their family members and giving their ages.

Telling what you have to do and what you are going to do
Tener que; Ir a

1. **Tener que** + *infinitive* (**-ar, -er,** or **-ir** form of the verb) means "to have to."

   Tengo que comprar un regalo.

2. **Ir a** + *infinitive* means "to be going to." It is used to express what is going to happen in the near future.

   Vamos a llegar mañana.
   Ella va a cumplir quince años.

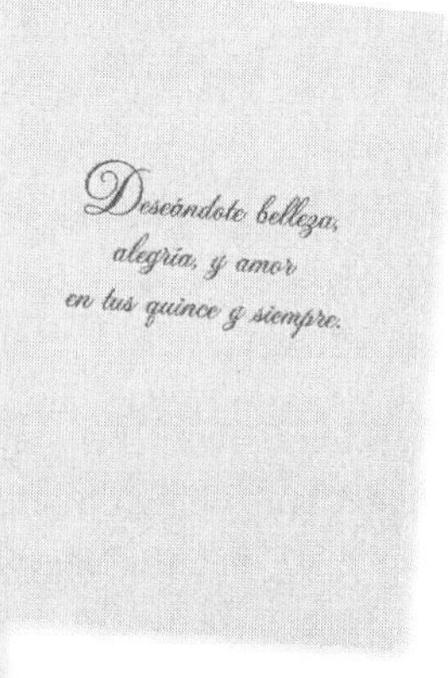

A HISTORIETA ¡Cuánto tengo que trabajar!

Contesten personalmente. *(Answer these questions about yourself.)*

1. ¿Tienes que trabajar mucho en la escuela?
2. Antes de la apertura de clases, ¿tienes que comprar materiales escolares?
3. ¿Tienes que comprar ropa también?
4. ¿Tienes que estudiar mucho?
5. ¿Tienes que leer muchos libros?
6. ¿Tienes que tomar apuntes?
7. ¿Tienes que escribir mucho?

CAPÍTULO 6
Estructura

Bell Ringer Review

Use BRR Transparency 6-4, or write the following on the board: Write the answer.

1. **¿Cuántos hermanos tienes?**
2. **¿Cuántos amigos muy buenos tienes?**
3. **¿Cuántos profesores tienes?**
4. **¿Cuántos años tienes?**

TEACHING STRUCTURE

Telling what you have to do and what you are going to do

A. Ask students to open their books to page 171. Read Steps 1 and 2 to them.

B. Have students name as many verbs as they can. Then have them make up simple sentences using theses verbs with **tengo que** or **no tengo que; voy a** or **no voy a.** This is an easy way to practice using the infinitive form of the verb along with another verb. The first time students do this, it is rather tricky for them.

A After going over **Práctica A,** have students tell anything else they have to do.

ANSWERS

Práctica

A
1. **Sí, (No, no) tengo que trabajar mucho en la escuela.**
2. **Sí, antes de la apertura de clases, tengo que comprar materiales escolares.**
3. **Sí, tengo que comprar ropa también.**
4. **Sí, (No, no) tengo que estudiar mucho.**
5. **Sí, (No, no) tengo que leer muchos libros.**
6. **Sí, (No, no) tengo que tomar apuntes.**
7. **Sí, (No, no) tengo que escribir mucho.**

Práctica

Writing Development

After doing **Práctica B,** have students write a short note to a friend. The note starts with: **Voy a dar una fiesta para...**

C Note how **Práctica C** combines **tener que** with **ir a** in a very natural, communicative context.

Actividades comunicativas

A and **B** These activities bring about very real communication. We very frequently tell people what we have to do, or explain why we are not going to do something.

B HISTORIETA Voy a dar una fiesta.

Contesten con **sí.** *(Answer with* sí.)

1. ¿Vas a dar una fiesta?
2. ¿Vas a dar la fiesta para Ángel?
3. ¿Ángel va a cumplir diecisiete años?
4. ¿Vas a invitar a sus amigos?
5. ¿Van Uds. a bailar durante la fiesta?
6. ¿Van a comer?

Estepona, España

C **¡Tenemos tanto que hacer!** Sigan el modelo. *(Follow the model.)*

ver la televisión / preparar la comida
No vamos a ver la televisión porque tenemos que preparar la comida.

1. escuchar discos compactos / estudiar
2. hablar por teléfono / escribir una composición
3. tomar seis cursos / sacar notas buenas
4. tomar apuntes / escuchar al profesor
5. ir a la fiesta / trabajar

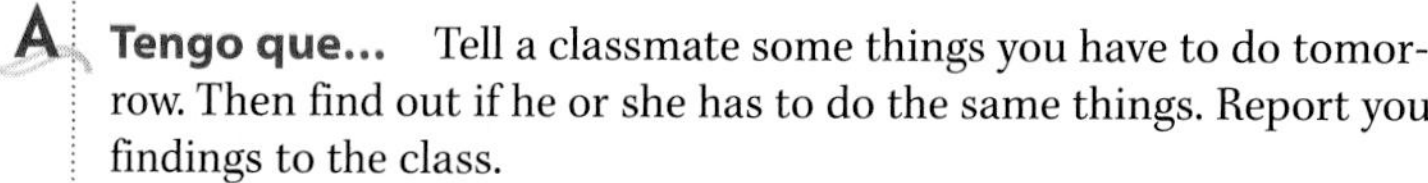

Actividades comunicativas

A **Tengo que...** Tell a classmate some things you have to do tomorrow. Then find out if he or she has to do the same things. Report your findings to the class.

B **No voy a...** Tell a classmate some things you're not going to do tomorrow because you have to do something else. Tell what you have to do. Your classmate will let you know if he or she is in the same situation.

ANSWERS

Práctica

B
1. **Sí, voy a dar una fiesta.**
2. **Sí, voy a dar la fiesta para Ángel.**
3. **Sí, Ángel va a cumplir diecisiete años.**
4. **Sí, voy a invitar a sus amigos.**
5. **Sí, vamos a bailar durante la fiesta.**
6. **Sí, vamos a comer.**

C
1. **No vamos a escuchar discos compactos porque tenemos que estudiar.**
2. **No vamos a hablar por teléfono porque tenemos que escribir una composición.**
3. **No vamos a tomar seis cursos porque tenemos que sacar notas buenas.**
4. **No vamos a tomar apuntes porque vamos a escuchar al profesor.**
5. **No vamos a ir a la fiesta porque vamos a trabajar.**

Actividades comunicativas

A Answers will vary, however, students should use the appropriate forms of **tener.**

B Answers will vary, however students should use the expressions **ir a** and **tener que.**

Telling what belongs to whom
Adjetivos posesivos

1. You use possessive adjectives to show possession or ownership. Like other adjectives, the possessive adjective must agree with the noun it modifies. The possessive adjectives **mi, tu,** and **su** have only two forms: singular and plural.

mi libro y mi revista	**mis libros y mis revistas**
tu libro y tu revista	**tus libros y tus revistas**
su libro y su revista	**sus libros y sus revistas**

2. The possessive adjective **su** can mean "his," "her," "their," or "your." Its meaning is usually obvious from the way it is used in the sentence. However, if it is not clear, **su** can be replaced by a prepositional phrase.

el libro { **de él** / **de ella** / **de Ud.**

el libro { **de ellos** / **de ellas** / **de Uds.**

3. The possessive adjective **nuestro** *(our)* has four forms.

nuestro apartamento	**nuestros libros**
nuestra casa	**nuestras revistas**

¿Lo sabes?

Vuestro is the possessive adjective used with **vosotros** in parts of Spain. **Vuestro,** like **nuestro,** has four forms.

Sevilla, España

Learning From Photos

Sevilla, España This photo was taken in the Barrio de Santa Cruz in Seville. This barrio is also called **la judería** because it is where many Jews lived prior to the Inquisition. It is a beautiful section with winding alleyways, cobblestoned squares, and whitewashed houses. There are many wrought-iron lanterns called **faroles,** which cast shadows on the whitewashed walls.

Bell Ringer Review

Use BRR Transparency 6-5, or write the following on the board: Write five things about your brother or sister. If you don't have a brother or sister, write five things about a good friend.

TEACHING STRUCTURE

Telling what belongs to whom

A. Have students point to themselves as they say **mi,** to a neighbor as they say **tu**, to themselves and someone else as they say **nuestro**, and to two neighbors as they say **su**.

B. Call on a student to read the examples in Step 1.

C. Write **su libro** on the board. Then repeat aloud all the phrases in Step 2 as you point to **su** to show students that it does, in fact, have several meanings.

D. Indicate to students that **nuestro** has four forms, the same as any other adjective that ends in **o**.

E. It is your decision regarding how thoroughly you teach the **vuestro** forms.

ABOUT THE SPANISH LANGUAGE

The possessive adjective **tu** is used with the subject **vos.**

Práctica

A Do **Práctica A** first with books closed. Call on individual students to answer one item each. Do the activity a second time, having one student respond to several consecutive items before calling on the next student.

B Have students look at a neighbor as they make up questions. Have them use the actual name of the neighbor, rather than **Lupita.**

C **PAIRED ACTIVITY** Have students work in pairs to prepare a mini-conversation.

Note This activity has students use a possessive adjective that is different from the subject. Students sometimes get the erroneous idea that they should always use the possessive adjective that corresponds to the subject of the sentence. For this reason, the type of material presented in this activity is quite important.

D You can do **Práctica D** with books closed or open.

Writing Development

Have students write a paragraph about their family and home based on their responses to **Práctica A.**

Additional Practice

¿Dónde está... ? Have students do the following: Think of a place in your house or apartment where your famly pet is hiding. Your partner will try to guess where the pet is. For example:

E1:¿Tu perro está en el jardín?
E2: No, no está en el jardín. (Sí está en el jardín.)

Práctica

A **HISTORIETA** Mi familia y mi casa

Contesten personalmente. *(Answer about your family and your home.)*

1. ¿Dónde está tu casa o tu apartamento?
2. ¿Cuántos cuartos tiene tu casa o tu apartamento?
3. Tu apartamento o tu casa, ¿es grande o pequeño(a)?
4. ¿Cuántas personas hay en tu familia?
5. ¿Dónde viven tus abuelos?
6. Y tus primos, ¿dónde viven?

B **Tengo una pregunta para ti.** Sigan el modelo. *(Follow the model.)*

la casa
Lupita, ¿dónde está tu casa?

1. el hermano
2. la hermana
3. los primos
4. los libros
5. la escuela
6. el/la profesor(a) de español

C **La verdad es que...** Preparen una conversación. *(Make up a conversation.)*

—¿Tienes tú mi libro?
—No. De ninguna manera. No tengo tu libro. La verdad es que tú tienes tu libro.

1. 
2. 
3. 
4. 

D **¿Cómo son sus parientes?** Sigan el modelo. *(Follow the model.)*

el hermano de Susana
Su hermano es muy simpático.

1. el hermano de Pablo
2. la amiga de Pablo
3. el primo de Carlos y José
4. la tía de Teresa y José
5. los tíos de Teresa y José
6. los padres de Ud.

ANSWERS

Práctica

A
1. Mi casa (apartamento) está en la calle ___.
2. Mi casa (apartamento) tiene ___ cuartos.
3. Mi apartamento (casa) es grande (pequeño[a]).
4. Hay ___ personas en mi familia.
5. Mis abuelos viven en ___.
6. Mis primos viven en ___.

B
1. Lupita, ¿dónde está tu hermano?
2. Lupita, ¿dónde está tu hermana?
3. Lupita, ¿dónde están tus primos?
4. Lupita, ¿dónde están tus libros?
5. Lupita, ¿dónde está tu escuela?
6. Lupita, ¿dónde está tu profesor(a) de español?

C
1. —¿Tienes mis revistas?
—No. De ninguna manera. No tengo tus revistas. La verdad es que tú tienes tus revistas.
2. —¿Tienes mi calculadora?
—No. De ninguna manera. No tengo tu calculadora. La verdad es que tú tienes tu calculadora.

(continued on page 175)

E **Historieta** Nuestra casa y nuestra escuela

Contesten personalmente. *(Answer about your family and friends.)*

1. Su casa (la casa de Uds.), ¿es grande o pequeña?
2. ¿Cuántos cuartos tiene su casa?
3. ¿Su casa está en la ciudad o en el campo?
4. ¿En qué calle está su escuela?
5. Su escuela, ¿es una escuela intermedia o una escuela superior?
6. En general, ¿sus profesores son simpáticos?
7. ¿Son interesantes sus cursos?
8. ¿Son grandes o pequeñas sus clases?

Madrid, España

Actividad comunicativa

A **Mi hermano y yo...** Work with a classmate. Tell him or her about yourself and a sibling, or your friend if you don't have a sibling. Then ask your classmate questions about his or her family. Here are some words you may want to use.

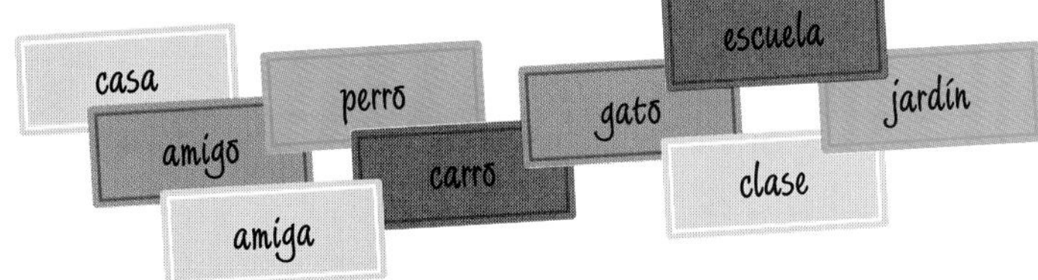

CAPÍTULO 6

Estructura

E It is recommended that you go over **Práctica E** first with books closed as students answer with the correct form of **nuestro.** Do the activity a second time with students reading in pairs. One reads the questions, and the other responds. You can do this as a paired activity or as a round-robin class activity.

¡OJO! All new material in the chapter has been presented. The sections that follow recombine and reintroduce the vocabulary and structures that have already been introduced.

ANSWERS CONTINUED

3. —¿Tienes mi disco compacto?
—No. De ninguna manera. No tengo tu disco compacto. La verdad es que tú tienes tu disco compacto.

4. —¿Tienes mis cuadernos?
—... No tengo tus cuadernos. La verdad es que tú tienes tus cuadernos.

D
1. Su hermano es muy simpático.
2. Su amiga es muy simpática.
3. Su primo es muy simpático.
4. Su tía es muy simpática.
5. Sus tíos son muy simpáticos.
6. Mis padres son muy simpáticos.

E
1. Nuestra casa es grande (pequeña).
2. Nuestra casa tiene ___ cuartos.
3. Nuestra casa está en la ciudad (el campo).
4. Nuestra escuela está en la calle ___.
5. Nuestra escuela es una escuela ___.
6. Sí (No), en general, nuestros profesores (no) son simpáticos.
7. Sí (No), nuestros cursos (no) son interesantes.
8. Nuestras clases son grandes (pequeñas).

Actividad comunicativa

A Encourage students to use possessive adjectives and the words in the colored boxes.

CAPÍTULO 6
Conversación

RESOURCES

- Audiocassette 4B/CD4
- CD-ROM, Disc 2, page 176

Bell Ringer Review

Use BRR Transparency 6-6, or write the following on the board: Write at least three things you have to do this weekend. Write three things you're going to do this afternoon.

TEACHING THE CONVERSATION

A. Tell students they are going to hear a conversation between two friends. One of them has to go somewhere. Have them listen for the place where he has to go and the reason why.

B. Have students close their books and listen to the recording of the conversation on Cassette 4B/Compact Disc 4.

C. Now have students open their books to page 176 and repeat the conversation after you line by line.

D. Call on pairs of students to read the conversation aloud with as much expression as possible.

E. After presenting the conversation, go over the **Después de conversar** activity. If students can answer the questions with relative ease, move on. Students should not be expected to memorize the conversation.

TECHNOLOGY OPTION

On the CD-ROM (Disc 2, page 176), students can watch a dramatization of this conversation. They can then play the role of either one of the characters and record themselves in the conversation.

Conversación

¿Tú tienes una hermana?

TADEO: ¿Vas a la fiesta de José Luis el viernes?
JAIME: ¡Ah! ¡Es verdad! José Luis va a dar una fiesta.
TADEO: ¡Hombre! ¿No vas?
JAIME: Pues, tengo que ir de compras. Tengo que comprar un regalo para mi hermana.
TADEO: ¿Tienes una hermana?
JAIME: Sí, y va a cumplir quince años.
TADEO: ¿Uds. van a dar una fiesta?
JAIME: ¡Claro! Vamos a tener una celebración.
TADEO: Pero, no es mañana, ¿verdad?
JAIME: No. Su fiesta es el sábado.
TADEO: Pues, tienes que ir a la fiesta de José Luis.

Después de conversar

Contesten. *(Answer.)*

1. ¿Con quién habla Tadeo?
2. ¿Adónde tiene que ir Jaime?
3. ¿Qué tiene que comprar?
4. ¿Por qué tiene que comprar un regalo para su hermana?
5. ¿Cuántos años tiene su hermana?
6. ¿Cuántos años va a cumplir el sábado?
7. ¿Van a dar una fiesta?
8. ¿Cuándo es la fiesta de su hermana?
9. ¿Cuándo es la fiesta de José Luis?

ANSWERS

Después de conversar

1. **Tadeo habla con Jaime.**
2. **Tiene que ir de compras.**
3. **Tiene que comprar un regalo para su hermana.**
4. **Tiene que comprar un regalo para su hermana porque su hermana va a cumplir quince años.**
5. **Su hermana tiene catorce años.**
6. **Va a cumplir quince años el sábado.**
7. **Sí, van a dar una fiesta.**
8. **La fiesta de su hermana es el sábado.**
9. **La fiesta de José Luis es el viernes.**

Actividades comunicativas

A **¿Qué casa?** You and your family are planning to spend a month in Peru. Which of the houses or apartments, as described in the newspaper ads, would suit your family best? Explain why.

B **¡Qué familia!** Work with a classmate. Make up an imaginary family. Describe each family member and tell what he or she has to do. Be as creative as possible.

1

RENTA

ALQUILER DE CASAS DEPARTAMENTOS Y RESIDENCIAS

En Lima, Callao y balnearios

1A.- CASAS

01 $ 1,500 2 chalets 21 Benavides colegio Humboldt Juana Larco Dammert 4 dorm. escritorio 9780150 o 9435188

01 CHACARILLA Maravillosa residencia 1 planta piscina 4 dormitorios 4 baños ideal diplomaticos funcionarios $ 2200 telefono 4613661.

ALQUILO casa 5 baños 3 salas comedor cocina 3 cocheras piscina 2 bares amoblada area de servicio lavanderia preferencia extranjeros Tf. 4469062 - 9940537

CHALET 2 plantas $ 300 Pueblo Libre 3 dormitorios sala comedor 2 baños lavanderia Telef. 4443394.

1B.- DEPARTAMENTOS

07 ALOJAMIENTO Temporal suite Los Pinos Pardo Miraflores departamentos full equipo 1 2 dormitorios cochera directo con departamentos cable VHS limpieza seguridad privacidad excelente ubicacion desde $ 45 diarios reservas 2421354 - 2421503 - 4477745

04 ALOJAMIENTO temporal San Isidro departamento independiente completamente equipado Tv cable limpieza diaria mínimo 1 semana T. 421-8092

02 VISTA AL MAR departamento nuevo 3 dormitorios 2 cocheras piscina jacuzzi c/s muebles $ 2,000 T. 445-8748

Pronunciación

Las consonantes b, v

There is no difference in pronunciation between a **b** and a **v** in Spanish. The **b** or **v** sound is somewhat softer than the sound of an English *b*. When making this sound, the lips barely touch. Imitate the following carefully.

ba	be	bi	bo	bu
bajo	**bebé**	**bicicleta**	**bonito**	**bueno**
bastante	**escribe**	**bien**	**recibo**	**bus**
trabaja	**recibe**	**biología**	**árbol**	**aburrido**
va	ve	vi	vo	vu
vamos	**verano**	**vive**	**vosotros**	**vuelo**
nueva	**venezolano**	**violín**	**voleibol**	

Repeat the following sentences.

El joven vive en la avenida Bolívar en Bogotá.
Bárbara trabaja los sábados en el laboratorio de biología.
La joven ve la bicicleta nueva en la televisión.

Learning From Realia

Residencias Have students look at the ads on page 177. Ask them what word is used for apartment in Peru **(departamento)**. Explain to students that Callao is a port city near Lima. **Balnearios** refers to those areas on the outskirts of Lima on the Pacific coast. Bordering Miraflores there is a group of beaches known as the Costa Verde. The Costa Verde is linked to Lima by a modern highway and the drive from the city to the coast is less than one-half hour.

ANSWERS

Actividades comunicativas

A Answers will vary, however students should be encouraged to use the verb **tener, tener que,** and **ir a** expressions, as well as possessive adjectives.

B Answers will vary. Encourage students to use the descriptive adjectives they have learned, as well as the expression **tener que.**

Actividades comunicativas

¡OJO! These **Actividades comunicativas** enable students to use the language on their own as if they were communicating in real-life situations.

B TECHNOLOGY OPTION In the CD-ROM version of **Actividad B** (Disc 2, page 177), students can interact with an on-screen native speaker and record their voice.

TEACHING PRONUNCIATION

A. Using Pronunciation Transparency P-6, model the first sentence in the Pronunciation section on page 177.

B. Now have students repeat the sounds and words carefully after you, or the recording on Cassette 4B/Compact Disc 4.

C. Have students open their books to page 177. Call on individuals to read the sentences carefully.

D. The words and sentences on page 177 can also be used for dictation.

TECHNOLOGY OPTION

In the CD-ROM version of the Pronunciation section (Disc 2, page 177), students will see an animation of the cartoon on this page. They can also listen to, record, and play back the sounds, words, and sentences presented here.

ABOUT THE SPANISH LANGUAGE

According to Spanish phonetics there is no difference between the sound of **b** and **v**. The phonetic symbol for each one is the same. In some areas, however, there is a very slight English sound given to **v**. The **b** and **v** cause quite a spelling problem for many people.

National Standards

Cultures

In the reading on page 178, students will learn about the importance of the family in Hispanic cultures. They will also learn about the role of the godparents.

TEACHING THE READING

Pre-reading

A. Have students open their books to page 178. Have them read the Reading Strategy and look at the photos, as the strategy suggests.

B. Have students scan the reading.

Reading

A. Call on individuals to read aloud. After every two or three sentences ask the questions from the **Después de leer** section.

B. After completing the reading, call on students to give some information about Hispanic families.

Post-reading

Have students do the **Después de leer** activity on page 179.

TECHNOLOGY OPTION

Students may listen to a recorded version of the **Lectura** on the CD-ROM, Disc 2, page 178.

Lecturas CULTURALES

Reading Strategy

Using background knowledge

When you are first assigned a reading, quickly look at the accompanying visuals to determine what the reading is about. Once you know what the topic is, spend a short time thinking about what you already know about it. If you do this, the reading will be easier to understand and you will more likely be able to figure out words you do not recognize.

LA FAMILIA HISPANA

Cuando un joven hispano habla de su familia, no habla solamente de sus padres y de sus hermanos. Habla de toda su familia—sus abuelos, tíos, primos, etc. Incluye también a sus padrinos—a su padrino y a su madrina.

¿Quiénes son los padrinos? Los padrinos son los que asisten al bebé durante el bautizo[1]. En la sociedad hispana, los padrinos forman una parte íntegra de la familia. Y la familia es una unidad muy importante en la sociedad hispana. Cuando hay una celebración familiar como un bautizo, una boda[2] o un cumpleaños, todos los parientes van a la fiesta. Y los padrinos también van a la fiesta.

[1]bautizo *baptism*
[2]boda *wedding*

Estepona, España

San Juan, Puerto Rico

Did You Know?

Apellidos You may wish to explain to students the system used for Hispanic names.

			Last name of father	Last name of mother
	Man	Julio	Guzmán	Echeverría
	Woman	Ana	Blanco	Robles
Julio and Ana marry:	**Man**	Julio Guzmán Echeverría		
	Woman	Ana Blanco de Guzmán		
Julio and Ana have children:	**Son**	José Guzmán Blanco		
	Daughter	Teresa Guzmán Blanco		

EXPANSION Have students write their names using this system.

Después de leer

A La familia hispana Contesten. *(Answer.)*

1. Cuando una persona hispana habla de su familia, ¿de quiénes habla?
2. ¿Quiénes son los padrinos?
3. ¿Son una parte importante de la familia los padrinos?
4. ¿Cuáles son algunas celebraciones familiares?
5. ¿Quiénes asisten a una celebración familiar?

La Sagrada Familia, Barcelona, España

Learning From Photos

La Sagrada Familia, Barcelona, España The complete name of this famous church in Barcelona is **Temple Expiatori de la Sagrada Familia.** Done by the famous Catalán architect Antoni Gaudí, the cathedral was not completed before Gaudí's untimely death in 1926 and it is still under construction. Gaudí was run over by a tram. He was not identified and died in a pauper's ward.

Independent Practice

Assign any of the following:

1. **Después de leer** activity, page 179
2. Workbook, **Un poco más,** pages 65–69
3. CD-ROM, Disc 2, pages 178–179

ANSWERS

Después de leer

A
1. **Habla de toda su familia—sus abuelos, tíos, primos, etc.**
2. **Los padrinos son los que asisten al bebé durante el bautizo.**
3. **Sí, los padrinos forman una parte íntegra de la familia.**
4. **Algunas celebraciones familiares son el bautizo, la boda y el cumpleaños.**
5. **Todos los parientes asisten a una celebración familiar.**

LECTURA OPCIONAL 1

National Standards

Comparisons
The reading and the related activity on this page about **la quinceañera** give students the opportunity to compare customs and celebrations in Hispanic cultures to their own.

If you have any Hispanic students in class have them describe any **quinceañera** celebrations they have attended.

TEACHING TIPS

A. This reading is optional. You may skip it completely, have the entire class read it, have only several students read it, or assign it for extra credit.

B. Have students look at the photograph. Note that **la quinceañera** is frequently dressed like a bride.

LECTURA OPCIONAL 1

LA QUINCEAÑERA

En los Estados Unidos celebramos la *Sweet Sixteen*. La *Sweet Sixteen* es una fiesta en honor de la muchacha que cumple dieciséis años.

En una familia hispana hay una gran celebración en honor de la quinceañera. ¿Quién es la quinceañera? La quinceañera es la muchacha que cumple quince años. La familia siempre da una gran fiesta en su honor. Todos los parientes y amigos asisten a la fiesta.

La quinceañera recibe muchos regalos. A veces los regalos son extraordinarios—como un viaje[1] a Europa o a los Estados Unidos, por ejemplo. Y si la quinceañera vive en los Estados Unidos es a veces un viaje a Latinoamérica o a España.

[1]viaje *trip*

En Tus Quince Años

Maracaibo, Venezuela

Después de leer

A ¿Una costumbre hispana o estadounidense? Lean las frases. *(Read the statements and tell whether each more accurately describes a Hispanic or an American custom. In some cases, it may describe a custom of both cultures.)*

1. Dan una fiesta en honor de una muchacha que cumple quince años.
2. Dan una fiesta en honor de la muchacha que cumple dieciséis años.
3. La muchacha recibe regalos para su cumpleaños.
4. La fiesta es principalmente para los amigos jóvenes de la muchacha.
5. Toda la familia asiste a la fiesta—los abuelos, los tíos, los padrinos.

ANSWERS

Después de leer

A
1. **Es una costumbre hispana.**
2. **Es una costumbre estadounidense.**
3. **Es una costumbre de las dos culturas.**
4. **Es una costumbre estadounidense.**
5. **Es una costumbre hispana.**

LECTURA OPCIONAL 2

LAS MENINAS

Todos tenemos fotos de nuestra familia, ¿no? Muchos tenemos todo un álbum. No hay nada más adorable que la foto de un bebé—sobre todo (especialmente) si el bebé es un hijo, sobrino o nieto, ¿verdad?

Muchas familias tienen retratos[1] de su familia—sobre todo, las familias nobles. Aquí tenemos el famoso cuadro *Las Meninas*[2]. El cuadro *Las Meninas* es del famoso artista español del siglo XVII, el pintor Diego Velázquez.

En su cuadro, *Las Meninas,* vemos a la hija del Rey[3] con sus damas y su perro. Vemos al pintor mismo de pie delante de su caballete[4]. Y en el cuadro hay algo maravilloso. Más atrás en el espejo[5] vemos el reflejo del Rey y la Reina. En el cuadro vemos a toda la familia real[6]: al padre, el Rey; a la madre, la Reina; a la hija, la princesa.

[1]retratos *portraits*
[2]Las Meninas *The ladies-in-waiting*
[3]Rey *King*
[4]caballete *easel*
[5]espejo *mirror*
[6]real *royal*

«Las Meninas» de Diego Velázquez

Después de leer

A Una familia real Contesten. *(Answer.)*

1. ¿Qué tienen muchas familias?
2. ¿Qué es una colección de fotos?
3. ¿Son adorables las fotos de un bebé?
4. ¿Tienen muchas familias retratos familiares también?
5. ¿Quién es el pintor de *Las Meninas?*
6. ¿Es español o latinoamericano Velázquez?
7. La muchacha en el cuadro, ¿es hija de quién?
8. ¿Dónde está el pintor en el cuadro?
9. ¿De quiénes hay un reflejo en el espejo?
10. ¿A quiénes vemos en el cuadro?

B *Las Meninas* Busquen a las personas en el cuadro. *(Find the following people in the painting.)*

1. el artista
2. la hija del Rey
3. las meninas o damas de la princesa
4. el Rey
5. el perro de la princesa
6. la madre de la princesa, la Reina

LECTURA OPCIONAL 2

TEACHING TIPS

A. You may want to use Fine Art Transparency F-4 with this reading. In the Transparency Binder, you will find additional background information about the painting, as well as related student activities.

B. Have students read the selection to themselves. Then have them do the **Después de leer** activities.

C. If you decide to do the **Conexiones** section one page 182 with the entire class, you may wish to include this reading as a part of it.

ANSWERS

Después de leer

A
1. **Muchas familias tienen fotos.**
2. **Una colección de fotos es un álbum.**
3. **Sí, las fotos de un bebé son adorables.**
4. **Sí, muchas familias tienen retratos familiares.**
5. **Diego Velázquez es el pintor de *Las Meninas.***
6. **Es español.**
7. **La muchacha en el cuadro es la hija del Rey.**
8. **El pintor está de pie delante de su caballete.**
9. **Hay un reflejo del Rey y de la Reina en el espejo.**
10. **Vemos a toda la familia real.**

B Have students point to each individual in the painting. You may want to project Fine Art Transparency F-4 so that everyone can see more clearly.

National Standards

Connections

This reading about painting and the photos of the famous works of art by Spanish and Latin American artists on pages 182–183 establish a connection with another discipline, allowing students to reinforce and further their knowledge of fine art through the study of Spanish.

¡OJO! The readings in the **Conexiones** section are optional. They focus on some of the major disciplines taught in schools and universities.

LAS BELLAS ARTES

EL ARTE

A. Have students read the introduction in English on page 182.

B. Give the students any information you like about the artists listed on page 182. (For additional information on the artists, see the Fine Art Connection on page 183 of this Teacher's Wraparound Edition.)

C. Model the new vocabulary words presented on page 182, then have students read the information on page 183.

TECHNOLOGY OPTION

You may wish to project Fine Art Transparencies F-5–F-9 as you do the reading. Students can also do the related activities that accompany the transparencies.

Conexiones

LAS BELLAS ARTES

EL ARTE

One may know a great deal or just a little about art. But almost everyone has at least some interest in art.

How often have we heard, "I may not know anything about art, but I certainly know what I like"?

There is no doubt that many of the world's great artists have come from Spain and Latin America. Do you recognize any of the following names?

El Greco, Velázquez, Murillo, Goya, Zurbarán, Sorolla, Picasso, Dalí, Miró, Rivera, Orozco, Siquieros, Kahlo, Tamayo, Botero.

Let's first read some information about art and then enjoy some famous works of Spanish and Latin American artists.

«Autorretrato» de Frida Kahlo

FINE ART CONNECTION

El Greco (1541–1614) was born in Greece, but painted in Spain. He made his paintings of saints and martyrs look supernatural.

Velázquez (1599–1660), born to a rich family in Seville, went to Madrid and became the painter of the court of Felipe IV.

Murillo (1617–1682) was born to a poor family in Seville. He was deeply religious and did many paintings for monasteries and convents.

Goya (1746–1828) was born in Aragón, Spain. During his lifetime he witnessed the brutality and suffering of war, which greatly influenced his works.

Zurbarán (1598–1664) was born in Badajoz, Spain. Many of his paintings have religious themes.

Sorolla (1863–1923) was born in Valencia. He did many portraits and scenes of Spain of his time.

Picasso (1881–1973) was born in Málaga. No artist achieved as much fame during his lifetime—or produced such a variety of artworks.

Dalí (1904–1989) was born in Cataluña. Many of his images are so bizarre that some have called him a madman.

(continued on page 183)

La pintura

El pintor
Antes de pintar, el pintor o artista tiene que preparar su lienzo. Tiene que colocar el lienzo en el caballete. El pintor escoge o selecciona el medio en que va a pintar. Los medios más populares son la acuarela[1], el óleo y el acrílico. El artista aplica los colores al lienzo con un pincel o una espátula.

El motivo o tema
Para el observador, el individuo que mira el cuadro, el motivo o tema de una obra de arte es el principal elemento de interés. Es la materia que pinta el artista—una persona, un santo, una escena, una batalla, un paisaje[2].

El estilo
El estilo es el modo de expresión del artista. En términos generales, clasificamos el estilo en figurativo o abstracto. Una obra figurativa presenta una interpretación literal o realista de la materia. El observador sabe[3] enseguida lo que ve en el cuadro.

Una obra de arte abstracto enfatiza o da énfasis al diseño más que a la materia. El artista no pinta la escena misma. Pinta algo que representa la escena o materia.

Aquí vemos unas obras famosas de algunos maestros de España y Latinoamérica.

«El dos de mayo» de Francisco de Goya

«Zapatistas» de José Clemente Orozco

«El entierro del Conde de Orgaz» de El Greco

[1]acuarela *watercolor*
[2]paisaje *landscape*
[3]sabe *knows*

Después de leer

A Tu pintura favorita Identifiquen el favorito. *(Identify your favorite.)*
Look at the paintings and tell which one is your favorite. Explain why it's your favorite. Do you think you prefer realistic art or abstract art?

Learning From Fine Art

«Zapatistas» In this painting we see the followers of Emiliano Zapata on their way to war. The plodding of the sad-faced peons and the rhythm created by their bodies leaning forward give the impression of a slow, steady march. The repeating hats, swords, and **sarapes** add to this feeling of movement. These peons are joined together to overcome their oppressors, the wealthy, powerful landowners.

«El entierro del conde de Orgaz» El Greco called this his most famous painting. It is divided into two parts, heaven and earth. Note the realistic portrayal of the people attending the burial of Orgaz in comparison to the elongated, mystical figures of heaven. Many think that the young boy on the lower right, who almost introduces us to the painting, is El Greco's son. The paper sticking out of the boy's pocket has his son's birthdate on it. Some think that El Greco himself is in the painting. They feel he is the thin man a bit left of center just above the fingers of an upturned hand. Note that these are the only two people looking out toward the viewer.

Fine Art Connection

Miró (1893–1983) was also born in Cataluña. He painted the world of dreams and the subconscious.

Rivera (1886–1957) was born in Mexico. He is one of the world's most famous muralists. His murals of revolutionary character deal with the history and social problems of Mexico.

Orozco (1883–1949) was also born in Mexico. Along with Diego Rivera and David Alfaro Siqueiros, he is one of the famed Mexican muralists. He used art to express his anger against all types of tyranny.

Siqueiros (1896–1974) was another Mexican muralist who was very involved in politics. He was imprisoned and driven into exile on several occasions.

Kahlo (1907–1954) Frida Kahlo, wife of the famous muralist Diego Rivera, was born in Mexico. Her own works have received worldwide acclaim in recent years. Kahlo, who had polio at age 6, was left a partial invalid for life after surviving a bus crash in her teens. She suffered constant pain and represented her pain by adding such things as thorn necklaces to her paintings. She painted numerous self-portraits.

Career Connection

Hablo español. Students who pursue careers in the humanities often need to have a reading knowledge of at least one foreign language in order to do research in their discipline. This is particularly true for students of art history, history, and literature.

RECYCLING

The **Actividades orales** and **the Actividad escrita** allow students to use the vocabulary and structures from this chapter in open-ended, real-life settings.

Actividades orales

¡OJO! Encourage students to say as much as possible when they do the **Actividades orales.** Tell them not to be afraid of making mistakes since the goal of the activities is real-life communication. If someone in the group makes an error, allow the others to politely correct him or her. Let students choose the activities they would like to particiapte in.

B Students can become extremely creative when doing **Actividad B**. You may wish to have some groups present their comments about each family to the entire class.

Student Portfolio

Have students keep a notebook containing their best written work from each chapter. These selected writings can be based on assignments from the Student Textbook and the Writing Activities Workbook. The four activities on page 185 are examples of writing assignments that may be included in each student's portfolio.

In the Workbook, students will develop an organized autobiography **(Mi autobiografía).** These workbook pages may also become a part of their portfolio. See the Teacher's Manual for more information on the Student Portfolio.

Culminación

Actividades orales

A **Fotos de la familia** Look at Anita Sepulveda's family photo album. Describe someone in the photos to a classmate. He or she will identify which person you're describing. Take turns.

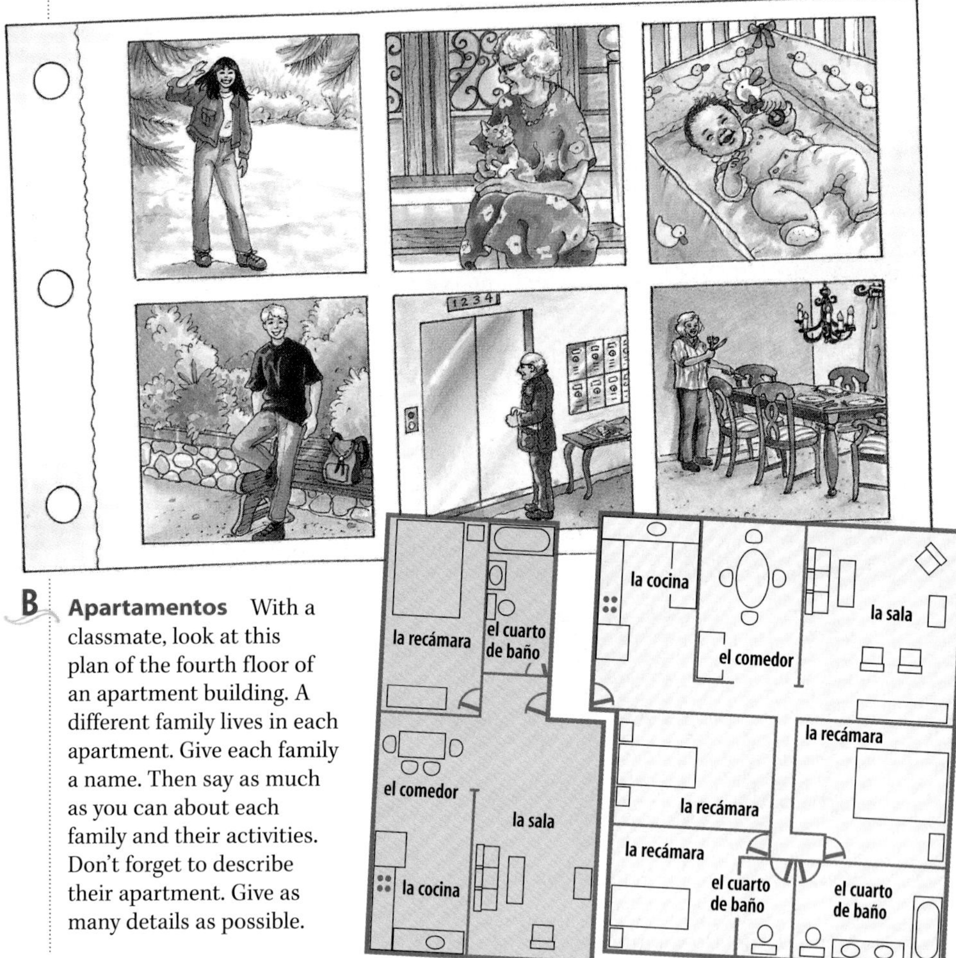

B **Apartamentos** With a classmate, look at this plan of the fourth floor of an apartment building. A different family lives in each apartment. Give each family a name. Then say as much as you can about each family and their activities. Don't forget to describe their apartment. Give as many details as possible.

ANSWERS

Actividades orales

A Answers will vary, however encourage students to use as much detail as possible when describing the photos.

B Answers will vary. Encourage students to be as creative as possible.

Independent Practice

Assign any of the following:

1. Activities, pages 184–185
2. Workbook, **Mi autobiografía,** page 70
3. Situation Cards
4. CD-ROM, Disc 2, Chapter 6, **Juego de repaso**

Actividades escritas

A **Mi familia y yo** You plan to spend next year as an exchange student in Argentina. You have to write a letter about yourself and your family to the agency in your community that selects the exchange students. Make your description as complete as possible.

B **Una fiesta** Look at the illustration of a birthday party. Write a paragraph about the party based on what you see.

C **La quinceañera** Your best friend Anita will soon be fifteen years old. Write out an invitation to her birthday party.

Writing Strategy

Ordering details

There are several ways to order details when writing. The one you choose depends on your purpose for writing. When describing a physical place, sometimes it is best to use spatial ordering. This means describing things as they actually appear—from left to right, from back to front, from top to bottom, or any other combination of logical order that works.

La casa de mis sueños

Write a description of your dream house. Be as complete as you can.

La Granja de San Ildefonso, Segovia

CAPÍTULO 6

Culminación

Actividades escritas

A and **B** Have students review the two vocabulary sections and the structures presented in this chapter before they begin to write.

TECHNOLOGY OPTION Students may use the Portfolio feature on the CD-ROM to write the letter in **Actividad A.**

C Have students read the **Conversación** on page 176 before they write their invitation.

Writing Strategy

Ordering details

A. Have students read the Writing Strategy on page 185.

B. Have students review the vocabulary presentation on pages 164–165, then have them do the writing activity.

TECHNOLOGY OPTION

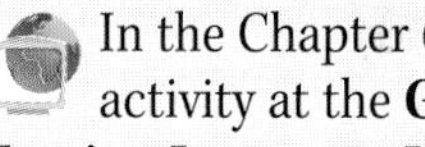

In the Chapter 6 Internet activity at the **Glencoe Foreign Language Web site (http://www.glencoe.com/sec/fl),** students visit real estate Web sites in the Spanish-speaking world and find a house or apartment to buy. You may wish to have students do the Internet activity, and then write the **La casa de mis sueños** as a follow-up. Students can also download and print out photos of their favorite house from the Internet.

ANSWERS

Actividades escritas

A Answers will vary.

B Answers will vary, however students might include such information as how old the person is, her name, what the people are doing at the party, and who the relatives are.

C Answers should include the person's name, as well as when, and where the party will take place.

Writing Strategy

Answers will vary.

CAPÍTULO 6
Vocabulario

ASSESSMENT RESOURCES

- Chapter Quizzes
- Testing Program
- Computer Testmaker
- Situation Cards
- Communication Transparency C-6
- Performance Assessment
- **Maratón mental** Videoquiz

VOCABULARY REVIEW

The words and phrases in the **Vocabulario** have been taught for productive use in this chapter. They are summarized here as a resource for both students and teacher. This list also serves as a convenient resource for the **Culminación** activities on pages 184 and 185. There are at least nine cognates in this vocabulary list. Have students find them.

Vocabulario

IDENTIFYING FAMILY MEMBERS

la familia
los parientes
el padre
la madre
el esposo, el marido
la esposa, la mujer
el/la hijo(a)
el/la hermano(a)
el/la abuelo(a)
el/la nieto(a)
el/la tío(a)
el/la sobrino(a)
el/la primo(a)
el gato
el perro
joven
viejo(a), anciano(a)

TALKING ABOUT FAMILY AFFAIRS OR EVENTS

el cumpleaños
el regalo
la celebración
tener
cumplir... años
invitar

IDENTIFYING ROOMS OF THE HOUSE

la sala
el comedor
la cocina
el cuarto, el dormitorio, la recámara
el cuarto de baño

TALKING ABOUT A HOME

la casa
el apartamento, el departamento
la calle
el jardín
el garaje
el carro
la planta baja
el piso
el ascensor
la escalera
privado(a), particular
alrededor de
cerca de
subir

DISCUSSING SOME HOME ACTIVITIES

el periódico
la revista
el libro
la película
la emisión deportiva
las noticias
ver la televisión
escribir una carta

For the Younger Student

Mi álbum de fotos If you think it's appropriate, ask students to bring in some family photos and have them talk about their family.

Learning From Photos

La familia real de España (page 187) The king and queen of Spain are **el rey Juan Carlos** and **la reina Sofía,** who is from Greece. Their son is **el príncipe Felipe.** Their daughters are **las Infantas Elena** and **Cristina.**

TECNOTUR

VIDEO

¡Buen viaje!

EPISODIO 6 ▸ La familia y su casa

Juan Ramón visita a la familia de Teresa.

Juan Ramón habla de las fotos de su familia que vive en Puerto Rico.

CD-ROM

Expansión cultural

La familia real de España

In this video episode Teresa's family welcomes Juan Ramón to their home in Madrid. To "rent" or "buy" your own house or apartment in a Spanish-speaking country, go to the Capítulo 6 Internet activity at the Glencoe Foreign Language Web site:

http://www.glencoe.com/sec/fl

Video Synopsis

In this episode, Juan Ramón meets Teresa's family—her mother, father, and little sister Pilar—at their home in Madrid. Teresa gives Juan Ramón a tour of the house and shows him his room. As Juan Ramón unpacks, he shares his photo album with Teresa. They go to the living room to look at the photos. Teresa seems to be especially interested in Juan Ramón's teen-age cousin Alvaro from Puerto Rico. Pilar interrupts the conversation with details about her up-coming birthday party.

OVERVIEW

This page previews three key multimedia components of the **Glencoe Spanish** series. Each reinforces the material taught in Chapter 6 in a unique manner.

VIDEO

The Video Program allows students to see how the chapter vocabulary and structures are used by native speakers within an engaging story line. For maximum reinforcement, show the video episode as a final activity for Chapter 6.

A. These two photos show highlights from the Chapter 6 video episode. Before watching it, ask the following: **¿Quiénes son las personas en la primera foto? ¿De dónde es Juan Ramón? En la segunda foto, ¿dónde están los jóvenes?**

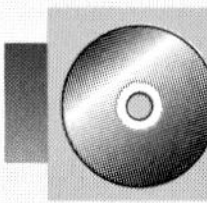

CD-ROM

A. The **Expansión cultural** photo shows the Royal Family of Spain. Have students read the caption on page 187.

B. In the CD-ROM version of **Expansión cultural** (Disc 2, page 187), students can listen to additional recorded information about the Royal Family.

INTERNET

Teacher Information and Student Worksheets for this activity can be accessed at the Web site.

Chapter 7 Overview ◆◆◆◆◆◆◆◆◆◆◆◆◆◆◆◆◆◆◆◆◆◆◆◆◆◆◆◆◆◆◆◆

SCOPE AND SEQUENCE pages 188–217

TOPICS	FUNCTIONS	STRUCTURE	CULTURE
◆ Team sports ◆ Physical activities	◆ How to talk about team sports and other physical activities ◆ How to tell what one wants to do or prefers to do ◆ How to discuss what one is able to do ◆ How to express what interests, bores, or pleases you	◆ Radical changing verbs **e → ie** ◆ Radical changing verbs **o → ue** ◆ **Interesar, aburrir,** and **gustar**	◆ El Real Madrid versus el Atlético de Madrid ◆ The World Cup of soccer ◆ The importance of soccer and baseball in the Spanish-speaking world ◆ The sport of **Jai alai** ◆ Archeological sites in Honduras, Mexico, and Puerto Rico ◆ Vistas de Puerto Rico

CHAPTER 7 RESOURCES

PRINT	MULTIMEDIA
Planning Resources	
Lesson Plans	Interactive Lesson Planner
Block Scheduling Lesson Plans	
Reinforcement Resources	
Writing Activities Workbook	Transparencies Binder
Student Tape Manual	Audiocassette/Compact Disc Program
Video Activities Booklet	Videocassette/Videodisc Program
Web Site User's Guide	Online Internet Activities
	Electronic Teacher's Classroom Resources
Assessment Resources	
Situation Cards	**Maratón mental** Mindjogger Videoquiz
Chapter Quizzes	Testmaker Computer Software (Macintosh/Windows)
Testing Program	Listening Comprehension Audiocassette/Compact Disc
Performance Assessment	Communication Transparency: C-7
Motivational Resources	
Expansion Activities	Café Glencoe: www.cafe.glencoe.com
	Keypal Internet Activities
Enrichment	
Spanish for Spanish Speakers	

Chapter 7 Planning Guide

SECTION	PAGES	SECTION RESOURCES
Vocabulario Palabras 1 **El fútbol**	190–193	Vocabulary Transparencies 7.1 Audiocassette 5A/ Compact Disc 4 Student Tape Manual, TE, pages 75–77 Workbook, pages 71–72 Chapter Quizzes, pages 32–33 CD-ROM, Disc 2, pages 190–193
Vocabulario Palabras 2 **El béisbol** **El básquetbol, El baloncesto**	194–197	Vocabulary Transparencies 7.2 Audiocassette 5A/ Compact Disc 4 Student Tape Manual, TE, pages 77–80 Workbook, page 73 Chapter Quizzes, pages 34–35 CD-ROM, Disc 2, pages 194–197
Estructura **Verbos de cambio radical e → ie en el presente** **Verbos de cambio radical o → ue en el presente** **Interesar, aburrir y gustar**	198–205	Workbook, pages 74–78 Audiocassette 5A/Compact Disc 4 Student Tape Manual, TE, pages 81–84 Chapter Quizzes, pages 36–37 Computer Testmaker CD-ROM, Disc 2, pages 198–205
Conversación **¿Quieres jugar?** **Pronunciación: Las consonantes s, c, z**	206–207	Audiocassette 5A/Compact Disc 4 Student Tape Manual, TE, pages 84–85 CD-ROM, Disc 2, pages 206–207
Lecturas culturales **El fútbol** **Deportes populares *(opcional)*** **El «Jai alai» o la pelota vasca *(opcional)***	208–211	Testing Program, pages 38–39 CD-ROM, Disc 2, pages 208–211
Conexiones **La arqueología *(opcional)***	212–213	Testing Program, page 39 CD-ROM, Disc 2, pages 212–213
Culminación **Actividades orales** **Actividades escritas** **Vocabulario** **Tecnotur**	214–217	**¡Buen viaje!** Video, Episode 7 Video Activities, pages 89–92 Internet Activities www.glencoe.com/sec/fl Testing Program, pages 35–38; 108; 140; 164 CD-ROM, Disc 2, pages 214–217

CAPÍTULO 7

OVERVIEW

In this chapter students will learn to discuss and describe team sports. To do this they will learn basic vocabulary related to soccer, basketball, and baseball. They will also learn the some stem-changing verbs—**empezar, querer, preferir, perder, volver, poder,** and **jugar.** Students will be able to use these verbs when talking about team sports.

They will also learn verbs such as **interesar, aburrir,** and **gustar** so they can tell what sports bore them or interest them and which sports they like. Students will also learn about the popularity of sports in various areas of the Spanish-speaking world.

National Standards

Communication
In Chapter 7 students will communicate in spoken and written Spanish on the following topics:

- describing team sports; namely, soccer, basketball, and baseball
- expressing interests, likes, and dislikes

Students will obtain and provide information, express personal preferences and dislikes, and engage in conversations about sports events as they fulfill the objectives listed on this page.

CAPÍTULO 7

Deportes de equipo

Objetivos

In this chapter you will learn to do the following:

- talk about team sports and other physical activities
- tell what you want to, begin to, and prefer to do
- talk about people's activities
- express what interests, bores, or pleases you
- discuss the role of sports in the Hispanic world

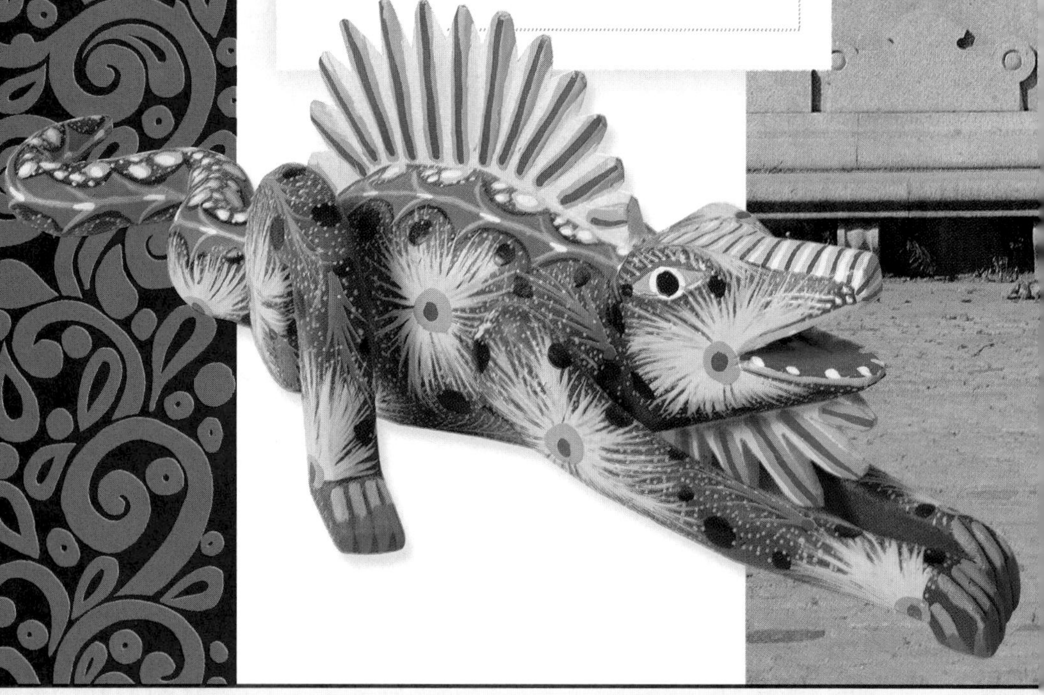

The **Glencoe Foreign Language Web site (http://www.glencoe.com/sec/fl)** offers three options that enable you and your students to experience the Spanish-speaking world via the Internet:

- The online **Actividades** are correlated to the chapters and utilize Hispanic Web sites around the world. For the Chapter 7 activity, see student page 217.
- The **Correspondencia electrónica** section provides information on how to set up a keypal (pen pal) exchange between your class and a class in the Spanish-speaking world.
- At **Café Glencoe,** the interactive "after-school" section of the site, you and your students can access a variety of additional online resources, including interactive games. The Chapter 7 crossword puzzle practices the chapter vocabulary and structures.

CAPÍTULO 7

Spotlight On Culture

Artefacto The beautifully painted animal is from Oaxaca, in southern Mexico.
Fotografía These young men are playing soccer in Retiro Park in Madrid. This park is a very popular gathering spot for both **madrileños** and tourists. Students will learn more about parks in the Spanish-speaking world in **¡Buen Viaje! Level 2.**

Pacing

Chapter 7 will require approximately seven to eight days. Pacing will vary according to the length of the class, the age of your students, and student aptitude.

Block Scheduling

The extended timeframe provided by block scheduling affords you the opportunity to implement a greater number of activities and projects to motivate and involve your students. See the Block Scheduling Lesson Plans Booklet for suggestions on how to present the chapter material within a block scheduling framework.

Chapter Projects

Los deportes Have students attend one of their school's athletic events. Then have them discuss it in Spanish. Their discussion should include the name of the sport, who the players are, how many players are on the team, and how good the team is.
Un reportaje Have students prepare a TV sports broadcast in Spanish. The broadcast can be an audio, video, or "live" broadcast.
Una entrevista Have students interview some of the school athletes who are taking Spanish. They can prepare a broadcast report on the interview. If the interviewee is in the class, the interview can be done "live."
Un artículo Have students prepare a short sports column in Spanish for the school newspaper. They could make this a regular feature.
¡Nachos! ¡Chorizo! ¡Churros! Have the Spanish Club sell some snacks at sporting events to raise money for a trip to a Spanish-speaking country. Easy snacks would be: **nachos (tortillitas con queso), chorizo, churros,** or **arroz y habichuelas (frijoles).**

CAPÍTULO 7
Vocabulario

PALABRAS 1

RESOURCES

-  Vocabulary Transparencies 7.1 (A & B)
- Student Tape Manual, TE, pages 75–77
- Audiocassette 5A/CD4
- Workbook, pages 71–72
- Quiz 1, pages 32–33
- CD-ROM, Disc 2, pages 190–193

Bell Ringer Review

Use BRR Transparency 7-1, or write the following on the board: Write three sentences about each of the following topics.

Mi casa
Mi familia

TEACHING VOCABULARY

A. Use Vocabulary Transparencies 7.1 (A & B) for the initial presentation of the new vocabulary.

B. After the oral presentation, as suggested in previous chapters, have students open their books and read the new vocabulary for additional reinforcement.

C. Project Vocabulary Transparency 7.1 A again and let students ask one another questions about what they see. For example, they might ask: **¿Cuántas personas hay en el equipo? ¿Qué tiene la muchacha en las manos? ¿Hay muchos espectadores en el estadio o pocos espectadores?**

Vocabulario

PALABRAS 1

El fútbol

Total Physical Response

TPR 1

Getting ready

Teach **rebotar** *(bounce)*, **pelota, tirar** *(throw)*, and **atrapar** *(catch)* by using the appropriate gestures as you say each word.

Begin

___ , levántate. Ven acá.
Cuenta: uno, dos, tres.
Ahora, toma la pelota.
Rebota la pelota cinco veces.
Ahora, tira la pelota. Tira la pelota a ___ .
___ , atrapa la pelota.
Y ahora, tira la pelota a ___ . Gracias.

TPR 2

The following TPR activity can be done with the entire class participating.

Begin

Indícame la mano derecha.
Indícame la mano izquierda.
Indícame la rodilla.
Indícame la pierna.
Levanta la mano derecha.
Y ahora levanta el pie derecho.
Levanta el pie izquierdo. Gracias.

19 noviembre
Real Madrid vs Barcelona

Hay un partido hoy.
Hay un partido entre el Real Madrid y el Barcelona.
El Real Madrid juega contra el Barcelona.

Los jugadores juegan (al) fútbol.
Un jugador lanza el balón.
Tira el balón con el pie.
El portero guarda la portería.

El segundo tiempo empieza.
Los dos equipos vuelven al campo.
El tanto queda empatado en cero.

El portero no puede bloquear (parar) el balón.
El balón entra en la portería.
González mete un gol.
Él marca un tanto.

El Real Madrid gana el partido.
El Barcelona pierde.
Pero el Barcelona no pierde siempre.
A veces gana.

D. Model the sentences under each illustration on page 191. Have students repeat the sentences. As they do, intersperse your presentation with questions such as the following:
¿Qué juegan los jugadores?
¿Qué lanza el jugador?
¿Tira el balón con la mano o con el pie?
¿Quién guarda la portería?
Have students answer with the complete sentence or sometimes have them use just the specific word or expression that responds to the question word.

ABOUT THE SPANISH LANGUAGE

- The verb **jugar** can be followed by **a** or the **a** can be eliminated. It is probably safe to say that the **a** is more commonly used in Spain but it is also heard in areas of Latin America.
- Another commonly used term for scoreboard is **el marcador.**
- **El partido** is used to refer to a sports match or game. **La partida** is used for a card game, for example.
- Note the use of the article **el** with **el Real Madrid** and **el Barcelona**. The article **el** is used because **el equipo** is understood. Later in the chapter students will see **la Argentina ante el Perú**, for example, when talking about the **Copa mundial**. The article refers to the country, not the team.

¡OJO! Práctica When students are doing the **Práctica** activities, accept any answer that makes sense. The purpose of these activities is to have students use the new vocabulary. They are not factual recall activities. Thus, do not expect students to remember specific information from the vocabulary presentation when answering. If you wish, have students use the photos on this page as a stimulus, when possible.

Historieta Each time **Historieta** appears, it means that the answers to the activity form a short story. Encourage students to look at the title of the **Historieta** since it can sometimes help them do the activity.

A and B After going over **Práctica A and B** on pages 192 and 193, call on one or more students to retell the stories in their own words.

Note Práctica A and B use only the third-person form of stem-changing verbs so that the students can immediately answer questions and speak without having to change endings. Students will learn how to manipulate the stem-changing verbs in the **Estructura** section of this chapter.

Writing Development

Have students write the answers to **Práctica A** in a paragraph to illustrate how all of the items tell a story.

Práctica

A HISTORIETA Un partido de fútbol

Contesten. *(Answer.)*

1. ¿Cuántos equipos de fútbol hay en el campo de fútbol?
2. ¿Cuántos jugadores hay en cada equipo?
3. ¿Qué tiempo empieza, el primero o el segundo?
4. ¿Vuelven los jugadores al campo cuando empieza el segundo tiempo?
5. ¿Tiene un jugador el balón?
6. ¿Lanza el balón con el pie o con la mano?
7. ¿Para el balón el portero o entra el balón en la portería?
8. ¿Mete el jugador un gol?
9. ¿Marca un tanto?
10. ¿Queda empatado el tanto?
11. ¿Quién gana, el Real Madrid o el Barcelona?
12. ¿Qué equipo pierde?
13. ¿Siempre pierde?

El estadio Atahualpa, Quito, Ecuador

ANSWERS

Práctica

A
1. **Hay dos equipos de fútbol en el campo de fútbol.**
2. **Hay once jugadores en cada equipo.**
3. **El primer (segundo) tiempo empieza.**
4. **Sí, los jugadores vuelven al campo cuando el segundo tiempo empieza.**
5. **Sí, un jugador tiene el balón. (No, un jugador no tiene el balón).**
6. **Lanza el balón con el pie.**
7. **El balón entra en la portería.**
8. **Sí, el jugador mete un gol.**
9. **Sí, marca un tanto.**
10. **No, el tanto no queda empatado.**
11. **El Real Madrid (El Barcelona) gana.**
12. **El Barcelona (El Real Madrid) pierde.**
13. **No, a veces gana.**

B **HISTORIETA** El fútbol

Contesten según se indica. *(Answer according to the cues.)*

1. ¿Cuántos jugadores hay en el equipo de fútbol? (once)
2. ¿Cuántos tiempos hay en un partido de fútbol? (dos)
3. ¿Quién guarda la portería? (el portero)
4. ¿Cuándo mete un gol el jugador? (cuando el balón entra en la portería)
5. ¿Qué marca un jugador cuando el balón entra en la portería? (un tanto)
6. En el estadio, ¿qué indica el tablero? (el tanto)
7. ¿Cuándo queda empatado el tanto? (cuando los dos equipos tienen el mismo tanto)

El equipo de Chile, La Copa mundial

Actividad comunicativa

A **Un partido de fútbol** Work with a classmate. Take turns asking and answering each other's questions about the illustration below.

CAPÍTULO 7

Vocabulario

Actividad comunicativa

¡OJO! Práctica versus Actividades comunicativas All activities which provide guided practice are labeled **Práctica.** The more open-ended communicative activities are labeled **Actividades comunicativas.**

Learning From Photos

El estadio Atahualpa, Quito, Ecuador (page 192) Have students look at this photo of the stadium in Quito. It will give them a feel for how the city is surrounded by mountains.

El equipo de Chile, La Copa mundial (page 193) Have students describe the uniform of the Chilean team. Have them describe anything else they see in the photo, using the vocabulary they learned in **Palabras 1.**

ANSWERS

Práctica

B
1. **Hay once jugadores en el equipo de fútbol.**
2. **Hay dos tiempos en un partido de fútbol.**
3. **El portero guarda la portería.**
4. **El jugador mete un gol cuando el balón entra en la portería.**
5. **Un jugador marca un tanto cuando el balón entra en la portería.**
6. **En el estadio el tablero indica el tanto.**
7. **El tanto queda empatado cuando los dos equipos tienen el mismo tanto.**

Actividad comunicativa

A Answers will vary. If students have difficulty, have them review the vocabulary on page 191.

Independent Practice

Assign any of the following:

1. Workbook, pages 71–72
2. Activities on student pages 192–193

CAPÍTULO 7 Vocabulario

PALABRAS 2

RESOURCES

- Vocabulary Transparencies 7.2 (A & B)
- Student Tape Manual, TE, pages 77–80
- Audiocassette 5A/CD4
- Workbook, page 73
- Quiz 2, pages 34–35
- CD-ROM, Disc 2, pages 194–197

Bell Ringer Review

Use BRR Transparency 7-2, or write the following on the board: Answer.

¿Sí o no?

1. **El jugador de fútbol tiene que tirar el balón con las dos manos.**
2. **Hay ocho tiempos en un partido de fútbol.**
3. **Hay once jugadores en un equipo de fútbol.**

TEACHING VOCABULARY

A. Model the new words and phrases on pages 194 and 195 using Vocabulary Transparencies 7.2 (A & B) and Audiocassette 5A/CD4.

B. Have students repeat each word or expression two or three times.

C. As you present the vocabulary with the overhead transparencies you may wish to ask the following questions:

¿Lleva un guante un jugador de béisbol?

¿Quién lanza la pelota, el pícher o el cátcher?

Si el bateador no batea la pelota, ¿quién devuelve la pelota?

¿De dónde batea el bateador la pelota?

(continued on page 195)

Vocabulario

PALABRAS 2

El béisbol

El pícher lanza la pelota.

El cátcher devuelve la pelota.

El bateador batea.
Batea un jonrón.
El jugador corre de una base a otra.

Total Physical Response

Getting ready

You may wish to bring in some props (glove, bat, baseball, basketball, hoop) to use with these activities.

TPR 1

Begin

(Estudiante 1), ven acá. Tú vas a ser el pícher. Ponte el guante.
Toma la pelota.
(Estudiante 2), ven acá. Tú vas a ser el bateador.
Toma el bate.
(Estudiante 1), tira la pelota a (Estudiante 2).
(Estudiante 2), pega a la pelota.
La pelota vuela. (Estudiante 2), corre.
Corre a la primera base.
Gracias, ___ y ___. Siéntense.

TPR 2

Begin

___ y ___, vengan aquí. Vamos a jugar al básquetbol.

(continued on page 195)

En un juego de béisbol hay nueve entradas.
Si después de la novena entrada el tanto queda empatado, el partido continúa.

La jugadora atrapa la pelota.
Atrapa la pelota con el guante.

CAPÍTULO 7

Vocabulario

Del platillo, ¿corre a la primera base o a la tercera base?
Cuando el bateador batea, ¿quién atrapa la pelota con frecuencia? ¿El receptor o el jardinero?

ABOUT THE SPANISH LANGUAGE

- As students will learn later in the chapter most baseball vocabulary is similar to the English because baseball is a sport that originated in the United States.
- **La pelota** refers to a small ball. **El balón** refers to a larger ball. A very small ball such as a golf ball is **la bola.**
- There is no definite rule as to when to use **el campo** vs. **la cancha**. In Spain, however, **el campo** is heard in many instances where **la cancha** would be preferred in Latin America.

Total Physical Response

(continued from page 194)
(Estudiante 1), toma el balón.
Dribla con el balón. Dribla cinco veces.
Y ahora, pasa el balón a (Estudiante 2).
(Estudiante 2), corre y dribla con el balón.
Tira el balón.
No, no encesta. Toma el balón de nuevo.
Dribla con el balón.
Tira el balón y encesta.
Gracias, ___ y ___ . Siéntense.

A, **B**, and **C** It is recommended that you go over the **Práctica** activities orally in class before assigning them for homework.

Writing Development

After going over **Práctica B**, have students write a short description of a basketball game.

Learning From Photos

San Juan, Puerto Rico Note the young women playing basketball. Until rather recently it was not very common to see women participating in sports in the Hispanic countries, particularly team sports. This is no longer the case. Women are participating in team sports such as basketball, baseball, and volleyball, as well as tennis and golf.

A Historieta El béisbol

Escojan la respuesta correcta.
(Choose the correct answer.)

1. Juegan al béisbol en ____ de béisbol.
   a. un campo **b.** una pelota **c.** una base
2. El pícher ____ la pelota.
   a. lanza **b.** encesta **c.** batea
3. El receptor atrapa la pelota en ____.
   a. una portería **b.** un cesto **c.** un guante
4. El jugador ____ de una base a otra.
   a. tira **b.** devuelve **c.** corre
5. En un partido de béisbol hay ____ entradas.
   a. dos **b.** nueve **c.** once

Monterrey, México

San Juan, Puerto Rico

B Historieta El baloncesto

Contesten. *(Answer.)*

1. ¿Es el baloncesto un deporte de equipo o un deporte individual?
2. ¿Hay cinco o nueve jugadores en un equipo de baloncesto?
3. Durante un partido de baloncesto, ¿los jugadores driblan con el balón o lanzan el balón con el pie?
4. ¿El jugador tira el balón en el cesto o en la portería?
5. ¿El encestado (canasto) vale dos puntos o seis puntos?

ANSWERS

Práctica

A
1. a
2. a
3. c
4. c
5. b

B
1. **El baloncesto es un deporte de equipo.**
2. **Hay cinco jugadores en un equipo de baloncesto.**
3. **Durante un partido de baloncesto los jugadores driblan con el balón.**
4. **El jugador tira el balón en el cesto.**
5. **El encestado (canasto) vale dos puntos.**

C **¿Qué deporte es?** Escojan. *(Choose.)*

1. El jugador lanza el balón con el pie.
2. Hay cinco jugadores en el equipo.
3. Hay nueve entradas en el partido.
4. El jugador corre de una base a otra.
5. El portero para o bloquea el balón.
6. El jugador tira el balón y encesta.

Actividad comunicativa

JUEGO **¿Qué deporte es?** Work with a classmate. Give him or her some information about a sport. He or she has to guess what sport you're talking about. Take turns.

C Have students do **Práctica C** with books open.

Actividad comunicativa

JUEGO This is a good activity to use when students need a "break" during the class period, or as an opening or closing activity.

Learning From Realia

Anuncios Have students look at the ads on page 197. Ask them what they think a **zapatillero** is. (shoe bag)
What do they get for free if they buy a pair of football shoes? (socks)
What's the word for football shoe? (**bota**)
The present exchange rate is about 145 **pesetas** to a dollar.
Ask them: **¿Cuestan las botas mucho o no?**
What is the abbreviation for **pesetas? (pts.)**

For the Younger Student

Mi atleta favorito You may wish to have students bring in pictures of their favorite sports figures. Have other students say something about them. Ask the student who brought in the photo or picture why he or she is so fond of this player: **¿Por qué eres (es Ud.) muy aficionado(a) a ___?**

ANSWERS

Práctica

C
1. **el fútbol**
2. **el baloncesto**
3. **el béisbol**
4. **el béisbol**
5. **el fútbol**
6. **el baloncesto**

RESOURCES

- Workbook, pages 74–78
- Student Tape Manual, TE, pages 81–84
- Audiocassette 5A/CD4
- Quizzes 3–4, pages 36–37
- Computer Testmaker
- CD-ROM, Disc 2, pages 198–205

Bell Ringer Review

Use BRR Transparency 7-3, or write the following on the board: Write at least three words associated with each sport.

el béisbol
el fútbol
el básquetbol

TEACHING STRUCTURE

Telling what you want or prefer

A. Write the verb forms on the board. Have students repeat them aloud.

B. You may wish to start with the **nosotros** form, to show that it is different.

C. Use different colored chalk for **nosotros** (and **vosotros**) to emphasize the difference in sound and spelling in comparison to the other forms.

D. Read the information to the students about the use of **a** + infinitive from the **¿Lo sabes?** box on page 198.

Estructura

Telling what you want or prefer
Verbos de cambio radical e → ie en el presente

1. There are certain groups of verbs in Spanish that have a stem change in the present tense. The verbs **empezar** *(to begin)*, **comenzar** *(to begin)*, **querer** *(to want)*, **perder** *(to lose)*, and **preferir** *(to prefer)* are stem-changing verbs. The **e** of the stem changes to **ie** in all forms except **nosotros** and **vosotros.** The endings are the same as those of regular verbs. Study the following forms.

INFINITIVE	empezar	querer	preferir
yo	empiezo	quiero	prefiero
tú	empiezas	quieres	prefieres
él, ella, Ud.	empieza	quiere	prefiere
nosotros(as)	empezamos	queremos	preferimos
vosotros(as)	*empezáis*	*queréis*	*preferís*
ellos, ellas, Uds.	empiezan	quieren	prefieren

2. The verbs **empezar, comenzar, querer,** and **preferir** are often followed by an infinitive.

Ellos quieren ir al gimnasio.
¿Por qué prefieres jugar al fútbol?

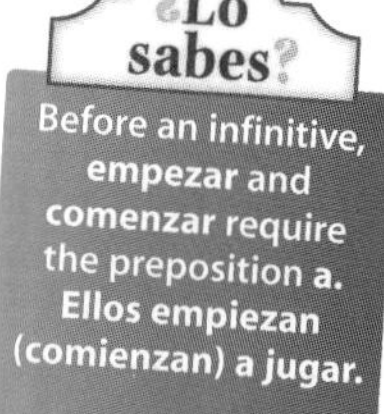

Lima, Perú

Learning From Photos

Lima, Perú Have students describe what they see in the photo on page 198. Ask them: **¿Son equipos profesionales o equipos de una escuela secundaria? ¿Hay muchos espectadores?**

Práctica

A HISTORIETA Queremos ganar.

Contesten. *(Answer.)*

1. ¿Empiezan Uds. a jugar?
2. ¿Empiezan Uds. a jugar a las tres?
3. ¿Quieren Uds. ganar el partido?
4. ¿Quieren Uds. marcar un tanto?
5. ¿Pierden Uds. a veces o ganan siempre?
6. ¿Prefieren Uds. jugar en el parque o en la calle?

Buenos Aires, Argentina

B HISTORIETA El partido continúa.

Formen oraciones según el modelo. *(Form sentences according to the model.)*

el segundo tiempo / empezar
El segundo tiempo empieza.

1. los jugadores / empezar a jugar
2. los dos equipos / querer ganar
3. ellos / preferir marcar muchos tantos
4. Sánchez / querer meter un gol
5. el portero / querer parar el balón
6. el equipo de Sánchez / no perder

C HISTORIETA ¿Un(a) aficionado(a) a los deportes?

Contesten personalmente. *(Answer these questions about yourself.)*

1. ¿Prefieres jugar al béisbol o al fútbol?
2. ¿Prefieres jugar con un grupo de amigos o con un equipo formal?
3. ¿Prefieres jugar en el partido o prefieres mirar el partido?
4. ¿Prefieres ser jugador(a) o espectador(a)?
5. ¿Siempre quieres ganar?
6. ¿Pierdes a veces?

Práctica

A B and C Each **Práctica** on this page tells a story. After going over the **Práctica** activities you can have students retell all the information in their own words.

Note In **Práctica A** and **C** you can ask the questions or have students do them as a paired activity. One student asks the questions and calls on another to respond. It is preferable to vary this procedure because it is more time consuming as a paired activity.

ANSWERS

Práctica

A
1. **Sí, (No, no) empezamos a jugar.**
2. **Sí, (No, no) empezamos a jugar a las tres.**
3. **Sí, (No, no) queremos ganar el partido.**
4. **Sí, queremos marcar un tanto.**
5. **Perdemos a veces. (Ganamos siempre.)**
6. **Preferimos jugar en el parque (la calle).**

B
1. **Los jugadores empiezan a jugar.**
2. **Los dos equipos quieren ganar.**
3. **Ellos prefieren marcar muchos tantos.**
4. **Sánchez quiere meter un gol.**
5. **El portero quiere parar el balón.**
6. **El equipo de Sánchez no pierde.**

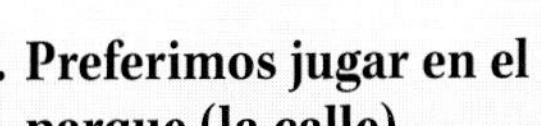

C
1. **Prefiero jugar al béisbol (fútbol).**
2. **Prefiero jugar con un grupo de amigos (un equipo formal).**
3. **Prefiero jugar en el partido (mirar el partido).**
4. **Prefiero ser jugador(a) (espectador[a]).**
5. **Sí, siempre quiero ganar. (No, no quiero ganar siempre.)**
6. **Sí, pierdo a veces. (No, no pierdo.)**

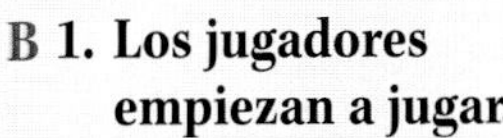

D This activity has students use different forms of the various stem-changing verbs.

Actividad comunicativa

A **EXPANSION** In addition to doing exactly what **Actividad A** calls for, you can also have students describe in their own words everything they see in each illustration.

Cooperative Learning

¿Cuál es tu deporte favorito? Each group chooses a leader who asks the others what their favorite sports are and whether they prefer to play sports, watch them on TV, or go to games. The leader will take notes and report to the class. You can follow up with a class survey, grouping names of students on the board according to their preferences, and then discuss the results.

D **HISTORIETA** ¿Baloncesto o béisbol?

Completen. *(Complete.)*

Rosita ___1___ (querer) jugar al baloncesto. Yo ___2___ (querer) jugar al béisbol. Y tú, ¿___3___ (preferir) jugar al baloncesto o ___4___ (preferir) jugar al béisbol? Si tú ___5___ (querer) jugar al béisbol, tú y yo ___6___ (ganar) y Rosita ___7___ (perder). Pero si tú ___8___ (querer) jugar al baloncesto, entonces tú y Rosita ___9___ (ganar) y yo ___10___ (perder).

Actividad comunicativa

A **¿Qué prefieres?** With a partner, look at the illustrations below. They each depict two activities. Find out from your partner which activity he or she prefers to do and which one he or she doesn't want to do. Take turns.

ANSWERS

Práctica

D
1. quiere
2. quiero
3. prefieres
4. prefieres
5. quieres
6. ganamos
7. pierde
8. quieres
9. ganan
10. pierdo

Actividad communicativa

A Answers will vary but may follow this model:

—¿Prefieres jugar al béisbol o prefieres mirar el partido de béisbol?

—Prefiero jugar al béisbol. No quiero mirar el partido de béisbol.

Describing more activities
Verbos de cambio radical o → ue en el presente

1. The verbs **volver** *(to return to a place)*, **devolver** *(to return a thing)*, **poder** *(to be able)*, and **dormir** *(to sleep)* are also stem-changing verbs. The **o** of the stem changes to **ue** in all forms except **nosotros** and **vosotros.** The endings are the same as those of regular verbs. Study the following forms.

INFINITIVE	volver	poder	dormir
yo	vuelvo	puedo	duermo
tú	vuelves	puedes	duermes
él, ella, Ud.	vuelve	puede	duerme
nosotros(as)	volvemos	podemos	dormimos
vosotros(as)	*volvéis*	*podéis*	*dormís*
ellos, ellas, Uds.	vuelven	pueden	duermen

2. The **u** in the verb **jugar** changes to **ue** in all forms except **nosotros** and **vosotros.**

jugar **juego, juegas, juega, jugamos,** ***jugáis,*** **juegan**

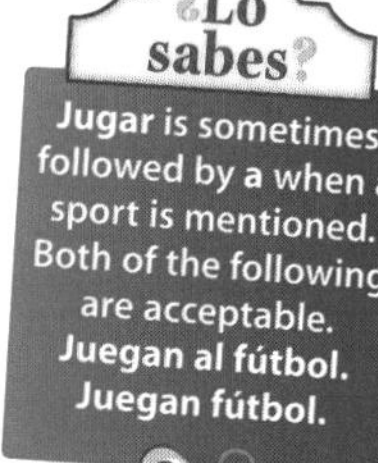

Jugar is sometimes followed by a when a sport is mentioned. Both of the following are acceptable.
Juegan al fútbol.
Juegan fútbol.

A HISTORIETA Un partido de béisbol

Contesten. *(Answer.)*

1. ¿Juegan Uds. al béisbol?
2. ¿Juegan Uds. con unos amigos o con el equipo de la escuela?
3. ¿Vuelven Uds. al campo después de cada entrada?
4. ¿Pueden Uds. continuar el partido si el tanto queda empatado después de la novena entrada?
5. ¿Duermen Uds. bien después de un buen partido de béisbol?

La Liga mexicana

Bell Ringer Review

Use BRR Transparency 7-4, or write the following on the board: Change the following to **nosotros.**

1. **Yo empiezo a jugar.**
2. **Yo quiero ganar.**
3. **Yo no pierdo.**

TEACHING STRUCTURE

Describing more activities

A. Write the verb forms from page 201 on the board and have students repeat them after you.

B. To give visual assitance for the spelling, use different colored chalk when writing the **nosotros** and **vosotros** forms on the board.

C. Have students open their books to page 201 and lead them through Steps 1 and 2.

A **Práctica A** can be done orally with books closed.

Writing Development

Have students write a paragraph about **un partido de béisbol** after going over **Práctica A.**

ANSWERS

Práctica

A
1. **Sí, (No, no) jugamos al béisbol.**
2. **Jugamos con unos amigos (con el equipo de la escuela).**
3. **Sí, volvemos al campo después de cada entrada.**
4. **Sí, podemos continuar el partido si el tanto queda empatado después de la novena entrada.**
5. **Sí, (No, no) dormimos bien después de un buen partido de béisbol.**

Estructura

Práctica

B After answering the questions in **Práctica B,** see whether students can make up similar questions using the verbs **querer, preferir,** and **poder.**

EXPANSION Ask students to describe the top photo, **Una clase de español en los Estados Unidos,** on page 202. **¿Leen o juegan los alumnos?**

Now, have students talk about their Spanish class. Encourage them to say as much as they can.

C In this activity students have to use all different forms of the various stem-changing verbs.

Actividad comunicativa

A Tell students to be as creative as possible. They can make up some outlandish reasons why they can't do something.

Class Motivator

¿Sí o no? Divide the class into two teams and play the following True/False game.

1. **Es necesario tener un cesto para jugar al voleibol.**
2. **Es necesario tener una red para jugar al voleibol.**
3. **El jugador de básquetbol puede correr con el balón en la mano.**
4. **El jugador de básquetbol tiene que driblar con el balón.**
5. **El balón de voleibol tiene que pasar por encima de la red.**
6. **El voleibol no puede tocar la red.**
7. **Los jugadores de básquetbol llevan guantes.**
8. **Los jugadores de béisbol corren de un canasto a otro.**

B HISTORIETA En la clase de español

Contesten. *(Answer.)*

1. ¿Juegas al Bingo en la clase de español?
2. ¿Juegas al Loto en la clase de español?
3. ¿Puedes hablar inglés en la clase de español?
4. ¿Qué lengua puedes o tienes que hablar en la clase de español?
5. ¿Duermes en la clase de español?
6. ¿Devuelve el/la profesor(a) los exámenes pronto?

Una clase de español en los Estados Unidos

C HISTORIETA Sí, pero ahora no puede.

Completen. *(Complete.)*

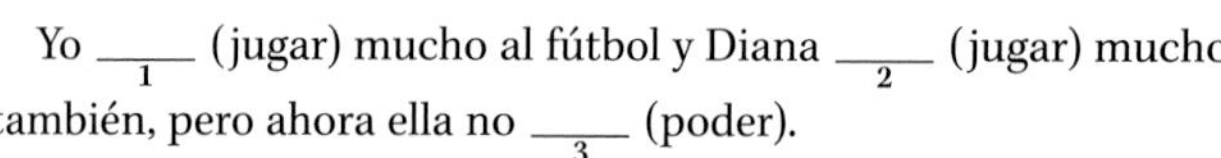

Yo ___ (1) (jugar) mucho al fútbol y Diana ___ (2) (jugar) mucho también, pero ahora ella no ___ (3) (poder).

—Diana, ¿por qué no ___ (4) (poder) jugar ahora?

—No ___ (5) (poder) porque ___ (6) (querer) ir a casa.

Sí, Diana ___ (7) (querer) ir a casa porque ella ___ (8) (tener) un amigo que ___ (9) (volver) hoy de Puerto Rico y ella ___ (10) (querer) estar en casa. Pero mañana todos nosotros ___ (11) (ir) a jugar. Y el amigo puertorriqueño de Diana ___ (12) (poder) jugar también. Su amigo ___ (13) (jugar) muy bien.

San Juan, Puerto Rico

Actividad comunicativa

A **Quiero pero no puedo.** A classmate will ask you if you want to do something or go somewhere. Tell him or her that you want to but you can't because you have to do something else. Tell what it is you have to do. Take turns asking and answering the questions.

ANSWERS

Práctica

B 1. **Sí, (No, no) juego al Bingo en la clase de español.**
2. **Sí, (No, no) juego al Loto en la clase de español.**
3. **Sí, (No, no) puedo hablar inglés en la clase de español.**
4. **Puedo (Tengo que) hablar español en la clase de español.**
5. **No, no duermo (Sí, duermo) en la clase de español.**
6. **Sí (No), el/la profesor(a) (no) devuelve los exámenes pronto.**

C 1. **juego** 2. **juega** 3. **puede** 4. **puedes** 5. **puedo** 6. **quiero** 7. **quiere** 8. **tiene** 9. **vuelve** 10. **quiere** 11. **vamos** 12. **puede** 13. **juega**

Actividad comunicativa

A Answers will vary. However, students will typically begin their question with: **¿Quieres + infinitive... ?** Their partner will answer with: **Sí, quiero... pero no puedo porque...**

Expressing what interests, bores, or pleases you
Interesar, aburrir y gustar

1. The verbs **interesar** and **aburrir** function the same in Spanish and English. Study the following examples.

¿Te aburre el arte?	*Does art bore you?*
No, el arte me interesa.	*No, art interests me.*
¿Te aburren los deportes?	*Do sports bore you?*
No, los deportes me interesan.	*No, sports interest me.*

¿Lo sabes?
Mí and ti are used after a preposition: para mí y para ti
A mí me gustan. ¿A ti también?

2. The verb **gustar** in Spanish functions the same as **interesar** and **aburrir**. **Gustar** conveys the meaning "to like," but its true meaning is "to please." The Spanish equivalent of "I like baseball" is "Baseball pleases me." Study the following examples.

¿Te gusta el béisbol? Ah, sí, me gusta mucho.
¿Te gustan los deportes? Sí, me gustan mucho.

3. The verb **gustar** is often used with an infinitive to tell what you like to do.

¿Te gusta jugar fútbol? Sí, me gusta jugar.
¿Te gusta comer? Sí, me gusta comer.

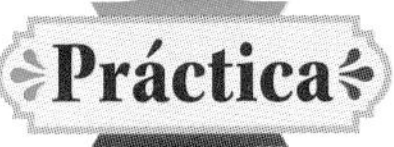

Práctica

A ¿Qué cursos te interesan y qué cursos te aburren?
Contesten. *(Answer.)*

1. ¿Te interesa la historia?
2. ¿Te interesa la geografía?
3. ¿Te interesa la biología?
4. ¿Te interesa la educación física?
5. ¿Te interesan las matemáticas?
6. ¿Te interesan las ciencias?
7. ¿Te interesan las lenguas?

Colegio San José, Málaga, España

Bell Ringer Review

Use BRR Transparency 7-5, or write the following on the board: Write down as many foods as you can remember.

TEACHING STRUCTURE

Expressing what interests, bores, or pleases you

¡OJO! English-speaking students often have a problem grasping the concept of **gustar.** Introducing **interesar** and **aburrir** in conjunction with **gustar** makes it much easier for students since we do have an exact parallel construction in English.

A. As you go over the explanation and **Práctica** activities, have students point to themselves as they say **me** and have them look at a friend as they say **te.**

Práctica

A Note that Items 1–4 have singular subjects and Items 5–7 have plural subjects. We have separated them to help students understand the concept.

ANSWERS

Práctica

A 1. Sí, (No, no) me interesa la historia. (No, me aburre la historia.)
2. Sí, (No, no) me interesa la geografía. (No, me aburre la geografía.)
3. Sí, (No, no) me interesa la biología. (No, me aburre la biología.)
4. Sí, (No, no) me interesa la educación física. (No, me aburre la educación física.)
5. Sí, (No, no) me interesan las matemáticas. (No, me aburren las matemáticas.)
6. Sí, (No, no) me interesan las ciencias. (No, me aburren las ciencias.)
7. Sí, (No, no) me interesan las lenguas. (No, me aburren las lenguas.)

Estructura

B thru **G** After going over **Práctica B–G** on pages 204 and 205, permit students to make up original sentences with **interesar**, **aburrir** and **gustar** using any vocabulary they know.

RECYCLING

All of these activities recycle vocabulary from the preceding chapters.

B **¿Te interesa o te aburre?** Sigan el modelo. *(Follow the model.)*

la biología
La biología me interesa. No me aburre.

1. el álgebra
2. la geometría
3. la historia
4. el español
5. la geografía

C **¿Te interesan o te aburren?** Sigan el modelo. *(Follow the model.)*

las películas
¿Te interesan las películas o te aburren?
Las películas me interesan. No me aburren.

1. los partidos de fútbol
2. las películas románticas
3. las emisiones deportivas
4. las noticias

D **Los deportes** Contesten. *(Answer.)*

1. ¿Te gusta el fútbol?
2. ¿Te gusta el béisbol?
3. ¿Te gusta el voleibol?
4. ¿Te gusta más el béisbol o el fútbol?
5. ¿Te gusta más el voleibol o el básquetbol?

Un flan

E **Los alimentos** Contesten. *(Answer.)*

1. ¿Te gusta la ensalada?
2. ¿Te gusta un sándwich de jamón y queso?
3. ¿Te gusta la sopa?
4. ¿Te gusta la carne?
5. ¿Te gustan las tortillas?
6. ¿Te gustan las enchiladas?
7. ¿Te gustan los frijoles?
8. ¿Te gustan los tomates?

ANSWERS

Práctica

B
1. **El álgebra me interesa. No me aburre.**
2. **La geometría me interesa. No me aburre.**
3. **La historia me interesa. No me aburre.**
4. **El español me interesa. No me aburre.**
5. **La geografía me interesa. No me aburre.**

C
1. **¿Te interesan los partidos de fútbol o te aburren? Los partidos de fútbol me interesan. No me aburren.**
2. **¿Te interesan las películas románticas o te aburren? Las películas románticas me interesan. No me aburren.**
3. **¿Te interesan las emisiones deportivas o te aburren? Las emisiones deportivas me interesan. No me aburren.**
4. **¿Te interesan las noticias o te aburren? Las noticias me interesan. No me aburren.**

D
1. **Sí, (No, no) me gusta el fútbol.**
2. **Sí, (No, no) me gusta el béisbol.**
3. **Sí, (No, no) me gusta el voleibol.**
4. **Me gusta más el béisbol (el fútbol).**
5. **Me gusta más el voleibol (el básquetbol).**

F **¿Te gusta la ropa?** Sigan el modelo. *(Follow the model.)*

¿Te gusta la gorra?
Sí, a mí me gusta.

G **¿Qué te gusta hacer?** Contesten. *(Answer.)*

1. ¿Te gusta cantar?
2. ¿Te gusta bailar?
3. ¿Te gusta comer?
4. ¿Te gusta leer?
5. ¿Te gusta más hablar o escuchar?
6. ¿Te gusta más jugar o ser espectador(a)?

Actividades comunicativas

A **¿Qué te interesa?** Work with a classmate. Take turns telling those things that interest you and those that bore you. Decide which interests you have in common.

B **Gustos** Get together with a classmate. Tell one another some things you like and don't like. The following are some categories you may want to explore. Decide whether you and your classmates have any of the same likes and dislikes.

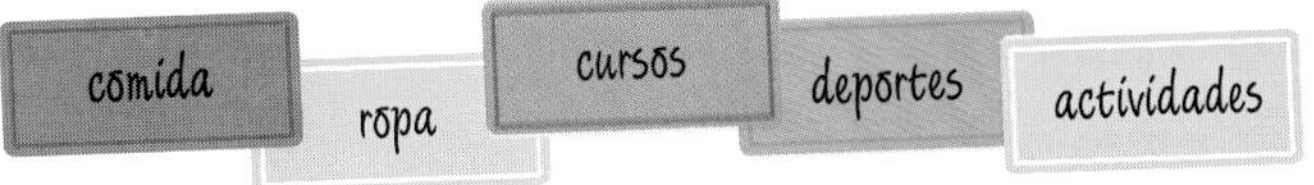

CAPÍTULO 7
Estructura

F After doing **Práctica F**, quickly review the colors students learned in Chapter 3.

G This can be done as a paired activity. Ask students to think of additional verbs of action they have learned. Write these on the board.

Actividades comunicativas

Let students select the activity they wish to take part in.

A **TECHNOLOGY OPTION** In the CD-ROM version of **Actividad A** (Disc 2, page 205), students may interact with an on-screen native speaker and record their conversation.

A and **B** **EXPANSION** After doing **Actividades A** and **B,** follow up by having each pair of students report to the class those things that interest them, those things that bore them, those things they like, and those they dislike.

¡OJO! All new material in the chapter has been presented. The sections that follow recombine and reintroduce the vocabulary and structures that have already been introduced.

ANSWERS CONTINUED

E
1. **Sí, (No, no) me gusta la ensalada.**
2. **Sí, (No, no) me gusta un sándwich de jamón y queso.**
3. **Sí, (No, no) me gusta la sopa.**
4. **Sí, (No, no) me gusta la carne.**
5. **Sí, (No, no) me gustan las tortillas.**
6. **Sí, (No, no) me gustan las enchiladas.**
7. **Sí, (No, no) me gustan los frijoles.**
8. **Sí, (No, no) me gustan los tomates.**

F
1. **¿Te gusta la camisa? Sí, a mí me gusta.**
2. **¿Te gustan los tenis? Sí, a mí me gustan.**
3. **¿Te gusta la falda? Sí, a mí me gusta.**
4. **¿Te gustan los zapatos? Sí, a mí me gustan.**
5. **¿Te gusta el pantalón? Sí, a mí me gusta.**
6. **¿Te gusta la chaqueta? Sí, a mí me gusta.**

G
1. **Sí, (No, no) me gusta cantar.**
2. **Sí, (No, no) me gusta bailar.**
3. **Sí, (No, no) me gusta comer.**
4. **Sí, (No, no) me gusta leer.**
5. **Me gusta más hablar (escuchar).**
6. **Me gusta más jugar (ser espectador[a]).**

Actividades comunicativas
A and B Answers will vary.

CAPÍTULO 7
Conversación

RESOURCES

- Audiocassette 5A/CD4
- CD-ROM, Disc 2, page 206

Bell Ringer Review

Use BRR Transparency 7-6, or write the following on the board: Write down two things that you like and two things that you don't like.

TEACHING THE CONVERSATION

A. Have students open their books to page 206. One half of the class will take the part of **Anita**, the other half will take the part of **Tomás**. Each half will read in unison.

B. Now, call on one individual to be **Anita** and another to be **Tomás**. Have them read the conversation aloud.

C. You may wish to play the recording on Cassette 5A/Compact Disc 4 for them.

D. Go over the **Después de conversar** activity.

E. Call on students to present a similar conversation of their own.

TECHNOLOGY OPTION

On the CD-ROM (Disc 2, page 206), students can watch a dramatization of this conversation. They can then play the role of either one of the characters, and record themselves in the conversation.

Conversación

¿Quieres jugar?

ANITA: Tomás, ¿prefieres el béisbol o el fútbol?
TOMÁS: ¿Yo? Yo prefiero el fútbol. Me gusta más que el béisbol.
ANITA: ¿Juegas fútbol?
TOMÁS: Sí, juego. Pero la verdad es que me gusta más ser espectador que jugador.
ANITA: ¿Es bueno el equipo de tu escuela?
TOMÁS: Sí, tenemos un equipo estupendo.
ANITA: ¿Son campeones?
TOMÁS: No, pero van a ganar el campeonato.

Después de conversar

Contesten. *(Answer.)*

1. ¿Prefiere Tomás el béisbol o el fútbol?
2. ¿Juega mucho al fútbol?
3. ¿Qué prefiere ser?
4. ¿Es bueno el equipo de su escuela?
5. ¿Qué va a ganar el equipo?

206 *doscientos seis* CAPÍTULO 7

ANSWERS

Después de conversar

1. **Tomás prefiere el fútbol.**
2. **No, no juega mucho al fútbol.**
3. **Prefiere ser espectador.**
4. **Sí, tiene un equipo estupendo.**
5. **El equipo va a ganar el campeonato.**

Actividades comunicativas

A **No soy muy aficionado(a) a...** Work with a classmate. Tell him or her what sport you don't want to play because you don't like it. Tell what you prefer to play. Then ask your classmate questions to find out what sports he or she likes.

B **Un partido de fútbol** You are at a soccer match with a friend (your classmate). He or she has never been to a soccer match before and doesn't understand the game. Your friend has a lot of questions. Answer the questions and explain the game. You may want to use some of the following words.

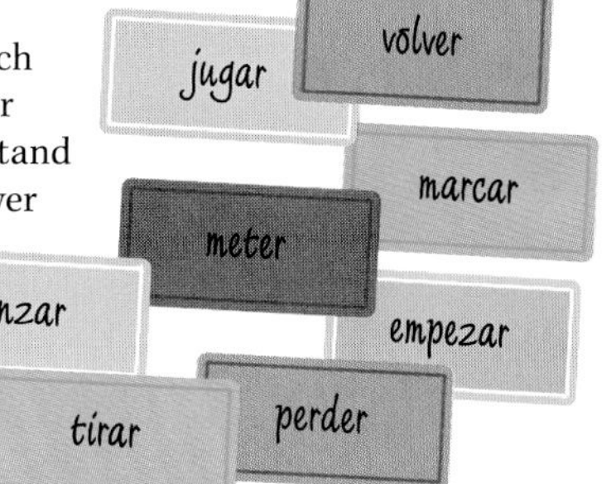

Pronunciación

Las consonantes s, c, z

The consonant **s** is pronounced the same as the *s* in *sing*. Repeat the following.

sa	se	si	so	su
sala	**base**	**sí**	**peso**	**su**
pasa	**serio**	**simpático**	**sopa**	**Susana**
saca	**seis**	**siete**	**sobrino**	

The consonant **c** in combination with **e** or **i (ce, ci)** is pronounced the same as an **s** in all areas of Latin America. In many parts of Spain, **ce** and **ci** are pronounced like the *th* in English. Likewise, the pronunciation of **z** in combination with **a, o, u (za, zo, zu)** is the same as an **s** throughout Latin America and as a **th** in most areas of Spain. Repeat the following.

za	ce	ci	zo	zu
cabeza	**cero**	**cinco**	**zona**	**zumo**
empieza	**encesta**	**ciudad**	**almuerzo**	**Zúñiga**

Repeat the following sentences.

González enseña en la sala de clase.
El sobrino de Susana es serio y sincero.
La ciudad tiene cinco zonas.
Toma el almuerzo a las doce y diez en la cocina.

Actividades comunicativas

A Have each pair of students report back to the class telling what sport(s) each partner prefers to play.

B If possible, have several pairs of students present their conversations to the entire class.

TEACHING PRONUNCIATION

A. Have students repeat the consonant sounds after you or the recording on Cassette 5A/Compact Disc 4. Have them imitate very carefully.

B. Be sure students do not make an English *z* sound when pronouncing words with the letter **z.**

C. Have students open their books to page 207. Call on individuals to read the sentences carefully.

D. The words and sentences presented here can also be used for dictation. It is important to bring these sounds and their spellings back frequently since they are very often misspelled.

TECHNOLOGY OPTION

In the CD-ROM version of the Pronunciation section (Disc 2, page 207), students will see an animation of the cartoon on this page. They can also listen to, record, and play back the sounds, words, and sentences presented here.

ANSWERS

Actvidades comunicativas

A Answers will vary.

B Answers will vary, but encourage students to use as many of the words in the colored boxes as possible.

National Standards

Cultures

The reading about soccer and the World Cup on page 208, and the related activities on page 209, give students an understanding of the importance of this sport in the Hispanic culture.

TEACHING THE READING

¡OJO! If your students are not interested in sports, you can go over the **Lectura** quickly. If your class is rather sports-minded, you may wish to do the **Lectura** more thoroughly.

Pre-reading

Give students a brief oral synopsis of the reading in Spanish.

Reading

A. Ask students to open their books to page 208. Call on individuals to read two or three sentences. After each student reads, ask the others follow-up questions. Continue in this manner through the entire reading.

B. Ask five or six questions that review the main points of the reading. The answers to these questions will give a coherent oral summary of the **Lectura**.

C. Call on a more able student to give a summary of the **Lectura** in his or her own words. Call on slower students to answer questions about the oral summary just given. Then have a slower student give an oral summary based on the summary of the more able student.

D. With more able classes, have students write their own summary. This should take approximately seven minutes.

Lecturas culturales

Reading Strategy

Scanning for specific information

Scanning for specific information means reading to find out certain details without concerning yourself with the other information in the passage. Some examples of scanning are looking up words in a dictionary or searching a television listing to find out when certain programs are on. Another example of scanning is reading articles to find out something specific, such as sports results.

EL FÚTBOL

La Liga española

Estamos en el estadio Santiago Bernabéu en Madrid. ¡Qué emoción! El Real Madrid juega contra el Atlético de Madrid. Quedan[1] dos minutos en el segundo tiempo. El partido está empatado en cero. ¿Qué va a pasar[2]? Da Silva pasa el balón a Casero. Casero lanza el balón con el pie izquierdo. El balón vuela[3]. El portero quiere parar el balón. ¿Puede o no? No, no puede. El balón entra en la portería. Casero mete un gol y marca un tanto. En los últimos dos minutos del partido, el equipo de Casero y da Silva gana. El Real Madrid derrota[4] al Atlético de Madrid uno a cero. El Real Madrid es triunfante, victorioso. Casero y da Silva son sus héroes.

La Copa mundial

Casero y da Silva son jugadores muy buenos y van a jugar en la Copa mundial. Pero da Silva no va a jugar con el mismo equipo que Casero. ¿Por qué? Porque da Silva no es español. Es del Brasil y en la Copa él va a jugar con el equipo del Brasil. Casero va a jugar con el equipo de España porque es español.

Cada cuatro años las estrellas[5] de cada país forman parte de un equipo nacional. Hay treinta y dos equipos nacionales que juegan en la Copa mundial. Los equipos de los treinta y dos países de todas partes del mundo compiten[6] para ganar la Copa y ser el campeón del mundo.

[1] Quedan *Remain*
[2] pasar *happen*
[3] vuela *flies*
[4] derrota *defeats*
[5] estrellas *stars*
[6] compiten *compete*

El estadio Santiago Bernabéu

Did You Know?

La Copa mundial The World Cup matches were played in the United States for the first time ever in 1994. The very first World Cup matches were held in Uruguay in 1930. The Uruguayan national team was the winner. Uruguay and Argentina have each won twice. Three-time winners are Italy and West Germany. Brazil has won the cup four times. The World Cup competition takes place every four years.

Independent Practice

Assign any of the following:

1. **Después de leer** activities, page 209
2. Workbook, **Un poco más**, pages 79–81
3. CD-ROM, Disc 2, pages 208–209

Después de leer

A **Lo mismo** Escojan la palabra equivalente. *(Choose the equivalent term.)*

1. la mayoría — a. victorioso
2. el vocabulario — b. tirar
3. lanzar — c. el o la que gana
4. el campeón — d. la mayor parte
5. triunfante — e. no permitir pasar, bloquear
6. el jugador — f. las palabras
7. parar — g. el miembro del equipo

B **Lo contrario** Escojan lo contrario. *(Choose the opposite.)*

1. el/la jugador(a) — a. primeros
2. últimos — b. derecho
3. izquierdo — c. el/la espectador(a)
4. gana — d. pierde
5. entra — e. sale

C **HISTORIETA El partido de fútbol**

Contesten. *(Answer.)*

1. ¿A qué juegan los dos equipos?
2. ¿Cuántos minutos quedan en el segundo tiempo?
3. ¿Quién pasa el balón?
4. ¿Quién lanza el balón?
5. ¿Cómo lanza el balón?
6. ¿Puede parar el balón el portero?
7. ¿Qué mete Casero?
8. ¿Qué marca?
9. ¿Qué equipo es victorioso?
10. ¿Quiénes son los héroes?

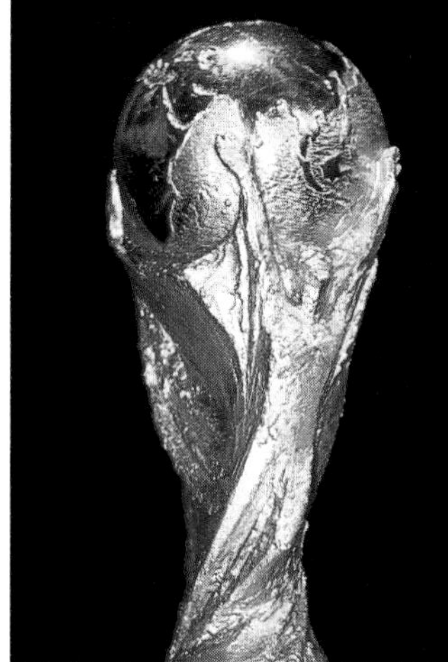

La Copa de la FIFA

D **La Copa mundial** Digan que sí o que no.

1. Los equipos juegan en la Copa mundial cada año.
2. Todos los jugadores de un equipo son de la misma nacionalidad.
3. Cada equipo que juega en la Copa representa un país.
4. Los equipos de veintidós naciones juegan en la Copa mundial.
5. Todos los equipos son de Europa.

Post-reading

A. Have students form three groups. Have each group write a brief news announcement for a different type of sporting event and present their announcement to the class.

B. Now have students do the **Después de leer** activities on page 209.

TECHNOLOGY OPTION

Students may listen to a recorded version of the **Lectura** on the CD-ROM, Disc 2, page 208.

Después de leer

A and **B** You may assign both of these activities before going over them in class.

C **Después de leer C** will help students prepare an oral or written summary of the **Lectura.**

D Have more able students give the correct answer to any false statements in this activity.

ANSWERS

Después de leer

A 1. d 2. f 3. b 4. c 5. a 6. g 7. e

B 1. c 2. a 3. b 4. d 5. e

C
1. Los dos equipos juegan al fútbol.
2. Quedan dos minutos en el segundo tiempo.
3. Da Silva pasa el balón.
4. Casero lanza el balón.
5. Lanza el balón con el pie izquierdo.
6. No, el portero no puede parar el balón.
7. Casero mete un gol.
8. Marca un tanto.
9. El Real Madrid es victorioso.
10. Casero y Da Silva son los héroes.

D
1. No, los equipos no juegan en la Copa mundial cada año.
2. Sí, todos los jugadores de un equipo son de la misma nacionalidad.
3. Sí, cada equipo que juega en la Copa representa un país.
4. No, los equipos de treinta y dos naciones juegan en la Copa mundial.
5. No, no todos los equipos son de Europa.

CAPÍTULO 7
Lecturas

LECTURA OPCIONAL 1

National Standards

Cultures

In the reading on this page students learn where soccer and baseball are popular in the Spanish-speaking world. They will demonstrate an understanding of the importance of these two sports in the Hispanic culture.

TEACHING TIPS

¡OJO! This reading on sports is optional. You may skip it completely, have the entire class read it, have only several students read it, or assign it for extra credit.

A. Have students read the passage quickly as they look at the photos that accompany it. Have students discuss whatever information they find interesting.

INFORMAL ASSESSMENT

You may wish to give students who read this selection the following quiz.

Answer.

1. **¿Dónde es popular el fútbol?**
2. **¿Tiene muchos aficionados?**
3. **¿Cuándo está lleno el estadio?**
4. **¿Dónde es popular el béisbol?**
5. **¿Por qué hay mucha influencia del inglés en el vocabulario del béisbol?**

LECTURA OPCIONAL 1

La Argentina vs. Croatia

La Liga mexicana

DEPORTES POPULARES

El fútbol

El fútbol es un deporte muy popular en todos los países hispanos. Los equipos nacionales tienen millones de aficionados. Cuando el equipo de un país juega contra el equipo de otro país, el estadio está lleno[1] de espectadores.

El béisbol

El béisbol no es un deporte popular en todos los países hispanos. Es popular en sólo algunos. El béisbol tiene o goza de popularidad en Cuba, Puerto Rico, la República Dominicana, Venezuela, Nicaragua, México y Panamá. Como el béisbol es esencialmente un deporte norteamericano, la mayoría del vocabulario del béisbol es inglés: las bases, el pícher, el out, el jonrón.

Muchos jugadores de béisbol de las Grandes Ligas son hispanos. Entre 1919 y hoy más de cien jugadores latinos juegan en la Serie Mundial.

[1]lleno *full*

Después de leer

A **¿Es la verdad o no?** Contesten con **sí** o **no.** *(Answer with* sí *or* no.)

1. El fútbol es un deporte popular en todas partes de Latinoamérica.
2. Casi todos los países tienen su equipo nacional de fútbol.
3. Cuando un equipo nacional juega contra otro equipo nacional—un equipo de otro país—hay muy poca gente en el estadio; hay muy pocos espectadores.
4. El béisbol es también un deporte popular en todos los países hispanos.
5. El béisbol es muy popular en los países del Caribe.
6. Muchos beisbolistas famosos de las Grandes Ligas de los Estados Unidos son de origen hispano o latino.

B **Las nacionalidades** Completen. *(Complete.)*

1. Un puertorriqueño es de ____.
2. Un cubano es de ____.
3. Un panameño es de ____ y un nicaragüense es de ____.
4. Un mexicano es de ____ y un dominicano es de la ____.

Did You Know?

El básquetbol After soccer, the sport that has reached worldwide popularity is basketball. The professional basketball league in Spain is one of the best in Europe. Many American college players that are not able to play in the NBA (National Basketball Association) in the U.S. are able to obtain lucrative contracts in European leagues, especially in Italy and Spain. The sport has reached its highest levels in Brazil in South America and in Puerto Rico in the Caribbean.

ANSWERS

Después de leer

A 1. Sí, el fútbol es un deporte popular en todas partes de Latinoamérica.

2. Sí, casi todos los países tiene su equipo nacional de fútbol.

3. No, cuando un equipo nacional juega contra otro equipo nacional el estadio está lleno de espectadores.

4. No, el béisbol no es un deporte popular en todos los países hispanos.

LECTURA OPCIONAL 2

El país vasco, España

EL «JAI ALAI» O LA PELOTA VASCA

Jai alai es una palabra vasca. El país vasco es una región del norte de España y del sudoeste de Francia. El jai alai tiene otro nombre—la pelota vasca. El jai alai es un juego vasco popular.

Juegan al jai alai o pelota vasca en una cancha. Los jugadores son «pelotaris». Llevan un pantalón blanco, una camisa blanca, una faja roja y alpargatas. Tienen una cesta. Usan la cesta para lanzar y recibir la pelota.

En la cancha de jai alai hay tres paredes[1]. El frontón es la pared delantera[2]. «Frontón» es también el nombre de toda la cancha. El jugador lanza la pelota con la cesta contra la pared. Cuando la pelota pega[3] contra el frontón y rebota[4] hacia el jugador, el «pelotari» tiene que devolver la pelota. ¡Y la pelota viaja[5] a unas ciento cincuenta millas por hora!

[1]paredes *walls*
[2]delantera *front*
[3]pega *hits*
[4]rebota *rebounds*
[5]viaja *travels*

Miami, Florida

Después de leer

A Jai alai Completen. *(Complete.)*

1. El jai alai o la ____ es un juego popular vasco.
2. Los pelotaris son ____ de jai alai.
3. Llevan un pantalón ____, una camisa ____ y una faja ____.
4. Los pelotaris no llevan zapatos cuando juegan. Llevan ____
5. Los pelotaris usan una ____ para lanzar y recibir la pelota.
6. El ____ es la cancha de jai alai.
7. En una cancha de jai alai hay tres ____.
8. El jugador tiene que ____ la pelota cuando pega contra el frontón.
9. En un juego de jai alai la pelota viaja a ____ millas por hora.

ANSWERS CONTINUED (PAGE 211)

5. **Sí, el béisbol es muy popular en los países del Caribe.**
6. **Sí, muchos beisbolistas famosos de las Grandes Ligas de los Estados Unidos son de origen hispano o latino.**

B
1. **Puerto Rico**
2. **Cuba**
3. **Panamá, Nicaragua**
4. **México, República Dominicana**

Después de leer

A
1. **pelota vasca**
2. **jugadores**
3. **blanco, blanca, roja**
4. **alpargatas**
5. **cesta**
6. **frontón**
7. **paredes**
8. **devolver**
9. **unas ciento cincuenta**

LECTURA OPCIONAL 2

TEACHING TIPS

¡OJO! This reading on **Jai alai** is optional. You may skip it completely, have the entire class read it, have only several students read it, or assign it for extra credit.

INFORMAL ASSESSMENT

You may wish to give the following quiz to students who read this selection.

Answer.

¿Dónde está el país vasco? ¿Cuál es otro nombre del *jai alai?*
¿Dónde juegan al jai alai?
¿Qué llevan los jugadores del jai alai?
¿Qué usan para lanzar la pelota?
¿Cuántas paredes tiene la cancha?
¿A cuántas millas por hora viaja la pelota cuando el jugador devuelve la pelota?

Did You Know?

Jai alai This sport is played in Florida and Connecticut. Rather than being called **jai alai** or **pelota vasca**, it is often called **frontón,** the name of the court.

HISTORY CONNECTION

El país vasco The Basque country has a great deal of beautiful scenery but it is also a very industrial area. The Basques, **los vascos,** speak a mystery language—**el vasco** in Spanish, **euskadi** in Basque. There is a strong separatist movement in the Basque country.

CAPÍTULO 7
Conexiones

National Standards

Connections
This reading about archeology establishes a connection with another discipline, allowing students to reinforce and further their knowledge of social sciences through the study of Spanish.

¡OJO! The readings in the **Conexiones** section are optional. They focus on the some of the major disciplines taught in schools and universities. The vocabulary is useful for discussing topics such as history, literature, art, economics, business, science, etc.

You may choose any of the following ways to do this reading on archeology with your students.

Independent reading Have students read the selections and do the post-reading activities as homework, which you collect. This option is least intrusive on class time and requires a minimum of teacher involvement.

Homework with in-class follow-up Assign the readings and post-reading activities as homework. Review and discuss the material with the students in class the next day.

Intensive in-class activity This option includes a pre-reading vocabulary presentation, in-class reading and discussion, assignment of the activities for homework, and a discussion of the assignment in class the following day.

Conexiones

Las ciencias sociales

La arqueología

Archeology is a fascinating field. Archeologists travel to every corner of the globe searching for places to excavate and study the ruins of ancient civilizations. There have been interesting archeological discoveries in Latin America where many pre-Colombian civilizations existed long before the arrival of the Spaniards. Let's read about some of these archeological sites. A few famous ones revealed some interesting information about sports and games in pre-Colombian cultures.

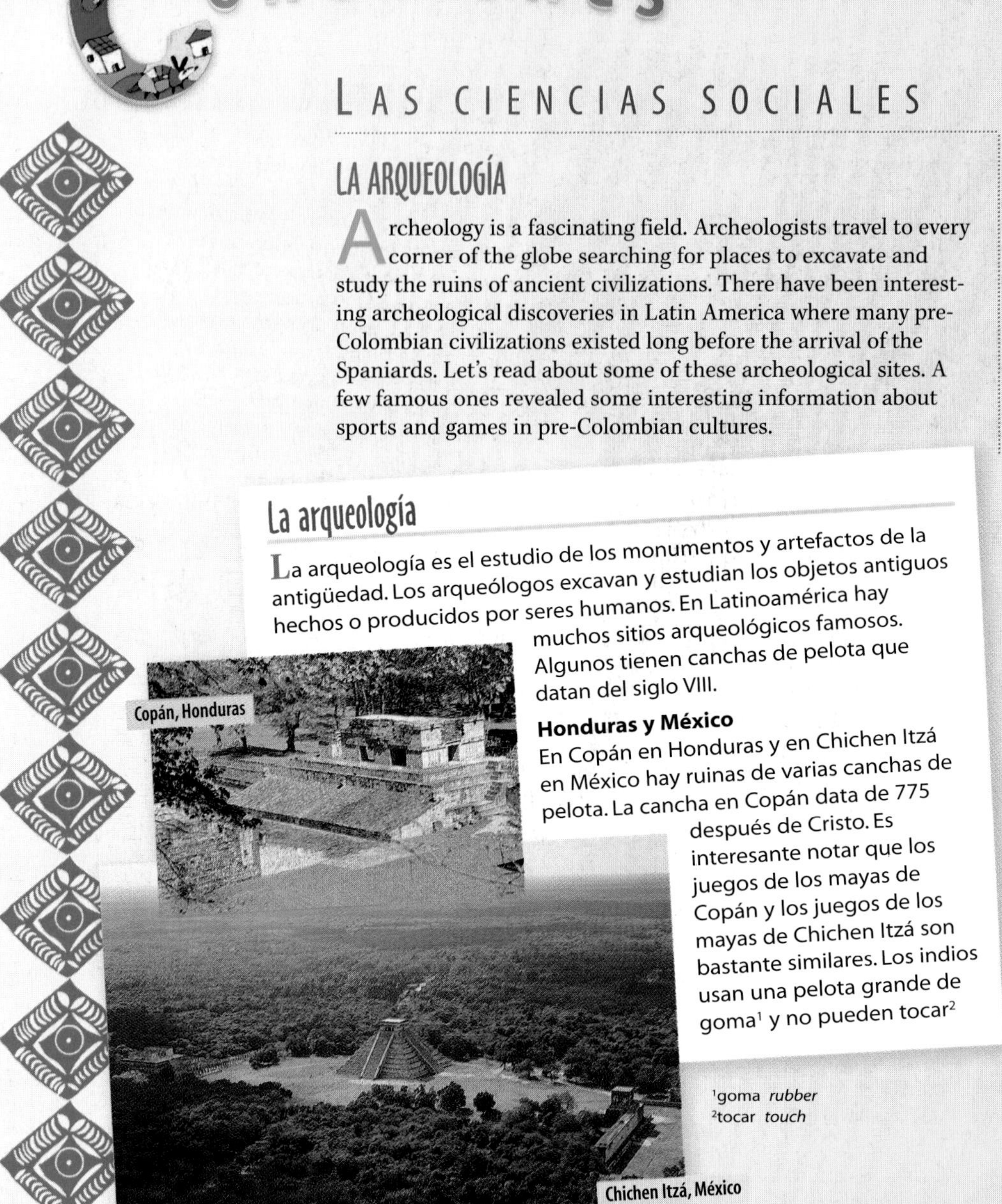

La arqueología

La arqueología es el estudio de los monumentos y artefactos de la antigüedad. Los arqueólogos excavan y estudian los objetos antiguos hechos o producidos por seres humanos. En Latinoamérica hay muchos sitios arqueológicos famosos. Algunos tienen canchas de pelota que datan del siglo VIII.

Honduras y México

En Copán en Honduras y en Chichen Itzá en México hay ruinas de varias canchas de pelota. La cancha en Copán data de 775 después de Cristo. Es interesante notar que los juegos de los mayas de Copán y los juegos de los mayas de Chichen Itzá son bastante similares. Los indios usan una pelota grande de goma[1] y no pueden tocar[2]

Copán, Honduras

Chichen Itzá, México

[1] goma *rubber*
[2] tocar *touch*

Learning From Photos

Chichen Itzá, México The ball game mentioned in the reading was played in the ball court pictured in the lower right hand corner of the photo of Chichen Itzá.

Copán, Honduras This is the ball court in Copán. It was here that the Mayan athletes played before thousands of spectators. The ball court dates from 775 A.D. and was built upon ruins of two former ball courts. The object of the game seems to have been to bounce the ball up the slanted walls and hit one of the carved, stone goals at the top. The players were not allowed to use their hands, arms, or feet. The ball was large and made of solid rubber. It appears that the game was somewhat a combination of football and handball. In the Copán museum there are scenes of the ballplayers in action.

la pelota con las manos. El juego es una diversión[3] pero en Chichen Itzá tiene también sentido religioso. Después del juego sacrifican a los jugadores que pierden.

Chichen Itzá, México

Puerto Rico

Recientemente hay una excavación arqueológica cerca de Ponce en Puerto Rico. ¿Y qué descubren? Descubren una cancha de pelota. Y el juego que juegan los indios taínos de Puerto Rico es parecido o similar al juego de los mayas de Centroamérica. El juego de los taínos es el batú. El batú es un juego de diversión pero tiene también sentido religioso. En el juego hay dos bandos o equipos. Juegan con una pelota de goma. Uno de los bandos lanza la pelota al otro bando. El otro bando tiene que devolver la pelota. Y no pueden usar las manos. Tienen que lanzar la pelota con la pierna, la rodilla o el brazo pero no pueden tocar la pelota con la mano. El equipo que deja rodar[4] la pelota por el suelo[5] el mayor número de veces[6] pierde el juego.

Ponce, Puerto Rico

[3]diversión *amusement*
[4]deja rodar *lets roll*
[5]suelo *ground*
[6]mayor número de veces *greatest number of times*

Después de leer

A ¡A discutir! Discutan. *(Discuss with your classmates.)*
There are many interesting and unbelievable things in this reading selection. This is particularly true when one realizes that the games took place centuries ago and that there is quite a distance between these areas of Central America and Puerto Rico. Discuss some of these interesting facts. You can have your discussion in English.

CAPÍTULO 7
Conexiones

LAS CIENCAS SOCIALES

LA ARQUEOLOGÍA

A. This selection makes students aware that in several areas of the Spanish-speaking world there are archeological sites that are as important and impressive as those in Greece, Italy, and Egypt.

B. Have students skim the reading to at least familiarize themselves with some of this interesting information. It is not necessary that they know it in depth.

Learning From Photos

Chichen Itzá, México The pyramid pictured here is **el Castillo,** which rises above all the other buildings in Chichen Itzá. On top of the castle there is a temple dedicated to Kukulcán, more commonly known in Central Mexico as Quetzalcóatl. Quetzalcóatl was the famous leader who was turned into a god and incarnated as a plumed serpent.

There are seven ball courts in Chichen Itzá. One is the largest in Mesoamerica. Its two parallel walls are 272 feet long. As stated in the reading, no hands were used in the game and it had religious as well as recreational significance. One of the bas-relief carvings depicts a player being decapitated.

Of sad interest to many interested in the environment, the western wall of the largest ball court has been blackened by acid rain blown over from the oil fields in the Gulf of Mexico.

Ponce, Puerto Rico This park in Ponce has many artifacts of the Taíno Indians.

Career Connection

La arquelogía Many important archeological sites and digs are located in the Spanish-speaking world. Students interested in a career in this area would need a reading knowledge of Spanish for research purposes and good verbal skills to communicate with native speakers in the field. Ask students to give examples of other famous archeological sites in the Hispanic world.

ANSWERS

Después de leer

A Discussion should focus on the following:

- The courts discovered at the archeological sites indicate that these games were played centuries ago.
- The game the Taíno Indians of Puerto Rico played was very similar to that of the Central American Mayas.
- In the game played by the Mayas of Chichen Itzá, the losers were sacrificed!

CAPÍTULO 7
Culminación

RECYCLING

The **Actividades orales** and the **Actividades escritas** allow students to use the vocabulary and structures from this chapter and earlier chapters in open-ended, real-life settings.

Actividades orales

¡OJO! Encourage students to say as much as possible when they do these activities. Tell them not to be afraid of making mistakes since the goal of the activities is real-life communication. If someone in the group makes an error, allow the others to politely correct him or her.

Let students choose the activities they would like to particpate in.

A and C

TECHNOLOGY OPTION Students may use the Portfolio feature on the CD-ROM and choose photos to use with **Actividades A** and **C.**

Student Portfolio

Have students keep a notebook containing their best written work from each chapter. These selected writings can be based on assignments from the Student Textbook and the Writing Activities Workbook. The activities on page 215 are examples of writing assignments that may be included in each student's portfolio.

In the Workbook, students will develop an organized autobiography **(Mi autobiografía).** These workbook pages may also become a part of their portfolio. See the Teacher's Manual for more information on the Student Portfolio.

Culminación

Actividades orales

A **Soy muy aficionado(a) a...** Name a sport that you really like. Then give a description of that sport.

B **Entrevista con el capitán** You are to interview the captain of one of the school's sports teams (your classmate) for the local Spanish language television station. Try to find out as much information as possible. Then change roles.

C **Los deportes** Pick your favorite sport. Get together with a classmate who likes the same sport as you. Take turns describing the sport you like best.

JUEGO **¡Adivina quién es!** Think of your favorite sports hero. Tell a classmate something about him or her. Your classmate will ask you three questions about your hero before guessing who it is. Then reverse roles and you guess who your classmate's hero is.

DON BALON LA REVISTA NÚMERO 1 DEL FÚTBOL

ANSWERS

Actividades orales

A Answers will vary. Encourage students to describe a team sport so they can use the chapter vocabulary.

B Answers will vary.

C Answers will vary.

Independent Practice

Assign any of the following:

1. Activities, pages 214–215
2. Workbook, **Mi autobiografía,** page 82
3. Situation Cards
4. CD-ROM, Disc 2, Chapter 7, **Juego de repaso**

Actividades escritas

A **Un reportaje** Work in groups of three. One of you is the captain of one of the school's teams. The other two are sports reporters for a Spanish newspaper. The two reporters will prepare an interview with the captain about the team's last game. The reporters will edit the information they get from the interview and write their report for tomorrow's paper. The report can be in the present tense.

B **Horario deportivo** There are several exchange students from Latin America at your school. Prepare for them your school's schedule of sporting events for the coming month. Prepare the chart in Spanish so they can refer to it easily.

DEPORTES

FÚTBOL

Los siguientes partidos de FÚTBOL corresponden a la Liga Nacional de Primera División.
Se recomienda consulten fechas por posibles cambios de fechas. / Please check dates for any changes.

• ESTADIO SANTIAGO BERNABÉU
P.º DE LA CASTELLANA, 104.
TEL.: 91 344 00 52. (METRO: SANTIAGO BERNABÉU).

4 Oct.
Real Madrid - Tenerife.

25 Oct.
Real Madrid - Racing.

• ESTADIO VICENTE CALDERÓN
VIRGEN DEL PUERTO, 67.
TEL.: 91 366 47 07. (METRO: PIRÁMIDES Y MARQUÉS DE VADILLO).

18 Oct.
Atlético de Madrid - Tenerife.

Writing Strategy

Gathering information

If your writing project deals with a topic you are not familiar with, you may need to gather information before you begin to write. Some of your best sources are the library, the Internet, and people who know something about the topic. Even if you plan to interview people about the topic, it may be necessary to do some research in the library or on the Internet to acquire enough knowledge to prepare good interview questions.

La Copa mundial

Many of you already know that the World Cup is a soccer championship. Try to give a description of the World Cup as best you can in Spanish. If you are not familiar with it, you will need to do some research. It might be interesting to take what you know or find out about the World Cup and compare it to the World Series in baseball. Gather information about both these championships and write a report.

CAPÍTULO 7
Culminación

Actividades escritas

A Be sure that within each group there is at least one student who is interested in sports. The other two students should write down their questions.

B Each sporting event should include the date, time, place, and the names of the two opposing teams.

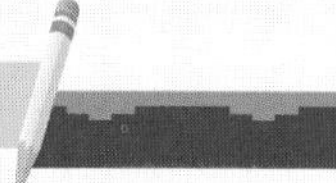

Writing Strategy

Gathering information

A. Have students read the Writing Strategy on page 215.

B. Encourage students to use the Internet as part of their research. Also encourage them to ask native Spanish speakers in their school or community about the World Cup.

ANSWERS

Actividades escritas
A and **B** Answers will vary.

Writing Strategy
Answers will vary, depending on the variety of information sources each student uses.

ASSESSMENT RESOURCES

- Chapter Quizzes
- Testing Program
- Computer Testmaker
- Situation Cards
- Communication Transparency C-7
- Performance Assessment
- **Maratón mental** Videoquiz

VOCABULARY REVIEW

The words and phrases in the **Vocabulario** have been taught for productive use in this chapter. They are summarized here as a resource for both students and teacher. This list also serves as a convenient resource for the **Culminación** activities on pages 214 and 215. There are approximately fourteen cognates in this vocabulary list. Have students find them.

Vocabulario

IDENTIFYING SPORTS

el fútbol
el béisbol
el básquetbol, el baloncesto

DESCRIBING A SPORTS EVENT IN GENERAL

el estadio
el/la espectador(a)
el campo
la cancha
el partido
el/la jugador(a)
el equipo
el tablero indicador
el tanto
empatado(a)
empezar, comenzar
tirar
lanzar
perder
ganar
entre
contra

DESCRIBING A FOOTBALL GAME

el fútbol
el balón
el tiempo
el/la portero(a)
la portería
jugar
bloquear
parar
marcar un tanto
meter un gol

DESCRIBING A BASEBALL GAME

el béisbol
el/la bateador(a)
el pícher, el lanzador
el cátcher, el receptor
el jardinero
el guante
el platillo
el jonrón
la base
la entrada
la pelota
el bate
batear
correr
atrapar
devolver

DESCRIBING A BASKETBALL GAME

el básquetbol, el baloncesto
el cesto, la canasta
driblar
pasar
encestar
meter

EXPRESSING LIKES AND INTERESTS

gustar
interesar
aburrir

IDENTIFYING SOME PARTS OF THE BODY

el pie
la pierna
la rodilla
la mano
el brazo
la cabeza

OTHER USEFUL EXPRESSIONS

poder
querer
volver
preferir
a veces
siempre
izquierdo(a)
derecho(a)

For the Younger Student

Tarjetas de colección Many younger students collect baseball and football cards. You may have them bring some to class and talk about their favorite teams and players.
Afiches Have groups of students make posters for a sports day at your school. They should include the date, event(s), team names, times, etc.
Biografías Have students choose their favorite athlete. Have them prepare a short biography about him or her.

Did You Know?

Los estadios de fútbol The largest sports stadiums in the world are soccer stadiums in Hispanic countries, with capacities in excess of 100,000 spectators. Among the largest stadiums are **el Estadio Azteca** in Mexico City (see page 217) and **el Estadio del Boca Juniors,** nicknamed **la Bombonera** *(The Candy Store),* in Buenos Aires.

TECNOTUR

VIDEO

¡Buen viaje!

EPISODIO 7 ▸ Deportes de equipo

Luis y Cristina visitan la pintoresca comunidad de Coyoacán, México.

También juegan al fútbol con unos amigos.

CD-ROM

Expansión cultural

El famoso estadio Azteca en la Ciudad de México

interNET CONNECTION

In this video episode Luis and Cristina talk about sports—which ones they like to play and which ones are popular in their countries. To find out more about sports in the Spanish-speaking world, go to the Capítulo 7 Internet activity at the Glencoe Foreign Language Web site:

http://www.glencoe.com/sec/fl

Video Synopsis

In this episode, Luis and Cristina are at the plaza in Coyoacán, a historic section of Mexico City. Luis joins a soccer game in progress while Cristina videotapes the action. Luis and Cristina then share information about the sports they like to play.

As they stroll through the square, the conversation turns to their school vacation. Cristina suddenly realizes that she left her camera on a bench in the plaza. They run back to retrieve it and discover that it is still recording. They then enjoy watching the playback.

CAPÍTULO 7

Tecnotur

OVERVIEW

This page previews three key multimedia components of the **Glencoe Spanish** series. Each reinforces the material taught in Chapter 7 in a unique manner.

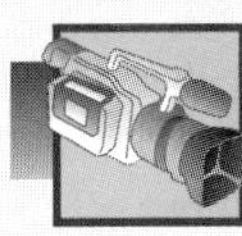

VIDEO

The Video Program allows students to see how the chapter vocabulary and structures are used by native speakers within an engaging story line. For maximum reinforcement, show the video episode as a final activity for Chapter 7.

A. In these two photos, we see Cristina and Luis in the section of Mexico City called Coyoacán. Ask them, **¿Son mexicanos Luis y Cristina? ¿De dónde es Cristina? ¿Qué toman en la primera foto? ¿Luis es un buen jugador de fútbol o no?**

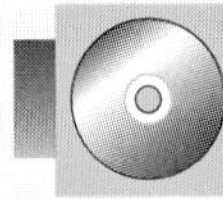

CD-ROM

A. The **Expansión cultural** photo is of the famous Azteca Stadium in Mexico City. Have students read the caption on page 217. Then have them say something about the photo.

B. In the CD-ROM version of **Expansión cultural** (Disc 2, page 217), students can listen to additional recorded information about this stadium.

INTERNET

Teacher Information and Student Worksheets for this activity can be accessed at the Web site.

RESOURCES

- Workbook: Self-Test 2, pp. 83–86
- CD-ROM, Disc 2, pp. 218–221
- Tests: Unit 2, pp. 40; 109; 141

OVERVIEW

This section reviews the salient points from Chapters 5–7. In the **Conversación** students will review sports vocabulary, regular **-ir** verbs, and some stem-changing verbs in context. In the **Estructura** sections, they will study the conjugations of regular **-er** and **-ir** verbs, stem-changing verbs, possessive adjectives, and the conjugations of verbs like **interesar, aburrir,** and **gustar.** They will practice these structures as they talk about a Spanish party.

TEACHING THE CONVERSATION

A. Have students open their books to page 218 and repeat the conversation after you in unison.

B. Then call on a pair of students to read the first half of the conversation.

C. Intersperse questions from the **Después de conversar** section.

D. Do the same with the second half of the conversation.

Learning From Realia

Bolívar vs. Cobreloa This ticket is for a game in Caracas. Tell students **Bs** stands for **bolívares**, the monetary unit of Venezuela.

Repaso CAPÍTULOS 5–7

Conversación

Un partido importante

JULIO: Alberto, Carlos y yo vamos al Café Miramar. ¿Quieres ir con nosotros?
ALBERTO: No, Julio, no puedo porque quiero ver el partido.
JULIO: ¿De qué partido hablas?
ALBERTO: Los Osos juegan contra los Tigres y mi equipo favorito son los Osos.
JULIO: ¿Vas al estadio a ver el partido?
ALBERTO: No. Las entradas (los boletos) cuestan mucho. Voy a ver el partido en la televisión.
JULIO: ¿A qué hora empieza?
ALBERTO: A las siete y media. ¿Quieres ver el partido también?
JULIO: Sí. ¿Dónde vives?
ALBERTO: Vivo en la calle Central, número 32.
JULIO: Bien. ¡Hasta pronto!

Después de conversar

A Los tres amigos Contesten. *(Answer.)*

1. ¿Adónde quieren ir los dos muchachos?
2. ¿Invitan a Alberto?
3. ¿Puede ir Alberto?
4. ¿Por qué no?
5. ¿Por qué no va al estadio?
6. ¿Dónde va a ver el partido?
7. ¿A qué hora empieza?
8. ¿Van los muchachos a casa de Alberto?

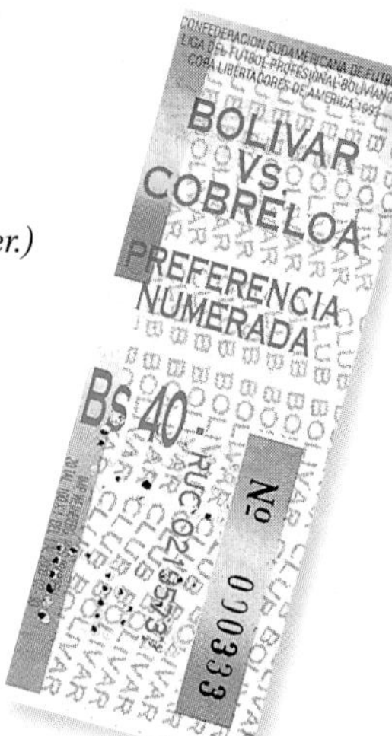

ANSWERS

Después de conversar

A
1. **Los dos muchachos quieren ir al Café Miramar.**
2. **Sí, invitan a Alberto.**
3. **No, no puede ir.**
4. **Quiere ver el partido de su equipo favorito.**
5. **No va al estadio porque las entradas cuestan mucho.**
6. **Va a ver el partido en la televisión.**
7. **Empieza a las siete y media.**
8. **Sí, los muchachos van a su casa.**

Estructura

Verbos en -er, -ir

Review the forms of regular **-er** and **-ir** verbs.

COMER	**como**	**comes**	**come**	**comemos**	***coméis***	**comen**
VIVIR	**vivo**	**vives**	**vive**	**vivimos**	***vivís***	**viven**

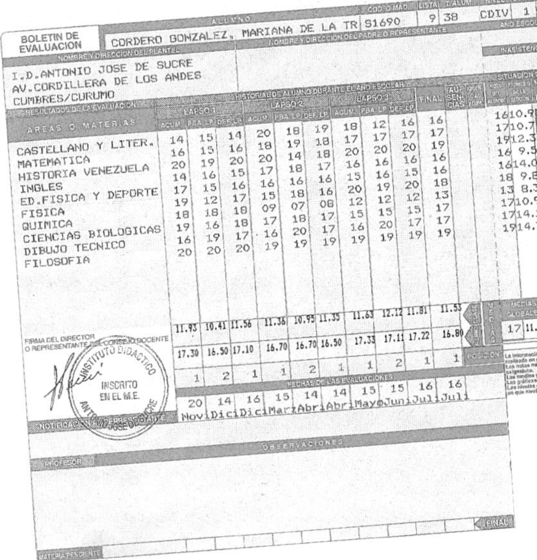

BOLETIN DE EVALUACION

ALUMNO: CORDERO GONZALEZ, MARIANA DE LA TR — COD. O MAD.: S1690 — LISTA: 9 — T. ALUM.: 38 — NIVEL: CDIV — CURSO: 1

NOMBRE Y DIRECCION DEL PLANTEL: I.D. ANTONIO JOSE DE SUCRE, AV. CORDILLERA DE LOS ANDES, CUMBRES/CURUMO

NOMBRE Y DIRECCION DEL PADRE O REPRESENTANTE

HISTORIAL DE ALUMNO DURANTE EL AÑO ESCOLAR

AREAS O MATERIAS	LAPSO 1 ACUM.	LAPSO 1 PBA. LP	LAPSO 1 DEF. LP	LAPSO 2 ACUM.	LAPSO 2 PBA. LP	LAPSO 2 DEF. LP	LAPSO 3 ACUM.	LAPSO 3 PBA. LP	LAPSO 3 DEF. LP	FINAL		
CASTELLANO Y LITER.	14	15	14	20	18	19	18	12	16	16	16	10.9
MATEMATICA	16	15	16	18	19	18	17	17	17	17	17	10.7
HISTORIA VENEZUELA	20	19	20	20	14	18	20	20	20	19	19	12.3
INGLES	14	16	15	17	18	17	16	16	16	16	16	9.5
ED. FISICA Y DEPORTE	17	15	16	16	16	16	15	16	15	16	16	14.0
FISICA	19	12	17	15	18	16	20	19	20	18	18	9.8
QUIMICA	18	18	18	09	07	08	12	12	12	13	13	8.3
CIENCIAS BIOLOGICAS	19	16	18	17	18	17	15	15	15	17	17	10.9
DIBUJO TECNICO	16	19	17	16	20	17	16	20	17	17	17	14.1
FILOSOFIA	20	20	20	19	19	19	19	19	19	19	19	14.7
MEDIAS	11.93	10.41	11.56	11.36	10.95	11.35	11.63	12.12	11.81	11.53		
	17.30	16.50	17.10	16.70	16.70	16.50	17.33	17.11	17.22	16.80		
POSICION	1	2	1	1	2	1	1	2	1	1		
FECHAS DE LAS EVALUACIONES	20 Novi	14 Dici	16 Dici	15 Marz	14 Abri	14 Abri	15 Mayo	15 Juni	16 Juli	16 Juli		

MEDIAS GLOBALES: 17 | 11.53

FIRMA DEL DIRECTOR O REPRESENTANTE DEL CONSEJO DOCENTE

INSTITUTO DIDACTICO ANTONIO JOSE DE SUCRE — INSCRITO EN EL M.E.

NOTIFICACION AL REPRESENTANTE

OBSERVACIONES

PROFESOR

MATERIA PENDIENTE

FINAL

Práctica

A Tú y tus amigos Contesten. *(Answer.)*

1. ¿Qué comes cuando vas a un café?
2. ¿Qué bebes cuando estás en un café?
3. ¿Qué aprenden tú y tus amigos en la escuela?
4. ¿Qué leen Uds. en la clase de inglés?
5. ¿Qué escriben Uds.?
6. ¿Comprenden los alumnos cuando el profesor de español habla?
7. ¿Reciben Uds. notas buenas en todas las asignaturas?

Verbos de cambio radical

1. Review the forms of stem-changing verbs.

e → ie

EMPEZAR	**empiezo**	**empiezas**	**empieza**	**empezamos**	***empezáis***	**empiezan**
PERDER	**pierdo**	**pierdes**	**pierde**	**perdemos**	***perdéis***	**pierden**

o → ue

VOLVER	**vuelvo**	**vuelves**	**vuelve**	**volvemos**	***volvéis***	**vuelven**
PODER	**puedo**	**puedes**	**puede**	**podemos**	***podéis***	**pueden**

2. Review the forms of the verb **tener.** Note that this verb also has a change in the stem.

TENER	**tengo**	**tienes**	**tiene**	**tenemos**	***tenéis***	**tienen**

CAPÍTULOS 5–7
Repaso

TEACHING STRUCTURE

Verbos en -er, -ir

A. Write the verbs on the board and have students read all forms aloud.

B. Have students give another **-er** and another **-ir** verb and supply the endings.

C. Now have students do **Práctica A** orally before assigning it for homework.

TEACHING STRUCTURE

Verbos de cambio radical

Follow the same procedure as outlined above to review these verbs. For additional practice, have students make up original sentences with each of the verbs before doing the **Práctica** on page 220.

ANSWERS

Práctica

A 1. Como ___ cuando voy a un café.
2. Bebo ___ cuando estoy en un café.
3. Aprendemos muchas cosas en la escuela.
4. Leemos novelas en la clase de inglés.
5. Escribimos composiciones.
6. Sí (No), los alumnos (no) comprenden cuando el profesor de español habla.
7. Sí (No), nosotros (no) recibimos notas buenas en todas las asignaturas.

CAPÍTULOS 5–7
Repaso

Práctica

B This activity practices the irregular stem-changing verbs in a sports context.

C After going over **Práctica C** call on a student to summarize the information in his or her own words.

TEACHING STRUCTURE

Adjetivos posesivos

Go over the forms of the possessive adjectives with the students. Ask them questions in Spanish to be sure they know the meaning of each word and how it is used—masculine, feminine, singular, or plural.

Práctica

D Have students provide the name of their town and street.

EXPANSION After going over **Práctica D**, have students describe their own home orally.

Learning From Photos

La Ciudad de México Students have already learned that **una colonia** is the word used to refer to the sections of Mexico City. Two very upscale **colonias** that have homes such as the one shown here are Chapultepec and Polanco.

Práctica

B HISTORIETA Un juego de béisbol

Completen. *(Complete.)*

El juego de béisbol ___1___ (empezar) a las tres y media. Habla Teresa:
—Hoy yo ___2___ (querer) ser la pícher.
La verdad es que Teresa ___3___ (ser) una pícher muy buena. Ella ___4___ (jugar) muy bien. Nosotros ___5___ (tener) un equipo bueno. Todos nosotros ___6___ (jugar) bien. Nuestro equipo no ___7___ (perder) mucho. Hoy yo ___8___ (tener) que jugar muy bien porque nuestro equipo no ___9___ (poder) perder. ___10___ (Tener) que ganar.

C Entrevista Contesten personalmente. *(Answer .)*

1. ¿Cuántos años tienes?
2. ¿Cuántos hermanos tienes?
3. ¿Cuántos años tienen ellos?
4. ¿Tienen Uds. un perro o un gato?

Adjetivos posesivos

Review the forms of possessive adjectives

mi, mis	**nuestro, nuestra, nuestros, nuestras**
tu, tus	
su, sus	**su, sus**

Práctica

D HISTORIETA Nuestra casa

Completen. *(Complete.)*

Vivo en ____. ___1___ casa está en la calle ____. ___2___ padres tienen un carro. Y yo tengo una bicicleta. ___3___ carro está en el garaje y ___4___ bicicleta está en el garaje también. Nosotros tenemos un perro. ___5___ perro está en el jardín. El jardín alrededor de ___6___ casa es bonito. Mi hermano y ___7___ amigos siempre juegan en el jardín.

La Ciudad de México

ANSWERS

Práctica

B
1. **empieza**
2. **quiero**
3. **es**
4. **juega**
5. **tenemos**
6. **jugamos**
7. **pierde**
8. **tengo**
9. **puede**
10. **Tiene**

C
1. **Tengo ___ años.**
2. **Tengo ___ hermanos. (No tengo hermanos.)**
3. Answers will vary.
4. **Sí, tenemos un perro (un gato). (No, no tenemos un perro [un gato].)**

D
1. (name of town), **Mi,** (Answers will vary.)
2. **Mis**
3. **Nuestro**
4. **mi**
5. **Nuestro**
6. **nuestra**
7. **sus**

Verbos como **interesar, aburrir, gustar**

Review the construction for verbs such as **gustar, interesar,** and **aburrir.**

¿Te gusta el arte?	**Sí, me gusta el arte.** **El arte me interesa mucho.** **No me aburre nada.**
¿Te gustan los deportes?	**Los deportes, sí, me gustan mucho.** **Los deportes me interesan.** **No me aburren nada.**

E **Información** Den cuantas respuestas posibles. *(Give as many answers as possible.)*

1. ¿Qué te gusta?
2. ¿Qué te interesa?
3. ¿Qué te aburre?

Actividad comunicativa

A **Una fiesta familiar** With a classmate, look at the illustration. Take turns describing the illustration, giving as much detail as you can.

CAPÍTULOS 5-7
Repaso

TEACHING STRUCTURE

Verbos como interesar, aburrir, gustar

A. Have students open their books to page 221 and read the explanation with them.

B. Have students identify the subject of each sentence. Point out to them that if the subject is plural, the verb is plural.

Práctica

E If students have problems doing **Práctica E**, review some of the **Práctica** in Chapter 7, pages 203–205.

Actividad comunicativa

A You can also have the students make up questions about the illustration. Then have them ask their classmates the questions.

Note: You may wish to do the second literary selection (pages 442–447) with students at this time.

Independent Practice

Assign any of the following:

1. Activities, pages 218–221
2. Workbook: Self-Test 2, pages 83–86
3. CD-ROM, Disc 2, pages 218–221
4. CD-ROM, Disc 2, Chapters 5–7, **Juegos de repaso**

ANSWERS

Práctica

E 1. Me gusta(n) ___. (___ me gusta[n].)
2. Me interesa(n) ___ (___ me interesa[n].)
3. Me aburre(n) ___. (___ me aburre[n].)

Actividad comunicativa

A Answers will vary. Students should use the vocabulary from Chapters 5 and 6.

VISTAS DE ESPAÑA

OVERVIEW

The **Vistas de España** were prepared by National Geographic Society. Their purpose is to give students greater insight, through these visual images, into the culture and people of Spain. Have students look at the photographs on pages 222–225 for enjoyment. If they would like to talk about them, let them say anything they can, using the vocabulary they have learned to this point.

National Standards

Cultures

The **Vistas de España** photos, and the accompanying captions, allow students to gain insights into the people and culture of Spain.

Learning From Photos

1. Plaza Mayor, Salamanca Salamanca is a lovely city of honey-colored sandstone buildings like the one we see in this photo. Although some argue that Seville and Santiago de Compostela may be more beautiful cities, no one disagrees that the Plaza Mayor of Salamanca is the most magnificent square in all of Spain. It was designed in 1729 and it is bordered by an arcade walkway lined with elegant boutiques and wonderful pastry shops. A walk around the square is a tradition loved by the locals and students alike. Salamanca is a university town. Alfonso IX de León founded the university in 1218. The first female university professor in Spain taught Latin there in the 15th century. It is possible that Cervantes and Hernán Cortés took some courses there.

(continued)

1. Plaza Mayor, Salamanca
2. Casares, Pueblo blanco, Andalucía
3. Romería, Sevilla
4. Arcos de la mezquita de Córdoba
5. El Alcázar de Segovia
6. Escuela andaluza del arte ecuestre, Jerez

222

Learning From Photos

2. Casares, Pueblo blanco, Andalucía The mountain village of Casares is high in the Sierra Bermeja above Estepona. The typical whitewashed Andalusian houses are perched on slopes. From the Moorish castle at the top of the mountain, there are views of orchards, olive gardens, and the Mediterranean in the distance.

3. Romería, Sevilla The **ferias** take place in Seville every April, usually two weeks after Easter. A typical day begins around noon with a parade. All around the city there are tents, both public and private, for parties. Dancers perform the classic **sevillanas,** the most popular modern **flamenco.**

(continued)

Learning From Photos

(continued)
6. Escuela andaluza del arte ecuestre, Jerez This school was founded by Álvaro Domecq of the Domecq sherry family in the 1970's. The prestigious riding school is housed on the grounds of a splendid 19th-century palace. The horses are a special breed called Cartujana. They are a cross between the Andalusian workhorse and the Arabian. Every Thursday skilled riders dressed in 18th-century riding gear demonstrate intricate riding techniques and jumping.

Learning From Photos

(continued from page 222)
4. Arcos de la mezquita de Córdoba The Mezquita de Córdoba was built between the 8th and 10th centuries. It is one of the most beautiful examples of Spanish Moorish architecture. As you enter the cathedral, some 850 columns of onyx, granite, and marble rise before you. Built as a mosque **(mezquita),** it has served as a cathedral since 1236. After the **Reconquista** the Christians basically left the building untouched. They simply began to use it as a Christian place of worship.

5. El Alcázar de Segovia This fortress probably dates from Roman times. Gutted by fire in 1862, the building was completely redone. The exterior is quite imposing, especially when seen from a distance, as in this photograph. *(continued)*

VISTAS DE ESPAÑA

Learning From Photos

1. Museo Guggenheim, Bilbao Bilbao, called **Bilbo** in Basque, is the capital of the Vizcaya province in the **País vasco.** Bilbao is at the center of a vast industrial area. The pride of Bilbao is the new (1997) Guggenheim Museum funded primarily by the Basque government. It is the newest in the family of museums, including two in New York City and one in Venice, managed by the Guggenheim Foundation. The museum rises from the banks of the **río Nervión** like a vast ship with billowing sails. The work of the acclaimed California architect, Frank Gehry, the building is considered one of the great architectural masterpieces of the late 20th century.

2. Málaga This port city on the Mediterranean claims the title of capital of the Costa del Sol, but tourists arrive at its airport and continue on to places such as Torremolinos or Marbella. The high-rises we see in the photo started to spring up in the 1970's. There is a great deal of urban sprawl but the old town **(casco viejo)** of Málaga is charming.

3. Paseo del Prado, Madrid In the center of the busy Plaza de Cibeles is the famous fountain depicting Sybil, the wife of Saturn. She is driving a chariot drawn by lions. This monument is beautifully lit at night. Loved by the **madrileños** and visitors alike, it has come to symbolize Madrid. During the Civil War citizens of Madrid risked their lives sandbagging the fountain as Nationalist aircraft bombed the city.

4. Barcos pesqueros, Palma de Mallorca Mallorca is the largest

(continued)

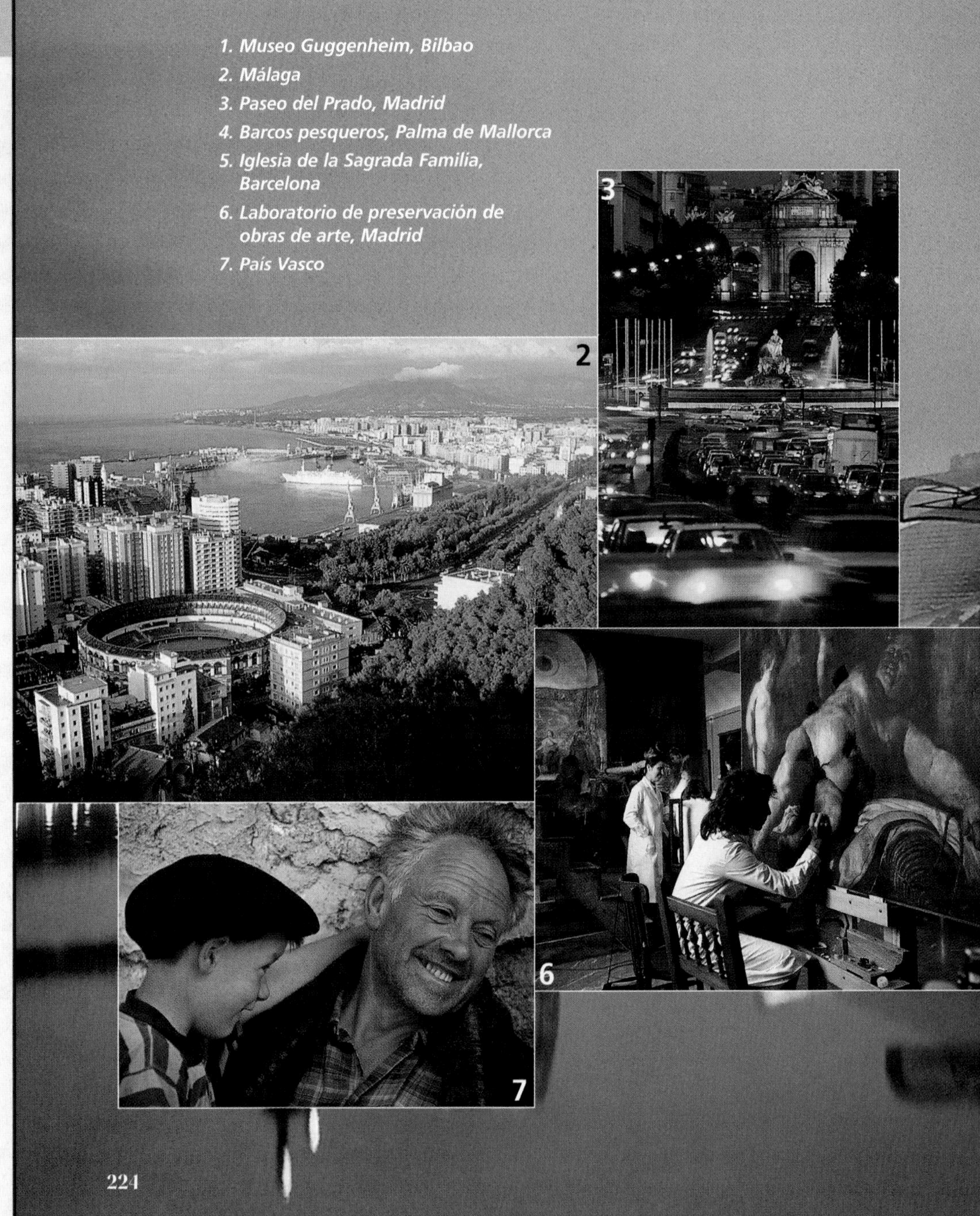

1. Museo Guggenheim, Bilbao
2. Málaga
3. Paseo del Prado, Madrid
4. Barcos pesqueros, Palma de Mallorca
5. Iglesia de la Sagrada Familia, Barcelona
6. Laboratorio de preservación de obras de arte, Madrid
7. País Vasco

NATIONAL GEOGRAPHIC SOCIETY

TEACHER'S CORNER

Index to NATIONAL GEOGRAPHIC MAGAZINE

The following articles may be used for research relating to this chapter:

- "Barcelona: Star of the New Europe," by T. D. Allman, December 1998.
- "Europe's First Family: The Basques," by Thomas J. Abercrombie, November 1995.
- "The New World of Spain," by Bill Bryson, April 1992.
- "Pizarro, Conqueror of the Inca," by John Hemming, February 1992.
- "When the Moors Ruled Spain," by Thomas J. Abercrombie, July 1988.
- "Madrid: The Change in Spain," by John J. Putman, February 1986.
- "The Indomitable Basques," by Robert Laxalt, July 1985.
- "Iberia's Vintage River," by Marion Kaplan, October 1984.
- "Catalonia: Spain's Country Within a Country," by Randall Peffer, January 1984.
- "The Genius of El Greco," by J. Carter Brown, June 1982.

VISTAS DE ESPAÑA

Learning From Photos

(continued from page 224)
of the Balearic islands. The others are Menorca, Ibiza, and Formentera. Although some small fishing villages still exist, the coastal beach areas have, for the most part, been developed for mass tourism.

5. Iglesia de la Sagrada Familia, Barcelona This famous church is still under construction. It was unfinished at the time of architect Antonio Gaudí's untimely death in 1926. This surreal creation brings about both shrieks of derision or sighs of rapture.

6. Laboratorio de preservación de obras de arte, Madrid In this photo we see a studio where artworks are being restored. Madrid is considered one of the major cultural centers of Europe. Some of its museums include the world-famous Prado, the Centro de Arte Reina Sofía, a museum of modern art, and the Museo Thyssen-Bornemisza.

7. País Vasco The Basques are a proud, industrious, and fiercely independent people. They have their own language, **euskera,** and refer to their region as **Euskadi.** Many Basque men still wear the **boina** that this young boy has on.

Products available from GLENCOE/MCGRAW-HILL

To order the following products, call Glencoe/McGraw-Hill at 1-800-334-7344.

CD-ROMs
- Picture Atlas of the World
- The Complete National Geographic: 109 Years of National Geographic Magazine

Software
- ZingoLingo: Spanish Diskettes

Transparency Set
- NGS PicturePack: Geography of Europe

Videodisc
- STV: World Geography (Volume 2: "Africa and Europe")

Products available from NATIONAL GEOGRAPHIC SOCIETY

NATIONAL GEOGRAPHIC SOCIETY

To order the following products, call National Geographic Society at 1-800-368-2728.

Books
- Exploring Your World: The Adventure of Geography
- National Geographic Satellite Atlas of the World

Chapter 8 Overview

SCOPE AND SEQUENCE pages 226–255

TOPICS	FUNCTIONS	STRUCTURE	CULTURE
◆ Minor illnesses ◆ Symptoms of a cold, flu, or fever ◆ Medical exams ◆ Parts of the body ◆ Prescriptions	◆ How to describe symptoms of a minor illness ◆ How to have a prescription filled at a pharmacy ◆ How to tell someone where you are from ◆ How to describe origin and location ◆ How to describe characteristics or conditions ◆ How to discuss what happens to you or to someone else	◆ **Ser** and **estar** ◆ **Me, te, nos**	◆ Patricia goes to the doctor with a minor illness ◆ Differences between pharmacies in the U.S. and pharmacies in Spanish-speaking countries ◆ A famous Cuban-American doctor: Antonio Gassett ◆ Information about nutrition in Spanish

CHAPTER 8 RESOURCES

PRINT	MULTIMEDIA
Planning Resources	
Lesson Plans Block Scheduling Lesson Plans	Interactive Lesson Planner
Reinforcement Resources	
Writing Activities Workbook Student Tape Manual Video Activities Booklet Web Site User's Guide	Transparencies Binder Audiocassette/Compact Disc Program Videocassette/Videodisc Program Online Internet Activities Electronic Teacher's Classroom Resources
Assessment Resources	
Situation Cards Chapter Quizzes Testing Program Performance Assessment	**Maratón mental** Mindjogger Videoquiz Testmaker Computer Software (Macintosh/Windows) Listening Comprehension Audiocassette/Compact Disc Communication Transparency: C-8
Motivational Resources	
Expansion Activities	Café Glencoe: **www.cafe.glencoe.com** Keypal Internet Activities
Enrichment	
Spanish for Spanish Speakers	

Chapter 8 Planning Guide

SECTION	PAGES	SECTION RESOURCES
Vocabulario Palabras 1 ¿Cómo está?	228–231	Vocabulary Transparencies 8.1 Audiocassette 5B/Compact Disc 5 Student Tape Manual, TE, pages 89–90 Workbook, pages 87–88 Chapter Quizzes, page 38 CD-ROM, Disc 3, pages 228–231
Vocabulario Palabras 2 En la consulta del médico En la farmacia	232–235	Vocabulary Transparencies 8.2 Audiocassette 5B/ Compact Disc 5 Student Tape Manual, TE, pages 91–92 Workbook, pages 89–90 Chapter Quizzes, page 39 CD-ROM, Disc 3, pages 232–235
Estructura Ser y estar Ser y estar Me, te, nos	236–243	Workbook, pages 91–93 Audiocassette 5B/Compact Disc 5 Student Tape Manual, TE, pages 93–96 Chapter Quizzes, page 40–42 Computer Testmaker CD-ROM, Disc 3, pages 236–243
Conversación En la consulta del médico Pronunciación: La consonante c	244–245	Audiocassette 5B/Compact Disc 5 Student Tape Manual, TE, pages 96–97 CD-ROM, Disc 3, pages 244–245
Lecturas culturales Una joven nerviosa La farmacia *(opcional)* Una biografía—El doctor Antonio Gassett *(opcional)*	246–249	Testing Program, pages 48–49 CD-ROM, Disc 3, pages 246–249
Conexiones La nutrición *(opcional)*	250–251	Testing Program, page 49 CD-ROM, Disc 3, pages 250–251
Culminación Actividades orales Actividades escritas Vocabulario Tecnotur	252–255	**¡Buen viaje!** Video, Episode 8 Video Activities, pages 93–96 Internet Activities www.glencoe.com/sec/fl Testing Program, pages 45–48; 110; 142; 165–166 CD-ROM, Disc 3, pages 252–255

CAPÍTULO 8

OVERVIEW

In this chapter students will learn to talk about routine illnesses and describe their symptoms to a doctor. They will use vocabulary associated with medical exams, prescriptions, and minor illnesses such as colds, flu, and headaches. Students will talk about themselves and others using the pronouns **me, te,** and **nos.** They will express characteristics and origin using the verb **ser,** and conditions and location using the verb **estar.**

The cultural focus of the chapter is on medical services and health problems in Spanish-speaking countries.

National Standards

Communication

In Chapter 8, students will communicate in spoken and written Spanish on the following topics:

- describing symptoms of minor ailments
- getting a prescription at a pharmacy
- expressing emotions and conditions

Students will obtain and provide information and engage in conversations dealing with health and health services as they fulfill the objectives listed on this page.

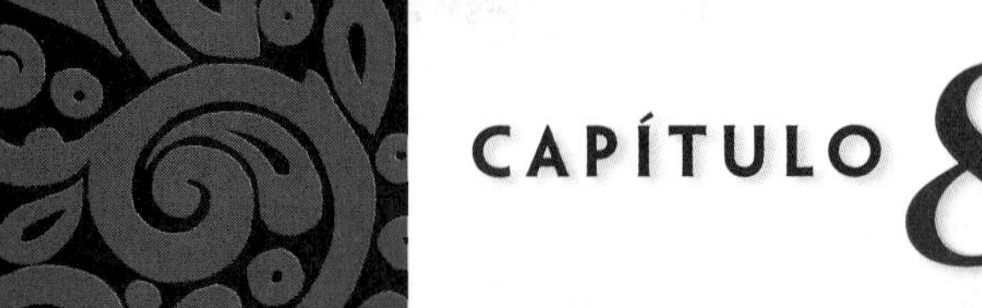

CAPÍTULO 8

La salud y el médico

Objetivos

In this chapter you will learn to do the following:

- explain a minor illness to a doctor
- describe some feelings
- have a prescription filled at a pharmacy
- describe characteristics and conditions
- tell where things are and where they're from
- tell where someone or something is now
- tell what happens to you or someone else

interNET CONNECTION

The **Glencoe Foreign Language Web site (http://www.glencoe.com/sec/fl)** offers three options that enable you and your students to experience the Spanish-speaking world via the Internet:

- The online **Actividades** are correlated to the chapters and utilize Hispanic Web sites around the world. For the Chapter 8 activity, see student page 255.
- The **Correspondencia electrónica** section provides information on how to set up a keypal (pen pal) exchange between your class and a class in the Spanish-speaking world.
- At **Café Glencoe,** the interactive "after-school" section of the site, you and your students can access a variety of additional online resources, including interactive games. The Chapter 8 click-and-drag game practices the difference between **ser** and **estar.**

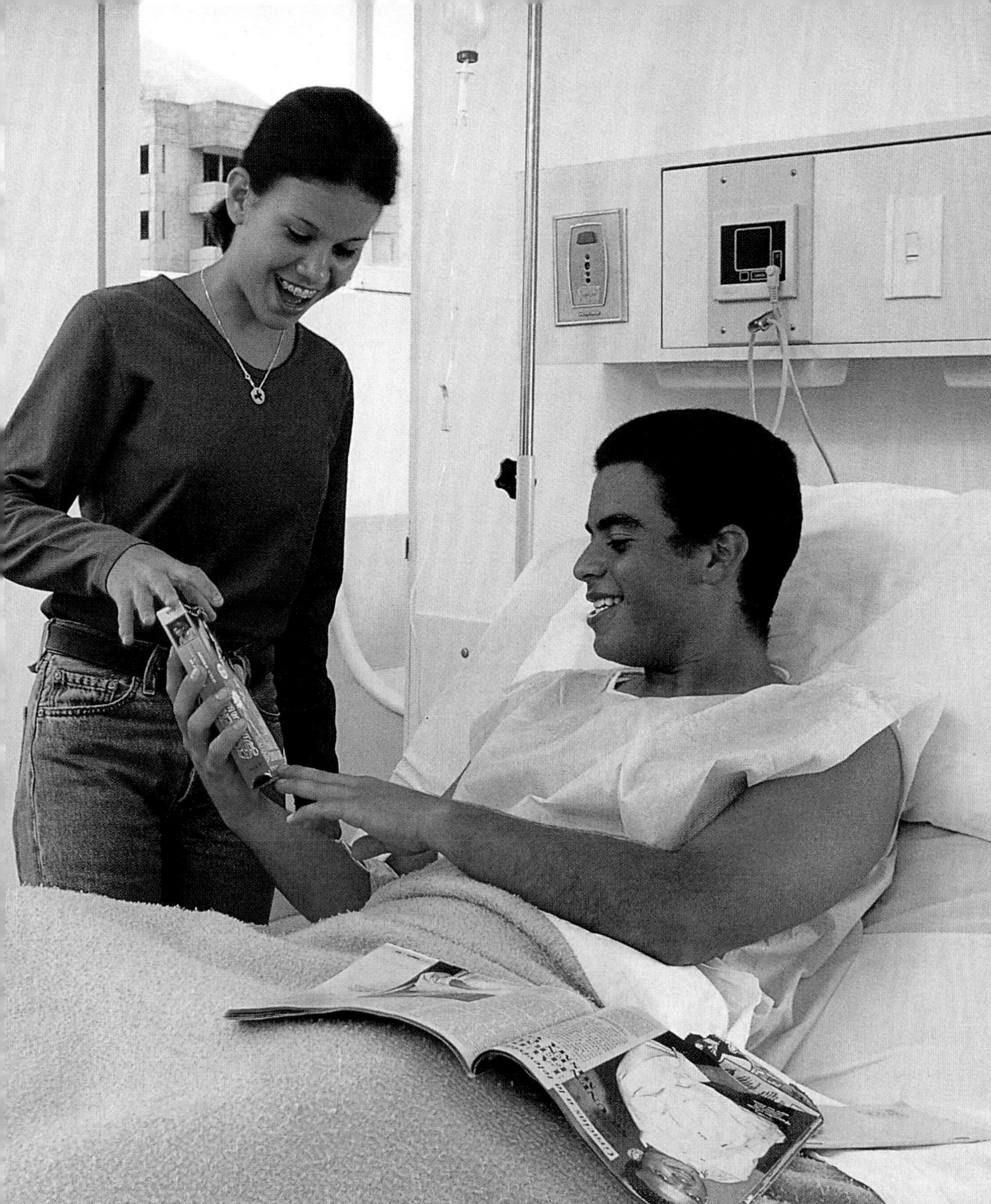

CAPÍTULO 8

Spotlight On Culture

Artefacto These decorative bowls on page 226 were made by Huichol Indians from the states of Jalisco and Nayarit, Mexico.
Fotografía This photo shows a young lady visiting a friend in a hospital in Caracas, Venezuela. Students may also find it interesting that the patient's room opens directly on the outdoors, rather than on an interior corridor.

Learning From Photos

Actividad Ask the following questions about the photo after presenting the new vocabulary on pages 228–229:
¿Quién está en el hospital, Irene o Carlos?
¿A quién visita Irene?
¿Qué opinas? ¿Está muy enfermo Carlos?
¿Tiene Carlos una revista?
¿Lee la revista?
¿Por qué no lee la revista? ¿Qué mira?
¿Es un videocasete?

Pacing

Chapter 8 will require approximately eight to ten days. Pacing will vary according to the length of the class, the age of your students, and student aptitude.

Chapter Projects

Primeros auxilios Obtain a video on first-aid, health, or nutrition in Spanish or English from the health department in your school. Use it as a springboard for discussing health and illnesses with the new vocabulary from this chapter.

Block Scheduling

See the Block Scheduling Lesson Plans Booklet for suggestions on how to present the chapter material within a block scheduling framework.

RESOURCES

- Vocabulary Transparencies 8.1 (A & B)
- Student Tape Manual, TE, pages 89–90
- Audiocassette 5B/CD5
- Workbook, pages 87–88
- Quiz 1, page 38
- CD-ROM, Disc 3, pages 228–231

Bell Ringer Review

Use BRR Transparency 8-1, or write the following on the board: Answer.

1. **¿Cuántos años tienes?**
2. **¿Tienes una familia grande o pequeña?**
3. **¿Cuántos hermanos tienes?**
4. **¿Cuántos son Uds. en la familia?**
5. **¿Tienen Uds. un perro o un gato?**

TEACHING VOCABULARY

A. Have students close their books. Present the vocabulary using Vocabulary Transparencies 8.1 (A & B).

B. Point to yourself as you teach the words **la garganta, la cabeza, el estómago.**

C. You can easily use gestures to teach the following words and expressions: **enfermo, cansado, contento, triste, nervioso, toser, estornudar, tener escalofríos, tener dolor de garganta, tener dolor de cabeza, tener dolor de estómago.**

D. Have students repeat the words and sentences on pages 228 and 229. Then have them open their books and read the new vocabulary aloud.

Vocabulario

¿Cómo está?

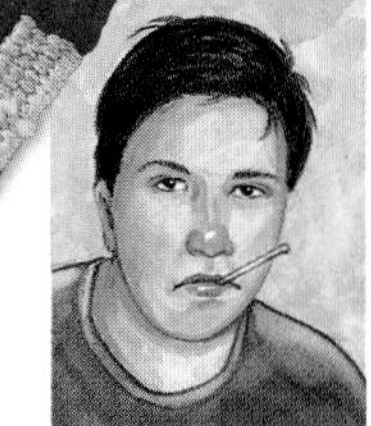
enfermo

cansada

contento

triste

nervioso

El pobre muchacho está enfermo.
Tiene fiebre.
Tiene la gripe.

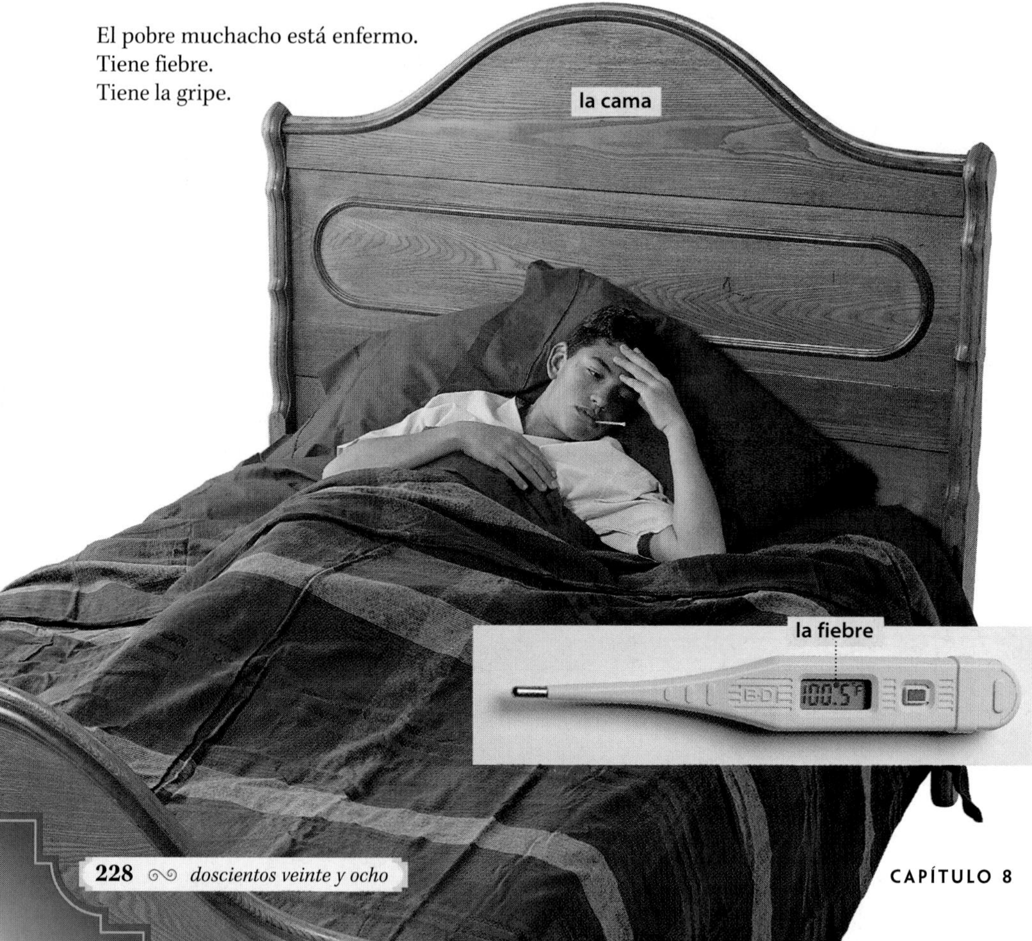

Total Physical Response

Begin

___, ven acá por favor. Imagínate que estás enfermo(a).
Indícame que estás cansado(a).
Indícame que tienes fiebre.
Indícame que tienes escalofríos.
Indícame que tienes dolor de garganta.
Indícame que tienes dolor de cabeza.
Indícame que tienes dolor de estómago.
Indícame que tienes tos.
Indícame que estás estornudando mucho.
Gracias, ___. Y ahora puedes regresar a tu asiento.

La muchacha tiene catarro.
Está resfriada.

El muchacho tiene tos.
Tiene dolor de garganta.

El muchacho tiene dolor de estómago.

La muchacha tiene dolor de cabeza.

El enfermo tiene que guardar cama.
Tiene escalofríos porque tiene fibre.
Él está de mal humor.
No está de buen humor.

ABOUT THE SPANISH LANGUAGE

- One can say either **Estoy resfriado(a)** or **Tengo un resfriado.**
- In some areas **la fiebre** is **la calentura**.
- Note that no article is used with the expression **guardar cama**. Note the difference between **estar en cama** *(to be in bed sick)*, **estar en la cama** *(to be in bed sleeping)*.
- You may wish to explain to students that one must be aware of false cognates. A very common way to say *to have a cold* is **estar constipado(a). Constipado** does not mean *constipated* as one would expect. The actual expression is **estar estreñido(a). Embarazada** is another false cognate. **Embarazada** means *pregnant*, not *embarrassed.*

VOCABULARY EXPANSION

Tourists often experience stomach problems when traveling. If you wish, you may give students the following expressions they may find very useful.

Tengo náuseas.
Tengo vómitos.
Tengo diarrea.
Estoy estreñido(a). *(constipated)*
Tengo calambres. *(cramps)*

Class Motivator

Simón dice After practicing the **Palabras 1** vocabulary, you may wish to play a game of **Simón dice**. Call the first round yourself and have the students act out the following:
Simón dice: Tienes dolor de cabeza.
Simón dice: Tienes dolor de garganta.
Simón dice: Tienes tos.
Simón dice: Tose.
Simón dice: Estornuda.
Simón dice: Tienes escalofríos.

CAPÍTULO 8
Vocabulario

¡OJO! **Práctica** When students are doing the **Práctica** activities, accept any answer that makes sense. The purpose of these activities is to have students use the new vocabulary. They are not factual recall activities. Thus, do not expect students to remember specific information from the vocabulary presentation when answering. If you wish, have students use the photos on this page as a stimulus, when possible.

Historieta Each time **Historieta** appears, it means that the answers to the activity form a short story. Encourage students to look at the title of the **Historieta** since it will sometimes help them do the activity. It is recommended that you go over the **Práctica** before assigning them for homework.

A and **B** Students can retell the stories in **Práctica A** and **B** in their own words.

Writing Development

Have students write the answers to **Práctica A** and **B** in a paragraph to illustrate how all of the items tell a story.

Learning From Realia

Formula 44M Have students look at the medicine bottle label on this page. With very minimal guessing they should be able to read and understand all the printed material.

Práctica

A **HISTORIETA** El pobre joven está enfermo.

Contesten.

1. ¿Está enfermo el pobre muchacho?
2. ¿Tiene la gripe?
3. ¿Tiene tos?
4. ¿Tiene dolor de garganta?
5. ¿Tiene fiebre?
6. ¿Tiene escalofríos?
7. ¿Tiene dolor de cabeza?
8. ¿Está siempre cansado?

Estepona, España

B **HISTORIETA** La pobre muchacha

Contesten.

San Miguel de Allende, México

1. ¿Está enferma la muchacha?
2. ¿Tiene tos?
3. ¿Estornuda mucho?
4. ¿Tiene dolor de cabeza?
5. ¿Está resfriada?
6. ¿Está en cama?
7. ¿Tiene que guardar cama?
8. ¿Qué opinión tienes? ¿Qué crees? ¿Está la muchacha de buen humor o de mal humor?

ANSWERS

Práctica

A
1. **Sí, el pobre muchacho está enfermo.**
2. **Sí, tiene la gripe.**
3. **Sí, (No, no) tiene tos.**
4. **Sí, (No, no) tiene dolor de garganta.**
5. **Sí, (No, no) tiene fiebre.**
6. **Sí, (No, no) tiene escalofríos.**
7. **Sí, (No, no) tiene dolor de cabeza.**
8. **Sí, (No, no) está siempre cansado.**

B
1. **Sí, la muchacha está enferma.**
2. **Sí, (No, no) tiene tos.**
3. **Sí, (No, no) estornuda mucho.**
4. **Sí, tiene dolor de cabeza.**
5. **Sí, está resfriada.**
6. **Sí, está en cama.**
7. **Sí, tiene que guardar cama.**
8. **Creo que la muchacha está de mal humor.**

C ¿Cómo está? Contesten según las fotos.

1. ¿Cómo está el joven? ¿Está triste o contento?

2. Y la joven, ¿cómo está? ¿Está triste o contenta?

3. El señor, ¿está bien o está enfermo?

4. Y la señora, ¿está nerviosa o está tranquila?

D ¿Cómo estás tú? Contesten personalmente.

1. ¿Cómo estás hoy?
2. Cuando estás enfermo(a), ¿estás de buen humor o estás de mal humor?
3. Cuando tienes dolor de cabeza, ¿estás contento(a) o triste?
4. Cuando tienes catarro, ¿siempre estás cansado(a) o no?
5. Cuando tienes catarro, ¿tienes fiebre y escalofríos?
6. Cuando tienes la gripe, ¿tienes fiebre y escalofríos?
7. ¿Tienes que guardar cama cuando tienes catarro?
8. ¿Tienes que guardar cama cuando tienes fiebre?

Actividad comunicativa

A ¿Qué te pasa? Work with a classmate. Ask your partner what's the matter—**¿Qué te pasa?** He or she will tell you. Then suggest something he or she can do to feel better. **¿Por qué no... ?** Take turns.

Práctica

C EXPANSION Ask for volunteers to imitate the people in **Actividad C.** Then have other students give the appropriate description. Have students do the same using the other words and expressions taught on pages 228–229.

D Práctica D can be done as an interview or a paired activity.

Actividad comunicativa

¡OJO! Práctica versus Actividades comunicativas All activities which provide guided practice are labeled **Práctica.** The more open-ended communicative activities are labeled **Actividades comunicativas.**

A Encourage students to be as creative as possible when doing this activity. They can have a lot of fun with it. Students should use the following model:
—¿Qué te pasa?
—Estoy nervioso(a) porque tengo un examen mañana.
—¿Por qué no vas al cine?

ANSWERS

Práctica

C **1. Está triste.** **2. Está contenta.** **3. Está enfermo.** **4. Está nerviosa.**

D **1. Estoy ___.**
2. Cuando estoy enfermo(a), estoy de mal humor.
3. Cuando tengo dolor de cabeza, estoy triste.
4. Cuando tengo catarro, siempre estoy cansado(a).
5. Sí (No), cuando tengo catarro, (no) tengo fiebre y escalofríos.
6. Sí, cuando tengo la gripe, tengo fiebre y escalofríos.
7. Sí, (No, no) tengo que guardar cama cuando tengo catarro.
8. Sí, tengo que guardar cama cuando tengo fiebre.

Actividad comunicativa

A Students should follow the model:
—¿Qué te pasa?
—*(response)*
—¿Por qué no ___?

Independent Practice

Assign any of the following:
1. Workbook, pages 87–88
2. Activities on pages 230–231
3. CD-ROM, Disc 3, pages 228–231

RESOURCES

- Vocabulary Transparencies 8.2 (A & B)
- Student Tape Manual, TE, pages 91–92
- Audiocassette 5B/CD5
- Workbook, pages 89–90
- Quiz 2, page 39
- CD-ROM, Disc 3, pages 232–235

Bell Ringer Review

Use BRR Transparency 8-2, or write the following on the board: Write some adjectives that describe your family doctor.

TEACHING VOCABULARY

A. Have students close their books. Present the new words using Vocabulary Transparencies 8.2 (A & B). As you point to each item, have students repeat the corresponding word or expression after you two or three times.

B. Have students keep their books closed. Dramatize the following words or expressions from **Palabras 2: abrir la boca, examinar los ojos, me duele la cabeza, me duele la garganta, me duele el pecho, me duele el estómago.**

C. Ask students to open their books to pages 232–233. Have them read along and repeat the new material after you or the recording on Cassette 5B/Compact Disc 5.

D. Make sure that students know the meaning of the cognates listed on page 233.

Vocabulario

En la consulta del médico

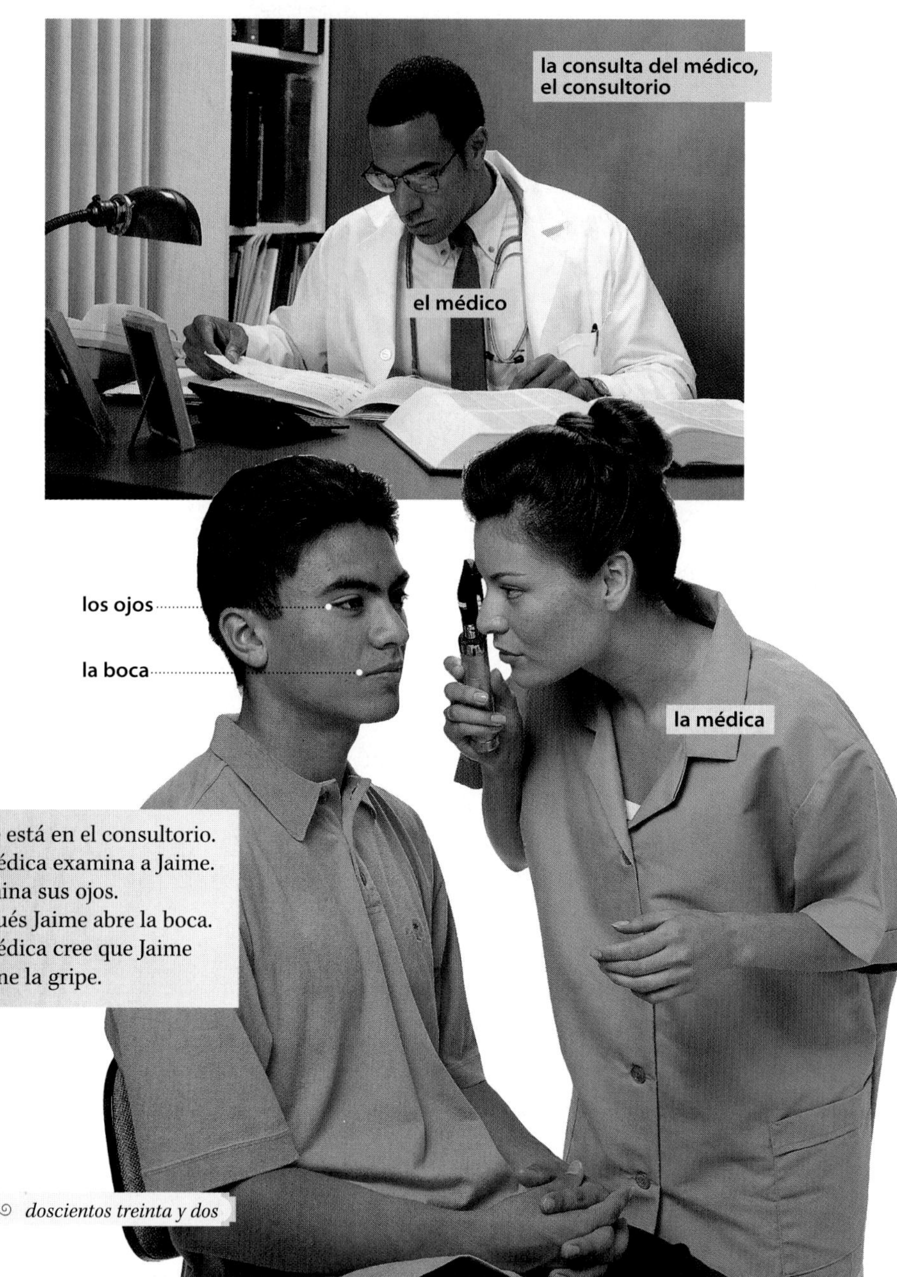

Jaime está en el consultorio.
La médica examina a Jaime.
Examina sus ojos.
Después Jaime abre la boca.
La médica cree que Jaime tiene la gripe.

Total Physical Response

Begin

(Estudiante 1), ven acá. Tú vas a ser el/la médico(a).
Y (Estudiante 2), ven acá. Tú vas a ser el/la enfermo(a).
(Estudiante 2), siéntate.
(Estudiante 2), indica al médico que te duele la garganta.
(Estudiante 2), abre la boca.
(Estudiante 1), examina la garganta.
(Estudiante 1), y ahora examina los ojos.
(Estudiante 1), dale una pastilla.
(Estudiante 2), toma la pastilla.

Me duele la cabeza.

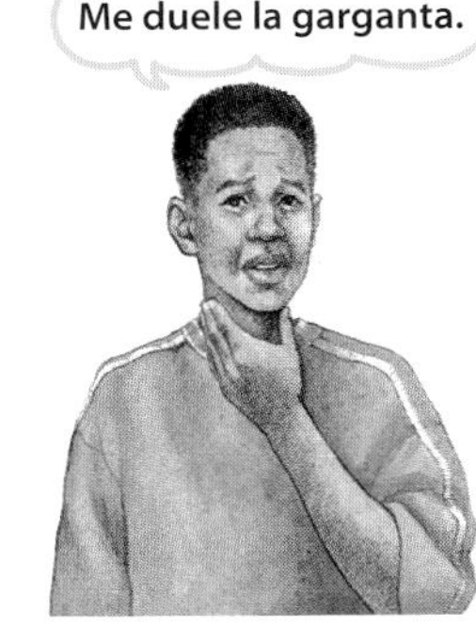

En la farmacia

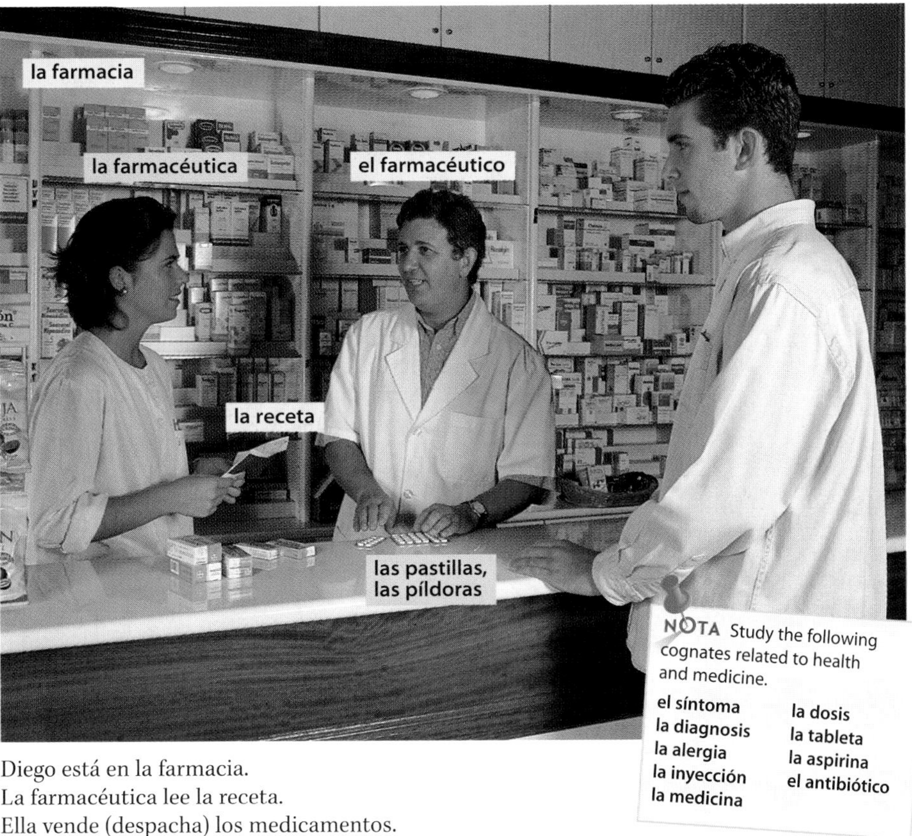

Diego está en la farmacia.
La farmacéutica lee la receta.
Ella vende (despacha) los medicamentos.

NOTA Study the following cognates related to health and medicine.

el síntoma	**la dosis**
la diagnosis	**la tableta**
la alergia	**la aspirina**
la inyección	**el antibiótico**
la medicina	

CAPÍTULO 8
Vocabulario

Did You Know?

Médicas Note that the doctor in the blue uniform on page 232 is a woman. In recent years in the United States, more and more women have entered the medical profession. In Spain and Latin America this is not a recent trend. There have always been a large number of female doctors.

RECYCLING

Bring back previously learned vocabulary by asking: **¿Dónde te duele?** and point to your arm, foot, finger, and hand.

ABOUT THE SPANISH LANGUAGE

- Other words that are used often in addition to **las pastillas** and **las píldoras** are: **los comprimidos, las tabletas, las cápsulas.**
- Explain to students that many nouns that end in **-ma** come from Greek and they are masculine and take the article **el: el problema, el programa, el síntoma, el drama.**
- Almost all nouns that end in **-osis** are feminine: **la dosis, la diagnosis, la prognosis, la tuberculosis.**

CAPÍTULO 8
Vocabulario

Práctica

A Have students act out **Práctica A** using as much expression as possible.

B Go over **Práctica B** once with the entire class. Then have students retell the story in their own words.

Learning From Photos

San Miguel de Allende, México Ask the following questions about the boy in the doctor's office (top photo).

¿Dónde está el muchacho?
¿Quién examina al muchacho? ¿El médico o la médica?
¿Qué abre el muchacho?
¿Lleva ella una máscara?

La farmacéutica Have students look at the pharmacist in the bottom photo. Note that she is wearing a type of smock or apron. The wearing of the smock, apron, or some type of uniform is more common in many professions in Spain and Latin America than in the United States. There are also many female pharmacists in both Spain and Latin America.

For the Younger Student

Está enfermo(a) Have students draw a picture of someone who isn't feeling too well. Then have them describe their pictures to the class, or have them write descriptions of their drawings.

Práctica

A **¿Qué te pasa?** Preparen una conversación según el modelo.

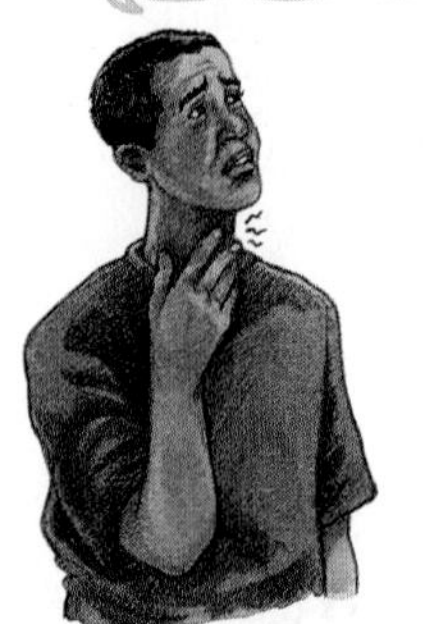

—¿Qué te pasa? ¿Tienes dolor de garganta?
—Sí, me duele mucho. ¡Qué enfermo(a) estoy!

1.

2.

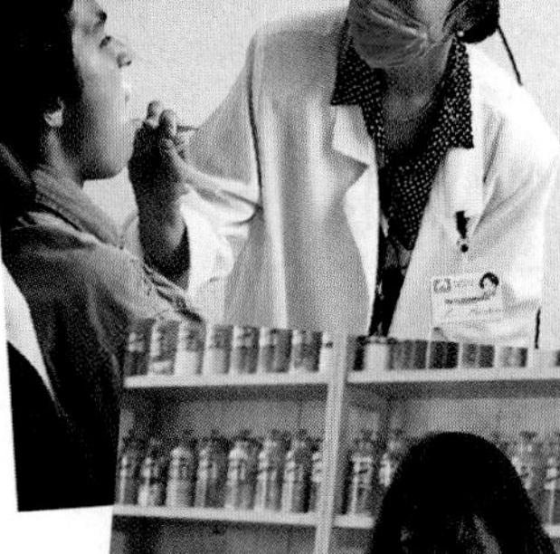

San Miguel de Allende, México

B **HISTORIETA En el consultorio**

Contesten.

1. ¿Dónde está Alberto? ¿En la consulta de la médica o en el hospital?
2. ¿Quién está enfermo? ¿Alberto o la médica?
3. ¿Quién examina a Alberto? ¿La médica o la farmacéutica?
4. ¿Qué examina la médica? ¿La cabeza o la garganta?
5. ¿Qué tiene que tomar Alberto? ¿Una inyección o una pastilla?
6. ¿Quién receta los antibióticos? ¿La médica o la farmacéutica?
7. ¿Adónde va Alberto con la receta? ¿A la clínica o a la farmacia?
8. ¿Qué despacha la farmacéutica? ¿Los medicamentos o las recetas?

ANSWERS

Práctica

A 1. **—¿Qué te pasa? ¿Tienes dolor de estómago?**
—Sí, me duele mucho. ¡Qué enfermo(a) estoy!

2. **—¿Qué te pasa? ¿Tienes dolor de cabeza?**
—Sí, me duele mucho. ¡Qué enfermo(a) estoy!

B 1. **Alberto está en la consulta de la médica.**
2. **Alberto está enfermo.**
3. **La médica examina a Alberto.**
4. **La médica examina la garganta.**
5. **Alberto tiene que tomar una pastilla (una inyección).**
6. **La médica receta los antibióticos.**
7. **Alberto va a la farmacia con la receta.**
8. **La farmacéutica despacha los medicamentos.**

C **HISTORIETA** Alberto está enfermo, el pobre.

Corrijan las oraciones.

1. Alberto está muy bien.
2. Alberto está en el hospital.
3. Alberto examina a la médica.
4. Alberto abre la boca y la médica examina los ojos.
5. La médica habla con Alberto de sus síntomas.
6. La farmacéutica receta unos antibióticos.
7. La médica despacha los medicamentos.
8. Alberto va al consultorio con la receta.

Actividades comunicativas

A **Buenos días, doctor.** Look at the illustration. Pretend you're the patient. Tell the doctor how you're feeling.

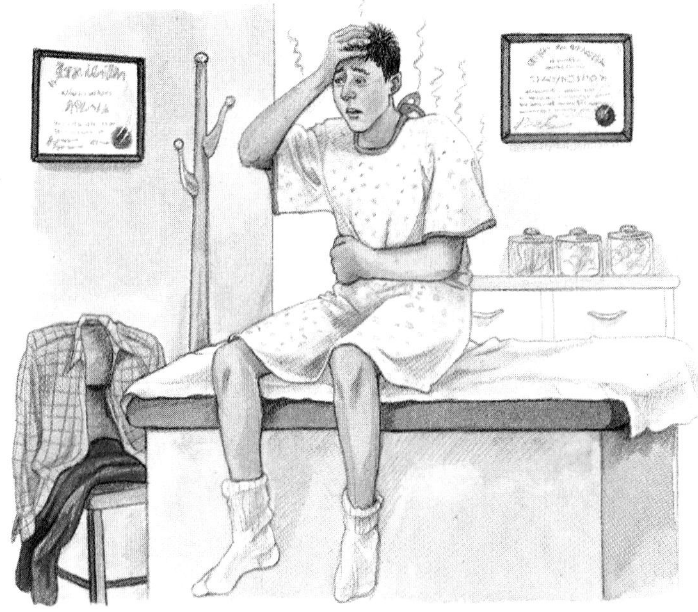

B **En la consulta del médico** Work with a classmate. You're sick with a cold or the flu. The doctor (your partner) will ask you questions about your symptoms. Answer the doctor's questions as completely as you can. Then change roles.

CAPÍTULO 8
Vocabulario

C Have students do **Práctica C** with books open. After you go over it once with the entire class, have students retell the story in their own words.

Actividades comunicativas

¡OJO! These activities encourage students to use the chapter vocabulary and grammar in open-ended situations. It is not necessary to have them do every activity. Choose the ones you consider most appropriate.

A and **B** You may have students present their conversations to the class.

EXPANSION

In **Actividad A** have individual students each come up with a symptom. See how many symptoms the class can come up with.

TECHNOLOGY OPTION

Students may use the Portfolio feature on the CD-ROM to record their conversations in **Actividad A.**

ANSWERS

Práctica

C
1. **Alberto está enfermo.**
2. **Alberto está en el consultorio (la consulta) de la médica.**
3. **La médica examina a Alberto.**
4. **Alberto abre la boca y la médica examina la garganta.**
5. **Alberto habla con la médica de sus síntomas.**
6. **La médica receta unos antibióticos.**
7. **La farmacéutica despacha los medicamentos.**
8. **Alberto va a la farmacia con la receta.**

Actividades comunicativas

A Students should use the vocabulary from **Palabras 1** and **2.** Answers will vary, but may include: **Tengo dolor de cabeza, tengo escalofríos, tengo dolor de estómago, etc.**

B Students will begin with either **Tengo la gripe** or **Estoy resfriado(a).** Then answers will vary.

CAPÍTULO 8
Estructura

RESOURCES

- Workbook, pages 91–93
- Student Tape Manual, TE, pages 93–96
- Audiocassette 5B/CD5
- Quizzes 3–5, pages 40–42
- Computer Testmaker
- CD-ROM, Disc 3, pages 236–243

Bell Ringer Review

Use BRR Transparency 8-3, or write the following on the board: Write as many words as you can that describe a person.

TEACHING STRUCTURE

Characteristics and conditions

¡OJO! Explain to students that the verb **ser** comes from the Latin verb **esse**, from which the English word *essence* is derived. The verb **ser** is therefore used to describe the essence of something, that which is inherent or characteristic.

The verb **estar**, on the other hand, is derived from Latin **stare**, from which the English word *state* is derived. **Estar** is therefore used to describe a state or a condition.

A. Read Steps 1 and 2 aloud.

B. Have students repeat the examples in Steps 1 and 2 as you write them on the board.

A You may wish to have students do **Práctica A** with books open. Students can do this as a paired activity.

Estructura

Characteristics and conditions
Ser y estar

1. In Spanish there are two verbs that mean "to be." They are **ser** and **estar.** These verbs have very distinct uses. They are not interchangeable. **Ser** is used to express a trait or characteristic that does not change.

Ella es muy sincera.
La casa de apartamentos es muy alta.

2. **Estar** is used to express a temporary condition or state.

Eugenio está enfermo.
Está cansado y nervioso.

La familia está contenta, San Miguel de Allende

A **Al contrario** Sigan el modelo.

1. Teresa es morena.
2. Justo es alto.
3. Héctor es feo.
4. Catalina es muy seria.
5. La clase de biología es aburrida.
6. Los cursos son fáciles.
7. Nuestro equipo de fútbol es malo.
8. Su familia es grande.

ANSWERS

Práctica

A
1. **Al contrario. No es morena. Teresa es rubia.**
2. **Al contrario. No es alto. Justo es bajo.**
3. **Al contrario. No es feo. Héctor es guapo.**
4. **Al contrario. No es muy seria. Catalina es muy cómica (graciosa).**
5. **Al contrario. No es aburrida. La clase de biología es interesante.**
6. **Al contrario. No son fáciles. Los cursos son difíciles.**
7. **Al contrario. No es malo. Nuestro equipo de fútbol es bueno.**
8. **Al contrario. No es grande. Mi familia es pequeña.**

B **Tu escuela y tus clases** Contesten.

1. ¿Cómo es tu escuela?
2. ¿Quién en la clase de español es rubio?
3. ¿Quién es moreno?
4. ¿Cuál es un curso interesante?
5. ¿Cuál es una clase aburrida?
6. ¿El equipo de qué deporte es muy bueno?

C **¿Cómo está o cómo es?** Describan a la persona en cada dibujo.

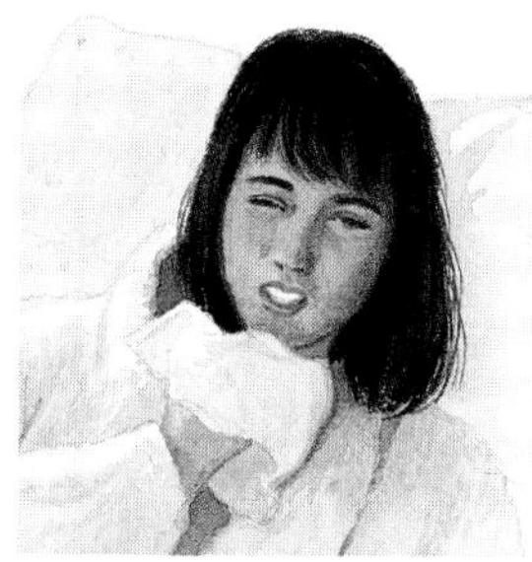

1. Antonia

2. Jorge

3. Beatriz

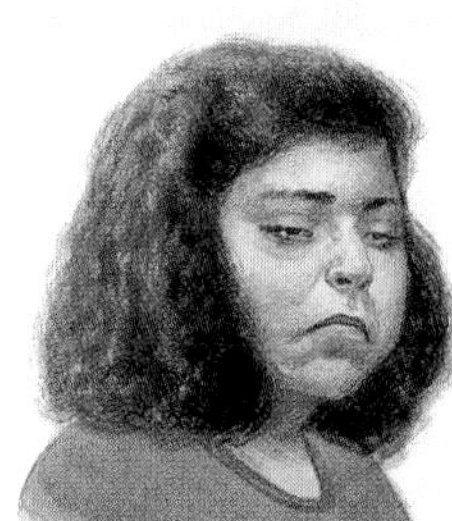

4. Teresa

5. Susana

D **¿Cómo eres?** Den una descripción personal.

INFOR-MED

La Medicina cada día avanza más en el desarrollo de nuevas formas de proteger la salud del ser humano. ¡Manténgase informado al respecto!

EXPANSION

Have students change the subjects in **Práctica A** on page 236 from singular to plural. This will review the forms of adjectives as well as the forms of the verb **ser.**

B After going over **Práctica B**, have students say as much as they can about their school or one of their classes.

C Note that **Práctica C** makes students come up with **ser** or **estar** on their own.

D See who can come up with the most complete description of him- or herself.

Learning From Realia

Infor-Med Have students read the Infor-Med ad and tell what it says in English.

ANSWERS

Práctica

B Answers will vary.

C Answers will vary, but may include:
1. **Antonia está resfriada (enferma).**
2. **Jorge está cansado (aburrido).**
3. **Beatriz está contenta.**
4. **Teresa está triste (cansada).**
5. **Susana es inteligente.**

D Answers will vary. Students can use adjectives that they learned in earlier chapters, including Chapter 1, page 38, as well as the words and expressions taught in this chapter.

Estructura

Práctica

E If necessary, have students quickly review the explanation of **ser** and **estar** on page 236 before beginning this activity.

EXPANSION Have students retell in their own words as much of the story from **Práctica E** as they can.

Actividades comunicativas

A Students will begin their conversations with: **¡Hola! ¿Cómo estás?** You may wish to have students read their descriptions to the class.

E **HISTORIETA Están enfermos.**

Completen con la forma correcta de **ser** o **estar.**

Rubén y Marisol ___(1) enfermos. Rubén no tiene energía. ___(2) muy cansado. ___(3) triste. Y Marisol tiene tos. Su garganta ___(4) muy roja. La mamá de Rubén y Marisol ___(5) muy nerviosa. Su papá ___(6) nervioso también porque sus dos hijos ___(7) enfermos. Pero su médico ___(8) muy bueno. El doctor Rodríguez ___(9) muy inteligente. Su consultorio ___(10) muy moderno. El doctor Rodríguez examina a Rubén y a Marisol. El médico habla:

—Uds. no ___(11) muy enfermos. Tienen la gripe. Aquí tienen unos antibióticos. Los antibióticos ___(12) muy buenos.

Ahora todos ___(13) muy contentos y los padres no ___(14) nerviosos. No ___(15) nerviosos porque Rubén no ___(16) muy enfermo y Marisol no ___(17) muy enferma. Dentro de poco, sus hijos van a ___(18) muy bien.

Actividades comunicativas

A **¿Por qué?** There is usually a reason for everything. Talk to a classmate. He or she will ask you how you're feeling. Answer and explain why you are feeling as you are. Some of the following words may be helpful to you.

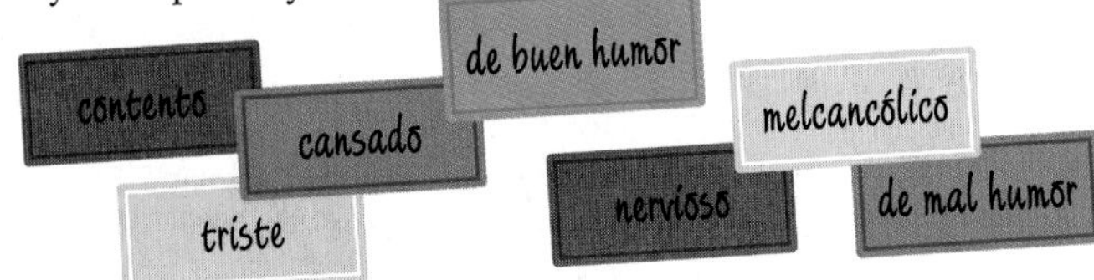

ANSWERS

Práctica

E
1. **están**
2. **Está**
3. **Está**
4. **está**
5. **está**
6. **está**
7. **están**
8. **es**
9. **es**
10. **es**
11. **están**
12. **son**
13. **están**
14. **están**
15. **están**
16. **está**
17. **está**
18. **estar**

Actividades communicativas

A Answers will vary. Encourage students to use as many words as possible from the colored boxes.

B **Virtudes y defectos** Work in small groups. Make a list of characteristics and personality traits. Divide them into two groups—**características positivas (virtudes)** and **características negativas (defectos).** Then have some fun. Make up a description of a person with many virtues. Make up another description of a person with many defects or faults. Be as creative as possible.

Origin and location
Ser y estar

1. The verb **ser** is used to express where someone or something is from.

La muchacha es de Cuba.
El café es de Colombia.

2. **Estar** is used to express where someone or something is located.

Los alumnos están en la escuela.
Los libros están en el salón de clase.

Santafé de Bogotá, Colombia

Práctica

A **¿De dónde es?** Contesten según el modelo.

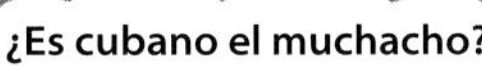

1. ¿Es colombiana la muchacha?
2. ¿Es guatemalteco el muchacho?
3. ¿Es puertorriqueña la joven?
4. ¿Es española la profesora?
5. ¿Es peruano el médico?
6. ¿Son venezolanos los amigos?
7. ¿Son chilenas las amigas?
8. ¿Son costarricenses los jugadores?

ANSWERS

Actividades comunicativas

B Answers will vary.

Práctica

A 1. **Sí, creo que es de Colombia.**
2. **Sí, creo que es de Guatemala.**
3. **Sí, creo que es de Puerto Rico.**
4. **Sí, creo que es de España.**
5. **Sí, creo que es del Perú.**
6. **Sí, creo que son de Venezuela.**
7. **Sí, creo que son de Chile.**
8. **Sí, creo que son de Costa Rica.**

B Find out which group has the longest list by having them read them aloud to the class.

Bell Ringer Review

Use BRR Transparency 8-4, or write the following on the board: Write the names of as many countries as you can in Spanish.

TEACHING STRUCTURE

Origin and location

¡OJO! You may wish to emphasize that **estar** is used with both permanent and temporary locations. For example: **Madrid está en España. Los alumnos de la señora Rivera están en Madrid ahora.**

A. Read Steps 1 and 2 with the students and have them read the model sentences aloud.

Práctica

A Have students do **Práctica A** as an oral paired activity. Be sure they know the meaning of **creo.** Say **Sí, creo que es de Cuba** as you shake your head and give an expression of belief but not absolute certainty. Say the model sentences with the appropriate intonation to indicate the naturalness of the exchange.

CAPÍTULO 8
Estructura

Writing Development

Have students write out **Práctica B** as a short letter.

C The purpose of **Práctica C** is to contrast the use of **ser** and **estar** and hopefully make it easy for students to understand the difference between origin and location.

Note You may have to supply some additional countries to enable students to respond to these questions. Or, you may ask students to name the countries that they wrote down for the Bell Ringer Review activity on page 239.

B HISTORIETA Una carta a un amigo

Completen la carta.

Caracas, Venezuela

Hola David,

¿Qué tal? ¿Cómo ___1___? Yo ___2___ muy bien. Yo ___3___ Alejandro Salas. ___4___ de Venezuela. Mi casa ___5___ en Caracas, la capital. ___6___ en la calle Rómulo Gallegos. Nuestro apartamento ___7___ moderno. Y ___8___ bastante grande. ___9___ en el quinto piso del edificio. El edificio ___10___ muy alto. Tiene muchos pisos. Me gusta nuestro apartamento.

David, ¿cómo ___11___ tu casa? ¿ ___12___ muy grande y moderna? Y tu familia, ¿ ___13___ grande o pequeña?

C **¿De dónde es y dónde está ahora?** Contesten.

1. Bernardo es de México pero ahora está en Venezuela.
   ¿De dónde es Bernardo?
   ¿Dónde está ahora?
   ¿De dónde es y dónde está?
2. Linda es de los Estados Unidos pero ahora está en Colombia.
   ¿De dónde es Linda?
   ¿Dónde está ahora?
   ¿De dónde es y dónde está?
3. La señora Martín es de Cuba pero ahora está en Puerto Rico.
   ¿De dónde es la señora Martín?
   ¿Dónde está ella ahora?
   ¿De dónde es y dónde está?

ANSWERS

Práctica

B
1. estás
2. estoy
3. soy
4. Soy
5. está
6. Está
7. es
8. es
9. Está
10. es
11. es
12. Es
13. es

C
1. Bernardo es de México.
   Ahora está en Venezuela.
   Es de México y ahora está en Venezuela.
2. Linda es de los Estados Unidos.
   Ahora está en Colombia.
   Es de los Estados Unidos y ahora está en Colombia.
3. La señora Martín es de Cuba.
   Ahora está en Puerto Rico.
   Es de Cuba y ahora está en Puerto Rico.

D Entrevista Contesten personalmente.

1. ¿Estás en la escuela ahora?
2. ¿Dónde está la escuela?
3. ¿En qué clase estás?
4. ¿En qué piso está la sala de clase?
5. ¿Está el/la profesor(a) en la clase también?
6. ¿De dónde es él/ella?
7. ¿Y de dónde eres tú?
8. ¿Cómo estás hoy?
9. Y el/la profesor(a), ¿cómo está?
10. ¿Y cómo es?

E HISTORIETA Un amigo, Ángel

Completen con **ser** o **estar.**

Ángel ___1___ un amigo muy bueno. ___2___ muy atlético y ___3___ muy inteligente. Además ___4___ sincero y simpático. Casi siempre ___5___ de buen humor. Pero hoy no. Al contrario, ___6___ de mal humor. ___7___ muy cansado y tiene dolor de cabeza. ___8___ enfermo. Tiene la gripe. ___9___ en casa. ___10___ en cama.

La casa de Ángel ___11___ en la calle 60. La calle 60 ___12___ en West New York. West New York no ___13___ en Nueva York. ___14___ en Nueva Jersey. Pero la familia de Ángel no ___15___ de West New York. Sus padres ___16___ de Cuba y sus abuelos ___17___ de España. Ellos ___18___ de Galicia, una región en el noroeste de España. Galicia ___19___ en la costa del Atlántico y del mar Cantábrico. Ángel tiene una familia internacional.

Pero ahora todos ___20___ en West New York y ___21___ contentos. Muchas familias en West New York ___22___ de ascendencia cubana. El apartamento de la familia de Ángel ___23___ muy bonito. ___24___ en el tercer piso y tiene una vista magnífica de la ciudad de Nueva York.

West New York, New Jersey

D and E You may have two students come to the front of the class and present **Práctica D** as an interview. This **Práctica** incorporates all uses of **ser** and **estar** as does **Práctica E.**

Did You Know?

Práctica E gives the students a great deal of cultural information. Many people from Galicia in Northwestern Spain migrated to the United States and areas of Latin America, particularly the Caribbean.

When many Cubans left Cuba for political reasons in the early 1960's, many went to Miami, Florida and to West New York, Union City, and Weehawkin, New Jersey on the palisades overlooking New York City. Many businesses became Cuban-owned and operated. Although there are still many people of Cuban descent in these communities, they have been joined by many others from Central and South America and the Dominican Republic.

ANSWERS

Práctica

D
1. **Sí, (No, no) estoy en la escuela ahora.**
2. **La escuela está en ___.**
3. **Estoy en la clase de ___.**
4. **La sala de clase está en el ___ piso.**
5. **Sí, el/la profesor(a) está en la clase también.**
6. **Él/Ella es de ___.**
7. **Yo soy de ___.**
8. **Estoy ___.**
9. **El/La profesor(a) está ___.**
10. **Es ___.**

E
1. **es**
2. **Es**
3. **es**
4. **es**
5. **está**
6. **está**
7. **Está**
8. **Está**
9. **Está**
10. **Está**
11. **está**
12. **está**
13. **está**
14. **Está**
15. **es**
16. **son**
17. **son**
18. **son**
19. **está**
20. **están**
21. **están**
22. **son**
23. **es**
24. **Está**

Bell Ringer Review

Use BRR Transparency 8-5, or write the following on the board: Write the Spanish names for as many parts of the body as you can.

TEACHING STRUCTURE

Telling what happens to whom

¡OJO! Only the pronouns **me, te,** and **nos** are presented in this chapter. At this point students do not have to distinguish between direct and indirect objects. The pronouns **lo, la, los, las** are presented in Chapter 9, and **le, les** in Chapter 10.

The pronouns **me, te, nos** are presented first because they are less complicated than the third-person pronouns. They are both direct and indirect objects. They are the only pronouns that are absolutely necessary for communication. For example, if asked a question with **te**, it is necessary to answer with **me**. When speaking in the third person, one could answer with a noun instead of a pronoun: **¿Invitaste a Juan? Sí, invité a Juan.**

A. Have students point to themselves as they say **me,** and point to or look at a friend as they say **te.**

B. Have students read the model sentences aloud. You can call on an individual to read them or have the entire class read them in unison.

A **Práctica A** can be done as a paired activity.

B Call on two students to present **Práctica B** as a mini-conversation.

Telling what happens to whom
Me, te, nos

Me, **te,** and **nos** are object pronouns. Note that the pronoun is placed right before the verb.

¿Te ve el médico?
Sí, el médico me ve. Me examina.
¿Te da una receta?
Sí, me da una receta.
Cuando tenemos la gripe, el médico nos receta antibióticos.

A HISTORIETA En el consultorio

Contesten.

1. ¿Estás enfermo(a)?
2. ¿Vas a la consulta del médico?
3. ¿Te ve el médico?
4. ¿Te examina?
5. ¿Te habla el médico?
6. ¿Te da una diagnosis?
7. ¿Te receta unas pastillas?
8. ¿Te despacha los medicamentos la farmacéutica?

B **Una invitación** Completen.

—Aquí tienes una carta. ¿Quién ___1___ escribe?
—Carlos ___2___ escribe.
—¿Ah, sí?
—Sí, ___3___ invita a una fiesta.
—¿___4___ invita a una fiesta?
—Sí, Carlos siempre ___5___ invita cuando tiene una fiesta.

ANSWERS

Práctica

A
1. **Sí, (No, no) estoy enfermo(a).**
2. **Sí, (No, no) voy a la consulta del médico.**
3. **Sí, (No, no) me ve el médico.**
4. **Sí, (No, no) me examina.**
5. **Sí, (No, no) me habla el médico.**
6. **Sí, (No, no) me da una diagnosis.**
7. **Sí, (No, no) me receta unas pastillas.**
8. **Sí (No), la farmacéutica (no) me despacha los medicamentos.**

B
1. **te**
2. **me**
3. **me**
4. **Te**
5. **me**

Actividad comunicativa

A **Preguntas y más preguntas** Work with a partner. Have some fun making up silly questions and giving answers. For example, **¿Te da una receta tu amigo cuando es tu cumpleaños?** Use as many of the following words as possible. Be original!

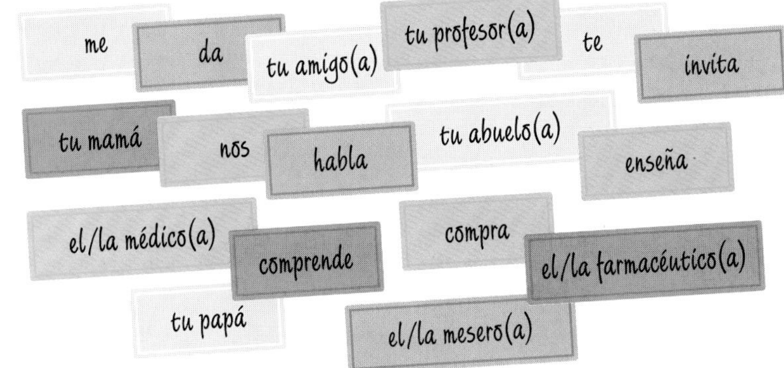

La Facultad de Medicina,Universidad de Madrid

CAPÍTULO 8
Estructura

Actividad comunicativa

A You may wish to do this activity with the entire class. As students give silly statements, the laughter of the other class members indicates comprehension. You can call on another student to correct the silly statement and say something that makes sense.

Learning From Photos

La Facultad de Medicina, Universidad de Madrid The University of Madrid has an excellent School of Medicine. You may wish to point out to teachers that the term *school* is **la facultad** in Spanish when referring to a *school* at a university.

¡OJO! All new material in the chapter has been presented. The sections that follow recombine and reintroduce the vocabulary and structures that have already been introduced.

ANSWERS

Actividad comunicativa

A Answers will vary. Encourage students to use as many words as possible from the colored boxes.

RESOURCES

- Audiocassette 5B/CD5
- CD-ROM, Disc 3, page 244

Bell Ringer Review

Use BRR Transparency 8-6, or write the following on the board:
Answer the following questions.

1. **¿Comes mucho cuando estás enfermo(a)?**
2. **¿Tienes mucho apetito cuando estás enfermo(a)?**
3. **¿Tomas muchos líquidos cuando estás enfermo(a)?**
4. **¿Guardas cama cuando estás enfermo(a)?**

TEACHING THE CONVERSATION

A. Tell students they will hear a conversation between Alejandro and a doctor. Have students close their books and listen as you read the conversation or play Cassette 5B/Compact Disc 5.
B. Have students keep their books closed as you reread the conversation to them, stopping after every three sentences to ask simple comprehension questions.
C. Have students open their books and read the conversation aloud.
D. Have them dramatize the conversation.
E. Have a student summarize the visit to the doctor in his or her own words.

TECHNOLOGY OPTION

On the CD-ROM (Disc 3, page 244), students can watch a dramatization of this conversation. They can then play the role of either one of the characters, and record themselves in the conversation.

Conversación

En la consulta del médico

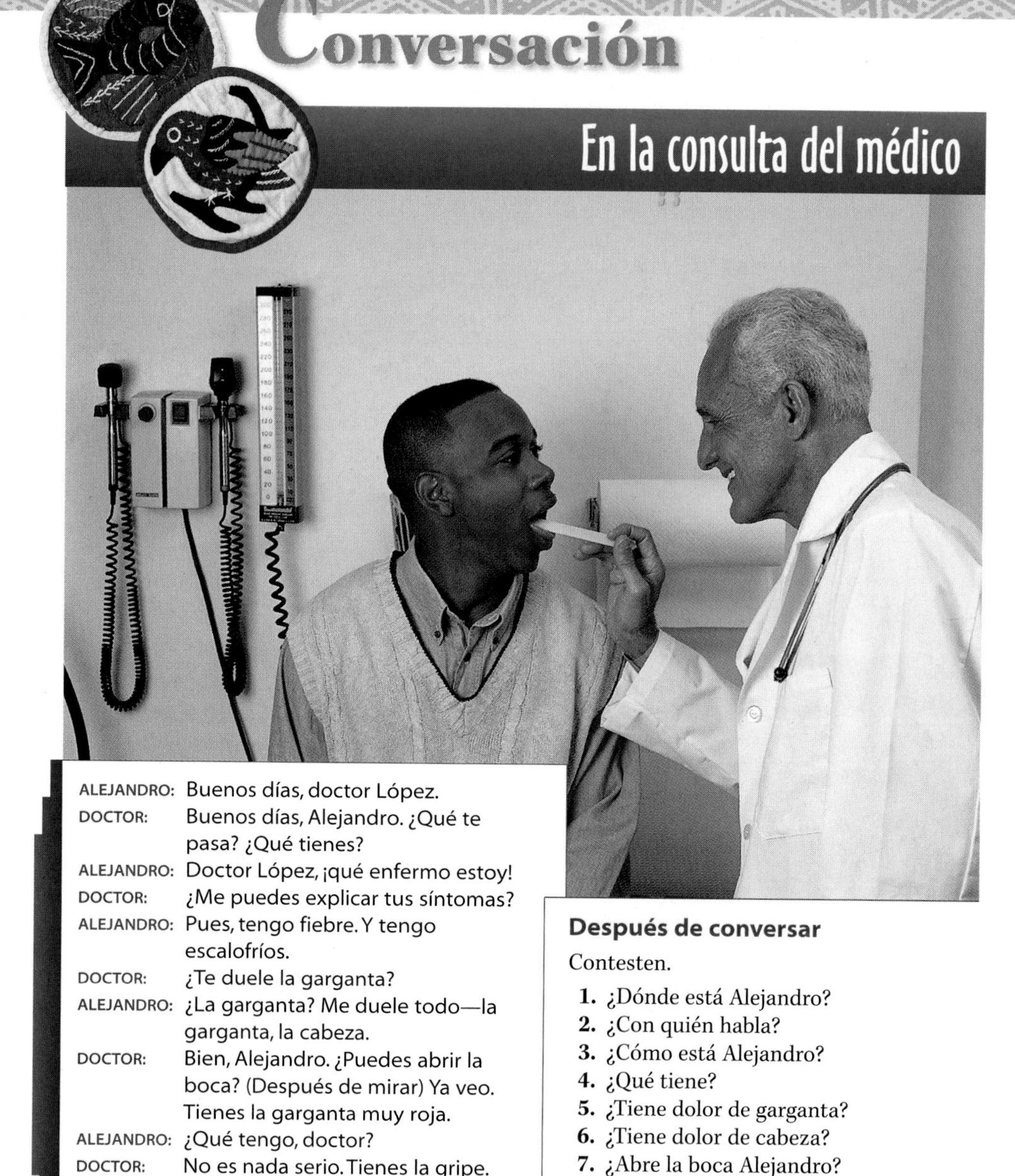

ALEJANDRO: Buenos días, doctor López.
DOCTOR: Buenos días, Alejandro. ¿Qué te pasa? ¿Qué tienes?
ALEJANDRO: Doctor López, ¡qué enfermo estoy!
DOCTOR: ¿Me puedes explicar tus síntomas?
ALEJANDRO: Pues, tengo fiebre. Y tengo escalofríos.
DOCTOR: ¿Te duele la garganta?
ALEJANDRO: ¿La garganta? Me duele todo—la garganta, la cabeza.
DOCTOR: Bien, Alejandro. ¿Puedes abrir la boca? (Después de mirar) Ya veo. Tienes la garganta muy roja.
ALEJANDRO: ¿Qué tengo, doctor?
DOCTOR: No es nada serio. Tienes la gripe. Te voy a recetar unos antibióticos. Dentro de dos días vas a estar muy bien.

Después de conversar

Contesten.

1. ¿Dónde está Alejandro?
2. ¿Con quién habla?
3. ¿Cómo está Alejandro?
4. ¿Qué tiene?
5. ¿Tiene dolor de garganta?
6. ¿Tiene dolor de cabeza?
7. ¿Abre la boca Alejandro?
8. ¿Qué examina el médico?
9. ¿Cómo está la garganta?
10. ¿Qué cree el médico que Alejandro tiene?

ANSWERS

Después de conversar

1. **Alejandro está en la consulta (el consultorio) del médico.**
2. **Habla con el médico (doctor).**
3. **Alejandro está enfermo.**
4. **Tiene fiebre y escalofríos.**
5. **Sí, tiene dolor de garganta.**
6. **Sí, tiene dolor de cabeza.**
7. **Sí, Alejandro abre la boca.**
8. **El médico examina la garganta de Alejandro.**
9. **La garganta está roja.**
10. **El médico cree que Alejandro tiene la gripe.**

Actividades comunicativas

A **¿Debes o no debes ser médico(a)?** Work with a classmate. Interview one another and decide who would be a good doctor. Make a list of questions for your interview. One question you may want to ask is: **¿Tienes mucha o poca paciencia?**

JUEGO **¿Quién es?** Play a guessing game with a classmate. Give some features and characteristics of someone in the class. Then tell how the person appears to be today. Your partner will guess who it is you are talking about. Then your partner will describe someone and it will be your turn to guess.

ALUMNO 1: **Es morena y alta. Está contenta hoy.**
ALUMNO 2: **¡Es Alicia!**
ALUMNO 1: **Sí, es ella.**

Pronunciación

La consonante c

You have already learned that **c** in combination with **e** or **i** (**ce, ci**) is pronounced like an **s**. The consonant **c** in combination with **a, o, u** (**ca, co, cu**) has a hard **k** sound. Since **ce, ci** have the soft **s** sound, **c** changes to **qu** when it combines with **e** or **i** (**que, qui**) in order to maintain the hard **k** sound. Repeat the following.

ca	que	qui	co	cu
cama	**que**	**equipo**	**como**	**cubano**
casa	**queso**	**aquí**	**médico**	
catarro	**parque**	**química**	**cocina**	
cansado	**pequeño**	**tranquilo**		
cabeza				
boca				

Repeat the following sentences.

El médico cubano está en la consulta pequeña.
El queso está en la cocina de la casa.
El cubano come el queso aquí en el parque pequeño.

Career Connection

Hablo español Because the Hispanic population in the United States is continually growing, Spanish is a very useful tool for communication in all areas of the medical profession. Ask students to think of several positions in the health care field where a knowledge of Spanish would be useful or essential. If possible, invite a bilingual health care professional to speak to your class on this topic.

ANSWERS

Actividades comunicativas
A Answers will vary.

EXPANSION

Have students present other versions of the conversation on page 244. The student playing the patient should give different symptoms. The "doctor" will have to change his or her responses accordingly.

Actividades comunicativas

A Note the career orientation of **Actividad A.**

JUEGO This game makes a nice end-of-class activity. It also recycles descriptive adjectives from Chapters 1 and 2.

TEACHING PRONUNCIATION

A. Remind students that the **c** sound is somewhat softer in Spanish than it is in English. Have them imitate your pronunciation or the pronunciation of the speaker on Cassette 5B/Compact Disc 5.

B. You may also use these words and sentences for a dictation.

C. To see if students are grasping this spelling concept, you may also wish to dictate the following words, which they do not know.

queda	**quiste**
cate	**quita**
coco	**quema**
quiosco	**coloca**
culebra	**loco**

TECHNOLOGY OPTION

In the CD-ROM version of the Pronunciation section (Disc 3, page 245), students will see an animation of the cartoon on this page. They can also listen to, record, and play back the sounds, words, and sentences presented here.

Bell Ringer Review

Use BRR Transparency 8-7, or write the following on the board: Rewrite these sentences. Change the singular object pronouns in the first two sentences to the plural form. In the second two sentences, change the plural forms to singular.

1. **Me duele la cabeza.**
2. **Me da una receta.**
3. **Nos invita a la fiesta.**
4. **El médico nos examina.**

National Standards

Cultures

The reading about a visit to the doctor on pages 246–247 and the related activities give students an understanding of daily life in the Spanish-speaking world.

Comparisons

Have students look at the prescription on page 246. It is from the Clínica Nuestra Señora de América. **La clínica** has quite a different meaning from the English word *clinic.* A **clínica** is very often a private hospital owned by either one or several doctors.

TEACHING THE READING

Pre-reading

A. Have students scan the passage to look for cognates.

B. Give students a brief synopsis of the **Lectura** in Spanish. Ask a few questions based on it.

Lecturas CULTURALES

Reading Strategy

Visualizing

As you are reading, try to visualize (or make a mental picture) of exactly what it is you are reading. Allow your mind to freely develop an image. This will help you to remember what you read. It may also help you identify with the subject you are reading about.

UNA JOVEN NERVIOSA

La pobre Patricia está muy enferma hoy. No tiene energía. Está cansada. Tiene dolor de garganta y tiene tos. Está de muy mal humor porque mañana tiene que jugar en un partido importante de fútbol. No quiere perder[1] el partido pero no puede jugar si está tan enferma y débil[2].

Pues, no hay más remedio para Patricia. Tiene que ir a ver al médico. Llega al consultorio.

[1]perder *to miss*
[2]débil *weak*

Madrid, España

Independent Practice

Assign any of the following:

1. **Después de leer** activity, page 247
2. Workbook, **Un poco más,** pages 94–97
3. CD-ROM, Disc 3, pages 246–247

En el consultorio Patricia habla con el médico. Explica que tiene un partido importante que no quiere perder. El médico examina a Patricia. Ella abre la boca y el médico examina la garganta. Sí, está un poco roja pero no es nada serio. Su condición no es grave.

Habla Patricia:

—Doctor, no puedo guardar cama. Tengo que jugar fútbol mañana.

—Patricia, estás muy nerviosa. Tienes que estar tranquila. No hay problema. Aquí tienes una receta. Vas a tomar una pastilla tres veces al día—una pastilla con cada comida. Mañana vas a estar mucho mejor[3] y no vas a perder tu partido. Y, ¡buena suerte[4]!

[3]mucho mejor *much better*
[4]buena suerte *good luck*

Madrid, España

Después de leer

A Pobre Patricia Contesten.

1. ¿Quién está enferma?
2. ¿Cuáles son sus síntomas?
3. ¿Está de buen humor o de mal humor?
4. ¿Por qué está nerviosa?
5. ¿Cuál es el único remedio para Patricia?
6. ¿Con quién habla Patricia en el consultorio?
7. ¿Qué examina el médico?
8. ¿Cómo está la garganta?
9. ¿Cómo es su condición?
10. ¿Tiene que guardar cama Patricia?
11. ¿Qué tiene que tomar?
12. ¿Cuándo tiene que tomar las pastillas?
13. ¿Cómo va a estar mañana?

Reading

Call on a student to read three or four sentences. Ask several questions to check comprehension before calling on the next student to read. Continue in this way until the selection has been completed.

Post-reading

Assign the reading selection and the **Despues de leer** activity on page 247 as homework. Go over the homework the next day in class.

TECHNOLOGY OPTION

Students may listen to a recorded version of the **Lectura** on the CD-ROM, Disc 3, pages 246–247.

Learning From Photos

Madrid, España Ask the following questions about the photo on this page:

¿Es una clínica o una farmacia?
¿Lleva uniforme la farmacéutica?
¿De qué color es?
¿Qué tiene la farmacéutica en la mano?

(You may wish to give the students the word for *box*, **la caja.**)

ANSWERS

Después de leer

A
1. **Patricia está enferma.**
2. **No tiene energía. Está cansada. Tiene dolor de garganta y tiene tos.**
3. **Está de muy mal humor.**
4. **Está nerviosa porque mañana tiene que jugar en un partido importante de fútbol y no puede jugar si está tan enferma y débil.**
5. **Tiene que ir a ver al médico.**
6. **Patricia habla con el médico en el consultorio.**
7. **El médico examina la garganta.**
8. **Está un poco roja pero no es nada serio.**
9. **Su condición no es grave.**
10. **No, no tiene que guardar cama.**
11. **Tiene que tomar las pastillas que receta el médico.**
12. **Tiene que tomar las pastillas tres veces al día—una pastilla con cada comida.**
13. **Mañana va a estar mucho mejor.**

LECTURA OPCIONAL 1

National Standards

Cultures

The reading about pharmacies and the related activities on this page give students an understanding of medical services in the Spanish-speaking world.

Comparisons

In this selection students learn that, unlike pharmacists in the United States, Spanish and Latin American pharmacists can dispense many medicines without a prescription. Pharmacists will also listen to a patient's symptoms and recommend a medicine.

TEACHING TIPS

¡OJO! This reading is optional. You may skip it completely, have the entire class read it, have only several students read it, or assign it for extra credit.

A. After the students read the selection, ask them to state the main difference between pharmacies in the United States and those in many Hispanic countries.

B. You may wish to use the **Después de leer** questions as an informal quiz to find out how well the students understood the reading.

Learning From Photos

Buenos Aires, Argentina This photo is of a traditional pharmacy sometimes called **un apotecario.** These traditional pharmacies sell only medical products. Some newer pharmacies, however, are now selling cosmetics too.

LA FARMACIA

En los Estados Unidos si uno quiere o necesita antibióticos, es necesario tener una receta. Es necesario visitar al médico para un examen. El médico receta los medicamentos y el paciente lleva la receta a la farmacia. El farmacéutico no puede despachar medicamentos sin la receta de un médico.

En muchos países hispanos no es necesario tener una receta para comprar antibióticos. Uno puede explicar sus síntomas al farmacéutico y él o ella puede despachar los medicamentos. Pero hay una excepción. Los farmacéuticos no pueden despachar medicamentos que contienen sustancias controladas como un narcótico o un medicamento con alcohol.

Y hay otra cosa importante. El precio[1] de las medicinas en los países hispanos es mucho más bajo que el precio de las mismas medicinas en los Estados Unidos.

[1]precio *price*

Buenos Aires, Argentina

Después de leer

A **¿Sí o no?** Digan que sí o que no.

1. El farmacéutico en los Estados Unidos no puede despachar medicamentos si el cliente no tiene una receta de su médico.
2. En Latinoamérica el médico despacha los medicamentos.
3. En Latinoamérica es necesario ir a una clínica por los antibióticos.
4. El farmacéutico en Latinoamérica puede despachar antibióticos sin una receta del médico.
5. El farmacéutico en Latinoamérica no puede vender medicamentos que contienen o llevan una droga o alcohol sin una receta.
6. Los medicamentos cuestan más en los países hispanos que en los Estados Unidos.

ANSWERS

Después de leer

A
1. **Sí.**
2. **No.**
3. **No.**
4. **Sí.**
5. **Sí.**
6. **No.**

LECTURA OPCIONAL 2

UNA BIOGRAFÍA—EL DOCTOR ANTONIO GASSETT

El doctor Antonio Gassett es de La Habana, Cuba. Recibe su bachillerato en ciencias en la Universidad de Belén, en Cuba. Más tarde estudia en la Facultad de Medicina de la Universidad de La Habana. Poco después, sale de[1] Cuba por motivos políticos. Va a Boston donde trabaja de técnico de laboratorio en la Fundación de Retina de Boston.

Le interesa mucho el trabajo con los ojos y decide estudiar oftalmología. Estudia en Harvard y en la Universidad de la Florida.

Hoy el doctor Gassett es una persona famosa. Descubre un método para tratar la córnea. Con el tratamiento del doctor Gassett muchas personas ciegas—que no pueder ver—recobran la vista[2]. El doctor recibe muchos premios[3] por sus investigaciones y descubrimientos[4].

La Habana, Cuba

[1]sale de *he leaves*
[2]recobran la vista *regain sight*
[3]premios *prizes, awards*
[4]descubrimientos *discoveries*

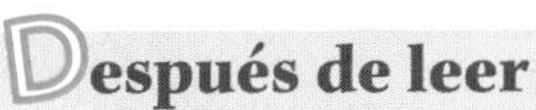

Después de leer

A Estudio de palabras Contesten.

1. The word **investigar** is a cognate of *investigate.* What does "to investigate" mean? In Spanish, **investigar** can mean both "to investigate" and "to do research." Related words are: **las investigaciones, el investigador.** Use these words in a sentence.
2. In the reading, find a word related to each of the following: **tratar, descubrir.**

B Palabras sinónimas Busquen una expresión equivalente.

1. obtiene su bachillerato
2. por razones políticas
3. le fascina el trabajo
4. es una persona célebre, renombrada

LECTURA OPCIONAL 2

National Standards

Cultures
In this selection students learn about an important contribution to medicine made by a Cuban-American.

TEACHING TIPS

¡OJO! This reading is optional. You may skip it completely, have the entire class read it, have only several students read it, or assign it for extra credit.

A. Have students read the selection silently. Ask them to give a one-sentence summary in Spanish of what Dr. Gassett's contribution to medicine is.

B. Now have them quickly do the **Después de leer** activities.

ANSWERS

Después de leer

A 1. In English, to investigate something means *to observe or study something closely* or *to conduct an official inquiry.* Answers will vary.
2. **el tratamiento, descubrimientos**

B 1. **recibe su bachillerato**
2. **por motivos políticos**
3. **le interesa mucho el trabajo**
4. **es una persona famosa**

CAPÍTULO 8
Conexiones

National Standards

Connections

This reading about nutrition establishes a connection with another discipline, allowing students to reinforce and further their knowledge of natural sciences through the study of Spanish.

LAS CIENCIAS NATURALES

LA NUTRICIÓN

¡OJO! The readings in the **Conexiones** section are optional. They focus on some of the major disciplines taught in schools and universities. The vocabulary is useful for discussing such topics as history, literature, art, economics, business, science, etc.

You may choose any of the following ways to do this reading on nutrition with your students.

Independent reading Have students read the selections and do the post-reading activities as homework, which you collect. This option is least intrusive on class time and requires a minimum of teacher involvement.

Homework with in-class follow-up Assign the readings and post-reading activities as homework. Review and discuss the material in class the next day.

Intensive in-class activity This option includes a pre-reading vocabulary presentation, in-class reading and discussion, assignment of the activities for homework, and a discussion of the assignment in class the following day.

Conexiones

LAS CIENCIAS NATURALES

LA NUTRICIÓN

Good nutrition is very important. What we eat can determine if we will enjoy good health or poor health. For this reason, it is most important to have a balanced diet and avoid the temptation to eat "junk food."

Read the following information about nutrition in Spanish. Before reading this selection, however, look at the following groups of related words. Often if you know the meaning of one word you can guess the meaning of several other words related to it.

varía, la variedad, la variación
activo, la actividad
los adolescentes, la adolescencia
proveen, la provisión, el proveedor
el consumo, consumir, el consumidor
elevar, la elevación, elevado

Comer bien

Es muy importante comer bien para mantener la salud. Cada día debemos[1] comer una variedad de vegetales, frutas, granos y cereales y carnes o pescado.

Calorías

El número de calorías que necesita o requiere una persona depende de su metabolismo, de su tamaño y de su nivel[2] de actividad física. Los adolescentes necesitan más calorías que los ancianos o viejos. Requieren más calorías porque son muy activos y están creciendo[3]. Una persona anciana de tamaño pequeño con un nivel bajo de actividad física requiere menos calorías.

[1]debemos *we should*
[2]nivel *level*
[3]creciendo *growing*

Class Motivator

La nutrición Those students who are interested in nutrition may prepare a food chart with the following heads.

Alimentos altos en calorías
Alimentos bajos en calorías
Grasas
Carbohidratos
Vitamina A
Vitamina B
Vitamina C
Vitamina D
Vitamina E

Under each heading they can put photos or drawings of the appropriate foods labeled in Spanish that they have already learned to identify.

Proteínas
Las proteínas son especialmente importantes durante los períodos de crecimiento. Los adolescentes, por ejemplo, deben comer comestibles o alimentos ricos[4] en proteínas porque están creciendo.

Carbohidratos
Los carbohidratos son alimentos como los espaguetis, las papas y el arroz. Los carbohidratos proveen mucha energía.

Grasas
Las grasas o lípidos son otra fuente[5] importante de energía. Algunas carnes contienen mucha grasa. Pero es necesario controlar el consumo de lípidos o grasa porque en muchos individuos elevan el nivel de colesterol.

Vitaminas
Las vitaminas son indispensables para el funcionamiento del organismo o cuerpo. ¿Cuáles son algunas fuentes de las vitaminas que necesita el cuerpo humano?

VITAMINA	FUENTE
A	vegetales, leche, algunas frutas
B	carne, huevos, leche, cereales, vegetales verdes
C	frutas cítricas, tomates, lechuga
D	leche, huevos, pescado
E	aceites[6], vegetales, huevos, cereales

Madrid, España

[4]ricos *rich* [5]fuente *source* [6]aceites *oils*

Después de leer

A La nutrición Contesten.

1. ¿Qué debemos comer cada día?
2. ¿De qué depende el número de calorías que requiere una persona?
3. ¿Quiénes requieren más calorías? ¿Por qué?
4. ¿Por qué necesitan los adolescentes alimentos ricos en proteínas?
5. ¿Qué proveen los carbohidratos?
6. ¿Por qué es necesario controlar el consumo de grasas o lípidos?

CAPÍTULO 8
Conexiones

RECYCLING

You may wish to have all students read this selection since so many are interested in good eating habits. This reading also serves to review and reinforce the names for many foods.

Additional Practice

Have students write out a balanced menu for **el desayuno, el almuerzo,** and **la cena** for one day. They should use the information they learned in the **Conexiones** reading when planning their meals.

ANSWERS

Después de leer

A 1. **Cada día debemos comer una variedad de vegetales, frutas, granos y cereales y carnes o pescado.**
2. **Depende de su metabolismo, de su tamaño y de su nivel de actividad.**
3. **Los adolescentes requieren más calorías porque son muy activos y están creciendo.**
4. **Los adolescentes deben comer alimentos ricos en proteínas porque están creciendo.**
5. **Los carbohidratos proveen mucha energía.**
6. **Es necesario controlar el consumo de grasas o lípidos porque en muchos individuos elevan el nivel de colesterol.**

CAPÍTULO 8
Culminación

RECYCLING

The **Actividades orales** and the **Actividad escrita** allow students to use the vocabulary and structure from this chapter and previous chapters in open-ended, real-life settings.

Actividades orales

A You may also wish to have one student act out the symptoms for the entire class as the other student describes them.

B For greater authenticity, have students write out a prescription on a piece of paper to use in the activity.

TECHNOLOGY OPTION In the CD-ROM version of **Actividad B,** Disc 3, page 252, students can interact with an on-screen, native speaker and record their voice.

C You may wish to have some groups present their skits to the entire class.

Student Portfolio

Have students keep a notebook containing their best written work from each chapter. These selected writings can be based on assignments from the Student Textbook and the Writing Activities Workbook. The activities on page 253 are examples of writing assignments that may be included in each student's portfolio.

In the Workbook, students will develop an organized autobiography **(Mi autobiografía).** These workbook pages may also become a part of their portfolio. See the Teacher's Manual for more information on this topic.

Culminación

Actividades orales

A **Todos están enfermos.** Work with a classmate. Choose one of the unfortunate people in the illustrations. Describe him or her. Your partner will guess which person you're describing and say what the matter is with that person. Take turns.

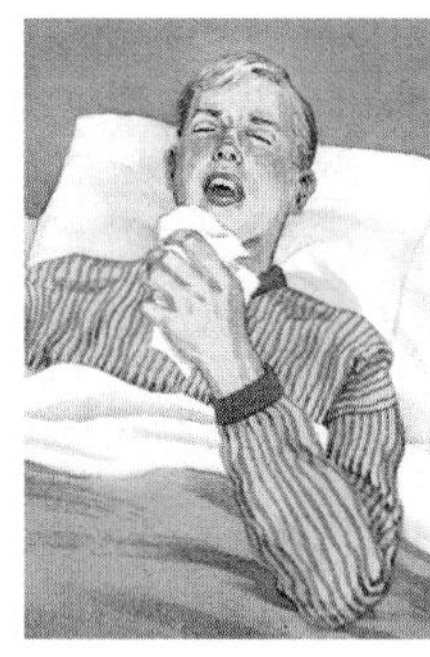
Paco

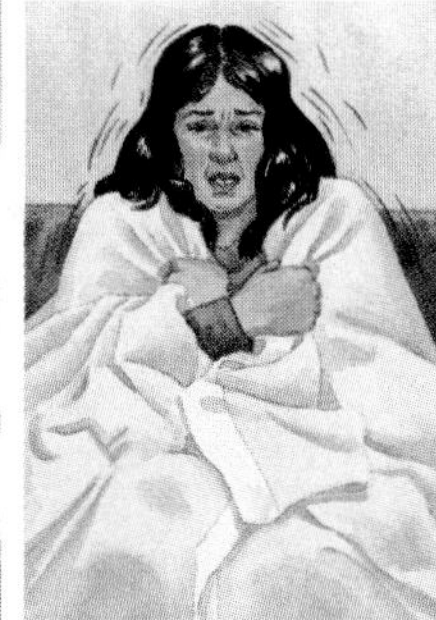
Gloria

Ana

David

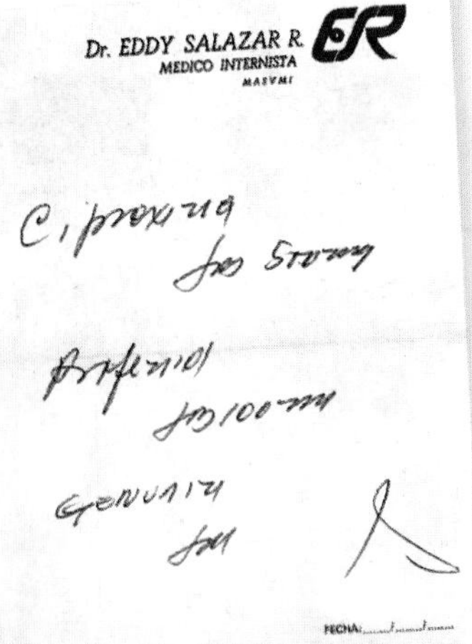

B **Aquí tengo una receta.** You are in a pharmacy in Panama. Your classmate will be the pharmacist. Make up a conversation about your prescription and why you need it. Take turns.

C **¡Qué enfermo(a) estoy!** With a partner, prepare a skit about a nervous person in a doctor's office. If you want, you can prepare the skit based on the story about **Una joven nerviosa.** Your skit can be about Patricia and her doctor.

JUEGO **Estoy muy mal hoy.** Work with a partner. Make gestures to indicate how you're feeling today. Your partner will ask you why you feel that way. Tell him or her. Be as creative and humorous as possible.

ANSWERS

Actividades orales

A Answers will vary. Be sure that students describe all four individuals.

B Answers will vary.

C Answers will vary.

Independent Practice

Assign any of the following:

1. Activities, pages 252–253
2. Workbook, **Mi autobiografía,** page 98
3. Situation Cards
4. CD-ROM, Disc 3, Chapter 8, **Juego de repaso**

Actividad escrita

A **¡Necesito un doctor!** Andrés is a Bolivian exchange student staying with you. He passes you the following note in class. You sense that he is a bit of a "worry wart." Send a note back to him. Let him know you can take him to your doctor after class. Reassure him that it's not so bad. Tell him something about a visit to your doctor.

¡Ay! ¡Qué enfermo estoy! Me duele todo —la cabeza, la garganta, el estómago. ¿Qué tengo? ¿Qué me pasa? Quiero hablar ahora con mis padres. Pero no puedo. Están en Bolivia. Tengo que ir al médico. ¡Ay, hombre!

Writing Strategy

Writing a personal essay

In writing a personal essay, a writer has several options: to tell a story, describe something, or encourage someone to think a certain way or to do something. Whatever its purpose, a personal essay allows a writer to express a viewpoint about a subject he or she has experienced. Your essay will be much livelier if you allow your enthusiasm to be obvious; do so by choosing interesting details and vivid words to relay your message.

El servicio en la comunidad

Your Spanish Club has a community service requirement. You have decided to work in the emergency room **(la sala de emergencia)** at your local hospital. You serve as a translator or intepreter for patients who speak only Spanish. Write a flyer for your Spanish Club. Tell about your experience with one or more patients. Give your feelings about the work you do and try to encourage other club members to volunteer their services, too.

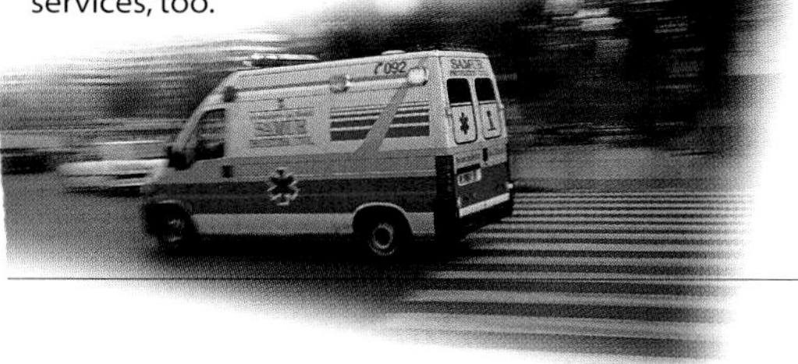

Actividad escrita

A TECHNOLOGY OPTION
Students can use the Portfolio feature on the CD-ROM to write this note.

Writing Strategy

Writing a personal essay

A. Have students read the Writing Strategy on page 253.

B. Have students refer to the **Vocabulario** on page 254 as they jot down ideas for their essay.

National Standards

Communities

The writing assignment on page 253 encourages students to use the language beyond the school setting.

ANSWERS

Actividad escrita

A Answers will vary. Students might use phrases such as: **Vamos al consultorio (médico) después de las clases. No es nada serio. Los médicos son muy buenos aquí.**

Writing Strategy

Answers will vary.

CAPÍTULO 8
Vocabulario

ASSESSMENT RESOURCES

- Chapter Quizzes
- Testing Program
- Computer Testmaker
- Situation Cards
- Communication Transparency C-8
- Performance Assessment
- **Maratón mental** Videoquiz

VOCABULARY REVIEW

The words and phrases in the **Vocabulario** have been taught for productive use in this chapter. They are summarized here as a resource for both students and teacher. This list also serves as a convenient resource for the **Culminación** activities on pages 252 and 253. Have the students look at the list. If there are any words they do not know, have them find them in the **Vocabulario** sections on pages 228–229 and 232–233. If absolutely necessary students can look up some words in the end vocabulary.

There are approximately fifteen cognates in this vocabulary list. Have students find them.

Vocabulario

DESCRIBING MINOR HEALTH PROBLEMS

la salud
la fiebre
los escalofríos
la gripe
el catarro
la tos
la energía
el dolor
enfermo(a)
cansado(a)
estornudar
estar resfriado(a)
toser

SPEAKING WITH THE DOCTOR

¿Qué te pasa?
la consulta, el consultorio
el/la médico(a)
el hospital
el síntoma
la diagnosis
la alergia
la inyección
Me duele...
Tengo dolor de...
creer
examinar
abrir la boca
guardar cama
recetar

DESCRIBING SOME EMOTIONS

contento(a)
triste
de buen humor, de mal humor
nervioso(a)
tranquilo(a)

IDENTIFYING MORE PARTS OF THE BODY

la garganta
los ojos
la boca
el estómago

SPEAKING WITH A PHARMACIST

la farmacia
el/la farmacéutico(a)
la receta
el medicamento, la medicina
la aspirina
el antibiótico
las pastillas, las píldoras, la tableta
la dosis
despachar, vender

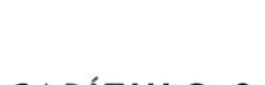

TECNOTUR

VIDEO

¡Buen viaje!

EPISODIO 8 ▸ La salud y el médico

Juan Ramón y Teresa hacen planes para ir a Segovia.

¿Es verdad que Pilar está enferma?

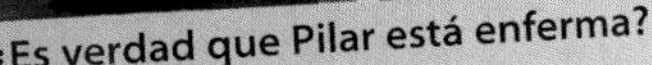

CD-ROM

Expansión cultural

La Puerta de Alcalá en la Plaza de la Independencia.

interNET CONNECTION

In this video episode Pilar seems to have the symptoms of a terrible illness until she hears what the pharmacist has to say! To find out whether or not you have a healthy lifestyle, go to the Capítulo 8 Internet activity at the Glencoe Foreign Language Web site:

http://www.glencoe.com/sec/fl

OVERVIEW

This page previews three key multimedia components of the **Glencoe Spanish** series. Each reinforces the material taught in Chapter 8 in a unique manner.

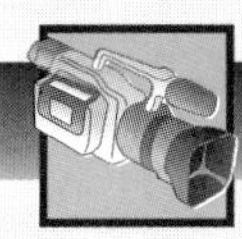

VIDEO

The Video Program allows students to see how the chapter vocabulary and structures are used by native speakers within an engaging story line. For maximum reinforcement, show the video episode as a final activity for Chapter 8.

A. Have students read the photo captions on page 255. From the information given, ask them why they think Pilar might be pretending to be sick.

B. Now show the Chapter 8 video episode. See the Video Activities Booklet for detailed suggestions for using this resource.

CD-ROM

A. The **Expansión cultural** photo shows an important landmark in Madrid. Have students read the caption on page 255.

B. In the CD-ROM version of **Expansión cultural** (Disc 3, page 255), students can listen to additional recorded information about the Puerta de Alcalá.

INTERNET

Teacher Information and Student Worksheets for this activity can be accessed at the Web site.

Video Synopsis

In this episode Juan Ramón and Teresa are discussing their upcoming trips to Segovia and Sevilla as they stroll through a downtown street in Madrid with Pilar. Pilar interrupts their conversation and makes it clear that she would like to go with them. When Teresa tells her she can't, Pilar suddenly begins to cough and tells her sister that she is feeling sick. Teresa and Juan Ramón rush her to a nearby pharmacy where it becomes obvious that Pilar is faking illness in order to get attention. At the prospect of taking large doses of medication, Pilar makes a miraculous recovery. She does, however, manage to exact a promise from her sister and Juan Ramón that they will be back in time for her birthday party on Sunday.

Chapter 9 Overview

SCOPE AND SEQUENCE pages 256–285

TOPICS	FUNCTIONS	STRUCTURE	CULTURE
◆ Summer and winter weather ◆ Summer and winter sports and leisure activities	◆ How to describe summer and winter weather ◆ How to talk about summer and winter sports such as swimming, tennis, and skiing ◆ How to relate actions and events that took place in the past ◆ How to refer to persons and things already mentioned	◆ **-ar** verbs in the preterite ◆ Direct object pronouns—**lo, la, los, las** ◆ **Ir** and **ser** in the preterite	◆ World-class beaches and resorts in the Spanish-speaking world ◆ Opposite seasons in the northern and southern hemispheres ◆ Snowboarding in Chile ◆ Weather and climate in the Spanish-speaking world

CHAPTER 9 RESOURCES

PRINT	MULTIMEDIA
Planning Resources	
Lesson Plans Block Scheduling Lesson Plans	Interactive Lesson Planner
Reinforcement Resources	
Writing Activities Workbook Student Tape Manual Video Activities Booklet Web Site User's Guide	Transparencies Binder Audiocassette/Compact Disc Program Videocassette/Videodisc Program Online Internet Activities Electronic Teacher's Classroom Resources
Assessment Resources	
Situation Cards Chapter Quizzes Testing Program Performance Assessment	**Maratón mental** Mindjogger Videoquiz Testmaker Computer Software (Macintosh/Windows) Listening Comprehension Audiocassette/Compact Disc Communication Transparency: C-9
Motivational Resources	
Expansion Activities	Café Glencoe: www.cafe.glencoe.com Keypal Internet Activities
Enrichment	
Spanish for Spanish Speakers	

Chapter 9 Planning Guide

SECTION	PAGES	SECTION RESOURCES
Vocabulario Palabras 1 El balneario La natación El tenis	258–261	Vocabulary Transparencies 9.1 Audiocassette 6A/ Compact Disc 5 Student Tape Manual, TE, pages 101–103 Workbook, pages 99–102 Chapter Quizzes, pages 43–44 CD-ROM, Disc 3, pages 258–261
Vocabulario Palabras 2 El invierno El tiempo en el invierno La estación de esquí	262–265	Vocabulary Transparencies 9.2 Audiocassette 6A/ Compact Disc 5 Student Tape Manual, TE, pages 103–105 Workbook, pages 103–104 Chapter Quizzes, pages 45–46 CD-ROM, Disc 3, pages 262–265
Estructura Pretérito de los verbos en -ar Pronombres—lo, la, los, las Ir y ser en el pretérito	266–273	Workbook, pages 105–110 Audiocassette 6A/Compact Disc 5 Student Tape Manual, TE, pages 105–107 Chapter Quizzes, pages 47–49 Computer Testmaker CD-ROM, Disc 3, pages 266–273
Conversación ¡A la playa! Pronunciación: La consonante g	274–275	Audiocassette 6A/Compact Disc 5 Student Tape Manual, TE, pages 107–108 CD-ROM, Disc 3, pages 274–275
Lecturas culturales Paraísos del mundo hispano Estaciones inversas *(opcional)* El «snowboarding» *(opcional)*	276–279	Testing Program, page 53 CD-ROM, Disc 3, pages 276–279
Conexiones El clima *(opcional)*	280–281	Testing Program, page 54 CD-ROM, Disc 3, pages 280–281
Culminación Actividades orales Actividades escritas Vocabulario Tecnotur	282–285	**¡Buen viaje!** Video, Episode 9 Video Activities, pages 97–100 Internet Activities www.glencoe.com/sec/fl Testing Program, pages 50–53; 111; 143; 167–168 CD-ROM, Disc 3, pages 282–285

CAPÍTULO 9

OVERVIEW

In this chapter students will learn to describe summer and winter weather and talk about summer and winter activities. To do this they will learn to use vocabulary associated with the beach, as well as with skiing. Students will also learn to narrate in the past. In order to do this they will learn the preterite of **-ar** verbs. Students will also learn about the many wonderful summer and winter resorts in the Spanish-speaking world.

National Standards

Communication

In Chapter 9, students will communicate in spoken and written Spanish on the following topics:

- summer weather and summer activities
- winter weather and winter activities

Students will also learn to narrate past events. They will obtain and provide information and engage in conversations about beach and ski resorts, water sports, tennis, and skiing as they fulfill the chapter objectives listed on this page.

CAPÍTULO 9
El verano y el invierno

Objetivos

In this chapter you will learn to do the following:

- describe summer and winter weather
- talk about summer activities and sports
- talk about winter sports
- discuss past actions and events
- refer to people and things already mentioned
- talk about resorts in the Hispanic world

The **Glencoe Foreign Language Web site (http://www.glencoe.com/sec/fl)** offers three options that enable you and your students to experience the Spanish-speaking world via the Internet:

- The online **Actividades** are correlated to the chapters and utilize Hispanic Web sites around the world. For the Chapter 9 activity, see student page 285.
- The **Correspondencia electrónica** section provides information on how to set up a keypal (pen pal) exchange between your class and a class in the Spanish-speaking world.
- At **Café Glencoe,** the interactive "after-school" section of the site, you and your students can access a variety of additional online resources, including interactive games.

CAPÍTULO 9

Spotlight On Culture

Artefacto The Peruvian poncho, made from beautiful, woven fabric, is worn in the Andean **altiplano**.

Fotografía The beach resort shown here is Benidorm, between Valencia and Alicante on the Costa Blanca. Benidorm has two white, crescent-shaped beaches. Like many of the other resorts on the Costa Blanca, it has become somewhat overdeveloped.

Learning From Photos

Benidorm, España Ask the following questions about the photo after presenting the vocabulary on pages 258–259:

¿Es grande o pequeña la playa?
¿Hay mucha gente en la playa?
¿Hay mucha gente en el mar?
¿Son grandes las olas?
¿Qué tiempo hace?

Pacing

Chapter 9 will require approximately eight to ten days. Pacing will vary according to the length of the class, the age of your students, and student aptitude.

Block Scheduling

See the Block Scheduling Lesson Plans Booklet for suggestions on how to present the chapter material within a block scheduling framework.

Chapter Projects

Mis vacaciones Have students share their family's vacation experiences by bringing in photos and vacation memorabilia. You may wish to group students according to their vacation destinations—mountains, beach, city, camping, etc.—and have each group tell as much as they can about their vacation there.

Un viaje ideal Have groups plan the ideal four-week vacation trip through a region of their choice in Spain or Latin America.

Un folleto Have students work in groups to prepare a brochure in Spanish about a winter resort, its features and weather. Have them include ads in the brochure for winter sports equipment and clothes.

Agencia de viaje Have students go to a travel agency to get some brochures on winter and summer resorts in the Spanish-speaking world. They can present their material to the class in Spanish or prepare a bulletin board display.

RESOURCES

- Vocabulary Transparencies 8.1 (A & B)
- Student Tape Manual, TE, pages 101–103
- Audiocassette 6A/CD5
- Workbook, pages 99–102
- Quiz 1, pages 43–44
- CD-ROM, Disc 3, pages 258–261

Bell Ringer Review

Use BRR Transparency 9-1, or write the following on the board:
Complete the following in the present.

1. **Yo mir__ un video en casa.**
2. **Mis amigos y yo (nosotros) escuch__ casetes.**
3. **Tú siempre habl__ por teléfono.**
4. **Mis amigos me visit__ en casa.**
5. **Tomás me invit__ a una fiesta.**

TEACHING VOCABULARY

A. It is recommended that you present the vocabulary initially with books closed as students focus their attention on Vocabulary Transparencies 9.1 (A & B). Point to each item and have the class repeat the word two or three times in unison. Ask questions such as **¿Es una plancha de vela? ¿Es una plancha de vela o una toalla playera? ¿Qué es?**

B. When presenting the sentences, break them into logical parts as in the following example: **Adriana y sus amigos fueron a la playa. Fueron a la playa el viernes.** Interspersе your presentation *(continued on page 259)*

Vocabulario

PALABRAS 1

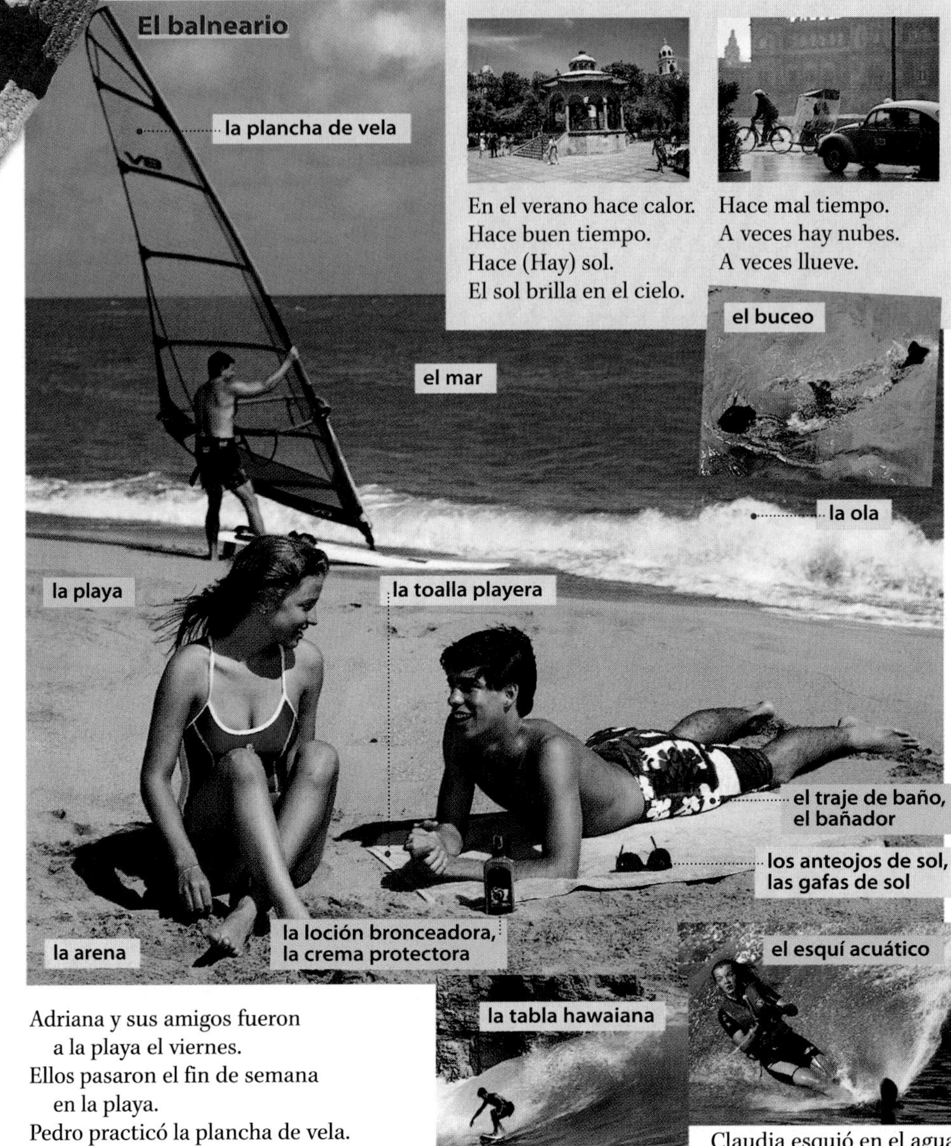

En el verano hace calor.
Hace buen tiempo.
Hace (Hay) sol.
El sol brilla en el cielo.

Hace mal tiempo.
A veces hay nubes.
A veces llueve.

Adriana y sus amigos fueron a la playa el viernes.
Ellos pasaron el fin de semana en la playa.
Pedro practicó la plancha de vela.
Diego buceó.
Carlos tomó el sol.

Alejandro practicó el surfing.

Claudia esquió en el agua.

Total Physical Response

TPR 1

Getting ready

You may want to bring in the following props to use in this activity: tube of sunscreen, tennis ball, tennis racquet. Demonstrate the following verbs using the appropriate gestures: **abre, ponte, tapa, rebota, golpea.**

Begin

___, ven acá. Aquí tienes un tubo de crema bronceadora.
___, abre el tubo.
Ponte la crema protectora en el brazo, en la pierna y en la cara.
Y ahora, tapa el tubo.
Pon el tubo en tu mochila.
Ahora, estás en la playa.
Pon la toalla playera en la arena.
Siéntate.
Toma el sol.
Ahora, levántate.
Ve al agua, al mar.
Nada.
Gracias, ___. Siéntate, por favor.

La natación

Sandra fue a la piscina.
Ella nadó en la piscina.

El tenis

Los amigos jugaron (al) tenis.
Jugaron tenis en una cancha al aire libre.
No jugaron en una cancha cubierta.
Jugaron singles, no dobles.
Un jugador golpeó la pelota.
La pelota pasó por encima de la red.

with questions building from simple to more complex. For example: **¿Fueron los amigos a la playa? ¿Quiénes fueron a la playa? ¿Fueron a la playa el lunes? ¿Cuándo fueron a la playa?**

C. Note that the preterite verbs are presented in the third person so students can use them immediately in answering questions without having to change the endings.

D. Dramatizations You can also use gestures or have students dramatize the following expressions: **usar la loción bronceadora, tomar el sol, esquiar en el agua, nadar, jugar (al) tenis.**

E. After the oral presentation of the vocabulary, have students open their books and read the material for additional reinforcement.

ABOUT THE SPANISH LANGUAGE

La piscina is the most commonly used word for swimming pool. **La alberca** is used in Mexico. You will also hear **la pila** which more frequently means *basin* or *trough.*

VOCABULARY EXPANSION

You may wish to teach some additional vocabulary related to the beach.

el malecón	*road that parallels the beach*
la silla playera	*beach chair*
la sombrilla	*umbrella*
correr las olas	*body surf*
alquilar (rentar) un barco	*to rent a boat*
pescar (ir a la pesca)	*to go fishing*

Total Physical Response

TPR 2

___, ven acá.
Toma la pelota.
Rebota la pelota.
Rebota la pelota una vez más.
Toma la raqueta.
Golpea la pelota con la raqueta.
Siéntate, por favor.
Gracias, ___.

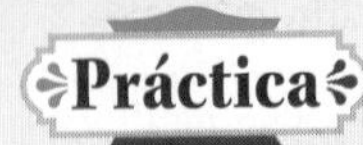

A **Práctica A** can be done first with books open for oral practice. You may then do it again with books closed for additional reinforcement.

B **Práctica B** should be done with books open.

C **EXPANSION** Ask students if they can think of additional items Claudia may have bought. **¿Qué más compró Claudia en la tienda?**

Geography Connection

San Juan, Puerto Rico San Juan, the capital of Puerto Rico, has some beautiful beaches. Many people erroneously think the beaches are on the Caribbean but they are not. San Juan is actually on the northeastern coast of Puerto Rico on the Atlantic Ocean. The Caribbean is on the southern coast of Puerto Rico, but there are actually more beaches on the northern or Atlantic coast.

Acapulco, México This beach resort is a sun worshipper's paradise on the Pacific coast 260 miles south of Mexico City. The natural setting is beautiful and the **Bahía de Acapulco** is one of the world's best natural harbors. There is almost constant sunshine and the temperature is in the 80's year-round.

Práctica

A HISTORIETA ¡A la playa!

Contesten con **sí**.

1. ¿Fue Isabel a la playa?
2. ¿Pasó el fin de semana allí?
3. ¿Nadó en el mar?
4. ¿Esquió en el agua?
5. ¿Buceó?
6. ¿Tomó el sol?
7. ¿Usó una crema protectora?

San Juan, Puerto Rico

Acapulco, México

B HISTORIETA El tiempo

Completen.

En el verano ___1___ calor. Hay ___2___. El sol brilla en el ___3___. Pero no hace buen tiempo siempre. A veces hay ___4___. Cuando hay ___5___, el cielo está nublado. No me gusta cuando ___6___ cuando estoy en la playa.

C ¿Qué compró Claudia? Contesten según los dibujos.

Claudia fue a la tienda. ¿Qué compró?

ANSWERS

Práctica

A 1. **Sí, Isabel fue a la playa.**
2. **Sí, pasó el fin de semana allí.**
3. **Sí, nadó en el mar.**
4. **Sí, esquió en el agua.**
5. **Sí, buceó.**
6. **Sí, tomó el sol.**
7. **Sí, usó una crema protectora.**

B 1. **hace**
2. **sol**
3. **cielo**
4. **nubes**
5. **nubes**
6. **llueve**

C 1. **anteojos de sol**
2. **un bañador (traje de baño)**
3. **una toalla playera**
4. **crema protectora (loción bronceadora)**

(PAGE 261)

D 1. **una playa**
2. **mar, mar**
3. **olas**
4. **nada, toma**
5. **La loción bronceadora (crema protectora)**

Cancún, México

D HISTORIETA El balneario

Completen.

1. Un balneario tiene ____.
2. El Mediterráneo es un ____ y el Caribe es un ____.
3. En un mar o en un océano hay ____.
4. En la playa la gente ____ y ____ el sol.
5. ____ da protección contra el sol.
6. Una persona lleva ____ y ____ cuando va a la playa.
7. Me gusta mucho ir a la playa en el ____ cuando hace ____ y hay mucho ____.
8. Si uno no vive cerca de la costa y no puede ir a la playa, puede nadar en ____.

E HISTORIETA Un juego de tenis

Contesten.

1. ¿Dónde jugaron los tenistas al tenis?
2. ¿Jugaron singles o dobles?
3. ¿Cuántas personas hay en la cancha cuando juegan dobles?
4. ¿Golpearon los tenistas la pelota?
5. ¿La pelota tiene que pasar por encima de la red?

Estepona, España

Actividades comunicativas

A **Vamos a la playa.** Work with a classmate. You are going to spend a day or two at the beach. Go to the store to buy some things you need for your beach trip. One of you will be the clerk and the other will be the shopper. Take turns.

B **¿Dónde vamos a jugar tenis?** Call some friends (your classmates) to try to arrange a game of doubles. Decide where you're going to play, when, and with whom.

CAPÍTULO 9
Vocabulario

D Do **Práctica D** first with books open.

E **Práctica E** can be done first with books open for oral practice. You can do it again with books closed for additional reinforcement.

Actividades comunicativas

¡OJO! **Práctica versus Actividades comunicativas** All activities which provide guided practice are labeled **Práctica.** The more open-ended communicative activities are labeled **Actividades comunicativas.**

A Each student should make a list of the items before beginning the paired activity. Ask several pairs to present their dialogues to the class.

TECHNOLOGY OPTION Students may use the Portfolio feature on the CD-ROM to record their conversation.

B Role-play this activity with one of your better students first.

Learning From Photos

Cancún, México This relatively new resort is one of the most popular tourist destinations in Mexico. Development started here in 1974. The resort was carved out of the jungle. The hotel area is on a 22-kilometer barrier reef off the Yucatán peninsula in the Caribbean. Cancún is also close to the fabulous Mayan ruins of Chichen Itzá, Tulum, and Cobá. The thatched roof cabanas you see in the photo are from pre-Hispanic days. They are called **palapas.** People sit under them for protection from the sun.

Estepona, España This lovely town is on the southern coast of Spain not too far from Málaga.

ANSWERS CONTINUED

Práctica

D 6. **un traje de baño (bañador), anteojos (gafas) de sol**
7. **verano, calor, sol**
8. **una piscina (alberca)**

E 1. **Los tenistas jugaron al tenis en una cancha al aire libre.**
2. **Jugaron dobles.**
3. **Hay cuatro personas en la cancha cuando juegan dobles.**
4. **Sí, los tenistas golpearon la pelota.**
5. **Sí, la pelota tiene que pasar por encima de la red.**

Actividades comunicativas

A Answers will vary; however, students will use the vocabulary presented on page 258.

B Answers will vary; however, students should use the vocabulary presented on page 259.

RESOURCES

- Vocabulary Transparencies 9.2 (A & B)
- Student Tape Manual, TE, pages 103–105
- Audiocassette 6A/CD5
- Workbook, pages 103–104
- Quiz 2, pages 45–46
- CD-ROM, Disc 3, pages 262–265

Bell Ringer Review

Use BRR Transparency 9-2, or write the following on the board: Write down at least three words related to each of the following sports.

el fútbol
el béisbol
el básquetbol
el tenis

TEACHING VOCABULARY

A. Have students close their books. Have them focus their attention on Vocabulary Transparencies 9.2 (A & B). Point to each item and have the class repeat the word two or three times in unison. Ask questions such as: **¿Es una esquiadora? ¿Lleva un anorak, guantes y botas? ¿Qué lleva?**

B. When presenting the sentences, break them into logical parts as in the following example: **En el invierno hace frío. Hace frío. Nieva, etc.** Intersperse with questions building from simple to more complex: **¿Hace frío en el invierno? ¿Cuando hace calor, en el invierno o en el verano? ¿Nieva o llueve en el invierno? ¿Cuándo nieva?**

(continued on page 263)

Vocabulario

El invierno

El tiempo en el invierno

En el invierno hace frío.
Nieva.
Hay mucha nieve.
La temperatura baja a cinco grados bajo cero.

Total Physical Response

TPR 1
Begin
___, levántate y ven acá, por favor.
Siéntate.
Vamos a hacer gestos.
Ponte las botas.
Ponte los esquís.
Y ahora levántate.
Ponte el anorak.
Ponte las gafas.
Toma el bastón.
Pon el bastón en la mano derecha.
Toma el otro bastón.
Pon este bastón en la mano izquierda.
Y ahora, esquía.
Gracias, ___. Ahora puedes regresar a tu asiento.
Siéntate, por favor.

CAPÍTULO 9
Vocabulario

La estación de esquí

Los esquiadores compraron los boletos en la ventanilla.

Ellos tomaron el telesilla para subir la montaña.

Bajaron la pista.
Esquiaron muy bien.
Bajaron la pista para expertos, no la pista para principiantes.

NOTA You may be familiar with the following expressions to talk about things that happen in the present. Look also at time expressions you use to talk about things that happened in the past.

EL PRESENTE	EL PASADO
hoy	ayer
esta noche	anoche
esta tarde	ayer por la tarde
esta mañana	ayer por la mañana
este año	el año pasado
esta semana	la semana pasada

C. After the oral presentation of the vocabulary, have students open their books and read the material for additional reinforcement.

ABOUT THE SPANISH LANGUAGE

- An airplane or train ticket is called **un billete** in Spain and **un boleto** throughout Latin America. **El ticket,** or any of its variations—**el tique, el tiqué, el tiquete—**is commonly used in Spain and throughout Latin America to refer to any small ticket that resembles a stub.
- **La boletería** is used throughout Latin America. It is not used in Spain.
- **El telesilla** is masculine because it is a compound noun.

VOCABULARY EXPANSION

You may wish to present some words related to ice skating.

el hielo	*ice*
el patinaje	*skating*
los patines	*skates*
patinar	*to skate*
la pista de patinaje, el patinadero	*skating rink*

Total Physical Response

TPR 2

Getting ready

Teach the expression **ponte en fila** by putting several students in a line. Also demonstrate **debajo del brazo** and **empieza a esquiar.**

Begin

___, levántate y ven acá, por favor.
Ponte en fila.
Espera el telesquí.
Siéntate en el telesquí.
Pon los bastones debajo del brazo izquierdo.
Adiós. Ahora estás en la parte superior de la montaña.
Bájate del telesquí.
Pon un bastón en la mano izquierda y otro en la mano derecha.
Empieza a esquiar.
Baja la pista.
Gracias, ___. Ahora puedes volver a tu asiento.

¡OJO! It is recommended that you go over the **Práctica** activities before assigning them for homework.

A Quickly review the weather expressions taught on pages 258 and 262 before doing **Práctica A**. Students should be able to give at least five or six weather expressions.

Writing Development

Students can write **Práctica A** and **B** in paragraph form.

Learning From Photos

Villarrica, Chile Villarrica is a town of 25,000 people in the famous Chilean lake region which borders Argentina. Villarrica is one of Chile's most famous resorts. In addition to skiing in the winter, people swim in the Andean waters of Lake Villarrica in the summer. Boating on the lake is also very popular. Not far from Lake Villarrica is **el volcán Villarrica.**

Práctica

Parque Nacional de Puyehue, Chile

A **¿Qué tiempo hace?**
Describan el tiempo en la foto.

Villarrica, Chile

B **HISTORIETA En una estación de esquí**
Contesten según se indica.

1. ¿Cuándo son populares las estaciones de esquí? (en el invierno)
2. ¿Qué tipo de pistas hay en una estación de esquí? (para expertos y para principiantes)
3. ¿Dónde compraron los esquiadores los tickets para el telesquí? (en la ventanilla)
4. ¿Qué tomaron los esquiadores para subir la montaña? (el telesilla)
5. ¿Qué bajaron los esquiadores? (la pista)

C **Me gusta esquiar.** Completen.

En el ___(1) hace frío. A veces nieva. Cuando hay mucha ___(2) me gusta ir a una ___(3) de esquí. Llevo mis ___(4), mis botas y los ___(5) y voy a las montañas. Tomo el ___(6) para subir la montaña. No soy un esquiador muy bueno. Siempre bajo una ___(7) para principiantes.

ANSWERS

Práctica

A Answers will vary, but may include the following: **Es el invierno. Hace frío. Hay mucha nieve. Hace sol. El sol brilla en el cielo.**

B
1. **Las estaciones de esquí son populares en el invierno.**
2. **En una estación de esquí hay pistas para expertos y pistas para principiantes.**
3. **Los esquiadores compraron los tickets para el telesquí en la ventanilla.**
4. **Los esquiadores tomaron el telesilla para subir la montaña.**
5. **Los esquiadores bajaron la pista.**

C
1. **invierno**
2. **nieve**
3. **estación**
4. **guantes**
5. **esquís**
6. **telesilla**
7. **pista**

Actividades comunicativas

A **¡A esquiar!** You're at a ski resort in Chile and have to rent **(alquilar)** some equipment for a day on the slopes. Tell the clerk (your partner) what you need. Find out whether he or she has what you need and how much it all costs.

B **En una estación de esquí** Have a conversation with a classmate. Tell as much as you can about what people do at a ski resort. Find out which one of you knows more about skiing. If skiing is a sport that is new to you, tell whether you think it would interest you.

C **¿A qué ciudad?** With a classmate, look at the following weather map that appeared in a Spanish newspaper. You are in Madrid and want to take a side trip. Since you both have definite preferences regarding weather, use the map to help you make a decision. After you choose a city to go to, tell what you are going to do there.

Actividades comunicativas

¡OJO! These activities encourage students to use the chapter vocabulary and structures in open-ended situations. It is not necessary to have them do all the activities. Allow students to select the activity or activities they wish to take part in.

A You may want to do **Actividad A** only with students who are interested in skiing. Determine how much each item will cost in dollars before students begin this activity.

B **EXPANSION** Have one partner try to convince the other that skiing is interesting. Have him or her give as many reasons as possible.

C Before doing **Actividad C,** review the meaning of the icons at the bottom of the weather map.

A and **C** You may wish to ask one of the groups doing **Actividad A** or **Actividad C** to volunteer and present the conversation to the entire class.

Learning From Realia

El Tiempo This weather map is from the newspaper **El ABC** in Madrid. You may wish to play the following True/False game.

1. **Hay sol en Málaga.**
2. **Llueve en Córdoba.**
3. **Llueve en Bilbao.**
4. **Está nublado (Hay nubes) al norte de Madrid.**
5. **Palma de Mallorca está en una isla.**
6. **Alicante está en una isla también.**
7. **Ceuta está en el norte de África.**

ANSWERS

Actividades comunicativas

A and **B** Answers will vary; however, students should use the vocabulary presented on pages 262–263.

C Answers will vary; however, the students' choice of city and plans should correspond to the weather conditions shown on the map.

RESOURCES

- Workbook, pages 105–110
- Student Tape Manual, TE, pages 105–107
- Audiocassette 6A/CD5
- Quizzes 3–5, pages 47–49
- Computer Testmaker
- CD-ROM, Disc 3, pages 266–273

Bell Ringer Review

Use BRR Transparency 9-3, or write the following on the board: Indicate if each of the following is associated with **el verano** or **el invierno.**

Bajan la pista.
Esquían.
Esquían en el agua.
Toman el telesilla.
Usan una toalla playera.
Bucean.

TEACHING STRUCTURE

Describing past actions

A. Have students open their books to page 266. Read Step 1 aloud. Then have the class repeat the two model sentences after you.

B. Write the verbs **hablar, tomar,** and **nadar** on the board. Have the class repeat each form after you. After you write the forms for one verb on the board, you may wish to have students provide the forms for the other verbs. For example, under **hablar**, write **hablé**. Underline the ending. Rather than give the endings for **tomar** and/or **nadar**, ask: If it's **hablé** for **hablar**, what's the form for **tomar? Nadar?** Have students repeat all forms.

(continued on page 267)

Estructura

Describing past actions
Pretérito de los verbos en -ar

1. You use the preterite to express actions that began and ended at a definite time in the past.

Ayer María pasó el día en la playa.
Yo, no. Pasé el día en la escuela.

2. The preterite of regular **-ar** verbs is formed by dropping the infinitive ending **-ar** and adding the appropriate endings to the stem. Study the following forms.

INFINITIVE	hablar	tomar	nadar	
STEM	habl-	tom-	nad-	ENDINGS
yo	hablé	tomé	nadé	-é
tú	hablaste	tomaste	nadaste	-aste
él, ella, Ud.	habló	tomó	nadó	-ó
nosotros(as)	hablamos	tomamos	nadamos	-amos
vosotros(as)	*hablasteis*	*tomasteis*	*nadasteis*	*-asteis*
ellos, ellas, Uds.	hablaron	tomaron	nadaron	-aron

3. Note that verbs that end in **-car, -gar,** and **-zar** have a spelling change in the **yo** form.

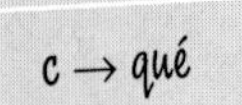

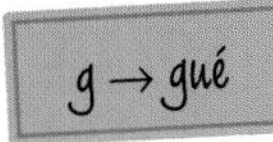

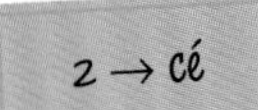

¿Marcaste un tanto?	**Sí, marqué un tanto.**
¿Llegaste a tiempo?	**Sí, llegué a tiempo.**
¿Jugaste (al) baloncesto?	**Sí, jugué (al) baloncesto.**
¿Empezaste a jugar?	**Sí, empecé a jugar.**

ANSWERS (PAGE 267)

Práctica

A
1. **Sí, ayer Rubén pasó la tarde en la playa.**
2. **Sí, (No, no) tomó mucho sol.**
3. **Sí, (No, no) usó crema protectora.**
4. **Sí, (No, no) nadó en el mar.**
5. **Sí, (No, no) buceó.**
6. **Sí, (No, no) esquió en el agua.**

B
1. **Los amigos compraron una raqueta.**
2. **Los jóvenes jugaron al tenis.**

Práctica

A HISTORIETA Una tarde en la playa

Contesten.

1. Ayer, ¿pasó Rubén la tarde en la playa?
2. ¿Tomó él mucho sol?
3. ¿Usó crema protectora?
4. ¿Nadó en el mar?
5. ¿Buceó?
6. ¿Esquió en el agua?

San Juan, Puerto Rico

B HISTORIETA Un partido de tenis

Contesten según se indica.

1. ¿Qué compraron los amigos? (una raqueta)
2. ¿A qué jugaron los jóvenes? (tenis)
3. ¿Jugaron en una cancha cubierta? (no, al aire libre)
4. ¿Golpearon la pelota? (sí)
5. ¿Jugaron singles o dobles? (dobles)
6. ¿Quiénes marcaron el primer tanto? (Alicia y José)
7. ¿Quienes ganaron el partido? (ellos)

MERIDIANO TELEVISIÓN

MAÑANA
06:00 Golf Boomme Valley Classic 2 Ronda
07:30 Formula 1 Gran Premio de Luxemburgo (En Vivo)
10:00 Máxima Velocidad
11:00 Mundo Marcial
11:30 Basket Nacional: Cocodrilos vs Tanqueros (En Vivo)

TARDE
01:30 Formula 1 Gran Premio de Luxemburgo
04:00 Fútbol Nacional: Caracas F.C. vs Minerven (En Vivo)
06:00 Supergolazo
06:30 Revista Semanal

NOCHE
07:00 Tenis Copa Davis USA vs Italia
09:00 Retrospectiva de Golf
09:30 Revista Semanal
10:00 Tercer Tiempo
10:30 Noticiero Meridiano
11:30 Wheelies

NOTA: Esta programación puede estar sujeta a cambios por motivos de fuerza mayor.

C HISTORIETA En casa

Contesten personalmente.

1. Anoche, ¿a qué hora llegaste a casa?
2. ¿Preparaste la comida?
3. ¿Estudiaste?
4. ¿Miraste la televisión?
5. ¿Escuchaste discos compactos?
6. ¿Hablaste por teléfono?
7. ¿Con quién hablaste?

D HISTORIETA Yo llegué al estadio.

Cambien **nosotros** en **yo**.

Ayer nosotros llegamos al estadio y empezamos a jugar fútbol. Jugamos muy bien. No tocamos el balón con las manos. Lo lanzamos con el pie o con la cabeza. Marcamos tres tantos.

C. For Step 3, have students look at the examples and point out the spelling changes.

TEACHING TIP

While going over Step 3 of the structure explanation, you may wish to review the following sound/spelling correspondences:
ca, que, qui, co cu
ga, gue, gui, go, gu
za, ce, ci, zo, zu
These explain the spelling of **jugó, jugué, buscó, busqué, empezó, empecé.**

Práctica

¡OJO! The **Práctica** activities on pages 267 and 268 build from easy to more complex. Some deal with one subject pronoun only. **Práctica G** on page 268 combines all subjects.

A, B, and C It is suggested you go over **Práctica A, B,** and **C** orally with books closed. You ask the questions and have students answer. Do these **Práctica** activities a second time with books open.

PAIRED ACTIVITIES **Práctica A, B,** and **C** can be done as paired activities. One student asks the question and calls on another to respond.

EXPANSION You can have students retell the story in each **Práctica** in their own words.

Writing Development

Students can also write **Práctica A, B,** and **C** in paragraph form.

ANSWERS CONTINUED

B
3. **No, jugaron al aire libre.**
4. **Sí, golpearon la pelota.**
5. **Jugaron dobles.**
6. **Alicia y José marcaron el primer tanto.**
7. **Ellos ganaron el partido.**

C
1. **Anoche llegué a casa a las ___.**
2. **Sí, (No, no) preparé la comida.**
3. **Sí, (No, no) estudié.**
4. **Sí, (No, no) miré la televisión.**
5. **Sí (No, no) escuché discos compactos.**
6. **Sí (No, no) hablé por teléfono.**
7. **Hablé con ___. (No hablé por teléfono.)**

D **Ayer yo llegué al estadio y empecé a jugar fútbol. Jugué muy bien. No toqué el balón con las manos. Lo lancé con el pie y con la cabeza. Marqué tres tantos.**

E Have pairs of students present **Práctica E** as a mini-conversation using as much expression as possible.

G Have students retell the story in **Práctica G** in their own words.

E El baloncesto Formen preguntas según el modelo.

Sigan el modelo.

¿Jugó Pablo?
A ver. Pablo, ¿jugaste?

1. ¿Jugó Pablo al baloncesto?
2. ¿Dribló con el balón?
3. ¿Pasó el balón a un amigo?
4. ¿Tiró el balón?
5. ¿Encestó?
6. ¿Marcó un tanto?

Málaga, España

F HISTORIETA Una fiesta

Sigan el modelo.

hablar
Mis amigos y yo hablamos durante la fiesta.

1. bailar
2. cantar
3. tomar un refresco
4. tomar fotos
5. escuchar música

Valdesquí, España

G HISTORIETA En una estación de esquí

Completen.

El fin de semana pasado José, algunos amigos y yo ___1___ (esquiar). ___2___ (Llegar) a la estación de esquí el viernes por la noche. Luego nosotros ___3___ (pasar) dos días en las pistas.

José ___4___ (comprar) un pase para el telesquí. Todos nosotros ___5___ (tomar) el telesquí para subir la montaña. Pero todos nosotros ___6___ (bajar) una pista diferente. José ___7___ (bajar) la pista para expertos porque él esquía muy bien. Pero yo, no. Yo ___8___ (tomar) la pista para principiantes. Y yo ___9___ (bajar) con mucho cuidado.

ANSWERS

Práctica

E 1. A ver. Pablo, ¿jugaste al baloncesto?
2. A ver. Pablo, ¿driblaste con el balón?
3. A ver. Pablo, ¿pasaste el balón a un amigo?
4. A ver. Pablo, ¿tiraste el balón?
5. A ver. Pablo, ¿encestaste?
6. A ver. Pablo, ¿marcaste un tanto?

F 1. Mis amigos y yo bailamos durante la fiesta.
2. Mis amigos y yo cantamos durante la fiesta.
3. Mis amigos y yo tomamos un refresco durante la fiesta.
4. Mis amigos y yo tomamos fotos durante la fiesta.
5. Mis amigos y yo escuchamos música durante la fiesta.

G 1. esquiamos 4. compró 7. bajó
2. Llegamos 5. tomamos 8. tomé
3. pasamos 6. bajamos 9. bajé

Actividades comunicativas

A **Pasaron el fin de semana en la playa.** Look at the illustration. Work with a classmate, asking and answering questions about what these Spanish friends did at the beach in Torremolinos.

B **Pasé un día en una estación de esquí.** You went on a skiing trip in the Sierra Nevada, Granada, Spain. You had a great time. Call your friend (a classmate) to tell him or her about your trip. Your friend has never been skiing so he or she will have a few questions for you.

Actividades comunicativas

¡OJO! These activities encourage students to use the chapter vocabulary and structures in open-ended situations. It is not necessary to have them do all the activities. Choose the ones you consider most appropriate. We have provided visuals with these activities to aid students to speak in the past using the preterite of **-ar** verbs only. It is important that we not give students activities that would force them to use unknown preterite forms, or the imperfect.

A Before students do this activity, you may want them to quickly review the vocabulary presented on pages 258 and 259. Now have students look at the illustrations and ask one another questions about them.

B In addition to using the illustrations, students can quickly review **Práctica G** on page 268 for some ideas regarding what to say.

Did You Know?

Estaciones de esquí Many people are surprised to learn that there are so many ski resorts in so many areas of Spain. There are major ski resorts in the Pyrenees, in the Sierra Nevada near Granada, and just north of Madrid in the Sierra de Guadarrama and Sierra de Gredos.

ANSWERS

Actividades comunicativas

A Answers will vary; however, students should use the vocabulary presented on pages 258–259. Answers should be expressed in the preterite.

B Answers will vary. Answers should be expressed using the preterite.

CAPÍTULO 9
Estructura

Bell Ringer Review

Use BRR Transparency 9-4, or write the following on the board:
Answer the following questions.

1. **¿Compraste un traje de baño nuevo?**
2. **¿Llevaste el traje de baño a la playa?**
3. **¿Nadaste?**
4. **¿Esquiaste en el agua también?**

TEACHING STRUCTURE

Referring to items already mentioned

A. Write several of the model sentences from Step 1 on the board. Draw a box around the direct object (noun). Now circle the direct object pronoun. Then draw a line from the box to the circle. This visual technique helps many students grasp the concept that one word replaces the other.

B. Have students open their books to page 270. Instead of providing, or having students read the information in Step 2, you may wish to have students come up with the answers: Does **lo** replace a masculine or feminine noun? What pronoun replaces a feminine noun?

Práctica

A Have students do **Práctica A** as a paired activity as shown in the model.

EXPANSION Have students hold up additional items they know. For example, **¿El lápiz? ¿El cuaderno? ¿El libro?**

Referring to items already mentioned
Pronombres—**lo, la, los, las**

1. The following sentences each have a direct object. The direct object is the word in the sentence that receives the action of the verb. The direct object can be either a noun or a pronoun.

Ella compró el bañador.	**Ella lo compró.**
Compró los anteojos de sol.	**Los compró en la misma tienda.**
¿Compró loción bronceadora?	**Sí, la compró.**
¿Compró las toallas en la misma tienda?	**No, no las compró en la misma tienda.**
¿Invitaste a Juan a la fiesta?	**Sí, lo invité.**
¿Invitaste a Elena?	**Sí, la invité.**

2. Note that **lo, los, la,** and **las** are direct object pronouns. They must agree with the noun they replace. They can replace either a person or a thing. The direct object pronoun comes right before the verb.

Ella compró el regalo.	**Ella lo compró.**
Invitó a Juan.	**Lo invitó.**
No miré la fotografía.	**No la miré.**
No miré a Julia.	**No la miré.**

A **¿Dónde está?** Sigan el modelo.

1. ¿El traje de baño?
2. ¿El tubo de crema?
3. ¿La pelota?
4. ¿La crema protectora?
5. ¿Los anteojos de sol?
6. ¿Los boletos?
7. ¿Los esquís acuáticos?
8. ¿Las toallas playeras?
9. ¿Las raquetas?
10. ¿Las tablas hawaianas?

ANSWERS

(PAGE 271)

Práctica

A 1. **Aquí lo tienes.**
2. **Aquí lo tienes.**
3. **Aquí la tienes.**
4. **Aquí la tienes.**
5. **Aquí los tienes.**
6. **Aquí los tienes.**
7. **Aquí los tienes.**
8. **Aquí las tienes.**
9. **Aquí las tienes.**
10. **Aquí las tienes.**

B All answers begin with: **¿Cuándo compraste...**
1. **—... la toalla playera?**
—La compré ayer.
—¿Dónde la compraste?
—La compré...
—¿Cuánto te costó?
—Me costó...
2. **—... los anteojos de sol?**
—Los compré ayer.
—¿Dónde los compraste?
—Los compré...

B De compras Sigan el modelo.

—¿Cuándo compraste los bastones?
—Los compré ayer.
—¿Dónde los compraste?
—Los compré en la tienda Padín.
—¿Cuánto te costaron?
—Me costaron ciento cinco pesos.

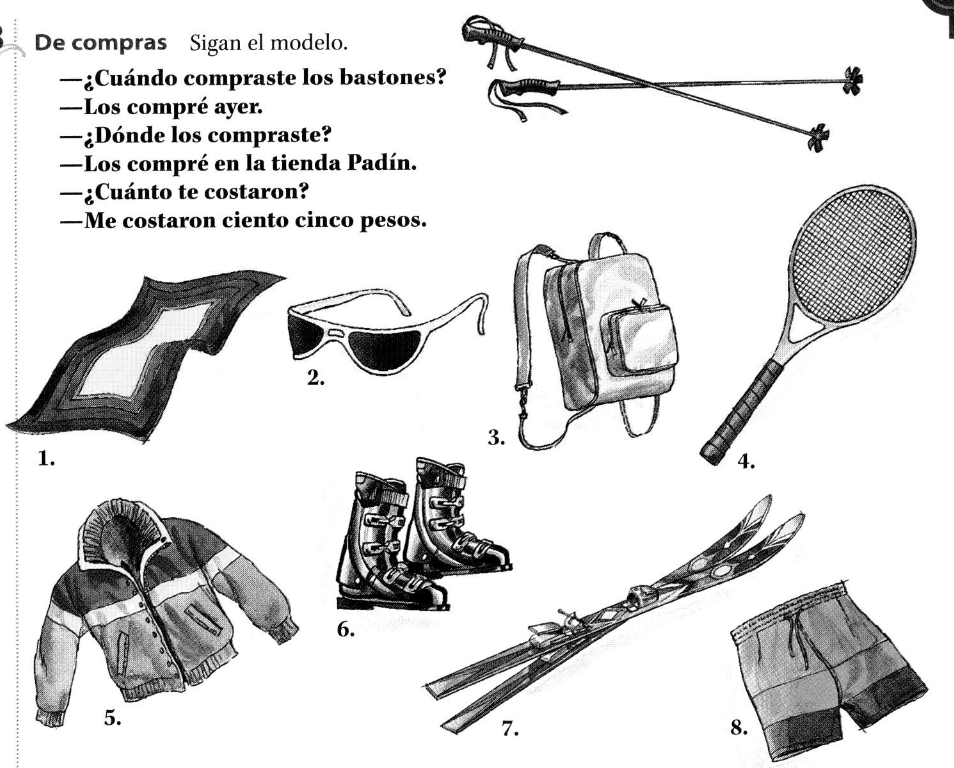

C Historieta Un regalo que le gustó

Completen.

Yo compré un regalo para Teresa. ___(1) compré en la tienda de departamentos Cortefiel. Compré unos anteojos de sol. A Teresa le gustaron mucho. Ella ___(2) llevó el otro día cuando fue a la piscina. Ella tiene algunas fotografías con sus anteojos de sol. Su amigo Miguel ___(3) tomó.

Madrid, España

Práctica

B Have students present each part of **Práctica B** as a mini-conversation between two people. Have students make up a price for each item in **Práctica B.**

C Have students retell the story in **Práctica C** in their own words.

Learning From Photos

Madrid, España Have students take turns describing the photo on page 271. This will review vocabulary taught in Chapter 3.

ANSWERS CONTINUED

—¿Cuánto te costaron?
—Me costaron...
3. —... la mochila?
—La compré ayer.
—¿Dónde la compraste?
—La compré...
—¿Cuánto te costó?
—Me costó...
4. —... la raqueta?
—La compré ayer.
—¿Dónde la compraste?
—La compré...
—¿Cuánto te costó?
—Me costó...
5. —... el anorak?
—Lo compré ayer.
—¿Dónde lo compraste?
—Lo compré...
—¿Cuánto te costó?
—Me costó...
6. —... las botas?
—Las compré ayer.
—¿Dónde las compraste?
—Las compré...
—¿Cuánto te costaron?
—Me costaron...
7. —... los esquís?
—Los compré ayer.
—¿Dónde los compraste?
—Los compré...
—¿Cuánto te costaron?
—Me costaron...
8. —... el traje de baño (bañador)?
—Lo compré ayer.
—¿Dónde lo compraste?
—Lo compré...
—¿Cuánto te costó?
—Me costó...

C 1. Lo
2. los
3. las

Estructura

D Students will answer with the appropriate direct object pronoun.

TEACHING STRUCTURE

Describing past actions

A. Ask students to open their books to page 272. As you go over the explanation, tell students that the meaning of the sentences makes it clear whether it is the verb **ser** or **ir**.

B. Have students repeat the verb forms on page 272 in unison.

C. In Step 2, call on a student to read the model sentences, or have the entire class repeat them.

D HISTORIETA Una fiesta

Contesten.

1. ¿Invitaste a Juan a la fiesta?
2. ¿Invitaste a Alejandra?
3. ¿Compraste los refrescos?
4. ¿Preparaste la ensalada?
5. ¿Tomó Pepe las fotografías de la fiesta?

Describing past actions
Ir y ser en el pretérito

1. The verbs **ir** and **ser** are irregular in the preterite tense. Note that they have identical forms.

INFINITIVE	ir	ser
yo	fui	fui
tú	fuiste	fuiste
él, ella, Ud.	fue	fue
nosotros(as)	fuimos	fuimos
vosotros(as)	*fuisteis*	*fuisteis*
ellos, ellas, Uds.	fueron	fueron

2. The context in which each verb is used in the sentence will clarify the meaning. The verb **ser** is not used very often in the preterite.

El Sr. Martínez fue profesor de español.
Él fue a España.
Mi abuela fue médica.
Mi abuela fue al consultorio de la médica.

ANSWERS

Práctica

D 1. Sí, (No, no) lo invité a la fiesta.
2. Sí, (No, no) la invité.
3. Sí, (No, no) los compré.
4. Sí, (No, no) la preparé.
5. Sí (No), Pepe (no) las tomó.

Práctica

A **¿Y tú?** Contesten personalmente.

1. Ayer, ¿fuiste a la escuela?
2. ¿Fuiste a la playa?
3. ¿Fuiste a la piscina?
4. ¿Fuiste al campo de fútbol?
5. ¿Fuiste a la cancha de tenis?
6. ¿Fuiste a las montañas?
7. ¿Fuiste a casa?
8. ¿Fuiste a la tienda?

B **¿Quién fue y cómo?** Contesten personalmente.

1. ¿Fuiste a la escuela ayer?
2. ¿Fue tu amigo también?
3. ¿Fueron juntos?
4. ¿Fueron en carro?
5. ¿Fue también la hermana de tu amigo?
6. ¿Fue ella en carro o a pie?

Actividad comunicativa

A **Anteayer** Work with a classmate. Ask whether he or she went to one of the places below the day before yesterday **(anteayer)**. Your partner will respond. Take turns asking and answering the questions.

Práctica

A and **B** Students very often confuse **fui** and **fue**. For this reason, **Práctica A** gives practice using **fui**. After you finish **Práctica A**, call on several students to retell the story in their own words. This will assist in evaluating whether they understand the difference between **fui** and **fue. Práctica B** starts with **fui** and then uses **fue** and **fueron**.

Actividad comunicativa

A Make sure students can identify each place illustrated: **la playa, la cancha de tenis, el consultorio del médico, la tienda de ropa, el restaurante**.

EXPANSION After students finish **Actividad A,** have them look at each illustration and say as much as they can about it.

¡OJO! All new material in the chapter has been presented. The sections that follow recombine and reintroduce the vocabulary and structures that have already been introduced.

ANSWERS

Práctica

A
1. **Sí (No), ayer (no) fui a la escuela.**
2. **Sí, (No, no) fui a la playa.**
3. **Sí, (No, no) fui a la piscina.**
4. **Sí, (No, no) fui al campo de fútbol.**
5. **Sí, (No, no) fui a la cancha de tenis.**
6. **Sí, (No, no) fui a las montañas.**
7. **Sí, (No, no) fui a casa.**
8. **Sí, (No, no) fui a la tienda.**

B
1. **Sí, (No, no) fui a la escuela ayer.**
2. **Sí (No), mi amigo (no) fue.**
3. **Sí, (No, no) fuimos juntos.**
4. **Sí, (No, no) fuimos en carro.**
5. **Sí (No), la hermana de mi amigo (no) fue.**
6. **Ella fue en carro (a pie).**

Actividad comunicativa

A Answers should follow this model:

1. **—___, ¿fuiste a la playa anteayer?**
   —Sí, (No, no) fui a la playa anteayer.

RESOURCES

- Audiocassette 6A/CD5
- CD-ROM, Disc 3, page 274

Bell Ringer Review

Use BRR Transparency 9-5, or write the following on the board:
Answer.

1. **¿Fuiste a la papelería? ¿Qué compraste allí?**
2. **¿Fuiste a la tienda de ropa? ¿Qué compraste?**
3. **¿Fuiste al mercado?¿Qué compraste?**

TEACHING THE CONVERSATION

A. Tell students they are going to hear a conversation between two young women, Gloria and Paula.
B. Have students close their books. Read the conversation to them or play Cassette 6A/CD5.
C. Have the class repeat the conversation once or twice in unison.
D. Call on pairs to read the conversation. Encourage them to be as animated as possible.
E. Change the names of the characters to boy's names. Have pairs act out the conversation for the class allowing them to make any changes that make sense.
F. After presenting the conversation, go over the **Después de conversar** activity. If students can answer the questions with relative ease, move on. Students should not be expected to memorize the conversation.

TECHNOLOGY OPTION

On the CD-ROM (Disc 3, page 274) students can watch a dramatization of this conversation. They can then play the role of either one of the characters, and record themselves in the conversation.

Conversación

¡A la playa!

GLORIA: ¿Adónde fuiste ayer?
PAULA: Pues, fui a la playa. Y no puedes imaginar lo que me pasó.
GLORIA: ¿Qué te pasó?
PAULA: Llegué a la playa sin mi traje de baño.
GLORIA: ¿Sin tu traje de baño?
PAULA: Sí, ¡sin mi traje de baño! Lo dejé en casa.
GLORIA: ¡Fuiste a la playa y dejaste tu traje de baño en casa! ¡Muy inteligente, Paula!
PAULA: Ah, pero lo pasé muy bien. Fui a nadar.
GLORIA: ¿Nadaste? ¿Sin traje de baño?
PAULA: Querer es poder. Fui al agua en mi blue jean.

Después de conversar

Contesten.

1. ¿Adónde fue Paula ayer?
2. ¿Llegó a la playa con su traje de baño?
3. ¿Dónde dejó su traje de baño?
4. Pero, ¿lo pasó bien en la playa?
5. ¿Nadó?
6. ¿Qué llevó cuando fue al agua?

ANSWERS

Después de conversar

1. **Paula fue a la playa ayer.**
2. **No, no llegó a la playa con su traje de baño.**
3. **Dejó su traje de baño en casa.**
4. **Sí, lo pasó bien en la playa.**
5. **Sí, nadó.**
6. **Llevó su blue jean cuando fue al agua.**

Actividades comunicativas

A **¿Qué tiempo hace?** Work with a classmate. One of you lives in tropical San Juan, Puerto Rico. The other lives in Buffalo, New York. Describe the winter weather where you live.

B **Fuimos de vacaciones.** Work with a classmate. Take turns telling one another what you did last summer. You may wish to use the following words.

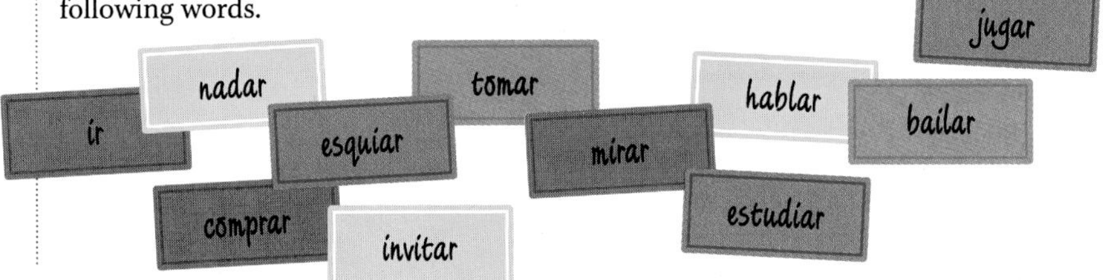

Pronunciación

La consonante g

The consonant **g** has two sounds, hard and soft. You will study the soft sound in Chapter 10. **G** in combination with **a, o, u, (ga, go, gu)** is pronounced somewhat like the *g* in the English word *go.* To maintain this hard **g** sound with **e** or **i,** a **u** is placed after the **g: gue, gui.** Repeat the following.

ga	gue	gui	go	gu
gafa	**Rodríguez**	**guitarra**	**goma**	**agua**
amiga	**guerrilla**	**guía**	**estómago**	**guante**
garganta			**tengo**	
paga			**juego**	
gato				

Repeat the following sentences.

El gato no juega en el agua.
Juego béisbol con el guante de mi amigo Rodríguez.
No tengo la guitarra de Gómez.

Actividades comunicativas

¡OJO! Although we want students to speak freely in these cooperative and communicative activities, they must take into account what students can realistically say based on their knowledge of the language. Since they now know the preterite of **-ar** verbs, students can discuss past events that call for **-ar** verbs. We have been careful not to give activities that would be impossible for students to do, such as discussing a past event that would necessitate the use of **comer**, irregular verbs, or the imperfect. These **Actividades comunicativas** incorporate all previously learned material, but do not frustrate students by leading them into errors that are beyond their control.

B **TECHNOLOGY OPTION**
Students may use the Portfolio feature on the CD-ROM to record their conversations in **Actividad B.**

TEACHING PRONUNCIATION

A. Have students carefully repeat **ga, gue, gui, go, gu** after you or the recording on Cassette 6A/CD 5.
Note English speakers tend to make the **g** sound too hard when speaking Spanish. As students repeat **ga, gue, gui, go, gu**, indicate to them that the sound is produced very softly toward the back of the throat.

B. Now have students repeat the words after you.

C. Use Pronunciation Transparency P-9 to model the first sentence: **El gato no juega en el agua.**

D. Have students open their books to page 275. Call on individuals to read the sentences carefully.

E. All model sentences on page 275 can be used for dictation.

Additional Practice

A escuchar Give students the following directions in order to practice auditory discrimination: *Listen to the following. If I am talking about the present, raise one hand. If I am talking about the past, raise both hands:*

Hablo.	**Miró.**
Nadó.	**Compro.**
Esquío.	**Pagó.**
Miro.	

ANSWERS

Actividades comunicativas

A Answers will vary. Students should use the appropriate weather expressions taught on pages 258 and 262.

B Answers will vary; however, all answers should be expressed in the preterite. Encourage students to use as many words as possible from the colored boxes.

CAPÍTULO 9
Lecturas

National Standards

Cultures

The reading about beach resorts in the Spanish-speaking world on page 276, and the related activities on page 277, allow students to find out more about famous tourist destinations in the Hispanic world.

TEACHING THE READING

Pre-reading

Have students scan the **Lectura** for cognates.

Reading

A. Have the class read the selection once silently.

B. Now call on individuals to read about four sentences each.

C. Ask comprehension questions based on each series of four sentences. For example, **¿En qué países hay playas fantásticas?**

D. Do the Reading Strategy on page 276.

Post-reading

A. If possible, bring in photos, slides, or videos of some popular beach resorts in Spain or Latin America. You may obtain videos from local travel agencies or the library. Additional information is available on the Internet.

B. Have students read the **Lectura** at home and write the answers to the **Después de leer** activities.

TECHNOLOGY OPTION

Students may listen to a recorded version of the **Lectura** on CD-ROM, Disc 3, pages 276–277.

Lecturas CULTURALES

Reading Strategy

Summarizing

When reading an informative passage, we try to remember what we read. Summarizing helps us to do this. The easiest way to summarize is to begin to read for the general sense and take notes on what you are reading. It is best to write a summarizing statement for each paragraph and then one for the entire passage.

PARAÍSOS DEL MUNDO HISPANO

¿Viajar[1] por el mundo hispano y no pasar unos días en un balneario? ¡Qué lástima[2]! En los países de habla española hay playas fantásticas. España, Puerto Rico, Cuba, México, Uruguay—todos son países famosos por sus playas.

En el verano cuando hace calor y un sol bonito brilla en el cielo, ¡qué estupendo es pasar un día en la playa! Y en lugares (sitios) como México, Puerto Rico y Venezuela, el verano es eterno. Podemos ir a la playa durante todos los meses del año.

Muchas personas toman sus vacaciones en una playa donde pueden disfrutar de[3] su tiempo libre. En la playa nadan o toman el sol. Vuelven a casa muy tostaditos o bronceados. Pero, ¡cuidado! Es necesario usar una crema protectora porque el sol es muy fuerte[4] en las playas tropicales.

[1]Viajar *To travel* [2]lástima *pity* [3]disfrutar de *enjoy* [4]fuerte *strong*

Nerja, España

Acapulco, México

GEOGRAPHY CONNECTION

Nerja, España This is a lovely resort on the Mediterranean Costa del Sol east of Málaga. In the summer months it is very popular with northern Europeans. Although Nerja is developing, much of its growth has been in the hills to the north of the sea. There are many new **urbanizaciones** *(planned communities),* which are quite popular with retirees.

San Juan, Puerto Rico
La playa de Varadero, Cuba
Punta del Este, Uruguay

Después de leer

A La palabra, por favor. Den la palabra apropiada.

1. un lugar que tiene playas donde la gente puede nadar
2. una cosa triste y desagradable
3. maravillosas, estupendas
4. célebres
5. lindo, hermoso
6. de y para siempre
7. regresan a casa

B En la playa Contesten.

1. ¿Qué hay en los países de habla española?
2. ¿Cuándo es estupendo pasar un día en la playa?
3. ¿Cómo disfruta de su tiempo la gente que va a la playa?
4. ¿Cómo es el sol en las playas tropicales?

Learning From Photos

La playa de Varadero, Cuba This area was the playground of the wealthy prior to the takeover by Castro. It is a beautiful beach and is frequented today by many Canadians and Europeans.
San Juan, Puerto Rico (See Geography Connection, page 260.)
Punta del Este, Uruguay This beautiful resort is on a peninsula that juts out into the sea where the Río de la Plata officially ends and the Atlantic begins. Punta del Este is surrounded by superb forests. In these forests there are beautiful mansions built by millionaires from Brazil and Argentina. On the western side of the peninsula is Playa Mansa where water is safe and calm. On the eastern side is the Playa Brava with its rough surf, dangerous for swimming but great for surfing.

Después de leer

A and **B** Allow students to refer to the reading for the answers, or you may use these activities as a testing device for factual recall.

ANSWERS

Después de leer

A 1. **un balneario**
2. **una lástima**
3. **fantásticas**
4. **famosos**
5. **bonito**
6 **eterno**
7. **vuelven a casa**

B 1. **Hay playas fantásticas en los países de habla española.**
2. **En el verano cuando hace calor y un sol bonito brilla en el cielo, es estupendo pasar un día en la playa.**
3. **Nadan o toman el sol.**
4. **El sol es muy fuerte en las playas tropicales.**

Independent Practice

Assign any of the following:
1. **Después de leer** activities, page 277
2. Workbook, **Un poco más,** pages 111–115
3. CD-ROM, Disc 3, pages 276–277

LECTURA OPCIONAL 1

National Standards

Cultures

The reading about winter resorts, and the related activities on this page, make students aware of the fact that the seasons are reversed in the northern and southern hemispheres.

Comparisons

This reading allows students to compare their activities with activities that their counterparts might engage in in South America.

TEACHING TIPS

¡OJO! This reading is optional. You may skip it completely, have the entire class read it, have only several students read it, or assign it for extra credit.

GEOGRAPHY CONNECTION

La Costa del Sol, España The Costa del Sol runs along the Mediterranean from the Cabo de Gata beyond Almería all the way to the tip of Tarifa beyond Gibraltar. The most popular resort area is located between Málaga and Estepona. Although many parts of this region are very beautiful, there is great concern that it has been overdeveloped.

Have students locate Málaga and the Costa del Sol on the map of Spain on page 463 or use the Map Transparency.

LECTURA OPCIONAL 1

ESTACIONES INVERSAS

Es el mes de julio. En España es el verano y la gente va a la playa a nadar. Y en la Argentina y Chile la gente va a las montañas a esquiar. ¿Cómo es que esquían en julio? Pues, el mes de julio es invierno. En el hemisferio sur las estaciones son inversas de las estaciones del hemisferio norte.

Los Andes, Chile

Después de leer

A ¿A esquiar o a nadar?

Contesten.

1. ¿Qué mes es?
2. ¿Qué estación es en España?
3. ¿Adónde va la gente?
4. ¿Qué estación es en la Argentina y Chile?
5. ¿Adónde va la gente?
6. En julio, ¿dónde nada la gente?
7. En julio, ¿dónde esquía la gente?

B ¿Qué estación es?

Explica por qué es invierno en julio en Chile y la Argentina.

La Costa del Sol, España

ANSWERS

Después de leer

A
1. **Es el mes de julio.**
2. **Es el verano.**
3. **La gente va a la playa.**
4. **Es el invierno.**
5. **La gente va a las montañas a esquiar.**
6. **La gente nada en el hemisferio norte.**
7. **La gente esquía en el hemisferio sur.**

B Es invierno en julio en Chile y la Argentina porque en el hemisferio sur las estaciones son inversas de las estaciones del hemisferio norte.

LECTURA OPCIONAL 2

EL «SNOWBOARDING»

¿Qué es el «snowboarding» o «el surf de nieve»? Es un deporte relativamente joven y nuevo. Es como el surfing—pero no sobre el agua. Practican el «snowboarding» sobre la nieve. Hay dos tipos o modalidades de surf de nieve—las carreras[1] y las exhibiciones.

Para practicar el «snowboarding», necesitas una tabla, un casco[2], guantes y rodilleras[3].

Sobre el skiboard—que es un tipo de tabla—el aficionado[4] hace unas piruetas y movimientos difíciles. El «snowboarding» es un deporte nuevo, pero ya hay competencias de «snowboarding» en los Juegos Olímpicos.

[1]carreras *races*
[2]casco *helmet*
[3]rodilleras *kneepads*
[4]aficionado *fan*

«Snowboarding» en Chile

Después de leer

A **¿Sí o no?** Digan que sí o que no.

1. El «snowboarding» es un deporte antiguo.
2. El «snowboarding» es como el surfing sobre el agua, pero los aficionados lo practican en la nieve.
3. Hay solamente un tipo de surf de nieve.
4. El skiboard es un tipo de tabla, similar a una tabla hawaiana.
5. El aficionado de «snowboarding» hace unas piruetas en el aire.

LECTURA OPCIONAL 2

TEACHING TIPS

¡OJO! This reading is optional. You may skip it completely, have the entire class read it, have only several students read it, or assign it for extra credit.

A. Find out if any of your students prefer snowboarding to skiing: **¿Prefieres el snowboarding o el esquí?** If any student indicates a preference for snowboarding, you may wish to ask this student to describe his or her experience, using the vocabulary learned in this chapter.

B. Quickly go over the **Después de leer** activities.

ANSWERS

Después de leer

A
1. **No.**
2. **Sí.**
3. **No.**
4. **Sí.**
5. **Sí.**

CAPÍTULO 9
Conexiones

National Standards

Connections

This reading about climate and weather in the Spanish-speaking world establishes a connection with another discipline, allowing students to reinforce and further their knowledge of social sciences through the study of Spanish.

¡OJO! The readings in the **Conexiones** section are optional. They focus on some of the major disciplines taught in schools and universities. The vocabulary is useful for discussing such topics as history, literature, art, economics, business, science, etc. You may choose any of the following ways to do this reading on climate and weather with your students.

Independent reading Have students read the selections and do the post-reading activities as homework, which you collect. This option is least intrusive on class time and requires a minimum of teacher involvement.

Homework with in-class follow-up Assign the readings and post-reading activities as homework. Review and discuss the material in class the next day.

Intensive in-class activity This option includes a pre-reading vocabulary presentation, in-class reading and discussion, assignment of the activities for homework, and a discussion of the assignment in class the following day.

LAS CIENCIAS SOCIALES

EL CLIMA

A. As students read about these climate zones, have them locate each area being discussed on the map of South America on page 464, or on the Map Transparency.

Conexiones

LAS CIENCIAS SOCIALES

EL CLIMA

We often talk about the weather, especially when on vacation. When planning a vacation trip, it's a good idea to take into account the climate of the area we are going to visit. When we talk about weather or climate, we must remember, however, that there is a difference between the two. Weather is the condition of the atmosphere for a short period of time. Climate is the term used for the weather that prevails in a region over a long period of time.

Let's read about weather and climate throughout the vast area of the Spanish-speaking world.

El Parque Nacional de los Glaciares, Argentina

El clima y el tiempo

El clima y el tiempo son dos cosas muy diferentes. El tiempo es la condición de la atmósfera durante un período breve o corto. El tiempo puede cambiar[1] frecuentemente. Puede cambiar varias veces en un solo día.

El clima es el término que usamos para el tiempo que prevalece[2] en una zona por un período largo. El clima es el tiempo que hace cada año en el mismo lugar.

Zonas climáticas

En el mundo de habla española hay muchas zonas climáticas. Mucha gente cree que toda la America Latina tiene un clima tropical, pero es erróneo. El clima de Latinoamérica varía de una región a otra.

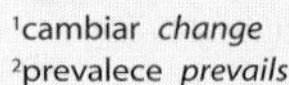

[1]cambiar *change*
[2]prevalece *prevails*

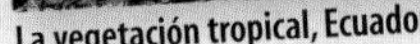

La vegetación tropical, Ecuador

El río Santiago Cayapas, Ecuador

El Amazonas
Toda la zona o cuenca amazónica es una región tropical. Hace mucho calor y llueve mucho durante todo el año.

Los Andes
En los Andes, aún en las regiones cerca de la línea ecuatorial, el clima no es tropical. En las zonas montañosas el clima depende de la elevación. En los picos andinos, por ejemplo, hace frío.

Los picos andinos cerca de Cuzco, Perú

Una aldea en las montañas, Urubamba, Perú

Clima templado
Algunas partes de la Argentina, Uruguay y Chile tienen un clima templado. España también tiene un clima templado. En una región de clima templado hay cuatro estaciones: el verano, el otoño, el invierno y la primavera. Y el tiempo cambia con cada estación. ¡Y una cosa importante! Las estaciones en la América del Sur son inversas de las de la América del Norte.

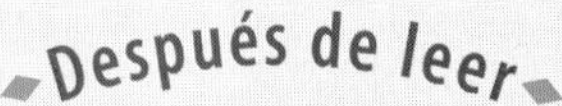

Después de leer

A **¿Sabes?** Contesten en inglés.

1. What's the difference between weather and climate?
2. What is an erroneous idea that many people have about Latin America?
3. How can it be cold in some areas that are actually on the equator?
4. What is a characteristic of a tropical area?
5. What is a characteristic of a region with a temperate climate?

B. Have students read the introduction in English on page 280. They should then proceed to the main reading.

ANSWERS

Después de leer

1. Weather is the condition of the atmosphere during a short period of time. It can change frequently. Climate is the weather prevailing in a region over a long period of time. It's the weather that a given place has every year.
2. Many people think all of Latin America has a tropical climate.
3. In mountainous areas the climate depends on the elevation.
4. It's hot all year and it rains a lot.
5. It has four seasons and the weather changes with each season.

CAPÍTULO 9
Culminación

RECYCLING

The **Actividades orales** and the **Actividad escrita** give students the opportunity to re-use, as much as possible, the vocabulary and structures from this chapter and earlier chapters in open-ended, real-life settings.

Actividades orales

¡OJO! Encourage students to say as much as possible when they do these activities. Tell them not to be afraid of making mistakes since the goal of the activities is real-life communication. If someone in the group makes an error, allow the others to politely correct him or her.

D TECHNOLOGY OPTION In the CD-ROM version of **Actividad D** (Disc 3, page 282), students can interact with an on-screen native speaker and record their voice.

Student Portfolio

Have students keep a notebook containing their best written work from each chapter. These selected writings can be based on assignments from the Student Textbook and the Writing Activities Workbook. The activities on page 283 are examples of writing assignments that may be included in each student's portfolio.

In the Workbook, students will develop an organized autobiography **(Mi autobiografía).** These workbook pages may also become a part of their portfolio. See the Teacher's Manual for more information on the Student Portfolio.

Culminación

Actividades orales

A ¿Qué tipo de vacación prefieres? Work with a classmate. Tell him or her where you like to go on vacation. Tell what you do there and some of the reasons why you enjoy it so much. Take turns.

B Unas vacaciones maravillosas Work with a classmate. Pretend you each have a million dollars. Take turns describing your millionaire's dream vacation.

C El norte y el sur Work with a classmate. One of you is from Santo Domingo in the Dominican Republic. The other is from Santiago, Chile. In as much detail as possible tell what each of you did in July in your area.

D El esquí You are at a café near the slopes of Bariloche in Argentina. You meet an Argentine skier (your partner). Find out as much as you can about each other's skiing habits and abilities.

San Carlos de Bariloche, Argentina

ANSWERS

Actividades orales

A and **B** Answers will vary; however, encourage students to make maximum use of the words and expressions they have learned thus far.

C Answers will vary. Have students refer to their maps of Central and South America when doing this activity.

D Answers will vary.

Actividad escrita

A Una tarjeta postal Look at these postcards. Choose one. Pretend you spent a week there. Write the postcard to a friend.

Cancún, México
Bariloche, Argentina

Writing Strategy

Comparing and contrasting

Before you begin to write a comparison of people, places, or things, you must be aware of how they are alike and different. When you compare, you are emphasizing similarities; when you contrast, you are emphasizing differences. Making a diagram or a list of similarities and differences is a good way to organize your details before you begin to write.

Irene y José Luis durante un día de julio

It's a typical July day. But Irene is in Santiago de Chile and José Luis is in Santiago de Compostela in Spain. The days are quite different in these two places. Write a comparison between a July day in Santiago de Chile and in Santiago de Compostela. Explain why the days are so different.

Because of the type of weather, Irene's activities on this day are probably different from those of José Luis. Explain what each one is doing. Are they wearing the same clothing or not?

Not everything is different, however. What are Irene and José Luis doing on this July day in two different places in spite of the different weather?

Independent Practice

Assign any of the following:
1. Activities, pages 282–283
2. Workbook, **Mi autobiografía,** page 116
3. Situation Cards
4. CD-ROM, Disc 3, Chapter 9, **Juego de repaso**

ANSWERS

Actividad escrita

A Answers will vary. Accept any answers that describe the location shown on the postcard.

Writing Strategy

Answers will vary, but students will indicate that in July it's summer in Spain and winter in Chile.

Actividad escrita

A TECHNOLOGY OPTIONS

Students may use the Portfolio feature on the CD-ROM to do **Actividad A.**

At **Café Glencoe (www.cafe.glencoe.com)** at the **Glencoe Foreign Language Web site,** students can actually send an electronic postcard.

Writing Strategy

Comparing and contrasting

A. Have students read the Writing Strategy on page 283. Then have students make a list of similarities and differences between a July day in Santiago de Chile and in Santiago de Compostela, Spain.

B. Have students refer to the maps of Spain and South America in their textbook on pages 463 and 464.

C. As students develop the last paragraph, remind them that much of their daily routine could be the same as those of the students they are describing.

Geography Connection

Bariloche, Argentina Bariloche is in the heart of the Argentine lake area on the southern end of Lago Nahuel Huapi. It resembles a European ski village with chalet-like houses made of wood and stone.

Bariloche is a ski resort in the winter. The snow festival is held every August. Fishing is great from mid-November to mid-March. In the summer, Bariloche is popular with campers, swimmers, and anglers.

CAPÍTULO 9
Vocabulario

ASSESSMENT RESOURCES

- Chapter Quizzes
- Testing Program
- Computer Testmaker
- Situation Cards
- Communication Transparency C-9
- Performance Assessment
- **Maratón mental** Videoquiz

VOCABULARY REVIEW

The words and phrases in the **Vocabulario** have been taught for productive use in this chapter. They are summarized here as a resource for both students and teacher. This list also serves as a convenient resource for the **Culminación** activities on pages 282 and 283. There are approximately 16 cognates in this vocabulary list. Have students find them.

Vocabulario

DESCRIBING THE BEACH

el balneario	la arena	el mar
la playa	la ola	la piscina, la alberca

DESCRIBING SUMMER WEATHER

el verano	el cielo	Hace buen (mal) tiempo.
la nube	Hace (Hay) sol.	Llueve.
estar nublado	Hace calor.	El sol brilla.

IDENTIFYING BEACH GEAR

el traje de baño, el bañador	los anteojos (las gafas) de sol	la plancha de vela
la loción bronceadora, la crema protectora	la toalla playera	la tabla hawaiana
	el esquí acuático	

DESCRIBING SUMMER AND BEACH ACTIVITIES

la natación	tomar el sol	pasar el fin de semana
el buceo	esquiar en el agua	practicar el surfing
nadar	bucear	

DESCRIBING A TENNIS GAME

el tenis	la raqueta	dobles
la cancha de tenis (al aire libre, cubierta)	la pelota	jugar (al) tenis
	la red	golpear la pelota
el/la tenista	singles	

DESCRIBING A SKI RESORT

la estación de esquí	el/la esquiador(a)	el telesquí, el telesilla
la ventanilla, la boletería	la montaña	el/la experto(a)
el ticket, el boleto	la pista	el/la principiante

IDENTIFYING SKI GEAR

el esquí	el bastón	el guante
la bota	el anorak	

DESCRIBING WINTER ACTIVITIES

esquiar	tomar (subir en) el telesilla	bajar la pista

DESCRIBING WINTER WEATHER

el invierno	el grado	Hace frío.
la nieve	bajo cero	Nieva.
la temperatura		

OTHER USEFUL EXPRESSIONS

ayer	por encima de

For the Younger Student

Balnearios y estaciones de esquí Have students prepare brochures for different resorts using information from the library or from the Internet. Use their brochures for a bulletin board display.

Critical Thinking Activity

Decision making, evaluating consequences Write the following on the board or on an overhead transparency:

1. **Maripaz va a la playa. Pero ella sabe que cada vez que va a la playa, no vuelve bronceada. Vuelve quemada. Es un problema para ella. Por consiguiente, ella debe comprar una crema protectora muy fuerte. Ella tiene 1.000 pesos. Quiere comprar un par de anteojos de sol que son fabulosos. Pero si ella compra los anteojos, no va a tener bastante dinero para comprar la crema protectora. ¿Qué debe ella hacer?**
2. **La tentación sale victoriosa. Maripaz compró los anteojos de sol y ella no va a cambiar sus planes. Va a ir a la playa. ¿Cuáles pueden ser las consecuencias de su decisión?**
3. **¿Qué otras alternativas tiene Maripaz?**

TECNOTUR

VIDEO

¡Buen viaje!

EPISODIO 9 ▸ El verano y el invierno

Cristina está de vacaciones con Isabel y su familia en Puerto Vallarta, México.

Un juego de voleibol en la playa cerca del hotel

CD-ROM

Expansión cultural

Puerto Vallarta es un centro turístico importante en la costa del Pacífico de México.

interNET CONNECTION

In this video episode Cristina and Isabel spend the afternoon at the beach in Puerto Vallarta. To find out today's weather in other Spanish-speaking cities, go to the Capítulo 9 Internet activity at the Glencoe Foreign Language Web site:

http://www.glencoe.com/sec/fl

Video Synopsis

This episode opens with Cristina sitting on a hotel beach in Puerto Vallarta, writing a postcard to her mother. The entire de la Rosa family is vacationing at the hotel. Isabel joins Cristina on the beach. They discuss clothes, apply sunscreen, then go for a walk along the beach, talking about summertime activities. Upon their return, Luis joins them, and invites them to play beach volleyball with his friends.

CAPÍTULO 9

Tecnotur

OVERVIEW

This page previews three key multimedia components of the **Glencoe Spanish** series. Each reinforces the material taught in Chapter 9 in a unique manner.

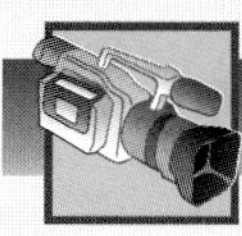

VIDEO

The Video Program allows students to see how the chapter vocabulary and structures are used by native speakers within an engaging story line. For maximum reinforcement, show the video episode as a final activity for Chapter 9.

A. These two photos show highlights from the Chapter 9 video episode. Before watching it, ask students what they see in these two photos: **¿Qué ven Uds. en las fotos?**

B. Now show the Chapter 9 video episode. See the Video Activities Booklet for detailed suggestions for using this resource.

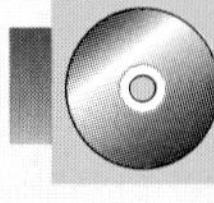

CD-ROM

A. The **Expansión cultural** photo shows a view of Puerto Vallarta, Mexico where Cristina, Isabel, and Luis spend their vacation. Have students read the caption on page 285.

B. In the CD-ROM version of **Expansión cultural,** students can listen to additional recorded information about Puerto Vallarta.

INTERNET

Teacher Information and Student Worksheets for this activity can be accessed at the Web site.

Chapter 10 Overview

SCOPE AND SEQUENCE pages 286–313

TOPICS	FUNCTIONS	STRUCTURE	CULTURE
◆ Attending cultural events ◆ Teen dating customs	◆ How to talk about going to cultural events and purchasing a ticket ◆ How to discuss movies, plays, and museums ◆ How to express cultural preferences ◆ How to relate actions or events that took place in the past ◆ How to tell for whom something is done	◆ **-er** and **-ir** verbs in the preterite ◆ Indirect object pronouns **le, les**	◆ Verónica talks about teen dating customs in the Spanish-speaking world compared to dating customs in the U.S. ◆ El Teatro Nacional, San José, Costa Rica ◆ ***La Zarzuela*** ◆ Palacio de Bellas Artes ◆ Music of the Spanish-speaking world ◆ The Ballet Folklórico de México

CHAPTER 10 RESOURCES

PRINT	MULTIMEDIA
Planning Resources	
Lesson Plans	Interactive Lesson Planner
Block Scheduling Lesson Plans	
Reinforcement Resources	
Writing Activities Workbook	Transparencies Binder
Student Tape Manual	Audiocassette/Compact Disc Program
Video Activities Booklet	Videocassette/Videodisc Program
Web Site User's Guide	Online Internet Activities
	Electronic Teacher's Classroom Resources
Assessment Resources	
Situation Cards	**Maratón mental** Mindjogger Videoquiz
Chapter Quizzes	Testmaker Computer Software (Macintosh/Windows)
Testing Program	Listening Comprehension Audiocassette/Compact Disc
Performance Assessment	Communication Transparency: C-10
Motivational Resources	
Expansion Activities	Café Glencoe: www.cafe.glencoe.com
	Keypal Internet Activities
Enrichment	
Spanish for Spanish Speakers	Fine Art Transparencies: F-10, F-11

Chapter 10 Planning Guide

SECTION	PAGES	SECTION RESOURCES
Vocabulario Palabras 1 **Al cine** **En el cine**	288–291	Vocabulary Transparencies 10.1 Audiocassette 6B/ Compact Disc 6 Student Tape Manual, TE, pages 113–116 Workbook, pages 117–118 Chapter Quizzes, page 50 CD-ROM, Disc 3, pages 288–291
Vocabulario Palabras 2 **En el museo** **En el teatro**	292–295	Vocabulary Transparencies 10.2 Audiocassette 6B/ Compact Disc 6 Student Tape Manual, TE, pages 117–118 Workbook, pages 118–120 Chapter Quizzes, pages 51–52 CD-ROM, Disc 3, pages 292–295
Estructura **Pretérito de los verbos en -er e -ir** **Complementos le, les**	296–301	Workbook, pages 121–124 Audiocassette 6B/Compact Disc 6 Student Tape Manual, TE, pages 119–121 Chapter Quizzes, pages 53–54 Computer Testmaker CD-ROM, Disc 3, pages 296–301
Conversación **¿Saliste?** **Pronunciación: Las consonantes j, g**	302–303	Audiocassette 6B/Compact Disc 6 Student Tape Manual, TE, pages 122–123 CD-ROM, Disc 3, pages 302–303
Lecturas culturales ***Dating*** **La zarzuela *(opcional)*** **El baile *(opcional)***	304–307	Testing Program, page 59 CD-ROM, Disc 3, pages 304–307
Conexiones **La música *(opcional)***	308–309	Testing Program, page 60 CD-ROM, Disc 3, pages 308–309
Culminación **Actividades orales** **Actividades escritas** **Vocabulario** **Tecnotur**	310–313	**¡Buen viaje!** Video, Episode 10 Video Activities, pages 101–105 Internet Activities www.glencoe.com/sec/fl Testing Program, pages 55–59; 112; 143; 169 CD-ROM, Disc 3, pages 310–313

CAPÍTULO 10

OVERVIEW

In this chapter students will learn to discuss several types of cultural activities. To do this they will learn basic vocabulary associated with movies, museums, and the theater. They will also continue to express themselves in the past by learning the preterite of **-er** and **-ir** verbs. The cultural focus of the chapter will be dating customs and cultural events in the Spanish-speaking world.

National Standards

Communication
In Chapter 10, students will communicate in spoken and written Spanish on the following topics:
- going to the movies
- visiting a museum
- attending a theater performance

Students will obtain and provide information about these topics and engage in conversations about their personal exposure to cultural events. They will also continue to learn to express themselves in the past.

Pacing

Chapter 10 will require approximately eight to ten days. Pacing will vary according to the length of the class, the age of your students, and student aptitude.

Block Scheduling

See the Block Scheduling Lesson Plans Booklet for suggestions on how to present the chapter material within a block scheduling framework.

CAPÍTULO 10
Diversiones culturales

Objetivos

In this chapter you will learn to do the following:

- discuss movies, museums, and theater
- discuss cultural events
- relate more past actions or events
- tell for whom something is done
- discuss some dating customs in the United States and compare them with those in Spanish-speaking countries
- talk about cultural activities that are popular in the Spanish-speaking world

interNET CONNECTION

The **Glencoe Foreign Language Web site (http://www.glencoe.com/sec/fl)** offers three options that enable you and your students to experience the Spanish-speaking world via the Internet:

- The online **Actividades** are correlated to the chapters and utilize Hispanic Web sites around the world. For the Chapter 10 activities, see student page 313.
- The **Correspondencia electrónica** section provides information on how to set up a keypal (pen pal) exchange between your class and a class in the Spanish-speaking world.
- At **Café Glencoe,** the interactive "after-school" section of the site, you and your students can access a variety of additional online resources, including interactive games.

doscientos ochenta y siete 287

CAPÍTULO 10

Spotlight On Culture

Artefacto The musical instruments shown here are two **zampoñas** and a **charango.** The colonists brought stringed instruments to the New World and the Indians were quick to adapt them to their own tastes. They used an armadillo shell as a sounding box and the end result was a **charango.** The **charango** is a small instrument similar to a ukulele, which helps give Andean music its distinctive sound. Today, many **charangos** are made from wood, as is the one shown here. The **zampoña** is a reed flute commonly used in Andean music.

Fotografía This photo shows the Prado Museum in Madrid. The building was originally commissioned by Carlos III in 1785 to house a natural history museum. When the Prado was completed in 1819, however, it became an art museum to exhibit the vast collection of the Spanish royalty. Painting represents one of Spain's greatest contributions to world cultures. The **Prado** collection includes the works of three great masters: **Francisco de Goya**, **Diego Velázquez,** and **El Greco,** as well as other masterpieces by Flemish and Italian artists. The room we see in this photo contains works by **El Greco**.

Chapter Projects

El arte hispánico Have groups research different Spanish and Latin American painters and/or sculptors. Each group can put on an art show using prints of the artists' most famous works.

TECHNOLOGY OPTIONS See the Chapter 10 Internet activity, **Una exposición de arte,** at the **Glencoe Foreign Language Web site** at **http://www.glencoe.com/sec/fl** for links, worksheets, and teacher information for this project.

El museo Visit a local museum so that students can see different styles of art and, hopefully, some work by Hispanic artists.

El video Show a Spanish movie (video) and discuss it with the students in class.

Visita al cine Organize a field trip to a local movie theater to see a Spanish film. If all of the Spanish classes at your school plan to go, you may be able to have the theater order the film of your choice for a special screening.

Learning From Photos

En el Prado After presenting the new vocabulary in this chapter, ask these questions about the photo on pages 286–287:

¿Dónde están las dos muchachas?
¿Mira el señor un cuadro?
El cuadro es de El Greco. ¿Es El Greco un artista español?

CAPÍTULO 10

Vocabulario

PALABRAS 1

RESOURCES

- Vocabulary Transparencies 10.1 (A & B)
- Student Tape Manual, TE, pages 113–116
- Audiocassette 6B/CD6
- Workbook, pages 117–118
- Quiz 1, page 50
- CD-ROM, Disc 3, pages 288–291

Bell Ringer Review

Use BRR Transparency 10-1, or write the following on the board: Complete the following in the past.

1. Yo ___ un video. (mirar)
2. Y yo ___ unos discos. (escuchar)
3. Luego, yo ___ al café. (ir)
4. En el café yo ___ con el mesero. (hablar)
5. Yo ___ un refresco. (tomar)

TEACHING VOCABULARY

A. Using Vocabulary Transparencies 10.1 (A & B), play the **Palabras 1** presentation on Cassette 6B/Compact Disc 6. Point to the appropriate illustration as you play the cassette.

B. Have students repeat each word or expression after you two or three times as you point to the corresponding item on the transparency.

C. Now call on individual students to point to the corresponding illustration on the transparency as you say the word or expression.

Vocabulario

PALABRAS 1

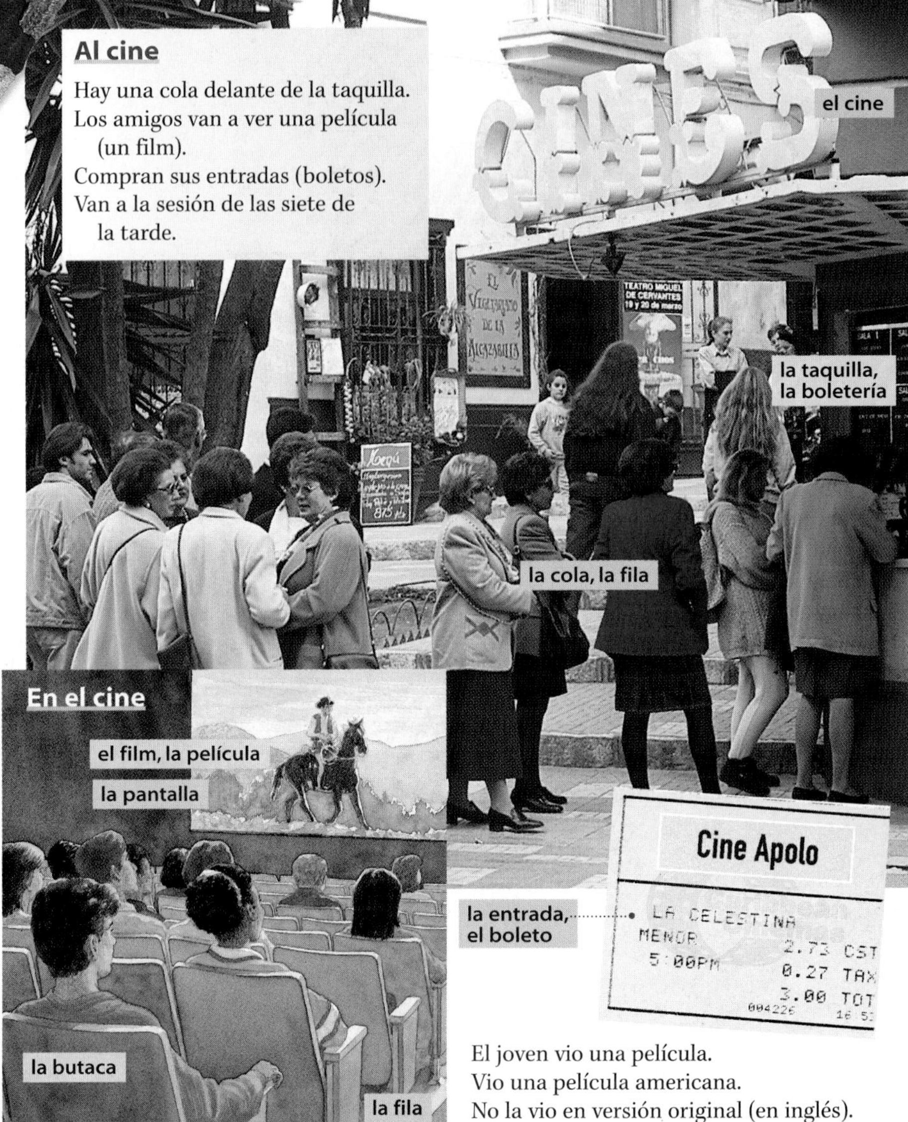

El joven vio una película.
Vio una película americana.
No la vio en versión original (en inglés).
La vio doblada al español.
Si la película no está doblada, lleva subtítulos.

Total Physical Response

Begin
___, levántate, por favor.
Ven acá. Imagínate que quieres ir al cine.
Ve por el autobús. Allí está.
¡Corre! ¡Anda rápido! Vas a perder el bus.
¡Ay! Perdiste el bus. Pero no hay problema.
Ve a la estación de metro.
Baja al metro.
Espera.
Aquí viene el metro. Sube.
El metro llega a la estación que quieres. Baja del metro.
Sube la escalera.
Allí está el cine. Ve a la taquilla.
Ponte en fila.
Indica a la taquillera que quieres una entrada.
Gracias, ___. Y ahora toma tu asiento.

Luego salió del cine.
¡Ay¡ Perdió el autobús (la guagua, el camión).

Como perdió el autobús, el joven fue a la estación de metro.
Subió al metro en la estación Insurgentes.
Volvió a casa en el metro.

NOTA The verb **salir** has several uses. Note the following meanings the verb can convey.

Diego salió anoche.
Diego went out last night.
Diego left last night.

Diego salió con Sandra.
Diego went out with (dated) Sandra.

Todo salió muy bien.
Everything turned out fine.

Vocabulario

¡OJO! Note that only the third-person singular forms of the preterite of **-er** and **-ir** verbs are used in the vocabulary presentation so that students can immediately answer questions and use the new vocabulary without having to make ending changes.

VOCABULARY EXPANSION

You may wish to give students the following additional vocabulary.

una película policíaca
una película documental
una película de amor (romántica)
una película de ciencia ficción
una película de aventuras (de acción)
una película de vaqueros (del oeste)

Did You Know?

Insurgentes This is one of the main subway stations in Mexico City. Mexico City's subway system is one of the world's best, as well as the safest and cheapest. The stations, many with marble, are immaculate and brightly lit. The trains are French designed and, like the famous Paris *métro,* they run very quietly on rubber tires. The Mexico City subway transports more than five million passengers daily.

ABOUT THE SPANISH LANGUAGE

- The ticket to a movie or theater is often referred to as **la entrada** rather than **el boleto** or **el billete. La localidad** is used for both a ticket or a seat in a theater.
- **La taquilla** is the most common word for a movie or theater ticket window. **La boletería** is used in Latin America, **la taquilla** in Spain. In some areas you also hear **la ventanilla.**
- The word **la fila** or **la cola** can be used for a line of people. **La cola** is heard more in Latin America, **la fila** in Spain.
- In addition to **la película** and **el film**, you will often hear and see **el filme**.
- In addition to **el autobús**, the shortened form **el bus** is more and more frequently heard. In the Caribbean area the word for *bus* is **la guagua**; in Mexico **el camión.** Other regional terms for *bus* are **el ómnibus**, **el micro**, **la góndola,** and **el colectivo.** (In many areas **colectivo** means a *public taxi;* in Argentina, however, it means *bus*).

¡OJO! **Práctica** When students are doing the **Práctica** activities, accept any answer that makes sense. The purpose of these activities is to have students use the new vocabulary. They are not factual recall activities. Thus, do not expect students to remember specific information from the vocabulary presentation when answering. If you wish, have students use the photo on this page as a stimulus, when possible.
Historieta Each time **Historieta** appears, it means that the answers to the activity form a short story. Encourage students to look at the title of the **Historieta** since it can sometimes help them do the activity.

A and **B** After going over **Práctica A** and **B** have students retell the stories in their own words. It is recommended that you go over all the activities once in class before assigning them for homework.

Writing Development

Have students write the answers to **Práctica A** and **B** in a paragraph to illustrate how all of the items tell a story.

Málaga, España

A **HISTORIETA** Al cine

Contesten.

1. ¿Fue Eduardo al cine?
2. ¿Compró su entrada en la taquilla?
3. ¿Fue a la sesión de las ocho de la tarde?
4. ¿Tomó una butaca en una fila cerca de la pantalla?
5. ¿Vio la película en versión original o doblada?
6. ¿A qué hora salió del cine?
7. ¿Perdió el autobús?
8. ¿Volvió a casa en el metro?

B **HISTORIETA** En la taquilla

Escojan.

1. La gente hace cola delante de ____.
   a. la pantalla b. la fila c. la taquilla
2. Compran ____ en la taquilla.
   a. butacas b. películas c. entradas
3. En el cine presentan o dan ____ americana.
   a. una entrada b. una película c. una novela
4. No es la versión original de la película. Está ____ al español.
   a. entrada b. doblada c. en fila
5. Los clientes entran en el cine y toman ____.
   a. una pantalla b. una entrada c. una butaca
6. Proyectan la película en ____.
   a. la pantalla b. la butaca c. la taquilla

Learning From Realia

Metro 10 viajes Ask students what **diez viajes** mean. What words tell you not to fold the subway ticket? Is it okay to throw the ticket away after one has entered the subway? The ticket on the right says **sencillo**. Can you guess what this means?

ANSWERS

Práctica

A
1. **Sí, Eduardo fue al cine.**
2. **Sí, compró su entrada en la taquilla.**
3. **Sí, (No, no) fue a la sesión de las ocho de la tarde.**
4. **Sí, (No, no) tomó una butaca en una fila cerca de la pantalla.**
5. **Vio la película doblada (en versión original).**
6. **Salió del cine a las ___.**
7. **Sí, (No, no) perdió el autobús.**
8. **Sí, (No, no) volvió a casa en el metro.**

B
1. **c**
2. **c**
3. **b**
4. **b**
5. **c**
6. **a**

C **Lo mismo** Den un sinónimo.
1. la película
2. el autobús
3. la boletería
4. la entrada

Actividades comunicativas

A **Vamos al cine.** Work with a classmate. Pretend you and your partner are making plans to go out tonight to a Spanish-language movie. Discuss your plans together.

La estación de metro en la Puerta del Sol, Madrid

B **Una encuesta** Work in groups of four. Conduct a survey. Find out the answers to the following:
- ¿Eres muy aficionado(a) al cine o no?
- ¿Cuántas películas ves en una semana?
- ¿Ves las películas en el cine o las alquilas (rentas) en una tienda de videos?

Compile the information and report the results of your survey to the class.

C If necessary, have students refer back to pages 288 and 289 to find the answers.

Actividades comunicativas

A **TECHNOLOGY OPTION** You may wish to have students do the Chapter 10 Internet activity in conjunction with this communicative activity. In that activity students can find out what movies are currently playing in a Spanish-speaking country. For more information, see the Internet Connection, page 313.

B Each group should appoint a leader to gather the information and report to the class. You may want to write these three questions on the board and have a student tally the results for the entire class.

ABOUT THE SPANISH LANGUAGE

The subway entrance is called **la boca del metro.**

Learning From Photos

La estación de metro en la Puerta del Sol, Madrid This is a very busy plaza with much vehicular and pedestrian traffic. A brass plaque in the plaza marks kilometer 0, the spot from which all distances in Spain are measured. The city's main subway interchange is below the Puerta del Sol. Many lines converge there.

Independent Practice

Assign any of the following:
1. Workbook, **Palabras 1,** pages 117–118
2. Activities, pages 290–291
3. CD-ROM, Disc 3, pages 288–291

Additional Practice

You may wish to ask students the following questions:
1. **¿Donde hay una cola?**
2. **¿Qué venden o despachan en la taquilla?**
3. **¿Dónde venden (despachan) las entradas?**
4. **¿Dónde proyectan la película en el cine?**

ANSWERS

Práctica

C 1. **el film**
2. **la guagua (el camión)**
3. **la taquilla**
4. **el boleto**

Actividades comunicativas

A Answers will vary; however, students should mention the name of the movie, what time it's playing, and how they will get to the movie.

B Answers will vary.

CAPÍTULO 10
Vocabulario
PALABRAS 2

RESOURCES

- Vocabulary Transparencies 10.2 (A & B)
- Student Tape Manual, TE, pages 117–118
- Audiocassette 6B/CD6
- Workbook, pages 118–120
- Quiz 2, pages 51–52
- CD-ROM, Disc 3, pages 292–295

Bell Ringer Review

Use BRR Transparency 10-2, or write the following on the board:
Rewrite the following in the past.
1. **Yo miro un video.**
2. **Yo escucho un disco nuevo.**
3. **Yo voy al café.**
4. **Yo tomo un refresco.**

¡OJO! In **Palabras 1** the preterite of **-er** and **-ir** verbs is presented in the **-ió** form. In **Palabras 2** the preterite of these verbs is presented in the **-ió** and **-ieron** forms. This enables you to ask questions immediately that students can answer without having to manipulate the verb endings. The other forms will be taught immediately afterwards in the **Estructura** section of this chapter.

TEACHING VOCABULARY

A. Have students close their books. Show Vocabulary Transparencies 10.2 (A & B). Point to each item and have students repeat the corresponding word or expression after you two or three times.

B. Ask questions of individual students such as the following: **¿Es el actor o la actriz? ¿Es el telón o la escena? ¿Quién es? ¿Qué es?** *(continued on page 293)*

Vocabulario
PALABRAS 2

En el museo

En el teatro

El autor escribió la obra.
Escribió una obra teatral.
García Lorca escribió la obra *Bodas de Sangre.*

Total Physical Response

Begin
___, levántate y ven acá, por favor.
Vas a hacer algunos gestos. ¿De acuerdo?
Muy bien, eres escultor(a). Haz una estatua.
Eres artista. Pinta un cuadro.
Eres actor (actriz). Entra en escena. Dile algo al público, a los espectadores.
Eres director(a) de orquesta. Dirige a la orquesta.
Ahora, eres espectador(a) al concierto.
Escucha la música de la orquesta.

Los actores dieron una representación de *Bodas de Sangre*.
Los actores entraron en escena.
El público vio el espectáculo.
Les gustó mucho (el espectáculo).
Todos aplaudieron. Los actores recibieron aplausos.

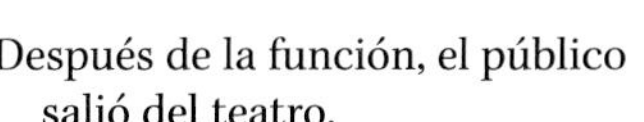

Después de la función, el público salió del teatro.

CAPÍTULO 10
Vocabulario

C. Have students open their books to page 292. Reinforce the new vocabulary by reading the words and sentences on pages 292–293, or play the recording on Cassette 6B/Compact Disc 6.

D. Point out to students that the photo of the man on page 292 is García Lorca.

National Standards

Cultures

In this chapter students will learn about the famous author García Lorca. García Lorca was born in 1898 in Granada. He was assassinated by anti-Republican rebels at the beginning of the Spanish Civil War in 1936. An extremely talented and brilliant writer, he is considered by many to be a "brilliantly endowed child of the muses." García Lorca was a poet, dramatist, artist, and musician. More has now been written about García Lorca than any other Spanish writer with the exception of Cervantes. He is also the most translated Spanish author of all time. His plays fill theaters all over the world.

ABOUT THE SPANISH LANGUAGE

You will sometimes hear **la audiencia** for *audience* but this use of the word is not correct. **El público** should be used. The definition of **audiencia** is: **Admisión de presencia de un príncipe o autoridad; obtener audiencia. Acto de oír los jueces a los litigantes. Tribunal que entiende en los pleitos.**

CAPÍTULO 10
Vocabulario

Práctica

A Students should answer in complete sentences. For example, **Los turistas fueron al museo.**

B Ask students to add any additional information as they do **Práctica B**. For example, for Item 1 they might say, **Hay muchos espectadores en el teatro.**

PAIRED ACTIVITY Have students work in pairs as they do this activity.

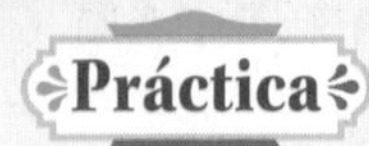

FINE ART CONNECTION

Fernando Botero Give students the following information: **Fernando Botero es un artista muy conocido. Nació en Medellín, Colombia, en 1932. En su obra combina lo mágico con lo real. Transforma retratos de grandes artistas e imágenes de las familias de la burguesía de Latinoamérica en cuadros y esculturas. Sus figuras son siempre grandes (gordas).** To show students one of Botero's paintings, **«Niños ricos»**, see **¡Buen viaje! Level 3,** Fine Art Transparency F-3.

Práctica

A HISTORIETA En el museo

Contesten según se indica.

1. ¿Adónde fueron los turistas? (al museo)
2. ¿Qué vieron? (una exposición de arte)
3. ¿Vieron unos cuadros de Botero, el artista colombiano? (sí)
4. ¿Qué más vieron de Botero? (unas estatuas en bronce)
5. ¿Les gustó la obra de Botero? (sí, mucho)

B **¿Qué es?** Identifiquen.

1.

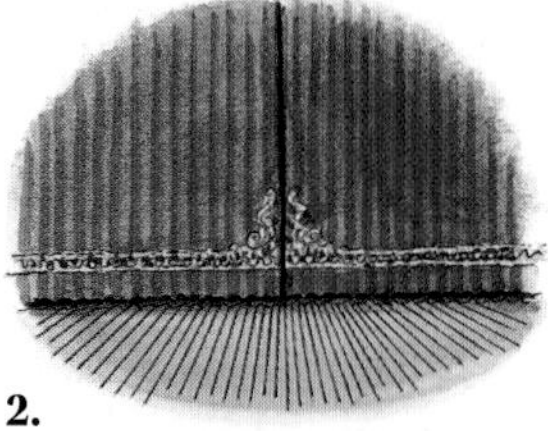
2.

3.

4.

5.

6.

7.

8.

9.

ANSWERS

Práctica

A
1. **Los turistas fueron al museo.**
2. **Vieron una exposición de arte.**
3. **Sí, vieron unos cuadros de Botero, el artista colombiano.**
4. **Vieron unas estatuas en bronce.**
5. **Sí, la obra de Botero les gustó mucho.**

B
1. **Es el teatro.**
2. **Es el telón.**
3. **Es la escena.**
4. **Es la taquilla (boletería).**
5. **Es el escenario.**
6. **Son los actores.**
7. **Es el museo.**
8. **Es una estatua.**
9. **Es un cuadro.**

C HISTORIETA Una noche en Buenos Aires

Contesten según se indica.

1. ¿Quiénes salieron anoche? (Susana y sus amigos)
2. ¿Adónde fueron? (al teatro Colón)
3. ¿Qué vieron? (una obra de García Lorca)
4. ¿Quién escribió la obra? (García Lorca)
5. ¿Le gustó la representación al público? (sí, mucho)
6. ¿Quiénes recibieron aplausos? (los actores)
7. ¿A qué hora salieron del teatro Susana y sus amigos? (a eso de las diez y media)
8. ¿Cómo volvieron a casa? (en taxi)

El Teatro Colón, Buenos Aires

D La palabra, por favor.

Escojan.

1. El ____ escribió la obra.
   a. actor **b.** autor **c.** artista
2. Cuando empieza el espectáculo, levantan ____.
   a. la pantalla **b.** el telón **c.** el escenario
3. El ____ es magnífico y muy bonito. Es una obra de arte.
   a. autor **b.** público **c.** escenario
4. Los ____ actuaron muy bien.
   a. autores **b.** actores **c.** escenarios
5. Al público le gustó mucho la representación y todos ____.
   a. aplaudieron **b.** salieron
   c. entraron en escena

El interior del Teatro Colón, Buenos Aires

Actividad comunicativa

A Me gusta ir al museo. Work with a classmate. One of you likes to go to museums and the other one finds them boring but really likes the theater. Discuss the reasons for your preferences.

National Standards

Comparisons
Have students look at the photo of the interior of the Teatro Colón. In Spain and Latin America the dress code is still quite formal for many cultural functions.

Actividad comunicativa

A Encourage students to use expressions such as **Me gusta ir a...** and **Me aburre porque...**

Learning From Photos

El Teatro Colón, Buenos Aires
El Teatro Colón is one of the world's leading opera houses. It hosts concerts and ballets from other countries but it also has its own ballet troupe, opera company, and symphony orchestra. The theater fills almost one square city block.

ANSWERS

C
1. **Susana y sus amigos salieron anoche.**
2. **Fueron al teatro Colón.**
3. **Vieron una obra de García Lorca.**
4. **García Lorca escribió la obra.**
5. **Sí, al público le gustó mucho la representación.**
6. **Los actores recibieron aplausos.**
7. **Susana y sus amigos salieron del teatro a eso de la diez y media.**
8. **Volvieron a casa en taxi.**

D
1. **b**
2. **b**
3. **c**
4. **b**
5. **a**

Actividad comunicativa

A Answers will vary; however, students may use expressions such as **me gusta** and **me aburre** in their answers.

RESOURCES

- Workbook, pages 121–124
- Student Tape Manual, TE, pages 119–121
- Audiocassette 6B/CD6
- Quizzes 3–4, pages 53–54
- Computer Testmaker
- CD-ROM, Disc 3, pages 296–301

Bell Ringer Review

Use BRR Transparency 10-3, or write the following on the board:
Complete in the present.

1. **Ellos ___ en una casa de apartamentos. (vivir)**
2. **Pero nosotros ___ en una casa privada. (vivir)**
3. **Ellos ___ a su apartamento en el ascensor. (subir)**
4. **Yo ___ en el comedor. (comer)**
5. **¿Dónde ___ tú? ¿En el comedor o en la cocina? (comer)**

TEACHING STRUCTURE

Telling what people did

A. Write the verbs from the first chart on page 296 on the board. Underline the endings and have students repeat each form after you.

B. After you have written a form for **comer**, for example, **yo comí**, you may wish to have students give you the forms for **volver, vivir,** and **subir**.

C. Point out to students that the preterite endings for the **-er** and **-ir** verbs are exactly the same.

D. Have students open their books to page 296 and go over the forms of **dar** and **ver** in Step 2 with them.

E. Have students read aloud the model sentences in Step 3.

Estructura

Telling what people did
Pretérito de los verbos en -er e -ir

1. You have already learned the preterite forms of regular **-ar** verbs. Study the preterite forms of regular **-er** and **-ir** verbs. Note that they also form the preterite by dropping the infinitive ending and adding the appropriate endings to the stem. The preterite endings of regular **-er** and **-ir** verbs are the same.

INFINITIVE	comer	volver	vivir	subir	
STEM	com-	volv-	viv-	sub-	ENDINGS
yo	comí	volví	viví	subí	-í
tú	comiste	volviste	viviste	subiste	-iste
él, ella, Ud.	comió	volvió	vivió	subió	-ió
nosotros(as)	comimos	volvimos	vivimos	subimos	-imos
vosotros(as)	*comisteis*	*volvisteis*	*vivisteis*	*subisteis*	*-isteis*
ellos, ellas, Uds.	comieron	volvieron	vivieron	subieron	-ieron

2. The preterite forms of the verbs **dar** and **ver** are the same as those of regular **-er** and **-ir** verbs.

INFINITIVE	dar	ver
yo	di	vi
tú	diste	viste
él, ella, Ud.	dio	vio
nosotros(as)	dimos	vimos
vosotros(as)	*disteis*	*visteis*
ellos, ellas, Uds.	dieron	vieron

3. Remember that the preterite is used to tell about an event that happened at a specific time in the past.

Ellos salieron anoche.
Ayer no comí en casa. Comí en el restaurante.
¿Viste una película la semana pasada?

ANSWERS (PAGE 297)

Práctica

A
1. **Sí, Carlos dio una fiesta.**
2. **Sí, (No, no) dio la fiesta para celebrar el cumpleaños de Teresa.**
3. **Sí (No), Carlos (no) escribió las invitaciones.**
4. **Sí (No), los amigos de Teresa (no) recibieron las invitaciones.**
5. **Sí (No), Teresa (no) vio a todos sus amigos en la fiesta.**
6. **Sí, (No, no) le dieron regalos a Teresa.**

Práctica

Málaga, España

A HISTORIETA Una fiesta fabulosa

Contesten.

1. ¿Dio Carlos una fiesta?
2. ¿Dio la fiesta para celebrar el cumpleaños de Teresa?
3. ¿Escribió Carlos las invitaciones?
4. ¿Recibieron las invitaciones los amigos de Teresa?
5. ¿Vio Teresa a todos sus amigos en la fiesta?
6. ¿Le dieron regalos a Teresa?
7. ¿Recibió Teresa muchos regalos?
8. Durante la fiesta, ¿comieron todos?
9. ¿A qué hora salieron de la fiesta?
10. ¿Volvieron a casa muy tarde?

B En la escuela Contesten personalmente.

1. ¿A qué hora saliste de casa esta mañana?
2. ¿Perdiste el bus escolar o no?
3. ¿Aprendiste algo nuevo en la clase de español?
4. ¿Escribiste una composición en la clase de inglés?
5. ¿Comprendiste la nueva ecuación en la clase de álgebra?
6. ¿Viste un video en la clase de español?
7. ¿A qué hora saliste de la escuela?
8. ¿A qué hora volviste a casa?

El Teatro Ayacucho, Caracas, Venezuela

C Al cine Sigan el modelo.

ir al cine
—¿Fuiste al cine?
—Sí, fui al cine.

1. ver una película en versión original
2. comprender la película en versión original
3. aplaudir
4. perder el autobús
5. volver a casa un poco tarde

Práctica

¡OJO! Note that the **Práctica** on pages 297–298 builds from simple to more complex. **Práctica A** reintroduces the third-person forms presented in the **Vocabulario. Práctica B** enables students to hear the **tú** form as they respond with the **yo** form. **Práctica C** makes them use both **tú** and **yo**. **Práctica D** and **E** together on page 298 make them use all forms.

A This activity recycles vocabulary from earlier chapters as it practices the preterite.

B **Práctica B** can be done as an interview. Have several students report back to the class after they have finished their interview.

C **Práctica C** can be done as a paired activity.

ANSWERS CONTINUED

A
7. Sí (No), Teresa (no) recibió muchos regalos.
8. Sí (No), durante la fiesta todos (no) comieron.
9. Salieron de la fiesta a (eso de) las ___.
10. Sí, (No, no) volvieron a casa muy tarde.

B
1. Salí de casa a (eso de) las ___ esta mañana.
2. Sí, (No, no) perdí el bus escolar.
3. Sí, (No, no) aprendí algo (nada) nuevo en la clase de español.
4. Sí, (No, no) escribí una composición en la clase de inglés.
5. Sí, (No, no) comprendí la nueva ecuación en la clase de álgebra.
6. Sí, (No, no) vi un video en la clase de español.
7. Salí de la escuela a (eso de) las ___.
8. Volví a casa a (eso de) las ___.

C
1. —¿Viste una película en versión original?
—Sí, vi una película en versión original.
2. —¿Comprendiste la película en versión original?
—Sí, comprendí la película en versión original.
3. —¿Aplaudiste?
—Sí, aplaudí.
4. —¿Perdiste el autobús?
—Sí, perdí el autobús.
5. —¿Volviste a casa un poco tarde?
—Sí, volví a casa un poco tarde.

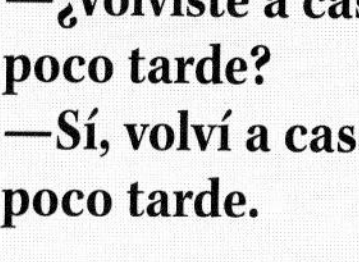

Writing Development

After going over **Práctica D** in class, have students write the information in their own words in paragraph form.

E Have students present **Práctica E** as a mini-conversation. Ask several pairs to present the conversation to the entire class.

Actividad comunicativa

¡OJO! This activity encourages students to use the chapter vocabulary and structures in open-ended situations. However, since students do not yet know the preterite of irregular verbs, be sure that they use the verbs in the colored boxes when doing **Actividad A.** This will deter them from trying to use unknown forms.

A Each student in the group should take turns asking someone else a question, using one of the words provided.

D HISTORIETA Al cine y al restaurante

Contesten.

1. ¿Salieron tú y tus amigos anoche?
2. ¿Vieron una película?
3. ¿Qué vieron?
4. ¿A qué hora salieron del cine?
5. ¿Fueron a un restaurante?
6. ¿Qué comiste?
7. Y tus amigos, ¿qué comieron?
8. ¿A qué hora volviste a casa?

Caracas, Venezuela

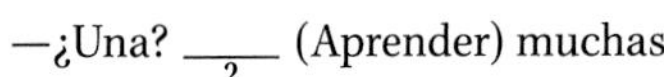

E HISTORIETA En la clase de español

Completen.

—Ayer en la clase de español, ¿___1 (aprender) tú una palabra nueva?

—¿Una? ___2 (Aprender) muchas.

—¿Les ___3 (dar) un examen el profesor?

—Sí, nos ___4 (dar) un examen.

—¿___5 (Salir) Uds. bien en el examen?

—Pues, yo ___6 (salir) bien pero otros no ___7 (salir) muy bien.

—Entonces tú ___8 (recibir) una nota buena, ¿no?

Actividad comunicativa

A **Ayer** Work in groups of four. Find out what you all did yesterday. Ask each other lots of questions and tabulate your answers. What did most of you do? Use the following words.

ANSWERS

Práctica

D
1. **Sí, mis amigos y yo salimos anoche.**
2. **Sí, vimos una película.**
3. **Vimos ___.**
4. **Salimos del cine a (eso de) las ___.**
5. **Sí, fuimos a un restaurante.**
6. **Comí ___.**
7. **Mis amigos comieron ___.**
8. **Volví a casa a (eso de) las ___.**

E
1. **aprendiste**
2. **Aprendí**
3. **dio**
4. **dio**
5. **Salieron**
6. **salí**
7. **salieron**
8. **recibiste**

Actividad comunicativa

A Answers will vary; however, students should use the verbs from the colored boxes in the preterite.

Telling what you do for others
Complementos le, les

1. You have already learned the direct object pronouns **lo, la, los,** and **las.** Now you will learn the indirect object pronouns **le** and **les.** Observe the difference between a direct object and an indirect object in the following sentences.

Juan lanzó la pelota. **Juan le lanzó la pelota a Carmen.**

In the preceding sentences, **la pelota** is the direct object because it is the direct receiver of the action of the verb **lanzó** *(threw).* **Carmen** is the indirect object because it indicates "to whom" the ball was thrown.

2. The indirect object pronoun **le** is both masculine and feminine. **Les** is used for both the feminine and masculine plural. **Le** and **les** are often used along with a noun phrase—**a Juan, a sus amigos.**

María le dio un regalo a Juan. **Juan le dio un regalo a María.**
María les dio un regalo a sus amigos. **Juan les dio un regalo a sus amigas.**

3. Since **le** and **les** can refer to more than one person, they are often clarified as follows:

Le hablé { **a él. / a ella. / a Ud.** } **Les hablé** { **a ellos. / a ellas. / a Uds.** }

A **¿Qué o a quién?** Indiquen el complemento directo y el indirecto.

1. Carlos recibió la carta.
2. Les vendimos la casa a ellos.
3. Vimos a Isabel ayer.
4. Le hablamos a Tomás.
5. ¿Quién tiene el periódico? Tomás lo tiene.
6. El profesor nos explicó la lección.
7. Ella le dio los apuntes a su profesor.
8. Ellos vieron la película en el cine.

Plaza Callao, Madrid, España

TEACHING STRUCTURE

Telling what you do for others

A. Write the following sentences on the board. The arrows will help students understand the concept of direct vs. indirect objects. **Juan lanzó → el balón a Carmen. Ella le dio → el regalo a su amiga**. As students look at these sentences, tell them that Juan doesn't throw Carmen. He throws the ball. To whom does he throw the ball? To Carmen. The ball is the direct object because it receives the action of the verb directly. Carmen is the indirect object because she receives the action of the verb indirectly.

B. Now have students open their books to page 299. Lead them through Steps 1–3 and the accompanying model sentences.

C. You may wish to write the model sentences from Step 2 on the board and underline the indirect object once and the direct object twice.

D. As you write the sentences from Step 2 on the board. Circle **le** and circle **a Juan**. Then draw arrows back and forth to indicate that they are the same person. This visual explanation helps many students.

Note Be sure that students learn that **le** and **les** are both masculine and feminine.

A **Práctica A** is a diagnostic tool to determine if students understand the concept of direct and indirect objects.

ANSWERS

Práctica

A
1. **la carta: complemento directo**
2. **Les, a ellos: complemento indirecto; la casa: complemento directo.**
3. **Isabel: complemento directo**
4. **Le, a Tomás: complemento indirecto**
5. **el periódico, lo: complementos directos**
6. **nos: complemento indirecto; la lección: complemento directo**
7. **le, a su profesor: complemento indirecto; los apuntes: complemento directo**
8. **la película: complemento directo**

CAPÍTULO 10
Estructura

¡OJO! It is recommended that you not wait for every student to use these pronouns perfectly. If certain students find the concept difficult, they can still function by answering with nouns. **¿Hablaste a Juan? Sí, hablé a Juan.** Direct and indirect objects will be reintroduced throughout this textbook series.

Práctica

B C and **E** Do **Práctica B, C,** and **E** on pages 300–301 orally with books closed. Then have students open their books and read these **Práctica** activities for additional reinforcement. When books are open, you can either ask the questions and have students answer, or have students do the activities in pairs.

D Have students present **Práctica D** as a mini-conversation.

Learning From Photos

El Museo del Prado In this photo we see an exterior view of the entrance to the Prado museum. For more information, see Spotlight on Culture, page 287.

B HISTORIETA Pobre Eugenio

Contesten según el dibujo.

1. ¿Qué le duele?
2. ¿Qué más le duele?
3. ¿Quién le examina la garganta?
4. ¿Quién le da la diagnosis?
5. ¿Qué le da la médica?
6. ¿Quién le da los medicamentos?

C Sí que le hablé. Contesten.

1. ¿Le hablaste a Rafael?
2. ¿Le hablaste por teléfono?
3. ¿Le diste las noticias?
4. ¿Y él les dio las noticias a sus padres?
5. ¿Les escribió a sus padres?
6. ¿Les escribió en inglés o en español?

D HISTORIETA Tiene que tener la dirección.

Completen.

—¿____(1) hablaste a Juan ayer?

—Sí, ____(2) hablé por teléfono y ____(3) hablé a Sandra también. ____(4) hablé a los dos.

—¿____(5) diste la dirección de Maricarmen?

—No, porque Adriana ____(6) dio la dirección. Y ____(7) dio su número de teléfono también.

El Museo del Prado, Madrid

ANSWERS

Práctica

B
1. **Le duele la garganta.**
2. Answers will vary.
3. **La médica le examina la garganta.**
4. **La médica le da la diagnosis.**
5. **La médica le da una receta.**
6. **El farmacéutico le da los medicamentos.**

C
1. **Sí, le hablé a Rafael.**
2. **Sí, le hablé por teléfono.**
3. **Sí, (No, no) le di las noticias.**
4. **Sí (No), él (no) les dio las noticias a sus padres.**
5. **Sí, (No, no) les escribió a sus padres.**
6. **Les escribió en inglés (español).**

D
1. **Le**
2. **le**
3. **le**
4. **Les**
5. **Les**
6. **les**
7. **les**

E **HISTORIETA** Juan es aficionado al arte.

Contesten.

1. ¿A Juan le interesa el arte?
2. ¿Le gusta ir a los museos?
3. ¿Le encantan las exposiciones de arte?
4. ¿Le gusta mucho la obra de Velázquez?
5. ¿Le gustan también los cuadros de Goya?
6. A sus amigos, ¿les interesa también el arte?
7. ¿Les gustan las obras de los muralistas mexicanos?

«La fragua de Vulcano» de Diego Velázquez

Actividad comunicativa

A **Regalos para todos** Work in pairs. Tell what each of the following people is like. Then tell what you buy or give to each one as a gift.

CAPÍTULO 10

Estructura

E **EXPANSION** Show Fine Art Transparency F-11 of this painting by Velázquez. You may wish to have students read the background information provided in the transparency package and have them do the related activities.

Actividad comunicativa

A Students should use **gustar** when telling what each person likes. They will use either **comprar** or **dar** when telling what they buy or give as a gift.

Learning From Photos

«La fragua de Vulcano» In 1629 Velázquez was sent on a trip to Italy to buy some works of art for the Royal collection. On this trip he went to Venice, Rome, and Naples, where he met Ribera, the Spanish painter. While in Italy he studied the Italian painters and worked to improve his ability to convey space. He painted **«La fragua de Vulcano»** during his stay. (For additional information on other paintings by Velázquez, see page 181 in the student textbook.)

¡OJO! All new material in the chapter has been presented. The sections that follow recombine and reintroduce the vocabulary and structures that have already been introduced.

ANSWERS

Práctica

E
1. **Sí, a Juan le interesa el arte.**
2. **Sí, le gusta ir a los museos.**
3. **Sí, le gustan las exposiciones de arte.**
4. **Sí, (No, no) le gusta mucho la obra de Velázquez.**
5. **Sí, (No, no) le gustan los cuadros de Goya.**
6. **Sí (No), a sus amigos (no) les interesa el arte.**
7. **Sí, (No, no) les gustan las obras de los muralistas mexicanos.**

Actividad comunicativa

A Answers may follow this model: **A mi papá le gusta la ropa. Le doy una corbata. (Le compro una corbata).**

RESOURCES

- Audiocassette 6B/CD6
- CD-ROM, Disc 3, page 302

TEACHING THE CONVERSATION

A. To vary the presentation, have students listen to the recording on Cassette 6B/Compact Disc 6 with books closed.
B. Ask students to tell you in one or two sentences what the conversation is about. This can be done in either Spanish or English.
C. Have students open their books. Give them two or three minutes to read the conversation silently.
D. Call on one student to read aloud the part of **Paco** and another the part of **Julia**.
E. Then go over the **Después de conversar** questions that follow.
F. Call on one student to retell the story of the conversation in narrative form.

Note If students can answer the **Después de conversar** questions with relative ease, move on. Students should not be expected to memorize the conversation.

TECHNOLOGY OPTION

On the CD-ROM (Disc 3, page 302), students can watch a dramatization of this conversation. They can then play the role of either one of the characters, and record themselves in the conversation.

Conversación

¿Saliste?

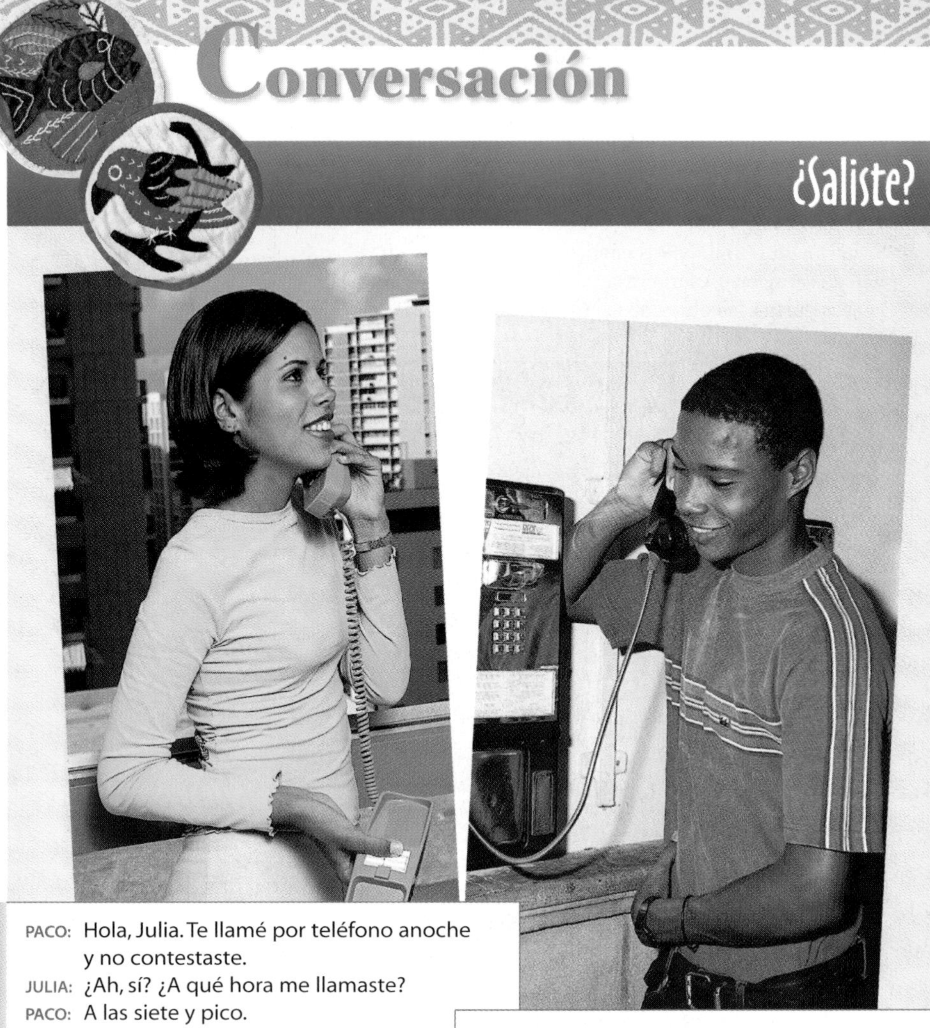

PACO: Hola, Julia. Te llamé por teléfono anoche y no contestaste.
JULIA: ¿Ah, sí? ¿A qué hora me llamaste?
PACO: A las siete y pico.
JULIA: Ay, no volví a casa hasta las ocho y media.
PACO: ¿Adónde fuiste?
JULIA: Pues, fui al cine con Felipe.
PACO: ¿Uds. fueron al cine y tú volviste a casa a las ocho y media? ¿Cómo puede ser?
JULIA: Pues, fuimos a la sesión de las cinco. Y después del cine comimos en Pizza Perfecta.

Después de conversar

Contesten.

1. ¿A quién telefoneó Paco?
2. ¿Ella contestó?
3. ¿A qué hora la llamó Paco?
4. ¿A qué hora volvió Julia a casa?
5. ¿Adónde fue?
6. ¿Con quién fue?
7. ¿A qué sesión fueron?
8. ¿Dónde comieron?

ANSWERS

Después de conversar

1. **Paco le telefoneó a Julia.**
2. **No, ella no contestó.**
3. **Paco la llamó a las siete y pico.**
4. **Julia no volvió a casa hasta las ocho y media.**
5. **Fue al cine.**
6. **Fue con Felipe.**
7. **Fueron a la sesión de las cinco.**
8. **Comieron en Pizza Perfecta.**

Additional Practice

Una llamada telefónica Have students work in pairs to make up a brief telephone conversation about any topic that interests them. Have several pairs present their conversation for the class. Students should use the conversation on page 302 as a model.

Actividades comunicativas

A **El viernes pasado y el viernes que viene** Get together with a group of classmates. Tell one another what you did last Friday night. Then tell what you're going to do next Friday night.

B **Un viaje escolar** The Spanish Club is going on a field trip. It's just in the planning stages. You may go to a museum that's showing the works of a Spanish artist, a Spanish-language movie, a Spanish play, or a Mexican or Spanish restaurant. Your Spanish teacher wants some input from you. With your classmates, discuss where you want to go and why.

C **¿Por qué volviste tan tarde?** You got home really late last night. One of your parents (your partner) wants to know why. He or she will ask a lot of questions. You'd better have some good answers!

Pronunciación

Las consonantes j, g

The Spanish **j** sound does not exist in English. In Spain, the **j** sound is very guttural. It comes from the throat. In Latin America, the **j** sound is much softer. Repeat the following.

ja	je	ji	jo	ju
Jaime	**Jesús**	**Jiménez**	**joven**	**jugar**
hija	**garaje**	**ají**	**viejo**	**junio**
roja			**trabajo**	**julio**
			ojos	

G in combination with **e** or **i (ge, gi)** has the same sound as **j.** For this reason you must pay particular attention to the spelling of the words with **je, ji, ge,** and **gi.** Repeat the following.

ge	gi
general	**biología**
gente	**alergia**
generoso	**original**
Insurgentes	

Repeat the following sentences.

El hijo del viejo general José trabaja en junio en Gijón.
El jugador juega en el gimnasio.
El joven Jaime toma jugo de naranja.

ANSWERS

Actividades comunicativas

A Answers will vary; however, students should use the preterite as well as **ir a** + infinitive in their answers.
B Answers will vary, according to the choices given. Each student in the group should have the opportunity to answer.
C Answers will vary.

Actividades comunicativas

A **Actividad A** contrasts past and future events.

B **TECHNOLOGY OPTION**
Students may use the Portfolio feature on the CD-ROM to write a composition about their field trip.

National Standards

Communities
By organizing a field trip to one of the locales suggested in **Actividad B,** you will give your students the opportunity to use their Spanish beyond the school setting.

C **TECHNOLOGY OPTION**
In the CD-ROM version of **Actividad C** (Disc 3, page 303), students can interact with an on-screen native speaker and record their voices.

TEACHING PRONUNCIATION

¡OJO! This is another sound that is radically different in Spain and Latin America. The sound of the letter **j** is extremely harsh in Spain, very guttural. It is similar to the German **ach.** In Latin America, however, it is a very soft sound. In many countries it is barely audible. Since the **g** and **j** can present spelling problems, it is recommended that you have students commit to memory the spelling of these words.

A. Have students carefully repeat the sounds **ja, je, ji, jo, ju; ge gi** after you or the recording on Cassette 6B/Compact Disc 6.
B. Now have them repeat the words and sentences.
C. Have students open their books to page 303. Call on individuals to read the sentences carefully.
D. You may use these sentences for dictation.

National Standards

Cultures

The reading about teen dating habits in the Spanish-speaking world on page 304 and the related activities on page 305 allow students to gain an understanding of the cultural practices that exist in the Spanish-speaking world.

Comparisons

The reading on this page allows students to make comparisons between dating customs and some teenage activites in the Spanish-speaking world and in the United States.

TEACHING THE READING

¡OJO! It is extremely difficult to generalize about dating customs these days in all the many areas of the Spanish-speaking world. The general statements in this **Lectura** hold true but there are some differences that must be taken into account. The more cosmopolitan an urban area is, the more students tend to pair off and date on their own. In small, rural areas, however, doing things in groups is still more common.

Pre-reading

A. Have students briefly discuss dating customs in the United States.

B. Tell them that they are going to read about dating customs in the Spanish-speaking world. Explain that dating customs are changing, but ask them to look for some differences between their dating customs and those of their Spanish-speaking counterparts. Also have them look for similarities.

(continued on page 305)

Lecturas CULTURALES

Reading Strategy

Recognizing text organization

Before you read a passage, try to figure out how the text is organized. If you can follow the organization of a text, you will understand the main ideas more quickly and be able to look for certain ideas and information more easily.

DATING

Algunas diferencias culturales son muy interesantes. Y las diferencias culturales pueden tener una influencia en la lengua que hablamos. Por ejemplo, *dating, boyfriend* y *girlfriend* son palabras que usamos mucho en inglés, ¿no? Y son palabras que no tienen equivalente en español. ¿Cómo es posible? Pues, vamos a hablar con Verónica. Ella es del Perú.

—Verónica, ¿saliste anoche?

—Sí, salí con un grupo de amigos de la escuela.

—¿Adónde fueron?

—Fuimos al cine. Vimos una película muy buena. Fue una película americana. La vimos en versión original con subtítulos en español.

—Verónica, ¿no sales a veces sola con un muchacho, con un amigo de la escuela?

—Pues, no mucho. Generalmente salimos en grupo. Pero es algo que está cambiando[1]. Está cambiando poco a poco[2]. Hoy en día una pareja[3] joven puede salir a solas. Podemos ir a un café, por ejemplo, a tomar un refresco. A veces vamos al cine o sólo damos un paseo[4] por el parque. Pero, para nosotros, es algo bastante nuevo.

[1]cambiando *changing*
[2]poco a poco *little by little*
[3]pareja *couple*
[4]damos un paseo *take a walk*

Marbella, España

Dating en Buenos Aires, Argentina

Did You Know?

Un novio o una novia Explain to students that **un novio** or **una novia** refers to a person whom you are dating exclusively. It implies a more serious relationship than our concept of "boyfriend" or "girlfriend."

Independent Practice

Assign any of the following:

1. Después de leer activities, page 305
2. Workbook, **Un poco más,** pages 125–127
3. CD-ROM, Disc 3, pages 304–305

Después de leer

A ***Dating*** Contesten.

1. ¿En qué lengua usamos las palabras *dating, boyfriend* y *girlfriend?*
2. ¿Tienen equivalente en español?
3. ¿Hay mucho *dating* entre los jóvenes de Latinoamérica y España?
4. ¿Ahora empiezan a salir en parejas?
5. Por lo general, ¿cómo salen?
6. ¿Con quién salió Verónica?
7. ¿Adónde fueron?
8. ¿Qué vieron?

B **Aquí** Contesten personalmente.

1. Donde tú vives, ¿salen los jóvenes con más frecuencia en grupos o en parejas?
2. Y tú, ¿sales a veces con sólo un(a) muchacho(a)?
3. ¿Adónde van?
4. ¿Pueden salir durante la semana?
5. ¿Qué noche salen?
6. ¿A qué hora tienes que estar en casa?

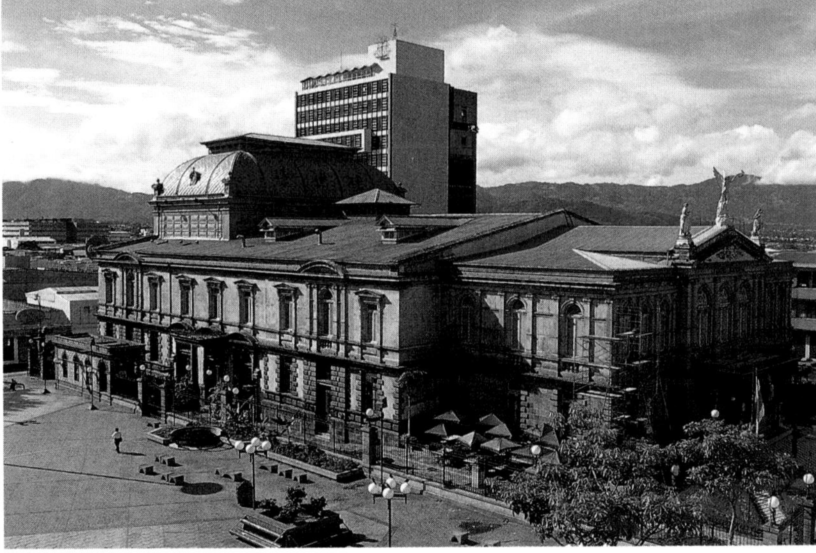

El Teatro Nacional, San José, Costa Rica

ANSWERS

Después de leer

A 1. **En inglés.**
2. **No, no tienen equivalente en español.**
3. **No, no hay mucho dating entre los jóvenes de Latinoamérica y España.**
4. **Sí, ahora empiezan a salir en parejas.**
5. **Por lo general, salen en grupo.**
6. **Verónica salió con un grupo de amigos de la escuela.**
7. **Fueron al cine.**
8. **Vieron una película americana.**

B 1. **Los jóvenes salen en grupos (en parejas).**
2. **Sí, salgo a veces con sólo un(a) muchacho(a). (No, no salgo con sólo un[a] muchacho[a].)**
3. **Vamos al cine (al partido de ___, a la casa de mis amigos, etc.).**
4. **Sí, (No, no) podemos salir durante la semana.**
5. **Salimos el viernes o el sábado.**
6. **Tengo que estar en casa a las ___.**

Reading

A. Have students open their books to page 304 and read the selection silently and quickly.

B. Call on an individual to read approximately half a paragraph. Then stop and ask pertinent comprehension questions.

Post-reading

After going over the **Lectura** in class, assign it for homework. Also assign the **Después de leer** activities on page 305. Go over them in class the next day.

TECHNOLOGY OPTION

Students may listen to a recorded version of the **Lectura** on the CD-ROM, Disc 3, pages 304–305.

Después de leer

A Allow students to refer to the reading to find the answers, or you may use this activity as a testing device for factual recall.

B Depending on the class, this topic may lead to a lively discussion involving all of your students.

Learning From Photos

El Teatro Nacional, San José, Costa Rica The Teatro Nacional in San José is extremely popular and beautiful. It houses the National Theater Company, the National Dance Company, and two orchestras. There are presentations of one kind or another almost every evening. At 10:30 on Sunday morning there is often a musical concert.

CAPÍTULO 10
Lecturas

LECTURA OPCIONAL 1

National Standards

Cultures

The reading about Spanish operetta, **la zarzuela,** and the related activity on this page give students an appreciation of one of the significant art forms of the Spanish-speaking world.

TEACHING TIPS

¡OJO! This reading is optional. You may skip it completely, have the entire class read it, have only several students read it, or assign it for extra credit.

A. Have students read the paragraph silently.

B. Do the **Después de leer** activity. This activity provides a quick and informal assessment of how well students understood this reading.

Learning From Realia

El Teatro de la Zarzuela is popular with both Spaniards and tourists. Because of the light nature of a **zarzuela,** it can be enjoyed even by those who have a limited knowledge of Spanish. Ask students the following questions about the ticket on page 306: **¿Cuánto costó la entrada?¿A qué hora es el espectáculo? ¿Qué número es la butaca?**

LECTURA OPCIONAL 1

LA ZARZUELA

Hay un género teatral exclusivamente español. Es la zarzuela. La zarzuela es una obra dramática muy ligera. No es profunda. Generalmente tiene un argumento[1] gracioso.

La zarzuela es un tipo de opereta. A veces, durante la presentación, los actores hablan y a veces cantan.

[1]argumento *plot*

Una zarzuela, Madrid, España

El Chaleco Blanco

La Gran Vía

Después de leer

A La zarzuela Digan que sí o que no.

1. La zarzuela es una novela española.
2. La zarzuela es un tipo de obra teatral.
3. En una zarzuela los actores no hablan, sólo bailan.
4. Una zarzuela es un tipo de opereta.
5. Los actores en una zarzuela hablan y cantan.
6. El tema o argumento de una zarzuela es siempre serio y profundo.

ANSWERS

Después de leer

A
1. No.
2. Sí.
3. No.
4. Sí.
5. Sí.
6. No.

LECTURA OPCIONAL 2

EL BAILE

El Ballet Folklórico de México goza de fama mundial. El espectáculo que presenta el Ballet Folklórico todos los domingos y miércoles en el Palacio de Bellas Artes es uno de los shows más populares de la Ciudad de México. La compañía baila una variedad de danzas regionales de México. A veces la coreografía del Ballet Folklórico de México es muy graciosa y divertida.

Hay también el Ballet Folklórico Nacional de México. Esta compañía presenta un programa auténtico y clásico de danzas mexicanas regionales en el Teatro de la Ciudad.

El Palacio de Bellas Artes, México

El Ballet Folklórico, México

Después de leer

A **Una comparación** Expliquen la diferencia entre El Ballet Folklórico de México y El Ballet Folklórico Nacional de México.

LECTURA OPCIONAL 2

National Standards

Cultures

The reading about the **Ballet Folklórico de México** and the related activity on this page familiarize students with a world-famous ballet company from Mexico and give them an appreciation of an important Mexican art form.

TEACHING TIPS

¡OJO! This reading is optional. You may skip it completely, have the entire class read it, have only several students read it, or assign it for extra credit.

Learning From Photos

El Palacio de Bellas Artes The Palacio de Bellas Artes was constructed as an opera house between 1904 and 1934. Construction on it was halted during the Mexican Revolution (1910–1917). Today the Palacio is a handsome theater, which houses the Ballet Folklórico de México and hosts other Mexican and international artists. The building is renowned for its architecture. It was designed by the Italian architect Adamo Boari. It also contains an impressive collection of paintings by Mexican artists including Rufino Tamayo and the famous muralists Rivera, Orozco, and Siqueiros.

ANSWERS

Después de leer

A Answers may include the following:
El Ballet Folklórico de México baila una variedad de danzas regionales de México en el Palacio de Bellas Artes. El Ballet Folklórico Nacional de México presenta una programa auténtico y clásico de danzas mexicanas regionales en el Teatro de la Ciudad.

CAPÍTULO 10
Conexiones

National Standards

Connections

This reading about music in the Spanish-speaking world establishes a connection with another discipline, allowing students to reinforce and deepen their knowledge of world music through the study of Spanish.

¡OJO! The readings in the **Conexiones** section are optional. They focus on some of the major disciplines taught in schools and universities. The vocabulary is useful for discussing such topics as history, literature, art, economics, business, science, etc.

See page 34 of this Teacher's Wraparound Edition for suggestions on how to present these **Conexiones** readings and the other optional readings in the book.

LAS BELLAS ARTES

LA MÚSICA

A. Most students will be familiar with these musical terms in English. Model the terms in Spanish and have students repeat after you.

B. Ask students to scan the readings on pages 308 and 309 and make a list of words they do not know. Explain the meaning of these words as a whole-class activity.

C. It is suggested that you play some recordings of the types of Spanish music discussed in this section. Ask a music teacher to help you assemble some selections from the Music Department's library.

TECHNOLOGY OPTION

Cassette 1A/Compact Disc 1 of the Audio Program features a variety of songs from the Spanish-speaking world that you might like to play for your students. The lyrics to these songs are in the Student Tape Manual, Teacher's Edition.

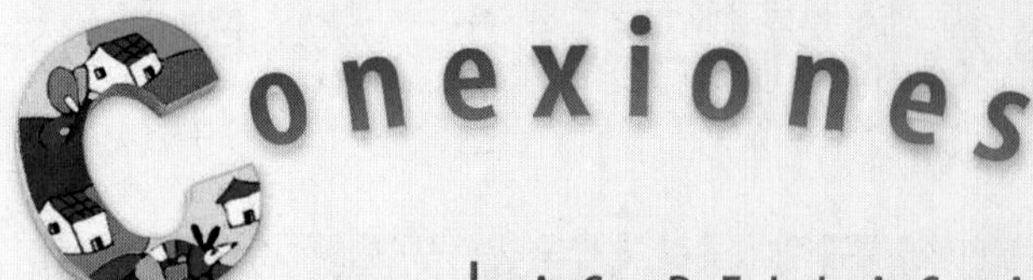

LAS BELLAS ARTES

LA MÚSICA

Music does not attempt to reproduce what we see in the world in such a tangible way as do painting and literature. Music is, and has been, however, an integral part of the daily lives of people in even the most primitive cultures.

First let's take a look at the many cognates that exist in the language of music. Then let's read some general information about music. Finally, let's take a look at some special music of the Hispanic world.

In addition, many names of musical instruments are cognates: **el piano, el órgano, el violín, la viola, la guitarra, la trompeta, el clarinete, el saxofón, la flauta, el trombón.**

Música y músicos

Instrumentos musicales
Clasificamos los instrumentos musicales en cuatro grupos. Son los instrumentos de cuerda, los instrumentos de viento, los instrumentos de metal y los instrumentos de percusión. Dividimos la orquesta en secciones de cuerda, viento, metal y percusión.

Una orquesta y una banda
¿Cuál es la diferencia entre una orquesta y una banda? En una banda no hay instrumentos de cuerda. No hay violines ni violas, por ejemplo.

Learning From Photos

Los instrumentos Have students look at the illustration on page 308 and the photos on page 309. Ask them to find and identify instruments from each of the following categories: **los instrumentos de cuerda, de viento, de metal y de percusión.**

La ópera
La ópera es una obra teatral. Pero en una ópera los actores no hablan. Cantan al acompañamiento de una orquesta.

La música popular
Además de[1] la música clásica hay muchas variaciones de música popular. De influencia afroamericana hay jazz y «blues». Hay «reggae» de Jamaica.

De las islas hispanohablantes de las Antillas hay salsa y merengue. Hay una relación íntima entre el canto (la canción) y la danza (el baile) en la música latinoamericana. Por ejemplo, en la lengua quechua del área andina, una sola palabra—taqui—significa «canción y baile».

Ejemplos de la música típica de Latinoamérica
Un instrumento muy popular entre los indios andinos es la flauta. El yaraví es una canción muy popular. En quechua esta palabra significa «lamento». Es una canción triste. A veces cantan un yaraví pero a veces sólo lo tocan en la flauta sin cantar.

Un instrumento popular de los indígenas de Guatemala es la marimba. Hay orquestas de marimba que van de un pueblo a otro para tocar en las fiestas locales.

La banda mariachi es un pequeño grupo de músicos ambulantes. Tocan guitarras, violines y trompetas. La música mariachi tiene su origen en Guadalajara, México, en el estado de Jalisco.

La salsa, el merengue y el mambo de Cuba, Puerto Rico y la República Dominicana son canciones y bailes.

El cante jondo es una canción triste y espontánea de los gitanos[2] andaluces. Es apasionada y emocional como lo es también el baile flamenco.

Murcia, España

[1]Además de *In addition to*
[2]gitanos *gypsies*

Después de leer

A ¿Cuáles son? Identifiquen.
1. algunos instrumentos de cuerda
2. algunos instrumentos de viento
3. algunos instrumentos de metal

B Distintos tipos de música
Expliquen la diferencia entre una orquesta y una banda.

C ¿Sabes? Contesten.
1. ¿Qué es una ópera?
2. ¿Cuáles son algunos tipos de música popular?
3. ¿Entre qué hay una relación íntima en la música latinoamericana?

National Standards

Communities
If you have any Hispanic students in class, ask if they know any dances from their countries that they could perform for the class, or any musical groups who might put on a performance.

You could also ask them to bring in recordings from home to share with the class.

Learning From Photos

Cuzco, Perú The Indians from Cuzco, Perú are playing **una flauta.** There are several different types of flutes. Some are made from wood and others are ceramic. Note that the flute being played here is a single tube. The **zampoña** on page 287 has several tubes and is played somewhat like a harmonica but with a very different sound.
Guatemala The Indian from Guatemala is playing a typical **marimba.**
México The Mexican group is a **mariachi** band.
Murcia, España The guitarists and singers from Spain are called **tunos. Los tunos** form **una tuna** or **una estudiantina,** which is a musical group traditionally made up of university students. These groups go to various locales in the community, stopping to sing and play at each location. In Spain they go from restaurant to restaurant or **mesón** to **mesón.** When they finish their performance, they pass around a tambourine and their audience makes a donation. The **tunos** are popular only in Spain and in one town in Mexico, Guanajuato.

ANSWERS

Después de leer

A **1. el violín, la viola, la guitarra**
2. el clarinete, el saxófono, la flauta
3. la trompeta, el trombón

B **En una banda no hay instrumentos de cuerda.**

C **1. Es una obra teatral pero los actores no hablan. Cantan al acompañamiento de una orquesta.**
2. Unos tipos de música popular son: jazz, blues, reggae, salsa y merengue.
3. Hay una relación íntima en la música latinoamericana entre el canto (la canción) y la danza (el baile).

CAPÍTULO 10
Culminación

RECYCLING

The **Actividades orales** and the **Actividad escrita** allow students to use the vocabulary and structures from this chapter in open-ended, real-life settings.

Actividades orales

¡OJO! Encourage students to say as much as possible when they do these activities. Tell them not to be afraid of making mistakes since the goal of the activities is real-life communication.

Let students choose the activities they would like to take part in.

A TECHNOLOGY OPTION
Students may use the Portfolio feature on the CD-ROM to record their conversations in **Actividad A.**

Student Portfolio

Have students keep a notebook containing their best written work from each chapter. These selected writings can be based on assignments from the Student Textbook and the Writing Activities Workbook. The two activities on page 311 are examples of writing assignments that may be included in each student's portfolio.

In the Workbook, students will develop an organized autobiography **(Mi autobiografía).** These workbook pages may also become a part of their portfolio. See the Teacher's Manual for more information on the Student Portfolio.

Culminación

Actividades orales

A **Diversiones** Work with a classmate. Pretend you're on vacation in Cancún, México. You meet a Mexican teenager (your partner) who's interested in what you do for fun in your free time **(cuando tienes tiempo libre).** Tell him or her about your leisure activities, then your partner will tell you what he or she does.

B **Un día en el museo** With a classmate, look at the illustrations below that tell a story about the day José and Ana spent at the museum last Saturday. Ask each other as many questions about each of the illustrations as you can. Then answer each other's questions.

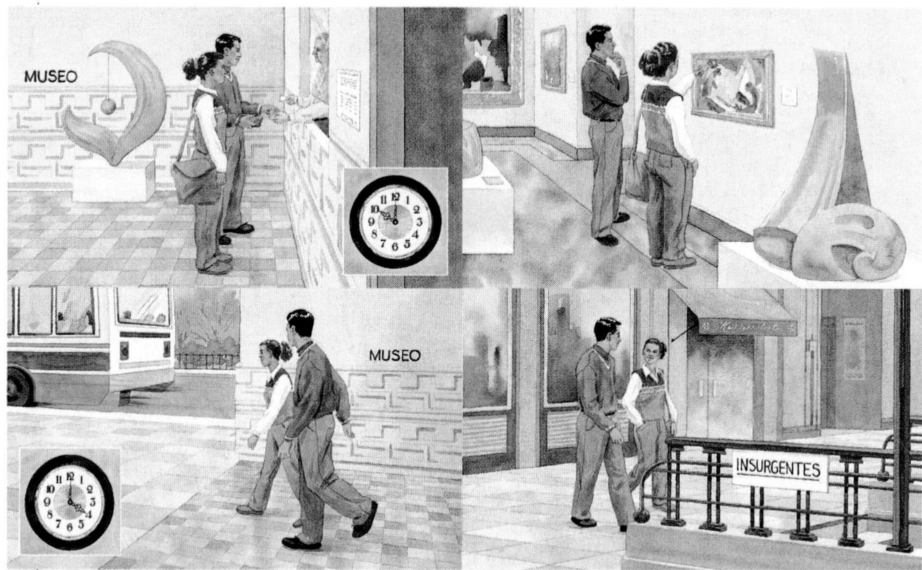

C **¡Vamos al cine!** With your classmates, see a Spanish film or play that is playing at a theater in your community. Afterwards, go out for a snack together and discuss the movie or play in Spanish. If there are no Spanish movies or plays in your community, try to rent a Spanish video that you can watch and discuss in class.

ANSWERS

Actividades orales

A Answers will vary. In addition to the leisure activities presented in this chapter, students might mention activities they learned to talk about in earlier chapters, such as listening to music, watching TV, going out to eat, playing sports, etc.

B Answers will vary; however, students should use the preterite in their answers.

C Answers will vary. The discussion may have to be conducted in English.

Independent Practice

Assign any of the following:

1. Activities, pages 310–311
2. Workbook, **Mi autobiografía,** page 128
3. Situation Cards
4. CD-ROM, Disc 3, Chapter 10, **Juego de repaso**

Actividad escrita

A **Una obra teatral** Prepare a poster in Spanish for your school play. Give all the necessary information to advertise **el espectáculo.**

Writing Strategy

Persuasive writing

Persuasive writing is writing that encourages a reader to do something or to accept an idea. Newspaper and magazine advertisements, as well as certain articles, are examples of persuasive writing. As you write, present a logical argument to encourage others to follow your line of thinking. Your writing should contain sufficient evidence to persuade readers to "buy into" what you are presenting. Explain how your evidence supports your argument; end by restating your argument.

Un reportaje

Your local newspaper has asked you to write an article to attract Spanish-speaking readers to a cultural event taking place in your hometown. You can write about a real or fictitious event. You have seen the event and you really liked it. Tell why as you try to convince or persuade your readers to go see it.

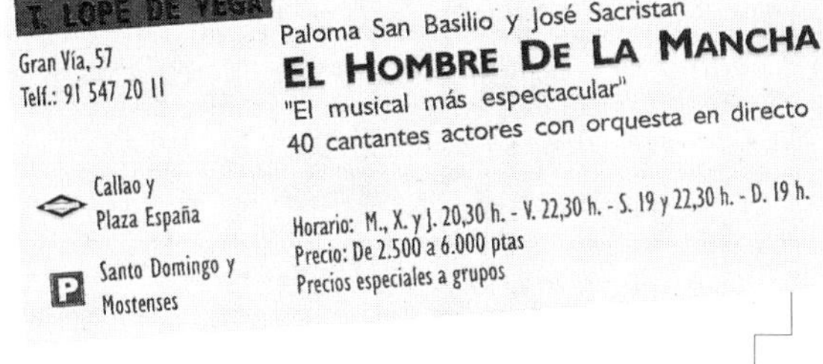

CAPÍTULO 10
Culminación

Actividad escrita

A Your class should ask students who are performing in the school play, and the Theatre Department for information for the posters. Display the best ones.

National Standards

Communities

If you are able to organize a field trip to a Spanish movie or play in your community, as suggested in **Actividad C** on page 310, you will give your students the opportunity to use their Spanish beyond the school setting.

Actividad A on this page encourages students to share their knowledge of Spanish with other students in their school.

Writing Strategy

Persuasive writing

A. Have students read the Writing Strategy on page 311.

B. Before students begin to write their letters, they should make a list of reasons why readers should see the event.

TECHNOLOGY OPTION Students can use the Portfolio feature on the CD-ROM to write this letter.

C. Even though *Man of La Mancha* is in English, you may want to play a song from the musical.

ANSWERS

Actividad escrita

A Posters should include the following information: **¿Qué es? ¿Cuánto es? ¿Dónde es? ¿Cuánto cuestan los boletos?**

Writing Strategy

Letters will vary in content, based on the event.

ASSESSMENT RESOURCES

- Chapter Quizzes
- Testing Program
- Computer Testmaker
- Situation Cards
- Communication Transparency C-10
- Performance Assessment
- **Maratón mental** Videoquiz

VOCABULARY REVIEW

The words and phrases in the **Vocabulario** have been taught for productive use in this chapter. They are summarized here as a resource for both students and teacher. This list also serves as a convenient resource for the **Culminación** activities on pages 310 and 311. There are approximately 15 cognates in this vocabulary list. Have students find them.

Vocabulario

DISCUSSING A MOVIE THEATER

el cine
la taquilla, la boletería
la entrada, el boleto
la sesión
la cola
la butaca
la fila
la pantalla
la película, el film
en versión original
con subtítulos
doblado(a)

DESCRIBING A MUSEUM VISIT

el museo
la exposición
el mural
el cuadro
la estatua
el/la artista
el/la escultor(a)

DESCRIBING A PLAY

el teatro
la escena
el escenario
el telón
el actor
la actriz
la representación
la obra teatral
el público

DESCRIBING CULTURAL EVENTS AND ACTIVITIES

una diversión cultural
ver una película (un espectáculo)
dar una representación
entrar en escena
aplaudir
salir del teatro

DISCUSSING TRANSPORTATION

perder el autobús (la guagua, el camión)
la estación de metro

OTHER USEFUL EXPRESSIONS

el/la joven
delante de
luego

For the Younger Student

¡Vamos a cantar! Ask the music teacher to come in and teach some of the songs from the Audio Program (Cassette 1A/CD1) to your students. If your students are musically inclined, you may wish to ask them if they would like to perform a Spanish song in the school concert.

HISTORY CONNECTION

El Alcázar de Segovia (page 313)
This fortress possibly dates from Roman times. It was expanded in the 14th and 15th centuries and completely redone in 1862 after being destroyed by fire when it was used as an artillery school. The beautiful towers of the Alcázar look as if they have been carved out of sugar.

TECNOTUR

EL VIDEO

¡Buen viaje!

EPISODIO 10 ▸ Diversiones culturales

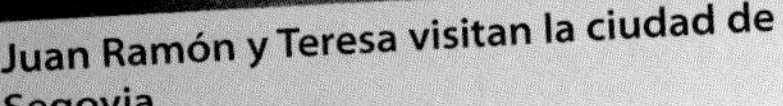

Juan Ramón y Teresa visitan la ciudad de Segovia.

Uno de los lugares interesantes que visitaron fue el famoso Alcázar de Segovia.

CD-ROM

Expansión cultural

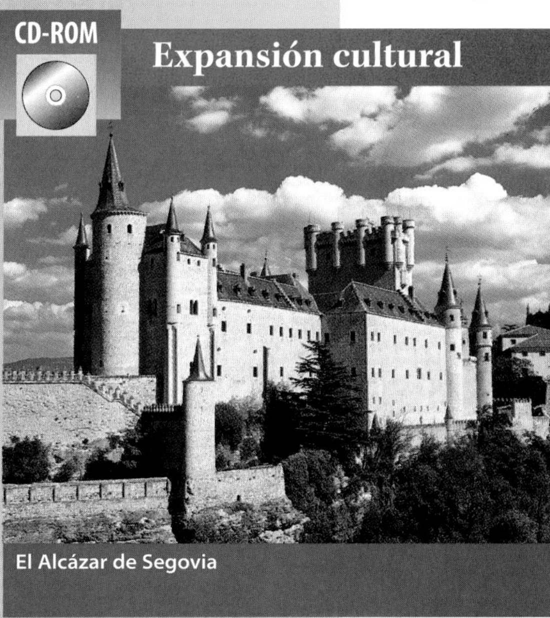

El Alcázar de Segovia

interNET CONNECTION

In this video episode Teresa and Juan Ramón discuss what cultural activities they enjoy and what they like to do on weekends when they go out with their friends. To find out what's playing at the movies tonight in a Spanish-speaking city, go to the Capítulo 10 Internet activity at the Glencoe Foreign Language Web site:

http://www.glencoe.com/sec/fl

Video Synopsis

This episode takes place in Segovia. Teresa and Juan Ramón discuss their itinerary as they stroll through the town. They check Juan Ramón's video camera along the way to make sure he is getting the footage. Then the conversation turns to museums and art. We find out that each one has a favorite artist. They stroll along again and discuss the activities they like to do with their friends. They finish their tour at the gardens of La Granja, where Juan Ramón enthusiastically teaches Teresa two dances from his native Puerto Rico, the salsa and the merengue.

OVERVIEW

This page previews three key multimedia components of the **Glencoe Spanish** series. Each reinforces the material taught in Chapter 10 in a unique manner.

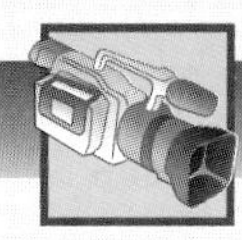

VIDEO

The Video Program allows students to see how the chapter vocabulary and structures are used by native speakers within an engaging story line. For maximum reinforcement, show the video episode as a final activity for Chapter 10.

A. These two photos shown highlights from the Chapter 10 video episode. Before watching it, ask students the following questions: **¿Es Segovia una ciudad moderna o antigua? ¿Cómo llegan al Alcázar, en carro o a pie?**

CD-ROM

A. The **Expansión cultural** photo shows a more complete view of **El Alcázar de Segovia** that Juan Ramón and Teresa visit.

B. In the CD-ROM version of **Expansión cultural,** students can listen to additional recorded information about **El Alcázar.**

INTERNET

Teacher Information and Student Worksheets for this activity can be accessed at the Web site.

Chapter 11 Overview

SCOPE AND SEQUENCE pages 314–341

TOPICS	FUNCTIONS	STRUCTURE	CULTURE
◆ Air travel ◆ Travel-related activities	◆ How to check in for a flight ◆ How to talk about services on board the plane ◆ How to talk about the plane crew ◆ How to get through the airport after deplaning ◆ How to tell what you and others are presently doing ◆ How to tell what you and others know	◆ **Hacer, poner, traer, salir** in the present ◆ The present progressive ◆ **Saber** and **conocer** in the present	◆ The importance of air travel in Latin America ◆ The Andes Mountains ◆ The Amazon River ◆ Comparing the flight time from New York to Madrid versus the flight time from Caracas to Buenos Aires ◆ The Nazca lines of Peru ◆ Everyday finances in the Spanish-speaking world ◆ Vistas de España

CHAPTER 11 RESOURCES

PRINT	MULTIMEDIA
Planning Resources	
Lesson Plans	Interactive Lesson Planner
Block Scheduling Lesson Plans	
Reinforcement Resources	
Writing Activities Workbook	Transparencies Binder
Student Tape Manual	Audiocassette/Compact Disc Program
Video Activities Booklet	Videocassette/Videodisc Program
Web Site User's Guide	Online Internet Activities
	Electronic Teacher's Classroom Resources
Assessment Resources	
Situation Cards	**Maratón mental** Mindjogger Videoquiz
Chapter Quizzes	Testmaker Computer Software (Macintosh/Windows)
Testing Program	Listening Comprehension Audiocassette/Compact Disc
Performance Assessment	Communication Transparency: C-11
Motivational Resources	
Expansion Activities	Café Glencoe: www.cafe.glencoe.com
	Keypal Internet Activities
Enrichment	
Spanish for Spanish Speakers	

Chapter 11 Planning Guide

SECTION	PAGES	SECTION RESOURCES
Vocabulario Palabras 1 **Antes del vuelo**	316–319	Vocabulary Transparencies 11.1 Audiocassette 7A/ Compact Disc 6 Student Tape Manual, TE, pages 127–129 Workbook, pages 129–130 Chapter Quizzes, page 55 CD-ROM, Disc 3, pages 316–319
Vocabulario Palabras 2 **Después del vuelo** **El vuelo** **La tripulación**	320–323	Vocabulary Transparencies 11.2 Audiocassette 7A/ Compact Disc 6 Student Tape Manual, TE, pages 129–131 Workbook, pages 131–132 Chapter Quizzes, page 56 CD-ROM, Disc 3, pages 320–323
Estructura **Hacer, poner, traer, salir en el presente** **El presente progresivo** **Saber y conocer en el presente**	324–329	Workbook, pages 133–137 Audiocassette 7A/Compact Disc 6 Student Tape Manual, TE, pages 131–133 Chapter Quizzes, pages 57–59 Computer Testmaker CD-ROM, Disc 3, pages 324–329
Conversación **Está saliendo nuestro vuelo.** **Pronunciación: La consonante r**	330–331	Audiocassette 7A/Compact Disc 6 Student Tape Manual, TE, pages 134–135 CD-ROM, Disc 3, pages 330–331
Lecturas culturales **El avión en la América del Sur** **Distancias y tiempo de vuelo *(opcional)*** **Las líneas de Nazca *(opcional)***	332–335	Testing Program, page 64 CD-ROM, Disc 3, pages 332–335
Conexiones **Las finanzas *(opcional)***	336–337	Testing Program, page 65 CD-ROM, Disc 3, pages 336–337
Culminación **Actividades orales** **Actividades escritas** **Vocabulario** **Tecnotur**	338–341	**¡Buen viaje!** Video, Episode 11 Video Activities, pages 106–109 Internet Activities www.glencoe.com/sec/fl Testing Program, pages 61–64; 113; 145; 170–171 CD-ROM, Disc 3, pages 338–341

OVERVIEW

In this chapter students will learn the vocabulary associated with air travel and airports. (Vocabulary for on board the plane is presented in **¡Buen viaje! Level 2**). In order to describe their travel, students will learn the present tense of verbs with a **g** in the **yo** form, as well as the present progressive.

Students will also learn about the importance of air travel in South America because of its geographical characteristics.

National Standards

Communication

In Chapter 11 students will communicate in Spanish on the following topics:

- checking in at the airport
- going through security and finding their departure gate
- going through customs and passport control
- claiming their bags

Students will obtain and provide information about taking a flight and about procedures at an airport. They will learn to engage in conversations with various types of airline employees.

CAPÍTULO 11

Un viaje en avión

Objetivos

In this chapter you will learn to do the following:

- check in for a flight
- talk about some services on board the plane
- get through the airport after deplaning
- tell what you or others are currently doing
- tell what you know and whom you know
- discuss the importance of air travel in South America

The **Glencoe Foreign Language Web site (http://www.glencoe.com/sec/fl)** offers three options that enable you and your students to experience the Spanish-speaking world via the Internet:

- The online **Actividades** are correlated to the chapters and utilize Hispanic Web sites around the world. For the Chapter 11 activity, see student page 341.
- The **Correspondencia electrónica** section provides information on how to set up a keypal (pen pal) exchange between your class and a class in the Spanish-speaking world.
- At **Café Glencoe,** the interactive "after-school" section of the site, you and your students can access a variety of additional online resources, including interactive games.

trescientos quince 315

CAPÍTULO 11

Spotlight On Culture

Artefacto The two decorative items we see here are Panamanian **molas.** A **mola** is a type of blouse popular particularly in Panama and Colombia. It is made of multicolored cloth. The designs on many **molas** are so beautiful that people use them as wall hangings.

The Cuna Indians of Panama are famous for their **molas.** In many areas the designs on a **mola** depict Christian, as well as local themes. This is true of many other Indian handicrafts. On a simple **mola,** for example, one might see a cross, a bird-god, and a political figure.

Fotografía This plane is landing at the airport in Santo Domingo in the Dominican Republic.

Pacing

Chapter 11 will require approximately eight to ten days. Pacing will vary according to the length of the class, the age of your students, and student aptitude.

Block Scheduling

The extended timeframe provided by block scheduling affords you the opportunity to implement a greater number of activities and projects to motivate and involve your students. See the Block Scheduling Lesson Plans Booklet for suggestions on how to present the chapter material within a block scheduling framework.

Chapter Projects

Pasaporte hispano Have each student create his or her Spanish passport. Have students fill out forms in Spanish with their name, address, nationality, birth date, metric weight, etc. Students could use a real photo or draw a picture of themselves. Covers can be made of construction paper.

Visita al aeropuerto If your students have had little opportunity to travel, you may want to plan a field trip to a nearby airport. This is a wonderful enrichment experience for some students. As you tour the airport, have them use as much of their Spanish vocabulary as possible.

CAPÍTULO 11
Vocabulario

PALABRAS 1

RESOURCES

- Vocabulary Transparencies 11.1 (A & B)
- Student Tape Manual, TE, pages 127–129
- Audiocassette 7A/CD6
- Workbook, pages 129–130
- Quiz 1, page 55
- CD-ROM, Disc 3, pages 316–319

Bell Ringer Review

Use BRR Transparency 11-1, or write the following on the board: Write a sentence using each of the following phrases.

en autobús
en carro (en coche)
en el bus escolar
en taxi
ir a pie

TEACHING VOCABULARY

A. Have students close their books. Using Vocabulary Transparencies 11.1 (A & B), introduce the words on pages 316–317. Have students repeat after you or Cassette 7A/Compact Disc 6 as you point to the illustrations.

B. Ask questions such as **¿Es la maletera? ¿Qué es? ¿Es la maletera del taxi?**

C. When presenting the contextualized sentences, you may wish to ask questions that progress from the simple to the more complex. For example: **¿Hace Clarita un viaje? ¿Quién hace un viaje? ¿Hace un viaje a España o a la América del Sur? ¿Adónde hace un viaje?**

Vocabulario

PALABRAS 1

Antes del vuelo

La agente revisa el pasaporte y el boleto.

Total Physical Response

Getting ready

If students don't already know the meaning of **llámalo, se para,** and **busca**, teach these expressions by using the appropriate gestures as you say each expression.

Begin

___, ven acá. Imagínate que vas a hacer un viaje. Tienes que ir al aeropuerto.
Aquí viene un taxi. Llámalo.
El taxi se para. Pon tu maleta en la maletera.
Abre la puerta.
Sube al taxi y siéntate.
Llegas al aeropuerto. Págale al taxista.
Dale el dinero.
Abre la puerta.
Baja (Bájate) del taxi.
Toma tu maleta.
Entra en el aeropuerto.
Mira la pantalla de salidas.
Busca el mostrador de la línea aérea.
Ve al mostrador de la línea aérea.
Pon tu maleta en la báscula.
Gracias, ___. Siéntate.

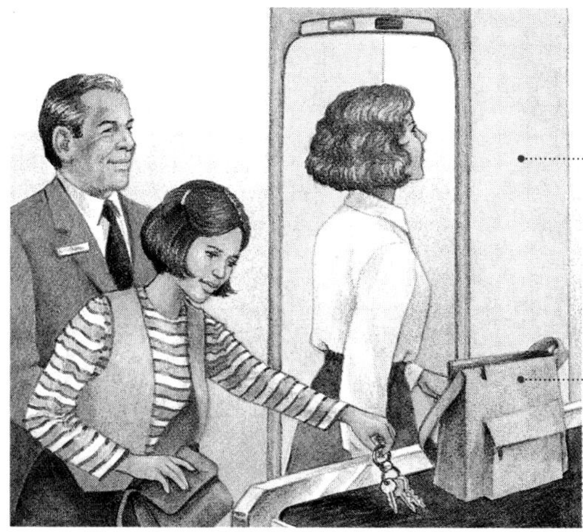

Los pasajeros están pasando por el control de seguridad.

Clarita hace un viaje en avión.
Hace un viaje a la América del Sur.
Toma un vuelo a Lima.
Clarita está facturando su equipaje.
Pone sus maletas en la báscula.
El agente pone un talón en cada maleta.

Los pasajeros están esperando en la puerta de salida.
El avión sale de la puerta número catorce.
El vuelo sale a tiempo.
No sale tarde. No sale con una demora.

ABOUT THE SPANISH LANGUAGE

You may wish to give students the following additional vocabulary and information concerning the words they have learned.

- **La tarjeta de embarque** is universally understood, as is **el pase de abordar.** Students will also hear **el pasabordo.**
- Explain to students that they are going to see and hear the words **el asiento** and **la plaza.** They both mean *seat* but **asiento** is more the *"physical" seat.* One will often hear: **Quiero una plaza en la sección de no fumar.**
- The older type of arrival and departure board is **el tablero**. The more modern airports have a TV screen, **la pantalla.**
- **El billete** is used in Spain for ticket**, el boleto** throughout Latin America.
- **La maletera** and **el maletero** are heard with equal frequency for the trunk of a car. **El baúl** is also used in certain areas.
- **El talón** is the baggage tag that is used for checked baggage. The personal identification tag is **una etiqueta**.
- The large scale shown in the illustration (page 317) is **una báscula. Básculas** have a flat surface and are usually used for heavier weights**. Una balanza** is a scale with weights on one end or the hanging scale used for produce.
- **Facturar** means to check luggage through to a destination. **Depositar** means to check something for safe-keeping, as in a checkroom.
- In Spanish there is no direct equivalent of *to check in.* What is heard is **Señores pasajeros, favor de presentarse en el mostrador.**

Cooperative Learning

Al aeropuerto Divide the class into three or four groups, depending on the class size. Each member of each group contributes two activities that could take place at an airport. Each group writes down all its activities and then pantomimes them in front of the class. Members of the other teams guess and say what they are doing in Spanish.

¡OJO! **Práctica** When students are doing the **Práctica** activities, accept any answer that makes sense. The purpose of these activities is to have students use the new vocabulary. They are not factual recall activities. Thus, do not expect students to remember specific information from the vocabulary presentation when answering. If you wish, have students use the photo on this page as a stimulus, when possible.
Historieta Each time **Historieta** appears, it means that the answers to the activity form a short story. Encourage students to look at the title of the **Historieta** since it can sometimes help them do the activity.

Writing Development

Have students write the answers to **Práctica A** in one paragraph to illustrate how all of the items tell a story.

B Students may have difficulty answering Item 4. Have them guess what **Lis** stands for.

C Have students refer to the boarding pass in **Práctica B** as they do **Práctica C.**

Learning From Realia

La tarjeta de embarque With regard to the boarding pass on page 318, the code **C** under **Clase** is for business class. Different carriers have different names for the categories. **Iberia** calls their business class **Clase preferente.**

Práctica

A HISTORIETA En el aeropuerto

Contesten.

1. ¿Hace Lupe un viaje a la América del Sur?
2. ¿Está en el aeropuerto?
3. ¿Está hablando con la agente de la línea aérea?
4. ¿Dónde pone sus maletas?
5. ¿Está facturando su equipaje a Bogotá?
6. ¿Pone la agente un talón en cada maleta?
7. ¿Revisa la agente su boleto?
8. ¿Tiene Lupe su tarjeta de embarque?
9. ¿De qué puerta va a salir su vuelo?

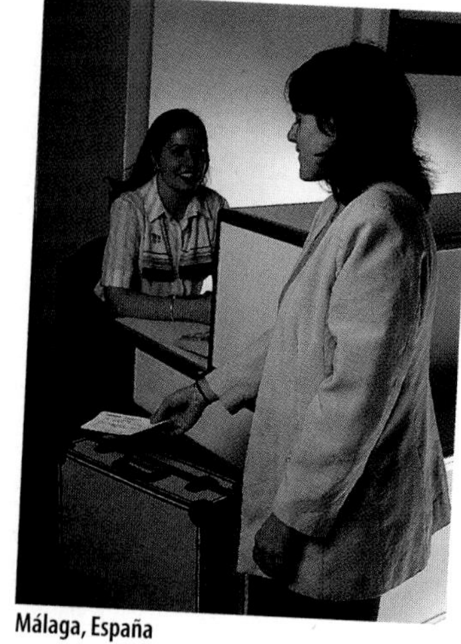

Málaga, España

B La tarjeta de embarque

Den la información siguiente.

1. el nombre de la línea aérea
2. el número del vuelo
3. el destino del vuelo
4. el aeropuerto de salida
5. la hora de embarque
6. la fecha del vuelo, el día que sale

C ¿Dónde está su asiento?

Completen según la tarjeta de embarque.

1. ¿Cuál es la letra del asiento que tiene el pasajero?
2. ¿En qué fila está el asiento?
3. ¿De qué puerta sale el avión?
4. ¿Tiene que conservar el pasajero la tarjeta durante el vuelo?
5. ¿Está su asiento en la sección de fumar o de no fumar?

ANSWERS

Práctica

A
1. **Sí, Lupe hace un viaje a la América del Sur.**
2. **Sí, está en el aeropuerto.**
3. **Sí, está hablando con la agente de la línea aérea.**
4. **Pone sus maletas en la báscula.**
5. **Sí, está facturando su equipaje a Bogotá.**
6. **Sí, la agente pone un talón en cada maleta.**
7. **Sí, la agente revisa su boleto.**
8. **Sí, Lupe tiene su tarjeta de embarque.**
9. **Su vuelo va a salir de la puerta número ___.**

B
1. **Iberia**
2. **(IB)3127**
3. **Madrid**
4. **Lisboa**
5. **12:45**
6. **22 de abril**

C
1. **La letra del asiento es A.**
2. **El asiento está en la fila 8.**
3. **El avión sale de la puerta 15.**
4. **Sí, el pasajero tiene que conservar la tarjeta durante el vuelo.**
5. **Su asiento está en la sección de no fumar.**

D Historieta Antes de la salida

Escojan.

1. ____ indica el asiento que tiene el pasajero a bordo del avión.
   a. El talón **b.** La tarjeta de embarque **c.** El boleto
2. Bogotá es ____ del vuelo.
   a. el número **b.** la ciudad **c.** el destino
3. Inspeccionan el equipaje de mano de los pasajeros en ____.
   a. el mostrador de la línea aérea **b.** el control de seguridad
   c. la puerta de salida
4. El vuelo para Bogotá sale ____ número cinco.
   a. del mostrador **b.** del control **c.** de la puerta
5. Los pasajeros están ____ por el control de seguridad.
   a. saliendo **b.** facturando **c.** pasando

Actividades comunicativas

A En el aeropuerto Work with a classmate. You're checking in at the airport for your flight to Quito, Ecuador. Have a conversation with the airline agent (your partner) at the ticket counter.

B Un vuelo Work with a classmate. Look at the following photograph. You are a passenger on this flight. Tell as much as you can about your experience at the airport.

D You may wish to have more able students make up a sentence using the incorrect choices from **Práctica D.**

Actividades comunicativas

¡OJO! Práctica versus Actividades comunicativas All activities which provide guided practice are labeled **Práctica.** The more open-ended communicative activities are labeled **Actividades comunicativas.**

A Students can review the illustration on page 316 to get them started.

TECHNOLOGY OPTION Students may use the Portfolio feature on the CD-ROM to do **Actividad A.**

B The most logical way to do this activity would be to use the preterite.

Independent Practice

Assign any of the following:
1. Workbook, **Palabras 1,** pages 129–130
2. Activities, pages 318–319
3. CD-ROM, Disc 3, pages 316–319

ANSWERS

Práctica

D 1. b
2. c
3. b
4. c
5. c

Actividades comunicativas

A Answers will vary.

B Answers will vary.

RESOURCES

- Vocabulary Transparencies 11.2 (A & B)
- Student Tape Manual, TE, pages 129–131
- Audiocassette 7A/CD6
- Workbook, pages 131–132
- Quiz 2, page 56
- CD-ROM, Disc 3, pages 320–323

Bell Ringer Review

Use BRR Transparency 11-2, or write the following on the board: Write down where some of your relatives live and what means of transportation you use to visit them.

TEACHING VOCABULARY

A. Have students look at Vocabulary Transparencies 11.2 (A & B) as they repeat each word or expression after you, or the recording on Cassette 7A/Compact Disc 6.

B. As you present the new vocabulary, you may intersperse comprehension questions. For example: **¿Los pasajeros tienen que pasar por el control de pasaportes? ¿Los pasajeros necesitan pasaporte cuando llegan de un país extranjero? ¿Qué abre la agente de aduana? ¿Qué inspecciona?**

Vocabulario

Después del vuelo

Cuando los pasajeros desembarcan, tienen que pasar por el control de pasaportes.
Tienen que pasar por el control de pasaportes cuando llegan de un país extranjero.

Los pasajeros están reclamando (recogiendo) sus maletas.

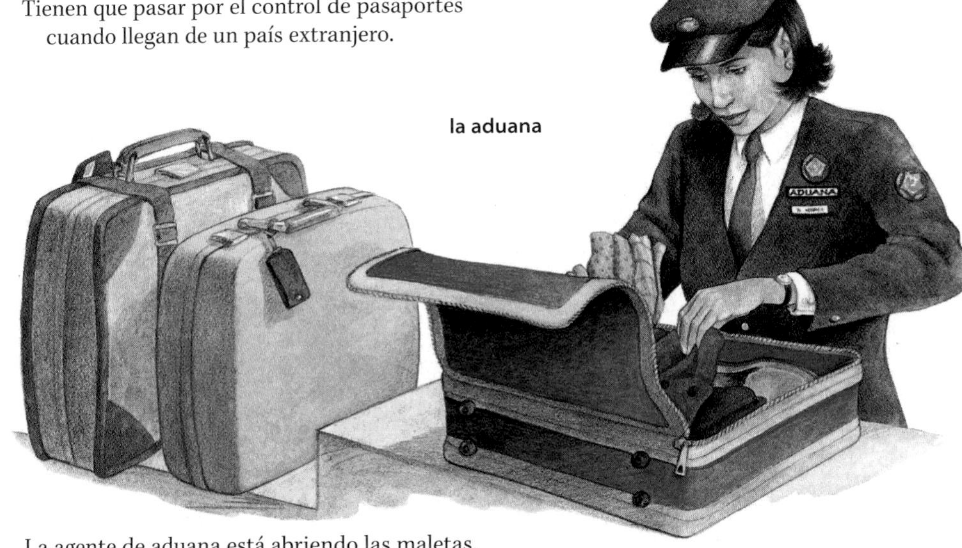

La agente de aduana está abriendo las maletas.
Está inspeccionando el equipaje.
Quiere saber lo que está en las maletas.

Total Physical Response

Begin

___, ven acá, por favor.
Tu vuelo está llegando. Vas a desembarcar.
Dile «adiós» a la asistente de vuelo.
Toma tu equipaje de mano.
Sal o baja del avión.
Aquí estás en el control de pasaportes.
Pasa por el control de pasaportes.
Dale tu pasaporte al agente.
Tienes que reclamar tu equipaje. Está llegando. Tienes dos maletas.
Aquí llega una de tus maletas. Toma tu maleta.
Aquí viene la otra. Tómala.
Ahora estás en la aduana.
Abre tu maleta para la agente de aduana.
Gracias, ___. Siéntate.

El vuelo

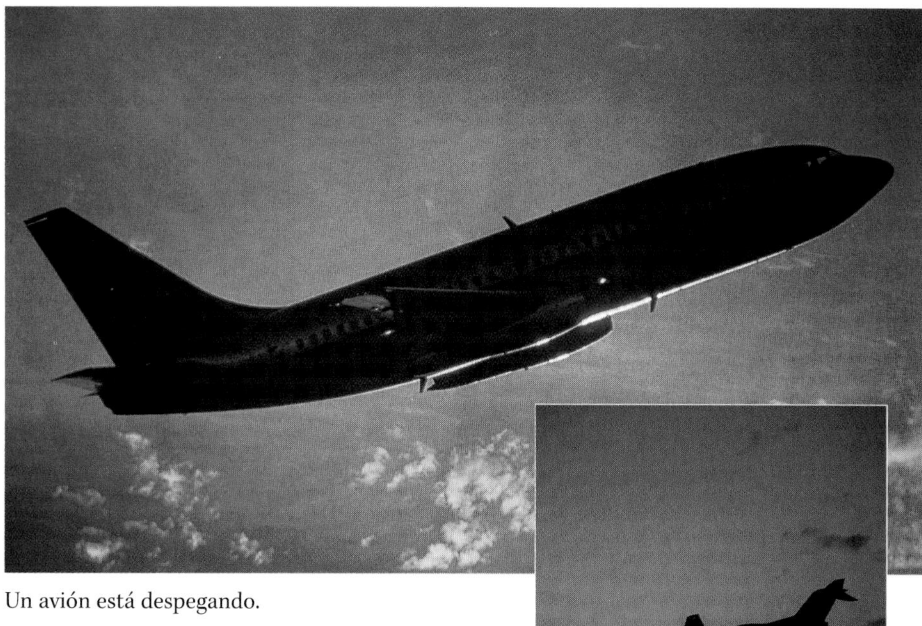

Un avión está despegando.

Otro avión está aterrizando.

La tripulación

La tripulación trabaja a bordo del avión.
Los asistentes de vuelo les dan la bienvenida a los pasajeros.

VOCABULARY EXPANSION

You may wish to teach students the following:

El avión sale para Madrid.
Es un vuelo *con destino* a Madrid.
El avión llega (viene) de Madrid.
Es un vuelo *procedente* de Madrid.

Did You Know?

En la aduana In recent years, customs formalities have become less complicated in many countries (but not all). In many cases, tourists with nothing to declare can follow a green arrow and pass though customs without having to open their suitcases.

Líneas aéreas Many airlines of Spain and Latin America are nationalized, that is, owned by the government. However, there is presently a move toward privatization of some national industries and the airline industry is one of them.

ABOUT THE SPANISH LANGUAGE

Other ways to express **el/la asistente de vuelo** are **el/la sobrecargo(a), el/la aeromozo(a). La azafata** is used in Spain for a female flight attendant. The original meaning of **azafata** was a *queen's lady-in-waiting.*

Práctica

A After going over **Práctica A,** have students retell the story in their own words.

B After going over **Práctica B,** have students correct the false statements.

Learning From Realia

Aeropuerto Madrid-Barajas
Ask students the following question: **¿Cuál es el nombre del aeropuerto de Madrid?**

Práctica

Málaga, España

A HISTORIETA La llegada

Contesten.

1. Cuando el avión aterriza, ¿abordan o desembarcan los pasajeros?
2. ¿Tienen que pasar por el control de pasaportes cuando llegan a un país extranjero?
3. ¿Van los pasajeros al reclamo de equipaje?
4. ¿Reclaman su equipaje?
5. ¿Tienen que pasar por la aduana?
6. ¿Abre las maletas el agente?

B **¿Sí o no?** Digan que sí o que no.

1. El avión aterriza cuando sale.
2. El avión despega cuando llega a su destino.
3. Un vuelo internacional es un vuelo que va a un país extranjero.
4. Los agentes de la línea aérea que trabajan en el mostrador en el aeropuerto son miembros de la tripulación.
5. La tripulación consiste en los empleados que trabajan a bordo del avión.

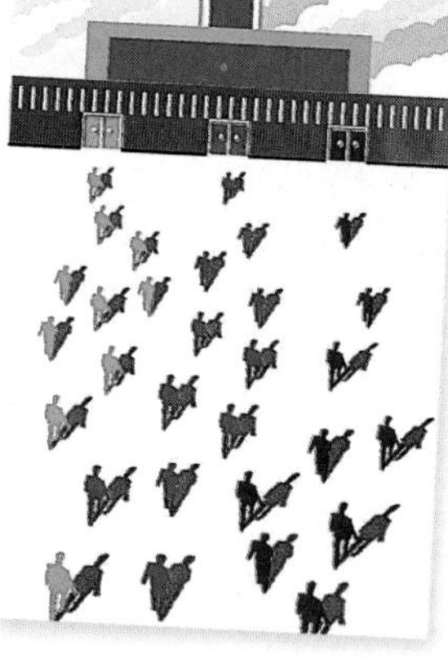

C **Pareo** Busquen una palabra relacionada.

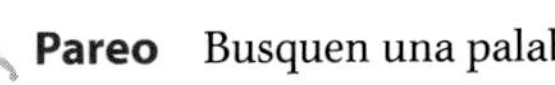

1. asistir	**a.** la llegada
2. controlar	**b.** la salida
3. reclamar	**c.** el asistente, la asistenta
4. inspeccionar	**d.** el despegue
5. despegar	**e.** el aterrizaje
6. aterrizar	**f.** el control
7. salir	**g.** la inspección
8. llegar	**h.** el reclamo
9. embarcar	**i.** el vuelo
10. volar	**j.** el embarque

ANSWERS

Práctica

A
1. **Cuando el avión aterriza, los pasajeros desembarcan.**
2. **Sí, tienen que pasar por el control de pasaportes cuando llegan a un país extranjero.**
3. **Sí, los pasajeros van al reclamo de equipaje.**
4. **Sí, reclaman su equipaje.**
5. **Sí, tienen que pasar por la aduana.**
6. **Sí, el agente abre las maletas.**

B
1. **No.**
2. **No.**
3. **Sí.**
4. **No.**
5. **Sí.**

C
1. **c**
2. **f**
3. **h**
4. **g**
5. **d**
6. **e**
7. **b**
8. **a**
9. **j**
10. **i**

Actividades comunicativas

A **¿Qué tenemos que hacer?** You're on a flight to Caracas. The person seated next to you (your partner) has never flown before. He or she is confused as to what you have to do when you get off the plane. Be as helpful as possible in answering his or her questions.

B **Un trabajo** Work with a classmate. You got a part-time job working at the airport because you can speak Spanish. You are called upon to help the Spanish-speaking passengers. In just one hour, the following situations need your attention. Help each of the following passengers.

1. A person is leaving on flight 125 for Chicago. He doesn't know if it's leaving on time. Help him out.
2. Another passenger is confused. He doesn't know his flight number to New York. Let him know what it is. Be extra helpful and let him know what time his flight leaves.
3. Another passenger is in a real hurry. She's changing **(cambiar)** flights and wants to know what gate to go to for her flight to Los Angeles. Tell her.
4. A young woman missed her flight and has to change her ticket. Go with her to the airline counter and explain to her what the agent says she has to do.

C **Una tarjeta de embarque** This is a boarding card for a flight you are about to take. Tell a classmate (your partner) all you can about your flight based on the information on the card.

Actividades comunicativas

A Tell students that in real life, this person could also be nervous or frightened. The partner who has never flown before should begin the conversation by saying: **Perdón, ¿qué tengo que hacer cuando desembarco del avión (cuando llegamos al aeropuerto)?**

B Students should take turns being the part-time worker and the passenger in distress. The student playing the passenger should explain briefly what the problem is in each case, according to the information provided on page 323.

C Students may need some help figuring out the codes on the Lan Chile boarding pass. See Learning From Realia below for the necessary information. Remind students that **18** means **kilos,** not pounds.

EXPANSION Have students figure out how much the two bags weigh in pounds (1 kilo = 2.2 lbs.).

Learning From Realia

Lan Chile Tell students that Lan Chile is the national airline carrier of Chile.

It will probably be necessary to explain some of the codes on this boarding pass, or you may wish to have students guess.

LPB **La Paz, Bolivia**
SCL **Santiago de Chile**
LA **Lan Chile**

The code **Y** under **clase** indicates coach class, as in the case of U.S. airlines.

ANSWERS

Actividades comunicativas

A Students should use the vocabulary from **Palabras 1** and **2.**

B Answers will vary.

C Answers will vary, but may include:
El avión sale de La Paz y va a Santiago.
El número del vuelo es LA961.
El avión sale de La Paz el 26 de enero a las 12:45 de la tarde.
La hora de embarque es a las 11:45.
El avión sale de la puerta P.
Mi asiento es 9A.
Tengo dos maletas. Pesan 18 kilos.

RESOURCES

- Workbook, pages 133–137
- Student Tape Manual, TE, pages 131–133
- Audiocassette 7A/CD6
- Structure Transparency S-11
- Quizzes 3–5, pages 57–59
- Computer Testmaker
- CD-ROM, Disc 3, pages 296–301

Bell Ringer Review

Use BRR Transparency 11-3, or write the following on the board:
Do the following.

1. Write down five things that you have.
2. Write down five things that you and a friend have to do.

TEACHING STRUCTURE

Telling what people do

A. Have students open their books to page 324. You may wish to say the infinitives aloud from Step 1.

B. Then point to yourself as you say **hago, pongo, traigo, salgo.**

C. Write the **yo** forms on the board and ask students what they have in common.

D. Have students repeat the **yo** forms.

E. Write the other forms on the board and indicate to students that they are the same as any regular **-er** or **-ir** verb they have already learned. These endings actually serve as a review of **-er** and **-ir** verbs.

F. For Step 2, have students repeat the forms of the verb **venir.** Point out that it has a **g** in the **yo** form; it also has a stem change, the same as **querer** or **preferir.**

G. Now lead students through Steps 3 and 4.

Estructura

Telling what people do
Hacer, poner, traer, salir en el presente

1. The verbs **hacer** *(to do, to make)*, **poner, traer** *(to bring)*, and **salir** have an irregular **yo** form. The **yo** form has a **g.** All other forms are the same as those of a regular **-er** or **-ir** verb.

INFINITIVE	hacer	poner	traer	salir
yo	hago	pongo	traigo	salgo
tú	haces	pones	traes	sales
él, ella, Ud.	hace	pone	trae	sale
nosotros(as)	hacemos	ponemos	traemos	salimos
vosotros(as)	*hacéis*	*ponéis*	*traéis*	*salís*
ellos, ellas, Uds.	hacen	ponen	traen	salen

2. The verb **venir** *(to come)* also has an irregular **yo** form. Note that in addition it has a stem change **e → ie** in all forms except **nosotros** and **vosotros.**

   VENIR **vengo** **vienes** **viene** **venimos** ***venís*** **vienen**

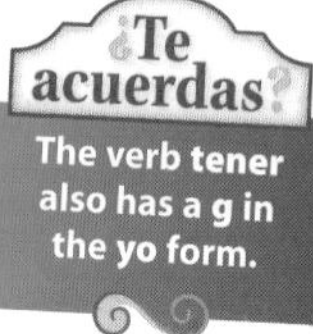

3. The verb **hacer** means "to do" or "to make." The question **¿Qué haces?** or **¿Qué hace Ud.?** means "What are you doing?" or "What do you do?" In Spanish, you will almost always answer these questions with a different verb.

   ¿Qué haces? Trabajo en el aeropuerto.

4. The verb **hacer** is used in many idiomatic expressions. An idiomatic expression is one that does not translate directly from one language to another. The expression **hacer un viaje** *(to take a trip)* is an idiomatic expression because in Spanish the verb **hacer** is used whereas in English we use the verb *to take.* Another idiomatic expression is **hacer la maleta** which means "to pack a suitcase."

"Transportación Terrestre Aeropuerto",
S.A. de C.V.
R.F.C. TTA - 880304 - 4R9
Alameda de León 1-G Tel. 4-43-50 Oaxaca,Oax.
Nº 15368 CLIENTE
Incluido Seguro del Viajero
Viaje Especial N$ 90.00
Nombre
Domicilio
ZONA 2 Fecha

Práctica

A HISTORIETA Un viaje en avión

Contesten.

1. ¿Haces un viaje?
2. ¿Haces un viaje a Europa?
3. ¿Haces un viaje a España?
4. ¿Sales para el aeropuerto?
5. ¿Sales en coche o en taxi?
6. ¿Traes equipaje?
7. ¿Pones el equipaje en la maletera del taxi?
8. En el aeropuerto, ¿pones el equipaje en la báscula?
9. ¿En qué vuelo sales?
10. ¿Sales de la puerta de salida número ocho?

Cádiz, España

B HISTORIETA Al aeropuerto

Sigan el modelo.

1. Ellos salen para el aeropuerto.
2. Ellos salen en taxi.
3. Ellos traen mucho equipaje.
4. Ellos ponen las maletas en la maletera.
5. Ellos salen a las seis.
6. Ellos vienen solos.

Práctica

A **Práctica A** focuses on the **yo** form to give students practice using the **g** form.

B This activity reviews the first- and third-person plural forms that students already know. You may wish to have students do **Práctica B** as a paired activity.

ANSWERS

Práctica

A
1. **Sí, hago un viaje.**
2. **Sí, hago un viaje a Europa.**
3. **Sí, hago un viaje a España.**
4. **Sí, salgo para el aeropuerto.**
5. **Salgo en coche (taxi).**
6. **Sí, traigo equipaje.**
7. **Sí, (No, no) pongo el equipaje en la maletera del taxi.**
8. **Sí, en el aeropuerto pongo el equipaje en la báscula.**
9. **Salgo en el vuelo número ___.**
10. **Sí, (No, no) salgo de la puerta de salida número ocho.**

B
1. **Ellos salen para el aeropuerto y nosotros también salimos para el aeropuerto.**
2. **Ellos salen en taxi y nosotros también salimos en taxi.**
3. **Ellos traen mucho equipaje y nosotros también traemos mucho equipaje.**
4. **Ellos ponen las maletas en la maletera y nosotros también ponemos las maletas en la maletera.**
5. **Ellos salen a las seis y nosotros también salimos a las seis.**
6. **Ellos vienen solos y nosotros también venimos solos.**

C **Práctica C** has students use all forms.

EXPANSION Have students retell the story from **Práctica C** in their own words.

Actividades comunicativas

RECYCLING

Actividad A allows students to use vocabulary from many of the preceding chapters. **Actividad B** reviews the weather expressions from Chapter 9.

A This activity gives students practice asking questions with **hacer** and answering with another verb. Tell students that while it is sometimes possible to answer with **hacer,** they will most often use another verb.

EXPANSION Have students make a list of each location mentioned in the colored boxes and write down one activity they do at each location. Have students exchange their lists and compare.

B One student will begin by asking the partner: **¿Qué haces cuando...?**

GEOGRAPHY CONNECTION

Marbella, España Marbella is a world-famous resort on the Costa del Sol. Although it is quite built up, it remains very upscale in comparison to its popular next-door neighbor Torremolinos.

C **HISTORIETA** Un viaje a Marbella

Completen.

Marbella, España

Yo ___1___ (hacer) un viaje a Marbella. Marbella ___2___ (estar) en la Costa del Sol en el sur de España. Mi amiga Sandra ___3___ (hacer) el viaje también. Nosotros ___4___ (hacer) el viaje en avión hasta Málaga y luego ___5___ (ir) a tomar el autobús a Marbella.

—¡Ay, ay, Sandra! Pero tú ___6___ (traer) mucho equipaje.

—No, yo no ___7___ (traer) mucho. ___8___ (Tener) sólo dos maletas. Tú exageras. Tú también ___9___ (venir) con mucho equipaje.

—¡Oye! ¿A qué hora ___10___ (salir) nuestro vuelo?

—No ___11___ (salir) hasta las seis y media. Nosotros ___12___ (tener) mucho tiempo.

Actividades comunicativas

A **¿Adónde vas y qué haces?** Work with a classmate. Ask one another about places you go to and what activities you do there. Below are suggestions for places you may want to find out about.

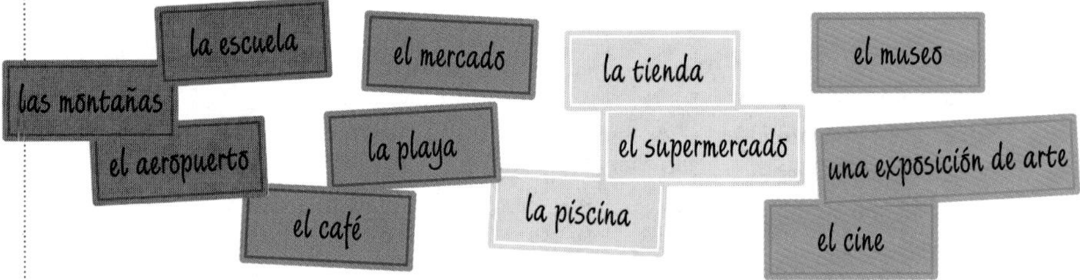

B **¿Qué haces cuando... ?** Work with a classmate. Find out what he or she does under the following weather conditions. Take turns asking and answering questions.

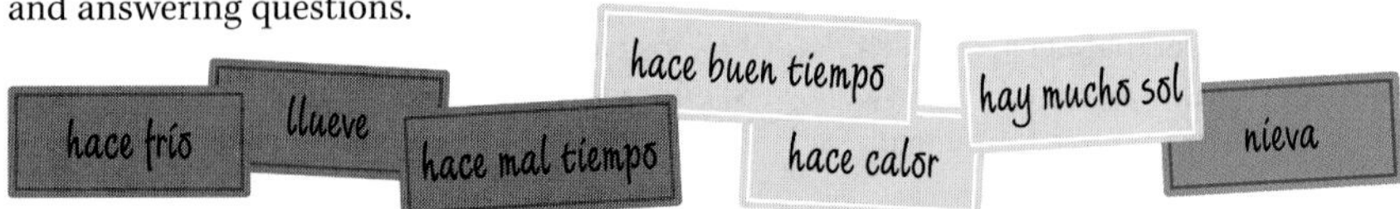

ANSWERS

Práctica

C 1. **hago**
2. **está**
3. **hace**
4. **hacemos**
5. **vamos**
6. **traes**
7. **traigo**
8. **Tengo**
9. **vienes**
10. **sale**
11. **sale**
12. **tenemos**

Actividades comunicativas

A Answers will vary; however, students will ask in the **tú** form, their partner will answer in the **yo** form.

B Answers will vary.

Describing an action in progress
El presente progresivo

1. The present progressive is used in Spanish to express an action that is presently going on, an action in progress. The present progressive is formed by using the present tense of the verb **estar** and the present participle—*speaking, doing*. To form the present participle of most verbs in Spanish you drop the ending of the infinitive and add **-ando** to the stem of **-ar** verbs and **-iendo** to the stem of **-er** and **-ir** verbs. Study the following forms of the present participle.

INFINITIVE	hablar	llegar	comer	hacer	salir
STEM	habl-	lleg-	com-	hac-	sal-
PARTICIPLE	hablando	llegando	comiendo	haciendo	saliendo

2. Note that the verbs **leer** and **traer** have a **y** in the present participle.

   leyendo **trayendo**

3. Study the following examples of the present progressive.

   ¿Qué está haciendo Isabel?
   Ahora está esperando el avión.
   Ella está mirando y leyendo su tarjeta de embarque.
   Y yo estoy buscando mi boleto.

Práctica

A HISTORIETA En el aeropuerto

Contesten según se indica.

1. ¿Adónde están llegando los pasajeros? (al aeropuerto)
2. ¿Cómo están llegando? (en taxi)
3. ¿Adónde están viajando? (a Europa)
4. ¿Cómo están haciendo el viaje? (en avión)
5. ¿Dónde están facturando el equipaje? (en el mostrador de la línea aérea)
6. ¿Qué está mirando el agente? (los boletos y los pasaportes)
7. ¿De qué puerta están saliendo los pasajeros para Madrid? (número siete)
8. ¿Qué están abordando? (el avión)

Madrid, España

Bell Ringer Review

Use BRR Transparency 11-4, or write the following on the board: Write a list of at least twenty action words you have learned so far in Spanish. Please keep these papers.

TEACHING STRUCTURE

Describing an action in progress

A. Have students open their books to page 327, and lead them through Step 1.

B. Give students other **-ar**, **-er**, and **-ir** verbs they know and have them give the present participle after they have seen how it is formed.

C. Now lead students through Steps 2 and 3 on page 327.

D. Have students take out their Bell Ringer Review paper (see above). Ask each student to choose a verb from the list and put it in the present progressive tense. For example: **Estoy bailando.**

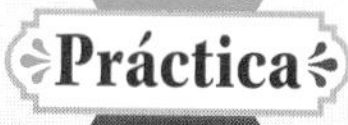

Práctica

A Have students retell the story from **Práctica A** in their own words.

Learning From Photos

Madrid, España Iberia is the name of the major Spanish air carrier. Explain to students that its name comes from the name of the peninsula where Spain is located.
España está en la península ibérica. Dos países forman la península ibérica. Son España y Portugal.
Explain to students that **los iberos** were the original inhabitants of Spain.

ANSWERS

Práctica

A
1. **Los pasajeros están llegando al aeropuerto.**
2. **Están llegando en taxi.**
3. **Están viajando a Europa.**
4. **Están haciendo el viaje en avión.**
5. **Están facturando el equipaje en el mostrador de la línea aérea.**
6. **El agente está mirando los boletos y los pasaportes.**
7. **Los pasajeros para Madrid están saliendo de la puerta número siete.**
8. **Están abordando el avión.**

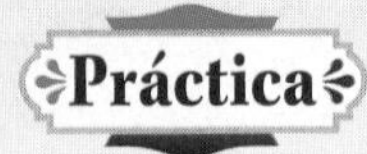

B Have students repeat **Práctica B,** this time adding a word or expression. For example: **Estoy viajando a España.**

TEACHING STRUCTURE

Telling what and whom you know

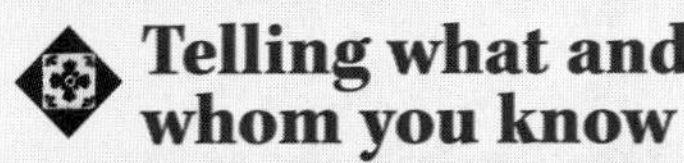

These verb forms should be easy for students since only the **yo** form is new. Students will, however, need constant reinforcement with **yo sé.**

A. Have students repeat **sé** and **conozco** as they point to themselves. Explain to them that once again they are going to learn two verbs that are irregular in the **yo** form only.

B. Have students open their books to page 328 and repeat all forms of the verbs in Step 1. You may also wish to write the forms on the board.

C. Lead students through Steps 2 and 3 concerning the specific uses of these verbs. Have students read all the model sentences aloud.

B **¿Qué estás haciendo?** Formen oraciones según el modelo.

Estoy viajando.
No estoy viajando.

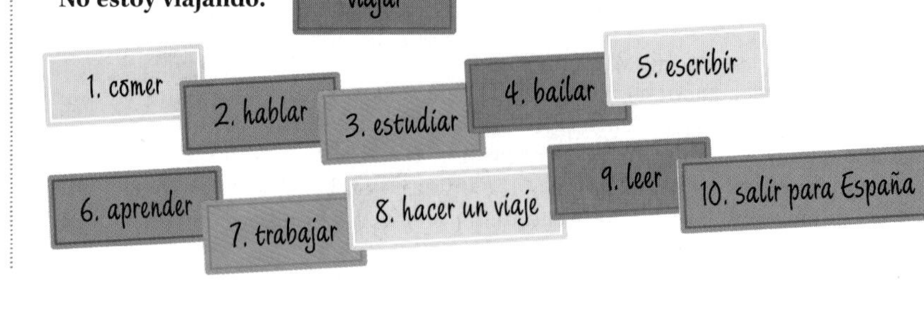

Telling what and whom you know
Saber y conocer en el presente

1. The verbs **saber** and **conocer** both mean "to know." Note that like many Spanish verbs they have an irregular **yo** form in the present tense. All other forms are regular.

INFINITIVE	saber	conocer
yo	sé	conozco
tú	sabes	conoces
él, ella, Ud.	sabe	conoce
nosotros(as)	sabemos	conocemos
vosotros(as)	*sabéis*	*conocéis*
ellos, ellas, Uds.	saben	conocen

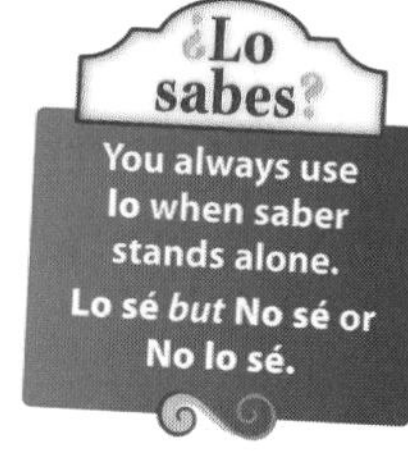

2. The verb **saber** means "to know a fact" or "to have information about something." It also means "to know how to do something."

Yo sé el número de nuestro vuelo.
Pero no sabemos a qué hora sale.
Yo sé esquiar y jugar tenis.

3. The verb **conocer** means "to know" in the sense of "to be acquainted with." It is used to talk about people and complex or abstract concepts rather than simple facts.

Yo conozco a Luis.
Teodoro conoce muy bien la literatura mexicana.

ANSWERS

Práctica

B All answers will include either **Estoy...** or **No estoy...**

1. **comiendo**
2. **hablando**
3. **estudiando**
4. **bailando**
5. **escribiendo**
6. **aprendiendo**
7. **trabajando**
8. **haciendo un viaje**
9. **leyendo**
10. **saliendo para España**

A **Mi vuelo** Contesten.

1. ¿Sabes el número de tu vuelo?
2. ¿Sabes a qué hora sale?
3. ¿Sabes de qué puerta va a salir?
4. ¿Sabes la hora de tu llegada a Cancún?
5. ¿Conoces al comandante del vuelo?
6. ¿Conoces a mucha gente en Cancún?

B **HISTORIETA Adela Del Olmo**

Completen con **saber** o **conocer**.

PEPITA: Sandra, ¿___1___ tú a Adela Del Olmo?
SANDRA: Claro que ___2___ a Adela. Ella y yo somos muy buenas amigas.
PEPITA: ¿___3___ tú que ella va a Panamá?
SANDRA: ¿Ella va a Panamá? No, yo no ___4___ nada de su viaje. ¿Cuándo va a salir?
PEPITA: Pues, ella no ___5___ exactamente qué día va a salir. Pero ___6___ que va a salir en junio. Ella va a hacer su reservación mañana. Yo ___7___ que ella quiere tomar un vuelo directo.
SANDRA: ¿Adela ___8___ Panamá?
PEPITA: Creo que sí. Pero yo no ___9___ definitivamente. Pero yo ___10___ que ella ___11___ a mucha gente en Panamá.
SANDRA: ¿Cómo es que ella ___12___ a mucha gente allí?
PEPITA: Pues, tú ___13___ que ella tiene parientes en Panamá, ¿no?
SANDRA: Ay, sí, es verdad. Yo ___14___ que tiene familia en Panamá porque yo ___15___ a su tía Lola. Y ___16___ que ella es de Panamá.

La Bahía de Panamá

Actividad comunicativa

JUEGO **Lo/La conozco muy bien.** Work with a classmate. Think of someone in the class whom you know quite well. Tell your partner some things you know about this person. Don't say who it is. Your partner will guess. Take turns.

ANSWERS

Práctica

A
1. **Sí, sé el número de mi vuelo.**
2. **Sí, sé a qué hora sale.**
3. **Sí, sé de qué puerta va a salir.**
4. **Sí, sé la hora de mi llegada a Cancún.**
5. **Sí, (No, no) conozco al comandante del vuelo.**
6. **Sí, (No, no) conozco a mucha gente en Cancún.**

B
1. **conoces**
2. **conozco**
3. **Sabes**
4. **sé**
5. **sabe**
6. **sabe**
7. **sé**
8. **conoce**
9. **sé**
10. **sé**
11. **conoce**
12. **conoce**
13. **sabes**
14. **sé**
15. **conozco**
16. **sé**

Práctica

A **Práctica A** focuses on the **yo** forms of **saber** and **concocer.**

B Since all the other forms of **saber** and **conocer** are the same as those of regular verbs, **Práctica B** makes students use all forms of these two verbs.

Actividad comunicativa

JUEGO This is a good activity to use as a warm-up at the beginning of the class hour.

¡OJO! There is no more new material in this chapter. The sections that follow recombine and reinforce the vocabulary and structures that have already been introduced.

Learning From Photos

La Bahía de Panamá Panama City is a very interesting city on the Bay of Panama on the Pacific Ocean. The original settlement, Vieja Panamá, was burned and sacked by the pirate Henry Morgan. There are still some ruins there. As this photo indicates, Panama City is also a city of modern high-rises: offices, banks, condominiums. The Casco Viejo of Panama City still maintains a colonial flavor with narrow streets of low white houses with iron balconies.

RESOURCES

- Audiocassette 7A/CD6
- CD-ROM, Disc 3, page 330

Bell Ringer Review

Use BRR Transparency 11-5, or write the following on the board:
Complete with personal information.
Yo quiero hacer un viaje a ___.
Yo quiero visitar a ___.
Yo voy a ir en ___.

TEACHING THE CONVERSATION

A. Tell students they are going to hear a conversation between a couple who are about to take a plane trip. They are at the airport.

B. Ask students to open their books to page 330 as you read the conversation aloud, or have them listen to the recording on Cassette 7A/Compact Disc 6.

C. Have several pairs of students role-play the conversation with their books open. Let students make any changes that make sense.

D. Extend the activity by having students make up their own dialogues based on the conversation at the airport.

E. After presenting the conversation, go over the **Después de conversar** activity. If students can answer the questions with relative ease, move on. Students should not be expected to memorize the conversation.

TECHNOLOGY OPTION

On the CD-ROM (Disc 3, page 330), students can watch a dramatization of this conversation. They can then play the role of either one of the characters, and record themselves in the conversation.

Conversación

Está saliendo nuestro vuelo.

Señores pasajeros. Su atención, por favor. La compañía de aviación anuncia la salida de su vuelo ciento seis con destino a Santafé de Bogotá. Embarque inmediato por la puerta de salida número seis.

ANTONIO: ¡Chist, Luisa! Están anunciando la salida de nuestro vuelo.
LUISA: Sí, lo sé. ¡Y Dios mío! ¿Antonio, sabes dónde está Fernando?
ANTONIO: Sí, tú conoces a Fernando. Llegó tarde otra vez. Todavía está facturando su equipaje.
LUISA: Hablando de equipaje, ¿tienes los talones para nuestras maletas?
ANTONIO: Sí, aquí están. Los tengo con los boletos.
LUISA: ¿De qué puerta sale nuestro vuelo?
ANTONIO: De la puerta número seis. Primero tenemos que pasar por el control de seguridad.
LUISA: ¡Vamos ya! No vamos a esperar a Fernando. Él puede perder el vuelo si quiere. Pero yo, no.

Después de conversar

Contesten.

1. ¿Está Fernando con Antonio y Luisa?
2. ¿Sabe Antonio dónde está Fernando?
3. ¿Qué está haciendo Fernando?
4. ¿Siempre llega tarde?
5. ¿Qué va a perder?

ANSWERS

Después de conversar

1. **No, Fernando no está con Antonio y Luisa.**
2. **Sí, Antonio sabe donde está Fernando.**
3. **Fernando está facturando su equipaje.**
4. **Siempre llega tarde.**
5. **Va a perder el vuelo.**

Career Connection

Hablo español. Because of the popularity of international travel (for business and pleasure) to and from the Spanish-speaking world, Spanish is an important communication tool. Have students make a list of at least four professions in the travel industry for which Spanish would be useful or necessary. Have students try to arrange interviews with some people in these professions.

Actividades comunicativas

A Un billete para Madrid Work with a classmate. You want to fly from Mexico City to Madrid. Call the airline to get a reservation. Your partner will be the reservation agent. Before you call, think about all the information you will need to give or get from the agent: date of departure, departure time, arrival time in Madrid, flight number, price.

B Antonio, Antonio Work with a classmate. You both know Antonio. He's a great guy, but he'll never get to the airport on time. He's always late. Have a conversation about Antonio. Tell some things you know about him that always make him late.

Pronunciación

La consonante r

When a word begins with an **r** (initial position), the **r** is trilled in Spanish. Within a word, **rr** is also trilled. The Spanish trilled **r** sound does not exist in English. Repeat the following.

ra	re	ri	ro	ru
rápido	**reclama**	**Ricardo**	**Roberto**	**Rubén**
raqueta	**recoger**	**rico**	**rojo**	**rubio**
párrafo	**corre**	**perrito**	**perro**	
		aterrizar	**catarro**	

The sound for a single **r** within a word (medial position) does not exist in English either. It is trilled less than the initial **r** or **rr**. Repeat the following.

ra	re	ri	ro	ru
demora	**arena**	**Clarita**	**maletero**	**Perú**
verano		**consultorio**	**número**	**Aruba**
para			**miro**	

Repeat the following sentences.

El mesero recoge los refrescos.
El perrito de Rubén corre en la arena.
El maletero corre rápido por el aeropuerto.
El avión para Puerto Rico aterriza con una demora de una hora.
El rico tiene una raqueta en el carro.

Did You Know?

La Cédula de Identidad Spaniards and other citizens of the European Union no longer need a passport to travel to nations within the EU. Each country in the European Union does require, however, that its citizens carry a national identification card. In Spain it is called the **Cédula de Identidad.** This ID card can be used for travel within the EU.

ANSWERS

Actvidades comunicativas

A Answers will vary; however, students should include the information called for in the activity.

B Answers will vary.

Actividades comunicativas

A Before beginning this activity, students should make a list in Spanish of the information they will need to give the airline agent (their partner).

B Use the conversation on page 330 as a model for this activity.

TEACHING PRONUNCIATION

¡OJO! The following information may help students pronounce the **r** sound correctly. Remember that this is an extremely difficult sound for Americans to make. Try to have students sound as native as possible. Do not frustrate a student who cannot pronounce perfectly. Many (or most) people do not, and a mild accent can be readily understood. Any native speaker will understand "**el caro**" as **el carro** even if the **r's** are mispronounced.

A. The Spanish **r** sound does not exist in English. A single **r** in medial position is pronounced like a soft **t** in English. The tongue hits the upper part of the mouth in a position similar to when we say "a lot of" *(a lotta)* very quickly in English.

B. Have students play a game trying to trill the initial **r** or the **rr**. Let them exaggerate as much as they wish and they may get it right.

C. Have students repeat the sounds and words after you or the recording on Cassette 7A/Compact Disc 6. Have them imitate very carefully.

D. Have students open their books to page 331. Call on individuals to read the sentences carefully.

E. All model sentences on page 331 can be used for dictation.

Bell Ringer Review

Use BRR Transparency 11-6, or write the following on the board: Write a list of the countries in South America that you know. Then give as many of their capitals as you can.

National Standards

Cultures

The reading about airline travel in South America on page 332 and the related activities on page 333 allow students to demonstrate an understanding of the importance of this mode of transportation on this continent.

TEACHING THE READING

Pre-reading

A. Ask which members of the class have traveled by air. Did they take a domestic or international flight? What are some of the differences between domestic and international air travel? What were the good points about their trip? The bad points?

B. Have students open their books to page 332. Do the Reading Strategy activity on this page. Then have students study the photos. Have them try to imagine what it is like to fly over the landscape they see in these photos.

Reading

Present the reading in two or three segments. Call on an individual to read three sentences. Then ask comprehension questions. For example, questions for the first paragraph may be:

¿Cuál es un medio de transporte importante en la América del Sur?

(continued on page 333)

Lecturas CULTURALES

Reading Strategy

Identifying the main idea

When reading, it is important to identify the main idea the author is expressing. Each paragraph usually discusses a different idea. The main idea is often found in the first or second sentence of a paragraph. Go through the reading quickly to find the main idea in each paragraph. Do not read every word. Once you know the main idea of the passage, go back and read it again more carefully.

EL AVIÓN EN LA AMÉRICA DEL SUR

El avión es un medio de transporte muy importante en la América del Sur. ¿Por qué? Pues, vamos a mirar un mapa del continente sudamericano. Van a ver que es un continente inmenso. Por consiguiente[1], toma mucho tiempo viajar de una ciudad a otra, sobre todo por tierra.

En la mayoría de los casos es imposible viajar de un lugar a otro por tierra. ¿Por qué? Porque es imposible cruzar[2] los picos de los Andes o la selva (jungla) tropical del río Amazonas. Por eso, a todas horas del día y de la noche, los aviones de muchas líneas aéreas están sobrevolando[3] el continente. Hay vuelos nacionales que enlazan[4] una ciudad con otra en el mismo país. Y hay vuelos internacionales que enlazan un país con otro.

[1]Por consiguiente *Consequently*
[2]cruzar *to cross*
[3]sobrevolando *flying over*
[4]enlazan *connect*

El río Amazonas

Los Andes, Patagonia

Independent Practice

Assign any of the following:

1. **Después de leer** activities, page 333
2. Workbook, **Un poco más,** pages 138–139
3. CD-ROM, Disc 3, pages 332–333

Después de leer

A **¿Sí o no?** Digan que sí o que no.

1. El continente sudamericano es muy pequeño.
2. El tren es un medio de transporte importante en la América del Sur.
3. En muchas partes de la América del Sur, es difícil viajar por tierra.
4. Los picos andinos son muy altos.
5. Las selvas tropicales están en los picos andinos.

B **Análisis** Contesten.

1. ¿Por qué es el avión un medio de transporte importante en la América del Sur?
2. ¿Por qué es imposible viajar por tierra de una ciudad a otra en muchas partes de la América del Sur?
3. ¿Cuál es la diferencia entre un vuelo nacional y un vuelo internacional?
4. ¿Cuál es la idea principal de esta lectura?

La selva amazónica cerca de Iquitos, Perú

ANSWERS

Después de leer

A 1. No.
2. No.
3. Sí.
4. Sí.
5. No.

B 1. El avión es un medio de transporte importante en la América del Sur porque es un continente inmenso.
2. Es imposible viajar por tierra en muchas partes de la América del Sur porque es imposible cruzar los picos de los Andes o las junglas de la selva tropical del río Amazonas.
3. Los vuelos nacionales enlazan una ciudad con otra en el mismo país. Los vuelos internacionales enlazan un país con otro.
4. El avión es muy importante como medio de transporte en la América del Sur.

¿Cómo es el continente sudamericano? ¿Toma mucho tiempo viajar de una ciudad a otra? ¿Por qué?

Post-reading

Have students explain in their own words why air travel is so important in South America.

TECHNOLOGY OPTION

Students may listen to a recording of the **Lectura** on the CD-ROM, Disc 3, page 332.

A and **B** Allow students to refer to the reading to look up the answers, or you may use these activities for informal assessment.

Geography Connection

El río Amazonas The Amazon is the longest river in South America. It flows through Brazil and has many tributaries in Colombia, Ecuador, and Peru. Other important rivers of South America are **el Magdalena** (Colombia), **el Orinoco** (Venezuela), **el Paraná** (Uruguay, Paraguay, and Argentina).

Have students locate these rivers on the map of South America on page 464 or on the Map Transparency.

LECTURA OPCIONAL 1

National Standards

Comparisons

This reading about travel time to various locales and the related activity on this page allow students to appreciate the immensity of the Spanish-speaking world.

¡OJO! Many people find the information about distances in this **Lectura** quite unbelievable. Even if you do not read this in-depth, you may wish to have students scan it just to get the basic idea.

TEACHING TIPS

This reading is optional. You may skip it completely, have the entire class read it, have only several students read it, or assign it for extra credit.

Después de leer

A Have students refresh their knowledge about the locations mentioned by looking at the maps on pages 463 and 464.

LECTURA OPCIONAL 1

DISTANCIAS Y TIEMPO DE VUELO

El aeropuerto JFK en Nueva York

Nueva York a Madrid

Los vuelos entre los Estados Unidos y Europa son muy largos, ¿no? El Atlántico es un océano grande. Para cruzar el océano Atlántico toma mucho tiempo. Pero los vuelos dentro de la América del Sur pueden ser muy largos también. Vamos a hacer algunas comparaciones.

Susana Rogers está abordando un jet en el aeropuerto internacional de John F. Kennedy en Nueva York. Va a ir a Madrid. Es un vuelo sin escala[1] y después de unas siete horas, el avión va a aterrizar en el aeropuerto de Barajas en Madrid.

El aeropuerto en Caracas, Venezuela

Caracas a Buenos Aires

A la misma hora que Susana está abordando el vuelo para Madrid, José Dávila está saliendo de Caracas, Venezuela. Él va a Buenos Aires, Argentina. Su vuelo es también un vuelo sin escala. ¿Sabe Ud. cuánto tiempo va a tomar? José va a llegar a Ezeiza, el aeropuerto de Buenos Aires, después de un vuelo de unas siete horas. Como ven Uds., hay muy poca diferencia entre el vuelo que cruza el océano de Nueva York a Madrid y el vuelo de Caracas a Buenos Aires.

[1]sin escala *nonstop*

Después de leer

A **¿Lo sabes?** Busquen la siguiente información.

1. el nombre de un océano
2. el nombre de un país
3. el nombre de una ciudad norteamericana
4. el nombre de una ciudad sudamericana
5. la duración del vuelo entre Nueva York y Madrid
6. la duración del vuelo entre Caracas y Buenos Aires

ANSWERS

Después de leer

A
1. **el Atlántico**
2. **los Estados Unidos (Venezuela, Argentina)**
3. **Nueva York**
4. **Caracas (Buenos Aires)**
5. **unas siete horas**
6. **unas siete horas**

Learning From Photos

El aeropuerto en Caracas, Venezuela
El aeropuerto internacional de Simón Bolívar serves Caracas. It is located on the coast in the suburb of **Maiquetía.**

LECTURA OPCIONAL 2

LAS LÍNEAS DE NAZCA

Un vuelo muy interesante es el vuelo en una avioneta de un solo motor sobre las figuras o líneas de Nazca. ¿Qué son las figuras de Nazca? En el desierto entre Nazca y Palpa en el Perú, hay toda una serie de figuras o dibujos misteriosos en la arena. Hay figuras de aves[1], peces[2] y otros animales. Hay también figuras geométricas—rectángulos, triángulos y líneas paralelas.

El origen de las figuras de Nazca es un misterio. No sabemos de dónde vienen. Pero sabemos que tienen unos tres o cuatro mil años de edad. Y son tan[3] grandes y cubren[4] un área tan grande que para ver las figuras bien es necesario tomar un avión. La avioneta para Nazca sale todos los días de Jorge Chávez, el aeropuerto internacional de Lima.

[1]aves *birds*
[2]peces *fish*
[3]tan *so*
[4]cubren *cover*

Después de leer

A Nazca Contesten.

1. ¿Sobre qué vuela la avioneta?
2. ¿Cuántos motores tiene la avioneta?
3. ¿Dónde están las figuras o líneas de Nazca?
4. ¿Están en un desierto las figuras?
5. ¿Es un misterio el origen de las figuras o sabemos de dónde vienen?
6. ¿Qué tipo de figuras o líneas hay?
7. ¿Cuántos años tienen?
8. ¿Cubren un área muy grande las líneas?
9. ¿De dónde salen los aviones para ver las líneas?

LECTURA OPCIONAL 2

National Standards

Cultures

The reading about the Nazca lines in Peru and the related activity on this page allow students to learn about one of the unsolved prehistoric mysteries in the Spanish-speaking world.

TEACHING TIPS

Use the questions in **Después de leer** to judge how well students understood the reading.

Learning From Photos

Las líneas de Nazca The Pan American Highway goes right through the area where the Nazca lines are located, but it is impossible to see them from the road. The purpose of the lines is unknown but they have caused a great deal of speculation. Some say they may have served as a calendar.

Unfortunately the Nazca lines suffered some damage in 1998 because of the flooding caused by El Niño.

ANSWERS

Después de leer

A
1. **La avioneta vuela sobre las figuras o líneas de Nazca.**
2. **La avioneta tiene sólo un motor.**
3. **Las figuras o líneas de Nazca están entre Nazca y Palpa en el Perú.**
4. **Sí, las figuras están en un desierto.**
5. **Es un misterio el origen de las figuras.**
6. **Hay figuras de aves, peces y otros animales. Hay también figuras geométricas.**
7. **Tienen unos tres o cuatro mil años.**
8. **Sí, las líneas cubren un área muy grande.**
9. **Los aviones salen de Jorge Chávez, el aeropuerto internacional de Lima.**

National Standards

Connections

This reading about finances establishes a connection with another discipline, allowing students to reinforce and further their knowledge of mathematics through the study of Spanish.

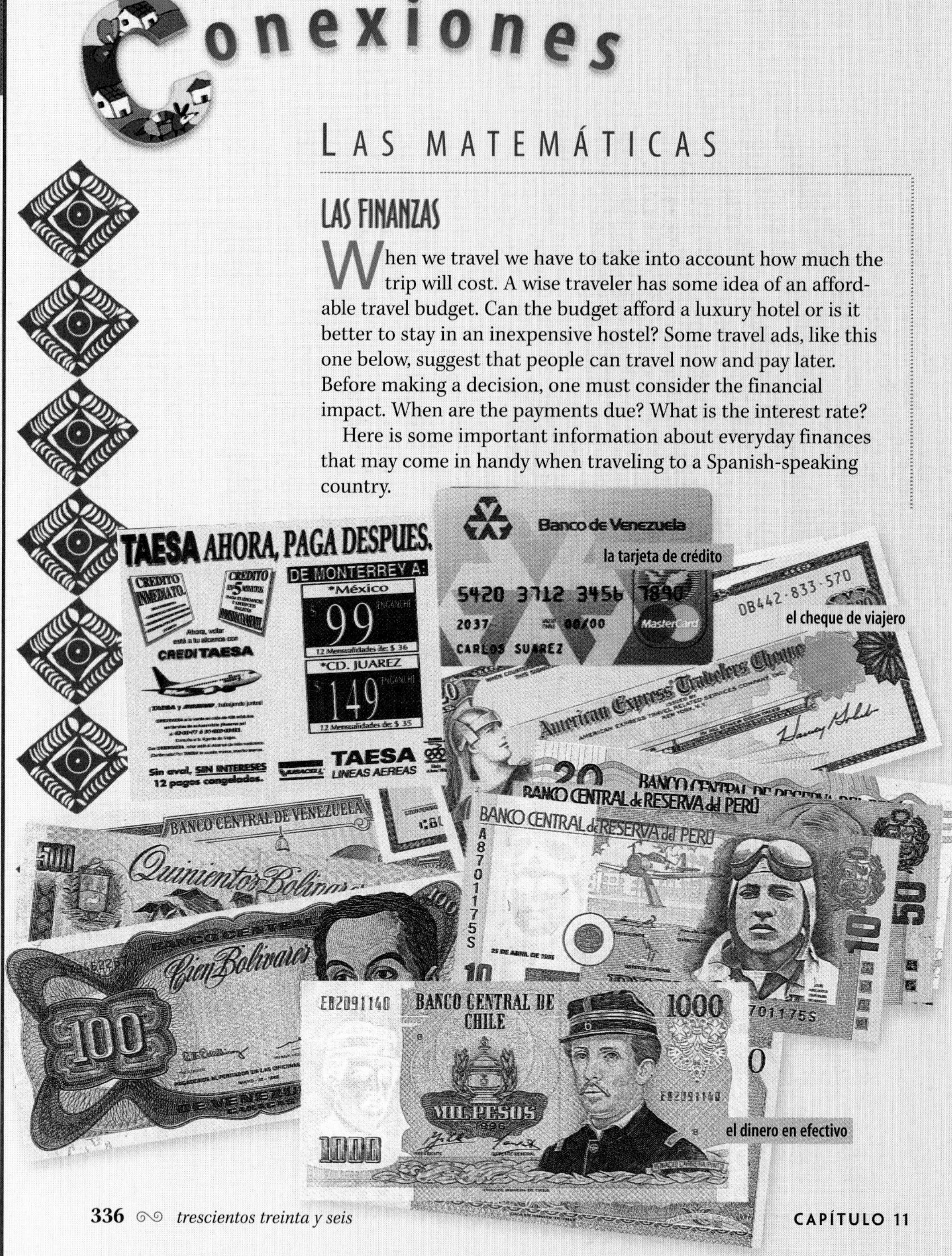

Conexiones

LAS MATEMÁTICAS

LAS FINANZAS

When we travel we have to take into account how much the trip will cost. A wise traveler has some idea of an affordable travel budget. Can the budget afford a luxury hotel or is it better to stay in an inexpensive hostel? Some travel ads, like this one below, suggest that people can travel now and pay later. Before making a decision, one must consider the financial impact. When are the payments due? What is the interest rate?

Here is some important information about everyday finances that may come in handy when traveling to a Spanish-speaking country.

la tarjeta de crédito

el cheque de viajero

el dinero en efectivo

336 *trescientos treinta y seis* CAPÍTULO 11

¡OJO! The readings in the **Conexiones** section are optional. They focus on some of the major disciplines taught in schools and universities. The vocabulary is useful for discussing such topics as history, literature, art, economics, business, science, etc.

You may choose any of the following ways to do this reading on finances with your students.

Independent reading Have students read the selections and do the post-reading activities as homework, which you collect. This option is least intrusive on class time and requires a minimum of teacher involvement.

Homework with in-class follow-up Assign the readings and post-reading activities as homework. Review and discuss the material in class the next day.

Intensive in-class activity This option includes a pre-reading vocabulary presentation, in-class reading and discussion, assignment of the activities for homework, and a discussion of the assignment in class the following day.

LAS MATEMÁTICAS

LAS FINANZAS

A. This reading contains some very useful vocabulary for any students interested in fields such as retailing, accounting, etc. The Vocabulary Expansion box on *(continued on page 337)*

VOCABULARY EXPANSION

el presupuesto	*budget*
los gastos	*expenses*
la factura	*bill*
una tarjeta de crédito	*credit card*
(el dinero) en efectivo	*cash*
cambiar dinero	*to change money*
el tipo de cambio	*exchange rate*
pagar a plazos	*to pay off (in installments)*
un pronto, un pie	*down payment*
una mensualidad	*monthly payment*
la tasa de interés	*interest rate*

Las finanzas

Madrid, España

Si vamos a hacer un viaje, es necesario saber cuánto va a costar. Es una buena idea preparar un presupuesto[1]. El presupuesto nos permite saber cuánto dinero tenemos y cuánto podemos gastar[2]. El presupuesto tiene que incluir los siguientes gastos[3]:

precio del vuelo
transporte local
hotel
comidas y refrescos
entradas
—museos, teatros

Cuando viajamos, podemos pagar nuestras cuentas o facturas con una tarjeta de crédito, cheques de viajero o (dinero) en efectivo.

En un país extranjero no vamos a pagar con dólares. Vamos a usar la moneda nacional—pesos o soles, por ejemplo. Tenemos que cambiar dinero. En México es necesario cambiar dólares en pesos. Antes de cambiar dinero, es importante saber el tipo de cambio[4].

Si decidimos pagar a plazos[5], es necesario pagar un pronto[6] (un pie, un enganche). Luego hay que hacer un pago cada mes—una mensualidad. Antes de decidir pagar algo a plazos, es necesario saber la tasa de interés[7] que tenemos que pagar. Todos debemos ser consumidores inteligentes porque la tasa de interés puede ser muy alta.

[1]presupuesto *budget*
[2]gastar *to spend*
[3]gastos *expenses*
[4]tipo de cambio *exchange rate*
[5]pagar a plazos *to pay in installments*
[6]pronto *down payment*
[7]tasa de interés *interest rate*

Después de leer

A La palabra, por favor. Completen.

1. El ____ nos indica cuánto dinero tenemos y cuánto podemos gastar en varias categorías.
2. El dinero que tenemos que pagar es un ____.
3. Los ____ no pueden exceder la cantidad de dinero que tenemos.
4. *VISA* es una ____.
5. Podemos pagar nuestras ____ con una tarjeta de crédito, ____ o ____.
6. En México tenemos que ____ dólares en pesos mexicanos. En España tenemos que ____ dólares en pesetas españolas.
7. Antes de cambiar dinero es necesario saber el ____.
8. Si uno decide comprar algo a plazos, es necesario pagar un ____ al principio.
9. Un pago mensual es una ____.
10. Si vamos a comprar algo a plazos, es siempre necesario saber la ____ que puede ser bastante alta.

page 336 contains some high-frequency financial terms that appear in the reading. You may want to go over them before beginning the reading.

B. Have students read the introduction in English on page 336.

C. Have students read the selection on page 337 and do the **Después de leer** activity that follows.

INFORMAL ASSESSMENT

You may wish to give the following quiz to students who have done the **Conexiones** section.

Answer.

¿Qué debemos preparar antes de hacer un viaje?
¿Qué nos permite saber el presupuesto?
¿Cuáles son algunos gastos que tenemos cuando viajamos?
¿Cómo podemos pagar nuestras cuentas o facturas?
¿Por qué tenemos que cambiar dinero?
Si vamos a pagar a plazos, ¿qué es necesario pagar enseguida?
¿Qué tenemos que saber antes de decidir de pagar algo a plazos?

ANSWERS

Después de leer

A
1. **presupuesto**
2. **gasto**
3. **gastos**
4. **tarjeta de crédito**
5. **cuentas (facturas), cheques de viajero, (dinero) en efectivo**
6. **cambiar, cambiar**
7. **tipo de cambio**
8. **pronto (pie, enganche)**
9. **mensualidad**
10. **tasa de interés**

CAPÍTULO 11
Culminación

RECYCLING

The **Actividades orales** and the **Actividad escrita** allow students to use the vocabulary and structures from this chapter in open-ended, real-life settings.

Actividades orales

A As students discuss this topic, they can make a list of things they have to do in preparation for their study abroad. Have several pairs read their list to the class at the end of this activity.

B Encourage students to be creative regarding their destinations!

TECHNOLOGY OPTION In the CD-ROM version of this activity, students can interact with an on-screen, native speaker and record their voices.

C This activity can be done individually, or students may prefer to plan their trip with a partner. Have students tell the class about their trip.

TECHNOLOGY OPTION The Internet is an excellent source for travel information.

National Standards

Communities Students who do **Actividad C** will find out more about the Spanish-speaking world by using resources in their community.

Culminación

Actividades orales

A **Un semestre en España** Work with a classmate. The two of you are leaving soon to spend a semester studying at a school in Seville, Spain. Discuss all the things you have to do to prepare for your upcoming experience—things you have to buy, travel arrangements you have to make, etc.

B **¿Adónde vas?** You just got to the airport and unexpectedly ran into a friend (your partner). Exchange information about the trip and flight each of you is about to take.

C **¡A planear un viaje!** Go to a travel agency in your community. Get some travel brochures and plan a trip. Tell all about your trip. Be sure to include how you will get from one place to another.

ANSWERS

Actividades orales

A Answers will vary.

B Answers will vary; however, students should give as many details about their flight as possible using the vocabulary from this chapter.

C Answers will vary.

Student Portfolio

Have students keep a notebook containing their best written work from each chapter. These selected writings can be based on assignments from the Student Textbook and the Writing Activities Workbook. The activities on page 339 are examples of writing assignments that may be included in each student's portfolio.

See the Teacher's Manual for more information on the Student Portfolio.

Actividad escrita

A **Un viaje en avión** You have a Venezuelan pen pal who is going to visit you this winter. This will be his or her first flight. Write your pen pal a letter and explain all the things he or she is going to experience before, during, and after the flight.

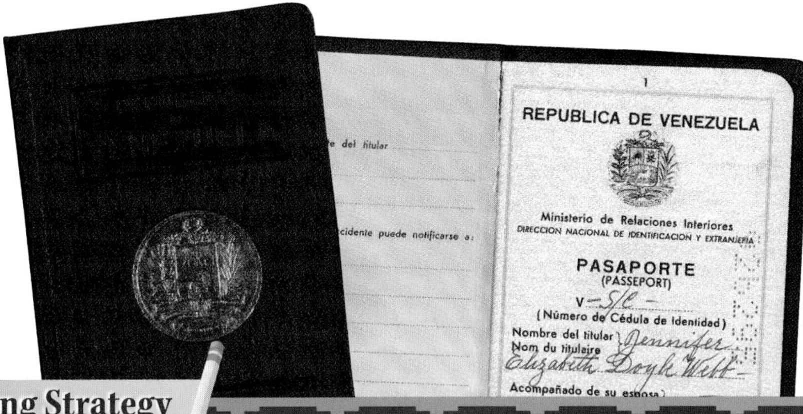

Writing Strategy

Answering an essay question

When writing an answer to an essay question, first read the question carefully to look for clues to determine how your answer should be structured. Then begin by restating the essay question in a single statement in your introduction. Next, support the statement in the body of the answer with facts, details, and reasons. Finally, close with a conclusion that summarizes your answer.

Un concurso

In order to win an all-expense-paid trip to the Spanish-speaking country of your choice, you have to write an essay in Spanish and send it to the company sponsoring the trip. Read the following essay questions and then write your answers. You really want to go, so be sure to plan your answers carefully and check your work.

¿A qué país quiere Ud. viajar? ¿Cómo quiere Ud. viajar? ¿Por qué quiere Ud. ir allí? ¿Qué quiere Ud. hacer allí? ¿Qué quiere aprender?

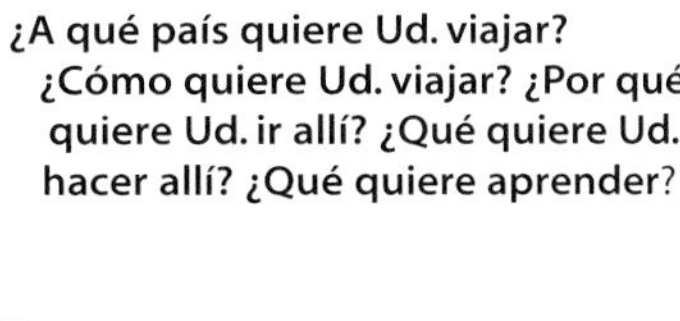

Actividad escrita

A In addition to describing what the pen pal is going to do at the airport, students may want to include the name of the city where the pen pal will land and what the weather is like there.

TECHNOLOGY OPTION Students can use the Portfolio feature on the CD-ROM to write this letter.

Writing Strategy

Answering an essay question

A. Have students read the Writing Strategy on page 339.

B. Encourage students to first make an outline that includes the elements mentioned in the Writing Strategy.

C. The illustration on page 339 suggests one reason for wanting to go to a Spanish-speaking country. However, students should be encouraged to give other reasons if they wish.

Independent Practice

Assign any of the following:

1. Activities, pages 338–339
2. Workbook, **Mi autobiografía,** page 142
3. Situation Cards
4. CD-ROM, Disc 3, Chapter 11, **Juego de repaso**

ANSWERS

Actividad escrita

A Answers will vary.

Writing Strategy

Answers will vary depending on the students' destinations and their reasons for wanting to go there.

CAPÍTULO 11
Vocabulario

ASSESSMENT RESOURCES

- Chapter Quizzes
- Testing Program
- Computer Testmaker
- Situation Cards
- Communication Transparency C-11
- Performance Assessment
- **Maratón mental** Videoquiz

VOCABULARY REVIEW

The words and phrases in the **Vocabulario** have been taught for productive use in this chapter. They are summarized here as a resource for both students and teacher. This list also serves as a convenient resource for the **Culminación** activities on pages 338 and 339. There are approximately twelve cognates in this vocabulary list. Have students find them.

Vocabulario

GETTING AROUND AN AIRPORT—DEPARTURE

el aeropuerto
el taxi
la línea aérea
el avión
el mostrador
el/la agente
el billete, el boleto
el pasaporte
la pantalla de salidas y llegadas
la tarjeta de embarque
el número del asiento
el número del vuelo
el destino
la puerta de salida, la sala de salida
la sección de no fumar
la báscula
el talón
la maleta
el/la maletero(a)
el/la pasajero(a)
el equipaje (de mano)
el control de seguridad

GETTING AROUND AN AIRPORT—ARRIVAL

el control de pasaportes
la aduana
el reclamo de equipaje

IDENTIFYING AIRLINE PERSONNEL

el/la agente
la tripulación
el/la comandante, el/la piloto
el/la copiloto
el asistente de vuelo
la asistente de vuelo

DESCRIBING AIRPORT ACTIVITIES

hacer un viaje
dar la bienvenida
salir a tiempo
tarde
con una demora
revisar el boleto
pasar por el control de seguridad
tomar un vuelo
facturar el equipaje
abrir las maletas
inspeccionar
abordar
desembarcar
despegar
aterrizar
reclamar (recoger) el equipaje

OTHER USEFUL EXPRESSIONS

el país
extranjero(a)
permitir
venir
poner
saber
conocer

For the Younger Student

Mi tarjeta de embarque Have students draw a boarding pass for the destination of their choice similar to the one on page 318 or page 323. Have them fill it in with the appropriate information and then have them tell all about it.

La pantalla de salidas y llegadas Have students draw an airport departure and arrival monitor screen similar to the one on page 316. Now have them work in pairs and ask each other questions about the information on it.

TECNOTUR

VIDEO

¡Buen viaje!

EPISODIO 11 ▸ Un viaje en avión

Luis tiene que volver a la Ciudad de México,...

...pero parece que hay un problema.

CD-ROM

Expansión cultural

Mexicana es una línea aérea de México.

In this video episode Luis misses his flight to Mexico City because of bad weather. To familiarize yourself with airports in the Spanish-speaking world, go to the Capítulo 11 Internet activity at the Glencoe Foreign Language Web site:

http://www.glencoe.com/sec/fl

Video Synopsis

In this episode Luis has to get back to Mexico City for a very important soccer match. Unfortunately for him, and his team, the weather in Mexico City is not good. When he gets to the Puerto Vallarta airport, he checks his luggage and discovers from the ticket agent that his flight has been delayed. Luis waits anxiously with Cristina and Isabel in the airport restaurant. At the end of the episode they hear that the flight has been cancelled.

CAPÍTULO 11

Tecnotur

OVERVIEW

This page previews three key multimedia components of the **Glencoe Spanish** series. Each reinforces the material taught in Chapter 11 in a unique manner.

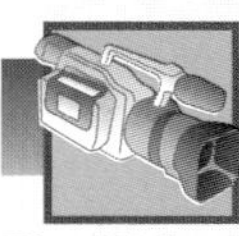

VIDEO

The Video Program allows students to see how the chapter vocabulary and structures are used by native speakers within an engaging story line. For maximum reinforcement, show the video episode as a final activity for Chapter 11.

A. Before viewing this episode, have students read the video photo captions on page 341. Ask them questions such as: **¿Dónde está Luis? ¿A dónde necesita volver?** Now ask them: **¿Cuál es su problema, en tu opinión?**

B. Now show the Chapter 11 video episode. See the Video Activities Booklet for detailed suggestions for using this resource.

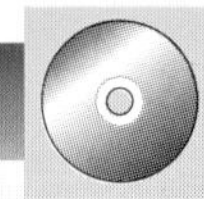

CD-ROM

A. Have students read the caption on the Mexicana brochure on page 341.

B. In the CD-ROM version of **Expansión cultural** (Disc 3, page 341), students can listen to additional recorded information about Mexicana Airlines.

INTERNET

Teacher Information and Student Worksheets for this activity can be accessed at the Web site.

CAPÍTULOS 8–11
Repaso

RESOURCES

- Workbook: Self-Test 3, pp. 143–148
- CD-ROM, Disc 3, pages 342–345
- Tests: Unit 3, pp. 66; 114; 146

OVERVIEW

This section reviews the salient points from Chapters 8–11. In the **Conversación** students will review health vocabulary, verbs with an irregular **yo** form, and the preterite in context. In the **Estructura** section, they will study the uses of **ser** vs. **estar,** the conjugations of irregular verbs, and the formation of the preterite. They will practice these structures as they talk about skiing, sports, and other leisure activities.

TEACHING THE CONVERSATION

A. Have students open their books to page 342. Ask two students to read the conversation aloud using as much expression as possible.

B. Go over the questions in the **Después de conversar** section.

Learning From Realia

Clínica médica Arabial Ask students to figure out what services are offered by this clinic in Granada.

Repaso CAPÍTULOS 8–11

Conversación

El pobre Juanito

ANITA: Juanito fue a Navacerrada a esquiar.

ANTONIO: Ah, sí. ¿Qué tal lo pasó?

ANITA: Muy bien. Pasó un fin de semana estupendo. Pero, ¿sabes dónde está ahora?

ANTONIO: No sé. No tengo idea.

ANITA: Pues, está en la consulta del médico.

ANTONIO: ¿Qué tiene? ¿Qué le pasó?

ANITA: No sé. Le duele mucho el estómago y no sabe si tiene fiebre.

ANTONIO: Pues, tú conoces a Juanito. Siempre está haciendo cosas que no debe hacer. ¿Qué comió?

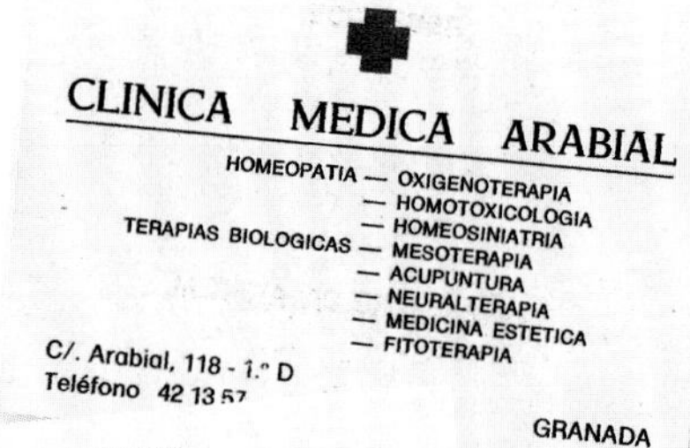

Después de conversar

A **El pobre Juanito** Contesten.

1. ¿Adónde fue Juanito?
2. ¿Por qué fue a Navacerrada?
3. ¿Qué tal fue el fin de semana?
4. ¿Dónde está Juanito ahora?
5. ¿Por qué? ¿Qué tiene?
6. ¿Qué está haciendo siempre Juanito?
7. ¿Comió algo malo Juanito?

ANSWERS

Después de conversar

A
1. **Juanito fue a Navacerrada.**
2. **A esquiar.**
3. **Pasó un fin de semana estupendo.**
4. **Juanito está en la consulta del médico.**
5. **Le duele mucho el estómago.**
6. **Siempre está haciendo cosas que no debe hacer.**
7. **No sabemos si Juanito comió algo malo.**

Estructura

Ser y estar

1. The verbs **ser** and **estar** both mean "to be." **Ser** is used to tell where someone or something is from. It is also used to describe an inherent trait or characteristic.

   Roberto es de Los Ángeles.
   Roberto es inteligente y guapo.

2. **Estar** is used to tell where someone or something is located. It is also used to describe a temporary condition or state.

   Ahora Roberto está en Madrid.
   Madrid está en España.
   Roberto está muy contento en Madrid.

3. **Estar** is used with a present participle to form the progressive tense.

   Estamos estudiando y aprendiendo mucho.

Nueva York

Práctica

A HISTORIETA Roberto

Completen con la forma apropiada de **ser** o **estar.**

Roberto _____ (1) de Caracas. Él _____ (2) muy simpático. _____ (3) muy gracioso también. Ahora él _____ (4) en Nueva York. _____ (5) estudiando en la universidad. Roberto _____ (6) muy contento en Nueva York.

Nueva York _____ (7) en el noreste de los Estados Unidos. Nueva York _____ (8) muy grande. _____ (9) muy interesante también. A Roberto le gusta mucho.

Hoy Roberto _____ (10) de mal humor. No _____ (11) muy contento. La nota que recibió en un curso no _____ (12) muy buena y Roberto _____ (13) muy inteligente.

Verbos irregulares en el presente

The following verbs all have an irregular **yo** form in the present tense. All other forms are regular.

HACER	**yo hago**	TRAER	**yo traigo**	SABER	**yo sé**
PONER	**yo pongo**	SALIR	**yo salgo**	CONOCER	**yo conozco**

CAPÍTULOS 8–11
Repaso

TEACHING STRUCTURE

Ser y estar

A. For review purposes, reverse the usual procedure and have students read the Spanish sentences and explain why either **ser** or **estar** is used.

B. Write **ser** and **estar** on the board and list their uses under the appropriate infinitive as students explain the rules.

A After going over **Práctica A**, have a student tell all about Roberto in his or her own words.

TECHNOLOGY OPTIONS Students may enjoy reviewing the difference between **ser** and **estar** by playing the Chapter 8 click-and-drag game at **Café Glencoe** at **www.cafe.glencoe.com**

TEACHING STRUCTURE

Verbos irregulares en el presente

Have students give all the forms of some of these verbs. Emphasize that all other forms are regular. Only **yo** is irregular.

ANSWERS

Práctica

A
1. es
2. es
3. Es
4. está
5. Está
6. está
7. está
8. es
9. Es
10. está
11. está
12. es
13. es

B **Práctica B** can be done as a paired activity.

TEACHING STRUCTURE

Los pronombres de complemento

A. Have students open their books to page 344. Read Steps 1–3 with them.

B. When going over Step 2, you may write the sentences on the board. Put a box around the direct object (noun) and draw an arrow from the noun to the pronoun as you box in the pronoun.

Práctica

C This is a point that students find quite difficult. It will be reinforced many times. If students have problems doing **Práctica C**, review some of the **Práctica** in Chapters 9 and 10.

Práctica

B **Entrevista** Contesten personalmente.

1. ¿Haces un viaje a Madrid?
2. ¿A qué hora sales para el aeropuerto?
3. ¿Pones las maletas en la maletera del carro?
4. ¿Traes mucho equipaje?
5. ¿Sabes a qué hora sale tu vuelo?
6. ¿Sabes el número del vuelo?
7. ¿Conoces Madrid?
8. ¿Sabes hablar español?

Los pronombres de complemento

1. The object pronouns **me, te,** and **nos** can function as either direct or indirect object pronouns. Note that the object pronouns in Spanish precede the conjugated verb.

¿*Te* vio Juan? **Sí, Juan *me* vio y *me* dio el libro.**

2. **Lo, los, la,** and **las** function as direct object pronouns only. They can replace persons or things.

Pablo compró *el boleto.*	**Pablo *lo* compró.**
Pablo compró *los boletos.*	**Pablo *los* compró.**
Elena compró *la raqueta.*	**Elena *la* compró.**
Elena compró *las raquetas.*	**Elena *las* compró.**
Yo vi a *los muchachos.*	**Yo *los* vi.**

3. **Le** and **les** function as indirect object pronouns only.

Yo *le* escribí una carta (a él, a ella, a Ud.).
Yo *les* escribí una carta (a ellos, a ellas, a Uds.).

Práctica

C **¡A esquiar!** Cambien los sustantivos en pronombres.

1. Llevo *los esquís* a la cancha.
2. También llevo *las botas.*
3. Compro *el boleto* en la taquilla.
4. Veo *a mi hermana* en el telesquí.
5. Doy *el boleto* a mi hermana.
6. Ella da *los esquís* a los muchachos.

Chacaltaya, una estación de esquí en Bolivia

ANSWERS

Práctica

B
1. **Sí, hago un viaje a Madrid.**
2. **Salgo para el aeropuerto a las ___.**
3. **Sí, (No, no) pongo las maletas en la maletera del carro.**
4. **Sí, (No, no) traigo mucho equipaje.**
5. **Sí, (No, no) sé a qué hora sale mi vuelo.**
6. **Sí, (No, no) sé el número del vuelo.**
7. **Sí, (No, no) conozco Madrid.**
8. **Sí, (No, no) sé hablar español.**

C
1. **Los llevo a la cancha.**
2. **También las llevo.**
3. **Lo compro en la taquilla.**
4. **La veo en el telesquí.**
5. **Lo doy a mi hermana.**
6. **Los da a los muchachos.**

El pretérito

1. The preterite is used to express an event that started and ended in the past. Review the forms of the preterite of regular verbs.

INFINITIVE	mirar	comer	vivir
yo	miré	comí	viví
tú	miraste	comiste	viviste
él, ella, Ud.	miró	comió	vivió
nosotros(as)	miramos	comimos	vivimos
vosotros(as)	*mirasteis*	*comisteis*	*vivisteis*
ellos, ellas, Uds.	miraron	comieron	vivieron

2. The forms of **ir** and **ser** in the preterite are identical. The meaning is made clear by the context of the sentence.

fui fuiste fue fuimos *fuisteis* fueron

D ¿Qué hicieron todos? Contesten.

1. ¿Fuiste al museo ayer?
   ¿Viste una exposición de arte?
   ¿Tomaste un refresco en la cafetería del museo?
2. ¿Salieron Uds. anoche?
   ¿Fueron al cine?
   ¿Tomaron el metro?
3. ¿Esquió Roberto?
   ¿Subió la pista en el telesilla?
   ¿Bajó la pista para expertos?
4. ¿Pasaron tus amigos el fin de semana en la playa?
   ¿Te escribieron una tarjeta postal?
   ¿Nadaron y tomaron el sol en la playa?

Actividades comunicativas

A Deportes The Latin American exchange student (your partner) at your school asks you what sports you played last year. Tell him or her and say which one you liked most and why. Then ask the exchange student the same questions.

B Diversiones Work with a classmate. Discuss what you each do when you have free time. Do you like to do the same activities?

CAPÍTULOS 8-11
Repaso

TEACHING STRUCTURE

El pretérito

A. Have students open their books to page 345. Write the verb forms from the chart on the board. Underline the endings.

B. Have the class repeat all forms of the same verb. Then have them read across—all the **yo** forms, all the **tú** forms, etc.

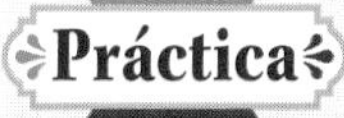

D The preterite will be reintroduced frequently. If students have problems doing **Práctica D**, review some of the **Práctica** in Chapters 9 and 10.

Actividades comunicativas

Allow students to select the activity they want to do.

Note: You may wish to do the third literary selection (pages 448–453) with students at this time.

ANSWERS

Práctica

D
1. **Sí, (No, no) fui al museo ayer.**
   Sí, (No, no) vi una exposición de arte.
   Sí, (No, no) tomé un refresco en la cafetería del museo.
2. **Sí, (No, no) salimos anoche.**
   Sí, (No, no) fuimos al cine.
   Sí, (No, no) tomamos el metro.
3. **Sí (No), Roberto (no) esquió.**
   Sí, (No, no) subió la pista en el telesilla.
   Sí, (No, no) bajó la pista para expertos.
4. **Sí (No), mis amigos (no) pasaron el fin de semana en la playa.**
   Sí, (No, no) me escribieron una tarjeta postal.
   Sí, nadaron y tomaron el sol en la playa.

Actividades comunicativas

A Answers will vary. Students should use the vocabulary from Chapters 9 and 10.

B Answers will vary. Students should use the vocabulary from Chapters 9, 10, and 11.

Independent Practice

Assign any of the following:
1. Activities, pp. 342–345
2. Workbook: Self-Test 3, pp. 143–148
3. CD-ROM, Disc 3, pp. 342–345
4. CD-ROM, Disc 3, Chapters 8–11, **Juegos de repaso**

VISTAS DE PUERTO RICO

OVERVIEW

The **Vistas de Puerto Rico** were prepared by National Geographic Society. Their purpose is to give students greater insight, through these visual images, into the culture and people of Puerto Rico. Have students look at the photographs on pages 346–349 for enjoyment. If they would like to talk about them, let them say anything they can, using the vocabulary they have learned to this point.

National Standards

Cultures
The **Vistas de Puerto Rico** photos, and the accompanying captions, allow students to gain insights into the people and culture of Puerto Rico.

1. Paseo de la Princesa, Viejo San Juan
2. Plaza de Armas, Viejo San Juan
3. Zona residencial, Viejo San Juan
4. Baile folklórico, Viejo San Juan
5. Coquí, Luquillo
6. Frutero, Viejo San Juan
7. Desfile de los Reyes Magos, Viejo San Juan

Learning From Photos

1. Paseo de la Princesa, Viejo San Juan Old San Juan is the most historic colonial area in the West Indies. It is situated on the western end of an islet. It is encircled by water—the Atlantic on the north and the lovely San Juan Bay on the south and west. The outer walls of the old city that we see here are formed by the ramparts of old Spanish fortresses.

El Paseo de la Princesa starts at the main square near the port. It passes in front of what was once one of the most feared prisons in the Caribbean, **la Princesa**. The Paseo continues and becomes a lovely walkway between the **murallas** and the Bay of San Juan. It is this section of the Paseo that we see here.

2. Plaza de Armas, Viejo San Juan The Plaza de Armas was the original main square of Old San Juan and the central hub of the city. The fountain has 19th-century statues representing the four seasons.

3. Zona residencial, Viejo San Juan This is a typical cobblestoned street in a lovely residential area of Old San Juan. Many of the buildings in the old section are undergoing beautiful restoration.

4. Baile folklórico, Viejo San Juan One of Puerto Rico's most notable exports is its music. The vibrant beats of the **salsa**, **bomba,** and **plena** are heard in many countries of the world. The **bomba** is African in origin. It was brought over by the slaves who worked on the sugar plantations. The **bomba** is described as a dialogue between dancer and

(continued)

VISTAS DE PUERTO RICO

Learning From Photos

(continued)
only and it appears that it cannot survive anywhere else, not even in the nearby Dominican Republic.

6. Frutero, Viejo San Juan The orange sellers can be found on the streets of San Juan and other towns of Puerto Rico. Their little wheel-like machine peels the orange to perfection.

7. Desfile de los Reyes Magos, Viejo San Juan As in many Spanish-speaking countries, children in Puerto Rico receive their Christmas gifts on January 6**, el día de los Reyes.** On this day, all over the island, there are many parades celebrating the bearing of the gifts by the Three Wise Men.

Learning From Photos

(continued from page 346)
drummer. The dance can go on as long as the dancer can continue to dance. The **plena** blends elements from Puerto Rico's many cultural backgrounds, including the music of the Taíno Indians. This type of music was first heard in Ponce.

5. Coquí, Luquillo The **coquí** is a tiny tree frog that has a distinctive cry from which it gets its name. Although the singing of the **coquí** can be heard in many areas of the island, one cannot miss it in areas such as El Yunque Rainforest where there are millions of **coquís**. The lovely **coquí** can be heard but not seen. Puerto Ricans are extremely fond of the **coquí,** who loves the island of Puerto Rico as much as the Puerto Ricans do. The **coquí** lives in Puerto Rico

(continued)

VISTAS DE PUERTO RICO

Learning From Photos

1. Vegetación tropical, Sierra de Cayey Puerto Rico has an extremely varied terrain. It has palm-lined beaches on four coasts and rugged mountain ranges in its interior. The Cordillera stretches across the central part of Puerto Rico. Its highest point is **Cerro de Punta** at 4,389 feet. Many people have weekend homes in the Cordillera, where the temperature is often 20 or more degrees lower than on the coast. From some heights one can look north and see the Atlantic, or look south and see the Caribbean.

2. Radiotelescopio, Arecibo The Arecibo Observatory has the world's largest and most sensitive radar/radio telescope. It features a 20-acre dish set in a sinkhole. It measures 1,000 feet in diameter and is 167 feet deep. It allows scientists to examine the ionosphere, the planets, and the moon. It has been used by scientists as part of the Search for Extraterrestrial Intelligence (SGTI). The Arecibo Observatory is called **un oído a los cielos,** *an ear to the heavens.*

3. Laguna del Condado, San Juan The Condado is an important tourist area of San Juan with luxury hotels and high-rise condominiums. Here we see the beach in front of one of the Condado hotels. Today the area around the Convention Center, including the hotels, is being completely renovated.

4. Museo de Arte, Ponce The building that houses this museum was donated to the people of Puerto Rico by Luis Ferré, a former governor. It has the finest *(continued)*

1. Vegetación tropical, Sierra de Cayey
2. Radiotelescopio, Arecibo
3. Laguna del Condado, San Juan
4. Museo de arte, Ponce
5. Cosecha de piñas, Manatí
6. Atleta puertorriqueña, San Juan
7. Catedral de Nuestra Señora de Guadalupe, Ponce

PUERTO RICO

NATIONAL GEOGRAPHIC SOCIETY

TEACHER'S CORNER

Index to NATIONAL GEOGRAPHIC MAGAZINE

The following articles may be used for research relating to this chapter:

- "The Uncertain State of Puerto Rico," by Bill Richards, April 1983.
- "Sailing a Sea of Fire," by Paul A. Zahl, July 1960.

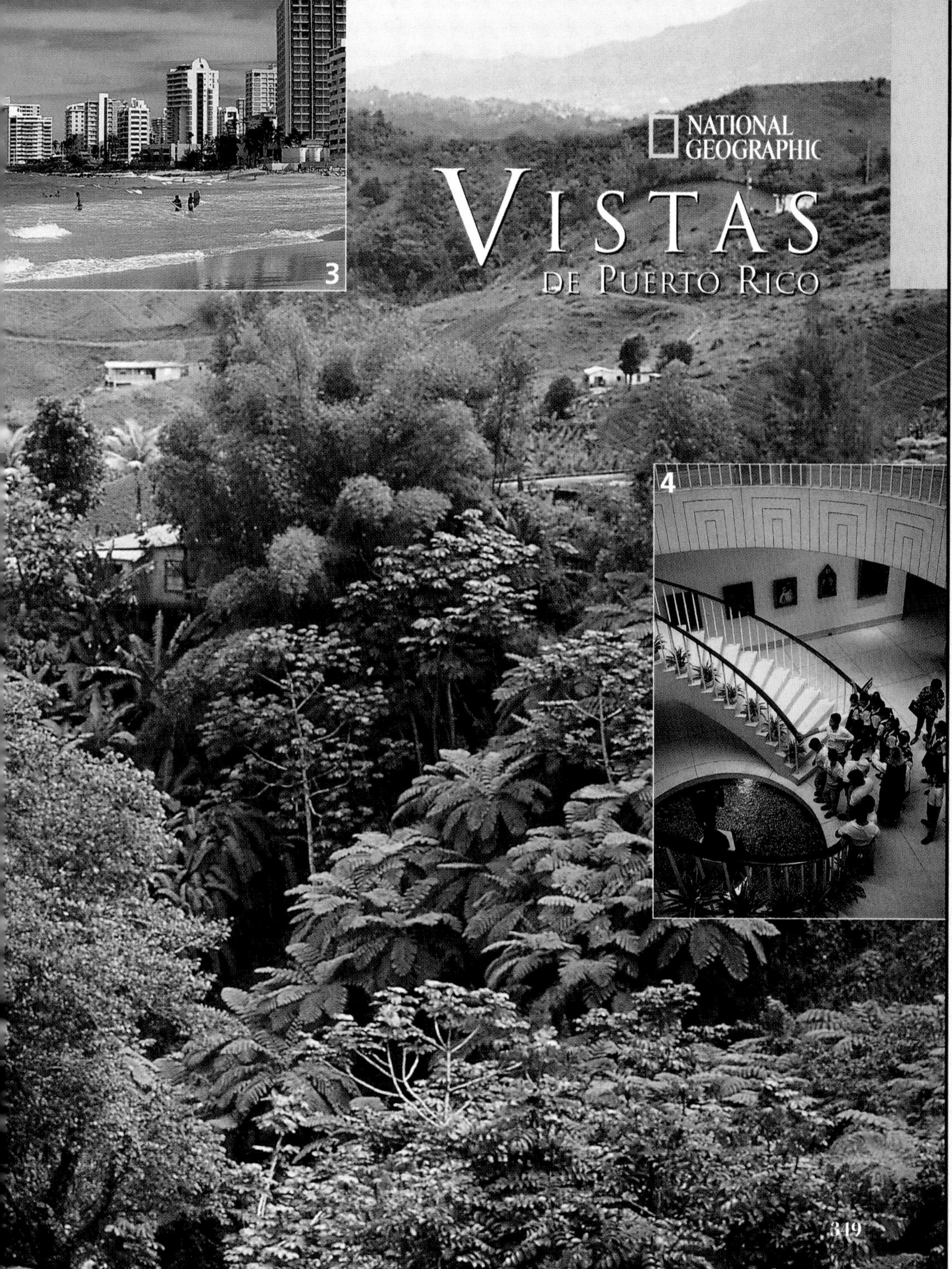

VISTAS DE PUERTO RICO

Learning From Photos

(continued from page 348)
collection of European and Latin American art in the Caribbean. The museum also has some of the best paintings of two noted Puerto Rican artists, Francisco Oller and José Campeche. The building was designed by Edward Durrell Stone, who also designed the JFK Center for the Performing Arts in Washington, D.C.

5. Cosecha de piñas, Manatí There are many pineapple plantations in this area on the northern coast between San Juan and Arecibo.

6. Atleta puertorriqueña, San Juan This young woman is wearing a tank top designed to look like the Puerto Rican flag, which is red, white, and blue with one star.

7. Catedral de Nuestra Señora de Guadalupe, Ponce Ponce is the second largest city in Puerto Rico. The cathedral is named after the patron saint of Mexico. In 1660, a rustic church was built where the cathedral stands today, but it was razed several times by fires and earthquakes. The present structure was built in 1931.

Products available from GLENCOE/MCGRAW-HILL

To order the following products, call Glencoe/McGraw-Hill at 1-800-334-7344.

CD-ROMs
- Picture Atlas of the World
- The Complete National Geographic: 109 Years of National Geographic Magazine

Software
- ZingoLingo: Spanish Diskettes

Transparency Set
- NGS PicturePack: Geography of North America

Products available from NATIONAL GEOGRAPHIC SOCIETY

NATIONAL GEOGRAPHIC SOCIETY

To order the following products, call National Geographic Society at 1-800-368-2728.

Books
- Exploring Your World: The Adventure of Geography
- National Geographic Satellite Atlas of the World

Chapter 12 Overview ◆◆◆◆◆◆◆◆◆◆◆◆◆◆◆◆◆◆◆◆◆◆◆◆◆◆◆◆◆◆◆◆

SCOPE AND SEQUENCE pages 350–377

TOPICS	FUNCTIONS	STRUCTURE	CULTURE
◆ Daily routines ◆ Grooming habits ◆ Camping	◆ How to describe personal grooming habits ◆ How to talk about your daily routine ◆ How to describe a backpacking trip ◆ How to tell about things you do for yourself ◆ How to discuss what others do for themselves	◆ Reflexive verbs ◆ Radical changing reflexive verbs	◆ Iván Orama describes a backpacking trip in Northern Spain ◆ Picos de Europa, Spain ◆ El Parque Nacional de Covadonga, Spain ◆ San Sebastián ◆ **El Camino de Santiago** in Northern Spain ◆ The Cathedral in Santiago de Compostela ◆ Ecology in the Spanish-speaking world

CHAPTER 12 RESOURCES

PRINT	MULTIMEDIA
Planning Resources	
Lesson Plans Block Scheduling Lesson Plans	Interactive Lesson Planner
Reinforcement Resources	
Writing Activities Workbook Student Tape Manual Video Activities Booklet Web Site User's Guide	Transparencies Binder Audiocassette/Compact Disc Program Videocassette/Videodisc Program Online Internet Activities Electronic Teacher's Classroom Resources
Assessment Resources	
Situation Cards Chapter Quizzes Testing Program Performance Assessment	**Maratón mental** Mindjogger Videoquiz Testmaker Computer Software (Macintosh/Windows) Listening Comprehension Audiocassette/Compact Disc Communication Transparency: C-12
Motivational Resources	
Expansion Activities	Café Glencoe: www.cafe.glencoe.com Keypal Internet Activities
Enrichment	
Spanish for Spanish Speakers	

Chapter 12 Planning Guide

SECTION	PAGES	SECTION RESOURCES
Vocabulario Palabras 1 **La rutina**	352–355	Vocabulary Transparencies 12.1 Audiocassette 7B/ Compact Disc 7 Student Tape Manual, TE, pages 138–140 Workbook, pages 149–150 Chapter Quizzes, pages 60–61 CD-ROM, Disc 4, pages 352–355
Vocabulario Palabras 2 **Una gira** **¿Qué ponen o llevan en la mochila?**	356–359	Vocabulary Transparencies 12.2 Audiocassette 7B/ Compact Disc 7 Student Tape Manual, TE, pages 141–142 Workbook, pages 151–152 Chapter Quizzes, page 62 CD-ROM, Disc 4, pages 356–359
Estructura **Verbos reflexivos** **Verbos reflexivos de cambio radical**	360–365	Workbook, pages 153–155 Audiocassette 7B/Compact Disc 7 Student Tape Manual, TE, pages 142–143 Structure Transparency S-12 Chapter Quizzes, pages 63–64 Computer Testmaker CD-ROM, Disc 4, pages 360–365
Conversación **¿A qué hora te despertaste?** **Pronunciación: La h, la y, la ll**	366–367	Audiocassette 7B/Compact Disc 7 Student Tape Manual, TE, pages 144–145 CD-ROM, Disc 4, pages 366–367
Lecturas culturales **Del norte de España** **El Camino de Santiago *(opcional)***	368–371	Testing Program, pages 73–74 CD-ROM, Disc 4, pages 368–371
Conexiones **La ecología *(opcional)***	372–373	Testing Program, page 74 CD-ROM, Disc 4, pages 372–373
Culminación **Actividades orales** **Actividades escritas** **Vocabulario** **Tecnotur**	374–377	**¡Buen viaje!** Video, Episode 12 Video Activities, pages 110–113 Internet Activities **www.glencoe.com/sec/fl** Testing Program, pages 71–73; 115; 147; 172 CD-ROM, Disc 4, pages 374–377

CAPÍTULO 12

OVERVIEW

In this chapter students will learn to discuss their daily routine with particular emphasis on hygiene. To do this they will learn reflexive verbs. The cultural focus is on the routine of the many young cyclists and backpackers who today follow the **Camino de Santiago** in Spain.

National Standards

Communication In Chapter 12 students will communicate in spoken and written Spanish on the following topics:

- daily routines
- taking care of oneself
- enjoying a good backpacking trip

Students will obtain and provide information about these topics and engage in conversations about everyday habits, including daily hygiene, as they fulfill the chapter objectives listed on this page.

CAPÍTULO 12

Una gira

Objetivos

In this chapter you will learn to do the following:

- describe your personal grooming habits
- talk about your daily routine
- tell some things you do for yourself
- talk about a backpacking trip

*inter*NET CONNECTION

The **Glencoe Foreign Language Web site (http://www.glencoe.com/sec/fl)** offers three options that enable you and your students to experience the Spanish-speaking world via the Internet:

- The online **Actividades** are correlated to the chapters and utilize Hispanic Web sites around the world. For the Chapter 12 activity, see student page 377.
- The **Correspondencia electrónica** section provides information on how to set up a keypal (pen pal) exchange between your class and a class in the Spanish-speaking world.
- At **Café Glencoe,** the interactive "after-school" section of the site, you and your students can access a variety of additional online resources, including interactive games.

CAPÍTULO 12

Spotlight On Culture

Artefacto The doll with the basket on her head is from Guatemala.
Fotografía The photo on this page was taken in the mountainous area called Picos de Europa in the province of Asturias (Spain). Even in the summer, some of the peaks that rise to over 2,640 meters (8,600 feet) are snow-covered. Also in this area is the beautiful **Parque Nacional de la Sierra de Covadonga**. It is connected to the town of Covadonga by a narrow lane.

Learning From Photos

El tiempo Have students look at the photo and describe the weather.

Pacing

Chapter 12 will require approximately eight to ten days. Pacing will vary according to the length of the class, the age of your students, and student aptitude.

Block Scheduling

The extended timeframe provided by block scheduling affords you the opportunity to implement a greater number of activities and projects to motivate and involve your students. See the Block Scheduling Lesson Plans Booklet for suggestions on how to present the chapter material within a block scheduling framework.

Chapter Projects

La buena higiene Have students prepare a booklet on good hygiene. Have them make a list of do's and don't's **(rutinas positivas/ rutinas negativas).** For example, under **rutinas positivas,** they might say, **cepillarse los dientes antes de acostarse.** Under **rutinas negativas,** they might say, **acostarse a medianoche.** Finally, students can compile a master list of good and bad habits of hygiene to display on a school bulletin board.

CAPÍTULO 12
Vocabulario
PALABRAS 1

RESOURCES

- Vocabulary Transparencies 12.1 (A & B)
- Student Tape Manual, TE, pages 138–140
- Audiocassette 7B/CD7
- Workbook, pages 149–150
- Quiz 1, pages 60–61
- CD-ROM, Disc 4, pages 352–355

Bell Ringer Review

Use BRR Transparency 12-1, or write the following on the board: Indicate if the following take place **en el verano, en el invierno o en las dos estaciones.**

1. **Los amigos esquían en el agua.**
2. **Los amigos bucean.**
3. **Los amigos nadan en el mar.**
4. **Los amigos nadan en una piscina cubierta.**
5. **Los amigos juegan tenis en una cancha al aire libre.**
6. **Los amigos bajan la pista para principiantes.**

TEACHING VOCABULARY

A. Have students close their books. Model the new words using Vocabulary Transparencies 12.1 (A & B). Point to each illustration and have the class repeat the corresponding word or expression after you or the recording on Cassette 7B/Compact Disc 7.

B. Now have students open their books and repeat the procedure as they read.

C. Act out the new words: **despertarse, levantarse, afeitarse, peinarse, lavarse, cepillarse, ponerse la ropa, sentarse.** *(continued on page 353)*

Vocabulario
PALABRAS 1

La rutina

El muchacho se llama José.

José se acuesta.
Se acuesta a las once de la noche.
Él se duerme enseguida.

La muchacha se despierta temprano.
Se levanta enseguida.

El muchacho se lava la cara.

El muchacho se afeita.
Se afeita con la navaja.

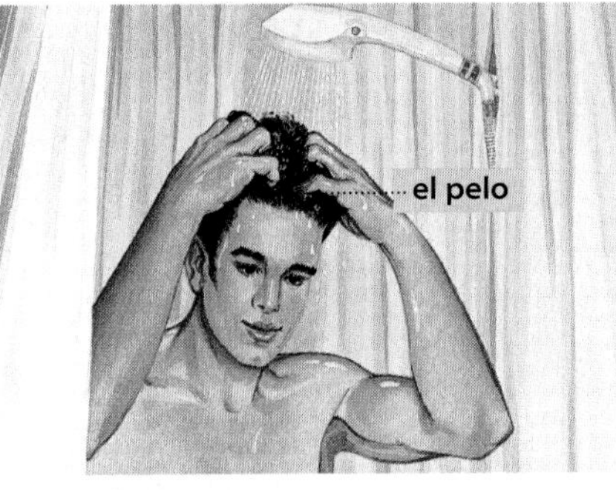

El muchacho toma una ducha.
El muchacho se lava el pelo.

La muchacha se baña.

Total Physical Response

Getting ready

You may use a chair for a bed. Bring in a mirror and an alarm clock. Or make a buzzing sound when you say **despertador.**

Begin

___, ven acá, por favor.
Son las siete de la mañana. Estás durmiendo.
Oyes el despertador. Te despiertas.
Te levantas. Vas al cuarto de baño.
Te lavas.
Te miras en el espejo.
Te cepillas los dientes.
Te peinas. Te pones la ropa.
Sales para la escuela.
Gracias, ___. Y ahora puedes regresar a tu asiento.

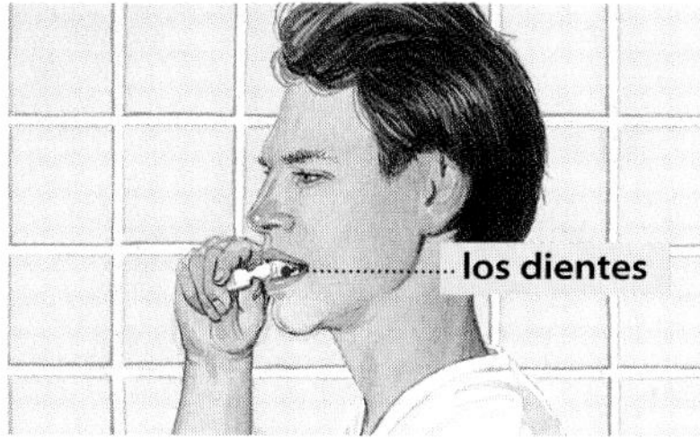

El muchacho se cepilla (se lava) los dientes.

La muchacha se maquilla.
Se pone el maquillaje.

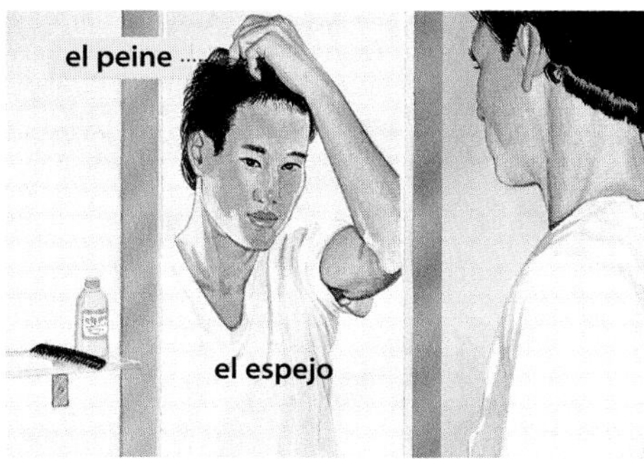

El muchacho se peina.
Se mira en el espejo cuando se peina.

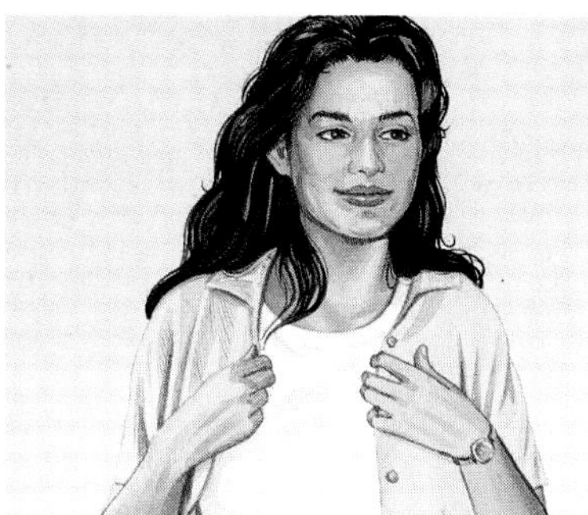

Ella se pone la ropa.

La muchacha se sienta a la mesa.
Toma el desayuno.
Se desayuna.

Did You Know?

El desayuno The breakfast the girl in the illustration is eating is typical of the U.S. and is becoming more common in many Hispanic countries. The usual breakfast in Spain and Latin America, however, continues to be **café con leche** with a great deal of **leche,** toast, and maybe juice or fruit. At mid-morning, people eat a sandwich or snack to tide themselves over until the midday meal.

Vocabulario

D. As you present the new vocabulary, ask questions such as the following: **¿La muchacha se despierta por la mañana o por la noche? Entonces, ¿ella se levanta o se acuesta? ¿Ella se levanta o se acuesta a las diez de la noche? ¿El muchacho se lava la cara o las manos? ¿Se cepilla los dientes?**

E. Call out the following verbs and have students pantomime each one: **despertarse, levantarse, lavarse, cepillarse los dientes, afeitarse.**

VOCABULARY EXPANSION

You may wish to teach students the following additional words so they can describe a typical U.S. breakfast: **huevos (fritos, revueltos, pasados por agua), tocino, jamón, salchicha, panqueques con jarabe** *(syrup).*

ABOUT THE SPANISH LANGUAGE

- The word for pajamas is **pijamas.**
- **Dientes** are *teeth* and **muelas** are *molars.* Both are often used as generic terms for teeth. A *toothache* is a **dolor de muelas**. You may wish to ask students what **diente** and **muela** mean in English. You may also ask them to identify the **dientes caninos** and the **incisivos.**
- The first meal of the day is breakfast, *to break a fast.* The same concept applies to the Spanish word. Ask students what the word for *a fast* would be in Spanish **(ayuno).** You will hear both **desayunar** and **desayunarse** when referring to breakfast.

¡OJO! **Práctica** When students are doing the **Práctica** activities, accept any answer that makes sense. The purpose of these activities is to have students use the new vocabulary. They are not factual recall activities. Thus, do not expect students to remember specific information from the vocabulary presentation when answering. If you wish, have students use the photos on this page as a stimulus, when possible.

Historieta Each time **Historieta** appears, it means that the answers to the activity form a short story. Encourage students to look at the title of the **Historieta** since it will sometimes help them do the activity.

A After going over **Práctica A,** have students retell the story in their own words.

EXPANSION Have students look at each photograph or illustration on page 354 and describe it in their own words.

Writing Development

Have students write the answers to **Práctica A** in a paragraph to illustrate how all of the items tell a story.

Práctica

A **HISTORIETA** Un día en la vida de…

Contesten según se indica.

1. ¿Cómo se llama el joven? (Paco)
2. ¿A qué hora se despierta? (a las seis y media)
3. ¿Cuándo se levanta? (enseguida)
4. ¿Adónde va? (al cuarto de baño)
5. ¿Qué hace? (se lava la cara y se cepilla los dientes)
6. Luego, ¿adónde va? (a la cocina)
7. ¿Se sienta a la mesa? (sí)
8. ¿Qué toma? (el desayuno)

B **¿Qué hace el muchacho o la muchacha?** Describan.

1.

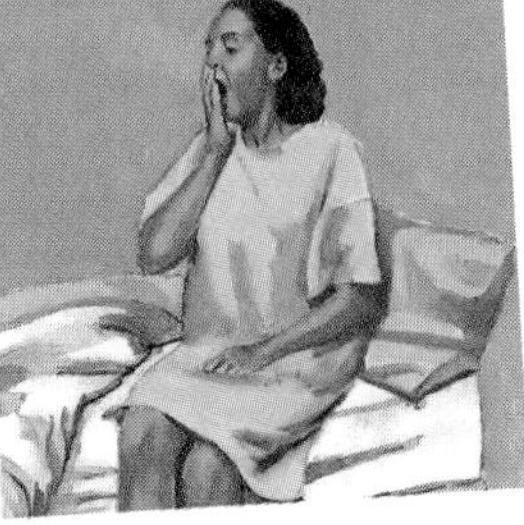

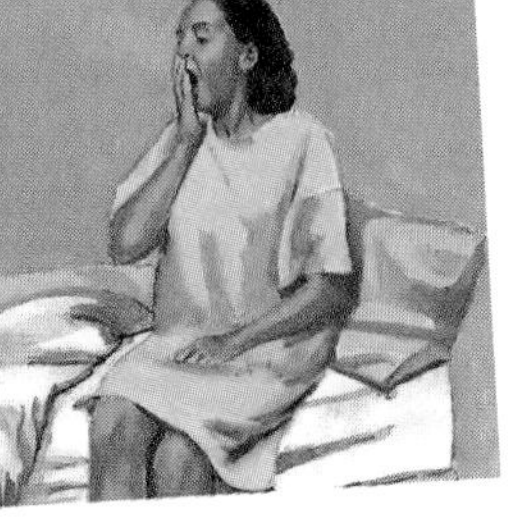

2.

3.

4.

5.

6.

ANSWERS

Práctica

A
1. **El joven se llama Paco.**
2. **Se despierta a las seis y media.**
3. **Se levanta enseguida.**
4. **Va al cuarto de baño.**
5. **Se lava la cara y se cepilla los dientes.**
6. **Luego va a la cocina.**
7. **Sí, se sienta a la mesa.**
8. **Toma el desayuno.**

B
1. **El muchacho se levanta.**
2. **La muchacha se acuesta.**
3. **La muchacha se peina.**
4. **El muchacho se lava el pelo.**
5. **La muchacha (se) desayuna (toma el desayuno).**
6. **El muchacho se afeita.**

C HISTORIETA Las actividades de Sarita

Completen.

Sarita ___1___ por la mañana. Ella ___2___ la cara y las manos. Ella ___3___ los dientes. Ella ___4___ el pelo. Ella ___5___ la ropa—un blue jean y una camiseta. Ella ___6___ en la cocina. Ella ___7___ a la mesa.

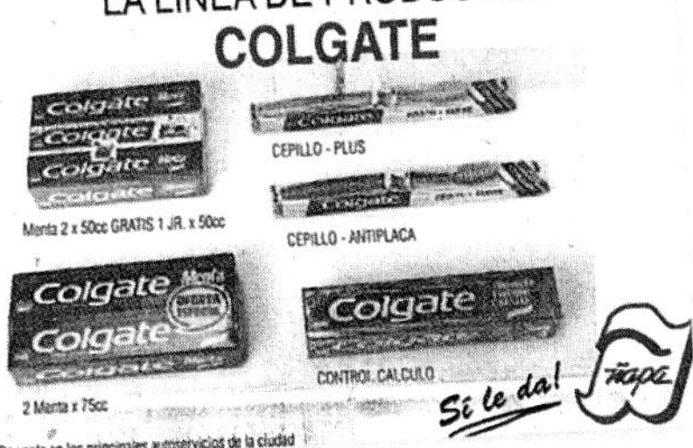

Málaga, España

D Entrevista

Contesten personalmente.

1. ¿Cómo te llamas?
2. ¿A qué hora tomas el desayuno?
3. ¿Tomas el desayuno en la cocina o en el comedor?
4. ¿Te gusta tomar un desayuno grande?
5. ¿Qué comes en el desayuno?
6. ¿Te gustan los cereales?

Actividad comunicativa

A La rutina Work with a classmate. Each of you will choose one family member and tell each other about that person's daily activities.

ANSWERS

Práctica

C
1. **se levanta (se despierta)**
2. **se lava**
3. **se cepilla**
4. **se peina (se cepilla, se lava)**
5. **se pone**
6. **se desayuna (se sienta)**
7. **se sienta (se desayuna)**

D
1. **Me llamo ___.**
2. **Tomo el desayuno a (eso de) las ___.**
3. **Tomo el desayuno en la cocina (el comedor).**
4. **Sí, (No, no) me gusta tomar un desayuno grande.**
5. **Como ___ y ___ en el desayuno.**
6. **Sí, (No, no) me gustan los cereales.**

Actividad comunicativa

A Answers will vary.

C After students do **Práctica C,** have them retell the story in their own words.

D **Práctica D** can be done in pairs as an interview. Encourage students to ask additional, related questions. For example: **¿Qué pones en el cereal? ¿fruta, leche o azúcar?**

EXPANSION See how many food items students can identify in the photo.

Actividad comunicativa

¡OJO! Práctica versus Actividades comunicativas All activities which provide guided practice are labeled **Práctica.** The more open-ended communicative activities are labeled **Actividades comunicativas.**

A The partner should take notes. At the end of the description he or she should refer to the notes and repeat what was said.

TECHNOLOGY OPTION
In the Chapter 12 video episode, Isabel describes her brother Luis' daily activities to Cristina. This video scene can serve as a model for **Actividad A.**

Learning From Realia

Los productos Colgate So many companies are multinational these days that it is very common to see U.S. products abroad. You may wish to bring in some Spanish magazines and have students find other ads in Spanish for American toiletries and beauty products.

RESOURCES

-  Vocabulary Transparencies 12.2 (A & B)
- Student Tape Manual, TE, pages 141–142
- Audiocassette 7B/CD7
- Workbook, pages 151–152
- Quiz 2, page 62
- CD-ROM, Disc 4, pages 356–359

Bell Ringer Review

Use BRR Transparency 12-2, or write the following on the board: Write sentences using the following expressions.

1. ir a la playa
2. tomar el sol
3. nadar
4. usar una crema protectora
5. ir a un restaurante

TEACHING VOCABULARY

A. Have students close their books. Present the vocabulary using Vocabulary Transparencies 12.2 (A & B). Have students repeat after you or the recording on Cassette 7B/Compact Disc 7.

B. As you present the vocabulary you may wish to ask the following questions:
¿Por dónde están viajando los amigos?
¿Quiénes están viajando?
¿Qué tipo de viaje están haciendo?
¿Está costando mucho dinero el viaje?
¿Cómo están pasando el viaje?
¿Se divierten mucho?
¿Duermen en el saco de dormir?
¿Duermen en su cuarto o al aire libre?

(continued on page 357)

Vocabulario

Una gira

Los amigos están viajando por España.
Están haciendo un viaje económico.
Lo están pasando muy bien.
Se divierten mucho.
Duermen en el saco de dormir.

el saco de dormir

Class Motivator

¿Qué llevas en la mochila? Put real items like those on page 357 in a bag or knapsack. You may want to include additional items, such as an alarm clock, a plastic safety razor, shaving cream, makeup, a comb, and a hand mirror. Now pass the knapsack around the room and have each student pull out an item and identify it. Divide the class and make this a contest to see which side can name the most items.

¿Qué ponen o llevan en la mochila?

Los amigos dan una caminata.
Algunos van a pie.
Y otros van en bicicleta.

Pasan la noche en un albergue para jóvenes.
Y a veces pasan la noche en un hostal o en una pensión.

CAPÍTULO 12
Vocabulario

C. After you have presented all the vocabulary, have students open their books and read the words and sentences for additional reinforcement.

ABOUT THE SPANISH LANGUAGE

- In addition to **el cepillo de dientes** you will also see and hear **el cepillo para los dientes.**
- **Un rollo de papel higiénico** is the most commonly used term. You will also hear **papel de baño** particularly among Spanish-speaking groups in the United States.
- **Una pastilla de jabón** is used in Spain.

VOCABULARY EXPANSION

You may wish to give students a few extra words that have to do with personal hygiene:

el desodorante *deodorant*
cortarse las uñas *trim your nails*
echarse perfume (colonia) *apply perfume (cologne)*

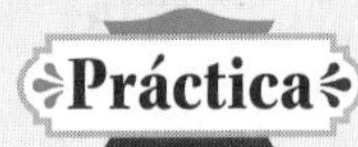

A **Práctica A** can be done as a game. Using a stopwatch, see who can identify the most items in the least amount of time.

Writing Development

After going over **Práctica B**, have students write the story in their own words in paragraph form.

RECYCLING

Quickly review the clothing items these students are wearing.

A **¿Qué pierde Pepe de la mochila?** Identifiquen.

Caracas, Venezuela

B **HISTORIETA Una gira**

Contesten.

1. ¿Hacen los jóvenes un viaje de lujo o un viaje económico?
2. ¿Por dónde están viajando?
3. ¿En qué llevan sus cosas?
4. ¿Cuáles son algunas cosas que ponen en la mochila?
5. ¿Cómo van de un lugar (sitio) a otro?
6. ¿En qué duermen a veces?
7. ¿Dónde pasan la noche de vez en cuando (a veces)?
8. ¿Se divierten?

ANSWERS

Práctica

A **Pepe pierde un cepillo, un rollo de papel higiénico, una navaja, un tubo de pasta dentífrica, una pastilla de jabón, un peine, un cepillo de dientes, crema de afeitar.**

B
1. **Los jóvenes hacen un viaje económico.**
2. **Están viajando por Caracas.**
3. **Llevan sus cosas en una mochila.**
4. **Algunas cosas que ponen en la mochila son: una botella de agua mineral, un tubo de pasta dentífrica, un cepillo de dientes, una barra (pastilla) de jabón, un rollo de papel higiénico y un cepillo.**
5. **Van de un lugar a otro en bicicleta.**
6. **A veces duermen en un saco de dormir.**
7. **De vez en cuando (A veces) pasan la noche en un albergue para jóvenes (en un hostal, una pensión).**
8. **Sí, se divierten mucho.**

C Historieta En el cuarto de baño

Completen.

1. El muchacho va a tomar una ducha. Necesita ____.
2. La muchacha quiere peinarse pero, ¿dónde está ____?
3. El muchacho va a afeitarse. Necesita ____.
4. Juanito quiere lavarse los dientes. ¿Dónde está ____?
5. No hay pasta dentífrica. Tengo que comprar otro ____.
6. No hay más jabón. Tengo que comprar otra ____.
7. Siempre uso ____ para lavarme el pelo.

Actividad comunicativa

A En la farmacia You're a clerk in a drugstore. A classmate is a Spanish-speaking customer who wants to buy the following toiletries. Have a conversation.

CAPÍTULO 12
Vocabulario

Actividad comunicativa

¡OJO! This activity encourages students to use the chapter vocabulary and structures in open-ended situations.

A As a preliminary step for this activity, quickly decide as a class how many **pesetas (pesos)** each item will cost approximately. Put the items and prices on the board so students can refer to them during the activity. You can have groups present their conversations to the class.

Additional Practice

Asociaciones Write the following list on the board: **el pelo, las manos, los ojos, la cara, los dientes.** Have students write down all the toiletries and verbs from this chapter that they associate with each word. For example, **el pelo: lavarse, peinarse, cepillarse, el peine, el champú.**

ANSWERS

C
1. **una barra (pastilla) de jabón**
2. **su peine**
3. **una navaja y crema de afeitar**
4. **su cepillo de dientes (pasta dentífrica)**
5. **tubo**
6. **barra (pastilla)**
7. **champú**

Actividad comunicativa

A Answers will vary; however, students should begin their conversation with the customary greetings, followed by **Quiero (Necesito) comprar...**

CAPÍTULO 12
Estructura

RESOURCES

- Workbook, pages 153–155
- Student Tape Manual, TE, pages 142–143
- Audiocassette 7B/CD7
-  Structure Transparency S-12
- Quizzes 3–4, pages 63–64
- Computer Testmaker
- CD-ROM, Disc 4, pages 360–365

 Bell Ringer Review

Use BRR Transparency 12-3, or write the following on the board: Answer.

1. **¿A qué hora sales de casa por la mañana?**
2. **¿Cómo vas a la escuela?**
3. **¿A qué horas llegas a la escuela?**
4. **¿Qué haces en la escuela?**
5. **¿Dónde tomas el almuerzo?**
6. **¿Qué haces después de las clases?**

TEACHING STRUCTURE

Telling what people do for themselves

A. Have students open their books to page 360 and look at the illustrations. You may also wish to use Structure Transparency S-12.

B. Ask students in which illustrations someone is doing something to himself (herself), and in which illustrations the person is doing something to someone (something) else.

C. Ask what additional word is used when the person is doing something to himself or herself. (**se**)

(continued on page 361)

Estructura

Telling what people do for themselves
Verbos reflexivos

1. Compare the following pairs of sentences.

Mariana baña al perro. **Mariana cepilla al perro.**

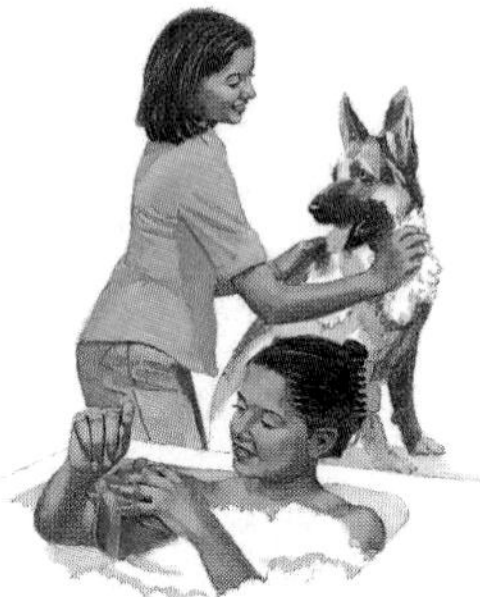

Mariana se baña. **Mariana se cepilla.**

In the sentences above the drawings, Mariana performs the action. The dog receives the action. In the sentences below the drawings, Mariana both performs and receives the action of the verb. For this reason the pronoun **se** must be used. **Se** refers back to Mariana in these sentences and is called a "reflexive pronoun." It indicates that the action of the verb is reflected back to the subject.

2. Study the forms of a reflexive verb.

INFINITIVE	lavarse	levantarse
yo	me lavo	me levanto
tú	te lavas	te levantas
él, ella, Ud.	se lava	se levanta
nosotros(as)	nos lavamos	nos levantamos
vosotros(as)	*os laváis*	*os levantáis*
ellos, ellas, Uds.	se lavan	se levantan

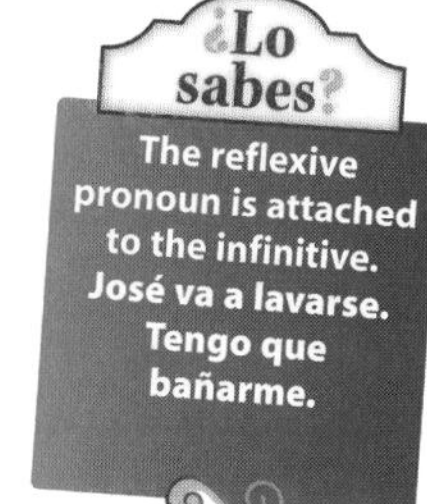

3. In the negative form, **no** is placed before the reflexive pronoun.

No te lavas las manos.
La familia Martínez no se desayuna en el comedor.

Did You Know?

El perro The word for *German shepherd* is **pastor alemán.** For the names of other breeds, see Learning From Photos on page 169.

Learning From Realia

La Montaña In the province of Asturias (Spain), the area that includes the Sierra and the Picos de Europa is referred to as **la Montaña.** As the brochure on page 361 indicates, it is a very popular area for hiking and many other outdoor activities.

4. In Spanish when you refer to parts of the body and articles of clothing, you often use the definite article, not the possessive adjective.

Él se lava la cara.
Me lavo los dientes.

A Historieta Teresa

Contesten.

1. ¿A qué hora se levanta Teresa?
2. ¿Se baña por la mañana o por la noche?
3. ¿Se desayuna en casa?
4. ¿Se lava los dientes después del desayuno?
5. ¿Se pone una chaqueta si sale cuando hace frío?

B El aseo Contesten personalmente.

1. ¿A qué hora te levantas? ¿Y a qué hora te levantaste esta mañana?
2. ¿Te bañas por la mañana o tomas una ducha? Y esta mañana, ¿te bañaste o tomaste una ducha?
3. ¿Te cepillas los dientes con frecuencia? ¿Cuántas veces te cepillaste los dientes hoy?
4. ¿Te desayunas en casa o en la escuela? Y esta mañana, ¿ dónde te desayunaste?
5. ¿Te afeitas o no? Y hoy, ¿te afeitaste?
6. ¿Te peinas con frecuencia? ¿Te miras en el espejo cuando te peinas? ¿Cuántas veces te peinaste hoy?

CAPÍTULO 12
Estructura

D. Explain to them that **se** is a reflexive pronoun and refers to the subject.
E. Then read the explanation that follows in Step 1 on page 360.
F. Call on students to read the model sentences under each illustration or have the class read them in unison.
G. Write the verbs **lavarse** and **levantarse** on the board. After you say **me lavo**, have students supply **me levanto**. Do the same with each subject.
H. Read Steps 3 and 4 and have the class read the model sentences aloud.
I. You may wish to give additional examples of verbs that can be both reflexive and nonreflexive.

Yo me lavo.	**Lavo mi carro.**
Él se acuesta.	**Él acuesta al bebé.**
Nos peinamos.	**Peinamos al gato.**

ABOUT THE SPANISH LANGUAGE

You may wish to explain the following to students:

Ellos se lavan la cara.
Ellos se ponen la chaqueta.

La cara and **la chaqueta** are in the singular because each person has only one face or one jacket. In English the plural forms are used because of the plural subject. You may also wish to point out to students that the possessive adjectives are not used in Spanish in these reflexive constructions as they are in English.

A You can do **Práctica A** with books closed and then with books open. Have students describe in their own words what Teresa does.

B **Práctica B** reinforces the use of the reflexive with both the present and the preterite.

ANSWERS

Práctica

A
1. Teresa se levanta a las ___.
2. Se baña por la mañana (por la noche).
3. Sí, (No, no) se desayuna en casa.
4. Sí, (No, no) se lava los dientes después del desayuno.
5. Sí, se pone una chaqueta si sale cuando hace frío.

B
1. Me levanto a (eso de) las ___. Esta mañana me levanté a las ___.
2. Me baño (Tomo una ducha) por la mañana. Esta mañana me bañé (tomé una ducha).
3. Sí, (No, no) me cepillo los dientes con frecuencia. Me cepillé los dientes ___ veces hoy.
4. Me desayuno en casa (en la escuela). Esta mañana me desayuné en casa (en la escuela).
5. Sí, (No, no) me afeito. Sí, (No, no) me afeité hoy.
6. Sí, (No, no) me peino con frecuencia. Sí, (No, no) me miro en el espejo cuando me peino. Hoy me peiné ___ veces. (Hoy no me peiné.)

Estructura

Práctica

C Remind students to use the definite article when referring to parts of the body, as seen in the model.

D Have students volunteer additional items. For example: **Ellos salen a las ocho. Ellos se acuestan a las diez.**

PAIRED ACTIVITIES

Have students do **Práctica C** and **D** as paired activities or mini-conversations.

C **¿Qué haces?** Sigan el modelo.

—¿Te lavas los dientes?
—Sí, me lavo los dientes.

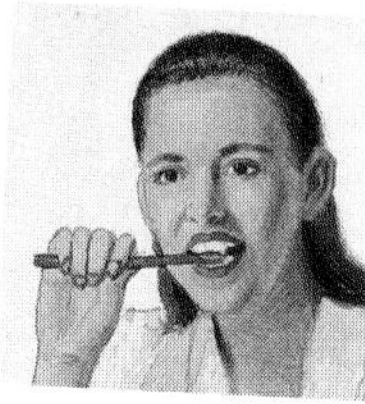

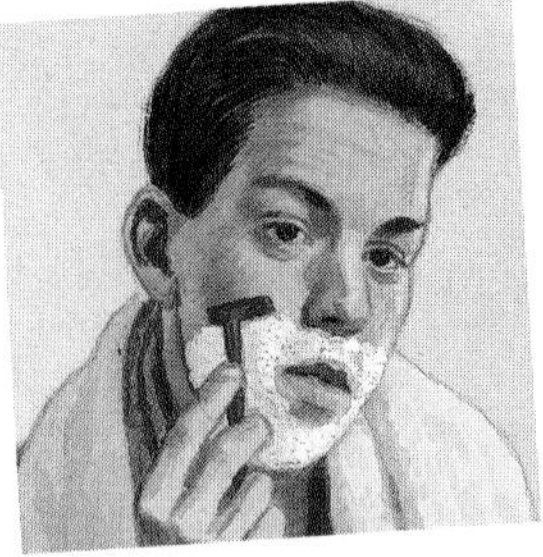

1.

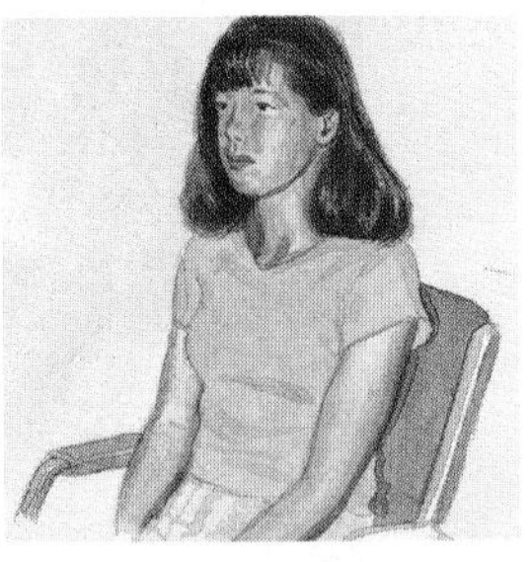

2.

3.

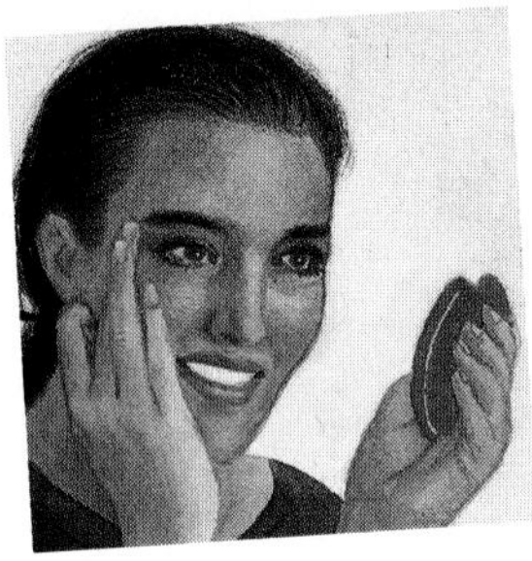

4.

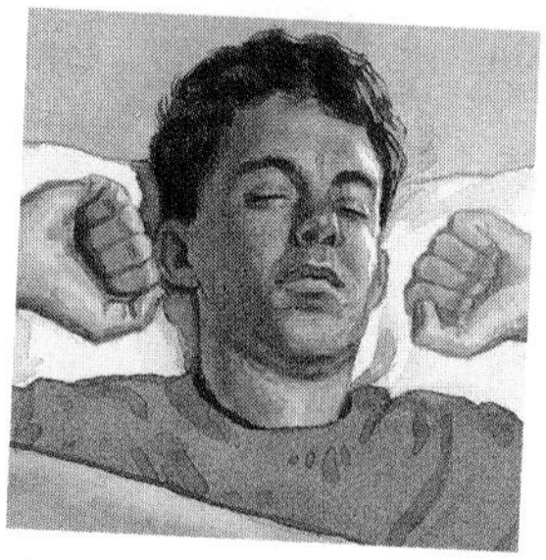

5.

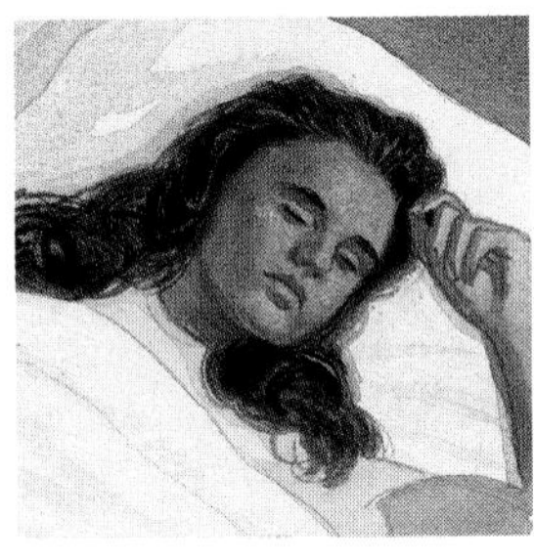

6.

D **¿Y Uds.?** Sigan el modelo.

1. Ellos se levantan a las seis y media.
2. Ellos se bañan a las siete menos cuarto.
3. Ellos se desayunan a las siete y media.

ANSWERS

Práctica

C 1. **¿Te afeitas? Sí, me afeito.**
2. **¿Te sientas? Sí, me siento.**
3. **¿Te lavas la cara? Sí, me lavo la cara.**
4. **¿Te maquillas? (Te pones el maquillaje?) Sí, me maquillo (me pongo el maquillaje).**
5. **¿Te despiertas? Sí, me despierto.**
6. **¿Te acuestas? Sí, me acuesto.**

D Answers will begin with:
Ah, sí. ¿Y a qué hora...
1. **... se levantan Uds.?**
—Nos levantamos a las seis y media también.
2. **... se bañan Uds.?**
—Nos bañamos a las siete menos cuarto también.
3. **... se desayunan Uds.?**
—Nos desayunamos a las siete y media también.

E **Nombres** Contesten.

1. ¿Cómo te llamas?
2. Y tu hermano(a), ¿cómo se llama?
3. ¿Cómo se llama tu profesor(a) de español?
4. ¿Y cómo se llaman tus abuelos?
5. Una vez más, ¿cómo te llamas?

F **¿Qué hacen todos?** Completen según las fotos.

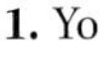

1. Yo
   Él
   Tú
   Ud.

2. Nosotros
   Ellos
   Uds.
   Él y yo

Actividades comunicativas

A **Me desayuno y luego...** Work in groups of three or four. Tell the order of your daily activities from morning to night. Do you all do everything in the same order? Does anyone do things really differently? What's the most common routine? What's the weirdest routine?

JUEGO **Me pongo...** Describe some clothing you're putting on. A classmate will guess where you are going or what you are going to do.

ANSWERS

E **1. Me llamo ___.**
2. Mi hermano(a) se llama ___. (No tengo un[a] hermano[a]).
3. Mi profesor(a) de español se llama ___.
4. Mis abuelos se llaman ___.
5. Me llamo ___.

F **1. Yo me lavo la cara.**
Él se lava la cara.
Tú te lavas la cara.
Ud. se lava la cara.

2. Nosotros nos peinamos.
Ellos se peinan.
Uds. se peinan.
Él y yo nos peinamos.

Actividades comunicativas

A Answers will vary. Students should come up with at least a dozen activities that they do from morning to night.

Estructura

E When doing **Práctica E**, you may wish to go around the room and ask each student **¿Cómo te llamas?** The more times they hear **Me llamo** ___, the better since students often put **es** after **me llamo.** Up to this point students have identified themselves by using **soy** to avoid this problem.

Actividades comunicativas

A **TECHNOLOGY OPTION**
In the CD-ROM version of **Actividad A** (Disc 4, page 363), students can interact with an on-screen native speaker and record their voices.

JUEGO This game gives students the opportunity to use vocabulary and structures from preceding chapters.

Additional Practice

Read this conversation to the class and then ask the questions that follow it.

—¿A qué hora te levantas, Carlos?
—¿Quieres saber a qué hora me levanto o a qué hora me despierto?
—¿A qué hora te levantas?
—Me levanto a las siete.
—¿Y a qué hora sales de la casa?
—Salgo a las siete y media. Me lavo, me cepillo los dientes, me afeito y tomo el desayuno en media hora.
—¿Y te pones la ropa también?
—Claro que me pongo la ropa.

Now ask the following questions:

1. **¿Cómo se llama el muchacho?**
2. **¿A qué hora se levanta?**
3. **¿Se cepilla los dientes?**
4. **¿Se afeita?**
5. **¿A qué hora sale de casa?**
6. **¿Se pone la ropa también?**

CAPÍTULO 12
Estructura

Bell Ringer Review

Use BRR Transparency 12-4, or write the following on the board:
Complete.

1. **Yo ___ (ir) a la playa pero mis amigos ___ (ir) a las montañas. Nosotros no ___ (querer) hacer la misma cosa.**
2. **Yo ___ (salir) ahora pero mis amigos no ___ (salir) ahora. Nosotros no ___ (poder) salir a la misma hora.**

TEACHING STRUCTURE

Telling what people do for themselves

¡OJO! There is actually no new concept here since students are already familiar with the stem-changing verbs and the reflexive pronouns.

A. Model the forms in the chart on page 364. Have students repeat after you.
B. Quickly go over the examples in Step 2.

Práctica

A You may wish to have students do this activity in pairs.

Telling what people do for themselves
Verbos reflexivos de cambio radical

1. The reflexive verbs **acostarse (o→ue)** and (**divertirse e→ie**) are stem-changing verbs. Study the following forms.

INFINITIVE	acostarse	divertirse
yo	me acuesto	me divierto
tú	te acuestas	te diviertes
él, ella, Ud.	se acuesta	se divierte
nosotros(as)	nos acostamos	nos divertimos
vosotros(as)	*os acostáis*	*os divertís*
ellos, ellas, Uds.	se acuestan	se divierten

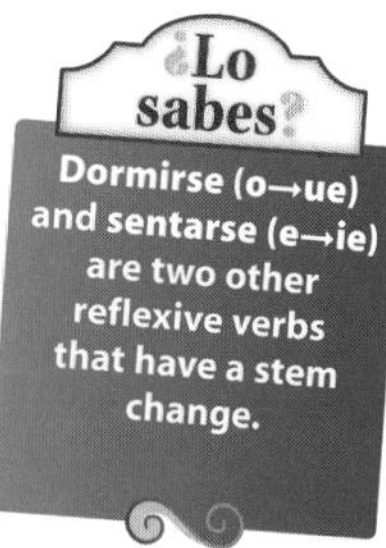

¿Lo sabes?
Dormirse (o→ue) and sentarse (e→ie) are two other reflexive verbs that have a stem change.

2. Many verbs in Spanish can be used with a reflexive pronoun. Often the reflexive pronoun gives a different meaning to the verb. Study the following examples.

María pone la blusa en la mochila.	*Mary puts the blouse in the backpack.*
María se pone la blusa.	*Mary puts on her blouse.*
María duerme ocho horas.	*Mary sleeps eight hours.*
María se duerme enseguida.	*Mary falls asleep immediately.*
María llama a Carlos.	*Mary calls Carlos.*
Ella se llama María.	*She calls herself Mary. (Her name is Mary.)*
María divierte a sus amigos.	*Mary amuses her friends.*
María se divierte.	*Mary amuses herself. (Mary has a good time.)*

Práctica

A ¿Cómo lo haces tú?
Contesten personalmente.

1. ¿Duermes en una cama o en un saco de dormir?
2. Cuando te acuestas, ¿te duermes enseguida?
3. Y cuando te despiertas, ¿te levantas enseguida?
4. ¿Te sientas a la mesa para tomar el desayuno?
5. ¿Te diviertes en la escuela?

Cataluña, España

ANSWERS

Práctica

A 1. **Duermo en una cama (un saco de dormir).**
2. **Sí (No), cuando me acuesto (no) me duermo enseguida.**
3. **Sí (No), cuando me despierto (no) me levanto enseguida.**
4. **Sí, (No, no) me siento a la mesa para tomar el desayuno.**
5. **Sí, (No, no) me divierto en la escuela.**

B HISTORIETA Duermo ocho horas.

Completen.

Cuando yo ___1___ (acostarse), yo ___2___ (dormirse) enseguida. Cada noche yo ___3___ (dormir) ocho horas. Yo ___4___ (acostarse) a las once y ___5___ (levantarse) a las siete de la mañana. Cuando yo ___6___ (despertarse), ___7___ (levantarse) enseguida. Pero cuando mi hermana ___8___ (despertarse), ella no ___9___ (levantarse) enseguida. Y mi hermano, cuando él ___10___ (acostarse), no ___11___ (dormirse) enseguida. Él pasa horas escuchando música en la cama. Así él ___12___ (dormir) solamente unas seis horas.

Actividades comunicativas

A ¿Lo está pasando bien? ¿Se divierte? Choose an illustration below and describe it. A classmate will tell which one you're describing and let you know whether he or she thinks the people are having fun. Take turns.

JUEGO ¿Qué tengo? You have something you have to use every day for part of your daily routine. Tell a classmate what it is. He or she will then guess what you do with it.

CAPÍTULO 12

Estructura

B This activity gives students practice using the **yo** and **él** forms of the stem-changing reflexive verbs.

Actividades comunicativas

A Partners should take turns describing each illustration.

JUEGO This is a good activity to use at the beginning or end of the class period.

EXPANSION To expand this activity, have students think of items they know from earlier chapters. For example: **Tengo unos discos compactos. Tengo un pasaporte, etc.** Have the class choose sides and make this a contest to see which side can think of the most items.

¡OJO! There is no more new material to present in this chapter. The sections that follow recombine and reinforce the vocabulary and structures that have already been introduced.

ANSWERS

Práctica

B
1. **me acuesto**
2. **me duermo**
3. **duermo**
4. **me acuesto**
5. **me levanto**
6. **me despierto**
7. **me levanto**
8. **se despierta**
9. **se levanta**
10. **se acuesta**
11. **se duerme**
12. **duerme**

Actividades comunicativas

A Descriptions of each illustration will vary.

RESOURCES

- Audiocassette 7B/CD7
- CD-ROM, Disc 4, page 366

Bell Ringer Review

Use BRR Transparency 12-5, or write the following on the board: Write three things you did this morning before leaving your house.

TEACHING THE CONVERSATION

A. Have students open their books to page 366 and scan the conversation.

B. Have them close their books. Read the conversation to them aloud or have them listen to the recording on Cassette 7B/Compact Disc 7.

C. Call on students to read aloud. One takes the part of **Timoteo**, the other takes the part of **Maripaz**.

D. After each third of the conversation, ask some comprehension questions from the **Después de conversar** section.

E. Have students who like to perform read the entire conversation aloud to the class using as much expression as possible.

F. After presenting the conversation, go over the **Después de conversar** activity. If students can answer the questions with relative ease, move on. Students should not be expected to memorize the conversation.

TECHNOLOGY OPTION

On the CD-ROM (Disc 4, page 366), students can watch a dramatization of this conversation. They can then play the role of either one of the characters and record themselves in the conversation.

Conversación

¿A qué hora te despertaste?

TIMOTEO: Maripaz, ¿a qué hora te despertaste esta mañana?
MARIPAZ: Esta mañana me levanté un poco tarde.
TIMOTEO: ¿Te levantaste tarde? ¿Por qué?
MARIPAZ: Porque anoche me acosté muy tarde.
TIMOTEO: ¿Por qué te acostaste tan tarde? ¿Saliste?
MARIPAZ: No, no salí. Pasé la noche estudiando. Hoy tengo un examen de álgebra. Estudié hasta la medianoche.
TIMOTEO: ¿Estudiaste hasta la medianoche?
MARIPAZ: Sí, y por lo general me despierto a las seis pero esta mañana no me desperté hasta las seis y media.
TIMOTEO: ¿Llegaste tarde a la escuela?
MARIPAZ: No, afortunadamente llegué a tiempo porque la clase de álgebra es mi primera clase.

Después de conversar

Contesten.

1. Esta mañana, ¿se levantó tarde o temprano Maripaz?
2. ¿Por qué se levantó tarde?
3. ¿Salió ella anoche?
4. ¿Cómo pasó la noche?
5. ¿Hasta qué hora estudió?
6. Por lo general, ¿a qué hora se despierta ella?
7. ¿A qué hora se despertó esta mañana?
8. ¿Llegó tarde a la escuela?
9. ¿Cuál es la primera clase de Maripaz?

ANSWERS

Después de conversar

1. **Esta mañana Maripaz se levantó un poco tarde.**
2. **Se levantó tarde porque anoche se acostó muy tarde.**
3. **No, ella no salió anoche.**
4. **Pasó la noche estudiando.**
5. **Estudió hasta la medianoche.**
6. **Por lo general se despierta a las seis.**
7. **Esta mañana no se despertó hasta las seis y media.**
8. **No, no llegó tarde a la escuela; llegó a tiempo.**
9. **La primera clase de Maripaz es la clase de álgebra.**

Actividades comunicativas

A **Me acosté muy tarde.** You got to bed really late last night and you're feeling tired. Tell a classmate why. Then he or she will ask you some questions about what you're doing today and how things are.

B **Vamos a dar una caminata.** You're planning to backpack through a Spanish-speaking country. Work with a classmate. Decide what country you want to go to. Then decide what you are going to take with you, how long you'll be away, how much money you'll need, and how you plan to get around.

Pronunciación

*La **h**, la **y**, la **ll***

The **h** in Spanish is silent. It is never pronounced. Repeat the following.

hijo	**hotel**	**higiénico**
hermano	**hace**	**hostal**

Y in Spanish can be either a vowel or a consonant. As a vowel, it is pronounced exactly the same as the vowel **i.** Repeat the following.

Juan y María
el jabón y el champú

Y is a consonant when it begins a word or a syllable. As a consonant, **y** is pronounced similarly to the *y* in the English word *yo-yo.* This sound has several variations throughout the Spanish-speaking world. Repeat the following.

ya **desayuno** **ayuda** **playa**

The **ll** is pronounced as a single consonant in Spanish. In many areas of the Spanish-speaking world, it is pronounced the same as the **y.** It too has several variations. Repeat the following.

llama	**botella**	**cepillo**	**toalla**
llega	**pastilla**	**rollo**	**lluvia**

Repeat the following sentences.

La hermana habla hoy con su hermano en el hotel.
Está lloviendo cuando ella llega a la calle Hidalgo.
El hombre lleva una botella de agua a la playa hermosa.

ANSWERS

Actividades comunicativas

A Answers will vary. Students can use the conversation on page 366 as a model for this activity.

B Answers will vary.

RECYCLING

Actividades A and B allow students to use a great deal of material from earlier chapters.

TEACHING PRONUNCIATION

¡OJO! In all areas of the Spanish-speaking world the **h** is silent. There are no exceptions. The **ll** and **y** have several variations. In most areas they are pronounced somewhat like the *yo* in the English word *yoyo*, or in the German word *ja*. In Argentina and Uruguay they are pronounced as a *j*, somewhat like the *j* in *Joe*. In Spain you will also hear a *j* sound, similar to the *y* sound Americans make when they pronounce quickly *didya*.

Tell students that it is not unusual for Spanish speakers to misspell words with **y** and **ll.** Since the two letters sound the same, they often mix them up. They will also omit the **h** in words that should have it. Students may find it reassuring that others sometimes have spelling problems too.

A. Have students very carefully repeat the sounds and words after you or the recording on Cassette 7B/Compact Disc 7.

B. Ask students to open their books to page 367. Call on individuals to read the sentences.

C. All model sentences on this page can be used for dictation.

TECHNOLOGY OPTION

In the CD-ROM version of the Pronunciation section (Disc 4, page 367), students will see an animation of the cartoon on this page. They can also listen to, record, and play back the sounds, words, and sentences presented here.

National Standards

Cultures

The reading on page 368 and the related activities on page 369 allow students to learn about a very popular hiking or biking trip through northern Spain that follows the old **Camino de Santiago**.

TEACHING THE READING

Pre-reading

A. Students should open their books to page 368.

B. Have them skim the passage as recommended in the Reading Strategy.

C. Have students go to the map of Spain on page 463. Indicate the area of Spain described in this reading. Point out San Sebastián and Santiago de Compostela.

Reading

As you go over each paragraph using any of the suggestions given throughout the textbook, you can call on a student to summarize the paragraph in his or her own words.

Post-reading

Have students do the **Después de leer** activities on page 369.

TECHNOLOGY OPTION

Students may listen to a recorded version of the **Lectura** on the CD-ROM, Disc 4, pages 368–369.

Lecturas CULTURALES

Reading Strategy

Skimming

There are several ways to read an article or a passage—each one with its own purpose. Skimming means reading quickly in order to find out the general idea of a passage. To skim means to read without paying careful attention to small details, noting only information about the main theme or topic. Sometimes a reader will skim a passage only to decide whether it's interesting enough to then read it in detail.

DEL NORTE DE ESPAÑA

¡Hola! Me llamo Iván Orama. Soy de San Juan, Puerto Rico. Pero ahora no estoy en Puerto Rico. Estoy en España donde un grupo de amigos de nuestro colegio estamos pasando el verano. Es una experiencia fabulosa. Nos divertimos mucho. ¿Me permites describir un día típico?

Esta mañana nos despertamos temprano. Todos nos levantamos enseguida. Con la mochila en la espalda[1] salimos de la pensión. Fuimos a una cafetería donde nos desayunamos. Yo tomé un jugo de china o, como lo llaman aquí en España, un zumo de naranja. Marta comió churros, una cosa típica española. Y los otros, no sé lo que comieron.

Cuando salimos del café, fuimos en nuestras bicicletas en dirección a Santiago de Compostela. Estamos siguiendo[2] más o menos el Camino[3] de Santiago.

[1]en la espalda *on our back*
[2]siguiendo *following*
[3]Camino *Way, Route*

Los Picos de Europa, España

El lago Enol en el Parque Nacional de Covadonga, España

Learning From Photos

Los Picos de Europa, España See Spotlight on Culture, page 351, for information about these mountains.

El lago Enol en el Parque Nacional de Covadonga, España In the **Parque Nacional de la Sierra de Covadonga** in Asturias there are two alpine lakes with cold, crystal-clear water. They are Lake Enol, seen here, and Lake Ercina. At a higher elevation there is a lookout called **el Mirador de la reina** from which one gets a view all the way to the ocean.

San Sebastián, España (page 369) This sophisticated city arcs around the lovely beach La Concha seen in the photo on this page. It is called La Concha because it has almost the exact same shape as a scallop shell. In the middle of the entrance to the Bay of Biscay there is a tiny island, **Isla de Santa Clara.** This island protects the city from the storms that come from the Bay of Biscay. La Concha is one of the calmest beaches on the northern coast of Spain.

El otro día pasamos un día estupendo en San Sebastián. Nos sentamos en la playa y nos bañamos en el mar Cantábrico. Te aseguro[4] que el agua del Cantábrico está mucho más fría que el agua del Caribe en nuestro Puerto Rico.

El lunes dimos una caminata por los Picos de Europa. Fue increíble. Los picos son tan altos que aún[5] en julio están cubiertos de nieve.

No sabemos cuándo vamos a llegar a Santiago. Pero lo estamos pasando muy bien. Nos divertimos mucho.

[4]Te aseguro *I assure you*
[5]aún *even*

San Sebastián, España

Después de leer

A Un día con los amigos Contesten.

1. ¿Cómo se llama el muchacho?
2. ¿De dónde es?
3. ¿Dónde está ahora?
4. ¿Con quiénes está?
5. ¿Qué están haciendo?
6. ¿Cuándo se levantaron esta mañana?
7. ¿Adónde fueron cuando salieron de la pensión?
8. ¿Qué comió Marta en el desayuno?

B Más sobre la caminata Escojan.

1. Cuando salieron del café, fueron ____.
   a. al albergue juvenil
   b. a San Sebastián
   c. hacia Santiago de Compostela
2. Pasaron el otro día ____.
   a. en la playa
   b. en el Camino de Santiago
   c. en el Cantábrico
3. Hay una playa bonita en ____.
   a. Santiago de Compostela
   b. los Picos de Europa
   c. San Sebastián
4. El agua del mar está fría en ____.
   a. el mar Cantábrico
   b. el mar Caribe
   c. los Picos de Europa
5. Los Picos de Europa están cubiertos de nieve porque ____.
   a. están cerca del mar Cantábrico
   b. son muy altos y allí hace mucho frío
   c. son increíbles

C La ruta Dibujen un mapa de la ruta de los jóvenes.

Después de leer

A and **B** **Después de leer A** and **B** may be used as testing devices to see how well students understood the **Lectura.**

C Have students trace the map of Spain on page 463 or use it as a model to draw an outline map of Spain for them.

History Connection

San Sebastián, España For centuries San Sebastián was a place of little importance. In 1845, however, Isabel II went to San Sebastián seeking relief from a skin ailment in the icy waters of the Atlantic. Much of the aristocracy of the time followed her to San Sebastián and in very little time the city became a favorite spot of the wealthy. To this day the city attracts an upscale group of Spanish summer vacationers who prefer the cooler weather and cultural events of San Sebastián to the hotter, sunnier beaches of the South.

ANSWERS

Después de leer

A
1. **El muchacho se llama Iván Orama.**
2. **Es de San Juan, Puerto Rico.**
3. **Ahora está en España.**
4. **Está con un grupo de amigos de su colegio.**
5. **Están pasando el verano en España.**
6. **Esta mañana se levantaron temprano.**
7. **Fueron a una cafetería cuando salieron de la pensión.**
8. **Marta comió churros.**

B
1. **c**
2. **a**
3. **c**
4. **a**
5. **b**

C The route should begin in San Sebastán and end in Santiago de Compostela. If students do the Chapter 12 Internet activity, they will be able to draw a much more detailed map. (See the Internet Connection, page 370.)

Independent Practice

Assign any of the following:

1. **Después de leer** activities, page 369
2. Workbook, **Un poco más,** pages 156–157
3. CD-ROM, Disc 4, pages 368–369

LECTURA OPCIONAL

National Standards

Cultures

This reading about **el Camino de Santiago** in northern Spain, and the related activities on page 371, allow students to learn about one of the historic pilgrimages that took place during the Middle Ages.

TEACHING TIPS

¡OJO! This reading is optional. You may skip it completely, have the entire class read it, have only several students read it, or assign it for extra credit.

A. Have students look at the photos on these two pages as they read about these places in the **Lectura.**

B. Have students discuss what information they find interesting.

LECTURA OPCIONAL

EL CAMINO DE SANTIAGO

Durante la Edad Media[1] hay tres peregrinaciones[2] famosas—la peregrinación a Jerusalén en Israel, la peregrinación a Roma y la peregrinación a Santiago de Compostela.

Santiago de Compostela está en Galicia, una región pintoresca en el noroeste de España. Galicia se parece más a[3] Irlanda que al resto de España. Llueve mucho en Galicia y todo es muy verde.

El Camino de Santiago es el camino que tomaron los peregrinos de la Edad Media. El camino empieza en los Pirineos, en el pueblo de Roncesvalles y termina en Santiago. Atraviesa o cruza todo el norte de España. ¿Por qué quieren ir a Santiago los peregrinos? Porque creen que allí está enterrado[4] el apóstol Santiago.

[1]Edad Media *Middle Ages*
[2]peregrinaciones *pilgrimages*
[3]se parece más a *looks more like*
[4]enterrado *buried*

La catedral en Santiago de Compostela

Una vista de Galicia

370 trescientos setenta — CAPÍTULO 12

HISTORY CONNECTION

La catedral en Santiago de Compostela This cathedral was built to be an impressive edifice. Have students try to imagine pilgrims walking across Spain some five centuries ago for thirty long days and finally arriving at the foot of this magnificent cathedral. Its size alone inspires awe.

interNET CONNECTION

The Chapter 12 Internet activity (see page 377) has students plan a trip along the **Camino de Santiago.** This is a good source for more information about the route. You may wish to do this activity as a follow-up to the readings on pages 368–371, or in conjunction with **Actividad B,** page 367, or **Actividad B,** page 375.

Los peregrinos viajan a pie (caminan) de un pueblo a otro. Cada día cubren un trecho[5] (tramo) fijo. Al final de cada trecho hay un hostal donde los peregrinos pueden pasar la noche. En el siglo XI hay hostales que pueden alojar[6] a unos mil peregrinos.

Una vez más el Camino de Santiago es muy popular. Hoy día muchos turistas toman la misma ruta. Pero no van a pie. Van en carro. Y muchos jóvenes van en bicicleta.

[5]trecho *stretch*
[6]alojar *lodge, accommodate*

Hostal de los Reyes Católicos, Santiago de Compostela

Después de leer

A Santiago de Compostela
Contesten.

1. ¿Dónde está Santiago de Compostela?
2. ¿En qué parte de España está Galicia?
3. ¿Por qué se parece mucho a Irlanda?
4. ¿Quién está enterrado en la catedral en Santiago de Compostela?

B ¿Qué sabes? Describan lo que aprendieron del Camino de Santiago.

Learning From Photos

Hostal de los Reyes Católicos, Santiago de Compostela
Another magnificent structure on the same square as the cathedral is the Hostal de los Reyes Católicos. It was constructed by Fernando and Isabel in 1499 in gratitude to Santiago for having expelled the Moors. It is the oldest hotel in the world, receiving guests for five centuries. It was a hospital for those who fell ill on the road during their pilgrimage. It remained a hospital until 1953 when it was converted into a luxurious **parador.** It is one of the most beautiful and famous of all the Spanish **paradores.** Students will learn more about these **paradores** in **¡Buen viaje! Level 2.**

Después de leer

A You may use this activity to assess how well your students understood the reading.

B Have each student say one thing about the reading

ANSWERS

Después de leer

A Answers will vary, but may include:
1. **Santiago de Compostela está en Galicia.**
2. **Está en el noroeste de España.**
3. **Se parece mucho a Irlanda porque llueve mucho en Galicia y todo es muy verde.**
4. **El apóstol Santiago está enterrado allí.**

B The description should be brief, rather than detailed.

CAPÍTULO 12
Conexiones

National Standards

Connections

This reading about ecology establishes a connection with another discipline, allowing students to reinforce and further their knowledge of natural sciences through the study of Spanish.

¡OJO! The readings in the **Conexiones** section are optional. They focus on some of the major disciplines taught in schools and universities. The vocabulary is useful for discussing such topics as history, literature, art, economics, business, science, etc.

You may choose any of the following ways to do this reading on ecology with your students.

Independent reading Have students read the selections and do the post-reading activities as homework, which you collect. This option is least intrusive on class time and requires a minimum of teacher involvement.

Homework with in-class follow-up Assign the readings and post-reading activities as homework. Review and discuss the material in class the next day.

Intensive in-class activity This option includes a pre-reading vocabulary presentation, in-class reading and discussion, assignment of the activities for homework, and a discussion of the assignment in class the following day.

Las ciencias naturales

La ecología

Even if you do not have students read this selection in-depth, you may have them skim it since the information is of interest to many. It will also expose

Conexiones

Las ciencias naturales

La ecología

Ecology is a subject of great interest to young people around the world. No one wants to wake up each morning and breathe polluted air. No one wants to hike along a river bank that is loaded with debris or swim in a contaminated ocean. As people travel around the world, they are appalled by the destruction they see done to the environment. We are all aware that urgent and dramatic steps must be taken to avert future ecological disasters.

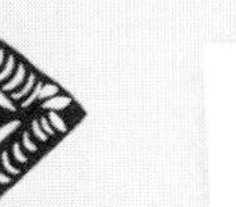

La contaminación del aire en la Ciudad de México

La ecología

El término «ecología» significa el equilibrio entre los seres vivientes—los seres humanos—y la naturaleza[1]. Hoy en día hay grandes problemas ecológicos en casi todas partes del mundo.

La contaminación del aire

La contaminación del medio ambiente[2] es el problema número uno. La contaminación de todos los tipos es la plaga de nuestros tiempos.

El aire que respiramos[3] está contaminado. Está contaminado principalmente por las emisiones de gases que escapan de los automóviles y camiones. Está contaminado también por el humo[4] que emiten las chimeneas de las fábricas[5] que queman[6] sustancias químicas.

Caracas, Venezuela

[1]naturaleza *nature*
[2]medio ambiente *environment*
[3]respiramos *we breathe*
[4]humo *smoke*
[5]fábricas *factories*
[6]queman *burn*

Learning From Photos

Fotografías For each photo on pages 372 and 373, have students choose one sentence from the reading that best describes that photo. For example, for Mexico City they might say: **La contaminación del medio ambiente es el problema número uno.**

El agua

Nuestras aguas están contaminadas también. Buques petroleros derraman[7] cantidades de petróleo cada año en nuestros mares y océanos. En las zonas industriales las fábricas echan los desechos[8] industriales en los ríos. Muchos de los desechos son tóxicos. Los ríos contaminados son portadores[9] de enfermedades serias.

El reciclaje

Hoy en día hay grandes campañas de reciclaje. El reciclaje consiste en recoger los desechos—papel, vidrio[10], metal—para transformar y poder utilizar estos productos de nuevo (una vez más).

Río de la Plata, Buenos Aires

Madrid, España

[7]Buques petroleros derraman *Oil tankers spill*
[8]desechos *wastes*
[9]portadores *carriers*
[10]vidrio *glass*

Después de leer

A En español, por favor. Busquen las palabras equivalentes en español.

1. ecology
2. ecological problems
3. air pollution
4. toxic wastes
5. recycling

B Para discutir Contesten.

1. ¿Está contaminado el aire donde Uds. viven?
2. ¿Hay mucha industria donde viven?
3. ¿Hay muchas fábricas?
4. ¿Hay muchos automóviles y camiones?
5. ¿Escapan gases de los automóviles?
6. ¿Hay campañas de reciclaje donde viven?

students to some current ecological terms that are useful for them to know, if only for receptive purposes.

A. Have students read the introduction in English on page 372.

B. Have students scan each reading section for cognates. Then have them do the reading again, this time for comprehension.

Después de leer

A This activity encourages students to look for cognates as they read.

B This activity is designed to encourage students to think about ecological conditions in their immediate community.

VOCABULARY EXPANSION

You may wish to give students a few extra words and phrases that are useful when talking about ecology and the environment:

el aumento de la temperatura global	*global warming*
la lluvia ácida	*acid rain*
la erosión	*erosion*
la energía solar	*solar energy*
la extinción	*extinction*
los fluorocarburos	*fluorocarbons*
la conservación	*conservation*

ANSWERS

Después de leer

A

1. **la ecología**
2. **problemas ecológicos**
3. **la contaminación del aire**
4. **los desechos tóxicos**
5. **el reciclaje**

B Answers will vary, but may include:

1. **Sí (No), el aire donde vivimos (no) está contaminado.**
2. **Sí, (No, no) hay mucha industria donde vivimos.**
3. **Sí, (No, no) hay muchas fábricas.**
4. **Sí, (No, no) hay muchos automóviles y camiones.**
5. **Sí, escapan gases de los automóviles.**
6. **Sí, (No, no) hay campañas de reciclaje donde vivimos.**

For the Younger Student

La ecología Have students identify an ecological problem at your school or in your community. Have them make a poster in Spanish identifying the problem and offering some solutions to it. Hang the posters up in the classroom or around the school. You might consider doing this for Earth Day.

CAPÍTULO 12
Culminación

RECYCLING

The **Actividades orales** and the **Actividades escritas** allow students to use the vocabulary and structures from this chapter in open-ended, real-life settings.

Actividades orales

A Encourage students to add as many details as possible as they describe each illustration. For example, in Illustration 1 they could say who the teens are, where they are, how old they are, etc.

B Students can also tell each other how their own routine changes on the weekend. For example: **Durante la semana me levanto a las seis pero los sábados me levanto a las nueve.**

TECHNOLOGY OPTION Students may use the Portfolio feature on the CD-ROM to record their conversations.

Student Portfolio

Have students keep a notebook containing their best written work from each chapter. These selected writings can be based on assignments from the Student Textbook and the Writing Activities Workbook. The activities on page 375 are examples of writing assignments that may be included in each student's portfolio.

In the Workbook, students will develop an organized autobiography **(Mi autobiografía).** These workbook pages may also become a part of their portfolio. See the Teacher's Manual for more information on the Student Portfolio.

Culminación

Actividades orales

A **Maricarmen se divierte.** Look at the illustrations below. Based on what you see in the illustrations, have a conversation with a classmate about Maricarmen's activities.

1.

2.
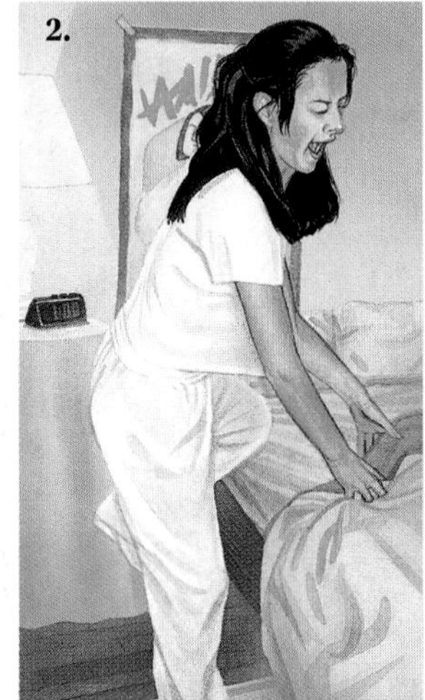

3.

4.
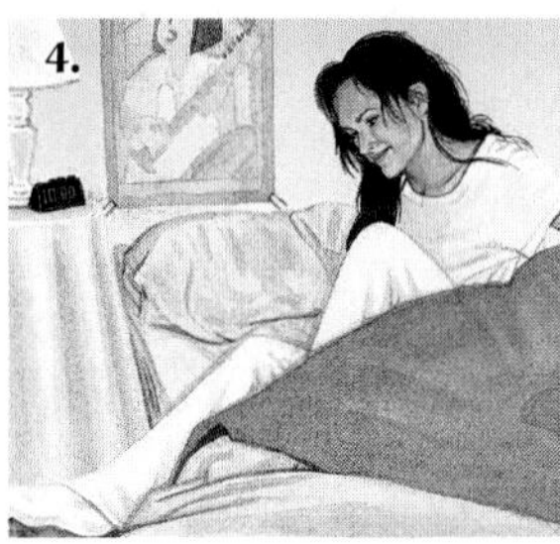

B **Durante la semana y los fines de semana** Most people like a change of pace on the weekend. Talk with a classmate about things that students do or don't do during the week. Your partner will say how that differs on the weekend and why. Take turns.

Durante la semana los alumnos se despiertan muy temprano.

Durante los fines de semana los alumnos se despiertan más tarde.

ANSWERS

Actividades orales

A Answers will vary. Students should describe the basic activity in each illustration, then add as many details as they can.

B Answers will vary.

Independent Practice

Assign any of the following:

1. Activities, pages 374–375
2. Workbook, **Mi autobiografía,** page 158
3. Situation Cards
4. CD-ROM, Disc 4, Chapter 12, **Juego de repaso**

Actividades escritas

A **Un día típico** Your Colombian pen pal is curious about your daily routine. Send him or her an e-mail describing all the activities you do on a typical day from the time you wake up to the time you go to bed.

B **Una gira** You backpacked around Spain for a month last summer. Write a Spanish-speaking friend a letter telling about your experience.

Writing Strategy

Taking notes

Taking notes gives you a written record of important information you may need for later use. When taking notes, write down key words and phrases as you continue to focus on what the speaker is still saying. When the speaker has finished, go back over your notes as soon as possible, highlighting the most important points and adding details to make them as complete as possible. If necessary, rewrite your notes, organizing them so they will be of utmost use to you.

Un trabajo de verano

You are working abroad this summer. You are going to help take care of two small children in Seville, Spain. The children's mother gives you many instructions about the children's routine and activities. Since you probably will not remember all she is telling you, you jot down notes. Take your notes and organize them to describe each child's day. Then write down your responsibilities—what it is you have to do.

CAPÍTULO 12
Culminación

Actividades escritas

A If students did **Actividad A,** page 363, they will be well-prepared to write this letter.

TECHNOLOGY OPTION

Go to the **Correspondencia electrónica** section at the **Glencoe Foreign Language Web site (http://www.glencoe.com/sec/fl)** to see the keypal activity for this chapter.

B **TECHNOLOGY OPTIONS**

If students do the Internet activity for this chapter (see the Internet Connection, page 377), they will be able to do this activity more easily.

Students may use the Portfolio feature on the CD-ROM to write this letter.

Writing Strategy

Taking notes

A. Have students read the Writing Strategy on page 375. You may wish to have them work in pairs to do this pre-writing activity. Students can take turns playing the role of the mother as the other takes notes. Encourage them to be as creative as possible when outlining the children's routine.

B. Students may want to arbitrarily assign Spanish names to the two children.

ANSWERS

Actividades escritas

A Students will typically answer by giving a description of a normal school day or a weekend day.

B Answers will vary.

Writing Strategy

Answers will vary, depending on the imagination and creativity of each student.

CAPÍTULO 12
Vocabulario

ASSESSMENT RESOURCES

- Chapter Quizzes
- Testing Program
- Computer Testmaker
- Situation Cards
- Communication Transparency C-12
- Performance Assessment
- **Maratón mental** Videoquiz

VOCABULARY REVIEW

The words and phrases in the **Vocabulario** have been taught for productive use in this chapter. They are summarized here as a resource for both students and teacher. This list also serves as a convenient resource for the **Culminación** activities on pages 374 and 375. There are approximately five cognates in this vocabulary list. Have students find them.

Vocabulario

STATING DAILY ACTIVITIES

la rutina
despertarse
levantarse
lavarse
bañarse
tomar una ducha
afeitarse
ponerse la ropa
mirarse
maquillarse
cepillarse
peinarse
sentarse
desayunarse
acostarse
dormirse
llamarse
divertirse

IDENTIFYING ARTICLES FOR GROOMING AND HYGIENE

la navaja
la crema de afeitar
el cepillo
el peine
el cepillo de dientes
el espejo
el maquillaje
una barra (una pastilla) de jabón
un tubo de pasta dentífrica
un rollo de papel higiénico
el champú

IDENTIFYING MORE PARTS OF THE BODY

la cara
los dientes
el pelo

IDENTIFYING MORE BREAKFAST FOODS

una botella de agua mineral
un vaso de jugo de naranja
el cereal
el pan tostado

DESCRIBING BACKPACKING

una gira
la mochila
el saco de dormir
el albergue para jóvenes
el hostal
la pensión
dar una caminata
ir en bicicleta

OTHER USEFUL EXPRESSIONS

el lugar
de vez en cuando

TECNOTUR

VIDEO ¡Buen viaje!

EPISODIO 12 ▸ Una gira

Isabel, Luis y Cristina hacen una gira por el campo.

Durante la gira los jóvenes preparan un desayuno.

CD-ROM Expansión cultural

Un desayuno mexicano

In this video episode Cristina, Isabel, and Luis go hiking and camping near Puerto Vallarta. To find out about some other interesting places to do these outdoor activities, go to the Capítulo 12 Internet activity at the Glencoe Foreign Language Web site:

http://www.glencoe.com/sec/fl

Video Synopsis

In this episode, Isabel, Luis, and Cristina go on a camping trip in the lush countryside near Puerto Vallarta. Isabel, who is not an outdoors type, is not a "happy camper." She is quite surprised to learn there is no shower available when she gets up in the morning! Once she has washed in a nearby stream and put on her makeup, however, Isabel feels like a "new person." Cristina, on the other hand, is very happy to hike and camp while visiting her Mexican friends. The girls eat a simple breakfast prepared by Cristina, while Isabel's brother Luis "sleeps in" in a nearby tent. The two girls talk about Luis' usual daily routine. At the end of this episode, Luis reluctantly wakes up to begin the day, as Cristina attempts to film him for their Web site project.

OVERVIEW

This page previews three key multimedia components of the **Glencoe Spanish** series. Each reinforces the material taught in Chapter 12 in a unique manner.

VIDEO

The Video Program allows students to see how the chapter vocabulary and structures are used by native speakers within an engaging story line. For maximum reinforcement, show the video episode as a final activity for Chapter 12.

A. Before viewing this episode, have students read the captions under the video stills on page 377. Ask them questions such as: **En la primera foto, ¿quiénes duermen? ¿Quién no duerme? ¿Es la mañana o la tarde? ¿Qué pasa en la segunda foto? ¿Comen fruta o cereal?**

B. Now show the Chapter 12 video episode. See the Video Activities Booklet for detailed suggestions for using this resource.

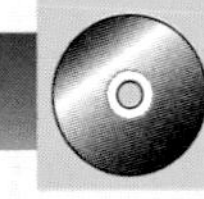

CD-ROM

A. Have students read the **Expansión cultural** photo caption on page 377. Then have them identify the items in the photo.

B. In the CD-ROM version of **Expansión cultural,** students can listen to additional recorded information about Mexican breakfasts.

INTERNET

Teacher information and Student Worksheets for this activity can be accessed at the Web site.

Chapter 13 Overview

SCOPE AND SEQUENCE pages 378–405

TOPICS	FUNCTIONS	STRUCTURE	CULTURE
◆ Train travel ◆ Travel-related activities	◆ How to use words and expressions related to train travel ◆ How to describe various types of trains and train services ◆ How to tell what people say ◆ How to talk about events or activities that took place at a definite time in the past	◆ **Hacer, querer,** and **venir** in the preterite ◆ Irregular verbs in the preterite ◆ **Decir** in the present	◆ José Luis and Maripaz take the AVE train to Seville ◆ Taking the train from Cuzco to Machu Picchu ◆ La Plaza de Armas, Cuzco ◆ Machu Picchu ◆ The 24-hour clock and the metric system

CHAPTER 13 RESOURCES

PRINT	MULTIMEDIA
Planning Resources	
Lesson Plans Block Scheduling Lesson Plans	Interactive Lesson Planner
Reinforcement Resources	
Writing Activities Workbook Student Tape Manual Video Activities Booklet Web Site User's Guide	Transparencies Binder Audiocassette/Compact Disc Program Videocassette/Videodisc Program Online Internet Activities Electronic Teacher's Classroom Resources
Assessment Resources	
Situation Cards Chapter Quizzes Testing Program Performance Assessment	**Maratón mental** Mindjogger Videoquiz Testmaker Computer Software (Macintosh/Windows) Listening Comprehension Audiocassette/Compact Disc Communication Transparency: C-13
Motivational Resources	
Expansion Activities	Café Glencoe: www.cafe.glencoe.com Keypal Internet Activities
Enrichment	
Spanish for Spanish Speakers	Fine Art Transparency: F-12

Chapter 13 Planning Guide

SECTION	PAGES	SECTION RESOURCES
Vocabulario Palabras 1 **En la estación de ferrocarril**	380–383	Vocabulary Transparencies 13.1 Audiocassette 8A/ Compact Disc 7 Student Tape Manual, TE, pages 147–150 Workbook, pages 159–160 Chapter Quizzes, page 65 CD-ROM, Disc 4, pages 380–383
Vocabulario Palabras 2 **En el tren**	384–387	Vocabulary Transparencies 13.2 Audiocassette 8A/ Compact Disc 7 Student Tape Manual, TE, pages 151–152 Workbook, pages 161–162 Chapter Quizzes, page 66 CD-ROM, Disc 4, pages 384–387
Estructura **Hacer, querer y venir en el pretérito** **Verbos irregulares en el pretérito** **Decir en el presente**	388–393	Workbook, pages 163–166 Audiocassette 8A/Compact Disc 7 Student Tape Manual, TE, pages 153–155 Chapter Quizzes, pages 67–69 Computer Testmaker CD-ROM, Disc 4, pages 388–393
Conversación **En la ventanilla** **Pronunciación: Las consonantes ñ, ch**	394–395	Audiocassette 8A/Compact Disc 7 Student Tape Manual, TE, pages 155–156 CD-ROM, Disc 4, pages 394–395
Lecturas culturales **En el AVE** **De Cuzco a Machu Picchu *(opcional)***	396–399	Testing Program, pages 77–78 CD-ROM, Disc 4, pages 396–399
Conexiones **Conversiones aritméticas *(opcional)***	400–401	Testing Program, page 78 CD-ROM, Disc 4, pages 400–401
Culminación **Actividades orales** **Actividades escritas** **Vocabulario** **Tecnotur**	402–405	**¡Buen viaje!** Video, Episode 13 Video Activities, pages 114–117 Internet Activities www.glencoe.com/sec/fl Testing Program, pages 75–77; 116; 148; 173–174 CD-ROM, Disc 4, pages 402–405

OVERVIEW

In this chapter students will learn to talk about a train trip. In order to do this they will learn vocabulary related to the train station and train travel. They will also continue to learn how to talk about past events by learning the preterite forms of some irregular verbs. The cultural focus of the chapter is on train travel in Spain and Latin America.

National Standards

Communication

In Chapter 13 students will communicate in spoken and written Spanish on the following topics:

- purchasing a train ticket and consulting a timetable
- getting through a train station
- traveling on board a train

Students will obtain and provide information about these topics and learn to engage in conversations with a ticket agent, train conductor, and fellow passengers as they fulfill the chapter objectives listed on this page.

Pacing

Chapter 13 will require approximately six to eight days. Pacing will vary according to the length of the class, the age of your students, and student aptitude.

Block Scheduling

See the Block Scheduling Lesson Plans Booklet for suggestions on how to present the chapter material within a block scheduling framework.

CAPÍTULO 13

Un viaje en tren

Objetivos

In this chapter you will learn to do the following:

- use expressions related to train travel
- purchase a train ticket and request information about arrival, departure, etc.
- talk about more past events or activities
- tell what people say
- discuss an interesting train trip in Spain

The **Glencoe Foreign Language Web site (http://www.glencoe.com/sec/fl)** offers three options that enable you and your students to experience the Spanish-speaking world via the Internet:

- The online **Actividades** are correlated to the chapters and utilize Hispanic Web sites around the world. For the Chapter 13 activity, see student page 405.
- The **Correspondencia electrónica** section provides information on how to set up a keypal (pen pal) exchange between your class and a class in the Spanish-speaking world.
- At **Café Glencoe,** the interactive "after-school" section of the site, you and your students can access a variety of additional online resources, including interactive games. The Chapter 13 crossword puzzle practices the chapter vocabulary and structures.

CAPÍTULO 13

Spotlight On Culture

Artefacto The decorative photo shows **castañuelas,** which are typically played during the dancing of flamenco. The fan, called **un abanico,** is also used in certain flamenco dances.
Fotografía This photo was taken at the **Estació de Sants** in Barcelona. Note that the name of the station is in **Catalán**. There are two other train stations in Barcelona.

Learning From Photos

La Estació de Sants You may wish to ask the following questions about the photo after presenting the new vocabulary on pages 380–381:
¿Dónde están los jóvenes?
¿Qué está mirando la muchacha?
¿El muchacho tiene un plano de qué ciudad?
¿Cómo se llama el periódico que tiene el muchacho?
¿Cuántos trenes ves en la foto?

Teacher Notes

Chapter Projects

Un viaje en tren Have groups plan a rail trip through Spain using a guide such as the one from Eurail (available at many travel agencies). Give them a time limit and have them include at least one overnight stay. They should plan arrival and departure times and the length of each stop on the itinerary. Groups can describe their trip to the class.
TECHNOLOGY OPTION In the Chapter 13 Internet activity students visit the RENFE Web site to plan a train trip in Spain. You may wish to have students do this activity as a project. (For more information, see the Internet Connection, page 405.)
Una ciudad Have the groups select one city from their itinerary and find out some information about it. They can do a brief report for a presentation to the class.

CAPÍTULO 13
Vocabulario

PALABRAS 1

RESOURCES

- Vocabulary Transparencies 13.1 (A & B)
- Student Tape Manual, TE, pages 147–150
- Audiocassette 8A/CD7
- Workbook, pages 159–160
- Quiz 1, page 65
- CD-ROM, Disc 4, pages 380–383

Bell Ringer Review

Use BRR Transparency 13-1, or write the following on the board: Complete the following sentences.

1. **Los pasajeros hacen ___ en el mostrador de la línea aérea.**
2. **Los pasajeros ___ su equipaje.**
3. **Los pasajeros en un aeropuerto tienen que pasar por ___.**
4. **Los pasajeros tienen que mostrar su ___.**

TEACHING VOCABULARY

A. Have students close their books. Present the vocabulary using Vocabulary Transparencies 13.1 (A & B).

B. Now have students open their books and repeat the new words and sentences after you or the recording on Cassette 8A/Compact Disc 7.

C. Have students act out the short dialogue on page 380.

Vocabulario

PALABRAS 1

En la estación de ferrocarril

Total Physical Response

TPR 1

Getting ready

A piece of paper with the word **maleta** written on it can represent a suitcase.

Begin

___, levántate y ven acá, por favor.
Vas a hacer algunos gestos. Aquí tienes una maleta.
Toma la maleta. Mira la maleta.
Abre la maleta. Pon la ropa en la maleta.
Cierra la maleta.
Ve al teléfono. Llama un taxi.
Toma la maleta y ve a la calle.
Espera el taxi.
El taxi llega. Pon la maleta en la maletera del taxi. Abre la puerta del taxi.
Sube al taxi. Siéntate.
Gracias, ___. Y ahora puedes volver a tu asiento.

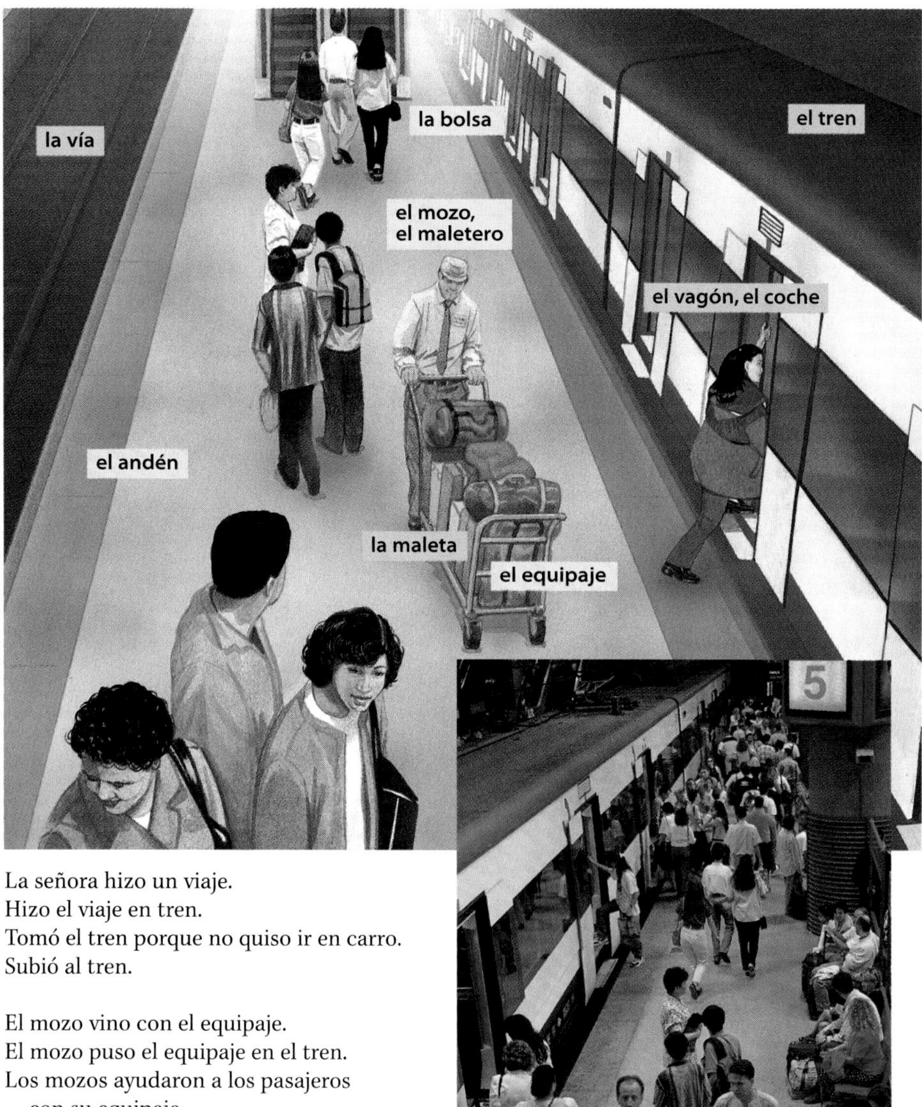

La señora hizo un viaje.
Hizo el viaje en tren.
Tomó el tren porque no quiso ir en carro.
Subió al tren.

El mozo vino con el equipaje.
El mozo puso el equipaje en el tren.
Los mozos ayudaron a los pasajeros con su equipaje.

El tren salió del andén número cinco.
Algunos amigos estuvieron en el andén.

D. As you present the new vocabulary, intersperse it with questions such as the following:
¿La muchacha compra un billete en primera o segunda clase?
¿Compra un billete sencillo o de ida y vuelta?
¿ Subió al tren o bajó del tren la señora?
¿Tiene el mozo bolsas y maletas?
¿Qué tiene el mozo?
¿Dónde puso el equipaje?
Have students answer with complete sentences or sometimes just have them use the specific word or phrase that responds to the question word.

ABOUT THE SPANISH LANGUAGE

- The word **el billete** is used in Spain**. El boleto** is used in Latin America. The expression *to buy a ticket* is **sacar un billete** in Spain and **comprar un boleto** in Latin America.
- **El tablero** is the word used for arrival or departure board. In some stations there is a modern type of TV screen that is called either **la pantalla** or **el monitor**.

INFORMAL ASSESSMENT

1. After presenting all the vocabulary from **Palabras 1,** show the Vocabulary Transparencies again and let students identify items at random.
2. Now have students make up questions about what they see on the transparencies. You may answer the questions or have them call on other students to answer.

Total Physical Response

TPR 2

Getting ready

Have your desk be **la ventanilla**. One student can be **el agente** and another student can be **el pasajero.** Numbers on the board can represent **los andenes.** A piece of paper with the word **boleto** or **billete** can be the ticket.

Begin

___, levántate y ven acá.
Ésta es la estación de ferrocarril.
Estamos en la sala de espera. Dame la maleta. Ve a la ventanilla. Compra un boleto.
Págale al agente.
Toma tu boleto. Mira el boleto.
Pon el boleto en tu bolsillo.
Ven acá. Toma la maleta.
Busca el andén número dos.
Ve al andén. Espera el tren.
Aquí viene el tren. Sube al tren.
Gracias, ___. Regresa a tu asiento.

¡OJO! **Práctica** When students are doing the **Práctica** activities, accept any answer that makes sense. The purpose of these activities is to have students use the new vocabulary. They are not factual recall activities. Thus, do not expect students to remember specific information from the vocabulary presentation when answering. If you wish, have students use the photos on this page as a stimulus, when possible.

Historieta Each time **Historieta** appears, it means that the answers to the activity form a short story. Encourage students to look at the title of the **Historieta** since it can sometimes help them do the activity. It is recommended that you go over all the **Práctica** in class before assigning them for homework.

A Have students retell the story from **Práctica A** in their own words.

B After completing **Práctica B**, have students ask questions about the incorrect choices from this activity.

Writing Development

Have students write the answers to **Práctica A** in a paragraph to illustrate how all of the items tell a story.

Práctica

A HISTORIETA En la estación de ferrocarril

Contesten según se indica.

1. ¿Cómo vino la señora a la estación? (en taxi)
2. ¿Dónde puso sus maletas? (en la maletera del taxi)
3. En la estación, ¿adónde fue? (a la ventanilla)
4. ¿Qué compró? (un billete)
5. ¿Qué tipo de billete compró? (de ida y vuelta)
6. ¿En qué clase? (segunda)
7. ¿Dónde puso su billete? (en su bolsa)
8. ¿Qué consultó? (el horario)
9. ¿Adónde fue? (al andén)
10. ¿De qué andén salió el tren? (del número dos)
11. ¿Por qué hizo la señora el viaje en tren? (no quiso ir en coche)

Atocha, una estación de ferrocarril en Madrid

En la estación de Atocha

B HISTORIETA Antes de abordar el tren

Escojan.

1. ¿Dónde espera la gente el tren?
   a. en la ventanilla **b.** en la sala de espera **c.** en el quiosco
2. ¿Dónde venden o despachan los billetes?
   a. en la ventanilla **b.** en el equipaje **c.** en el quiosco
3. ¿Qué venden en el quiosco?
   a. boletos **b.** maletas **c.** periódicos y revistas
4. ¿Qué consulta el pasajero para verificar la hora de salida del tren?
   a. la llegada **b.** la vía **c.** el horario
5. ¿Quién ayuda a los pasajeros con el equipaje?
   a. el mozo **b.** el tablero **c.** el andén
6. ¿De dónde sale el tren?
   a. de la ventanilla **b.** del andén **c.** del tablero

ANSWERS

Práctica

A
1. **La señora vino a la estación en taxi.**
2. **Puso sus maletas en la maletera del taxi.**
3. **En la estación fue a la ventanilla.**
4. **Compró un billete.**
5. **Compró un billete de ida y vuelta.**
6. **Compró un billete en segunda.**
7. **Puso su billete en su bolsa.**
8. **Consultó el horario.**
9. **Fue al andén.**
10. **El tren salió del andén número dos.**
11. **La señora hizo el viaje en tren porque no quiso ir en coche.**

B
1. **b**
2. **a**
3. **c**
4. **c**
5. **a**
6. **b**

C  HISTORIETA El billete del tren

Contesten.

Billete y Reserva

71 CIF G28016749

093318713003 01210

00030 A5PE0933 00000000 1302 14:39

AVE

Nombre :								
Tren	Clase	Fecha	Salida	Llegada	Coche	Plaza	Departamento	
LAN30	1	06/07	15.30	16.19	0007	070	NO FUMA	

De PTA.ATOCHA A CDAD.REAL

Tarifa 410 TARIFA GENERAL

Forma de pago METALICO — Total pts ****2450 — Incluido SOV e IVA

EL CONTROL DE ACCESO AL TREN SE CIERRA DOS MINUTOS ANTES DE LA SALIDA

0030 A5PE0933 00000000 1302 14:39

093318713003 01210

Tren LAN30 Fecha 06/07

Coche 0007 Plaza 070

1:410

Total pts ****2450

1. ¿De qué estación sale el tren?
2. ¿Adónde va el tren?
3. ¿Cuál es la fecha del billete?
4. ¿A qué hora sale el tren?
5. ¿Está el asiento en la sección de fumar o de no fumar?
6. ¿Qué clase de billete es?
7. ¿Con qué pagó el/la pasajero(a)?

Actividad comunicativa

A **RENFE (Red Nacional de Ferrocarriles Españoles)**
You're in Spain and you want to visit one of the cities on the map. A classmate will be the ticket agent. Get yourself a ticket and ask the agent any questions you have about your train trip.

ANSWERS

Práctica

C **1. El tren sale de la estación de Atocha.**
2. El tren va a Ciudad Real.
3. La fecha del billete es 06/07.
4. El tren sale a las 15:30.
5. El asiento está en la sección de no fumar.
6. Es un billete de segunda clase.
7. El/La pasajero(a) pagó en metálico.

Actividad comunicativa

A Answers will vary.

CAPÍTULO 13
Vocabulario

Learning From Realia

Billete y Reserva Have students look at the train ticket on this page. Ask them to guess what the word **metálico** means under **Forma de pago.** What do we say in English instead of **metálico?** *(cash)*

Actividad comunicativa

¡OJO! **Práctica versus Actividades comunicativas** All activities which provide guided practice are labeled **Práctica.** The more open-ended communicative activities are labeled **Actividades comunicativas.**

A You may wish to have some students present their skits to the class.

TECHNOLOGY OPTION In the Chapter 13 Internet activity students visit the RENFE Web site to plan a train trip in Spain. You may wish to have students do the Internet activity first and then have them do **Actividad A,** using the real information from the site. (See the Internet Connection, page 405.)

Learning From Photos

Atocha, una estación de ferrocarril en Madrid Until recently Atocha was falling into disuse and serving very few destinations. There was even talk of closing the station. Instead the station was completely renovated for the inauguration of the high speed AVE train in 1992. Today it serves points south and east of Madrid. Chamartín station serves trains heading north and to Barcelona. The Norte station is primarily for local trains serving the western suburbs.

CAPÍTULO 13
Vocabulario
PALABRAS 2

RESOURCES

- Vocabulary Transparencies 13.2 (A & B)
- Student Tape Manual, TE, pages 151–152
- Audiocassette 8A/CD7
- Workbook, pages 161–162
- Quiz 2, page 66
- CD-ROM, Disc 4, pages 384–387

Bell Ringer Review

Use BRR Transparency 13-2, or write the following on the board: Complete the following.

La compañía de aviación anuncia la ___ de su ___ 102 con ___ a Madrid. Pasajeros deben abordar por la ___ número tres. Embarque inmediato.

TEACHING VOCABULARY

A. Have students close their books. Present the vocabulary, using Vocabulary Transparencies 13.2 (A & B). Have students repeat each word or expression two or three times after you or Cassette 8A/Compact Disc 7.

B. Ask the following questions as you present the vocabulary: **¿Los jóvenes están en el tren o están en la ventanilla? ¿Qué tiene que ver el revisor? ¿Hay muchos o pocos asientos libres en el coche? ¿Los pasajeros toman asiento o se sientan en el pasillo? ¿Qué hacen los pasajeros en el coche-cama? ¿En el coche-comedor? ¿El tren sale a tiempo o sale tarde? ¿Sale con retraso? ¿Dónde bajan los pasajeros?**

Vocabulario

PALABRAS 2

En el tren

Total Physical Response

Getting ready

Set up an area in front of the classroom as **el tren** and place three chairs together. Tell students that those chairs are the seats in the train. Then call on one student to act as **el/la pasajero(a).**

Begin

___, levántate y ven acá, por favor.
Sube al tren. Busca tu asiento.
Pon tu maleta en el asiento. Abre la maleta.
Saca un libro de la maleta.
Cierra la maleta.
Pon la maleta en el compartimiento.
Siéntate. Toma tu asiento.
Abre tu libro. Lee el libro.
Gracias, ___. Y ahora puedes volver a tu asiento.

El tren salió a tiempo.
No salió tarde.
No salió con retraso (con una demora).

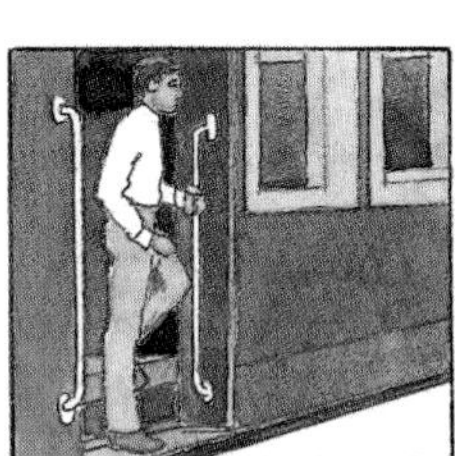

bajar(se) del tren

transbordar

Los pasajeros van a bajar en la próxima parada (estación).
Van a transbordar en la próxima parada.

ABOUT THE SPANISH LANGUAGE

Note that we have used the expression **bajar del tren**, which is grammatically correct. In many areas of Latin America one will hear **bajarse del tren**. In contemporary novels, you sometimes see both **bajar** and **bajarse** in the same work.

A B and C After going over **Práctica A, B, and C** students can summarize all the information in their own words.

Did You Know?

En tren Students have already learned about the importance of air travel in South America in Chapter 11.

Train travel in South America can be very interesting but in many areas it is not convenient (and in some cases it is nonexistent). In addition to long distances, there are often mechanical delays, flooding during the rainy season, and rugged terrain, all of which can make travel slow and tedious. The railway service is fairly good in Argentina and Chile. Most of Chile's 5,200 miles of track run north to south.

Práctica

A HISTORIETA En el tren

Contesten.

1. Cuando llegó el tren a la estación, ¿subieron los pasajeros a bordo?
2. ¿El tren salió tarde?
3. ¿Con cuántos minutos de demora salió?
4. ¿Vino el revisor?
5. ¿Revisó él los boletos?

Santiago, Chile

Madrid, España

B HISTORIETA El tren

Contesten según la foto.

1. ¿Tiene el tren compartimientos?
2. ¿Tiene el coche o vagón un pasillo central o lateral?
3. ¿Cuántos asientos hay a cada lado del pasillo?
4. ¿Hay asientos libres o están todos ocupados?
5. ¿Está completo el tren?
6. ¿Hay pasajeros de pie en el pasillo?

C HISTORIETA Un viaje en tren

Completen.

1. Entre Granada y Málaga el tren local hace muchas ____.
2. No hay un tren directo a Benidorm. Es necesario cambiar de tren. Los pasajeros tienen que ____.
3. Los pasajeros que van a Benidorm tienen que ____ en la próxima ____ o ____.
4. ¿Cómo lo sabes? El ____ nos informó que nuestro tren no es directo.

ANSWERS

Práctica

A
1. **Sí, cuando el tren llegó a la estación, los pasajeros subieron a bordo.**
2. **Sí (No), el tren (no) salió tarde.**
3. **Salió con una demora de ____ minutos.**
4. **Sí, el revisor vino.**
5. **Sí, él revisó los boletos.**

B
1. **No, el tren no tiene compartimientos.**
2. **El coche (vagón) tiene un pasillo central.**
3. **Hay dos asientos a cada lado del pasillo.**
4. **Hay asientos libres.**
5. **No, el tren no está completo.**
6. **No, no hay pasajeros de pie en el pasillo.**

C
1. **paradas**
2. **transbordar**
3. **transbordar, parada, estación**
4. **revisor**

Actividades comunicativas

A **¿Qué tienes que hacer?** Work with a classmate. You are spending a month in Madrid and your Spanish hosts are taking you to San Sebastián. You're trying to pack your bags and their child (your partner) has a lot of questions. Answer his or her questions and try to be patient. The child has never taken a train trip before.

Madrid

San Sebastián

B **De Santiago a Puerto Montt** You're planning a trip from Santiago de Chile to Puerto Montt. A classmate will be your travel agent. Get as much information as you can about the trip from Santiago to Puerto Montt. It gets rather cold and windy there and it rains a lot. You may want to find out if there are frequent delays. The following are some words and expressions you may want to use with the travel agent.

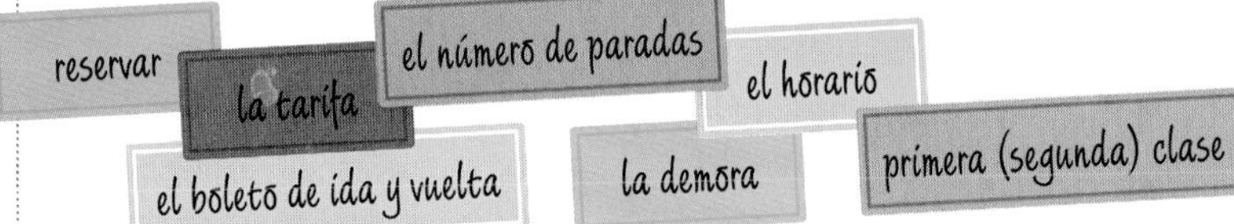

Learning From Photos

Madrid This view of Madrid is looking up the Gran Vía from Cibeles. The Gran Vía is a very busy street with hotels, night clubs, clothing stores, jewelery stores, bookstores, and **cafeterías.**

San Sebastián For information on San Sebastián, see Learning From Photos, Chapter 12, page 368.

ANSWERS

Actividades comunicativas

A Answers will vary. Students should use the vocabulary from **Palabras 1** and **2.**

B Answers will vary. Students should use as many words as possible from the colored boxes.

Actividades comunicativas

¡OJO! These activities encourage students to use the chapter vocabulary and structures in open-ended situations. It is not necessary to have them do all the activities. Choose the ones you consider most appropriate.

A Before students begin this activity, have them make a list of questions they will ask. You may wish to have students present their conversations to the class.

B Have students working on **Actividad B** locate **Puerto Montt** on the map of South America on page 464.

Geography Connection

Puerto Montt You may either have students look up some information on Puerto Montt on the Internet or give them the following information.

Puerto Montt is a city of some 120,000 inhabitants, many of German descent. A large number of its small houses are unpainted and one can see the Germanic influence in the architecture. In bakery shop windows there are still signs in Spanish and German—**Pasteles** and **Kuchen.**

Puerto Montt is the northernmost town in Chilean Patagonia. The weather can be very harsh with strong winds and a great deal of rain. The train trip to Puerto Montt from Santiago takes 20 hours.

RESOURCES

- Workbook, pages 163–166
- Student Tape Manual, TE, pages 153–155
- Audiocassette 8A/CD7
- Quizzes 3–5, pages 67–69
- Computer Testmaker
- CD-ROM, Disc 4, pages 388–393

Bell Ringer Review

Use BRR Transparency 13-3, or write the following on the board: Write original sentences using each of the following expressions in the present tense.

hacer un viaje
poner la ropa en la maleta
salir para la estación de ferrocarril
venir en tren

TEACHING STRUCTURE

Relating more past actions

A. Have students open their books to page 388. Read Steps 1 and 2 to the class.

B. Have the class repeat the verb forms aloud.

C. Call on an individual to read the model sentences.

D. Point out to students that all these irregular verbs have the ending **e** in the **yo** form.

Note Many of the verbs students will be learning in this chapter are not used very frequently in the preterite. For this reason, it is recommended that you do not spend a great deal of time on this topic. The most important verbs are **venir, hacer,** and **poner.**

Estructura

Relating more past actions
Hacer, querer y venir en el pretérito

1. The verbs **hacer, querer,** and **venir** are irregular in the preterite. Note that they all have an **i** in the stem and the endings for the **yo, él, ella,** and **Ud.** forms are different from the endings of regular verbs.

INFINITIVE	hacer	querer	venir
yo	hice	quise	vine
tú	hiciste	quisiste	viniste
él, ella, Ud.	hizo	quiso	vino
nosotros(as)	hicimos	quisimos	vinimos
vosotros(as)	*hicisteis*	*quisisteis*	*vinisteis*
ellos, ellas, Uds.	hicieron	quisieron	vinieron

2. The verb **querer** has several special meanings in the preterite.

Quise ayudar. *I tried to help.*
No quise ir en carro. *I refused to go by car.*

Práctica

A HISTORIETA ¿Cómo viniste?

Contesten.

1. ¿Viniste a la estación en taxi?
2. ¿Viniste en un taxi público o privado?
3. ¿Hiciste el viaje en tren?
4. ¿Hiciste el viaje en el tren local?
5. ¿Lo hiciste en tren porque no quisiste ir en coche?

Lima, Perú

ANSWERS

Práctica

A
1. **Sí, vine a la estación en taxi.**
2. **Vine en un taxi público.**
3. **Sí, hice el viaje en tren.**
4. **Sí, (No, no) hice el viaje en el tren local.**
5. **Sí, lo hice en tren porque no quise ir en coche. (No, no lo hice en tren porque quise ir en coche.)**

Learning From Photos

Lima, Perú You may wish to ask the following questions about the photo:
¿Cómo se llama la estación de ferrocarril en Lima?
¿Está hablando el joven con el taxista?
¿Cuántas maletas tiene el joven?

B **No quisieron.** Completen.

1. —Ellos no ___1___ (querer) hacer el viaje.
   —¿No lo ___2___ (querer) hacer?
   —No, de ninguna manera.
   —Pues, ¿qué pasó entonces? ¿Lo ___3___ (hacer) o no lo ___4___ (hacer)?
   —No lo ___5___ (hacer).
2. —¿Por qué no ___6___ (venir) Uds. esta mañana?
   —Nosotros no ___7___ (venir) porque no ___8___ (hacer) las reservaciones.
3. —Carlos no ___9___ (querer) hacer la cama.
   —Entonces, ¿quién la ___10___ (hacer)?
   —Pues, la ___11___ (hacer) yo.
   —¡Qué absurdo! ¿Tú la ___12___ (hacer) porque él no la ___13___ (querer) hacer?

Actividades comunicativas

A **¡Rebelde!** A friend of yours (your classmate) is in trouble with his or her parents because he or she didn't do as told. Find out what your friend didn't do and why. Use the model as a guide.

hacer la maleta
reservar un taxi
comprar los billetes
llamar a los parientes
hacer las reservaciones
leer el horario

B **¿Qué hiciste durante el fin de semana?** With a classmate, take turns asking each other what you and other friends did over the weekend.

CAPÍTULO 13
Estructura

A **Práctica A** on page 388 practices the **tú** and **yo** forms.

B Have students present **Práctica B** as a series of mini-conversations.

Actividades comunicativas

¡OJO! These activities encourage students to use the chapter vocabulary and structures in open-ended situations. It is not necessary to have them do all the activities. Choose the ones you consider most appropriate.

A Ask for volunteers to role-play the model dialogue. Have them do one or two examples from the handwritten list on the right before students work on their own in pairs.

EXPANSION Encourage students to come up with their own list of things they were supposed to do.

B This is a good warm-up activity to begin the class period. Students might begin by saying: **¿Qué hiciste durante el fin de semana?** or **¿Qué hicieron Uds. durante el fin de semana?**

ANSWERS

Práctica

B
1. **quisieron**
2. **quisieron**
3. **hicieron**
4. **hicieron**
5. **hicieron**
6. **vinieron**
7. **vinimos**
8. **hicimos**
9. **quiso**
10. **hizo**
11. **hice**
12. **hiciste**
13. **quiso**

Actividades comunicativas

A Answers will vary, but should follow the model.

B Answers will vary.

CAPÍTULO 13
Estructura

Bell Ringer Review

Use BRR Transparency 13-4, or write the following on the board:

1. Write three things you have to do.
2. Write three things you can do.
3. Write three things you want to do.
4. Write three things you know how to do.

TEACHING STRUCTURE

Describing more past actions

A. Have students open their books to page 390. Read Steps 1 and 2 to the class.
B. Have the class repeat the verb forms from the chart.
C. Call on an individual to read the model sentences in Step 2.

Fine Art Connection

«Vista de Toledo» de El Greco

Show Fine Art Transparency F-12 of this painting by El Greco from the Transparency Binder. You may wish to have students read the background information accompanying this transparency, and have them do the related activities.

EXPANSION Have students look at a photo of Toledo today. Ask them if they see a resemblance between today's photo and El Greco's painting done about four centuries ago.

Describing more past actions
Verbos irregulares en el pretérito

1. The verbs **estar, andar,** and **tener** are irregular in the preterite. They all have a **u** in the stem. Study the following forms.

INFINITIVE	estar	andar	tener
yo	estuve	anduve	tuve
tú	estuviste	anduviste	tuviste
él, ella Ud.	estuvo	anduvo	tuvo
nosotros(as)	estuvimos	anduvimos	tuvimos
vosotros(as)	*estuvisteis*	*anduvisteis*	*tuvisteis*
ellos, ellas, Uds.	estuvieron	anduvieron	tuvieron

2. The verb **andar** means "to go," but not to a specific place. The verb **ir** is used with a specific place.

Fueron a Toledo.
They went to Toledo.

Anduvieron por las plazas pintorescas de Toledo.
They wandered through (walked around) the picturesque squares of Toledo.

«Vista de Toledo» de El Greco

About the Spanish Language

In Spain the verb **andar** means *to walk.* **Caminar** is used in Latin America. **Ir a pie** means *to go on foot* and **dar un paseo** or **pasear(se)** means *to take a walk.*

3. The verbs **poder, poner,** and **saber** are also irregular in the preterite. Like the verbs **estar, andar,** and **tener,** they all have a **u** in the stem. Study the following forms.

INFINITIVE	poder	poner	saber
yo	pude	puse	supe
tú	pudiste	pusiste	supiste
él, ella, Ud.	pudo	puso	supo
nosotros(as)	pudimos	pusimos	supimos
vosotros(as)	*pudisteis*	*pusisteis*	*supisteis*
ellos, ellas, Uds.	pudieron	pusieron	supieron

4. Like **querer,** the verbs **poder** and **saber** have special meanings in the preterite.

Pude parar. *(After trying hard) I managed to stop.*
No pude parar. *(I tried but) I couldn't stop.*
Yo lo supe ayer. *I found it out (learned it) yesterday.*

A **HISTORIETA ¿Dónde está mi tarjeta de identidad estudiantil?**

Contesten según se indica.

1. ¿Estuviste ayer en la estación de ferrocarril? (sí)
2. ¿Tuviste que tomar el tren a Toledo? (sí)
3. ¿Pudiste comprar un billete de precio reducido? (no)
4. ¿Tuviste que presentar tu tarjeta de identidad estudiantil? (sí)
5. ¿Dónde la pusiste? (no sé)
6. ¿La perdiste? (sí, creo)
7. ¿Cuándo supiste que la perdiste? (cuando llegué a la estación)

Toledo, España

D. Have the class repeat the verb forms from the chart in Step 3.
E. Point out to students that all these irregular verbs have a **u** in the stem.
F. Call on an individual to read the model sentences from Step 4.

A Allow students to refer to the verb charts on these two pages as they do the activity.

Writing Development

Have students write a note telling someone what happened in **Práctica A.**

Toledo, España Toledo is one of the most magnificent cities in Spain. The rock on which it stands was inhabited in prehistoric times. The Romans came in 192 B.C. and built a large fort where the Alcázar now stands. Toledo was inhabited by the Iberians, Romans, Visigoths, and the Moors who arrived early in the 8th century.

Alfonso VI, aided by El Cid, took Toledo from the Moors in 1085. During the Renaissance Toledo was a center of humanism. It began, however, to decline in the 16th century. The expulsion of the Jews in 1492 had severe economic consequences, and the decision in 1561 to make Madrid the center of the court led to its political decline. The years El Greco spent in Toledo (1572 to his death in 1614) were the years of Toledo's decline.

ANSWERS

Práctica

A
1. **Sí, ayer estuve en la estación de ferrocarril.**
2. **Sí, tuve que tomar el tren a Toledo.**
3. **No, no pude comprar un billete de precio reducido.**
4. **Sí, tuve que presentar mi tarjeta de identidad estudiantil.**
5. **No sé dónde la puse.**
6. **Sí, creo que la perdí.**
7. **Supe que la perdí cuando llegué a la estación.**

CAPÍTULO 13
Estructura

B For additional practice, have students retell the story in their own words.

TEACHING STRUCTURE

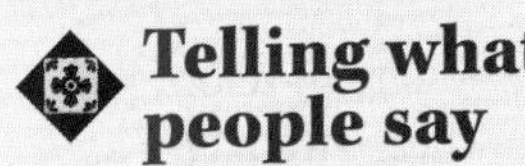

Telling what people say

A. Have students open their books to page 392 and repeat the forms of the verb **decir** after you.

B. Write the forms of the verb on the board. Underline the stem for each form.

C. Now do the **Práctica** on page 393.

Learning From Realia

Banco de Guatemala The **quetzal** is the monetary unit of Guatemala. The **quetzal** is a multicolored bird and it is the national symbol of Guatemala.

Ask students: **¿Cuántos quetzales hay en la página 392?**

B HISTORIETA **En el mercado**

Completen.

El otro día yo ___1___ (estar) en el mercado de Chichicastenango, en Guatemala. Ramón ___2___ (estar) allí también. Nosotros ___3___ (andar) por el mercado pero no ___4___ (poder) comprar nada. No es que no ___5___ (querer) comprar nada, es que no ___6___ (poder) porque ___7___ (ir) al mercado sin un quetzal.

Chichicastenango, Guatemala

Telling what people say
Decir en el presente

The verb **decir** *(to say)* is irregular in the present tense. Study the following forms.

INFINITIVE	decir
yo	digo
tú	dices
él, ella, Ud.	dice
nosotros(as)	decimos
vosotros(as)	*decís*
ellos, ellas, Uds.	dicen

ANSWERS

Práctica

B 1. estuve
2. estuvo
3. anduvimos
4. pudimos
5. quisimos
6. pudimos
7. fuimos

A **¿Qué dices?** Sigan el modelo.

¿Qué dices de la clase de español?

Pues, yo digo que es fantástica. Estoy aprendiendo mucho.

1. ¿Qué dices de la clase de matemáticas?
2. ¿Qué dices de la clase de inglés?
3. ¿Qué dices de la clase de biología?
4. ¿Qué dices de la clase de educación física?
5. ¿Qué dices de la clase de historia?

B **¿Qué dicen todos?** Completen con la forma apropiada del presente de **decir.**

Yo ___(1) que quiero ir en tren pero Elena me ___(2) que prefiere tomar el avión. Ella y Tomás también ___(3) que no hay mucha diferencia entre la tarifa del avión y la tarifa del tren.

—¿Qué ___(4) tú?

—Yo ___(5) que es mejor ir en tren.

—Bien. Tú y yo ___(6) la misma cosa. Estamos de acuerdo.

CAPÍTULO 13
Estructura

A Have students do **Práctica A** as a mini-conversation, working in pairs.

EXPANSION Have students think of additional topics to talk about, such as their school teams and clubs. For example:

—¿Qué dices del equipo de fútbol?
—Pues, yo digo que es fantástico porque está ganando.

B This activity uses all forms of **decir.**

¡OJO! There is no more new material to present in this chapter. The sections that follow recombine and reinforce the vocabulary and structures that have already been introduced.

Learning From Realia

Museo nacional del ferrocarril This museum is in Madrid. Ask students: **¿Tienes que pagar por la entrada?**

ANSWERS

Práctica

A All answers follow the model.

B
1. **digo**
2. **dice**
3. **dicen**
4. **dices**
5. **digo**
6. **decimos**

RESOURCES

- Audiocassette 8A/CD7
- CD-ROM, Disc 4, page 394

Bell Ringer Review

Use BRR Transparency 13-5, or write the following on the board: Write four things passengers must do when they check in at an airport.

TEACHING THE CONVERSATION

A. Have students close their books. Read the conversation to them or play Cassette 8A/Compact Disc 7.

B. Have the class repeat each line after you once.

C. Call on two students to read the conversation with as much expression as possible.

D. After completing the conversation, have students summarize it in their own words.

E. After presenting the conversation, go over the **Después de conversar** activity. If students can answer the questions with relative ease, move on. Students should not be expected to memorize the conversation.

TECHNOLOGY OPTION

On the CD-ROM (Disc 4, page 394), students can watch a dramatization of this conversation. They can then play the role of either one of the characters and record themselves in the conversation.

Learning From Photos

En la ventanilla The photo on this page was taken at the Toledo train station, which has beautiful mosaics and tilework.

Conversación

En la ventanilla

PASAJERA: Un billete para Madrid, por favor.
AGENTE: ¿Sencillo o de ida y vuelta?
PASAJERA: Sencillo, por favor.
AGENTE: ¿Para cuándo, señorita?
PASAJERA: Para hoy.
AGENTE: ¿En qué clase, primera o segunda?
PASAJERA: En segunda. ¿Tiene Ud. una tarifa reducida para estudiantes?
AGENTE: Sí. ¿Tiene Ud. su tarjeta de identidad estudiantil?
PASAJERA: Sí, aquí la tiene Ud.
AGENTE: Con el descuento son tres mil pesetas.
PASAJERA: ¿A qué hora sale el próximo tren?
AGENTE: Sale a las veinte y diez del andén número ocho.
PASAJERA: Gracias.

Después de conversar

Contesten.

1. ¿Dónde está la señorita?
2. ¿Adónde va?
3. ¿Qué tipo de billete quiere?
4. ¿Para cuándo lo quiere?
5. ¿En qué clase quiere viajar?
6. ¿Es alumna la señorita?
7. ¿Hay una tarifa reducida para estudiantes?
8. ¿Qué tiene la señorita?
9. ¿Cuánto cuesta el billete con el descuento estudiantil?
10. ¿A qué hora sale el tren?
11. ¿De qué andén sale?

ANSWERS

Después de conversar

1. **La señorita está en la ventanilla.**
2. **Va a Madrid.**
3. **Quiere un billete sencillo.**
4. **Lo quiere para hoy.**
5. **Quiere viajar en segunda (clase).**
6. **Sí, la señorita es alumna.**
7. **Sí, hay una tarifa reducida para estudiantes.**
8. **La señorita tiene su tarjeta de identidad estudiantil.**
9. **Con el descuento estudiantil el billete cuesta tres mil pesetas.**
10. **El tren sale a las veinte y diez.**
11. **Sale del andén número ocho.**

Actividades comunicativas

A **El horario** Look at the train schedule. With a classmate, ask and answer as many questions as you can about it.

B **Vamos a Barcelona.** You and a classmate are spending a semester in Spain. You will be going to Barcelona for a couple of days. One of you is going to fly and the other is going to take the train. Compare your trips: time, cost, and what you have to do the day of departure.

RENFE
Madrid
Toledo
Válido desde el 29 de mayo
24 de septiembre d

TIPO DE TREN	REGIONAL	REGIONAL	REGIONAL	REGIONAL	REGIONAL
PRESTACIONES	2.ª	2.ª	2.ª	2.ª	2.ª
ORIGEN		■	■	MADRID CH. 9.25	■
MADRID-ATOCHA VILLAVERDE BAJO LOS ANGELES SAN CRISTOBAL DE LOS ANGELES GETAFE-INDUSTRIAL PINTO VALDEMORO CIEMPOZUELOS ARANJUEZ CASTILLEJO-AÑOVER VILLAMEJOR ALGODOR TOLEDO-INDUSTRIAL TOLEDO	■ 6.20 6.37 6.50	7.20 7.28 7.30 7.33 7.36 7.41 7.47 7.52 8.03 8.13 8.22 8.29 8.36	8.25 8.33 8.35 8.38 8.41 8.46 8.52 8.57 9.08 9.16 9.44	9.39 10.11 10.40	10.55 11.03 11.05 11.08 11.11 11.16 11.22 11.27 11.38 11.53 12.02 12.09 12.16
DESTINO	■	■	■	■	■
OBSERVACIONES	L M X J V S – (1)	Diario (2)	L M X J V – – (4)	– – – – – S D (3)	Diario

OBSERVACIONES:
(1) No circula 25-VII y 15-VIII.
(2) Efectua parada en Santa Catalina (7.26).
(3) Circula 25-VII y 15-VIII.
(4) No circula 25-VII y 15-VIII. Diario hasta Aranjuez.
(5) Efectua parada en Santa Catalina (14.31).

(L) Lunes
(M) Martes
(X) Miércoles
(J) Jueves
(V) Viernes
(S) Sábado
(D) Domingo

PRONUNCIACIÓN

Las consonantes ñ, ch

The **ñ** is a separate letter of the Spanish alphabet. The mark over it is called a **tilde.** Note that it is pronounced similarly to the *ny* in the English word *canyon.* Repeat the following.

señor	**otoño**	**España**
señora	**pequeño**	**cumpleaños**
año		

Ch is pronounced much like the **ch** in the English word *church.* Repeat the following.

coche	**chaqueta**
chocolate	**muchacho**

Repeat the following sentences.

El señor español compra un coche cada año en el otoño.
El muchacho chileno duerme en una cama pequeña en el coche-cama.
El muchacho pequeño lleva una chaqueta color chocolate.

Actividades comunicativas

A Give students a few minutes to study the train schedule before they begin the activity.

B Students should write down their answers and then compare notes with their partners.

TECHNOLOGY OPTION Students may use the Portfolio feature on the CD-ROM to record their conversation.

TEACHING PRONUNCIATION

A. Most students have no particular problem with these sounds. Have them pronounce each word carefully after you or the recording on Cassette 8A/ Compact Disc 7.

B. Have students open their books to page 395. Call on individuals to read the words and sentences.

C. All model sentences on page 395 can be used for dictation.

TECHNOLOGY OPTION

In the CD-ROM version of the Pronunciation section (Disc 4, page 395), students will see an animation of the cartoon on this page. They can also listen to, record, and play back the words and sentences presented here.

ANSWERS

Actvidades comunicativas

A Answers will vary.

B Answers should include the time of departure, the cost of the trip, and a brief description of what they have to do the day they leave.

National Standards

Cultures

The reading about the AVE train in Spain and the related activities on page 397 allow students to demonstrate an understanding of the importance of train travel in Spain.

TEACHING THE READING

Pre-reading

A. Have students open their books to page 396 and read the information in the Reading Strategy.

B. Tell them that the illustration at the bottom of the page is of **un ave**.

C. Then have them scan the **Lectura** and the photos to look for the connection between the bird and the train.

D. Have students locate Madrid and Sevilla on the map of Spain on page 463.

Reading

A. Call on a student to read three or four sentences aloud.

B. Intersperse the oral reading with comprehension questions from **Después de leer Activity A,** page 397.

Post-reading

A. Assign the reading and the **Después de leer** activities on page 397 for homework.

B. Have a student summarize the reading selection in his or her own words.

TECHNOLOGY OPTION

Students may listen to a recorded version of the **Lectura** on the CD-ROM, Disc 4, pages 396–397.

Lecturas CULTURALES

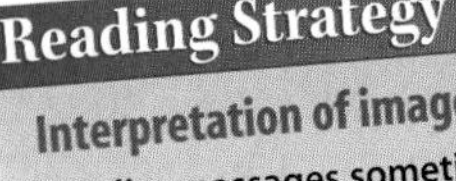

Reading Strategy

Interpretation of images

Reading passages sometimes use images as a symbol to create an impression. Many times these images are animals. If you are able to identify an image, it is helpful to stop for a moment and think about the qualities and characteristics of the particular symbol the author is using in his or her imagery. Then when you have finished reading, go back and think about how the two images being compared are alike.

EN EL AVE

José Luis y su hermana, Maripaz, pasan dos días en Sevilla. Vinieron a visitar a sus abuelos. El viaje que hicieron de Madrid, donde viven, fue fantástico. Tomaron el tren y llegaron a Sevilla en sólo dos horas y quince minutos. Salieron de Atocha en Madrid a las 17:00 y bajaron del tren en Sevilla a las 19:15. ¿Es posible recorrer el trayecto[1] Madrid–Sevilla en dos horas quince minutos? Es una distancia de 538 kilómetros. ¡Es increíble!

[1]recorrer el trayecto *cover the route*

A bordo del AVE

Independent Practice

Assign any of the following:

1. **Después de leer** activities, page 397
2. Workbook, **Un poco más,** pages 167–169
3. CD-ROM, Disc 4, pages 396–397

Sí, es increíble, pero es verdad. El nuevo tren español de alta velocidad es uno de los trenes más rápidos del mundo. Viaja a 250 kilómetros por hora. El tren se llama el AVE. ¿Por qué el AVE? Porque el tren vuela como un ave o pájaro.

José Luis y Maripaz tomaron el AVE. Según ellos, el viaje fue fantástico. ¿Por qué? Primero la velocidad. Pero el tren es también muy cómodo[2]. Lleva ocho coches en tres clases. Los pasajeros pueden escuchar música estereofónica o mirar tres canales de video. El tren también dispone de[3] teléfono por si acaso[4] un pasajero quiere o necesita hacer una llamada telefónica.

[2]cómodo *comfortable*
[3]dispone de *has available*
[4]por si acaso *in case*

Plaza de España, Sevilla

Torre del Oro, Sevilla

Plaza de España, Sevilla

Después de leer

A Una visita a los abuelos Contesten.

1. ¿Quiénes hicieron un viaje de Madrid a Sevilla?
2. ¿Quiénes vinieron a Sevilla, José Luis y su hermana o sus abuelos?
3. ¿Cómo hicieron el viaje?
4. ¿Qué tal fue el viaje?
5. ¿Cuánto tiempo tardó el viaje?
6. ¿A qué hora salieron de Madrid?
7. ¿A qué hora llegaron a Sevilla?

B Información Busquen la información.

1. uno de los trenes más rápidos del mundo
2. el nombre del tren
3. el número de coches que lleva el tren
4. el número de clases que tiene
5. algunas comodidades que el tren ofrece a los pasajeros

HISTORY CONNECTION

Plaza de España, Sevilla The grandiose structure on the Plaza de España was designed by the architect Aníbal González. It was Spain's pavillion at the 1929 Hispanic-American Exhibition Fair. There are four bridges over the ornamental lake. One of the bridges is seen here. Each bridge represents one of the medieval kingdoms of the Iberian peninsula.

Torre del Oro, Sevilla For information about the Torre del Oro, see History Connection, Chapter 4, page 111.

Después de leer

A Allow students to refer to the reading to look up the answers, or you may use this activity as a testing device for factual recall.

B Have individual students read the appropriate phrase or sentence aloud. Make sure all students find the information in the **Lectura.**

ANSWERS

Después de leer

A
1. **José Luis y su hermana, Maripaz, hicieron un viaje de Madrid a Sevilla.**
2. **José Luis y su hermana vinieron a Sevilla.**
3. **Hicieron el viaje en el tren.**
4. **El viaje fue fantástico.**
5. **El viaje tardó dos horas quince minutos.**
6. **Salieron de Madrid a las 17:00.**
7. **Llegaron a Sevilla a las 19:15.**

B
1. **el tren español de alta velocidad**
2. **el AVE**
3. **ocho**
4. **tres**
5. **música estereofónica, tres canales de video, teléfono**

LECTURA OPCIONAL

National Standards

Cultures

This reading about Machu Picchu in Peru and the related activities on page 399 allow students to develop an appreciation for one of the unique archeological sites in the Spanish-speaking world.

TEACHING TIPS

¡OJO! This reading is optional. You may skip it completely, have the entire class read it, have only several students read it, or assign it for extra credit.

A. Have students locate Cuzco on the map of South America on page 464, or use the Map Transparency.

B. Have students read the passage quickly as they look at the photos that accompany it. The photos will increase their comprehension because students will be able to visualize what they are reading about.

C. Have students discuss the information that they find interesting.

VIDEO CONNECTION

Machu Picchu The **¡Buen viaje! Level 3 Video Program** has a segment on Machu Picchu. You may want to show this video in connection with this reading.

LECTURA OPCIONAL

DE CUZCO A MACHU PICCHU

Un viaje muy interesante en tren es el viaje de Cuzco a Machu Picchu en el Perú. Cada día a las siete de la mañana, un tren de vía estrecha[1] sale de la estación de San Pedro en Cuzco y llega a Machu Picchu a las diez y media. Cuzco está a unos 3.500 metros sobre el nivel del mar. El tren tiene que bajar a 2.300 metros para llegar a Machu Picchu. Tiene que bajar 1.200 metros y en el viaje de regreso tiene que subir 1.200 metros.

Pero, ¿quiénes toman el tren para ir a Machu Picchu? Es un tren que lleva a muchos turistas que quieren ir a ver las famosas ruinas de los incas. Machu Picchu es una ciudad entera, totalmente aislada[2] en un pico andino al borde de[3] un cañón. Un dato histórico increíble es que los españoles no descubrieron a Machu Picchu durante su conquista

[1]de vía estrecha *narrow gauge*
[2]aislada *isolated*
[3]al borde de *on the edge of*

El valle del Urubamba, Perú

La Plaza de Armas, Cuzco

Machu Picchu

del Perú. Los historiadores creen que Machu Picchu fue el último refugio de los nobles incas al escaparse[4] de los españoles.

Machu Picchu fue descubierto por Hiram Bingham, el explorador y senador de los Estados Unidos, en 1911. ¿Cómo llegó Bingham a Machu Picchu en 1911? ¡A pie! Y aún hoy hay sólo dos maneras de ir a Machu Picchu—a pie o en el tren que sale a las siete y media de Cuzco.

[4]al escaparse *upon escaping*

Después de leer

A **¿Sí o no?** Digan que sí o que no.

1. Machu Picchu está a una altura más elevada que Cuzco.
2. El tren que va de Machu Picchu a Cuzco tiene que subir 1.200 metros.
3. El viaje de Cuzco a Machu Picchu toma tres horas y media.
4. Hay muy pocos turistas en el tren a Machu Picchu.
5. En Machu Picchu hay ruinas famosas de los incas.
6. Machu Picchu fue una ciudad de los incas.
7. Los españoles descubrieron la ciudad de Machu Picchu durante su conquista del Perú.
8. Hiram Bingham fue un senador de los Estados Unidos.
9. Él también fue a Machu Picchu en tren.

ANSWERS

Después de leer

A
1. No.
2. Sí.
3. Sí.
4. No.
5. Sí.
6. Sí.
7. No.
8. Sí.
9. No.

LECTURA OPCIONAL

INFORMAL ASSESSMENT

You may use the **Después de leer** activity as a testing device to see how well students understood the reading selection.

Learning From Photos

Machu Picchu, Perú The top photo on page 398, taken through a stone portal or doorway, gives us a beautiful view of one of the many terraces at Machu Picchu. Many of the original stone buildings have been reconstructed. However, since the original roofs were made of thatch, they have not been rebuilt.

El tren a Machu Picchu (page 398) This is the train that takes tourists from Cuzco to Machu Picchu.

El valle del Urubamba, Perú (page 398) This valley is referred to as the "Sacred Valley of the Incas." The name "Inca" originally applied to the royal family only. Today it is used to describe the people as a whole.

La Plaza de Armas, Cuzco (page 398) Cuzco is a city of 200,000 people. Its population is a blend of Indian, **mestizo,** and Spanish cultures. In the days of the Incas, the Plaza de Armas was called Huacaypata. This square was lined with the sumptuous palaces of the dead and mummified Incas, and with the imperial residences of the living Incas. Today, the palaces have been replaced by Spanish mansions. The first floors of these mansions are occupied by small stores and restaurants.

CAPÍTULO 13
Conexiones

National Standards

Connections

This reading about the 24-hour clock and the metric system establishes a connection with another discipline, allowing students to reinforce and further their knowledge of mathematics through the study of Spanish.

Comparisons

This reading allows students to compare the U.S. system of measurement with the metric system, which is used in most of the Spanish-speaking world.

¡OJO! The readings in the **Conexiones** section are optional. They focus on some of the major disciplines taught in schools and universities. The vocabulary is useful for discussing such topics as history, literature, art, economics, business, science, etc. You may choose any of the following ways to do this reading on mathematical conversions with your students.

Independent reading Have students read the selections and do the post-reading activities as homework, which you collect. This option is least intrusive on class time and requires a minimum of teacher involvement.

Homework with in-class follow-up Assign the readings and post-reading activities as homework. Review and discuss the material in class the next day.

Intensive in-class activity This option includes a pre-reading vocabulary presentation, in-class reading and discussion, assignment of the activities for homework, and a discussion of the assignment in class the following day.

Conexiones

LAS MATEMÁTICAS

CONVERSIONES ARITMÉTICAS

When traveling through many of the Spanish-speaking countries, you will need to make some mathematical conversions. For example, train as well as plane schedules and hours for formal events, radio, and television are given using the twenty-four-hour clock. The metric system rather than the English system is used for weights and measures. Let's take a look at some of the conversions that must be made.

La hora

Cuando lees el horario para el tren o un anuncio para un programa cultural, dan la hora usando las 24 horas. La una (1:00) es la una de la mañana y las doce (12:00) es el mediodía. Las trece (13:00), una hora después del mediodía, es la una de la tarde y las veinticuatro horas (00:00) es la medianoche.

Nuestros amigos José Luis y Maripaz salieron de Madrid a las 17:00 y llegaron a Sevilla a las 19:15. Es decir que salieron de Madrid a las 5:00 de la tarde y llegaron a las 7:15 de la tarde.

HORARIOS

MADRID Puerta de Atocha CADIZ	LLANO	
NUMERO DE TREN / DIAS DE CIRCULACION	9220 LMXJVSD	41 (1) LMXJVSD
MADRID Puerta de Atocha	10:05	16:05
CIUDAD REAL	11:06	17:06
PUERTOLLANO	* 11:23	* 17:23
CORDOBA	12:12	18:11
SEVILLA Santa Justa	13:19	19:26
JEREZ DE LA FRONTERA	14:16	20:23
EL PUERTO DE STA. MARIA	14:27	20:36
SAN FERNANDO DE CADIZ	14:41	20:50
CADIZ	14:55	21:05

CADIZ MADRID Puerta de Atocha		LLANO
NUMERO DE TREN / DIAS DE CIRCULACION	42 (2) LMXJVSD	9233 LMXJVSD
CADIZ	08:00	16:25
SAN FERNANDO DE CADIZ	08:13	16:36
EL PUERTO DE STA. MARIA	08:26	16:48
JEREZ DE LA FRONTERA	08:36	16:59
SEVILLA Santa Justa	09:43	17:57
CORDOBA	* 10:50	* 19:03
PUERTOLLANO	11:42	19:52
CIUDAD REAL	11:59	20:09
MADRID Puerta de Atocha	13:02	21:10

MADRID Puerta de Atocha HUELVA	LLANO
NUMERO DE TREN / DIAS DE CIRCULACION	9220 LMXJVSD
MADRID Puerta de Atocha	10:05
CIUDAD REAL	11:06
PUERTOLLANO	* 11:23
CORDOBA	12:12
LA PALMA DEL CONDADO (*)	14:05
HUELVA	14:30

HUELVA MADRID Puerta de Atocha	LLANO
NUMERO DE TREN / DIAS DE CIRCULACION	9233 LMXJVSD
HUELVA	16:55
LA PALMA DEL CONDADO	17:19
CORDOBA	* 19:03
PUERTOLLANO	19:52
CIUDAD REAL	20:09
MADRID Puerta de Atocha	21:10

(*) La Palma no admite viajeros destino Huelva.

TIPO DE RESTAURACION: SNACK

* El servicio de restauración en el asiento se realiza únicamente entre las estaciones señaladas.

OBSERVACIONES
(1) Procede de Barcelona, Zaragoza.
(2) Continúa a Zaragoza, Barcelona.

El sistema métrico—pesos y medidas[1]

Pesos

Las medidas tradicionales para peso en los Estados Unidos son la onza, la libra y la tonelada. En el sistema métrico decimal, las medidas para peso están basadas en el kilogramo, o kilo.

[1]pesos y medidas *weights and measures*

ABOUT THE SPANISH LANGUAGE

Terms from the English system—**el pie, la yarda, el galón—**are very seldom heard in Spanish.

Hay mil gramos en un kilo. El kilo es igual a 2,2 libras. Una libra estadounidense es un poco menos de medio kilo.

Líquidos
Las medidas para líquidos en los Estados Unidos son la pinta, el cuarto y el galón. En el sistema métrico es el litro. Un litro contiene un poco más que un cuarto.

Distancia y altura
Para medir la distancia y la altura en los Estados Unidos usamos la pulgada, el pie, la yarda y la milla. El sistema métrico usa el metro. El metro es un poco más que una yarda. Un kilómetro (mil metros) es 0,621 millas—un poco más que media milla.

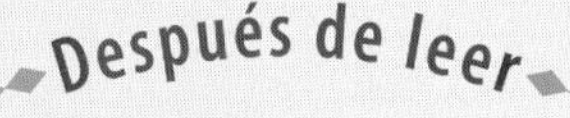

Después de leer

A La hora Read the schedule on page 400 and give the arrival and departure times of the trains using our system.

B El sistema métrico Contesten según las fotografías.

1. ¿Cuánto cuesta un litro de gasolina?
2. ¿Cuál es el límite de velocidad?
3. ¿Cuánto cuesta un litro de leche?
4. ¿Cuánto cuesta un kilo de carne?

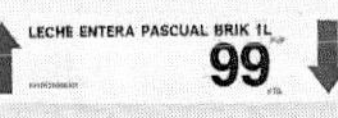

CAPÍTULO 13
Conexiones

LAS MATEMÁTICAS
CONVERSIONES ARITMÉTICAS

¡OJO! The material in this section will probably be of more interest to students who like math and science. It is, however, useful for all because, when travelling through most areas of the Spanish-speaking world, one has to use the metric system.

A. Have students read the introduction in English on page 400.

B. Now have them read the selection quickly. Students should already be familiar with the metric terms used in the reading.

C. Explain to students that here are some basic strategies to use when reading unfamiliar material. They should learn to: (1) recognize cognates and (2) derive meaning from context.

D. Now do the **Después de leer** activities.

ANSWERS

Después de leer

A Answers will vary.

B
1. **Un litro de gasolina super cuesta 118.6 pts.**
2. **El límite de velocidad es de 60 kilómetros por hora.**
3. **Un litro de leche cuesta 99 pts.**
4. **Un kilo de carne cuesta 1395 pts.**

RECYCLING

The **Actividades orales** and the **Actividad escrita** allow students to use the vocabulary and structures from this chapter in open-ended, real-life settings.

Actividades orales

¡OJO! Encourage students to say as much as possible when they do these activities. Tell them not to be afraid of making mistakes since the goal of the activities is real-life communication. If someone in the group makes an error, allow the others to politely correct him or her.

Let students choose the activities they would like to do.

A You may wish to assign one type of travel to each group.

B **TECHNOLOGY OPTION**
In the CD-ROM version of this activity (Disc 4, page 402), students can interact with an on-screen native speaker and record their voice.

Student Portfolio

Have students keep a notebook containing their best written work from each chapter. These selected writings can be based on assignments from the Student Textbook, the Writing Activities Workbook, and the Communication Activities Masters. The two activities on page 403 are examples of writing assignments that may be included in each student's portfolio.

In the Workbook, students will develop an organized autobiography **(Mi autobiografía).** These workbook pages may also become a part of their portfolio. See the Teacher's Manual for more information on the Student Portfolio.

Culminación

Actividades orales

A **El tren, el bus o el avión** Work in groups of three or four. Discuss the advantages **(las ventajas)** and the disadvantages **(las desventajas)** of bus, train, and air travel. In your discussion, include such things as speed, price, location of stations, and anything else you consider important.

B **¿Qué vamos a hacer?** You and a classmate are on a bus on the way to the train station in Madrid. There's an awful traffic jam **(un tapón, un atasco).** You know you are going to miss your train. Discuss your predicament with one another and figure out what you can do.

La estación de ferrocarril, Málaga

ANSWERS

Actividades orales

A Answers will vary.

B Answers will vary.

Independent Practice

Assign any of the following:
1. Activities, pages 402–403
2. Workbook, **Mi autobiografía,** page 170
3. Situation Cards
4. CD-ROM, Chapter 13, **Juego de repaso**

Actividad escrita

A **En la estación de ferrocarril** Look at the illustrations and write a paragraph about them.

Writing Strategy

Writing a descriptive paragraph

Your overall goal in writing a descriptive paragraph is to enable the reader to visualize your scene. To achieve this you must select and organize details that create an impression. Using a greater number of specific nouns and vivid adjectives will make your writing livelier.

Un viaje excelente

Write about a trip you took to a place you love. The place can be real or imaginary. Describe how and where you went, and when. Then describe what the weather is like in that place and what clothing you need there. Continue by writing about what you saw and how you got to each place you visited. In your description of the place, try to make your readers understand what it is about the place that you think is so great.

CAPÍTULO 13
Culminación

Actividad escrita

A You may wish to have students work in pairs to write this paragraph.

Writing Strategy

Writing a descriptive paragraph

A. Have students read the Writing Strategy on page 403.

B. Your students may enjoy writing about a trip to Machu Picchu or one of the other beautiful tourist destinations in the Spanish-speaking world. To help stimulate your students' "creative juices," have them find a photo in the textbook of a place they'd like to visit. Ask them to look at the photo for inspiration as they do the Writing Strategy activity on page 403.

ANSWERS

Actividad escrita

A Answers will vary.

Writing Strategy

Answers will vary.

ASSESSMENT RESOURCES

- Chapter Quizzes
- Testing Program
- Computer Testmaker
- Situation Cards
- Communication Transparency C-13
- Performance Assessment
- **Maratón mental** Videoquiz

VOCABULARY REVIEW

The words and phrases in the **Vocabulario** have been taught for productive use in this chapter. They are summarized here as a resource for both students and teacher. This list also serves as a convenient resource for the **Culminación** activities on pages 402 and 403. There are approximately four cognates in this vocabulary list. Have students find them.

Vocabulario

GETTING AROUND A TRAIN STATION

la estación de ferrocarril
la ventanilla
el billete, el boleto
  sencillo
  de ida y vuelta
la sala de espera
el mozo, el maletero
el equipaje
la maleta
la bolsa
el tablero de llegadas,
  de salidas
el horario
el quiosco
el tren
el andén
la vía
en segunda (clase)
en primera (clase)

DESCRIBING ACTIVITIES AT A TRAIN STATION

bajar(se) del tren
subir al tren
transbordar
salir a tiempo
  con retraso, con una demora

ON BOARD THE TRAIN

el coche, el vagón
el pasillo
el compartimiento
el asiento, la plaza
  libre
  ocupado(a)
  reservado(a)
completo(a)
el coche-cama
el coche-comedor, el coche-cafetería
la litera
el revisor
la parada
en la próxima parada

TECNOTUR

VIDEO ¡Buen viaje!

EPISODIO 13 ▸ Un viaje en tren

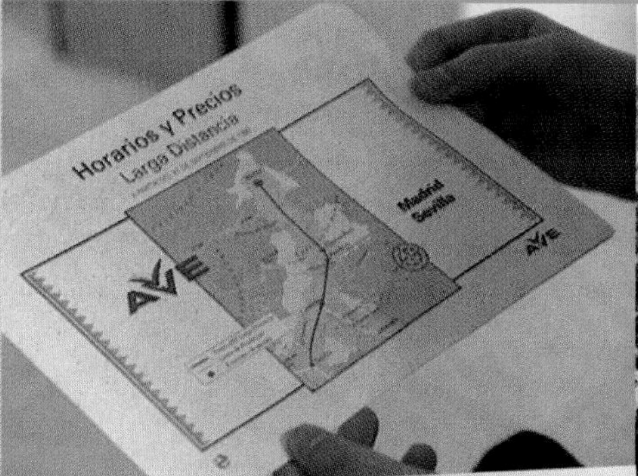

Juan Ramón y Teresa hacen un viaje en tren a Sevilla.

En Sevilla visitan varios lugares interesantes.

CD-ROM Expansión cultural

Muchos españoles creen que Sevilla es la ciudad más bonita del mundo.

interNET CONNECTION

In this video episode, Juan Ramón and Teresa take the AVE from Madrid to Seville. To plan your own train trip, go to the Capítulo 13 Internet activity at the Glencoe Foreign Language Web site:

http://www.glencoe.com/sec/fl

Video Synopsis

In this episode Juan Ramón and Teresa take the AVE train from the Atocha station in Madrid to Sevilla. They purchase their tickets and get on board. During the trip Juan Ramón tapes the train, the countryside, and Teresa. While on board they discuss whether Sevilla or San Juan, Puerto Rico, is the most beautiful city in the world. When in Sevilla Juan Rámon films various sites for the Web page. On the night train back to Madrid, Juan Rámon shares his impressions with us of the AVE and Sevilla.

OVERVIEW

This page previews three key multimedia components of the **Glencoe Spanish** series. Each reinforces the material taught in Chapter 13 in a unique manner.

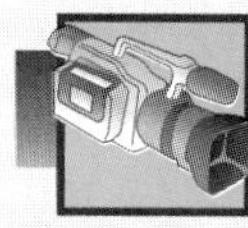

VIDEO

The Video Program allows students to see how the chapter vocabulary and structures are used by native speakers within an engaging story line. For maximum reinforcement, show the video episode as a final activity for Chapter 13.

A. Before viewing this episode, have students read the video photo captions. Ask: **¿Cómo se llama el tren? ¿De qué ciudad sale el tren?**

B. Now show the Chapter 13 video episode. See the Video Activities Booklet for detailed suggestions for using this resource.

CD-ROM

A. Have students read the **Expansión cultural** photo caption on page 405.

B. In the CD-ROM version of **Expansión cultural** (Disc 4, page 405), students can listen to additional recorded information about Sevilla.

INTERNET

Teacher Information and Student Worksheets for this activity can be accessed at the Web site.

Chapter 14 Overview

SCOPE AND SEQUENCE pages 406–431

TOPICS	FUNCTIONS	STRUCTURE	CULTURE
◆ Restaurants ◆ Foods and eating utensils	◆ How to order food or beverage at a restaurant ◆ How to identify eating utensils and dishes ◆ How to make a reservation at a restaurant ◆ How to explain how you like certain foods prepared ◆ How to talk about present and past events and activities	◆ Stem-changing verbs in the present ◆ Stem-changing verbs in the preterite	◆ Typical cuisine from Mexico ◆ Typical cuisine from Spain ◆ Typical foods from the Caribbean ◆ Regional vocabulary in the Spanish-speaking world ◆ Vistas del Ecuador

CHAPTER 14 RESOURCES

PRINT	MULTIMEDIA
Planning Resources	
Lesson Plans	Interactive Lesson Planner
Block Scheduling Lesson Plans	
Reinforcement Resources	
Writing Activities Workbook	Transparencies Binder
Student Tape Manual	Audiocassette/Compact Disc Program
Video Activities Booklet	Videocassette/Videodisc Program
Web Site User's Guide	Online Internet Activities
	Electronic Teacher's Classroom Resources
Assessment Resources	
Situation Cards	**Maratón mental** Mindjogger Videoquiz
Chapter Quizzes	Testmaker Computer Software (Macintosh/Windows)
Testing Program	Listening Comprehension Audiocassette/Compact Disc
Performance Assessment	Communication Transparency: C-14
Motivational Resources	
Expansion Activities	Café Glencoe: www.cafe.glencoe.com
	Keypal Internet Activities
Enrichment	
Spanish for Spanish Speakers	Fine Art Transparencies: F-13, F-14

Chapter 14 Planning Guide

SECTION	PAGES	SECTION RESOURCES
Vocabulario Palabras 1 **En el restaurante**	408–411	Vocabulary Transparencies 14.1 Audiocassette 8B/ Compact Disc 8 Student Tape Manual, TE, pages 159–161 Workbook, pages 171–172 Chapter Quizzes, page 70 CD-ROM, Disc 4, pages 408–411
Vocabulario Palabras 2 **Más alimentos o comestibles**	412–415	Vocabulary Transparencies 14.2 Audiocassette 8B/ Compact Disc 8 Student Tape Manual, TE, pages 161–164 Workbook, pages 173–174 Chapter Quizzes, pages 71–72 CD-ROM, Disc 4, pages 412–415
Estructura **Verbos con el cambio e → i en el presente** **Verbos con el cambio e → i, o → u en el pretérito**	416–419	Workbook, pages 175–176 Audiocassette 8B/Compact Disc 8 Student Tape Manual, TE, pages 164–165 Chapter Quizzes, pages 73–74 Computer Testmaker CD-ROM, Disc 4, pages 416–419
Conversación **En el restaurante** **Pronunciación: La consonante x**	420–421	Audiocassette 8B/Compact Disc 8 Student Tape Manual, TE, pages 166–167 CD-ROM, Disc 4, pages 420–421
Lecturas culturales **La comida mexicana** **La comida española *(opcional)*** **La comida del Caribe *(opcional)***	422–425	Testing Problem, pages 81–82 CD-ROM, Disc 4, pages 422–425
Conexiones **El lenguaje *(opcional)***	426–427	Testing Problem, page 82 CD-ROM, Disc 4, pages 426–427
Culminación **Actividades orales** **Actividades escritas** **Vocabulario** **Tecnotur**	428–431	**¡Buen viaje!** Video, Episode 14 Video Activities, pages 118–122 Internet Activities **www.glencoe.com/sec/fl** Testing Program, pages 79–81; 117; 149; 175 CD-ROM, Disc 4, pages 428–431

CAPÍTULO 14

OVERVIEW

In this chapter students will learn how to order food in a restaurant. To do this they will learn expressions needed to speak with a server, vocabulary associated with utensils, and additional items of food. They will continue to narrate in the present and past by learning the present and preterite of stem-changing verbs they can use at a restaurant—**pedir, servir, repetir.** The cultural focus of the chapter is on some typical cuisines of the Spanish-speaking world.

National Standards

Communication
In Chapter 14 students will learn to communicate in spoken and written Spanish on the following topics:
- ordering a meal
- describing a restaurant experience
- discussing cuisines of the Spanish-speaking world

Students will obtain and provide information about these topics and engage in conversations that would typically take place at a restaurant as they fulfill the chapter objectives listed on this page.

Pacing

Chapter 14 will require approximately six to eight days. Pacing will vary according to the length of the class, the age of your students, and student aptitude.

Block Scheduling

See the Block Scheduling Lesson Plans Booklet for suggestions on how to present the chapter material within a block scheduling framework.

CAPÍTULO 14

En el restaurante

Objetivos

In this chapter you will learn to do the following:
- order food or a beverage at a restaurant
- identify eating utensils and dishes
- identify more foods
- make a reservation at a restaurant
- talk about present and past events
- describe some cuisines of the Hispanic world

interNET CONNECTION

The **Glencoe Foreign Language Web site** (**http://www.glencoe.com/sec/fl**) offers three options that enable you and your students to experience the Spanish-speaking world via the Internet:
- The online **Actividades** are correlated to the chapters and utilize Hispanic Web sites around the world. For the Chapter 14 activity, see student page 431.
- The **Correspondencia electrónica** section provides information on how to set up a keypal (pen pal) exchange between your class and a class in the Spanish-speaking world.
- At **Café Glencoe,** the interactive "after-school" section of the site, you and your students can access a variety of additional online resources, including interactive games. In Chapter 14, the click-and-drag game practices the table setting.

cuatrocientos siete 407

CAPÍTULO 14

Spotlight On Culture

Artefacto The Andean area has produced the most superb folk art of the South American continent. The pre-Columbian peoples of the area excelled in weaving, pottery-making, and gold- and silver-smithing. It is said that Peru's artisans may produce the most interesting and varied crafts on the continent, and some of the finest in the world. On page 406 we see a Peruvian carved gourd.

There is a wonderful exhibit of pre-Columbian artifacts at the Museo de Antropología y Arqueología in Lima.

Fotografía The restaurant shown on this page is also in Lima.

Learning From Photos

Al restaurante Ask the following questions about the photo after presenting the new vocabulary in this chapter:

¿Es un restaurante económico o elegante?

¿Lleva un smoking el mesero?

¿Está poniendo la mesa el mesero?

Identifica todo lo que ves en la mesa.

¿Cuántas personas hay en la familia que está en el restaurante?

¿Cómo está vestido el papá? ¿Qué lleva?

¿Qué leen la mamá y el papá?

Chapter Projects

Visita a un restaurante hispano Plan a class outing to an inexpensive restaurant that serves food from a Spanish-speaking country. If possible, distribute the restaurant's menu in advance so students can think about what they will order. You may also have them use the menus to practice ordering in Spanish.

La cocina hispana Prepare a dish from one of the Spanish-speaking countries, or have students prepare some Hispanic foods and bring them to class. A number of typical dishes are described in this chapter. Students can go to the library to find recipes for these dishes.

TECHNOLOGY OPTION The **¡Buen viaje! Level 2,** Chapter 10 Internet activity utilizes Hispanic cuisine Web sites. If you are looking for recipes, you and your students may want to access the links for this activity. See page 406 for the address of the **Glencoe Foreign Language Web site.**

CAPÍTULO 14
Vocabulario

PALABRAS 1

RESOURCES

-  Vocabulary Transparencies 14.1 (A & B)
- Student Tape Manual, TE, pages 159–161
- Audiocassette 8B/CD8
- Workbook, pages 171–172
- Quiz 1, page 70
- CD-ROM, Disc 4, pages 408–411

Bell Ringer Review

Use BRR Transparency 14-1, or write the following on the board: Write a list of the foods you have learned.

TEACHING VOCABULARY

A. Have students close their books. Show Vocabulary Transparencies 14.1 (A & B). Point to individual items and have students repeat each word or expression two or three times affter you or Cassette 8B/Compact Disc 8.

B. Intersperse the presentation with simple questions that enable students to use the new words. For example: **¿Tienes hambre? ¿Quieres comer? ¿Tienes sed? ¿Qué pone el mesero? ¿Usas la taza para beber o para cortar la carne?** Have students answer with complete sentences or sometimes have them use just the word or expression that responds to the question.

C. After presenting the vocabulary orally, have students open their books and read the new vocabulary aloud. You can have the class read in chorus or call on individuals to read. Intersperse with questions such as those outlined above.

Vocabulario

PALABRAS 1

En el restaurante

El mesero pone la mesa.

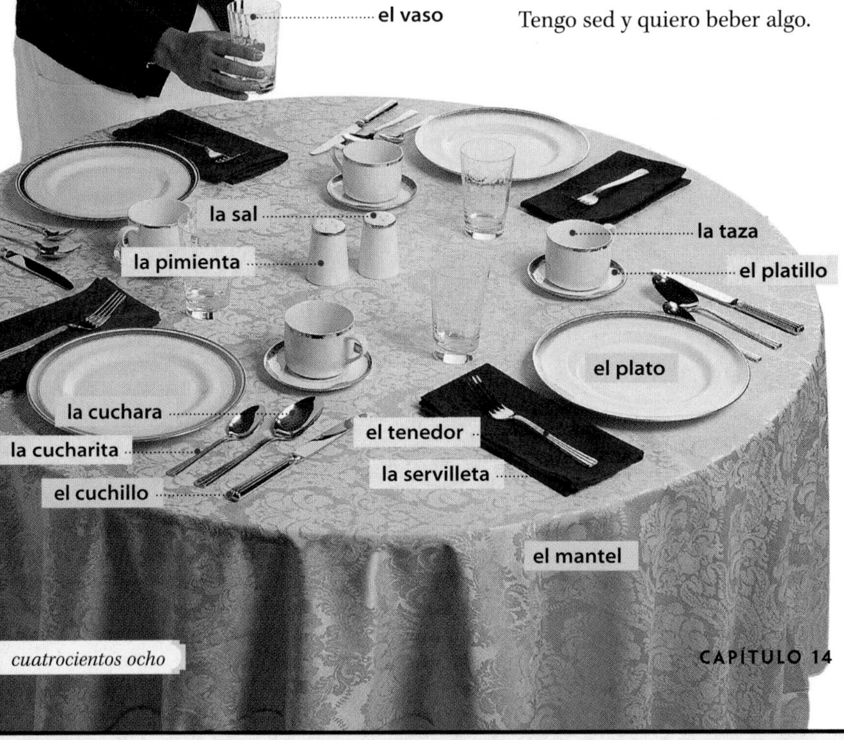

Tengo hambre y quiero comer.

Tengo sed y quiero beber algo.

Total Physical Response

Getting ready

Teach the following words by using the appropriate gestures as you say each expression: **cubre, dobla, a la derecha, a la izquierda, deja.**

TPR 1

Begin

___, ven acá, por favor.
Vas a poner la mesa.
Cubre la mesa con un mantel.
Dobla las servilletas.
Pon un plato en la mesa.
Luego pon la cucharita y el cuchillo a la derecha.
Pon el tenedor a la izquierda. Gracias, ___.

TPR 2

Begin

___, ven acá, por favor.
Vas a hacer unos gestos.
Toma el menú. Abre el menú.
Lee el menú. Cierra el menú.
Corta la carne con el cuchillo. Come.
Bebe. Deja una propina para el mesero.
Gracias, ___. Regresa a tu asiento.

La señorita pide el menú.

El cocinero fríe las papas.
Está friendo las papas.

El mesero le sirve la comida.

La señorita pide la cuenta.
El servicio no está incluido.
Ella deja una propina.

CAPÍTULO 14
Vocabulario

Additional Practice

Tengo hambre You may have students make up a brief conversation using the words **hambre** and **sed.** For example:
¿Sabes? Tengo hambre.
¿Ah sí? ¿Qué quieres comer?
Pues, creo que voy a pedir ___.

ABOUT THE SPANISH LANGUAGE

- The word **mesero** is used in Latin America. **Camarero** is used in Spain.
- The word **el menú** is universally understood. Other words frequently used for **menú** are **la minuta** and **la carta.**
- We have presented the words **sal** and **pimienta** but not **el salero, el pimentero** since the words are hardly ever used. One would say: **Sal, por favor.**

For the Younger Student

Poner la mesa You may wish to bring in silverware and have students set a table as they learn to identify each item.

TECHNOLOGY OPTION The Chapter 14 click-and-drag game at **Café Glencoe (www.cafe.glencoe.com)** practices the table setting.

Did You Know?

Pimienta, por favor. In Spain and many countries of Latin America a salt shaker is put on the table, but not a pepper shaker or pepper mill. If you want pepper you have to ask for it. The only exception would be some international restaurants and hotels.

¡OJO! **Práctica** When students are doing the **Práctica** activities, accept any answer that makes sense. The purpose of these activities is to have students use the new vocabulary. They are not factual recall activities. Thus, do not expect students to remember specific information from the vocabulary presentation when answering. If you wish, have students use the photos on this page as a stimulus, when possible.

Historieta Each time **Historieta** appears, it means that the answers to the activity form a short story. Encourage students to look at the title of the **Historieta** since it will sometimes help them do the activity.

A Have students work with a partner.

EXPANSION Ask students to volunteer additional items. For example: **Para tomar una limonada, una sopa, etc.**

B After going over **Práctica B,** have students retell the story in their own words.

Writing Development

Have students write the answers to **Práctica B** in a paragraph to illustrate how all of the items tell a story.

Learning From Realia

Alkalde The name of the restaurant on the check is Alkalde. It is a Basque restaurant. The Basques are considered to be the best cooks in Spain.

A **¿Qué necesitas?** Contesten según el modelo.

¿Para tomar leche?
Para tomar leche necesito un vaso.

1. ¿Para tomar agua?
2. ¿Para tomar café?
3. ¿Para comer la ensalada?
4. ¿Para comer el postre?
5. ¿Para cortar la carne?

Madrid, España

B **HISTORIETA En el restaurante**

Contesten.

1. ¿Cuántas personas hay en la mesa?
2. ¿Tiene hambre María?
3. ¿Pide María el menú?
4. ¿Le trae el menú el mesero?
5. ¿Qué pide María?
6. ¿El mesero le sirve?
7. ¿El mesero le sirve bien?
8. Después de la comida, ¿le pide la cuenta al mesero?
9. ¿Le trae la cuenta el mesero?
10. ¿Paga con su tarjeta de crédito María?
11. ¿María le da (deja) una propina al mesero?
12. Después de la comida, ¿tiene hambre María?

ANSWERS

Práctica

A
1. **Para tomar agua necesito un vaso.**
2. **Para tomar café necesito una taza.**
3. **Para comer la ensalada necesito un tenedor.**
4. **Para comer el postre necesito una cucharita (un tenedor).**
5. **Para cortar la carne necesito un cuchillo.**

B
1. **Hay una persona en la mesa.**
2. **Sí, María tiene hambre.**
3. **Sí, María pide el menú.**
4. **Sí, el mesero le trae el menú.**
5. **María pide ___.**
6. **Sí, el mesero le sirve.**
7. **Sí, el mesero le sirve bien.**
8. **Sí, le pide la cuenta al mesero después de la comida.**
9. **Sí, el mesero le trae la cuenta.**
10. **Sí (No), María (no) paga con su tarjeta de crédito.**
11. **Sí, María le da (deja) una propina al mesero.**
12. **No, María no tiene hambre después de la comida.**

C Palabras relacionadas Busquen una palabra relacionada.

1. la mesa — a. el servicio
2. la cocina — b. la bebida
3. servir — c. el cocinero
4. freír — d. la comida
5. comer — e. el mesero
6. beber — f. frito

Alcalá de Henares, España

D HISTORIETA El mesero pone la mesa.

Completen.

1. Para comer, los clientes necesitan ____, ____, ____ y ____.
2. Dos condimentos son la ____ y la ____.
3. El mesero cubre la mesa con ____.
4. En la mesa el mesero pone una ____ para cada cliente.
5. El niño pide un ____ de leche y sus padres piden una ____ de café.
6. Ellos tienen ____ y piden una botella de agua mineral.

Actividad comunicativa

A En el restaurante Look at the advertisement for a restaurant in Santiago de Chile. Tell as much as you can about the restaurant based on the information in the advertisement. A classmate will tell whether he or she wants to go to the restaurant and why.

CAPÍTULO 14
Vocabulario

C This activity helps students learn to identify word families.

Actividad comunicativa

¡OJO! Práctica versus Actividades comunicativas All activities which provide guided practice are labeled **Práctica.** The more open-ended communicative activities are labeled **Actividades comunicativas.**

A Students should base their descriptions on both the descriptive paragraph and the two photos in this ad. Explain to the class that the phrase **e informal** is not a spelling error. After they have done **Palabras 2,** pages 412–413, see how many seafood items they can identify in this ad.

Learning From Realia

Aquí está Coco There is something in this ad that would tell you that the restaurant must be in South America. What is it? **(del Pacífico Sur)**

ANSWERS

Práctica

C
1. **e**
2. **c**
3. **a**
4. **f**
5. **d**
6. **b**

D
1. **un plato, un tenedor, un cuchillo, una cucharita (una cuchara)**
2. **sal, pimienta**
3. **un mantel**
4. **servilleta**
5. **vaso, taza**
6. **sed**

Actividad comunicativa

A Answers will vary; however, students should mention the type of dishes served **(pescados y mariscos)** and whether the restaurant is formal or informal.

Independent Practice

Assign any of the following:
1. Workbook, pages 171–172
2. Activities, pages 410–411
3. CD-ROM, Disc 4, pages 408–411

CAPÍTULO 14
Vocabulario
PALABRAS 2

RESOURCES

- Vocabulary Transparencies 14.2 (A & B)
- Student Tape Manual, TE, pages 161–164
- Audiocassette 8B/CD8
- Workbook, pages 173–174
- Quiz 2, pages 71–72
- CD-ROM, Disc 4, pages 412–415

Bell Ringer Review

Use BRR Transparency 14-2, or write the following on the board:
Complete with the past tense.

1. **Anoche yo no ___ en casa. (comer)**
2. **Mis amigos y yo ___ en un restaurante. (comer)**
3. **Yo ___ al restaurante en el metro pero mis amigos ___ el autobús. (ir, tomar)**
4. **El mesero nos ___ un servicio muy bueno. (dar)**

TEACHING VOCABULARY

A. Have students close their books. Then model the new vocabulary on pages 412–413 using Vocabulary Transparencies 14.2 (A & B). Have students repeat each word or expression two or three times after you or the recording on Cassette 8B/Compact Disc 8.

B. Clarify any cuts of meat that are not evident. For example, students may not know the following: **carne de res** *(beef)*, **ternera** *(veal)*, **cerdo** *(pork)*, **cordero** *(lamb)*.

C. Have students read the dialogue on page 413 aloud, using as much expression as possible. You may want to have several students perform the telephone conversation for the class.

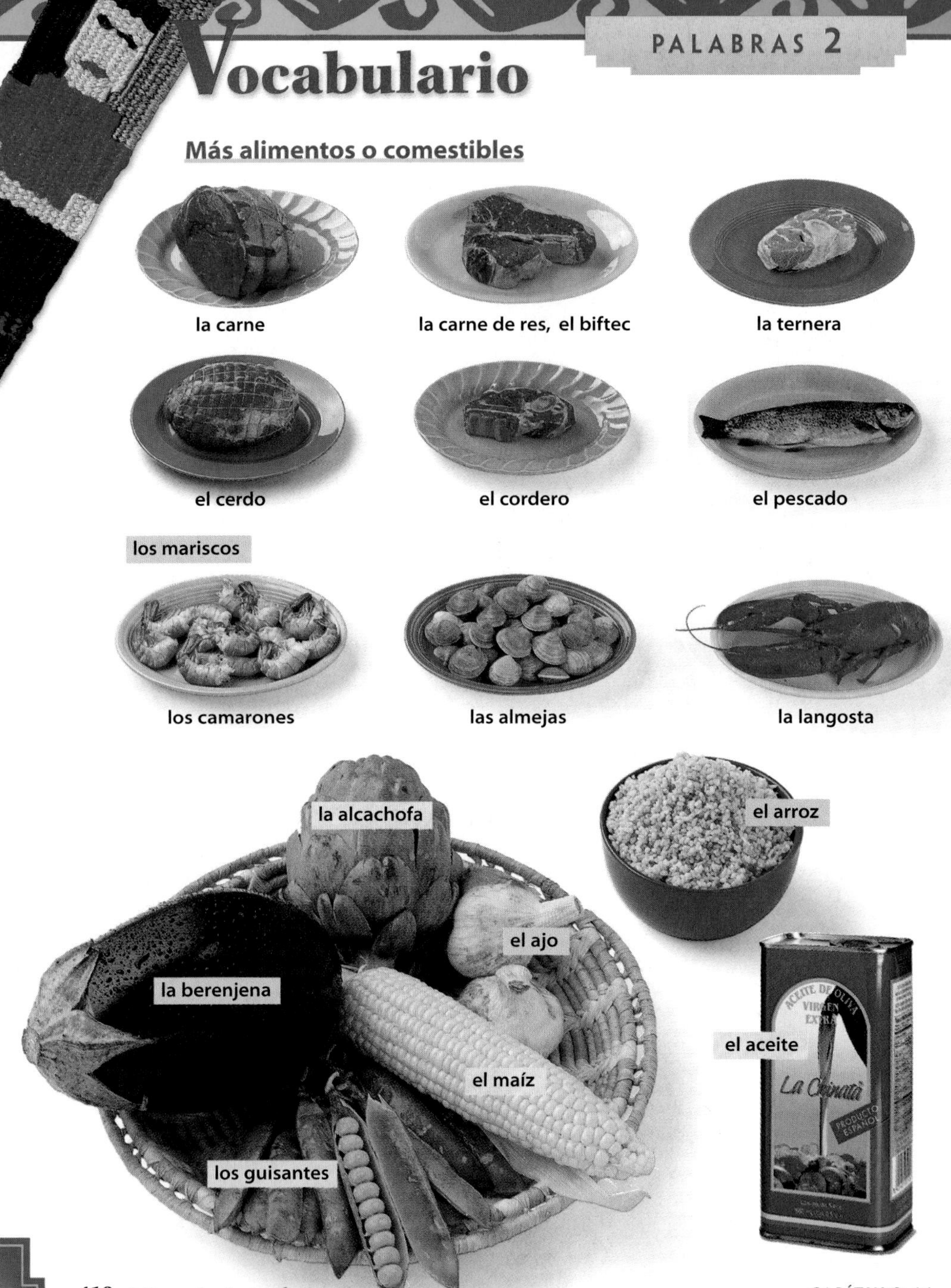

Total Physical Response

Begin
(Estudiante 1), levántate y ven acá, por favor.
Estamos en el restaurante Mendoza.
Siéntate, (Estudiante 1).
Toma el menú.
Ábrelo.
Lee el menú.
Llama al mesero.
(Estudiante 2), ven acá. Tú vas a ser el mesero.
(Estudiante 1), pídele al mesero lo que quieres comer.
(Estudiante 2), escribe lo que pide.
Ve a la cocina.
Vuelve con la comida.
Sirve la comida.
Pon los platos en la mesa.
(Estudiante 1), come.

Ah, tenemos un problema. Pediste la carne bien hecha y el mesero te sirvió la carne casi cruda. Llama al mesero.

(continued on page 413)

CAPÍTULO 14
Vocabulario

La joven pidió un biftec.
El mesero sirvió el biftec.
La comida está rica, deliciosa.

ABOUT THE SPANISH LANGUAGE

- Explain to students the difference between **La comida está buena** and **La comida es buena. (La comida está buena significa que la comida está deliciosa, que está muy rica, que tiene buen sabor. La comida es buena significa que es buena para la salud. Contiene vitaminas, etc.)**
- **El maíz** is the most universal word for corn. In Mexico, however, you will hear **elote** and in certain areas of South America **el choclo.**
- In addition to **la alcachofa** you will also hear **la cotufa.**
- There are several ways to say *shrimp*. There are some differences in type and size but words you will hear in addition to **el camarón** are **la gamba** (usually small shrimp in Spain), **el langostino** (large, but not a lobster) and **la quisquilla.**
- There are many ways to say *steak* in Spanish. **Biftec** and **bistec** are commonly used. You will also hear **filete** and **entrecote**. **Filete**, however, can be a filet of any type of meat or fish. **El entrecote** is meat only. The word **lomo** refers to any cut from the loin area. **Lomo de carne de res** is similar to a sirloin steak. **Solomillo** or **lomo fino** is similar to a tenderloin or filet mignon. In many areas of Latin America **el churrasco** is a grilled steak.

Total Physical Response

(Estudiante 2), ve a la mesa.
(Estudiante 1), dale el plato.
Pide la cuenta.
Mira la cuenta.
Saca el dinero de tu bolsillo o de tu cartera.
Paga.
Levántate.
Sal del restaurante.
Gracias, (Estudiante 1). Ahora puedes volver a tu asiento.
Y tú también, (Estudiante 2). Gracias.

VOCABULARY EXPANSION

You may wish to introduce the following expressions:

bien hecho(a), cocido(a)	*well done*
a término medio	*medium*
casi crudo, no muy cocido(a)	*rare*

A waiter will frequently ask
¿Qué les apetece?
(What would you like to order?)

CAPÍTULO 14
Vocabulario

Práctica

¡OJO! It is recommended that you go over all the **Práctica** in class before assigning them for homework.

A After doing **Práctica A,** go back to page 412 and ask students whether or not they like the other food items on that page.

B After doing **Práctica B,** have one or two students retell the story in his or her own words.

Learning From Photos

Caracas, Venezuela Have students describe what they see in these Venezuelan photos in their own words.

Práctica

A **¿Te gusta(n) o no te gusta(n)?** Contesten según las fotos.

B **Historieta** Cenó en el restaurante.

Contesten.

1. ¿Fue Victoria al restaurante anoche?
2. ¿Quién le sirvió?
3. ¿Pidió Victoria un biftec?
4. ¿Pidió también una ensalada?
5. ¿Le sirvió el mesero una ensalada de lechuga y tomate?
6. ¿Le sirvió una comida deliciosa o una comida mala?

Caracas, Venezuela

ANSWERS

Práctica

A
1. (No) me gusta el biftec.
2. (No) me gusta el pescado.
3. (No) me gustan los camarones (las gambas).
4. (No) me gusta la ensalada.
5. (No) me gusta el maíz.
6. (No) me gustan las almejas.

B
1. Sí, Victoria fue al restaurante anoche.
2. El mesero le sirvió.
3. Sí (No), Victoria (no) pidió un biftec.
4. Sí, (No, no) pidió una ensalada.
5. Sí (No), el mesero (no) le sirvió una ensalada de lechuga y tomate.
6. Le sirvió una comida deliciosa (mala).

C **¿Qué te gusta?** Contesten personalmente.

1. ¿Te gusta la ensalada?
2. ¿Te gusta la ensalada con aceite y vinagre?
3. ¿Te gusta el biftec?
4. ¿Te gusta el sándwich de jamón y queso? ¿Te gusta más con pan tostado?
5. ¿Te gusta la tortilla de queso?
6. ¿Te gustan los huevos con jamón?

Actividades comunicativas

A **Una reservación** You call a restaurant in Buenos Aires. The headwaiter (a classmate) answers. Make a reservation for yourself and a group of friends.

B **¿Qué recomienda Ud.?**
Here's a menu from a very famous restaurant in Madrid. In fact, it's the oldest restaurant in the city, dating from 1725. There are many items on the menu that you will be able to recognize. A classmate will be the server. Ask what he or she recommends and then order.

CARTA
I.V.A. 7% INCLUIDO

RESTAURANT
3ª Categoría

ENTRADAS

Jugos de tomate, naranja ... 395
Pimientos asados con bacalao ... 960
Lomo ibérico de bellota ... 2.260
Jamón ibérico de bellota ... 2.475
Surtido ibérico de bellota ... 2.115
Melón con jamón ... 2.095
Queso (manchego) ... 875
Ensalada riojana ... 930
Ensalada de lechuga y tomate ... 475
ENSALADA BOTIN (con pollo y jamón) ... 1.195
Ensalada de rape y langostinos ... 2.575
Ensalada de endivias con perdiz ... 2.075
Morcilla de Burgos ... 725
Croquetas de pollo y jamón ... 875
Manitas de cochinillo rebozadas ... 785
Salmón ahumado ... 1.990

SOPAS

Sopa al cuarto de hora (de pescados) ... 1.590
SOPA DE AJO CON HUEVO ... 580
Caldo de ave ... 480
Gazpacho ... 800

HUEVOS

Revuelto de la casa (morcilla y patatas) ... 830
Huevos revueltos con espárragos trigueros ... 995
Huevos revueltos con salmón ahumado ... 1.050
Tortilla de gambas ... 1.050

VERDURAS

Espárragos con mahonesa ... 1.335
Menestra de verduras salteadas con jamón ibérico ... 1.170
Alcachofas salteadas con jamón ibérico ... 885
Judías verdes con jamón ibérico ... 885
Setas a la segoviana ... 965
Patatas fritas ... 370
Patatas asadas ... 370

PESCADOS

Angulas ... (según mercado)
ALMEJAS BOTIN ... 2.355
Langostinos con mahonesa ... 3.730
Gambas al ajillo ... 2.695
Gambas a la plancha ... 2.695
Cazuela de pescados ... 2.825
Rape en salsa ... 2.610
Merluza al horno o frita ... 3.085
Lenguado frito, al horno o a la plancha (pieza) ... 2.495
Calamares fritos ... 1.565
CHIPIRONES EN SU TINTA (arroz blanco) ... 1.640

ASADOS Y PARRILLAS

COCHINILLO ASADO ... 2.315
CORDERO ASADO ... 2.500
Pollo asado 1/2 ... 950
Pollo en cacerola 1/2 ... 1.260
Perdiz estofada (pieza) ... 2.460
Filete de ternera a la plancha ... 1.850
Escalope de ternera ... 1.880
Ternera asada con guisantes ... 1.880
Solomillo a la plancha ... 2.695
SOLOMILLO BOTIN (al champiñón) ... 2.695
"Entrecotte" de cebón a la plancha ... 2.530

POSTRES

Cuajada ... 645
Tarta helada ... 650
Tarta de la casa (crema y bizcocho) ... 660
Tarta de chocolate ... 715
Tarta de frambuesa ... 805
Pastel ruso (crema de praliné) ... 785
Flan de la casa ... 415
Flan de la casa con nata ... 675
Helado de chocolate o caramelo ... 510
Helado de vainilla con salsa de chocolate ... 520
Surtido de buñuelos ... 855
Hojaldre de crema ... 725
Piña natural al dry-sack ... 605
Fresón con nata ... 765
Sorbete de limón ... 580
Melón ... 640
Bartolillos (sábados y domingos) ... 715

MENU DE LA CASA
(Primavera - Verano)
Precio: 4.080 ptas.
Gazpacho campero
Cochinillo asado
Helado

CAFE 215 - PAN 100 - MANTEQUILLA 125
HORAS DE SERVICIO: ALMUERZO, de 1:00 A 4:00 - CENA, de 8:00 A 12:00
ABIERTO TODOS LOS DIAS
HAY HOJAS DE RECLAMACION

C Students can do this activity in pairs.

EXPANSION You can have students expand **Práctica C** into a mini-conversation:
—¿Te gusta la ensalada?
—Sí, mucho. ¿Y a ti te gusta?
—Sí, me gusta. (No, no me gusta.)

Actividades comunicativas

¡OJO! These activities encourage students to use the chapter vocabulary and grammar in open-ended situations. It is not necessary to have them do all the activities. Choose the ones you consider most appropriate.

A Students should use the dialogue on page 413 as their model.

B The famous **Casa de Botín** restaurant specializes in **cordero asado** and **cochinillo asado. Cochinillo** is called **lechón** in Latin America. You may also wish to point out that the word **carta** is used here, rather than **menú.**

ANSWERS

Práctica

C
1. **Sí, (No, no) me gusta la ensalada.**
2. **Sí, (No, no) me gusta la ensalada con aceite y vinagre.**
3. **Sí, (No, no) me gusta el biftec.**
4. **Sí, (No, no) me gusta el sándwich de jamón y queso. Sí, (No, no) me gusta más con pan tostado.**
5. **Sí, (No, no) me gusta la tortilla de queso.**
6. **Sí, (No, no) me gustan los huevos con jamón.**

Actividades comunicativas

A Answers will vary.

B Answers will vary depending on what students choose from the menu.

RESOURCES

- Workbook, pages 175–176
- Student Tape Manual, TE, pages 164–165
- Audiocassette 8B/CD8
- Quizzes 3–4, pages 73–74
- Computer Testmaker
- CD-ROM, Disc 4, pages 416–419

Bell Ringer Review

Use BRR Transparency 14-3, or write the following on the board:
Answer the following questions.

1. ¿Te gusta la carne?
2. ¿Te gustan los mariscos?
3. ¿Cuáles son algunas legumbres que te gustan?
4. ¿Te gusta el postre?
5. ¿Qué te gusta beber?

TEACHING STRUCTURE

Describing more present activities

A. Have students open their books to page 416. Write the verb forms on the board. Underline the stem and have students repeat each form after you.

B. Note Oral practice with these verbs is important because, if students pronounce them correctly, they will be inclined to spell them correctly.

C. When going over the verb **seguir**, review with students the following sound-spelling correspondence: **ga, gue, gui, go, gu.**

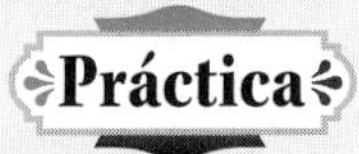

A Students will answer using the **yo** form.

Estructura

Describing more present activities
Verbos con el cambio e → i en el presente

1. The verbs **pedir, servir, repetir, freír, seguir** *(to follow),* and **vestirse** *(to get dressed)* are stem-changing verbs. The **e** of the infinitive stem changes to **i** in all forms of the present tense except the **nosotros** and **vosotros** forms. Study the following forms. Note the spelling of **seguir.**

INFINITIVE	pedir	servir	seguir	vestirse
yo	pido	sirvo	sigo	me visto
tú	pides	sirves	sigues	te vistes
él, ella, Ud.	pide	sirve	sigue	se viste
nosotros(as)	pedimos	servimos	seguimos	nos vestimos
vosotros(as)	*pedís*	*servís*	*seguís*	*os vestís*
ellos, ellas, Uds.	piden	sirven	siguen	se visten

A **Lo que yo pido** Digan si piden lo siguiente o no.

1.

2.

3.

4.

5.

6.

ANSWERS

Práctica

A All answers begin with **Sí, (No, no) pido...**
1. **... una langosta.**
2. **... queso.**
3. **... papas.**
4. **... un pollo.**
5. **... una botella de agua mineral.**
6. **... una ensalada.**

B **Lo que pedimos en el restaurante** Sigan el modelo.

1. A Teresa le gustan los mariscos. ¿Qué pide ella?
2. A Carlos le gusta el biftec. ¿Qué pide él?
3. A mis amigos les gustan las legumbres. ¿Qué piden ellos?
4. A mis padres les gusta mucho la ensalada. ¿Qué piden ellos?
5. Nos gusta el postre. ¿Qué pedimos?
6. Nos gustan las tortillas. ¿Qué pedimos?
7. ¿Qué pides cuando tienes sed?
8. ¿Qué pides cuando tienes hambre?

C **HISTORIETA** Vamos al restaurante.

Completen.

Cuando mi amiga y yo ___1___ (ir) al restaurante, nosotros ___2___ (pedir) casi siempre una hamburguesa. Yo la ___3___ (pedir) con lechuga y tomate y ella la ___4___ (pedir) con queso. A mi amiga le ___5___ (gustar) mucho las papas fritas. Ella ___6___ (decir) que le ___7___ (gustar) más cuando el cocinero las ___8___ (freír) en aceite de oliva.

D **Entrevista** Contesten personalmente.

1. Cuando vas a un restaurante, ¿qué pides?
2. ¿Pides papas? Si no pides papas, ¿pides arroz?
3. ¿Qué más pides con la carne y las papas o el arroz?
4. ¿Quién te sirve en el restaurante?
5. Si te sirve bien, ¿qué le dejas?

Marbella, España

Actividad comunicativa

A **¿Por qué no pides... ?** You're in a restaurant with a friend (a classmate). You are hungry and thirsty, but you don't know what to order. Your friend will suggest something. Then you decide.

B **Práctica B** reviews the use of **gustar** as it practices stem-changing verbs.

C After going over **Práctica C,** students can summarize the information in their own words.

D **Práctica D** may be done in pairs.

Actividad comunicativa

A In this activity, the first student can begin by asking: **¿Te gusta(n)... ?** or **¿Por qué no pides... ?**

TECHNOLOGY OPTION Students can use the Portfolio feature on the CD-ROM to record this conversation.

ANSWERS

Práctica

B
1. Ella pide mariscos.
2. Él pide biftec.
3. Ellos piden legumbres
4. Ellos piden ensalada.
5. Pedimos postre.
6. Pedimos tortillas.
7. Cuando tengo sed pido ___.
8. Cuando tengo hambre pido ___.

C
1. vamos
2. pedimos
3. pido
4. pide
5. gustan
6. dice
7. gustan
8. fríe

D
1. Cuando voy a un restaurante, pido ___.
2. Sí, (No, no) pido papas. Sí, si no pido papas, pido arroz. (No, si no pido papas, no pido arroz.)
3. Pido ___.
4. El mesero me sirve en el restaurante.
5. Si me sirve bien le dejo una propina.

Actividad comunicativa

A Answers will vary.

 Bell Ringer Review

Use BRR Transparency 14-4, or write the following on the board: Unscramble the following sentences.

1. **tacos/los/sirve/restaurante/el mesero/en el**
2. **pimienta/pide/Juan/sal/la/y/la**
3. **y/el/Sofía/fríen/pescado/papas/las/y Jaime**

TEACHING STRUCTURE

Describing more activities in the past

A. Have students repeat the verb forms shown in the charts on page 418, paying particular attention to the stem changes and correct pronunciation.

A The items in **Práctica A** describe an unfortunate experience in a restaurant.

EXPANSION After going over **Práctica A,** have students make up original stories about a horrible experience in a restaurant. This will be done as a narrative.

Note This is a good preparatory activity for **Actividad comunicativa A,** page 419. In that activity students "converse" with the restaurant manager about a problem with their meal and the service.

Describing more activities in the past
Verbos con el cambio e → i, o → u en el pretérito

1. The verbs **pedir, repetir, freír, servir,** and **vestirse** have a stem change in the preterite. The **e** of the infinitive stem changes to **i** in the **él** and **ellos** forms.

INFINITIVE	pedir	repetir	vestirse
yo	pedí	repetí	me vestí
tú	pediste	repetiste	te vestiste
él, ella, Ud.	pidió	repitió	se vistió
nosotros(as)	pedimos	repetimos	nos vestimos
vosotros(as)	*pedisteis*	*repetisteis*	*os vestisteis*
ellos, ellas, Uds.	pidieron	repitieron	se vistieron

2. The verbs **preferir, divertirse,** and **dormir** also have a stem change in the preterite. The **e** in **preferir** and **divertirse** changes to **i** and the **o** in dormir changes to **u** in the **él** and **ellos** forms.

INFINITIVE	preferir	divertirse	dormir
yo	preferí	me divertí	dormí
tú	preferiste	te divertiste	dormiste
él, ella, Ud.	prefirió	se divirtió	durmió
nosotros(as)	preferimos	nos divertimos	dormimos
vosotros(as)	*preferisteis*	*os divertisteis*	*dormisteis*
ellos, ellas, Uds.	prefirieron	se divirtieron	durmieron

HISTORIETA Servicio bueno o malo

Contesten según se indica.

1. ¿Qué pediste en el restaurante? (una ensalada)
2. ¿Cómo la pediste? (sin aceite y vinagre)
3. ¿Cuántas veces repetiste «sin aceite y vinagre»? (dos veces)
4. Y, ¿cómo sirvió el mesero la ensalada? (con aceite y vinagre)
5. ¿Qué hiciste? (pedí otra ensalada)
6. ¿Qué pidió tu amigo? (puré de papas)
7. ¿Y qué pasó? (el cocinero frió las papas)
8. ¿Qué sirvió el mesero? (papas fritas)
9. ¿Pidieron Uds. una bebida? (sí)
10. ¿Qué pidieron para beber? (una limonada)
11. ¿Qué sirvió el mesero? (un té)
12. ¿Le dieron Uds. una propina al mesero? (no)

ANSWERS

Práctica

A
1. **Pedí una ensalada en el restaurante.**
2. **La pedí sin aceite y vinagre.**
3. **Repetí «sin aceite y vinagre» dos veces.**
4. **El mesero sirvió la ensalada con aceite y vinagre.**
5. **Pedí otra ensalada.**
6. **Mi amigo pidió puré de papas.**
7. **El cocinero frió las papas.**
8. **El mesero sirvió papas fritas.**
9. **Sí, pedimos una bebida.**
10. **Pedimos una limonada.**
11. **El mesero sirvió un té.**
12. **No, no le dimos una propina al mesero.**

B HISTORIETA Preparando la comida

Completen con el pretérito.

Anoche mi hermano y yo ___1___ (preparar) la comida para la familia. Yo ___2___ (freír) el pescado. Mi hermano ___3___ (freír) las papas. Mamá ___4___ (poner) la mesa. Y papá ___5___ (servir) la comida. Todos nosotros ___6___ (comer) muy bien. A todos nos ___7___ (gustar) mucho el pescado. Mi hermano y mi papá ___8___ (repetir) el pescado. Luego yo ___9___ (servir) el postre, un sorbete. Después de la comida mi hermano tomó una siesta. Él ___10___ (dormir) media hora. Yo no ___11___ (dormir). No me gusta dormir inmediatamente después de comer.

Valparaíso, Chile

Actividad comunicativa

A Lo siento mucho. You're in a restaurant and you're fed up with the waiter. He hasn't done a thing right. Call over the manager (a classmate) and tell him or her all that happened. He or she will apologize and say something to try to make you happy.

CAPÍTULO 14

Estructura

B After doing **Práctica B,** have several students retell the story in their own words.

Learning From Photos

Valparaíso, Chile Have students describe the family members and their activities in the photo on page 419.

Actividad comunicativa

A Have students examine the illustration accompanying **Actividad A** carefully. There are quite a few things that have gone wrong! Before students begin to work on their conversations, you may wish to ask them to describe the people in the illustration and have them say what's wrong. See who can come up with the longest list.

¡OJO! There is no more new material to present in this chapter. The sections that follow recombine and reinforce the vocabulary and structures that have already been introduced.

ANSWERS

Práctica

B
1. **preparamos**
2. **freí**
3. **frió**
4. **puso**
5. **sirvió**
6. **comimos**
7. **gustó**
8. **repitieron**
9. **serví**
10. **durmió**
11. **dormí**

Actividad comunicativa

A Answers will vary.

RESOURCES

- Audiocassette 8B/CD8
- CD-ROM, Disc 4, page 420

Bell Ringer Review

Use BRR Transparency 14-5, or write the following on the board: Write three things you would possibly say to or ask a waiter at a café.

TEACHING THE CONVERSATION

A. Have students close their books. Tell them that they will hear a conversation between Teresa, Paco, and a waiter. Then read the conversation to them or play Cassette 8B/Compact Disc 8.

B. After introducing the conversation, you may wish to set up a café in the classroom and have groups of students perform the conversation for the class.

C. Have students summarize the conversation in their own words.

D. After presenting the conversation, go over the **Después de conversar** activity. If students can answer the questions with relative ease, move on. Students should not be expected to memorize the conversation.

TECHNOLOGY OPTION

On the CD-ROM (Disc 4, page 420), students can watch a dramatization of this conversation. They can then play the role of either of the characters and record themselves in the conversation.

Conversación

En el restaurante

TERESA: ¿Tiene Ud. una mesa para dos personas?
MESERO: Sí, señorita. Por aquí, por favor.
TERESA: ¿Es posible tener un menú en inglés?
MESERO: Sí, ¡cómo no!
PACO: Teresa, no necesito un menú en inglés. Lo puedo leer en español.
(El mesero les da un menú en inglés.)
PACO: No sé por qué ella me pidió un menú en inglés.
MESERO: No hay problema. Le traigo uno en español.
PACO: Gracias.
TERESA: Pues, Paco, ¿qué vas a pedir?
PACO: Para mí, la especialidad de la casa.
TERESA: Yo también pido la especialidad de la casa.

Después de conversar

Completen.

1. ¿Para cuántas personas quiere la mesa Teresa?
2. ¿Tiene el mesero una mesa libre?
3. ¿Qué tipo de menú pide Teresa?
4. ¿Necesita un menú en inglés Paco?
5. ¿Sabe él por qué ella le pidió un menú en inglés?
6. ¿Qué va a pedir Paco?
7. Y Teresa, ¿qué pide ella?

ANSWERS

Después de conversar

1. **Teresa quiere la mesa para dos personas.**
2. **Sí, el mesero tiene una mesa libre.**
3. **Teresa pide un menú en inglés.**
4. **No, Paco no necesita un menú en inglés.**
5. **No, no sabe por qué ella le pidió un menú en inglés.**
6. **Paco va a pedir la especialidad de la casa.**
7. **Ella también pide la especialidad de la casa.**

Actividades comunicativas

A **Fuimos al restaurante.** You and your parents went to a restaurant last night. A classmate will ask you questions about your experience. Answer him or her.

B **Preferencias** Work with a classmate and discuss whether you prefer to eat at home or in a restaurant. Give reasons for your preferences.

PRONUNCIACIÓN

La consonante x

An x between two vowels is pronounced much like the English x but a bit softer. It's like **a gs: examen → eg-samen.** Repeat the following.

exacto **examen**
éxito **próximo**

When x is followed by a consonant, it is often pronounced like an s. Repeat the following.

extremo **explicar** **exclamar**

Repeat the following sentence.

El extranjero exclama que baja en la próxima parada.

Actividades comunicativas

A Students can base their answers on any outing to a restaurant with their parents. They may wish to use the conversation on page 420 as a model.

B Students should use the verb **preferir** for this exchange.

TECHNOLOGY OPTION In the CD-ROM version of this activity (Disc 4, page 421), students can interact with an on-screen native speaker and record their voices.

TEACHING PRONUNCIATION

¡OJO! Whenever **x** is followed by a consonant in Spanish, it is pronounced as **s.** There are no exceptions to this rule.

There is, however, a variation in the pronunciation of **x** between two vowels. In some areas the **x** in the word **exacto,** for example, is pronounced like **s (esacto),** and in others it is **gs (eg-sacto).**

A. Have students repeat the words after you or the recording on Cassette 8B/ Compact Disc 8. Have them imitate very carefully.

B. Have students open their books to page 421. Call on individuals to read the words and sentence carefully.

C. All model sentences on page 421 can be used for dictation.

TECHNOLOGY OPTION

In the CD-ROM version of the Pronunciation section (Disc 4, page 421), students will see an animation of the cartoon on this page. They can also listen to, record, and play back the words vowels, words, and sentences presented here.

Learning From Realia

Si tienes hambre, llámanos Have students take a look at the ad to see how much of the vocabulary they already know. Ask if they can guess what **a domicilio** means *(home delivery).* The expression for *take out* is **para llevar.**

ANSWERS

Actividades comunicativas

A Answers will vary.

B Answers will vary; however, students will typically begin the conversation by asking: **¿Prefieres comer en casa o en el restaurante?**

National Standards

Cultures

The reading about Mexican cuisine on page 422 and the related activity on page 423 familiarize students with typical Mexican food and dishes.

TEACHING THE READING

Pre-reading

A. Have students open their books and do the Reading Strategy activity on page 422. Then ask them what they think the reading is about.

B. Have students tell some things they already know about Mexican food.

Reading

A. Now have students open their books. Call on individuals to read.

B. Intersperse oral reading with some comprehension questions. Then continue reading.

Post-reading

A. Have students tell what they see on the plate at the bottom of the page.

B. Go over the **Después de leer** activity orally on page 423. Then assign it for homework. Go over the activity again the following day.

TECHNOLOGY OPTION

Students may listen to a recorded version of the **Lectura** on the CD-ROM, Disc 4, page 422.

Lecturas CULTURALES

Reading Strategy

Thinking while reading

Good readers always think while reading. They think about what the passage might be about after reading the title and looking at the visuals. They predict, create visual images, compare, and check for understanding, and continually think while the author is explaining.

LA COMIDA MEXICANA

Es muy difícil decir lo que es la comida hispana porque la comida varía mucho de una región hispana a otra.

Aquí en los Estados Unidos la comida mexicana es muy popular. Hay muchos restaurantes mexicanos. Algunos sirven comida típicamente mexicana y otros sirven variaciones que vienen del suroeste de los Estados Unidos donde vive mucha gente de ascendencia mexicana.

La base de muchos platos mexicanos es la tortilla. La tortilla es un tipo de panqueque. Puede ser de harina[1] de maíz o de trigo[2]. Con las tortillas, los mexicanos preparan tostadas, tacos, enchiladas, etc. Rellenan[3] las tortillas de pollo, carne de res o frijoles y queso.

[1]harina *flour*
[2]trigo *wheat*
[3]Rellenan *They fill*

San Miguel de Allende, México

Learning From Photos

San Miguel de Allende, México Ask the following questions about the photo:

¿Dónde está la señora? ¿Está en la cocina o en el comedor?

¿Qué está haciendo ella? ¿Tortillas o arroz?

¿De qué son las tortillas? ¿De papas o de maíz?

Independent Practice

Assign any of the following:

1. **Después de leer** activities, page 423
2. Workbook, **Un poco más,** pages 177–179
3. CD-ROM, Disc 4, pages 422–423

Después de leer

A La comida mexicana Contesten.

1. ¿Varía mucho la cocina hispana de una región a otra?
2. ¿Dónde es popular la comida mexicana?
3. ¿De dónde vienen muchas variaciones de la cocina mexicana?
4. ¿Qué sirve de base para muchos platos mexicanos?
5. ¿Qué es una tortilla? ¿De qué puede ser?
6. ¿De qué rellenan las tortillas?

SECRETARIA DE EDUCACION, CULTURA Y RECREACION
MUSEO CASA
"DIEGO RIVERA"
GUANAJUATO, GTO.
COOPERACION N$ 5.00

«El cultivo del maíz» de Diego Rivera

Después de leer

A Allow students to refer to the story to look up the answers, or you may use this activity as a testing device for factual recall.

FINE ART CONNECTION

«El cultivo del maíz» de Diego Rivera Throughout his life Diego Rivera was vitally interested in the suffering of Mexico's poor. Ask the class why he would do a painting depicting someone cultivating corn. (Corn is extremely important to Mexico because it is the sustenance for Mexico's poor. Corn is for Mexico what potatoes, bread, or rice would be to people in other parts of the world.)

EXPANSION Show Fine Art Transparency F-13 of this painting by Diego Rivera, from the Transparency Binder. You may wish to have students read the background information accompanying this transparency and have them do the related activities.

ANSWERS

Después de leer

A
1. **Sí, la comida hispana varía mucho de una región a otra.**
2. **La comida mexicana es popular aquí en los Estados Unidos.**
3. **Vienen del suroeste de los Estados Unidos.**
4. **La tortilla sirve de base para muchos platos mexicanos.**
5. **Una tortilla es un tipo de panqueque. Puede ser de harina de maíz o de harina de trigo.**
6. **Rellenan las tortillas de pollo, carne de res o frijoles y queso.**

Lectura opcional 1

National Standards

Cultures
This reading about Spanish cuisine and the related activities on this page familiarize students with some typical foods from Spain.

TEACHING TIPS

¡OJO! This reading is optional. You may skip it completely, have the entire class read it, have only several students read it, or assign it for extra credit.

A. Have students read the passage quickly as they look at the photos that accompany it. The photos will increase comprehension because students can visualize what they are reading about.

B. Have students discuss what information they find interesting.

Learning From Photos

Barcelona, España Have students look at the three photos on this page to see how many items they can identify.

Lectura opcional 1

LA COMIDA ESPAÑOLA

En España, como en México, hay tortillas también. Pero hay una gran diferencia entre una tortilla mexicana y una tortilla española. La tortilla española no es de maíz. El cocinero español prepara la tortilla con huevos. La tortilla española, que es muy típica, lleva patatas (papas) y cebollas[1].

La cocina española es muy buena y muy variada. Como España es un país que tiene mucha costa, muchos platos españoles llevan marisco y pescado. Y los cocineros preparan muchos platos con aceite de oliva.

[1]cebollas *onions*

Barcelona, España

Después de leer

A **La cocina española** Contesten.

1. ¿Cuál es la diferencia entre una tortilla española y una tortilla mexicana?
2. ¿Qué lleva la típica tortilla a la española?
3. ¿Por qué llevan marisco y pescado muchos platos españoles?
4. ¿Qué usan muchos cocineros españoles para preparar una comida?

ANSWERS

Después de leer

A
1. **La tortilla española no es de maíz. El cocinero español la prepara con huevos.**
2. **Lleva patatas y cebollas.**
3. **Muchos platos españoles llevan marisco y pescado porque España es un país que tiene mucha costa.**
4. **Usan aceite de oliva para preparar una comida.**

LECTURA OPCIONAL 2

LA COMIDA DEL CARIBE

En el Caribe, en Puerto Rico, Cuba y en la República Dominicana, la gente come muchos mariscos y pescado. Es natural porque Puerto Rico, Cuba y la República Dominicana son islas. Pero la carne favorita de la región es el puerco o el lechón[1]. No hay nada más delicioso que un buen lechón asado[2]. Sirven el lechón con arroz, frijoles (habichuelas) y tostones. Para hacer tostones el cocinero corta en rebanadas[3] un plátano, una banana grande, verde y dura. Luego fríe las rebanadas en manteca[4].

[1]lechón *suckling pig*
[2]asado *roast*
[3]rebanadas *slices*
[4]manteca *lard*

Humacao, Puerto Rico

Después de leer

A ¿Lo sabes? Busquen la información.

1. algunos países de la región del Caribe
2. por qué come la gente muchos mariscos y pescado en la región del Caribe
3. una carne favorita de los puertorriqueños, cubanos y dominicanos
4. lo que sirven con el lechón asado
5. lo que son tostones

GEOGRAPHY CONNECTION

Humacao, Puerto Rico This town is on the western coast of Puerto Rico. The well-known resort and condominium complex **Palmas del Mar** is in Humacao.

ANSWERS

Después de leer

A
1. **Puerto Rico, Cuba y la República Dominicana**
2. **porque son islas**
3. **el puerco o el lechón**
4. **arroz, frijoles (habichuelas) y tostones**
5. **rebanadas de plátano fritas en manteca**

LECTURA OPCIONAL 2

National Standards

Cultures
This reading about Caribbean cuisine and the related activities on page 425 familiarize students with some typical foods from the Spanish-speaking countries of the Caribbean.

TEACHING TIPS

¡OJO! This reading is optional. You may skip it completely, have the entire class read it, have only several students read it, or assign it for extra credit.

A. Have students read the selection to themselves.

B. Now have students do the **Después de leer** activity on page 425.

Learning From Photos

Los platos del Caribe Have students look at the top photo on this page. Point out to them that the dish in the foreground contains **arroz, tostones,** and **habichuelas rosadas.** Tell them that red beans are favored in Puerto Rico and black beans are favored in Cuba.

On the plate in the background to the right, there are **tostones, arroz blanco,** and **asopao. Asopao** is a type of stew made with rice. It has more liquid than a **paella**. There are **asopaos de pollo, de camarones,** and **de jueyes** *(land crabs).*

National Standards

Connections

This reading about linguistic differences in the Spanish-speaking world establishes a connection with another discipline, allowing students to reinforce and further their knowledge of the humanities through the study of Spanish.

Comparisons

This reading on regional differences in pronunciation and vocabulary in Spanish and the related activities, which illustrate the same concepts in English, give students a better understanding of the nature of language.

¡OJO! The readings in the **Conexiones** section are optional. They focus on some of the major disciplines taught in schools and universities. The vocabulary is useful for discussing such topics as history, literature, art, economics, business, science, etc.

You may choose any of the following ways to do this reading on linguistic differences in the Spanish-speaking world.

Independent reading Have students read the selections and do the post-reading activities as homework, which you collect. This option is least intrusive on class time and requires a minimum of teacher involvement.

Homework with in-class follow-up Assign the readings and post-reading activities as homework. Review and discuss the material in class the next day.

Intensive in-class activity This option includes a pre-reading vocabulary presentation, in-class reading and discussion, assignment of the activities for homework, and a discussion of the assignment in class the following day.

Conexiones

LAS HUMANIDADES

EL LENGUAJE

As we already know, Spanish is a language that is spoken in many areas of the world. In spite of the fact that the Spanish-speaking world covers a large area of the globe, it is possible to understand a speaker of Spanish regardless of where he or she is from. Although there are regional differences, these differences do not cause serious comprehension problems.

However, pronunciation does change from area to area. For example, people from San Juan, Puerto Rico; Buenos Aires, Argentina; and Madrid, Spain have pronunciations that are quite different one from the other. However, the same is true of English. People from New York, Memphis, and London also have a distinct pronunciation but they can all understand one another.

The use of certain words will also change from one area to another. This is particularly true in the case of words for foods. Let's look at some regional differences with regard to vocabulary.

Regionalismos

Comestibles

En España son patatas y en todas partes de Latinoamérica son papas.

En casi todas partes es el maíz pero en México es el maíz o el elote y en Chile es el choclo.

En España son cacahuetes; en muchas partes de Latinoamérica son cacahuates pero en el Caribe son maní.

En muchas partes es jugo de naranja pero en Puerto Rico es jugo de china y en España es zumo de naranja.

Las judías verdes tienen muchos nombres. Además de judías verdes son habichuelas tiernas, chauchas, vainitas, ejotes y porotos.

Cosas que no son comestibles
Tomamos el autobús en España, el camión en México y la guagua en el Caribe y en las Islas Canarias.

En España todos duermen en el dormitorio o en la habitación. En México duermen en la recámara y, en muchas partes, en el cuarto o en el cuarto de dormir.

En España sacas un billete en la ventanilla y en Latinoamérica compras un boleto en la ventanilla o en la boletería.

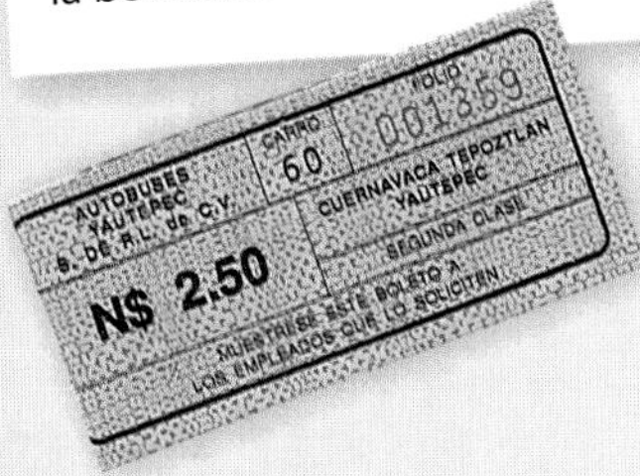

Después de leer

A Hispanohablantes If any of your classmates are native speakers of Spanish, ask them to compare the way they say things. Have them share this information with you.

B El inglés There are variations in the use of English words. Discuss the following terms and where they might be heard.

1. bag, sack
2. soda, pop
3. elevator, lift
4. line, queue
5. pram, baby carriage
6. truck, lorry
7. traffic circle, rotary, roundabout
8. subway, underground

CAPÍTULO 14
Conexiones

LAS HUMANIDADES
EL LENGUAJE

A. Have students read the introduction in English on page 426.

B. You may wish to have students skim this section for general interest.

C. For a more in-depth treatment, have students identify each illustrated item of food on page 426. Then have them give the additional regional names for each item. Now do the same with regard to the nonfood items in the photos on page 427.

Después de leer

B Ask students whether they know of additional examples in English. They might mention: purse/pocketbook.

For the Native Speaker

¿Cómo lo dices? Have native speakers make a list of at least twenty common items of food and clothing. Then have each student compare his or her list with those of the other native speakers in the class. Finally, have them make a list of the items that have different names.

ANSWERS

Después de leer

A Answers will vary. Have native speakers give a brief report to the class.

B Answers will include the following:

1. **bag: U.S.**
   sack: UK
2. **soda: East and West Coasts, South**
   pop: Midwest
3. **elevator: U.S.**
   lift: UK
4. **line: U.S.**
   queue: UK
5. **pram: UK**
   baby carriage: U.S.
6. **truck: U.S.**
   lorry: UK
7. **traffic circle: U.S.**
   rotary: New England states, Canada
   roundabout: UK
8. **subway: US**
   underground: UK

CAPÍTULO 14
Culminación

RECYCLING

The **Actividades orales** and the **Actividad escrita** allow students to use the vocabulary and structures from this chapter in open-ended, real-life settings.

Actividades orales

¡OJO! Encourage students to say as much as possible when they do these activities. Tell them not to be afraid of making mistakes since the goal of the activities is real-life communication. If someone in the group makes an error, allow the others to politely correct him or her.

Let students choose the activities they would like to do.

A This activity is an excellent follow-up to the readings in Chapter 14, pages 422–425.

B **TECHNOLOGY OPTION** In the Chapter 14 Internet activity, students visit the Web sites of Spanish restaurants and "order" a meal. You may want to do this activity prior to your field trip. This activity will help familiarize students with restaurant food vocabulary. (See the Internet Connection, page 431.)

National Standards

Communities

Actividad B allows students to use their knowledge of Spanish beyond the school setting to order a meal in a Spanish restaurant.

JUEGO This is a good activity to use when students need a "break" during the class period, or as an opening or closing activity.

Culminación

Actividades orales

A **Fuimos al restaurante.** Get together with a classmate and describe some dishes from different areas of the Spanish-speaking world. Then decide what kind of restaurant or restaurants you want to go to. Tell why.

B **¡A comer!** You and your classmates, accompanied by your teacher, go to a Spanish restaurant in your community and order your meal in Spanish. Try to speak only Spanish during your meal.

JUEGO **La comida** Mention a food category, such as meat, seafood, fruit, vegetable. Your partner will give the name of a food that belongs in that category. Take several turns each. Try to use as much of the food vocabulary you've learned as possible.

ANSWERS

Actividades orales

A Answers will vary. Students might use the names of foods and dishes from the readings on pages 422–425.

B Answers will vary, depending on the type of restaurant and its menu selections.

Student Portfolio

Have students keep a notebook containing their best written work from each chapter. These selected writings can be based on assignments from the Student Textbook and the Writing Activities Workbook. The activities on page 429 are examples of writing assignments that may be included in each student's portfolio.

See the Teacher's Manual for more information on the Student Portfolio.

Actividad escrita

A **Comidas buenas y ricas** Prepare the menu for several Spanish meals—**el desayuno, el almuerzo,** and **la cena.** Then present your menus to the class. Have the class vote on whether or not they would order your meals. Then decide who in the class should open a restaurant.

Writing Strategy

Writing a letter of complaint

When you write a letter of complaint, you must clearly identify the problem and suggest solutions; you should use a businesslike tone. You might be angry when you write a letter of complaint. But to be effective, you must control your emotions since your goal is to get the problem corrected. Your tone of voice is reflected in writing as much as it is in speech; your results will be better if you address the situation calmly and reasonably. In addition, it is important that the letter be addressed to the person who has the most authority.

¡Qué desastre!

Pretend you went to a restaurant where you had a very bad experience. The waiter didn't serve you what you ordered nor the way you ordered it. Write a letter to the management complaining about the food and the service.

CAPÍTULO 14 Culminación

Actividad escrita

A Students can use the food items taught in Chapter 5 (page 156), as well as those taught in this chapter. Encourage students to list only those foods that they know how to say in Spanish.

Writing Strategy

Writing a letter of complaint

A. Have students do the Writing Strategy activity on page 429. Based on the strategy, ask students which statement in the Critical Thinking Activity below would be most effective when writing a letter of complaint.

Critical Thinking Activity

Drawing conclusions

1. **Tuvimos que esperar cinco minutos para la mesa y no pudimos leer el menú en español.**
2. **Nos gustó la comida, pero hay un problema con el servicio.**
3. **¡Su restaurante es horrible!**

TECHNOLOGY OPTION

¡Qué desastre! Students can use the Portfolio feature on the CD-ROM to write the letter in the Writing Strategy activity.

Independent Practice

Assign any of the following:

1. Activities, pages 428–429
2. Workbook, **Mi autobiografía,** page 180
3. Situation Cards
4. CD-ROM, Disc 4, Chapter 14, **Juego de repaso**

ANSWERS

Actividad escrita

A Answers will vary. The selections for each meal should be logical.

Writing Strategy

Answers will vary depending on the creativity and imagination of each student. The illustration on page 429 gives clues as to what students could say in their letter.

CAPÍTULO 14
Vocabulario

ASSESSMENT RESOURCES

- Chapter Quizzes
- Testing Program
- Computer Testmaker
- Situation Cards
- Communication Transparency C-14
- Performance Assessment
- **Maratón mental** Videoquiz

VOCABULARY REVIEW

The words and phrases in the **Vocabulario** have been taught for productive use in this chapter. They are summarized here as a resource for both students and teacher. This list also serves as a convenient resource for the **Culminación** activities on pages 428 and 429. There are approximately eight cognates in this vocabulary list. Have students find them.

Vocabulario

GETTING ALONG AT A RESTAURANT

el restaurante
la mesa
el/la mesero(a),
el/la camarero(a)
el/la cocinero(a)
el menú
la cuenta
la tarjeta de crédito
la propina
el dinero

IDENTIFYING A PLACE SETTING

el vaso
la taza
el platillo
el plato
el tenedor
el cuchillo
la cucharita
la cuchara
el mantel
la servilleta

DESCRIBING SOME RESTAURANT ACTIVITIES

poner la mesa
pedir
servir
freír
repetir
reservar
tener hambre
tener sed

DESCRIBING FOOD

rico(a), delicioso(a)

IDENTIFYING MORE FOODS

la carne
la carne de res, el biftec
la ternera
el cerdo
el cordero
el pescado
los mariscos
los camarones
las almejas
la langosta
el ajo
la berenjena
la alcachofa
el arroz
el maíz
la sal
la pimienta
el aceite
el vinagre

TECNOTUR

VIDEO

¡Buen viaje!

EPISODIO 14 ▸ En el restaurante

Cristina, Isabel y Luis van a un restaurante.

Después del almuerzo los jóvenes miran los videos que reciben de España.

CD-ROM

Expansión cultural

La Casa de los Azulejos en la Ciudad de México es un restaurante muy popular.

interNET CONNECTION

In this video episode, Cristina, Isabel, and Luis are having lunch at a restaurant in Mexico. To visit some restaurants in cities in the Spanish-speaking world, go to the Capítulo 14 Internet activity at the Glencoe Foreign Language Web site:

http://www.glencoe.com/sec/fl

Video Synopsis

While on vacation in Puerto Vallarta, Luis, Cristina, and Isabel go out to lunch at an international restaurant. The waiter shows them to a table, then returns a few minutes later to take their order. All three decide on typical Mexican dishes. Isabel makes some comments about the table setting.

During lunch, they decide to look at some of the video clips that Juan Ramón has sent from Spain. In these clips we see Juan Ramón and Teresa in various locations in Spain.

CAPÍTULO 14

Tecnotur

OVERVIEW

This page previews three key multimedia components of the **Glencoe Spanish** series. Each reinforces the material taught in Chapter 14 in a unique manner.

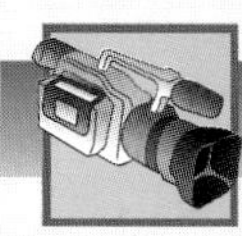

VIDEO

The Video Program allows students to see how the chapter vocabulary and structures are used by native speakers within an engaging story line. For maximum reinforcement, show the video episode as a final activity for Chapter 14.

A. Before viewing this episode, have students read the video photo captions. Ask them the following questions: **En la primera foto, ¿qué hacen? ¿Leen el menú? Y en la segunda foto, ¿de quiénes son los videos que reciben de España?**

B. Now show the Chapter 14 video episode. See the Video Activities Booklet for detailed suggestions for using this resource.

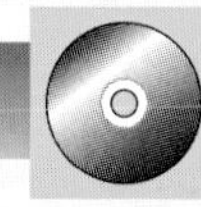

CD-ROM

A. Have students read the **Expansión cultural** photo caption on page 431.

B. In the CD-ROM version of **Expansión cultural** (Disc 4, page 431), students can listen to additional recorded information about the Casa de los Azulejos in Mexico City.

INTERNET

Teacher Information and Student Worksheets for this activity can be accessed at the Web site.

RESOURCES

- Workbook: Self-Test 4, pp. 181–184
- CD-ROM, Disc 4, pp. 432–435
- Tests: Unit 4, pp. 83; 118; 150

OVERVIEW

This section reviews the salient points from Chapters 12–14. In the **Conversación** students will review train travel vocabulary, reflexive verbs, and irregular verbs in the preterite in context. In the **Estructura** section, they will study the conjugations of irregular verbs and stem-changing verbs in the preterite. They will also review reflexive verbs in the present tense. They will practice these structures as they talk about their daily routines and what they eat every day.

TEACHING THE CONVERSATION

A. Have students open their books to page 432. Call on two students to read the conversation aloud.

B. Ask the questions from the **Después de conversar** section.

Learning From Realia

RENFE Have students look for the information that tells them this ticket is for a sleeper **(Billete Coches-cama)**. Where does it indicate for how many people the compartment is? **(Doble familiar)**.
RENFE means **la Red Nacional de Ferrocarriles Españoles.**

Repaso CAPÍTULOS 12–14

Conversación

El viaje en tren

ALBERTO: ¿Te gustó el viaje que hiciste en tren?
MARÍA: Sí, bastante. Dormí bien en la litera.
ALBERTO: ¿Te desayunaste en el tren?
MARÍA: No, porque llegamos a Madrid a las seis y media.
ALBERTO: Y, ¿a qué hora salieron de San Sebastián?
MARÍA: Salimos de San Sebastián a las veinte cuarenta.

Después de conversar

A Contesten.

1. ¿A María le gustó el viaje que hizo en tren?
2. ¿Cómo durmió en la litera?
3. ¿Se desayunó en el tren?
4. ¿A qué hora llegaron a Madrid?
5. ¿A qué hora salieron de San Sebastián?

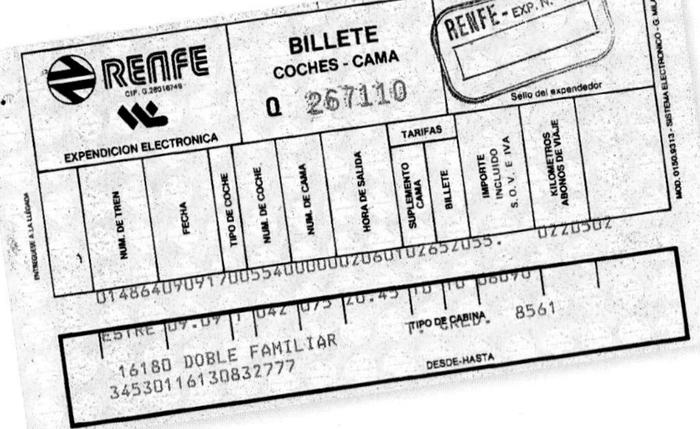

ANSWERS

Después de conversar

A

1. **Sí, a María le gustó el viaje bastante.**
2. **Durmió bien en la litera.**
3. **No se desayunó en el tren.**
4. **Llegaron a Madrid a las seis y media.**
5. **Salieron de San Sebastián a las veinte cuarenta.**

Estructura

Verbos irregulares en el pretérito

Review the preterite forms of the following irregular verbs.

HACER	**hice**	**hiciste**	**hizo**	**hicimos**	***hicisteis***	**hicieron**
QUERER	**quise**	**quisiste**	**quiso**	**quisimos**	***quisisteis***	**quisieron**
VENIR	**vine**	**viniste**	**vino**	**vinimos**	***vinisteis***	**vinieron**
ANDAR	**anduve**	**anduviste**	**anduvo**	**anduvimos**	***anduvisteis***	**anduvieron**
ESTAR	**estuve**	**estuviste**	**estuvo**	**estuvimos**	***estuvisteis***	**estuvieron**
TENER	**tuve**	**tuviste**	**tuvo**	**tuvimos**	***tuvisteis***	**tuvieron**
PODER	**pude**	**pudiste**	**pudo**	**pudimos**	***pudisteis***	**pudieron**
PONER	**puse**	**pusiste**	**puso**	**pusimos**	***pusisteis***	**pusieron**
SABER	**supe**	**supiste**	**supo**	**supimos**	***supisteis***	**supieron**

A HISTORIETA En la estación de ferrocarril

Completen con la forma apropiada del pretérito.

El otro día yo ___1___ (tener) que ir a Toledo. Carlos ___2___ (ir) también. Nosotros ___3___ (estar) en la estación de ferrocarril. Carlos ___4___ (hacer) cola en la ventanilla. Él me ___5___ (dar) mi billete y yo lo ___6___ (poner) en mi bolsa. Nosotros ___7___ (estar) en el andén. Cuando ___8___ (venir) el tren, yo no ___9___ (poder) hallar mi billete. No sé dónde lo ___10___ (poner). No sé dónde está.

Verbos de cambio radical

1. Some verbs have a stem change in both the present and preterite tenses. Verbs like **pedir (i, i)** change the **e** to **i** in both the present and preterite.

PRESENT	**pido**	**pides**	**pide**	**pedimos**	***pedís***	**piden**
PRETERITE	**pedí**	**pediste**	**pidió**	**pedimos**	***pedisteis***	**pidieron**

TEACHING STRUCTURE

Verbos irregulares en el pretérito

Have students open their books to page 433. Ask them to look at these verbs. You may also have them repeat them aloud. Many of these verbs, however, are not frequently used in the preterite.

A After students do **Práctica A,** you may wish to have them retell the story in their own words.

TEACHING STRUCTURE

Verbos de cambio radical

A. Go over Steps 1–3 on pages 433–434 with the students. Have them carefully repeat the verbs after you.

B. Explain to students that if they pronounce these verbs correctly, they will have no trouble spelling them.

ANSWERS

Práctica

A
1. **tuve**
2. **fue**
3. **estuvimos**
4. **hizo**
5. **dio**
6. **puse**
7. **estuvimos**
8. **vino**
9. **pude**
10. **puse**

Práctica

B and C If students have problems doing **Práctica B** and **C**, review some of the **Práctica** in Chapters 13 and 14.

D After going over **Práctica D** have students retell the story in their own words.

Note: You may wish to do the fourth literary selection (pages 454–459) with students at this time.

2. Verbs like **preferir (ie, i)** change the **e** to **ie** in the present; they change **e** to **i** in the preterite.

PRESENT	**prefiero**	**prefieres**	**prefiere**	**preferimos**	***preferís***	**prefieren**
PRETERITE	**preferí**	**preferiste**	**prefirió**	**preferimos**	***preferisteis***	**prefirieron**

3. Verbs like **dormir (ue, u)** change the **o** to **ue** in the present; they change **o** to **u** in the preterite.

PRESENT	**duermo**	**duermes**	**duerme**	**dormimos**	***dormís***	**duermen**
PRETERITE	**dormí**	**dormiste**	**durmió**	**dormimos**	***dormisteis***	**durmieron**

Práctica

B Información Completen con el presente.

1. Yo te ____ el café y tú me ____ el postre. Nosotros nos ____. (servir)
2. Tú lo ____ y yo lo ____. Nosotros dos lo ____. (preferir)
3. Ellos lo ____ y yo lo ____. Todos nosotros lo ____. (repetir)
4. Él ____ enseguida y yo ____ enseguida. Todos ____ enseguida. (dormirse)

C Información Completen.

1. Yo pedí un biftec y Ud. ____ un biftec también.
2. Yo freí el biftec y Ud. también lo ____.
3. Nosotros les servimos a todos los clientes y Uds. también les ____ a todos.
4. Seguimos trabajando en el comedor hasta las once y Uds. también ____ trabajando hasta las once.

D HISTORIETA En un restaurante mexicano

Contesten.

1. ¿Quién pidió tacos, tú o tu amigo?
2. ¿Quién pidió enchiladas?
3. ¿Sirvieron las enchiladas con mucho queso?
4. ¿Pediste arroz y frijoles también?
5. ¿Frió el cocinero los frijoles?
6. ¿Sirvió el mesero la ensalada con la comida?
7. Después de comer, ¿dormiste?
8. Y tu amigo, ¿durmió él también?

Comida mexicana en el restaurante «La Fonda», San Miguel de Allende

ANSWERS

Práctica

B
1. **sirvo, sirves, servimos**
2. **prefieres, prefiero, preferimos**
3. **repitan, repito, repetimos**
4. **se duerme, me duermo, nos dormimos**

C
1. **pidió**
2. **frió**
3. **sirvieron**
4. **siguieron**

D
1. **Yo pedí (Mi amigo pidió) tacos.**
2. **Yo pedí (Mi amigo pidió) enchiladas.**
3. **Sí, (No, no) sirvieron las enchiladas con mucho queso.**
4. **Sí, (No, no) pedí arroz y frijoles.**
5. **Sí (No), el cocinero (no) frió los frijoles.**
6. **Sí (No), el mesero (no) sirvió la ensalada con la comida.**
7. **Sí, (No, no) dormí.**
8. **Sí (No), mi amigo (no) durmió.**

Verbos reflexivos

The subject of a reflexive verb both performs and receives the action of the verb. Each subject has its corresponding reflexive pronoun.

INFINITIVE	levantarse	acostarse
yo	me levanto	me acuesto
tú	te levantas	te acuestas
él, ella, Ud.	se levanta	se acuesta
nosotros(as)	nos levantamos	nos acostamos
vosotros(as)	*os levantáis*	*os acostáis*
ellos, ellas, Uds.	se levantan	se acuestan

E **¿Y tú?** Contesten personalmente.

1. ¿A qué hora te acuestas?
2. ¿Te duermes enseguida?
3. Y, ¿a qué hora te despiertas?
4. ¿Te levantas enseguida?
5. ¿Cuántas horas duermes?

F **¿Y ellos?** Escriban las respuestas de Práctica A, cambiando **yo** a **mis hermanos.**

Actividades comunicativas

A **Un día típico** Work with a classmate. Compare a typical day in your life with a typical day in your partner's life.

B **Comidas** Work with a classmate. Ask your partner about the meals he or she ate yesterday. Which meals did he or she eat, at what time, and what foods? Your partner will answer and tell you what he or she liked and didn't like to eat. Take turns.

Tapas, Estepona, España

CAPÍTULOS 12-14
Repaso

TEACHING STRUCTURE

Verbos reflexivos

Have students read the reflexive verb forms aloud.

Práctica

E and F If students have problems doing **Práctica E** and **F,** review some of the **Práctica** in Chapter 12.

Actividades comunicativas

These activities contrast the use of the present **(Actividad A)** and the preterite **(Actividad B).**

Learning From Photos

Tapas, Estepona, España
Tapas are delicious little dishes that are eaten before lunch and before dinner. They are most often taken at a **taberna** or café. Some people, especially tourists and students, will make an inexpensive meal out of **tapas.**

ANSWERS

Práctica

E
1. **Me acuesto a las ___.**
2. **Sí, (No, no) me duermo enseguida.**
3. **Me despierto a las ___.**
4. **Sí, (No, no) me levanto enseguida.**
5. **Duermo ___ horas.**

F
1. **Mis hermanos se acuestan a las ___.**
2. **Sí, (No, no) se duermen enseguida.**
3. **Se despiertan a las ___.**
4. **Sí, (No, no) se levantan enseguida.**
5. **Duermen ___ horas.**

Actividades comunicativas

A Answers will vary. Students will use reflexive verbs.

B Answers will vary. Students will use the preterite and the food vocabulary from Chapter 14.

Independent Practice

Assign any of the following:
1. Activities, pp. 432–435
2. Workbook: Self-Test 4, pp. 181–185
3. CD-ROM, Disc 4, pp. 432–435
4. CD-ROM, Disc 4, Chapters 12–14, **Juegos de repaso**

VISTAS DE ECUADOR

OVERVIEW

The **Vistas de Ecuador** were prepared by National Geographic Society. Their purpose is to give students greater insight, through these visual images, into the culture and people of Ecuador. Have students look at the photographs on pages 436–439 for enjoyment. If they would like to talk about them, let them say anything they can, using the vocabulary they have learned to this point.

National Standards

Cultures
The **Vistas de Ecuador** photos, and the accompanying captions, allow students to gain insights into the people and culture of Ecuador.

Learning From Photos

1. Cosecha de cebada, provincia de Chimborazo The province of Chimorazo is the geographical center of Ecuador. It is a mostly rural, agricultural region with the highest percentage (70%) of indigenous people in the country. Riobamba is its principal city. The Volcán Chimborazo, the highest mountain peak in Ecuador, is in this province. Some of the highest farms in the world, with the hardiest of farmers, are on the slopes of Chimborazo. Farming here is limited to traditional techniques that have been practiced for centuries.

2. Mujer en un mercado, Saquisili The tiny village of Saquisili has a thriving market that takes place on Thursday. At this market you see people buying and selling practical items for daily use, not tourist trinkets.

(continued)

1. *Cosecha de cebada, provincia de Chimborazo*
2. *Mujer en un mercado, Saquisilí*
3. *Selva tropical cerca del río Coca*
4. *Nueva catedral, Cuenca*
5. *Plaza de la Independencia, Quito*
6. *Iguanas marinas, Islas Galápagos*
7. *Confección de sombreros de jipijapa, Cuenca*

436

Learning From Photos

Note that the woman in the photo is wearing the typical garb of the region, including the hat.

3. Selva tropical cerca del río Coca Ecuador is divided into three distinct geographical zones. **El litoral** along the Pacific coast, **la sierra** or the **altiplano andino,** and **el oriente. El oriente** is the eastern region of the country with tropical rainforests along the banks of Amazon tributaries. It is an area of exotic vegetation and rare, unusual birds and mammals. Some areas of **el oriente** are inaccessible.

4. Nueva catedral, Cuenca Cuenca, with over 350,000 inhabitants, is the third largest city in Ecuador. It is a modern metropolis that also has narrow, cobblestoned streets,

(continued)

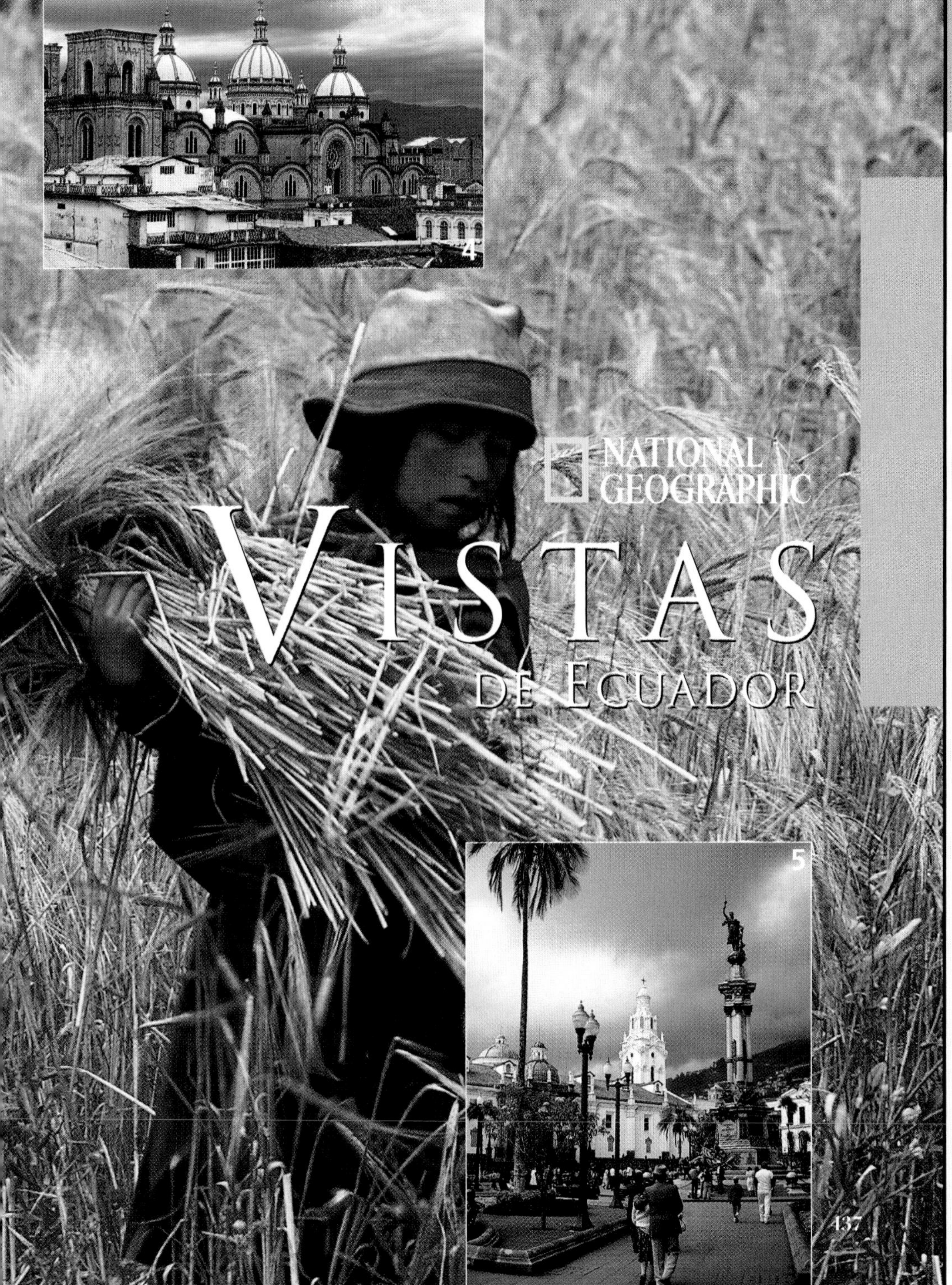

VISTAS DE ECUADOR

Learning From Photos

(continued)
wonderful place for strolling or having a picnic lunch. The cathedral in the photo is the third one built on this site. Construction started on the first cathedral the day Quito was founded. The second one was built in 1667. It was extensively remodeled after a major earthquake in 1755, but some of the work on this third cathedral was not finished until 1930.

6. Iguanas marinas, Islas Galápagos The famous Galapagos Islands are 960 kilometers off the coast of Ecuador. There are 60 named islands, islets, and rocks ranging from Isla Isabel (128 km. long) to tiny rock ledges. The Galapagos are the most volcanically active islands in the world. These islands have been recognized for years as a priceless and unique part of the world's natural heritage.

7. Confección de sombreros de jipijapa, Cuenca The hats we see being made here from **jipijapa** reeds are the famous Panama hats. Panama hats are woven from these plant fibers and they are made only in Ecuador. They are called *Panama hats* because they were provided to workers building the Panama Canal. The hats achieved their greatest fame in the late 19th and early 20th centuries when U.S. presidents, European royalty, and members of high society sported *Panamas.*

Learning From Photos

(continued from page 436)
whitewashed buildings with tile roofs and wooden balconies. The Plaza Abdón Calderón is the main square in colonial Cuenca. On the square is the old cathedral, El Sagrario, and the new cathedral, the Catedral de la Inmaculada Concepción. Construction began on the new cathedral (pictured here) in 1885. The cathedral, which holds 10,000 people, is made of brick and has beautiful sky-blue domes. Its interior is done in alabaster and pink marble.

5. Plaza de la Independencia, Quito In the center of this square in Quito there is a monument to Ecuador's independence. Between the wide walks there are beautiful patches of garden with very tall palm trees and attractive street lamps. The square is a

(continued)

VISTAS DE ECUADOR

Learning From Photos

1. Volcán Cotopaxi The superb Cotopaxi National Park, located some 60 kilometers south of Quito, surrounds the Cotopaxi volcano, Ecuador's second highest mountain (5,897 meters) and its highest active volcano. On a clear day the magnificent snow-capped Cotopaxi is visible from Quito.

2. Ciudad de Guayaquil Guayaquil is the major port and largest city of Ecuador. Situated on the Guayas River, its inhabitants are called **guayaquileños** or more familiarly, **guayacos**. Guayaquil is the economic hub of Ecuador. It is responsible for over 40% of the nation's industrial output, and almost 100% of the country's agricultural exports. Guayaquil is a city of bustling activity.

3. Perforación petrolera, río Napo The Napo River, in the northern part of **el oriente,** is sometimes as wide as one kilometer but it is quite shallow. There is a fair amount of oil exploration in this area. The major city in the region is Coca. It's a rather muddy city with the feel of an oil boomtown. In the **río Napo** area there are many lodges for people who enjoy exploring the jungle.

4. Alfombras hechas a mano, mercado de Otavalo Otavalo, a lovely town north of Quito, is famous for its market.

The **otavaleños** are attractive people with typical Andean features. As you can see in the photograph, the women dress in long, dark skirts with beautiful white blouses. They often wear long shawls in which they carry

(continued)

1. *Volcán Cotopaxi*
2. *Ciudad de Guayaquil*
3. *Perforación petrolera, río Napo*
4. *Alfombras hechas a mano, mercado de Otavalo*
5. *Envase del camarón, Guayaquil*
6. *Islas Galápagos*
7. *Plantación bananera, provincia de Guayas*

NATIONAL GEOGRAPHIC SOCIETY

TEACHER'S CORNER

Index to NATIONAL GEOGRAPHIC MAGAZINE

The following articles may be used for research relating to this chapter:

- "Simón Bolivar," by Bryan Hodgson, March 1994.
- "El Niño's Ill Wind," by Thomas Y. Canby, February 1984.
- "Ecuador—Low and Lofty Land Astride the Equator," by Loren McIntyre, February 1968.

Learning From Photos

(continued from page 438)
their purchases. Unlike women in other Andean areas, they do not wear hats. The **otavaleños** are world famous for all types of woven articles, including rugs, ponchos, and blankets.

5. Envase del camarón, Guayaquil Shrimp and tuna are two of Ecuador's major exports. There has been an on-going dispute over "national" waters. The Ecuadorian government states that the national waters extend 200 miles into the Pacific.

6. Islas Galápagos The Galapagos Islands are inhabited by species of wildlife that are so unique that almost half of them cannot be found anywhere else in the world. **Galápagos** are very large, lethargic tortoises that sun themselves on the rocks. Unfortunately they are almost extinct today thanks to the human predators who hunted them prior to the time of strict environmental regulations.

7. Plantación bananera, provincia de Guayas Ecuador is the world's largest banana exporter. Grown in all five provinces of **el litoral** bananas are shipped through the port of Guayaquil.

Products available from GLENCOE/MCGRAW-HILL

To order the following products, call Glencoe/McGraw-Hill at 1-800-334-7344.

CD-ROMs
- Picture Atlas of the World
- The Complete National Geographic: 109 Years of National Geographic Magazine

Software
- ZingoLingo: Spanish Diskettes

Transparency Set
- NGS PicturePack: Geography of South America

Videodisc
- STV: World Geography (Volume 3: "South America and Antarctica")

Products available from NATIONAL GEOGRAPHIC SOCIETY

NATIONAL GEOGRAPHIC SOCIETY

To order the following products, call National Geographic Society at 1-800-368-2728.

Books
- Exploring Your World: The Adventure of Geography
- National Geographic Satellite Atlas of the World

Video
- South America ("Nations of the World" Series)

Literatura 1

RESOURCES

- CD-ROM, Discs 1, 2, 3, 4, pages 440–441

¡OJO! The exposure to literature early in one's study of a foreign language should be a pleasant experience. As students read these selections it is not necessary that they understand every word. Explain to them that they should try to enjoy the experience of reading literature in a new language. As they read they should look for the following:

- who the main characters are
- what they are like
- what they are doing—the plot
- what happens to them—the outcome of the story

VERSOS SENCILLOS

TEACHING VOCABULARY

A. Present the new vocabulary using the teaching suggestions given in the regular chapters in this textbook.

B. Quickly go over **Práctica A** with the class.

VERSOS SENCILLOS
de José Martí

Vocabulario

A **¿Sí o no?** Digan que sí o que no.

1. Una rosa es una flor bonita.
2. El corazón es un órgano vital.
3. Damos la mano a un amigo.

ANSWERS

Práctica

A 1. Sí.
2. Sí.
3. Sí.

La Habana, Cuba

VERSOS SENCILLOS
de José Martí

INTRODUCCIÓN José Martí (1853–1895) es cubano. Es un hombre muy famoso. Es poeta y es también un héroe. Durante toda la vida Martí lucha[1] por la independencia de Cuba.

Estudia en Madrid y en Zaragoza en España. José Martí admira mucho a la España artística y humana. Pero ataca la España política porque su país, Cuba, en aquel entonces[2] es una colonia de España.

Martí pasa mucho tiempo en varias repúblicas hispanoamericanas—México, Guatemala, Venezuela y Honduras. «De América soy hijo»—proclama Martí. Pasa también unos catorce años en los Estados Unidos. Publica *Versos sencillos* en Nueva York en 1891.

Versos sencillos es una colección de poemas (poesías).

[1]**lucha** *fights* [2]**en aquel entonces** *at that time*

Versos sencillos

Cultivo una rosa blanca,
en julio como en enero
para el amigo sincero
que me da su mano franca.

Y para el cruel que me arranca°
el corazón con que vivo,
cardo ni ortiga° cultivo
cultivo la rosa blanca.

arranca *pulls out*

cardo ni ortiga *thistle nor nettle*

Después de leer

A En inglés, por favor. Contesten.

1. Is the theme of this short poem gardening, friendship, or roses?
2. What two types of people does the poet speak about?
3. In your own words in English, explain how the poet tells us that he treats all people equally.
4. How does the poet express "all the time"?

Class Motivator

Using the Song Cassette 1A/Compact Disc 1 from the Audio Program, play the song ***Guantanamera.*** Have students sing the words in the poem on page 441 to the melody. Explain to students that, although Pete Seeger composed the melody, the words to the song ***Guantanamera*** were taken from ***Versos sencillos.***

ANSWERS

Después de leer

1. friendship
2. a sincere friend, a cruel person
3. Answers will vary.
4. He says, " in July as in January."

Literatura 1

DISCUSSING LITERATURE

INTRODUCCIÓN

A. You may go over the **Introducción** with the students or you may decide to omit it and just have them read the poem.

B. You can ask the following questions about the **Introducción. ¿De qué nacionalidad es José Martí? ¿Qué es José Martí? ¿Martí lucha por la independencia de qué país? ¿Dónde estudia? ¿A qué España admira Martí? ¿A qué España ataca Martí? Durante la vida de Martí, ¿qué es Cuba?**

Versos sencillos

A. Have students close their books. Explain the meaning of **cardo** and **ortiga** to them.

B. Read the poem to the class. Use as much expression as you can. Hold out your hand as you say **me da su mano franca.** Gesture pulling out your heart as you say: **me arranca el corazón.** Smile as you say: **cultivo la rosa blanca.**

C. Have students open their books to page 441. Have them read the poem once in unison. Give them a couple of minutes to read the poem silently and then call on an individual to read aloud.

D. You can ask the following: **¿Qué cultiva el autor? ¿Cuándo cultiva la rosa blanca? ¿Para quién cultiva una rosa blanca? Para una persona cruel, ¿cultiva un cardo o una ortiga? ¿Qué cultiva para una persona cruel?**

E. Go over the **Después de leer** activity and have students answer in English.

TECHNOLOGY OPTION

Students can listen to a recording of this poem on the CD-ROM, Discs 1, 2, 3, 4, page 441.

RESOURCES

- CD-ROM, Discs 1, 2, 3, 4, pages 442–445

«UNA MONEDA DE ORO»

TEACHING VOCABULARY

A. Have students open their books to page 442. Have them repeat the new vocabulary words and sentences after you.

B. It is not necessary that students become as thoroughly familiar with this vocabulary as with the vocabulary in a typical chapter. It is presented to help students understand the reading but it is not necessary that they learn the vocabulary for productive purposes. High-frequency words will be reintroduced as new vocabulary in **¡Buen Viaje! Levels 2** and **3.**

Literatura 2

«UNA MONEDA DE ORO»

de Francisco Monterde

Vocabulario

Es temprano por la noche (8:30).
Hay una moneda en el suelo.

La moneda refleja la luz de la luna.
Un señor halla la moneda.

La señora enciende la luz.

Ella cose el bolsillo porque tiene un agujero.

La señora cuelga el chaleco en la silla.

El señor esconde la moneda.
Mete la moneda debajo del mantel.

El señor levanta el mantel.
Debajo del mantel hay dinero.
El señor está muy alegre.

Es la Navidad.
El señor recoge el juguete.
La niña está dormida.

Práctica

A **¿Sabes la palabra?** Escojan.

1. El ____ de diciembre es la Navidad.
   a. veinticinco **b.** veinticuatro
2. Los niños reciben ____ para la Navidad.
   a. sillas **b.** juguetes
3. Él tiene que coser el bolsillo porque tiene ____.
   a. un agujero **b.** una moneda
4. El señor no pierde la moneda. ____ la moneda.
   a. Busca **b.** Halla
5. La señora cuelga ____ en la silla.
   a. el chaleco **b.** el mantel
6. ¿Ellos van a ver la moneda? No, no quiero. Voy a ____ la moneda.
   a. recoger **b.** esconder
7. En la mano hay cinco ____.
   a. monedas **b.** dedos

B **La moneda** Contesten.

1. ¿Dónde está el señor? (en el parque)
2. ¿Qué parte del día es? (la noche)
3. ¿Qué halla el señor? (una moneda)
4. ¿Recoge la moneda? (sí)
5. ¿De qué es la moneda? (de oro)
6. ¿Qué refleja la moneda? (la luna)

Literatura 2

Práctica

A and **B** Quickly go over these activities orally to be sure that students will understand the words in the reading.

ANSWERS

Práctica

A
1. a
2. b
3. a
4. b
5. a
6. b
7. b

B
1. El señor está en el parque.
2. Es la noche.
3. El señor halla una moneda.
4. Sí, recoge la moneda.
5. La moneda es de oro.
6. La moneda refleja la luna.

Literatura 2

DISCUSSING LITERATURE

¡OJO! This reading is OPTIONAL. You may present the story thoroughly as a class activity or you may have some or all students merely read it on their own. If you present the story as a class activity you may wish to vary presentation procedures from section to section. Some options are:

- Students read silently.
- Students repeat after you in unison.
- Call on individuals to read aloud
- When dialogue appears in the story, call on students to take parts.

With any of the above procedures, intersperse some comprehension questions. Call on a student or students to give a brief synopsis of a section in Spanish.

«Una moneda de oro»

A. Before reading this selection you may wish to give students the following introduction in English to set the scene and help them understand the story: "We are going to read a story about a poor family in Mexico. A certain holiday is coming up. Just before the holiday something exciting happens to the father."

B. If you are presenting the story as a class activity, you can use many gestures or expressions to help students with comprehension. Examples:

Section 1 Pick up a coin. Look at it with an amazed, excited face. Caress the coin.

Section 2 If you have a pocket, put the coin in it. Take it out and check your pocket for a hole. Nod no and put the coin back. Indicate that you are doubtful. Look at the coin again and cheer up.

«UNA MONEDA DE ORO»
de Francisco Monterde

INTRODUCCIÓN Francisco Monterde es de México. Nace en 1894. Es poeta, dramaturgo y novelista. Es también cuentista. Publica una colección de cuentos[1] en 1943. Sus cuentos presentan un estudio serio de la historia de México.

Aquí tenemos el cuento «Una moneda de oro». Es un cuento sencillo[2] y tierno[3]. El autor habla de una pobre familia mexicana del campo.

[1]**cuentos** *stories* [2]**sencillo** *simple* [3]**tierno** *tender*

«Una moneda de oro»

1

Es una Navidad alegre para el pobre. El pobre es Andrés. No tiene dinero y no tiene trabajo desde el otoño.

Es temprano por la noche. Andrés pasa por el parque. En el suelo ve una moneda que refleja la luz de la luna. —¿Es una moneda de oro?—pregunta Andrés. —Pesa° mucho. ¡Imposible! No puede ser una moneda de oro. Es sólo una medalla.

Andrés sale del parque y examina la moneda. No, no es una medalla. Es realmente una moneda de oro. Andrés acaricia° la moneda. ¡Es muy agradable su contacto!

Pesa *It weighs*

acaricia *caresses*

2

Con la moneda entre los dedos, mete la mano derecha en el bolsillo de su pantalón. No, no puede meter la moneda en el bolsillo. Tiene miedo° de perder la moneda. Examina el bolsillo. No, no tiene agujeros. No hay problema. Puede meter la moneda en el bolsillo. No va a perder la moneda.

Andrés va a casa a pie. Anda rápido. La moneda de oro salta° en el bolsillo. El pobre Andrés está muy contento.

Luego tiene una duda. ¿Es falsa la moneda? Andrés tiene una idea. Va a entrar en una tienda. Va a comprar algo. Y va a pagar con la moneda. Si el dependiente acepta la moneda, es buena, ¿no? Y si no acepta la moneda, ¿qué? Andrés reflexiona. No, no va a ir a la tienda. Prefiere ir a casa con la moneda. Su mujer va a estar muy contenta.

Tiene miedo *He is afraid*

salta *jumps around*

3

Su casa es una casa humilde. Tiene sólo dos piezas o cuartos. Cuando llega a casa, su mujer no está. No está porque cada día tiene que ir a entregar° la ropa que cose para ganar unos pesos.

Andrés enciende una luz. Pone la moneda en la mesa. En unos momentos oye° a su mujer y a su hija. Ellas vuelven a casa. Esconde la moneda debajo del mantel.

La niña entra. Andrés toma la niña en sus brazos. Luego llega su mujer. Tiene una expresión triste y melancólica. —¿Tienes trabajo?—pregunta ella. —Hoy no puedo comprar pan. No me pagan cuando entrego la costura°.

Andrés no contesta. Levanta el mantel. Su mujer ve la moneda. Toma la moneda en las manos. —¿Quién te da la moneda?

—Nadie°—Andrés habla con su mujer. Explica cómo halla la moneda en el parque.

La niña toma la moneda y empieza a jugar con la moneda. Andrés tiene miedo. No quiere perder la moneda. Puede irse por° un agujero.

Andrés toma la moneda y pone la moneda en uno de los bolsillos de su chaleco. —¿Qué compramos con la moneda?—pregunta Andrés.

—No compramos nada. Tenemos que pagar mucho—suspira su mujer.

—Debemos° mucho.

—Es verdad—contesta Andrés. —Pero hoy es Nochebuena°. Tenemos que celebrar.

—No—contesta su mujer. —Primero tenemos que pagar el dinero que debemos.

entregar *return, deliver*

oye *he hears*

costura *sewing*

Nadie *No one*

irse por *slip through*

Debemos *We owe*

Nochebuena *Christmas Eve*

Una casa humilde, México

Section 3 Put the coin on a table. Cover it with anything that can be a tablecloth.
Tell the class you are now **la niña**. Take the coin and play with it. If you have a jacket, look annoyed, take the jacket off and hang it over the chair.
(continued on page 446)

Literatura 2

DISCUSSING LITERATURE

Section 4 Look all over for the coin. Search all the clothing you have on. Show your empty hands. Be **la niña**. Sit on a chair. Wake up. Stretch your arms and make a noise with the coin under the table.

Después de leer

Note Each of the four **Después de leer** activities corresponds to a different section of the reading. **Después de leer A** corresponds to Section 1, **B** to Section 2, **C** to Section 3, and **D** to Section 4.

As you finish each section of the story you can go over the corresponding activity.

TECHNOLOGY OPTION

Students can listen to a recording of this story on the CD-ROM, Discs 1, 2, 3, 4, pages 444–446.

Andrés está un poco malhumorado. Se quita° el chaleco y el saco. Cuelga el chaleco y el saco en la silla.

—Bueno, Andrés. Si quieres, puedes ir a comprar algo. Pero tenemos que guardar lo demás°.

Andrés acepta. Se pone° el chaleco y el saco y sale de casa.

Se quita *He takes off*
guardar lo demás *keep the rest*
Se pone *He puts on*

En la calle Andrés ve a su amigo Pedro.

—¿Adónde vas? ¿Quieres ir a tomar algo?

Andrés acepta. Los amigos pasan un rato en un café pequeño. Beben y hablan. Y luego Andrés sale. Va a la tienda. Sólo va a comprar comida para esta noche. Y un juguete para la niña.

Andrés compra primero los alimentos. El paquete está listo°. Andrés busca la moneda. Busca en el chaleco. No está. Busca en el saco. No está. Busca en su pantalón. La moneda no está en ninguno de sus bolsillos. El pobre Andrés está lleno de terror. Tiene que salir de la tienda sin la comida.

Una vez más está en la calle. Vuelve a casa. Llega a la puerta. No quiere entrar. Pero tiene que entrar. Entra y ve a la niña dormida con la cabeza entre los brazos sobre la mesa. Su mujer está cosiendo a su lado.

—La moneda...

—¿Qué?

—No tengo la moneda.

—¿Cómo?

La niña sobresalta°. Abre los ojos. Baja los brazos y bajo la mesa Andrés y su mujer oyen el retintín° de la moneda de oro.

¡Qué contentos están Andrés y su mujer! Recogen la moneda que la niña había escamoteado° del chaleco cuando estaba colgado en la silla.

listo *ready*
sobresalta *jumps up*
retintín *jingle*
había escamoteado *had secretly taken out*

Después de leer

A Comprensión Contesten.

1. ¿Quién es el pobre?
2. ¿Por qué no tiene dinero?
3. ¿Por dónde pasa Andrés?
4. ¿Qué ve en el suelo?
5. ¿Es una moneda de oro o es una medalla?

B Andrés y la moneda Escojan.

1. ¿Por qué no debe Andrés meter la moneda en el bolsillo de su pantalón?
   a. Porque el bolsillo tiene un agujero.
   b. Porque puede perder la moneda.
   c. Porque la moneda es muy grande.

ANSWERS

Después de leer

A
1. **El pobre es Andrés.**
2. **Porque no tiene trabajo desde el otoño.**
3. **Andrés pasa por el parque.**
4. **Ve una moneda en el suelo.**
5. **Es una moneda de oro.**

B
1. **b**
2. **a**
3. **b**
4. **b**
5. **a**
6. **c**

2. Cuando Andrés examina el bolsillo, ¿qué decide?
   a. Puede meter la moneda en el bolsillo porque no tiene agujero.
   b. Va a perder la moneda.
   c. La moneda de oro es sólo una medalla.
3. ¿Cómo va Andrés a casa?
   a. Salta.
   b. A pie y rápido.
   c. Con miedo.
4. ¿Qué duda tiene Andrés?
   a. Si tiene que comprar algo.
   b. Si la moneda es falsa o no.
   c. Si su pantalón tiene un agujero.
5. Si compra algo en una tienda, ¿por qué quiere pagar con la moneda?
   a. Si el dependiente acepta la moneda, no es falsa.
   b. Porque la moneda es falsa y Andrés no quiere la moneda.
   c. Porque no tiene dinero.
6. ¿Qué decide Andrés?
   a. Decide que la moneda es falsa.
   b. Decide que no necesita nada.
   c. Decide que no va a la tienda. Prefiere ir a casa.

Una vista del campo, México

La Navidad, México

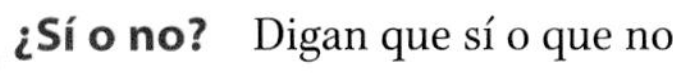

C **¿Sí o no?** Digan que sí o que no.

1. La casa de Andrés es muy humilde.
2. La casa tiene cuatro piezas.
3. Cuando llega Andrés, su mujer cose.
4. Su mujer cose para ganar dinero.
5. Su mujer y su hija vuelven a casa.
6. Andrés toma a su mujer en sus brazos.
7. Su mujer está muy contenta.
8. Hoy ella compra pan.
9. Cuando Andrés levanta el mantel, su mujer ve la moneda.
10. La niña empieza a jugar con la moneda.
11. Andrés quiere comprar algo para celebrar la Navidad.
12. Su mujer quiere comprar mucho.
13. Por fin Andrés puede ir a la tienda a comprar algo.

D **Andrés sale.** Contesten.

1. ¿A quién ve Andrés en la calle?
2. ¿Adónde van los dos?
3. Luego, ¿adónde va Andrés?
4. ¿Qué va a comprar?
5. ¿Qué busca Andrés?
6. ¿Qué no puede hallar?
7. ¿Qué ve cuando entra en la casa?
8. ¿Dónde está la moneda?

ANSWERS

Después de leer

C
1. Sí.
2. No.
3. No.
4. Sí.
5. Sí.
6. No.
7. No.
8. No.
9. Sí.
10. Sí.
11. Sí.
12. No.
13. Sí.

D
1. Andrés ve a su amigo Pedro.
2. Los dos van a un café pequeño.
3. Andrés va a la tienda.
4. Va a comprar comida para la noche y un juguete para la niña.
5. Andrés busca la moneda.
6. No puede hallar la moneda.
7. Ve a la familia.
8. La moneda está bajo la mesa.

RESOURCES

- CD-ROM, Discs 1, 2, 3, 4, pages 448–453

«La camisa de Margarita»

TEACHING VOCABULARY

A. Have students open their books to page 448. Have them repeat the new vocabulary words and sentences after you.

B. Students merely need to be familiar with the vocabulary to help them understand the story. This vocabulary does not have to be a part of their active, productive vocabulary. All high-frequency words will be reintroduced in **¡Buen viaje! Levels 2** and **3** as new vocabulary.

«LA CAMISA DE MARGARITA»
de Ricardo Palma

Vocabulario

Es un galán.
Es un señor muy elegante.
Es soltero. No tiene esposa.
No está casado.

Los jóvenes están enamorados.
El joven le echa flores a la señorita.
La joven le flecha el corazón al joven.
Los jóvenes tienen una sonrisita.

A and B Quickly go over these activities orally to be sure that students will understand the words in the reading.

El sacerdote habla con los recién casados. Están en la iglesia.

el suegro el padre del marido o de la mujer
el sacerdote un padre (religioso) católico
el pobretón un muchacho pobre que no tiene dinero
el chisme la historieta, un rumor
los muebles la silla, la mesa, la cama, etc., son muebles
altivo arrogante
con mucha plata que tiene mucho dinero, rico

NOTA In this story you will come across the following words that describe money used in Peru in the eighteenth century. From the context of the reading you will be able to tell which were of little value and which were of great value. It is not necessary for you to learn these words: **un ochavo, un real, un maravedí, un duro, un morlaco.**

Práctica

A Contesten según los dibujos.

1. ¿Es un tipo galán el joven?
2. ¿Es un poco altivo?
3. ¿Es soltero?
4. ¿Tiene esposa?
5. ¿Está enamorado el joven?
6. ¿Que le echa a la señorita?
7. ¿Qué tiene en la cara?
8. ¿Tiene la señorita una cadena de diamantes en el cuello?

B Expresen de otra manera.

1. Él no tiene mujer. No está casado.
2. Es un señor elegante.
3. Es un tipo muy arrogante.
4. No es un joven que tiene mucho dinero.
5. No sé si es verdad. Es un rumor.

ANSWERS

Práctica

A
1. **Sí, el joven es un tipo galán.**
2. **Sí, es un poco altivo.**
3. **Sí, es soltero.**
4. **No, no tiene esposa.**
5. **Sí, está enamorado.**
6. **Le echa flores a la señorita.**
7. **Tiene una sonrisita.**
8. **No, la señorita no tiene una cadena de diamantes en el cuello.**

B
1. **Él es soltero.**
2. **Es un galán.**
3. **Es muy altivo.**
4. **Es un pobretón.**
5. **Es un chisme.**

DISCUSSING LITERATURE

INTRODUCCIÓN

You may go over the **Introducción** with the class or you may decide to omit it and just have them read the story.

«La camisa de Margarita»

A. Tell students they are going to read a story that takes place in the colonial days, the 1600's, in Lima, Peru. The families involved are quite wealthy but there is a discussion about a wedding dress. You'll find out why.

B. You may wish to have students take a few minutes to read each section silently before going over it orally in class.

C. Since this reading is rather long you may wish to go over only certain sections orally and have students read the other sections silently.

D. Call on a more able student to give a synopsis of each section. This helps less able students understand the selection.

E. Here are some additional hints to help you teach the various sections of the reading:

Section 1

1. Tell students **colector** is a tax collector.
2. **El Callao** is the port for Lima, Peru.
3. Ask students if they know what **arrogante** means. If they don't, put on an arrogant air.

Section 2

1. Ask what they think the symbolism is behind the expression **le flecha al corazón.**

(continued on page 451)

«LA CAMISA DE MARGARITA»
de Ricardo Palma

INTRODUCCIÓN Ricardo Palma es uno de los hombres más famosos de letras peruanas de todos los tiempos. Él da origen a un nuevo género literario—la tradición. La tradición es una anécdota histórica.

Ricardo Palma publica sus *Tradiciones peruanas* en diez tomos de 1872 a 1910. Las tradiciones presentan la historia del Perú desde la época precolombina hasta la guerra con Chile (1879–1883). Las tradiciones más interesantes y más famosas son las tradiciones que describen la época colonial. «La camisa de Margarita» es un ejemplo de una tradición de la época colonial.

«La camisa de Margarita»

1

Cuando las señoras viejas de Lima quieren describir algo que cuesta mucho, ¿qué dicen? Dicen: —¡Qué! Si esto es más caro que la camisa de Margarita Pareja.

Margarita Pareja es por los años 1765 la hija mimada° de don Raimundo Pareja, un colector importante del Callao. La muchacha es una de estas limeñitas que es tan bella que puede cautivar° al mismo diablo°. Tiene unos ojos negros cargados° de dinamita que hacen explosión sobre el alma° de los galanes limeños.

Llega de España un arrogante joven llamado don Luis de Alcázar. Don Luis tiene en Lima un tío aragonés, don Honorato. Don Honorato es solterón y es muy rico. Si el tío es rico, no lo es el joven. No tiene ni un centavo.

mimada *spoiled*
cautivar *captivate, charm*
diablo *devil*
cargados *charged*
alma *soul*

2

En la procesión de Santa Rosa, Alcázar conoce a la linda Margarita. La muchacha le flecha el corazón. El joven le echa flores. Ella no le contesta ni sí ni no. Pero con sonrisitas y otras armas del arsenal femenino le da a entender al joven que es plato muy de su gusto.

Los enamorados olvidan° que existe la aritmética. Don Luis no considera su presente condición económica un obstáculo. Va al padre de Margarita y le pide su mano°. Al padre de Margarita, don Raimundo, no le gusta nada la petición del joven arrogante. Le dice que Margarita es demasiado joven para tomar marido.

olvidan *forget*
le pide su mano *asks for her hand*

Pero la edad de su hija no es la verdadera razón. Don Raimundo no quiere ser suegro de un pobretón. Les dice la verdad a algunos de sus amigos. Uno de ellos va con el chisme al tío aragonés. El tío, que es un tipo muy altivo, se pone° furioso.

—¡Cómo! ¡Desairar° a mi sobrino! No hay más gallardo en todo Lima. Ese don Raimundo va a ver...

se pone *becomes*
Desairar *To snub*

3

Y la pobre Margarita se pone muy enferma. Pierde peso° y tiene ataques nerviosos. Sufre mucho. Su padre se alarma y llama a varios médicos y curanderos. Todos declaran que la única medicina que va a salvar a la joven no se vende en la farmacia. El padre tiene que permitir a la muchacha casarse° con el varón de su gusto.

Don Raimundo va a la casa de don Honorato. Le dice: —Ud. tiene que permitir a su sobrino casarse con mi hija. Porque si no, la muchacha va a morir.

—No puede ser—contesta de la manera más desagradable el tío. —Mi sobrino es un pobretón. Lo que Ud. debe buscar para su hija es un hombre con mucha plata.

El diálogo entre los dos es muy borrascoso°.

—Pero, tío, no es cristiano matar° a quien no tiene la culpa°—dice don Luis.

peso *weight*
casarse *to marry*
borrascoso *stormy*
matar *kill*
culpa *blame*

Iglesia de San Francisco, Lima, Perú

Literatura 3

2. Explain: **Los enamorados olvidan que existe la aritmética. → Los jóvenes olvidan o no quieren aceptar que es necesario tener dinero para vivir.**
3. Tell students the uncle makes up an excuse. Ask them what the excuse is.
4. Have students explain in English how Don Honorato, Don Luis' uncle, finds out what's going on.

Section 3

1. Explain: **El varón es una persona de sexo masculino.**
2. **morir → no va a vivir**

Literatura 3

DISCUSSING LITERATURE

Section 4

1. Have students take a look at the sidenotes before reading.
2. Explain that **la puesta** refers to what she is wearing.

—¿Tú quieres casarte con esa joven?

—Sí, de todo corazón, tío y señor.

—Pues bien, muchacho. Si tú quieres, consiento. Pero con una condición. Don Raimundo me tiene que jurar° que no va a regalar un ochavo a su hija. Y no le va a dejar un real en la herencia—. Aquí empieza otra disputa.

jurar *to swear*

4

—Pero, hombre, mi hija tiene veinte mil duros de dote°.

—Renunciamos a la dote. La niña va a venir a casa de su marido con nada más que la ropa que lleva o tiene puesta°.

—Entonces me permite regalar a mi hija los muebles° y el ajuar (vestido) de novia.

—Ni un alfiler°.

—Ud. no es razonable, don Honorato. Mi hija necesita llevar una camisa para reemplazar la puesta.

—Bien, Ud. le puede regalar la camisa de novia y se acaba°.

Al día siguiente don Raimundo y don Honorato van a la Iglesia de San Francisco a oír misa°. En el momento que el sacerdote eleva la Hostia, dice el padre de Margarita: —Juro no dar a mi hija más que la camisa de novia.

Y don Raimundo cumple con° su promesa. Ni en la vida ni en la muerte le da después a su hija un maravedí.

Los encajes° de Flandes que adornan la camisa de la novia cuestan dos mil setecientos duros. El cordoncillo que ajusta al cuello es una cadena de brillantes que tienen un valor de treinta mil morlacos.

Los recién casados hacen creer al tío aragonés que la camisa no vale° nada. Porque don Honorato es tan testarudo°, que a saber el valor real de la camisa, le hace al sobrino divorciarse.

Ahora sabemos por qué es muy merecida° la fama que tiene la camisa nupcial de Margarita Pareja.

dote *dowry*
tiene puesta *has on*
muebles *furniture*
alfiler *pin*
se acaba *that's it*
oír misa *to hear mass*
cumple con *fulfills*

Palacio arzobispal, Lima

encajes *lace*
vale *is worth*
testarudo *hard-headed*
merecida *deserved*

Después de leer

A Margarita Pareja Contesten.

1. ¿Quiénes dicen: —¡Qué! ¡Si esto es más caro que la camisa de Margarita Pareja—?
2. ¿Quién es Margarita Pareja?
3. ¿Cómo es Margarita?
4. ¿Quién llega al Perú?
5. ¿De dónde viene?
6. ¿Quién es?
7. ¿Cómo es el tío?
8. ¿Cómo es el sobrino?

B Don Luis Completen.

1. Don Luis conoce a Margarita en ____.
2. Margarita le ____. Y don Luis le ____.
3. Don Luis no considera su condición económica ____.
4. Don Luis va al padre de Margarita y ____.
5. Al padre no le gusta nada ____.
6. No le gusta la petición porque ____.
7. Cuando el tío sabe lo que dice don Raimundo, él se pone ____.

Palacio arzobispal, Lima

C En español, por favor. Contesten en español.

1. What happens to Margarita?
2. What medicine does she need?
3. Why does the young man's uncle say his nephew cannot marry Margarita?
4. Under what condition does the uncle consent?

D En tus propias palabras In your own words in English, explain the ending of this story. What does Margarita's father do?

Plaza de Armas, Lima

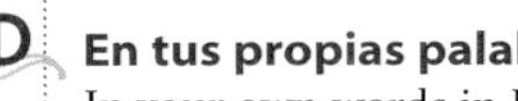

Literatura 3

Después de leer

Note Each of the four **Después de leer** activities corresponds to a different section of the reading. **Después de leer A** corresponds to Section 1, **B** to Section 2, **C** to Section 3, and **D** to Section 4.

As you finish each section of the story you can go over the corresponding activity.

TECHNOLOGY OPTION

Students can listen to a recording of this story on the CD-ROM, Discs 1, 2, 3, 4, pages 450–452.

Learning From Photos

Palacio arzobispal, Lima The Palace of the Archbishop and the other beautiful buildings in Lima pictured here were all constructed during the colonial period.

ANSWERS

Después de leer

A
1. Las señoras viejas de Lima.
2. Es la hija mimada de don Raimundo Pareja.
3. Es tan bella que puede cautivar al mismo diablo.
4. Un arrogante joven llamado don Luis de Alcázar.
5. De España.
6. Es sobrino de don Honorato.
7. El tío es solterón y muy rico.
8. El sobrino no tiene ni un centavo.

B
1. la procesión de Santa Rosa
2. flecha el corazón/echa flores
3. un obstáculo
4. le pide su mano
5. la petición del joven arrogante
6. no quiere ser suegro de un pobretón
7. furioso

C
1. Margarita se pone muy enferma.
2. La única medicina que necesita es casarse.
3. El tío del joven dice que su sobrino no puede casarse con Margarita porque es un pobretón.
4. Con la condición de que don Raimundo jure que no va a regalar un ochavo a su hija y no le va a dejar un real en la herencia.

D Answers will vary.

RESOURCES

- CD-ROM, Discs 1, 2, 3, 4, pages 454–459

¡OJO! You can present this story to the entire class, or have students read it silently and do the **Después de leer** activities on their own.

El Quijote

TEACHING VOCABULARY

A. Have students open their books to page 454. Have them repeat the new vocabulary words after you.

B. Quickly go over the **Práctica** on page 455 orally to ascertain that the students can recognize the vocabulary for receptive purposes.

EL QUIJOTE

de Miguel de Cervantes Saavedra

Vocabulario

Class Project

Una representación You may have students work in groups and prepare a play entitled **Don Quijote y los molinos de viento**. This episode lends itself to some very funny skits. Students can present their play to the entire class, other Spanish classes, or to the Spanish Club.

un(a) vecino(a) una persona que vive cerca, en la misma calle, por ejemplo
sabio(a) inteligente, astuto(a)
espantoso horrible, terrible
a toda prisa muy rápido
de nuevo otra vez
socorrer ayudar, dar auxilio o ayuda
no les hizo caso no les prestó atención

A Don Quijote y Sancho Panza Contesten.

1. ¿Es don Quijote delgado o gordo?
2. ¿Quién es gordo?
3. ¿Quién es un caballero andante?
4. ¿Quién es su escudero?
5. ¿Quién tiene una lanza?
6. ¿Quién tiene un caballo?
7. Y Sancho Panza, ¿qué tiene él?
8. ¿Tiene aspas un molino de viento?

B ¿Cómo son? Describan a don Quijote y a Sancho Panza.

C ¿Cómo se dice? Expresen de otra manera.

1. Ellos viven en *una región rural.*
2. Fue una aventura *horrible.*
3. Él salió *rápido.*
4. No le *prestó atención* a su vecino.
5. Él es un señor *inteligente y astuto.*
6. Él lo hizo *otra vez.*
7. Trató pero no pudo *ayudar* a su vecino.

Literatura 4

Did You Know?

El Quijote It is claimed that after the Bible, ***El Quijote*** is the most widely read book in the world.

Práctica

B EXPANSION If any of your students are artistic, ask them to draw a picture of Don Quijote and/or Sancho Panza. Have them describe their picture either orally or in written form.

ANSWERS

Práctica

A
1. **Don Quijote es delgado.**
2. **Sancho Panza es gordo.**
3. **Don Quijote es un caballero andante.**
4. **Sancho Panza es su escudero.**
5. **Don Quijote tiene una lanza.**
6. **Don Quijote tiene un caballo.**
7. **Sancho Panza tiene un asno.**
8. **Sí, un molino de viento tiene aspas.**

B Answers will vary.

C
1. **el campo**
2. **espantoso**
3. **a toda prisa**
4. **hizo caso**
5. **sabio**
6. **de nuevo**
7. **socorrer**

Literatura 4

DISCUSSING LITERATURE

INTRODUCCIÓN

You may go over the **Introducción** with the class or you may decide to omit it and just have them read the story.

El Quijote

A. As you present this reading there are many opportunities to use gestures to assist students with comprehension. Some examples are:
Don Quijote los atacó. (Attack two chairs.)
Puso su lanza en el aspa. (Put a long ruler or pointer through the space in the back of a chair.)
Vino un viento fuerte. (Make a howling sound.)
El viento movió el aspa. (Move your hand in a circular motion.)

B. You may wish to have students take a few minutes to read each section silently before going over it orally in class.

C. Since this reading is rather long you may wish to go over only certain sections orally and just have students read the others silently.

D. Call on a more able student to give a synopsis of each section. This helps less able students understand the selection.

EL QUIJOTE
de Miguel de Cervantes Saavedra

INTRODUCCIÓN La obra más famosa de todas las letras hispanas es la novela *El ingenioso hidalgo don Quijote de la Mancha* de Miguel de Cervantes Saavedra.

Los dos personajes principales de la novela son don Quijote y Sancho Panza. Don Quijote, un hombre alto y delgado, es un caballero andante. Es un idealista que quiere conquistar todos los males[1] del mundo. Su escudero, Sancho Panza, es un hombre bajo y gordo. Él es un realista puro. Siempre trata de desviar[2] a don Quijote de sus ilusiones y aventuras.

[1]**males** *evils*
[2]**trata de desviar** *tries to dissuade*

El Quijote

1

Un día, don Quijote salió de su pueblo en la región de la Mancha. Un idealista sin par°, don Quijote salió en busca de aventuras para conquistar los males del mundo. Es el trabajo de un verdadero caballero andante. Pero después de unos pocos días, don Quijote volvió a casa porque hizo su primera expedición sin escudero. No hay caballero andante sin escudero—sobre todo un caballero andante de la categoría de don Quijote.

Cuando volvió a su pueblo, empezó a buscar un escudero. Por fin encontró a un vecino, Sancho Panza, un hombre bajo y gordo. Salió por segunda vez, esta vez acompañado de su escudero. Don Quijote montó a su caballo, Rocinante, y Sancho lo siguió° montado en su asno.

sin par *without equal*
siguió *followed*

2

Los dos hicieron muchas expediciones por la región de la Mancha. El idealista don Quijote hizo muchas cosas que no quiso hacer el realista Sancho Panza. Más de una vez Sancho le dijo: —Pero, don Quijote, noble caballero y fiel compañero. Vuestra merced° está loco. ¿Por qué no dejamos° con estas tonterías°? ¿Por qué no volvemos a casa? Yo quiero comer. Y quiero dormir en mi cama.

Don Quijote no les hizo mucho caso a los consejos° de Sancho. Uno de los episodios más famosos de nuestro estimado caballero es el episodio de los molinos de viento.

Vuestra Merced *Your Highness*
no dejamos con *put an end to*
tonterías *foolish things*
consejos *advice*

◆3◆

Del buen suceso que el valeroso don Quijote tuvo en la espantable y jamás imaginada aventura de los molinos de viento.

En esto descubrieron treinta o cuarenta molinos de viento que hay en aquel campo; y así como° don Quijote los vio, dijo a su escudero: —¡Sancho! ¡Mira! ¿Tú ves lo que veo yo?

así como *as soon as*

—No, Vuestra Merced. No veo nada.

—Amigo Sancho, ¿no ves allí unos treinta o más gigantes que vienen hacia nosotros a hacer batalla?

—¿Qué gigantes?

—Aquellos que allí ves, de los brazos largos.

—Don Quijote. No son gigantes. Son simples molinos de viento. Y lo que en ellos parecen° brazos son aspas.

parecen *appear to be*

—Bien parece, Sancho, que tú no sabes nada de aventuras. Ellos son gigantes. Y si tienes miedo...

—¡Don Quijote! ¿Adónde va Vuestra Merced?

Molinos de viento, La Mancha, España

4

¿Adónde fue don Quijote? Él fue a hacer batalla con los terribles gigantes. Gigantes como éstos no deben ni pueden existir en el mundo. En nombre de Dulcinea, la dama de sus pensamientos°, don Quijote los atacó. Puso su lanza en el aspa de uno de los molinos. En el mismo instante vino un viento fuerte. El viento movió el aspa. El viento la revolvió con tanta furia que hizo pedazos° de la lanza de don Quijote y levantó a don Quijote en el aire.

dama de sus pensamientos *lady of his dreams*

pedazos *pieces*

A toda prisa el pobre Sancho fue a socorrer a su caballero andante. Lo encontró° en el suelo muy mal herido°.

encontró *found*
herido *wounded*

—Don Quijote, no le dije a Vuestra Merced que no vio gigantes. Vio simples molinos de viento. No puedo comprender por qué los atacó.

—Sancho, tú no sabes lo que dices. Son cosas de guerra° que tú no comprendes. Tú sabes que tengo un enemigo. Mi enemigo es el horrible pero sabio monstruo Frestón. Te dije las cosas malas que él hace. Y ahora convirtió a los gigantes en molinos de viento.

guerra *war*

—Yo no sé lo que hizo vuestro enemigo, Frestón. Pero yo sé lo que le hizo el molino de viento.

Sancho levantó a don Quijote del suelo. Don Quijote subió de nuevo sobre Rocinante. Habló más de la pasada aventura pero Sancho no le hizo caso. Siguieron el camino hacia Puerto Lápice en busca de otras jamás imaginadas aventuras.

Plaza de España, Madrid

For the Younger Student

Don Quijote y los molinos de viento Some students may enjoy drawing Don Quijote attacking the windmills. Using their drawing, they can describe the episode in their own words, either orally or in writing.

Class Motivator

¡Vamos a cantar! After reading this passage, you may wish to play some songs from the show *Man of La Mancha*.

Después de leer

A Don Quijote y Sancho Panza Escojan.

1. Don Quijote es ____.
   a. un realista
   b. un idealista
   c. un escudero
2. Don Quijote salió de su pueblo ____.
   a. en busca de la Mancha
   b. en busca de un escudero
   c. en busca de aventuras
3. Don Quijote volvió a casa para ____.
   a. comenzar su primera expedición
   b. buscar un escudero
   c. ver a Dulcinea
4. Sancho Panza es ____.
   a. un caballero andante también
   b. un idealista sin par
   c. un vecino de don Quijote
5. Sancho Panza tiene ____.
   a. un asno
   b. un caballo
   c. una lanza

B ¿Sí o no? Digan que sí o que no.

1. Don Quijote y Sancho Panza hicieron sólo dos expediciones.
2. Sancho le dice a don Quijote que está loco.
3. Don Quijote siempre quiere volver a casa.
4. Un episodio famoso del Quijote es el episodio de los molinos de viento.

C Los molinos de viento Completen.

1. Don Quijote ve unos treinta o cuarenta ____.
2. Sancho no ve ____.
3. Según don Quijote, los ____ quieren hacer ____.
4. Según don Quijote, los ____ que ve tienen ____ largos.
5. Según Sancho, no son gigantes. Don Quijote ve unos ____ y no tienen brazos. Tienen ____.

D La batalla Contesten.

1. ¿Contra quiénes fue don Quijote a hacer batalla?
2. ¿En dónde puso su lanza?
3. ¿Qué hizo mover al aspa?
4. ¿Revolvió rápidamente el aspa?
5. ¿Adónde levantó a don Quijote?
6. ¿Dónde encontró Sancho a don Quijote?
7. ¿Quién convirtió a los gigantes en molinos de viento?
8. Cuando Sancho levantó a don Quijote del suelo, ¿volvieron a casa?
9. Después de este episodio, ¿admite don Quijote que los gigantes son molinos de viento?

Literatura 4

Después de leer

Note Each of the four **Después de leer** activities corresponds to a different section of the reading. **Después de leer A** corresponds to Section 1, **B** to Section 2, **C** to Section 3, and **D** to Section 4.

As you finish each section of the story you can go over the corresponding activity.

TECHNOLOGY OPTION

Students can listen to a recording of this story on the CD-ROM, Discs 1, 2, 3, 4, pages 456–458.

ANSWERS

Después de leer

A 1. b
2. c
3. b
4. c
5. a

B 1. No.
2. Sí.
3. No.
4. Sí.

C 1. gigantes
2. nada
3. gigantes, batalla
4. gigantes, brazos
5. molinos de viento, aspas

D 1. Don Quijote fue a hacer batalla con los terribles gigantes.
2. En el aspa de uno de los molinos.
3. Un viento fuerte hizo mover al aspa.
4. Sí, el aspa revolvió rápidamente.
5. Levantó a don Quijote en el aire.
6. Sancho encontró a don Quijote en el suelo.
7. El sabio monstruo Frestón.
8. No, no volvieron a casa.
9. No, don Quijote no admite que los gigantes son molinos de viento.

Apéndices

cuatrocientos sesenta y uno 461

El mundo hispánico

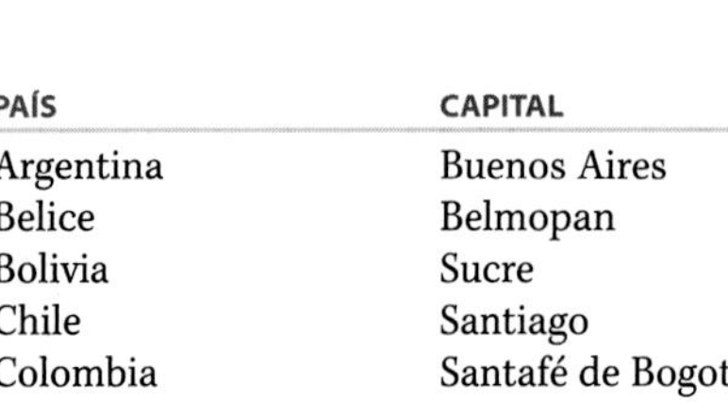

PAÍS	CAPITAL
Argentina	Buenos Aires
Belice	Belmopan
Bolivia	Sucre
Chile	Santiago
Colombia	Santafé de Bogotá
Costa Rica	San José
Cuba	La Habana
Ecuador	Quito
El Salvador	San Salvador
España	Madrid
Guatemala	Guatemala
Honduras	Tegucigalpa
México	México
Nicaragua	Managua
Panamá	Panamá
Paraguay	Asunción
Perú	Lima
Puerto Rico	San Juan
República Dominicana	Santo Domingo
Uruguay	Montivideo
Venezuela	Caracas

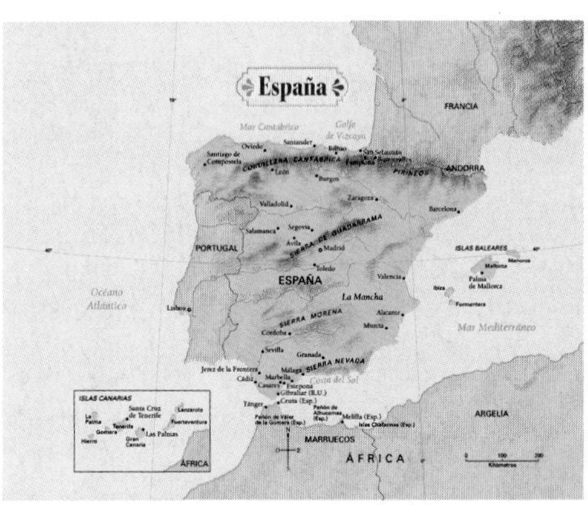

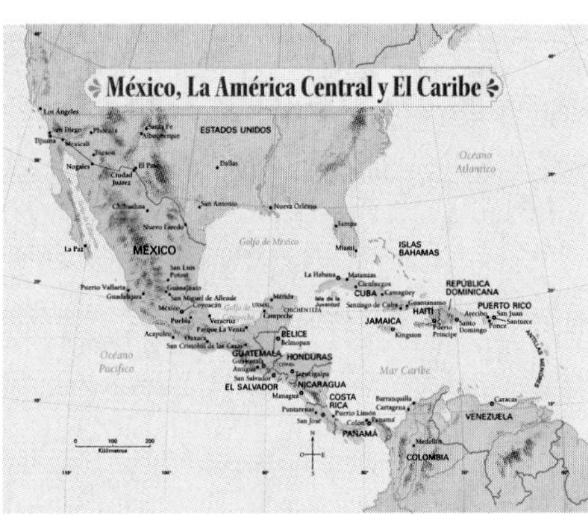

España
FRANCIA
Mar Cantábrico
Golfo de Vizcaya
Santiago de Compostela
Oviedo
Santander
Bilbao
San Sebastián
Pamplona
Roncevalles
CORDILLERA CANTÁBRICA
PIRINEOS
ANDORRA
León
Burgos
Zaragoza
Ebro
Barcelona
Valladolid
Río Duero
Salamanca
Segovia
SIERRA DE GUADARRAMA
Ávila
Madrid
PORTUGAL
ISLAS BALEARES
Menorca
Mallorca
Palma de Mallorca
Ibiza
Formentera
Tajo
Toledo
Río
ESPAÑA
Guadiana
Valencia
Océano Atlántico
Lisboa
Río
La Mancha
Alicante
SIERRA MORENA
Murcia
Mar Mediterráneo
Córdoba
Guadalquivir
Río
Sevilla
Granada
SIERRA NEVADA
Jerez de la Frontera
Málaga
Cádiz
Marbella
Casares
Estepona
Costa del Sol
Gibraltar (R.U.)
Tánger
Ceuta (Esp.)
Peñón de Alhucemas (Esp.)
Melilla (Esp.)
Peñón de Vélez de la Gomera (Esp.)
Islas Chafarinas (Esp.)
ARGELIA
MARRUECOS
ÁFRICA
N
O
E
S
10°
0°
40°
0 100 200
Kilómetros
ISLAS CANARIAS
La Palma
Hierro
Gomera
Tenerife
Santa Cruz de Tenerife
Gran Canaria
Las Palmas
Lanzarote
Fuerteventura
ÁFRICA

La América del Sur
Mar Caribe
Océano Atlántico
Océano Pacífico
Maracaibo
Caracas
VENEZUELA
GUYANA
Georgetown
SURINAM
Paramaribo
Cayena
GUAYANA FRANCESA
Medellín
Santafé de Bogotá
Cali
COLOMBIA
Islas Galápagos (Ecuador)
Otavalo
Quito
Volcán Cotopaxi
ECUADOR
Guayaquil
Cuenca
Iquitos
Río Amazonas
CORDILLERA DE LOS ANDES
PERÚ
Lima
Miraflores
MACHU PICCHU
Cuzco
BRASIL
Brasilia
BOLIVIA
La Paz
Sucre
ATACAMA DESERT
PARAGUAY
Asunción
São Paulo
Río de Janeiro
Vicuña
Córdoba
Rosario
URUGUAY
Valparaíso
Santiago
Buenos Aires
Montevideo
ARGENTINA
Mar del Plata
CHILE
Puerto Montt
Bariloche
PATAGONIA
Islas Malvinas (R.U.)
Punta Arenas
0 500 1000 Kilómetros
N O E S
464 cuatrocientos sesenta y dos
EL MUNDO HISPÁNICO

México, La América Central y El Caribe

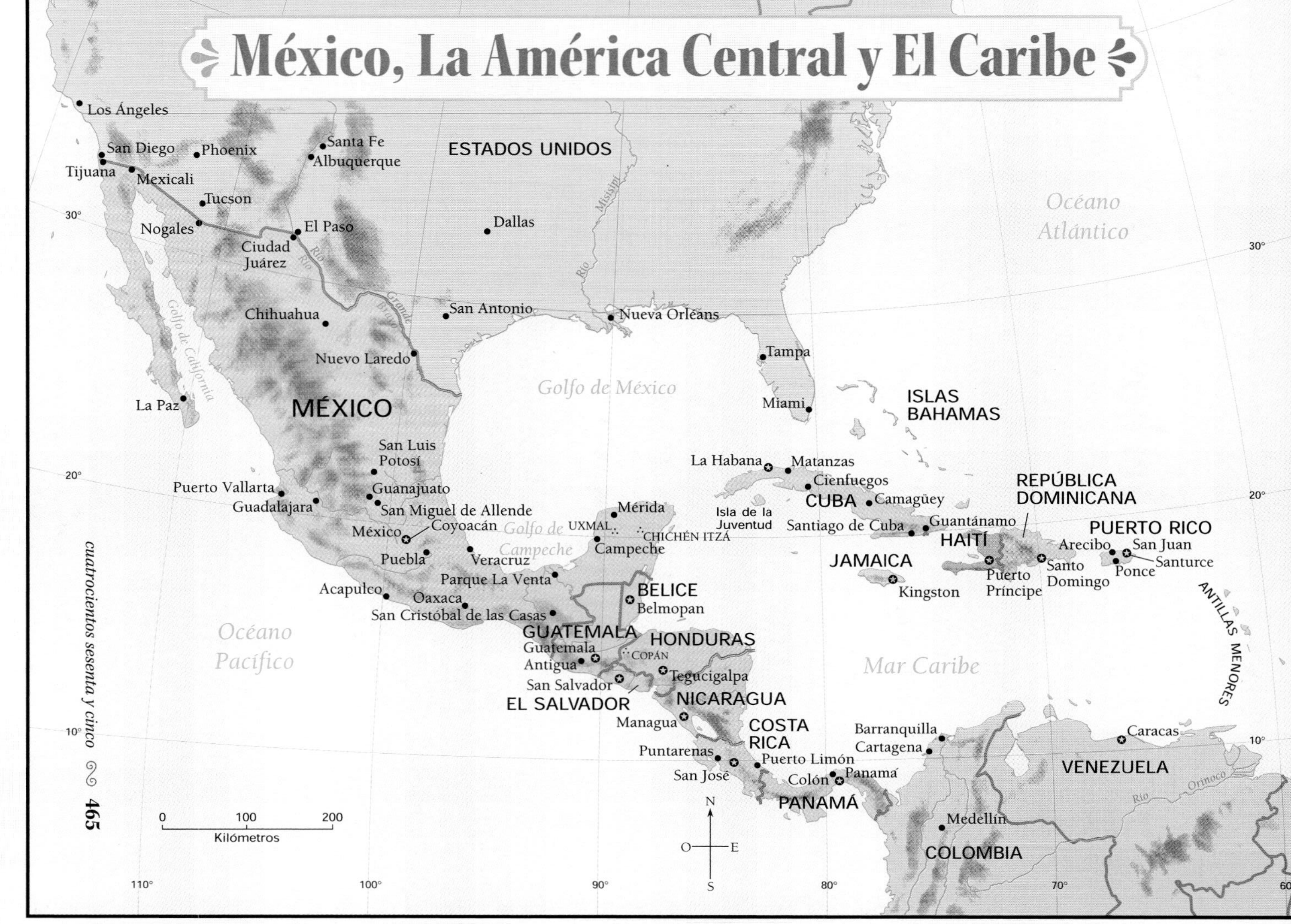

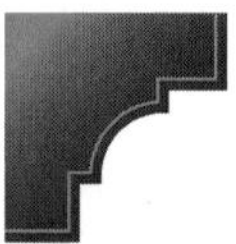

Verbos

Verbos regulares			
INFINITIVO	**hablar** *to speak*	**comer** *to eat*	**vivir** *to live*
PRESENTE PROGRESIVO	estar hablando	estar comiendo	estar viviendo
PRESENTE	yo hablo tú hablas él, ella, Ud. habla nosotros(as) hablamos *vosotros(as) habláis* ellos, ellas, Uds. hablan	yo como tú comes él, ella, Ud. come nosotros(as) comemos *vosotros(as) coméis* ellos, ellas, Uds. comen	yo vivo tú vives él, ella, Ud. vive nosotros(as) vivimos *vosotros(as) vivís* ellos, ellas, Uds. viven
PRETÉRITO	yo hablé tú hablaste él, ella, Ud. habló nosotros(as) hablamos *vosotros(as) hablasteis* ellos, ellas, Uds. hablaron	yo comí tú comiste él, ella, Ud. comió nosotros(as) comimos *vosotros(as) comisteis* ellos, ellas, Uds. comieron	yo viví tú viviste él, ella, Ud. vivió nosotros(as) vivimos *vosotros(as) vivisteis* ellos, ellas, Uds. vivieron

Verbos regulares con cambio en la primera persona singular *(Regular verbs with stem change in the first person singular)*			
INFINITIVO	**conocer** *to know*	**salir** *to leave*	**ver** *to see*
PRESENTE PROGRESIVO	estar conociendo	estar saliendo	estar viendo
PRESENTE	yo conozco	yo salgo	yo veo

Verbos con cambio radical
(Stem-changing verbs)

INFINITIVO	**preferir**[1] **(e>ie)** *to prefer*	**volver**[2] **(o>ue)** *to return*	**pedir**[3] **(e>i)** *to ask for*
PRESENTE PROGRESIVO	estar prefiriendo	estar volviendo	estar pidiendo
PRESENTE	yo prefiero tú prefieres él, ella, Ud. prefiere nosotros(as) preferimos *vosotros(as) preferís* ellos, ellas, Uds. prefieren	yo vuelvo tú vuelves él, ella, Ud. vuelve nosotros(as) volvemos *vosotros(as) volvéis* ellos, ellas, Uds. vuelven	yo pido tú pides él, ella, Ud. pide nosotros(as) pedimos *vosotros(as) pedís* ellos, ellas, Uds. piden
PRETÉRITO	yo preferí tú preferiste él, ella, Ud. prefirió nosotros(as) preferimos *vosotros(as) preferisteis* ellos, ellas, Uds. prefirieron	yo volví tú volviste él, ella, Ud. volvió nosotros(as) volvimos *vosotros(as) volvisteis* ellos, ellas, Uds. volvieron	yo pedí tú pediste él, ella, Ud. pidió nosotros(as) pedimos *vosotros(as) pedisteis* ellos, ellas, Uds. pidieron

[1] Verbos similares: *sugerir*
[2] Verbos similares: *morir, jugar*
[3] Verbos similares: *freír, repetir, seguir, servir*

Verbos irregulares

INFINITIVO	**andar** *to walk*	**dar** *to give*	**decir** *to tell, to say*
PRESENTE PROGRESIVO	estar andando	estar dando	estar diciendo
PRESENTE	yo ando tú andas él, ella, Ud. anda nosotros(as) andamos *vosotros(as) andáis* ellos, ellas, Uds. andan	yo doy tú das él, ella, Ud. da nosotros(as) damos *vosotros(as) dais* ellos, ellas, Uds. dan	yo digo tú dices él, ella, Ud. dice nosotros(as) decimos *vosotros(as) decís* ellos, ellas, Uds. dicen
PRETÉRITO	yo anduve tú anduviste él, ella, Ud. anduvo nosotros(as) anduvimos *vosotros(as) anduvisteis* ellos, ellas, Uds. anduvieron	yo di tú diste él, ella, Ud. dio nosotros(as) dimos *vosotros(as) disteis* ellos, ellas, Uds. dieron	yo dije tú dijiste él, ella, Ud. dijo nosotros(as) dijimos *vosotros(as) dijisteis* ellos, ellas, Uds. dijeron

Verbos irregulares

INFINITIVO	**empezar** *to begin*	**estar** *to be*	**hacer** *to do*
PRESENTE PROGRESIVO	estar empezando		estar haciendo
PRESENTE	yo empiezo tú empiezas él, ella, Ud. empieza nosotros(as) empezamos *vosotros(as) empezáis* ellos, ellas, Uds. empiezan	yo estoy tú estás él, ella, Ud. está nosotros(as) estamos *vosotros(as) estáis* ellos, ellas, Uds. están	yo hago tú haces él, ella, Ud. hace nosotros(as) hacemos *vosotros(as) hacéis* ellos, ellas, Uds. hacen
PRETÉRITO	yo empecé tú empezaste él, ella, Ud. empezó nosotros(as) empezamos *vosotros(as) empezasteis* ellos, ellas, Uds. empezaron	yo estuve tú estuviste él, ella, Ud. estuvo nosotros(as) estuvimos *vosotros(as) estuvisteis* ellos, ellas, Uds. estuvieron	yo hice tú hiciste él, ella, Ud. hizo nosotros(as) hicimos *vosotros(as) hicisteis* ellos, ellas, Uds. hicieron
INFINITIVO	**ir** *to go*	**poder** *to be able*	**poner** *to put*
PRESENTE PROGRESIVO	estar yendo	estar pudiendo	estar poniendo
PRESENTE	yo voy tú vas él, ella, Ud. va nosotros(as) vamos *vosotros(as) vais* ellos, ellas, Uds. van	yo puedo tú puedes él, ella, Ud. puede nosotros(as) podemos *vosotros(as) podéis* ellos, ellas, Uds. pueden	yo pongo tú pones él, ella, Ud. pone nosotros(as) ponemos *vosotros(as) ponéis* ellos, ellas, Uds. ponen
PRETÉRITO	yo fui tú fuiste él, ella, Ud. fue nosotros(as) fuimos *vosotros(as) fuisteis* ellos, ellas, Uds. fueron	yo pude tú pudiste él, ella, Ud. pudo nosotros(as) pudimos *vosotros(as) pudisteis* ellos, ellas, Uds. pudieron	yo puse tú pusiste él, ella, Ud. puso nosotros(as) pusimos *vosotros(as) pusisteis* ellos, ellas, Uds. pusieron

Verbos irregulares

INFINITIVO	**querer** *to want*	**saber** *to know*	**ser** *to be*
PRESENTE PROGRESIVO	estar queriendo	estar sabiendo	estar siendo
PRESENTE	yo quiero tú quieres él, ella, Ud. quiere nosotros(as) queremos *vosotros(as) queréis* ellos, ellas, Uds. quieren	yo sé tú sabes él, ella, Ud. sabe nosotros(as) sabemos *vosotros(as) sabéis* ellos, ellas, Uds. saben	yo soy tú eres él, ella, Ud. es nosotros(as) somos *vosotros(as) sois* ellos, ellas, Uds. son
PRETÉRITO	yo quise tú quisiste él, ella, Ud. quiso nosotros(as) quisimos *vosotros(as) quisisteis* ellos, ellas, Uds. quisieron	yo supe tú supiste él, ella, Ud. supo nosotros(as) supimos *vosotros(as) supisteis* ellos, ellas, Uds. supieron	yo fui tú fuiste él, ella, Ud. fue nosotros(as) fuimos *vosotros(as) fuisteis* ellos, ellas, Uds. fueron
INFINITIVO	**tener** *to have*	**traer** *to bring*	**venir** *to come*
PRESENTE PROGRESIVO	estar teniendo	estar trayendo	estar viniendo
PRESENTE	yo tengo tú tienes él, ella, Ud. tiene nosotros(as) tenemos *vosotros(as) tenéis* ellos, ellas, Uds. tienen	yo traigo tú traes él, ella, Ud. trae nosotros(as) traemos *vosotros(as) traéis* ellos, ellas, Uds. traen	yo vengo tú vienes él, ella, Ud. viene nosotros(as) venimos *vosotros(as) venís* ellos, ellas, Uds. vienen
PRETÉRITO	yo tuve tú tuviste él, ella, Ud. tuvo nosotros(as) tuvimos *vosotros(as) tuvisteis* ellos, ellas, Uds. tuvieron	yo traje tú trajiste él, ella, Ud. trajo nosotros(as) trajimos *vosotros(as) trajisteis* ellos, ellas, Uds. trajeron	yo vine tú viniste él, ella, Ud. vino nosotros(as) vinimos *vosotros(as) vinisteis* ellos, ellas, Uds. vinieron

Verbos reflexivos

INFINITIVO	**lavarse** *to wash oneself*		
PRESENTE PROGRESIVO	estar lavándose		
PRESENTE	yo me lavo tú te lavas él, ella, Ud. se lava nosotros(as) nos lavamos *vosotros(as) os laváis* ellos, ellas, Uds. se lavan		
PRETÉRITO	yo me lavé tú te lavaste él, ella, Ud. se lavó nosotros(as) nos lavamos *vosotros(as) os lavasteis* ellos, ellas, Uds. se lavaron		

Verbos reflexivos con cambio radical

INFINITIVO	**acostarse (o>ue)** *to go to bed*	**despertarse (e>ie)** *to wake up*	**dormirse (o>ue, u)** *to fall asleep*
PRESENTE PROGRESIVO	estar acostándose	estar despertándose	estar durmiéndose
PRESENTE	yo me acuesto tú te acuestas él, ella, Ud. se acuesta nosotros(as) nos acostamos *vosotros(as) os acostáis* ellos, ellas, Uds. se acuestan	yo me despierto tú te despiertas él, ella, Ud. se despierta nosotros(as) nos despertamos *vosotros(as) os despertáis* ellos, ellas, Uds. se despiertan	yo me duermo tú te duermes él, ella, Ud. se duerme nosotros(as) nos dormimos *vosotros(as) os dormís* ellos, ellas, Uds. se duermen
PRETÉRITO	yo me acosté tú te acostaste él, ella, Ud. se acostó nosotros(as) nos acostamos *vosotros(as) os acostasteis* ellos, ellas, Uds. se acostaron	yo me desperté tú te despertaste él, ella, Ud. se despertó nosotros(as) nos despertamos *vosotros(as) os despertasteis* ellos, ellas, Uds. se despertaron	yo me dormí tú te dormiste él, ella, Ud. se durmió nosotros(as) nos dormimos *vosotros(as) os dormisteis* ellos, ellas, Uds. se durmieron
INFINITIVO	**divertirse (e>ie, i)** *to enjoy oneself*	**sentarse** *to sit down*	**vestirse (e>i, i)** *to dress oneself*
PRESENTE PROGRESIVO	estar divirtiéndose	estar sentándose	estar vistiéndose
PRESENTE	yo me divierto tú te diviertes él, ella, Ud. se divierte nosotros(as) nos divertimos *vosotros(as) os divertís* ellos, ellas, Uds. se divierten	yo me siento tú te sientas él, ella, Ud. se sienta nosotros(as) nos sentamos *vosotros(as) os sentáis* ellos, ellas, Uds. se sientan	yo me visto tú te vistes él, ella, Ud. se viste nosotros(as) nos vestimos *vosotros(as) os vestís* ellos, ellas, Uds. se visten
PRETÉRITO	yo me divertí tú te divertiste él, ella, Ud. se divirtió nosotros(as) nos divertimos *vosotros(as) os divertisteis* ellos, ellas, Uds. se divirtieron	yo me senté tú te sentaste él, ella, Ud. se sentó nosotros(as) nos sentamos *vosotros(as) os sentasteis* ellos, ellas, Uds. se sentaron	yo me vestí tú te vestiste él, ella, Ud. se vistió nosotros(as) nos vestimos *vosotros(as) os vestistéis* ellos, ellas, Uds. se vistieron

Vocabulario español–inglés

The **Vocabulario español–inglés** contains all productive and receptive vocabulary from the text. The reference numbers following each productive entry indicate the chapter and vocabulary section in which the word is introduced. For example, **3.2** means that the word was taught in **Capítulo 3, Palabras 2. BV** refers to the preliminary **Bienvenidos** lessons. Words without a chapter reference indicate receptive vocabulary (not taught in the **Palabras** sections).

A

a at; to
  a bordo de aboard, on board, **11.2**
  a eso de at about (time), **4.1**
  a fines de at the end of
  a la española Spanish style
  a pie on foot, **4.1**
  a plazos in installments
  a solas alone
  a tiempo on time, **11.1**
  a veces sometimes, **7.1**
  a ver let's see
abordar to get on, board
abril April, **BV**
abrir to open, **8.2**
abstracto(a) abstract
la **abuela** grandmother, **6.1**
el **abuelo** grandfather, **6.1**
los **abuelos** grandparents, **6.1**
abundante plentiful
aburrido(a) boring, **2.1**
aburrir to bore
la **academia** academy, school
acariciar to caress
el **acceso** access
el **aceite** oil, **14.2**
aceptar to accept
el **acompañamiento** accompaniment
acompañar to accompany
acordarse (ue) to remember
acostarse (ue) to go to bed, **12.1**
el **acrílico** acrylic
la **actividad** activity
activo(a) active
el **actor** actor, **10.2**
la **actriz** actress, **10.2**
la **acuarela** watercolor
acuático(a): el esquí acuático water-skiing, **9.1**
acuerdo: de acuerdo OK, all right
adaptar to adapt
además moreover; besides
¡Adiós! Good-bye! **BV**
adivinar to guess
admirar to admire
admitir to admit
el/la **adolescente** adolescent, teenager
la **adolescencia** adolescence
¿adónde? where?, **1.1**
adorable adorable
adorar to adore
adornar to adorn
la **aduana** customs, **11.2**
aérea: la línea aérea airlines
el **aeropuerto** airport, **11.1**
afeitarse to shave, **12.1**
  la crema de afeitar shaving cream, **12.1**
aficionado(a) a fond of, **10.1**
el/la **aficionado(a)** fan (sports)
africano(a) African
afroamericano(a) African-American
afortunadamente fortunately
el/la **agente** agent, **11.1**
  el/la agente de aduana customs agent, **11.2**
agosto August, **BV**
agradable pleasant
el **agua** *(f.)* water, **9.1**
  el agua mineral mineral water, **12.2**
  esquiar en el agua to water-ski, **9.1**
el **agujero** hole
ahora now, **4.2**
el **aire** air
  al aire libre outdoor *(adj.)*
el **ají** chili pepper
el **ajo** garlic, **14.2**
el **ajuar de novia** trousseau
ajustar to adjust
al to the
  al aire libre outdoor *(adj.)*
  al contrario on the contrary
  al principio at the beginning
alarmarse to be alarmed
la **alberca** swimming pool, **9.1**
el **albergue para jóvenes (juvenil)** youth hostel, **12.2**
el **álbum** album
la **alcachofa** artichoke, **14.2**
el **alcohol** alcohol
alegre happy
el **alemán** German, **2.2**
la **alergia** allergy, **8.2**
el **álgebra** algebra, **2.2**
algo something, **5.2**

¿Algo más? Anything else?, **5.2**
algunos(as) some, **4.1**
el **alimento** food, **14.2**
allí there
almacenar to store
la **almeja** clam, **14.2**
el **almuerzo** lunch, **5.2**
tomar el almuerzo to have, eat lunch
la **alpargata** sandal
alquilar to rent
alrededor de around, **6.2**
los **alrededores** outskirts
altivo arrogant, haughty
alto(a) tall, **1.1**; high, **4.2**
en voz alta aloud
la nota alta high grade, **4.2**
la **altura** height
el/la **alumno(a)** student, **1.1**
amarillo(a) yellow, **3.2**
amazónico(a) Amazonian
ambicioso(a) hardworking, **1.1**
ambulante itinerant
la **América Central** Central America
la **América del Norte** North America
la **América del Sur** South America
americano(a) American, **1.1**
el/la **amigo(a)** friend, **1.1**
el **análisis** analysis
analítico(a) analytical
analizar to analyze
anaranjado(a) orange, **3.2**
anciano(a) old, **6.1**
el/la **anciano(a)** old person
andaluz(a) Andalusian
andante: el caballero andante knight errant
andar to walk, to go to
el **andén** railway platform, **13.1**
andino(a) Andean
la **anécdota** anecdote
el **animal** animal
anoche last night, **9.2**
el **anorak** parka, **9.2**
la **Antártida** Antarctic
anteayer the day before yesterday
los **anteojos de sol** sunglasses, **9.1**
antes de before, **5.1**
el **antibiótico** antibiotic, **8.2**
la **antigüedad** antiquity
antiguo(a) old, ancient
anunciar to announce
el **anuncio** announcement
el **año** year, **BV**
cumplir... años to be . . . years old
el año pasado last year, **9.2**
este año this year, **9.2**
tener... años to be . . . years old, **6.1**
el **apartamento** apartment, **6.2**
la casa de apartamentos apartment house, **6.2**
apasionado(a) passionate
la **apertura: la apertura de clases** beginning of the school year
aplaudir to applaud, **10.2**
el **aplauso** applause, **10.2**
recibir aplausos to receive applause, **10.2**
aplicar to apply
el **apóstol** apostle
aprender to learn, **5.1**
el **apunte: tomar apuntes** to take notes, **4.2**
aquel that
en aquel entonces at that time
aquí here
Aquí tiene (tienes, tienen)... Here is (are) . . .
por aquí right this way
aragonés(a) from Aragon (Spain)
el **árbol** tree
el **arco** arc
el **área** *(f.)* area
la **arena** sand, **9.1**
argentino(a) Argentinian, **2.1**
el **argumento** plot
la **aritmética** arithmetic, **2.2**
el **arma** *(f.)* weapon
la **arqueología** archeology
arqueológico(a) archeological
el/la **arqueólogo(a)** archeologist
arrancar to pull out
arrogante arrogant
el **arroyo** stream, brook
el **arroz** rice, **5.2**
el **arsenal** arsenal
el **arte** *(f.)* art, **2.2**
las bellas artes fine arts
el **artefacto** artifact
el/la **artista** artist, **10.2**
artístico(a) artistic
la **ascendencia** background
el ascensor elevator, **6.2**
así so, **12**
el **asiento** seat, **11.1**
el número del asiento seat number, **11.1**
la **asignatura** subject, discipline, **2.1**
el/la **asistente de vuelo** flight attendant, **11.2**
asistir to attend
el **asno** donkey
el **aspa** *(f.)* sail (of a windmill)
la **aspirina** aspirin, **8.2**
astuto(a) astute
atacar to attack
el **ataque** attack
la **atención: prestar atención** to pay attention, **4.2**
aterrizar to land, **11.2**
atlético(a) athletic
la **atmósfera** atmosphere
atrapar to catch, **7.2**
atrás behind, in the rear
atravesar (ie) to cross
el **atún** tuna, **5.2**
aún even
austral former Argentine unit of currency
auténtico(a) authentic
el **autobús** bus, **10.1**
perder el autobús (la guagua, el camión) to miss the bus, **10.1**
el/la **autor(a)** author, **10.2**
el **autoretrato** self-portrait
el **ave** *(f.)* bird
la **aventura** adventure
la **aviación** aviation
el **avión** airplane, **11.1**
la **avioneta** small airplane
ayer yesterday, **9.2**
ayer por la mañana yesterday morning, **9.2**

ayer por la tarde yesterday afternoon, 9.2
ayudar to help, 13.1
azul blue, 3.2

B
el bachillerato bachelor's degree
la bacteria bacteria
la bahía bay
bailar to dance, 4.2
el baile dance
bajar to lower; to go down, 9.2; to get off, 13.2
bajar(se) del tren to get off the train, 13.2
bajo: bajo cero below zero, 9.2
bajo(a) short, 1.1; low, 4.2
la planta baja ground floor, 6.2
la nota baja low grade, 4.2
el balneario beach resort, 9.1
el balón ball, 7.1
tirar el balón to throw (kick) the ball, 7.2
el baloncesto basketball, 7.2
la banana banana
la banda music band
el bando team
el bañador bathing suit 9.1
bañarse to take a bath, 12.1
el baño bathroom, 6.2; bath
el cuarto de baño bathroom, 6.2
el traje de baño bathing suit, 9.1
barato(a) cheap, inexpensive, 3.2
la barra: la barra de jabón bar of soap, 12.2
basado(a) based (on)
basar to base
basarse to be based
la báscula scales, 11.1
la base base, 7.2; basis
básico(a) basic
el básquetbol basketball, 7.2
la cancha de básquetbol basketball court. 7.2
bastante enough, rather, quite, 1.1
el bastón ski pole, 9.2
la batalla battle
el bate bat, 7.2
el/la bateador(a) batter, 7.2
batear to hit (sports), 7.2
el batú Taíno Indian game
el bautizo baptism
el/la bebé baby
beber to drink, 5.1
la bebida beverage, drink
el béisbol baseball, 7.2
el campo de béisbol baseball field, 7.2
el juego de béisbol baseball game, 7.2
el/la jugador(a) de béisbol baseball player, 7.2
el/la beisbolista baseball player
bello(a) beautiful, pretty, 1.1
las bellas artes fine arts
la berenjena eggplant, 14.2
la bicicleta bicycle
ir en bicicleta to go by bike, 12.2
bien fine, well, BV
muy bien very well, BV
la bienvenida: dar la bienvenida to welcome, 11.2
el biftec steak, 14.2
bilingüe bilingual
el billete ticket, 11.1
el billete sencillo one-way ticket, 13.1
el billete de ida y vuelta round-trip ticket, 13.1
la biografía biography
la biología biology, 2.2
biológico(a) biological
el/la biólogo(a) biologist
blanco(a) white, 3.2
el bloc writing pad, 3.1
bloquear to stop, block, 7.1
el blue jean jeans, 3.2
la blusa blouse, 3.2
la boca mouth, 8.2
el bocadillo sandwich, 5.1
la boletería ticket window, 9.2
el boleto ticket, 9.2
el bolígrafo ballpoint pen, 3.1
la bolsa bag, 5.2; pocketbook, 13.1
el bolsillo pocket
bonito(a) pretty, 1.1
la bota boot, 9.2
el bote can, 5.2
la botella: la botella de agua mineral bottle of mineral water, 12.2
el brazo arm, 7.1
breve brief
brillante bright
brillar to shine, 9.1
el bronce bronze, 10.2
bronceado(a) tan
bronceador(a): la loción bronceadora suntan lotion, 9.1
bucear to dive; to swim underwater, 9.1
el buceo diving, underwater swimming, 9.1
buen good
estar de buen humor to be in a good mood, 8.1
Hace buen tiempo. The weather is nice., 9.1
bueno(a) good, 1.2
Buenas noches. Good evening., BV
Buenas tardes. Good afternoon., BV
Buenos días. Hello, Good morning., BV
sacar una nota buena to get a good grade, 4.2
el bus bus, 4.1
el bus escolar school bus, 4.1
busca: en busca de in search of
buscar to look for, 3.1
la butaca seat (theater), 10.1

C
el caballero knight
el caballero andante knight errant
el caballete easel
la cabeza head, 7.1
el cacahuete (cacahuate) peanut
cada each, every, 1.2
la cadena chain (necklace)
el café coffee, BV; café, 5.1
el café al aire libre outdoor café
el café con leche coffee with milk, 5.1

el café solo black coffee, **5.1**
la **cafetería** cafeteria
la **caja** cash register, **3.1**
los **calcetines** socks, **3.2**
la **calculadora** calculator, **3.1**
calcular to calculate
el **cálculo** calculus, **2.2**
el **calle** street, **6.2**
el **calor: Hace calor.** It's hot., **9.1**
la **caloría** calorie
calzar to take, wear (shoe size), **3.2**
la **cama** bed, **8.1**
guardar la cama to stay in bed, **8.1**
hacer la cama to make the bed
el/la **camarero(a)** waiter, waitress, **5.1**
el **camarón** shrimp, **14.2**
cambiar to change; exchange
cambiar de tren to change trains (transfer), **13.2**
caminar to walk
la **caminata: dar una caminata** to take a hike, **12.2**
el **camino** trail, path
el **camión** bus (Mex.), **10.1**
la **camisa** shirt, **3.2**
la **camiseta** T-shirt, undershirt, **3.2**
la **campaña** campaign
el/la **campeón(a)** champion
el **campeonato** championship
el **campo** country; field
el campo de béisbol baseball field, **7.2**
el campo de fútbol soccer field, **7.1**
la casa de campo country home
el **canal** channel (TV)
la **canasta** basket, **7.2**
el **canasto** basket, **7.2**
la **cancha** court, **7.2**
la cancha cubierta enclosed court, **9.1**
la cancha de básquetbol basketball court, **7.2**
la cancha de tenis tennis court, **9.1**
la **canción** song
cansado(a) tired, **8.1**
cantar to sing, **4.2**
el **cante jondo** traditional flamenco singing
la **cantidad** amount
el **canto** singing
el **cañón** canyon
la **capital** capital
el/la **capitán** captain
el **capítulo** chapter
la **cara** face, **12.1**
el **carbohidrato** carbohydrate
cardinal: los punto cardinales cardinal points
el **cardo** thistle
el **Caribe** Caribbean
el mar Caribe Caribbean Sea
la **carne** meat, **5.2**
la carne de res beef, **14.2**
caro(a) expensive, **3.2**
la **carpeta** folder, **3.1**
el **carro** car, **4.1**
en carro by car, **4.1**
la **carta** letter, **6.2**
la **casa** home, house, **6.2**
la casa de apartamentos (departamentos) apartment house, **6.2**
la casa de campo country home
la casa privada (particular) private house, **6.2**
en casa at home
casado(a): estar casado(a) to be married
el **casete** cassette, **4.2**
casi almost, practically
el **caso** case
el **catarro** cold (illness), **8.1**
tener catarro to have a cold, **8.1**
el/la **cátcher** catcher, **7.2**
la **catedral** cathedral
la **categoría** category
católico(a) Catholic
catorce fourteen, **BV**
la **celebración** celebration
celebrar to celebrate
célebre famous
la **célula** cell
celular cellular
la **cena** dinner, **5.2**
cenar to have dinner
el **centavo** penny
central central
el **centro** center
cepillarse to brush one's hair, **12.1**
cepillarse los dientes to brush one's teeth, **12.1**
el **cepillo** brush, **12.2**
el cepillo de dientes toothbrush, **12.2**
cerca de near, **6.2**
el **cerdo** pig (pork), **14.2**
el **cereal** cereal, **5.2**
cero zero, **BV**
la **cesta** basket (jai alai)
el **cesto** basket, **7.2**
el **chaleco** vest
el **chalet** chalet
el **champú** shampoo, **12.2**
¡Chao! Good-bye!, **BV**
la **chaqueta** jacket, **3.2**
la **chaucha** string beans
el **cheque de viajero** traveler's check
chileno(a) Chilean
la **chimenea** chimney
la **china** orange (fruit)
el **chisme** piece of gossip
¡chist! shh!
el **choclo** corn
el **chocolate: de chocolate** chocolate *(adj.)*, **5.1**
el **churro** (type of) doughnut
el **cielo** sky, **9.1**
las **ciencias** science, **2.2**
las ciencias naturales natural sciences
las ciencias sociales social sciences, **2.2**
el/la **científico(a)** scientist
científico(a) scientific
cien(to) one hundred, **3.2**
cinco five, **BV**
el **cine** movie theater, **10.1**
cincuenta fifty, **2.2**
el **círculo** circle
la **ciudad** city
el **clarinete** clarinet
¡claro! certainly!, of course!
la **clase** class (school) **2.1;** class (ticket). **13.1**

la apertura de clases beginning of the school year
la sala de clase classroom, **4.1**
el salón de clase classroom, **4.1**
primera clase first-class, **13.1**
segunda clase second-class, **13.1**
clásico(a) classic
clasificar to classify
el/la **cliente** customer, **5.1**
el **clima** climate
climático(a) climatic
la **clínica** clinic
el **club** club, **4.2**
el Club de español Spanish Club, **4.2**
el **coche** car, **4.1;** train car, **13.2**
en coche by car, **4.1**
el **coche-cafetería** cafeteria (dining) car, **13.2**
el **coche-cama** sleeping car, **13.2**
el **coche-comedor** dining car, **13.2**
la **cocina** kitchen, **6.2**
el/la **cocinero(a)** cook, **14.1**
la **coincidencia** coincidence
la **cola** line (queue), **10.1**
hacer cola to stand in line, **10.1**
la **colección** collection
el **colector** collector
el **colegio** school, **1.1**
el **colesterol** cholesterol
colgar (ue) to hang
colocar to put, place
colombiano(a) Colombian, **1.1**
la **colonia** suburb, colony
el **color** color, **3.2**
¿De qué color es? What color is it?, **3.2**
de color marrón brown, **3.2**
el/la **comandante** captain, **11.2**
el **comedor** dining room, **6.2**
comenzar (ie) to begin
comer to eat, **5.1**
el **comestible** food, **14.2**
cómico(a) funny, **1.1**
la **comida** food, meal, **5.2**
como like; as; since, **1.2**
¿cómo? how?, what?, **1.1**
¿Cómo está... ? How is. . . ?, **8.1**
¡Cómo no! Of course!
el **comodidad** comfort
compacto(a): el disco compacto compact disk, CD, **4.2**
el/la **compañero(a)** friend, **1.2**
la **compañía** company
la **comparación** comparison
comparar to compare
la **competencia** competition
la **competición** competition, contest
competir (i, i) to compete
completo(a) full (train), **13.2**
la **composición** composition
la **compra: ir de compras** to go shopping, to shop, **5.2**
comprar to buy, **3.1**
comprender to understand, **5.1**
la **computadora** computer
con with
con mucha plata rich
¿con quién? with whom?
con retraso with a delay, **13.2**
con una demora with a delay, **11.1**
el **conde** count
el **concierto** concert
la **condición** condition
el **condimento** seasoning
el **condominio** condominium
conectar to connect
la **conferencia** lecture
Conforme. Agreed, Fine., **14.2**
congelado(a): los productos congelados frozen food, **5.2**
el **conjunto** set, collection
conocer to know, to be familiar with, **11.1**
la **conquista** conquest
conquistar to conquer
consentir (ie, i) to allow, tolerate
conservar to save
considerar to consider
consistir (en) to consist of
la **consulta: la consulta del médico** doctor's office, **8.2**
consultar to consult, **13.1**
el **consultorio** medical office, **8.2**
el/la **consumidor(a)** consumer
el **consumo** consumption
consumir to consume
el **contacto** touch
la **contaminación** pollution
contaminado(a) polluted
contaminar to pollute
contener to contain
contento(a) happy, **8.1**
contestar to answer
el **continente** continent
continuar to continue, **7.2**
contra against, **7.1**
el **control** inspection, **11.1**
el control de pasaportes passport inspection, **11.1**
el control de seguridad security check, **11.1**
controlar to control
conversar to talk, speak
convertir (ie, i) to convert, transform
la **copa: la Copa mundial** World Cup
copiar to copy
el/la **copiloto** copilot, **11.2**
el **corazón** heart
la **corbata** tie, **3.2**
el **cordero** lamb, **14.2**
el **cordoncillo** piping (embroidery)
la **coreografía** choreography
la **córnea** cornea
el **coro** choir, chorus
el **correo: el correo electrónico** e-mail, electronic mail
correr to run, **7.2**
cortar to cut
la **cortesía** courtesy, **BV**
corto(a) short, **3.2**
el pantalón corto shorts, **3.2**
la **cosa** thing
coser to sew
la **costa** coast
costar (ue) to cost, **3.1**

costarricense Costa Rican
la **costumbre** custom
la **costura** sewing
crear to create
crédito: la tarjeta de crédito credit card, **14.1**
creer to believe, **8.2;** to think so
el **crecimiento** growth
la **crema: la crema de afeitar** shaving cream, **12.1**
la crema protectora sunblock, **9.1**
criollo(a) Creole
cristiano(a) Christian
cruzar to cross
el **cuaderno** notebook, **3.1**
el **cuadro** painting, **10.2**
¿cuál? which?, what?, **BV**
¿Cuál es la fecha de hoy? What is today's date?, **BV**
¿cuáles? which ones?, what?
cuando when, **4.2**
¿cuándo? when?, **4.1**
¿cuánto? how much?, **3.1**
¿A cuánto está(n)... ? How much is (are) . . . ?, **5.2**
¿Cuánto es? How much does it cost?, **3.1**
¿Cuánto cuesta(n)... ? How much do(es) . . . cost?, **3.1**
¿cuántos(as)? how many?, **2.1**
cuarenta forty, **2.2**
el **cuarto** room, bedroom **6.2;** quarter
el cuarto de baño bathroom, **6.2**
el cuarto de dormir bedroom
menos cuarto a quarter to (the hour)
y cuarto a quarter past (the hour)
cuarto(a) fourth, **6.2**
cuatro four, **BV**
cuatrocientos(as) four hundred, **3.2**
cubano(a) Cuban
cubanoamericano(a) Cuban-American
cubrir to cover
la **cuchara** tablespoon, **14.1**
la **cucharita** teaspoon, **14.1**
el **cuchillo** knife, **14.1**
el **cuello** neck
la **cuenca** basin
la **cuenta** bill, check, **5.1**
el/la **cuentista** short-story writer
el **cuento** story
la **cuerda** string (instrument)
el **cuerpo** body
¡cuidado! careful!
con mucho cuidado very carefully
cultivar to cultivate
el **cumpleaños** birthday, **6.1**
cumplir: cumplir... años to be . . . years old, **6.1**
el/la **curandero(a)** folk healer
el **curso** course, class, **2.1**
el curso obligatorio required course
el curso opcional elective course

D

la **dama** lady-in-waiting, woman
la **danza** dance
dar to give, **4.2**
dar a entender to imply that
dar auxilio to help
dar énfasis to emphasize
dar la mano to shake hands
dar un examen to give a test, **4.2**
dar una fiesta to give (throw) a party, **4.2**
dar una representación to put on a performance, **10.2**
datar to date
los **datos** data, information
de of, from, for, **BV**
de... a... from (time) to (time), **2.2**
de joven as a young person
De nada. You're welcome., **BV**
de ninguna manera by no means, **1.1**
de vez en cuando sometimes
debajo (de) under, below
deber must; should; to owe
decidir to decide
décimo(a) tenth, **6.2**
decir to say, **13**
¡Diga! Hello! (answering the telephone—Spain), **14.2**
declarar to declare
el **dedo** finger
el **defecto** fault, flaw
definitivamente once and for all
dejar to leave (something), **14.1;** to let, allow
del of the, from the
delante de in front of, **10.1**
delantero(a) front
delgado(a) thin
delicioso(a) delicious
demás other, rest
demasiado too much
la **demora: con una demora** with a delay, **11.1**
dentífrico(a): la pasta dentífrica toothpaste, **12.2**
dentro de within
dentro de poco soon
el **departamento** apartment, **6.2**
la casa de departamentos apartment house, **6.2**
depender (de) to depend (on)
el/la **dependiente(a)** employee, **3.1**
el **deporte** sport, **7.1**
el deporte de equipo team sport
el deporte individual individual sport
deportivo(a) (related to) sports, **6.2**
la emisión deportiva sports program (TV), **6.2**
derecho(a) right, **7.1**
derrotar to defeat
desagradable unpleasant
desamparado(a): los niños desamparados homeless children

desayunarse to eat breakfast, **12.1**
el **desayuno** breakfast, **5.2**
tomar el desayuno to eat breakfast, **12.1**
el/la **descendiente** descendant
describir to describe
descubrir to discover
el **descuento** discount
desde since
desear to want, wish, **3.2**
¿Qué desea Ud.? May I help you? (in a store), **3.2**
los **desechos** waste
desembarcar to disembark, **11.2**
el **desierto** desert
despachar to sell, **8.2**
despertarse (ie) to wake up, **12.1**
despegar to take off (airplane), **11.2**
después (de) after, **5.1;** later
el **destino** destination, **11.1**
con destino a to
devolver (ue) to return (something), **7.2**
el **día** day, **BV**
Buenos días. Good morning., **BV**
hoy (en) día nowadays, these days
¿Qué día es (hoy)? What day is it (today)?, **BV**
la **diagnosis** diagnosis, **8.2**
el **diálogo** dialog
el **diamante** diamond
dibujar to draw
el **dibujo** drawing
diciembre December, **BV**
diecinueve nineteen, **BV**
dieciocho eighteen, **BV**
dieciséis sixteen, **BV**
diecisiete seventeen, **BV**
el **diente**: **cepillarse los dientes** to brush one's teeth, **12.1**
el cepillo de dientes toothbrush, **12.2**
diez ten
la **diferencia** difference
diferente different
difícil difficult, **2.1**
¡Diga! Hello! (telephone), **14.2**
diminuto(a) tiny, minute
la **dinamita** dynamite
el **dinero** money, **14.1**
el dinero en efectivo cash
¡Dios mío! Gosh!
la **dirección** address; direction
en dirección a toward
directo(a) direct
el/la **director(a)** director, principal
la **disciplina** subject area (school), **2.2**
el **disco**: **el disco compacto** compact disk, CD, **4.2**
discutir to discuss
el/la **diseñador(a)** designer
el **diseño** design
disfrutar to enjoy
la **disputa** quarrel, argument
el **disquete** diskette, **3.1**
la **distancia** distance
la **diversión** amusement
divertido(a) fun, amusing
divertirse (ie, i) to enjoy oneself, **12.2**
dividir to divide
la **división** division
divorciarse to get divorced
doblado(a) dubbed, **10.1**
dobles doubles, **9.1**
doce twelve, **BV**
la **docena** dozen
el/la **doctor(a)** doctor
el **dólar** dollar
doler (ue) to hurt, **8.2**
Me duele(n)... My . . . hurt(s) me, **8.2**
el **dolor** pain, ache, **8.1**
el dolor de cabeza headache, **8.1**
el dolor de estómago stomachache, **8.1**
el dolor de garganta sore throat, **8.1**
Tengo dolor de... I have a pain in my . . . , **8.2**
doméstico(a) domestic
la economía doméstica home economics, **2.2**
el **domingo** Sunday, **BV**
dominicano(a) Dominican, **2.1**
la República Dominicana Dominican Republic
don courteous way of addressing a male
donde where, **1.2**
¿dónde? where?, **1.2**
dormido(a) asleep
dormir (ue, u) to sleep
el saco de dormir sleeping bag, **12.2**
dormirse (ue, u) to fall asleep, **12.1**
el **dormitorio** bedroom, **6.2**
dos two, **BV**
doscientos(as) two hundred, **3.2**
la **dosis** dose, **8.2**
el/la **dramaturgo(a)** playwright
driblar to dribble, **7.2**
la **droga** drug
la **ducha** shower, **12.1**
tomar una ducha to take a shower, **12.1**
la **duda** doubt
dulce: **el pan dulce** sweet roll, **5.1**
la **duración** duration
durante during
duro(a) hard, difficult, **2.1**

E

echar to throw
echar (tomar) una siesta to take a nap
echarle flores to pay someone a compliment
la **ecología** ecology
ecológico(a) ecological
la **economía** economics; economy
la economía doméstica home economics, **2.2**
económico(a) economical, **12.2**
la **ecuación** equation
ecuatoriano(a) Ecuadorean, **2.1**
la **edad** age
el **edificio** building
la **educación** education
la educación física physical education, **2.2**
efectivo: **en efectivo** in cash

478

el **ejemplo: por ejemplo** for example
el **ejote** string beans
el the *(m. sing.),* **1.1**
él he, **1.1**
electrónico(a) electronic
el correo electrónico e-mail, electronic mail
la **elevación** elevation
elevado(a) elevated
elevar to elevate
ella she, **1.1**
ellos(as) they, **2.1**
el **elote** corn (Mex.)
embarcar to board, **11.2**
embarque: la tarjeta de embarque boarding pass, **11.1**
la puerta de embarque departure gate
la **emisión** program (TV), **6.2;** emission
la emisión deportiva sports program, **6.2**
emitir to emit
la **emoción** emotion
emocional emotional
empatado(a) tied (score), **7.1**
El tanto queda empatado. The score is tied., **7.1**
empezar (ie) to begin, **7.1**
el/la **empleado(a)** employee, **3.1**
en in; on
en aquel entonces at that time
en punto on the dot, sharp, **4.1**
el/la **enamorado(a)** sweetheart, lover
encantador(a) charming
encantar to delight
encender (ie) to light
encima: por encima de above, **9.1**
la **energía** energy
encestar to put in (make) a basket, **7.2**
encontrar (ue) to find
el/la **enemigo(a)** enemy
enero January, **BV**
el **énfasis: dar énfasis** to emphasize
enfatizar to emphasize
la **enfermedad** illness
enfermo(a) sick, **8.1**
el/la **enfermo(a)** sick person, **8.1**
el **enganche** down payment
enlatado(a) canned
la **ensalada** salad, **5.1**
enseguida right away, immediately, **5.1**
enseñar to teach, **4.1**
entero(a) entire, whole
enterrar (ie) to bury
el **entierro** burial
entonces then
en aquel entonces at that time
la **entrada** inning, **7.2**; admission ticket, **10.1**
entrar to enter, **4.1**
entrar en escena to come (go) on stage, **10.2**
entre between, **7.1**
entregar to deliver
la **entrevista** interview
enviar to send
envuelto(a) wrapped
el **episodio** episode
la **época** period of time, epoch
el **equilibrio** equilibrium
el **equipaje** baggage, luggage, **11.1**
el equipaje de mano carry-on luggage, **11.1**
el **equipo** team, **7.1**; equipment
el deporte de equipo team sport, **7.2**
erróneo(a) wrong, erroneous
la **escala** stopover
la **escalera** stairway, **6.2**
los **escalofríos** chills, **8.1**
escamotear to secretly take
escapar to escape
la **escena** scene
entrar en escena to come (go) on stage, **10.2**
el **escenario** scenery, set (theater), **10.2**
escoger to choose
escolar (related to) school, **2.1**
el bus escolar school bus, **4.1**
el horario escolar school schedule
los materiales escolares school supplies, **3.1**
la vida escolar school life
esconder to hide
escribir to write, **5.1**
escuchar to listen (to), **4.2**
el **escudero** squire, knight's attendant
la **escuela** school, **1.1**
la escuela intermedia middle school
la escuela primaria elementary school
la escuela secundaria high school, **1.1**
la escuela superior high school
el/la **escultor(a)** sculptor, **10.2**
la **escultura** sculpture
esencialmente essentially
eso: a eso de at about (time), **4.1**
el **espagueti** spaghetti
espantoso frightful
la **España** Spain, **1.2**
el **español** Spanish, **2.2**
español(a) Spanish *(adj.)*
la **espátula** palette knife, spatula
especial special
la **especialidad** specialty
especialmente especially
el **espectáculo** show, **10.2**
ver un espectáculo to see a show, **10.2**
el/la **espectador(a)** spectator, **7.1**
el **espejo** mirror, **12.1**
espera: la sala de espera waiting room, **13.1**
esperar to wait (for), **11.1**
espontáneo(a) spontaneous
la **esposa** wife, spouse, **6.1**
el **esposo** husband, spouse, **6.1**
el **esquí** skiing, **9.2;** ski
el esquí acuático waterskiing, **9.1**
el/la **esquiador(a)** skier, **9.2**
esquiar to ski, **9.2**
esquiar en el agua to water-ski, **9.1**
la **estación** season, **BV;** resort; station, **10.1**

la estación de esquí ski resort, **9.2**
la estación de ferrocarril train station, **13.1**
la estación de metro subway station, **10.1**
el **estadio** stadium, **7.1**
el **estado** state
los Estados Unidos United States
estadounidense from the United States
estar to be, **4.1**
estar resfriado(a) to have a cold, **8.1**
la **estatua** statue, **10.2**
el **este** east
estereofónico(a) stereo
el **estilo** style
estimado(a) esteemed
el **estómago** stomach, **8.1**
estornudar to sneeze, **8.1**
la **estrategia** strategy
la **estrella** star
la **estructura** structure
el/la **estudiante** student
estudiantil (relating to) student
estudiar to study, **4.1**
el **estudio** study
estupendo(a) stupendous
eterno(a) eternal
étnico(a) ethnic
la **Europa** Europe
exactamente exactly
exagerar to exaggerate
el **examen** test, exam, **4.2**
examinar to examine, **8.2**
la **excavación** excavation
excavar to dig, excavate
exceder to exceed
excelente excellent
la **excepción** exception
exclamar to exclaim
exclusivamente exclusively
la **exhibición** exhibition
existir to exist
el **éxito** success
la **expedición** expedition
la **experiencia** experience
el/la **experto(a)** expert, **9.2**
explicar to explain, **4.2**
el/la **explorador(a)** explorer
la **explosión** explosion
la **exposición (de arte)** (art) exhibition, **10.2**
la **expresión: el modo de expresión** means of expression
extranjero(a) foreign
el país extranjero foreign country, **11.2**
el/la **extranjero(a)** foreigner
extraordinario(a) extraordinary

F

la **fábrica** factory
fabuloso(a) fabulous
fácil easy, **2.1**
la **factura** invoice
facturar el equipaje to check luggage, **11.1**
la **Facultad** school (of a university)
la **faja** sash
la **falda** skirt, **3.2**
la **fama** fame
la **familia** family, **6.1**
familiar (related to the) family
famoso(a) famous, **1.2**
fantástico(a) fantastic, **1.2**
el/la **farmacéutico(a)** druggist, pharmacist, **8.2**
la **farmacia** drugstore, **8.2**
fascinar to fascinate
febrero February, **BV**
la **fecha** date, **BV**
¿Cuál es la fecha de hoy? What is today's date?, **BV**
feo(a) ugly, **1.1**
la **fiebre** fever, **8.1**
tener fiebre to have a fever, **8.1**
fiel faithful
la **fiesta** party
dar una fiesta to give (throw) a party, **4.2**
la **figura** figure
figurativo(a) figurative
fijo(a) fixed
la **fila** line (queue); row (of seats), **10.1**
el **film** film, **10.1**
el **fin** end
a fines de at the end of
el fin de semana weekend, **BV**
el **final: al final (de)** at the end (of)
las **finanzas** finances
la **física** physics, **2.1**
físico(a): la educación física physical education, **2.2**
flaco(a) thin, **1.2**
la **flauta** flute
flechar to become enamored of (to fall for)
la **flor** flower
formar to make up, to form
la **foto** photo
la **fotografía** photograph
el **francés** French, **2.2**
franco(a) frank, candid, sincere
la **frase** phrase, sentence
frecuentemente frequently
freír (i, i) to fry, **14.1**
fresco(a) fresh
el **frijol** bean, **5.2**
el **frío: Hace frío.** It's cold., **9.2**
frito(a) fried, **5.1**
las papas fritas French fries, **5.1**
el **frontón** wall (of a jai alai court)
la **fruta** fruit, **5.2**
la **fuente** source
fuerte strong
fumar: la sección de (no) fumar (no) smoking area, **11.1**
la **función** performance, **10.2**
el **funcionamiento** functioning
la **fundación** foundation
fundar to found, establish
la **furia** fury
furioso(a) furious
el **fútbol** soccer, **7.1**
el campo de fútbol soccer field, **7.1**
el **futuro** future

G

las **gafas de sol** sunglasses, **9.1**
el **galán** beau, heartthrob
el **galón** gallon
gallardo(a) gallant, fine-looking

480

ganar to win, **7.1**; to earn
la **ganga** bargain
el **garaje** garage, **6.2**
la **garganta** throat, **8.1**
el **gas** gas
gastar to spend
el/la **gato(a)** cat, **6.1**
general: en general generally
por lo general in general
generalmente usually, generally
el **género** genre
generoso(a) generous, **1.2**
la **gente** people
la **geografía** geography, **2.2**
la **geometría** geometry, **2.2**
geométrico(a) geometric
el **gigante** giant
el **gimnasio** gymnasium
la **gira** tour, **12.2**
el **gol**: **meter un gol** to score a goal, **7.1**
el **golfo** gulf
golpear to hit, 9.2
la **goma: la goma de borrar** eraser, **3.1**
gordo(a) fat, **1.2**
la **gorra** cap, hat, **3.2**
gozar to enjoy
Gracias Thank you., **BV**
gracioso(a) funny, **1.1**
el **grado** degree (temperature), **9.2**
la **gramática** grammar
el **gramo** gram
gran, grande big, large, great
las Grandes Ligas Major Leagues
el **grano** grain
la **grasa** fat
grave serious, grave
la **gripe** flu, **8.1**
gris gray, **3.2**
el **grupo** group
la **guagua** bus (P.R., Cuba), **10.1**
el **guante** glove, **7.2**
guapo(a) handsome, **1.1**
guardar to guard, **7.1**; to keep
guardar cama to stay in bed, **8.1**
guatemalteco(a) Guatemalan
la **guerra** war
la **guerrilla** guerrilla
el/la **guía** tour guide
el **guisante** pea, **5.2**
la **guitarra** guitar
gustar to like, to be pleasing
el **gusto** pleasure
Mucho gusto. Nice to meet you.

H

la **habichuela** bean, **5.2**
la habichuela tierna string bean
la **habitación** bedroom
el/la **habitante** inhabitant
habla: los países de habla española Spanish-speaking countries
hablar to speak, talk, **3.1**
hace: Hace buen tiempo. The weather is nice., **9.1**
Hace calor. It's hot., **9.1**
Hace frío. It's cold., **9.2**
Hace mal tiempo. The weather is bad., **9.1**
Hace sol. It's sunny., **9.1**
hacer to do, to make
hacer caso to pay attention
hacer la cama to make the bed,
hacer la maleta to pack one's suitcase
hacer un viaje to take a trip, **11.1**
hacia toward
hallar to find
la **hamburguesa** hamburger, **5.1**
hambe: tener hambre to be hungry, **14.1**
hasta until, **BV**
¡Hasta luego! See you later!, **BV**
¡Hasta mañana! See you tomorrow!, **BV**
¡Hasta pronto! See you soon!, **BV**
hay there is, there are, **BV**
hay que one must
Hay sol. It's sunny., **9.1**
No hay de qué. You're welcome., **BV**
hecho(a) made
helado(a): el té helado iced tea, **5.1**
el **helado** ice cream, **5.1**
el helado de chocolate chocolate ice cream, **5.1**
el helado de vainilla vanilla ice cream, **5.1**
el **hemisferio norte** northern hemisphere
el **hemisferio sur** southern hemisphere
la **herencia** inheritance
la **hermana** sister, **6.1**
el **hermano** brother, **6.1**
hermoso(a) beautiful, pretty, **1.1**
el/la **héroe** hero
higiénico(a): el papel higiénico toilet paper, **12.2**
la **hija** daughter, **6.1**
el **hijo** son, **6.1**
los hijos children, **6.1**
hispano(a) Hispanic
hispanoamericano(a) Spanish-American
hispanohablante Spanish-speaking
el/la **hispanohablante** Spanish speaker
la **historia** history, **2.2**; story
el/la **historiador(a)** historian
histórico(a) historical
la **historieta** little story
la **hoja**: **la hoja de papel** sheet of paper, **3.1**
¡Hola! Hello!, **BV**
el **hombre** man
¡hombre! good heavens!, you bet!
honesto(a) honest, **1.2**
el **honor** honor
la **hora** hour; time
¿A qué hora? At what time?, **2.2**
¿Qué hora es? What time is it?, **2.2**
la hora de salida departure hour
el **horario** schedule, **13.1**
el horario escolar school schedule
horrible horrible

el **hospital** hospital
la **Hostia** Host (relig.)
el **hostal** inexpensive hotel, **12.2**
el **hotel** hotel
hoy today, **BV**
hoy (en) día nowadays, these days
el **huarache** sandal
el **huevo** egg, **5.2**
humano(a): el ser humano human being
humilde humble
el **humor** mood, **8.1**
estar de buen humor to be in a good mood, **8.1**
estar de mal humor to be in a bad mood, **8.1**
el **huso horario** time zone

I

ida: de ida y vuelta round-trip (ticket), **13.1**
la **idea** idea
ideal ideal, **1.2**
el/la **idealista** idealist
la **iglesia** church
igual equal
la **ilusión** illusion
imaginado(a) imagined, dreamed of
imaginar to imagine
importante important
imposible impossible
la **impresora** printer
el/la **inca** Inca
incluido(a): ¿Está incluido el servicio? Is the tip included?, **5.1**
incluir to include, **5.1**
increíble incredible
la **independencia** independence
el **indicador: el tablero indicador** scoreboard, **7.1**
indicar to indicate, **11.1**
indígena native, indigenous
el/la **indígena** native person
indio(a) Indian
indispensable indispensable
individual individual
el deporte individual individual sport
el **individuo** individual
industrial industrial
la **influencia** influence
la **información** information
informar to inform, **13.2**
la **informática** computer science, **2.2**
el **inglés** English, **2.2**
inmediatamente immediately
inmediato(a) immediate
inmenso(a) immense
inspeccionar to inspect, **11.1**
el **instante** instant
la **instrucción** instruction
el **instrumento** instrument
el instrumento musical musical instrument
íntegro(a) integral
inteligente intelligent, **2.1**
el **interés** interest
interesante interesting, **2.1**
interesar to interest
intermedio(a): la escuela intermedia middle school
internacional international
la **interpretación** interpretation
íntimo(a) intimate
inverso(a) reverse
la **investigación** investigation
el/la **investigador(a)** researcher
el **invierno** winter, **BV**
la **invitación** invitation
invitar to invite, **6.1**
la **inyección** injection, **8.2**
ir to go, **4.1**
ir a + *infinitive* to be going to (do something)
ir a pie to go on foot, to walk **4.1**
ir de compras to go shopping, **5.2**
ir en bicicleta to go by bicycle, **12.2**
ir en carro (coche) to go by car, **4.1**
ir en tren to go by train
la **isla** island
italiano(a) Italian
izquierdo(a) left, **7.1**

J

el **jabón** soap, **12.2**
la barra (pastilla) de jabón bar of soap, **12.2**
jamás never
el **jamón** ham, **5.1**
el **jardín** garden, **6.2**
el/la **jardinero(a)** outfielder, **7.2**
el **jet** jet
el **jonrón** home run, **7.2**
joven young, **6.1**
de joven as a young person
el/la **joven** youth, young person, **10.1**
la **judía: la judía verde** green bean, **5.2**
el **juego** game
el juego de béisbol baseball game, **7.2**
el juego de tenis tennis game, **9.1**
los Juegos Olímpicos Olympic Games
el **jueves** Thursday, **BV**
el/la **jugador(a)** player, **7.1**
el/la jugador(a) de béisbol baseball player, **7.2**
jugar (ue) to play, **7.1**
jugar (al) béisbol (fútbol, baloncesto, etc.) to play baseball (soccer, basketball, etc.) **7.1**
el **jugo** juice
el jugo de naranja orange juice, **12.1**
el **juguete** toy
julio July, **BV**
la **jungla** jungle
junio June, **BV**
junto(a) together
juvenil: el albergue juvenil youth hostel, **12.2**

K

el **kilo** kilogram, **5.2**
el **kilómetro** kilometer

L

la the *(f. sing.)*, **1.1**; it, her *(pron.)*
el **laboratorio** laboratory
el **lado** side

el **lago** lake
el **lamento** lament
la **lana** wool
la **langosta** lobster, **14.2**
la **lanza** lance
el/la **lanzador(a)** pitcher, **7.2**
lanzar to throw, **7.1**
el **lápiz** pencil, **3.1**
largo(a) long, **3.2**
las them *(f. pl.) (pron.)*
la **lata** can, **5.2**
lateral side *(adj.)*, **13.2**
el **latín** Latin, **2.2**
latino(a) Latin *(adj.)*
Latinoamérica Latin America, **1.1**
latinoamericano(a) Latin American
lavarse to wash oneself, **12.1**
lavarse los dientes to brush one's teeth, **12.1**
le to him, to her; to you *(formal) (pron.)*
la **lección** lesson, **4.2**
la **leche** milk
el café con leche coffee with milk, **5.1**
el **lechón** suckling pig
la **lechuga** lettuce, **5.2**
la **lectura** reading
leer to read, **5.1**
la **legumbre** vegetable, **14**
la **lengua** language, **2.2**
el **lenguaje** language
les to them; to you *(formal pl.) (pron.)*
la **letra** letter (of alphabet)
levantar to lift
levantarse to get up, **12.1**
el/la **libertador(a)** liberator
la **libra** pound
libre free, **5.1**
al aire libre outdoor *(adj.)*
el **libro** book, **3.1**
el **liceo** high school
el **lienzo** canvas (painting)
la **liga** league
las Grandes Ligas Major Leagues
ligero(a) light (cheerful)
limeño(a) from Lima (Peru)
la **limonada** lemonade, **BV**
lindo(a) pretty, **1.1**
la **línea** line
la línea aérea airline
la línea ecuatorial equator
la línea paralela parallel line
la línea telefónica telephone line
el **lípido** lipid, fat
líquido(a) liquid
listo(a) ready
la **litera** berth, **13.2**
literal literal
literario(a) literary
la **literatura** literature, **2.1**
el **litro** liter
llamado(a) called
llamar to call
llamarse to be named, to call oneself, **12.1**
la **llegada** arrival, **11.1**
llegar to arrive, **4.1**
lleno(a) full
llevar to carry, **3.1**; to wear, **3.2**; to bring, **6.1**; to bear; to have (subtitles, ingredients, etc.)
llover (ue) to rain
Llueve. It's raining., **9.1**
la **lluvia** rain
lo it; him *(m. sing.) (pron.)*
lo que what, that which
local local, **13.2**
la **loción: la loción bronceadora** suntan lotion, **9.1**
loco(a) insane
los them *(m. pl.) (pron.)*
el **loto** lotto
luchar to fight
luego later; then, **BV**
¡Hasta luego! See you later!, **BV**
el **lugar** place
lujo: de lujo deluxe
lujoso(a) luxurious
la **luna** moon
el **lunes** Monday, **BV**
la **luz** light

M

la **madre** mother, **6.1**
madrileño(a) native of Madrid
la **madrina** godmother
el/la **maestro(a)** teacher; master
magnífico(a) magnificent
el **maíz** corn, **14.2**
mal bad, **14.2**
estar de mal humor to be in a bad mood, **8.1**
Hace mal tiempo. The weather's bad., **9.1**
la **maleta** suitcase, **11.1**
la **maletera** trunk (of a car), **13.1**
el/la **maletero(a)** porter, **11.1**
malhumorado(a) bad-tempered
malo(a) bad, **2.1**
sacar una nota mala to get a bad grade, **4.2**
la **mamá** mom
la **manera** way, manner, **1.1**
de ninguna manera by no means, **1.1**
el **maní** peanut
la **mano** hand, **7.1**
dar la mano to shake hands
el **mantel** tablecloth, **14.1**
mantener to maintain
la **manzana** apple, **5.2**
mañana tomorrow, **BV**
¡Hasta mañana! See you tomorrow!, **BV**
la **mañana** morning
de la mañana A.M. (time), **2.2**
por la mañana in the morning
el **mapa** map
el **maquillaje** makeup, **12.1**
poner el maquillaje to put one's makeup on, **12.1**
maquillarse to put one's makeup on, **12.1**
el **mar** sea, **9.1**
el mar Caribe Caribbean Sea
maravilloso(a) marvelous
el **marcador** marker, **3.1**
marcar: marcar un tanto to score a point, **7.1**
el **marido** husband, **6.1**
los **mariscos** shellfish, **5.2**
marrón: de color marrón brown, **3.2**
el **martes** Tuesday, **BV**

marzo March, **BV**
más more, **2.2**
más tarde later
más o menos more or less
la **masa** mass
las **matemáticas** mathematics, **2.1**
la **materia** matter, subject
el **material: los materiales escolares** school supplies, **3.1**
el **matrimonio** marriage
el/la **maya** Maya
mayo May, **BV**
mayor greater
la mayor parte the greater part, the most
la **mayoría** majority
me me *(pron.)*
la **medalla** medal
media: y media half-past (time), **2.2**
la **medianoche** midnight, **2.2**
el **medicamento** medicine (drugs), **8.2**
la **medicina** medicine (discipline), **8.2**
el/la **médico(a)** doctor, **8.2**
la **medida** measurement
el **medio** medium, means
el medio de transporte means of transportation
medio(a) half, **5.2**
media hora half an hour
el **mediodía** noon
medir (i, i) to measure
melancólico(a) melancholic
menos less, fewer
menos cuarto a quarter to (the hour)
la **mensualidad** monthly installment
el **menú** menu, **5.1**
el **mercado** market, **5.2**
el **merengue** merengue
la **merienda** snack, **4.2**
tomar una merienda to have a snack, **4.2**
la **mermelada** marmalade
el **mes** month, **BV**
la **mesa** table, **5.1**; plateau
la **mesera** waitress, **5.1**
el **mesero** waiter, **5.1**
el/la **mestizo(a)** mestizo
el **metabolismo** metabolism
el **metal: instrumentos de metal** brass (instruments in orchestra)
meter to put, place, **7.1**
meter un gol to score a goal, **7.1**
el **método** method
el **metro** subway, **10.1;** meter
mexicano(a) Mexican, **1.1**
mexicanoamericano(a) Mexican-American
la **mezcla** mixture
mi my
mí (to) me *(pron.)*
el **microbio** microbe
microscópico(a) microscopic
el **microscopio** microscope
el **miedo** fear
tener miedo to be afraid
el **miembro** member, **4.2**
mientras while
el **miércoles** Wednesday, **BV**
mil (one) thousand, **3.2**
la **milla** mile
el **millón** million
el **minuto** minute
mirar to look at, watch, **3.1**
mirarse to look at oneself, **12.1**
¡Mira! Look!
mismo(a) same, **2.1;** itself
el **misterio** mystery
misterioso(a) mysterious
mixto(a) co-ed (school)
la **mochila** backpack, **3.1;** knapsack, **12.2**
la **modalidad** mode, type
el/la **modelo** model
el **módem** modem
moderno(a) modern
el **modo** manner, way
el modo de expresión means of expression
el **molino de viento** windmill
el **momento** moment
la **moneda** coin, currency
el **monitor** monitor
monocelular single-celled
el **monstruo** monster
la **montaña** mountain, **9.2**
montañoso(a) mountainous
montar (caballo) to mount, get on (horse)
el **monumento** monument
moreno(a) dark, brunette, **1.1**
morir (ue, u) to die
el **mostrador** counter, **11.1**
el **motivo** reason, motive; theme
el **motor** motor
mover (ue) to move
el **movimiento** movement
el **mozo** porter, **13.1**
la **muchacha** girl, **1.1**
el **muchacho** boy, **1.1**
mucho(a) a lot; many, **2.1**
Mucho gusto. Nice to meet you.
los **muebles** furniture
la **muerte** death
la **mujer** wife, **6.1**
el/la **mulato(a)** mulatto
la **multiplicación** multiplication
multiplicar to multiply
mundial worldwide, (related to the) world
la Copa mundial World Cup
la Serie mundial World Series
el **mundo** world
todo el mundo everyone
el **mural** mural, **10.2**
el/la **muralista** muralist, **10**
el **museo** museum, **10.2**
la **música** music, **2.2**
el/la **músico(a)** musician
muy very, **BV**
muy bien very well, **BV**

N

nacer to be born
nacido(a) born
nacional national
la **nacionalidad** nationality, **1.2**
¿de qué nacionalidad? what nationality?
nadar to swim, **9.1**
el **narcótico** narcotic
nada nothing, **5.2**
De nada. You're welcome., **BV**
Nada más. Nothing else., **5.2**

Por nada. You're welcome., **BV**
nadie no one
la **naranja** orange, **5.2**
la **natación** swimming, **9.1**
natural: los recursos naturales natural resources, **2.1**
las ciencias naturales natural sciences
la **navaja** razor, **12.1**
navegar to navigate
navegar por la red to surf the Net
la **Navidad** Christmas
necesario(a) necessary
necesitar to need, **3.1**
negro(a) black, **3.2**
nervioso(a) nervous, **8.1**
nevar (ie) to snow, **9.2**
la **nieta** granddaughter, **6.1**
el **nieto** grandson, **6.1**
la **nieve** snow, **9.2**
ninguno(a) not any, none
de ninguna manera by no means, **1.1**
el/la **niño(a)** child
los niños desamparados homeless children
el **nivel** level
no no, **BV**
No hay de qué. You're welcome., **BV**
no hay más remedio there's no other alternative
noble noble
la **noche** night, evening
Buenas noches. Good night., **BV**
esta noche tonight, **9.2**
de la noche P.M. (time), **2.2**
por la noche in the evening, at night
la **Nochebuena** Christmas Eve
el **nombre** name
¿a nombre de quién? in whose name?, **14.2**
el **noroeste** northwest
el **norte** north
norteamericano(a) North American
nos (to) us *(pl. pron.)*
nosotros(as) we, **2.2**
la **nota** grade, **4.2**
la nota buena (alta) good (high) grade, **4.2**
la nota mala (baja) bad (low) grade, **4.2**
sacar una nota buena (mala) to get a good (bad) grade, **4.2**
notable notable
notar to note
las **noticias** news, **6.2**
novecientos(as) nine hundred, **3.2**
la **novela** novel
el/la **novelista** novelist
noveno(a) ninth, **6.2**
noventa ninety, **2.2**
noviembre November, **BV**
el/la **novio(a)** boyfriend/girlfriend; fiancé(e)
la **nube** cloud, **9.1**
Hay nubes. It's cloudy., **9.1**
nublado(a) cloudy, **9.1**
nuestro(a) our
nueve nine, **BV**
nuevo(a) new
de nuevo again
el **número** number, **1.2; size** (shoes), **3.2**
el número del asiento seat number, **11.1**
el número del vuelo flight number, **11.1**
nupcial nuptial, wedding
la **nutrición** nutrition

O

el **objeto** object
obligatorio(a): el curso obligatorio required course
la **obra** work
la obra de arte work of art
la obra dramática play
la obra teatral play, **10.2**
la **observación** observation
el/la **observador(a)** observer
observar to observe
el **obstáculo** obstacle
obtener to obtain
el **océano** ocean
ochenta eighty, **2.2**
ocho eight, **BV**
ochocientos(as) eight hundred, **3.2**
octavo(a) eighth, **6.2**
octubre October, **BV**
ocupado(a) occupied, taken, **5.1**
el **oeste** west
oficial official
ofrecer to offer
la **oftalmología** ophthalmology
oír to hear
el **ojo** eye, **8.2**
la **ola** wave, **9.1**
el **óleo** oil
la **oliva: el aceite de oliva** olive oil
once eleven, **BV**
la **onza** ounce
opcional: el curso opcional elective course
la **ópera** opera
el/la **operador(a)** operator
la **opereta** operetta
opinar to think
oralmente orally
la **orden** order (restaurant), **5.1**
el **ordenador** computer
el **orfanato** orphanage
el **organismo** organism
el **órgano** organ
el **origen** origin
original: en versión original in its original (language) version, **10.1**
el **oro** gold
la **orquesta** orchestra
la orquesta sinfónica symphonic orchestra
la **ortiga** nettle
oscuro(a) dark
otavaleño(a) of or from Otavalo, Ecuador
el **otoño** autumn, **BV**
otro(a) other, another
¡oye! listen!

P

la **paciencia** patience
el/la **paciente** patient
el **padre** father, **6.1**
el padre (religioso) father (relig.)

los padres parents, **6.1**
el **padrino** godfather
los padrinos godparents
pagar to pay, **3.1**
la **página** page
la página Web Web page
el **pago** payment
el pago mensual monthly payment
el **país** country, **11.2**
el país extranjero foreign country
el **paisaje** landscape
el **pájaro** bird
la **palabra** word
el **pan**: **el pan dulce** sweet roll, **5.1**
el pan tostado toast, **5.2**
panameño(a) Panamanian, **2.1**
el **panqueque** pancake
la **pantalla** screen, **10.1**
la pantalla de salidas y llegadas arrival and departure screen, **11.1**
el **pantalón** pants, trousers, **3.2**
el pantalón corto shorts, **3.2**
la **papa** potato, **5.1**
las papas fritas French fries, **5.1**
el **papá** dad
el **papel** paper, **3.1**
el papel higiénico toilet paper, **12.2**
la hoja de papel sheet of paper, **3.1**
la **papelería** stationery store, **3.1**
el **paquete** package, **5.2**
el **par**: **el par de tenis** pair of tennis shoes, **3.2**
el **paraíso** paradise
para for
¿para cuándo? for when?, **14.2**
la **parada** stop, **13.2**
parar to stop, to block, **7.1**
parecerse to look like
parecido(a) similar
la **pared** wall
la **pareja** couple
el/la **pariente** relative, **6.1**
el **parque** park
el **párrafo** paragraph
la **parte** part
la mayor parte the greatest part, the most
por todas partes everywhere
particular private, **6.2**
la casa particular private house, **6.2**
particularmente especially
el **partido** game, **7.1**
pasado(a) past; last
el (año) pasado last (year)
el/la **pasajero(a)** passenger, **11.1**
el **pasaporte** passport, **11.1**
pasar to pass, **7.2**; to spend; to happen
Lo están pasando muy bien. They're having a good time., **12.2**
pasar por to go through, **11.1**
¿Qué te pasa? What's the matter (with you)?, **8.1**
el **pase** pass (permission)
el **pasillo** aisle, **13.2**
la **pasta dentrífica** toothpaste, **12.2**
la **pastilla** pill, **8.2**
la pastilla de jabón bar of soap, **12.2**
la **patata** potato
pedir (i, i) to ask for, **14.1**
peinarse to comb one's hair, **12.1**
el **peine** comb, **12.1**
la **película** film, movie, **6.2**
ver una película to see a film, **10.1**
el **pelo** hair, **12.1**
la **pelota** ball, **7.2**
la pelota vasca jai alai
el/la **pelotari** jai alai player
la **península** peninsula
el **pensamiento** thought
pensar (ie) to think
la **pensión** boarding house, **12.2**
pequeño(a) small, **2.1**
la **percusión** percussion
perder (ie) to lose, **7.1; to** miss, **10.2**
perder el autobús (la guagua, el camión) to miss the bus, **10.2**
Perdón. Excuse me.
el/la **peregrino(a)** pilgrim
perezoso(a) lazy, **1.1**
el **período** period
el **periódico** newspaper, **6.2**
permitir to permit, **11.1**
pero but
el **perrito** puppy
el **perro** dog, **6.1**
la **persona** person, **1.2**
el **personaje** character
peruano(a) Peruvian
pesar to weigh
el **pescado** fish, **5.2**
la **peseta** Spanish unit of currency
el **peso** peso (monetary unit of several Latin American countries), **BV;** weight
la **petición** petition
el **petróleo** petroleum, oil
petrolero(a) oil
el **piano** piano
el/la **pícher** pitcher, **7.2**
el **pico** peak, mountain
y pico just after (time)
el **pie** foot, **7.1;** down payment
a pie on foot, **4.1**
de pie standing
la **pierna** leg, **7.1**
la **pieza** room
la **píldora** pill, **8.2**
el/la **piloto** pilot, **11.2**
la **pimienta** pepper, **14.1**
el **pincel** brush, paintbrush
la **pinta** pint
pintar to paint
el/la **pintor(a)** painter
pintoresco(a) picturesque
la **pintura** painting
la **pirueta** pirouette, maneuver
la **piscina** swimming pool, **9.1**
el **piso** floor, **6.2**; apartment
la **pista** (ski) slope, **9.2**
la **pizarra** chalkboard, **4.2**
el **pizarrón** chalkboard, **4.2**
la **pizza** pizza, **BV**
la **plaga** plague, menace
la **plancha de vela** sailboard, **9.1**

486

practicar la plancha de vela to go windsurfing, **9.1**
planear to plan
la **planta** floor, **6.2;** plant
la planta baja ground floor, **6.2**
la **plata** money (income)
el **plátano** banana, plantain, **5.2**
el **platillo** base, **7.2;** saucer, **14.1**
el **plato** plate, dish, **14.1**
la **playa** beach, **9.1**
playera: la toalla playera beach towel, **9.1**
la **plaza** plaza, square; seat, **13.2**
la **pluma** pen, **3.1**
la **población** population, people
pobre poor
el/la **pobre** the poor boy (girl)
le **pobretón** poor man
poco(a) little, few, **2.1**
un poco (de) a little
poder (ue) to be able, **7.1**
el **poema** poem
la **poesía** poetry
el **poeta** poet
político(a) political
el **pollo** chicken, **5.2**
el **poncho** poncho, shawl, wrap
poner to put, **11.1**
poner la mesa to set the table, **14.1**
ponerse to put on, **12.1**
ponerse el maquillaje to put on makeup, **12.1**
ponerse la ropa to dress oneself, to put on clothes, **12.1**
popular popular, **2.1**
la **popularidad** popularity
por for
por aquí over here
por ciento percent
por ejemplo for example
por eso therefore, for this reason, that's why
por favor please, **BV**
por fin finally
por hora per hour
por la noche in the evening
por lo general in general
Por nada. You're welcome., **BV**
¿por qué? why?
por tierra overland
el **poroto** string bean
porque because
la **portería** goal line, **7.1**
el/la **portero(a)** goalkeeper, goalie, **7.1**
la **posibilidad** possibility
posible possible
el **postre** dessert, **5.1**
practicar to practice
practicar el surfing (la plancha de vela, etc.) to go surfing (windsurfing, etc.), **9.1**
precolombino(a) pre-Columbian
el **precio** price
preferir (ie, i) to prefer
la **pregunta** question
preguntar to ask (a question)
el **premio: el Premio Nóbel** Nobel Prize
preparar to prepare
presentar to present; to show (movie)
la **presentación** presentation
prestar: prestar atención to pay attention, **4.2**
prevalecer to prevail
primario(a): la escuela primaria elementary school
la **primavera** spring, **BV**
primero(a) first, **BV**
en primera (clase) first-class, **13.1**
el/la **primo(a)** cousin, **6.1**
la **princesa** princess
principalmente mainly
el/la **principiante** beginner, **9.2**
prisa: a toda prisa as fast as possible
privado(a) private
la casa privada private house, **6.2**
el **problema** problem
procesar to process
la **procesión** procession
proclamar to proclaim
producido(a) produced
el **producto** product, **5.2**
los productos congelados frozen food, **5.2**
el/la **profesor(a)** teacher, professor, **2.1**
profundo(a) deep
el **programa** program
la **promesa** promise
pronto: ¡Hasta pronto! See you soon!, **BV**
la **propina** tip, **14.1**
la **protección** protection
protector(a): la crema protectora sunblock, **9.1**
la **proteína** protein
el **protoplasma** protoplasm
el/la **proveedor(a)** provider
proveer to provide
la **provisión** provision
próximo(a) next,**13.2**
en la próxima parada at the next stop, **13.2**
proyectar to project, **10.1**
publicar to publish
público(a) public
el **publico** audience, **10.2**
el **pueblo** town
el **puerco** pork
la **puerta** door; gate, **11.1**
la puerta de salida departure gate, **11.1**
puertorriqueño(a) Puerto Rican
pues well
la **pulgada** inch
el **punto: en punto** on the dot, sharp, **4.1**
los puntos cardinales cardinal points
el **puré de papas** mashed potatoes
puro(a) pure

Q

qué what; how, **BV**
¡Qué absurdo! How absurd!
¡Qué enfermo(a) estoy! I'm so sick!
¿Qué tal? How are you?, **BV**
¿Qué te pasa? What's the matter (with you)?, **8.2**
quechua Quechuan
quedar to remain, **7.1**

querer (ie) to want, wish
el **queso** cheese, **5.1**
el **quetzal** quetzal (money)
¿quién? who?, **1.1**
¿quiénes? who? *(pl.)*, **2.1**
la **química** chemistry, **2.2**
químico(a) chemical
quince fifteen, **BV**
la **quinceañera** fifteen-year-old (girl)
quinientos(as) five hundred, **3.2**
quinto(a) fifth, **6.2**
el **quiosco** newsstand, **13.1**
Quisiera... I would like . . . , **14.2**
quitarse to take off

R

rápido quickly
la **raqueta** racket (sports), **9.1**
el **rato** while
el **ratón** mouse
la **razón** reason
razonable reasonable
real royal
realista realistic
el/la **realista** realist
realmente really
rebotar to rebound
la **recámara** bedroom, **6.2**
el/la **receptor(a)** catcher, **7.2**
la **receta** prescription, **8.2**
recetar to prescribe, **8.2**
recibir to receive, **5.1**
el **reciclaje** recycling
recién recently
recientemente recently
reclamar to claim (luggage), **11.2**
el **reclamo de equipaje** baggage claim, **11.2**
recoger to pick up
recoger el equipaje to claim one's luggage, **11.2**
el **rectángulo** rectangle
el **recurso**: **los recursos naturales** natural resources
la **red** net, **9.1**
navegar por la red to surf the Net
reducido(a) reduced (price)
reemplazar to replace
reflejar to reflect
el **reflejo** reflection
reflexionar to reflect
el **refresco** drink, beverage, **5.1**
el **refugio** refuge
regalar to give
el **regalo** gift, **6.1**
la **región** region
regional regional
el **regionalismo** regionalism
regresar to return
regreso: el viaje de regreso return trip, trip back
regular regular, average, **2.2**
la **reina** queen
la **relación** relation
relacionado(a) related
relativamente relatively
religioso(a) religious
rellenar to fill
el **remedio** solution
renombrado(a) well-known
rentar to rent
renunciar to renounce, give up
repetir (i, i) to repeat; to take seconds (meal)
el **reportaje** report
la **representación** performance (theater), **10.2**
dar una representación to put on a performance, **10.2**
representar to represent
la **República Dominicana** Dominican Republic
requerir (ie, i) to require
la **reservación** reservation
reservado(a) reserved, **13.2**
reservar to reserve, **14.2**
resfriado(a): estar resfriado(a) to have a cold, **8.1**
el/la **residente** resident
resolver (ue) to solve
la **respuesta** answer
restar to subtract
el **restaurante** restaurant, **14.1**
el **resto** rest, remainder
la **retina** retina
el **retintín** jingle
el **retrato** portrait
el **retraso: con retraso** with a delay, late, **13.2**
revisar to inspect, **11.1**
revisar el boleto to check the ticket, **11.1**
el/la **revisor(a)** (train) conductor, **13.2**
la **revista** magazine, **6.2**
revolver (ue) to turn around
el **rey** king
rico(a) rich; delicious, **14.2**
el/la **rico(a)** rich person
el **río** river
rodar (ue) to roll
la **rodilla** knee, **7.1**
rojo(a) red, **3.2**
el **rollo de papel higiénico** roll of toilet paper, **12.2**
romántico(a) romantic
la **ropa** clothing, **3.2**
la tienda de ropa clothing store, **3.2**
la **rosa** rose
rosado(a) pink, **3.2**
rubio(a) blond, **1.1**
la **ruina** ruin
el **rumor** rumor
rural rural
la **ruta** route
la **rutina** routine, **12.1**

S

el **sábado** Saturday, **BV**
saber to know (how), **11.2**
sabio(a) wise
sabroso(a) delicious
sacar to get, **4.2**
sacar un billete to buy a ticket
sacar una nota buena (mala) to get a good (bad) grade, **4.2**
el **sacerdote** priest
el **saco** jacket
el saco de dormir sleeping bag, **12.2**
sacrificar to sacrifice
la **sal** salt, **14.1**
la **sala** room; living room, **6.2**
la sala de clase classroom, **4.1**
la sala de espera waiting room, **13.1**

la sala de salida departure area,**11.1**
la **salida** departure, **11.1**
la hora de salida departure hour, **13.1**
la pantalla de llegadas y salidas arrival and departure screen, **11.1**
la sala de salida departure area, **11.1**
salir to leave, **10.1;** to go out; to turn out
salir a tiempo to leave on time, **11.1**
salir bien (en un examen) to do well (on an exam)
salir tarde to leave late, **11.1**
el **salón**: **el salón de clase** classroom, **4.1**
saltar to jump
la **salud** health
el **saludo** greeting, **BV**
salvar to save
el **sándwich** sandwich, **BV**
la **sangre** blood
el **santo** saint
el **saxofono** saxophone
la **sección de (no) fumar** (no) smoking section, **11.1**
secundario(a): la escuela secundaria high school, **1.1**
sed: tener sed to be thirsty, **14.1**
seguir (i, i) to follow, **14**
según according to
segundo(a) second, **6.2**
el segundo tiempo second half (soccer), **7.1**
en segunda (clase) second-class, **13.1**
la **seguridad: el control de seguridad** security (airport), **11.1**
seis six, **BV**
seiscientos(as) six hundred, **3.2**
la **selección** selection
seleccionar to select
la **selva** jungle
la **semana** week, **BV**
el fin de semana weekend, **BV**
el fin de semana pasado last weekend
la semana pasada last week, **9.2**
el/la **senador(a)** senator
sencillo(a): el billete sencillo one-way ticket, **13.1**
sentarse (ie) to sit down, **12.1**
el **sentido** meaning, significance
el **señor** sir, Mr., gentleman, **BV**
la **señora** Ms., Mrs., madam, **BV**
la **señorita** Miss, Ms., **BV**
septiembre September, **BV**
séptimo(a) seventh, **6.2**
ser to be
el **ser: el ser humano** human being
el ser viviente living creature, being
la **serie: la Serie mundial** World Series
serio(a) serious, **1.1**
el **servicio** service, tip, **5.1**
¿Está incluido el servicio? Is the tip included?, **5.1**
la **servilleta** napkin, **14.1**
servir (i, i) to serve, **14.1**
sesenta sixty, **2.2**
la **sesión** show (movies), **10.1**
setecientos(as) seven hundred, **3.2**
setenta seventy, **2.2**
sexto(a) sixth, **6.2**
el **show** show
si if
sí yes
siempre always, **7.1**
de siempre y para siempre eternally, forever
la **sierra** sierra, mountain range
siete seven, **BV**
el **siglo** century
el **significado** meaning
significar to mean
siguiente following
la **silla** chair
similar similar
simpático(a) nice, **1.2**
simple simple
sin without
sin escala nonstop
sincero(a) sincere, **1.2**
singles singles, **9.1**
el **síntoma** symptom, **8.2**
el **sistema métrico** metric system
el **sitio** place
sobre on top of; over; on, about
sobre todo especially
sobresaltar to jump up
la **sobrina** niece, **6.1**
el **sobrino** nephew, **6.1**
social: las ciencias sociales social sciences
la **sociedad** society
la **sociología** sociology
socorrer to help
el **sol** Peruvian coin; sun, **9.1**
Hace (Hay) sol. It's sunny., **9.1**
tomar el sol to sunbathe,**9.1**
solamente only
soler (ue) to be accustomed to, tend to
sólo only
solo(a) alone
a solas alone
el café solo black coffee, **5.1**
soltero(a) single, bachelor
la **solución** solution
el **sombrero** hat
la **sonrisita** little smile
el **sorbete** sherbet, sorbet, **14**
la **sopa** soup, **5.1**
el/la **sordo(a)** deaf
su his, her, their, your
subir to go up, **6.2;** to board, to get on
subir al tren to get on, to board the train, **13.1**
el **subtítulo** subtitle, **10.1**
con subtítulos with subtitles, **10.1**
el **suburbio** suburb
suceso: el buen suceso great event
sudamericano(a) South American

el **sudoeste** southwest
el **suegro** father-in-law
el **suelo** ground
el **sueño** dream
sufrir to suffer
sumar to add
superior: la escuela superior high school
el **supermercado** supermarket, **5.2**
el **sur** south
el **surf de nieve** snowboarding
el **surfing** surfing, **9.1**
practicar el surfing to surf, **9.1**
el **suroeste** southwest
el **surtido** assortment
sus their, your *(pl.)*, **6.1**
suspirar to sigh
la **sustancia: la sustancia controlada** controlled substance

T

el **T-shirt** T-shirt, **3.2**
la **tabla: la tabla hawaiana** surfboard, **9.1**
el **tablero** board, **7.1**
el tablero de llegadas arrival board, **13.1**
el tablero de salidas departure board, **13.1**
el tablero indicador scoreboard, **7.1**
la **tableta** pill, **8.2**
taíno(a) Taino
tal: ¿Qué tal? How are you?, **BV**
la **talla** size, **3.2**
el **talón** luggage claim ticket, **11.1**
el **tamal** tamale, **BV**
el **tamaño** size, **3.2**
también also
tan so
el **tango** tango
el **tanto** point, **7.1**
marcar un tanto to score a point
tanto(a) so much
la **taquilla** box office, **10.1**
tardar to take time
tarda el viaje the trip takes (+ time)
tarde late
la **tarde** afternoon
Buenas tardes. Good afternoon., **BV**
esta tarde this afternoon, **9.2**
por la tarde in the afternoon
la **tarifa** fare, rate
la **tarjeta** card, **11.1**
la tarjeta de crédito credit card, **14.1**
la tarjeta de embarque boarding pass, **11.1**
la tarjeta de indentidad estudiantil student I.D. card
el **taxi** taxi, **11.1**
la **taza** cup, **14.1**
te you *(fam. pron.)*
el **té** tea, **5.1**
el té helado iced tea, **5.1**
teatral theatrical, **10.2**
el **teatro** theater, **10.2**
salir del teatro to leave the theater, **10.2**
el **teclado** keyboard
el/la **técnico(a)** technician
la **tecnología** technology
telefonear to telephone
telefónico(a) (related to the) telephone
la línea telefónica telephone line
el **teléfono** telephone
hablar por teléfono to talk on the phone
el **telesilla** chairlift, **9.2**
el **telesquí** ski lift, **9.2**
la **televisión** television, **6.2**
el **telón** curtain (stage), **10.2**
el **tema** theme, subject
la **temperatura** temperature, **9.2**
templado(a) temperate
temprano early, **12.1**
el **tenedor** fork, **14.1**
tener (ie) to have, **6.1**
tener... años to be . . . years old, **6.1**
tener hambre to be hungry, **14.1**
tener miedo to be afraid
tener que to have to
tener sed to be thirsty, **14.1**
el **tenis** tennis, **9.1**
los **tenis** tennis shoes, **3.2**
el par de tenis pair of tennis shoes, **3.2**
el/la **tenista** tennis player
tercer(o)(a) third, **6.2**
la **terminal** terminal
terminar to end
el **término** term
la **ternera** veal, **14.2**
la **terraza** terrace (sidewalk café)
terrible terrible
el **terror** terror, fear
la **tía** aunt, **6.1**
el **ticket** ticket, **9.2**
el **tiempo** time; weather, **9.1;** half (game)
a tiempo on time, **11.1**
el segundo tiempo second half (game), **7.1**
la **tienda** store, **3.2**
la tienda de departamentos department store
la tienda de ropa clothing store, **3.2**
la tienda de videos video store
tierno(a) tender
la **tierra: por tierra** by land, overland
el **tilde** accent
tímido(a) timid, shy, **1.2**
el **tío** uncle, **6.1**
los tíos aunt and uncle, **6.1**
típicamente typically
típico(a) typical
el **tipo** type
tirar to kick, **7.1**
tirar el balón to kick (throw) the ball, **7.2**
la **toalla playera** beach towel, **9.1**
tocar to touch; to play (music)
todavía yet, still
todo: todo el mundo everyone
todos(as) everybody, **2.2;** everything, all
por todas partes everywhere

tomar to take, **4.1**
tomar agua (leche, café) to drink water (milk, coffee)
tomar apuntes to take notes, **4.2**
tomar el bus (escolar) to take the (school) bus, **4.1**
tomar el desayuno to eat breakfast, **12.1**
tomar el sol to sunbathe, **9.1**
tomar fotos to take photos
tomar un jugo to drink some juice
tomar un refresco to have (drink) a beverage
tomar un vuelo to take a flight, **11.1**
tomar una ducha to take a shower, **12.1**
tomar una merienda to have a snack, **4.2**
el **tomate** tomato
el **tomo** volume
la **tonelada** ton
tonto(a) foolish
la **tortilla** tortilla, **5.1**
la **tos** cough, **8.1**
tener tos to have a cough, **8.1**
toser to cough, **8.1**
la **tostada** toast
tostadito(a) sunburned, tanned
tostado(a): el pan tostado toast, **5.2**
el **tostón** fried plantain slice
totalmente totally, completely
tóxico(a) toxic
trabajar to work, **3.2**
el **trabajo** work
la **tradición** tradition
tradicional traditionally
traer to bring, **14.1**
el **tráfico** traffic
el **traje** suit, **3.2**
el traje de baño bathing suit, **9.1**
el traje de gala evening gown, dress
el **tramo** stretch
tranquilo(a) peaceful; calm; quiet
transbordar to transfer, **13.2**
transformar to transform
transmitir to send, to transmit
el **transporte** transportation
el **tratamiento** treatment
tratar to treat; to try
trece thirteen, **BV**
treinta thirty, **BV**
treinta y uno thirty-one, **2.2**
el **tren** train, **13.2**
el tren directo nonstop train, **13.2**
el tren local local train, **13.2**
tres three, **BV**
trescientos(as) three hundred, **3.2**
el **triángulo** triangle
la **tripulación** crew, **11.2**
triste sad, **8.1**
triunfante triumphant
el **trombón** trombone
la **trompeta** trumpet
tropical tropical
tu your *(sing. fam.)*
tú you *(sing. fam.)*
el **tubo: el tubo de pasta dentífrica** tube of toothpaste, **12.2**
el/la **turista** tourist, **10.2**

U

Ud., usted you *(sing. form.)* **3.2**
Uds., ustedes you *(pl.)*, **2.2**
último(a) last
un a, **1.1**
la **una** one o'clock, **2.2**
único(a) only
la **unidad** unit
el **uniforme** uniform
la **universidad** university
universitario(a) (related to) university
uno(a) one, a, **BV**
unos(as) some
urbano(a) urban
usar to wear (size), **3.2;** to use
utilizar to use

V

la **vacación** vacation
el **vagón** train car, **13.1**
la **vainilla: de vainilla** vanilla *(adj.)*, **5.1**
la **vainita** string bean
¡vale! OK!
valer to be worth
valeroso(a) brave
el **valor real** true value
vamos a let's go
la **variación** variation
variado(a) varied
variar to vary, change
la **variedad** variety
verios(as) various
el **varón** male
vasco(a) Basque
la pelota vasca jai alai
el **vaso** (drinking) glass, **12.1**
el/la **vecino(a)** neighbor
el **vegetal** vegetable, **5.2**
el/la **vegetariano(a)** vegetarian
veinte twenty, **BV**
veinticinco twenty-five, **BV**
veinticuatro twenty-four, **BV**
veintidós twenty-two, **BV**
veintinueve twenty-nine, **BV**
veintiocho twenty-eight, **BV**
veintiséis twenty-six, **BV**
veintisiete twenty-seven, **BV**
veintitrés twenty-three, **BV**
veintiuno twenty-one, **BV**
la **velocidad** speed
vender to sell, **5.2**
venezolano(a) Venezuelan
venir to come, **11.1**
el viernes (sábado, etc.) que viene next Friday (Saturday, etc.)
la **ventanilla** ticket window, **9.2**
ver to see; to watch, **5.1**
el **verano** summer, **BV**
¡verdad! that's right (true)!
verdadero(a) true
verde green, **3.2**
la judía verde green bean, **5.2**
verificar to verify, **13.1**

la **versión: en versión original** in (its) original version, **10.1**
el **vestido** dress
vestirse (i, i) to get dressed
la **vez** time
a veces at times, sometimes, **7.1**
de vez en cuando now and then
una vez más one more time, again
la **vía** track, **13.1**
viajar to travel
viajar en avión to travel by air, **11.1**
el **viaje** trip
el viaje de regreso return trip
hacer un viaje to take a trip, **11.1**
victorioso(a) victorious
la **vida** life
la vida escolar school life
el **video** video
viejo(a) old, **6.1**
el/la **viejo(a)** old person
el **viento** wind
el **viernes** Friday, **BV**
el **vinagre** vinegar
la **viola** viola
el **violín** violin, **2.1**
visible visible
visitar to visit
vital vital
la **vitamina** vitamin
viviente: el ser viviente living creature, being
vivir to live, **5.2**
vivo(a) living, alive
la **vocal** vowel
volar (ue) to fly
el **voleibol** volleyball
volver (ue) to return, **7.1**
volver a casa to return home, **10.2**
la **voz** voice
en voz alta aloud
el **vuelo** flight, **11.1**
el número del vuelo flight number, **11.1**
tomar un vuelo to take a flight, **11.1**
el vuelo nacional domestic flight

Y

y and, **BV**
y cuarto a quarter past (the hour)
y media half past (the hour)
y pico just after (the hour)
ya already; now
la **yarda** yard
yo I, **1.1**
el **yogur** yogurt

Z

la **zanahoria** carrot, **5.2**
la **zapatería** shoe store
el **zapato** shoe, **3.2**
la **zona** zone, area, neighborhood
el **zumo de naranja** orange juice

492

Vocabulario inglés–español

The **Vocabulario inglés-español** contains all productive vocabulary from the text. The reference numbers following each entry indicate the chapter and vocabulary section in which the word is introduced. For example, **2.2** means that the word first appeared actively in **Capítulo 2, Palabras 2. BV** refers to the preliminary **Bienvenidos lessons.** Words without a chapter reference indicate receptive vocabulary (not taught in the **Palabras** sections).

A

a un(a)
able: to be able poder (ue), **7.1**
aboard a bordo de, **11.2**
about (time) a eso de, **4.1**
above por encima de
abstract abstracto(a)
academy la academia
to **accept** aceptar
access el acceso
to **accompany** acompañar
according to según
ache doler
My . . . aches Me duele... , **8.2**
acrylic el acrílico
activity la actividad
actor el actor, **10.2**
actress la actriz, **10.2**
to **adapt** adaptar
to **add** sumar
to **adjust** ajustar
to **admire** admirar
admission ticket la entrada, **10.1**
to **admit** admitir
adorable adorable
to **adore** adorar
to **adorn** adornar
adventure la aventura
African africano(a)
after después de, **5.1**; **(time)** y
It's ten after one. Es la una y diez.
afternoon la tarde
Good afternoon. Buenas tardes., **BV**
in the afternoon por la tarde
this afternoon esta tarde, **9.2**
against contra, **7.1**
agent el/la agente, **11.1**
customs agent el/la agente de aduana, **11.1**
agreed conforme, **14.2**
air el aire
open-air (outdoor) café (market) el café (mercado) al aire libre
airline la línea aérea
airplane el avión, **11.1**
by plane en avión, **11.1**
airport el aeropuerto, **11.1**
aisle el pasillo, **13.2**
a lot muchos(as), **2.1**; mucho, **3.2**
alarmed: to be alarmed alarmarse
album el álbum
algebra el álgebra, **2.2**
alive vivo(a)
all todos(as)
All right. De acuerdo.
allergy la alergia, **8.2**
to **allow** dejar; consentir (ie, i)
almost casi
alone solo(a)
aloud en voz alta
also también, **1.2**
always siempre, **7.1**
A.M. de la mañana
American americano(a)
amusement la diversión
analysis el análisis
analytical analítico(a)
to **analyze** analizar
ancient antiguo(a)
and y, **BV**
Andean andino(a)
anecdote la anécdota
animal el animal
another otro(a)
answer la respuesta
to **answer** contestar
Antarctic la Antártida
antibiotic el antibiótico, **8.2**
antiquity la antigüedad
Anything else? ¿Algo más?, **5.2**
apartment el apartamento, el piso, el departamento, **6.2**
apartment house la casa de apartamentos (apartamentos), **6.2**
to **applaud** aplaudir, **10.2**
applause el aplauso, **10.2**
apple la manzana, **5.2**
to **apply** aplicar
April abril, **BV**
Aragon: from Aragon (Spain) aragonés(a)
arc el arco
archeological arqueológico(a)
archeologist el/la arqueólogo(a)
archeology la arqueología
area el área *(f.)*, la zona

Argentinian argentino(a), **2.1**
argument la disputa
arithmetic la aritmética, **2.2**
arm el brazo, **7.1**
around alrededor de, **6.2; (time)** a eso de, **4.1**
arrival la llegada, **11.1**
arrival and departure screen la pantalla de salidas y llegadas, **11.1**
arrival board el tablero de llegadas, **13.1**
to **arrive** llegar, **4.1**
arrogant altivo, arrogante
arsenal el arsenal
art el arte, **(f.) 2.2**
artichoke la alcachofa, **14.2**
artifact el artefacto
artist el/la artista, **10.2**
artistic artístico(a)
as como
to **ask (a question)** preguntar
to **ask for** pedir (i, i), **14.1**
asleep dormido(a)
aspirin la aspirina, **8.2**
assortment el surtido
astute astuto(a)
at a, en
at about (time) a eso de, **4.1**
at home en casa, **6.2**
at night por la noche
at that time en aquel entonces
at the end of a fines de
at what time? ¿a qué hora?, **10.1**
athletic atlético
attack el ataque
to **attack** atacar
to **attend** asistir
attention: to pay attention prestar atención, **4.2**
audience el público, **10.2**
August agosto, **BV**
aunt la tía, **6.1**
aunt(s) and uncle(s) los tíos, **6.1**
Australia la Australia
author el/la autor(a), **10.2**
autumn el otoño, **BV**
average regular, **2.2**

B
baby el/la bebé
background la ascendencia
backpack la mochila, **3.1**
bacteria la bacteria
bad malo(a), **2.1**
to be in a bad (good) mood estar de mal (buen) humor, **8.1**
back to school la apertura de clases
bag la bolsa, **5.2**
baggage el equipaje, **11.1**
baggage claim el reclamo de equipaje, **11.2**
carry-on baggage el equipaje de mano, **11.1**
ball (basketball, soccer) el balón, **7.1; (tennis, baseball)** la pelota , **7.2**
to throw (kick) the ball tirar el balón, **7.2**
ballpoint pen el bolígrafo, **3.1**
banana el plátano, **5.2**
baptism, el bautizo
bar: bar of soap la barra de jabón, la pastilla de jabón, **12.2**
bargain la ganga
base (baseball) la base, **7.2**
baseball el béisbol, **7.2**
baseball field el campo de béisbol, **7.2**
baseball game el juego de béisbol, **7.2**
baseball player el/la jugador(a) de béisbol, **7.2;** el/la beisbolista
basic básico(a)
basket (basketball) el cesto, la canasta, **7.2**
to make a basket encestar, meter el balón en el cesto, **7.2**
basketball el básquetbol, el baloncesto, **7.2**
basketball court la cancha de básquetbol, **7.2**
Basque vasco(a)
bat el bate, **7.2**
bathing suit el traje de baño, el bañador, **9.1**

bathroom el baño, el cuarto de baño, **6.2**
batter el/la bateador(a), **7.2**
battle la batalla
bay la bahía
to **be** ser, **1.1;** estar, **4.1**
to be able poder (ue), **7.1**
to be accustomed to soler (ue)
to be afraid tener miedo
to be born nacer
to be going to ir a
to be hungry tener hambre, **14.1**
to be included estar incluido, **14.1**
to be named (called) llamarse, **12.1**
to be pleasing gustar
to be thirsty tener sed, **14.1**
to be tied (score) quedar empatado, **7.1**
to be worth valer, **7.2**
to be . . . years old tener... años, **6.2;** cumplir... años
beach la playa, **9.1**
beach resort el balneario, **9.1**
beach towel la toalla playera, **9.1**
bean el frijol, la habichuela, **5.2**
green bean la judía verde, **5.2**
beau el galán
beautiful hermoso(a), bello(a), **1.1**
because porque
to **bear (name)** llevar (el nombre)
bed la cama, **8.1**
to make the bed hacer la cama
to stay in bed guardar cama, **8.1**
bedroom la recámara, el dormitorio, el cuarto (de dormir), **6.2**
beef la carne de res, **14.2**
before antes de, **5.1**
to **begin** comenzar (ie); empezar (ie), **7.1**
beginner el/la principiante, **9.2**

beginning: beginning of school la apertura de clases
behind atrás
being: human being el ser humano
living being el ser viviente
to **believe** creer, **8.2**
below debajo (de); bajo
below zero bajo cero, **9.2**
berth la litera, **13.2**
between entre, **7.1**
beverage el refresco, **5.1**
bicycle la bicicleta
to go by bicycle ir en bicicleta, **13.2**
big grande, **2.1**
bilingual bilingüe
bill la cuenta, **5.1**
biography la biografía
biological biológico(a)
biologist el/la biólogo(a)
biology la biología, **2.1**
birthday el cumpleaños, **6.1**
black negro(a), **3.2**
black coffee el café solo, **5.1**
to **block** bloquear, parar, **7.1**
blond rubio(a), **1.1**
blood la sangre
blouse la blusa, **3.2**
blue azul, **3.2**
blue jeans el blue jean, **3.2**
board: arrival board el tablero de llegadas, **13.1; departure board** el tablero de salidas, **13.1**
to **board** embarcar, **11.2;** abordar; **(the train)** subir al tren, **13.1**
boarding el embarque
boarding house la pensión, **12.2**
boarding pass la tarjeta de embarque, **11.1**
book el libro, **3.1**
boot la bota, **9.2**
to **bore** aburrir
boring aburrido(a), **2.1**
born nacido(a)
bottle la botella, **12.2**
boy el muchacho, **1.1**
boyfriend/girlfriend el/la novio(a)
brave valeroso(a)
bread el pan, **5.1**
breakfast el desayuno, **5.2**
to eat breakfast desayunarse, tomar el desayuno, **12.1**
bright brillante
to **bring** llevar, **6.1;** traer, **14.1**
broadcast la emisión, **6.2**
sports broadcast la emisión deportiva, **6.2**
bronze el bronce, **10.2**
brook el arroyo
brother el hermano, **6.1**
brown de color marrón, **3.2**
brunette moreno(a), **1.1**
brush el cepillo, **12.2**
to **brush one's hair** cepillarse, **12.1**
to **brush one's teeth** cepillarse (lavarse) los dientes, **12.1**
building el edificio
bus el bus, **4.1;** el autobús (la guagua [P.R., Cuba], el camión [Mex.]), **10.1**
school bus el bus escolar, **4.1**
to miss the bus perder el autobús (la guagua, el | camión), **10.1**
but pero
to **buy** comprar, **3.1**
by (plane, car, bus, etc.) en (avión, carro, autobús, etc.)

C

cafe el café, **BV**
cafeteria la cafetería
to **calculate** calcular
calculator la calculadora, **3.1**
calculus el cálculo, **2.2**
called llamado(a)
can el bote, la lata, **5.2**
candid franco(a)
canned enlatado(a)
cap la gorra, **3.2**
capital la capital
captain el/la capitán; el/la comandante, **11.2**
car el carro, el coche, **4.1**
by car en carro, en coche, **4.1**
cafeteria car el coche-cafetería, **13.2**
dining car el coche-comedor, **13.2**
sleeping car el coche-cama, **13.2**
train car el coche, el vagón, **13.2**
card la tarjeta, **11.1**
credit card la tarjeta de crédito, **14.1**
cardinal: cardinal points los puntos cardinales
careful! ¡cuidado!
carefully: very carefully con mucho cuidado
to **caress** acariciar
Caribbean el Caribe
carrot la zanahoria, **5.2**
to **carry** llevar, **3.1**
carry-on luggage el equipaje de mano, **11.1**
case el caso
cash register la caja, **3.1**
cassette el casete, **4.2**
cat el/la gato(a), **6.1**
to **catch** atrapar, **7.2**
catcher el/la receptor(a), el/la cátcher, **7.2**
Catholic católico(a)
to **celebrate** celebrar
celebration la celebración
cell la célula
cellular celular
center el centro
central central, **13.2**
Central America la América Central
century el siglo
cereal el cereal, **5.2**
certainly! ¡claro!
chain (necklace) la cadena
chair la silla
chairlift el telesilla, **9.2**
chalet el chalet
chalkboard la pizarra, el pizarrón, **4.2**
champion el/la campeón(a)
championship el campeonato
to **change** cambiar
to change trains (transfer) cambiar de tren, transbordar, **13.2**

chapter el capítulo
character el personaje
charming encantador(a)
cheap barato(a), **3.2**
check la cuenta, **5.1**
to **check luggage** facturar el equipaje, **11.1**
to **check one's ticket** revisar el boleto, **11.1**
cheese el queso, **5.1**
chemical químico(a)
chemistry la química, **2.2**
chicken el pollo, **5.2**
child el/la niño(a)
children los niños, **6.1**
homeless children los niños desamparados
Chilean chileno(a)
chills: to have chills tener escalofríos, **8.1**
chocolate chocolate, **5.1**
chocolate ice cream el helado de chocolate, **5.1**
choir el coro
to **choose** escoger
chorus el coro
Christian cristiano(a)
Christmas la Navidad
Christmas Eve la Nochebuena
church la iglesia
circle el círculo
city la ciudad
to **claim (luggage)** reclamar (el equipaje), **11.2**
clam la almeja, **14.2**
class la clase, el curso, **2.1**
first class primera clase, en primera, **13.1**
second class segunda clase, en segunda, **13.1**
to **classify** clasificar
classroom la sala de clase, el salón de clase, **4.1**
clinic la clínica
cloth el lienzo
clothing la ropa, **3.2**
clothing store la tienda de ropa, **3.2**
cloud la nube, **9.1**
cloudy: to be cloudy estar nublado, **9.1**
It's cloudy. Hay nubes., **9.1**
club el club, **4.2**
Spanish Club el Club de español, **4.2**
coast la costa
co-ed mixto(a)
coffee el café, **BV**
black coffee, el café solo, **5.1**
coffee with milk el café con leche, **5.1**
cognate la palabra afina
coin la moneda
coincidence la coincidencia
cold (illness) el catarro, **8.1**
to have a cold tener catarro, estar resfriado(a), **8.1**
cold: It's cold. Hace frío., **9.2**
collection la colección, el conjunto
collector el colector
Colombian colombiano(a), **1.1**
colonial colonial
colony la colonia
color el color, **3.2**
What color is . . . ? ¿De qué color es... ?, **3.2**
comb el peine, **12.2**
to **comb one's hair** peinarse, **12.1**
to **come** venir
to come (go) on stage entrar en escena, **10.2**
compact disk el disco compacto, **4.2**
to **compare** comparar
to **compete** competir (i, i)
competition la competición
complete completo(a), **13.2**
compliment: to pay someone compliments echarle flores
composition la composición
computer el ordenador, la computadora
computer science la informática, **2.2**
concert el concierto
condominium el condominio
conductor (train) el/la revisor(a), **13.2**
confirmed bachelor el solterón
to **connect** conectar
to **conquer** conquistar
to **conserve** conservar, **11.1**
to **consider** considerar
to **consist of** consistir (en)
to **consult** consultar
consultation la consulta, **8.2**
contest la competición
continent el continente
to **continue** continuar, **7.2**
to **convert** convertir (ie, i)
cook el/la cocinero(a), **14.1**
copilot el/la copiloto, **11.2**
to **copy** copiar
corn el maíz, **14.2**
to **cost** costar (ue), **3.1**
How much does . . . cost? ¿Cuánto cuesta(n)... ?, **3.1**
Costa Rican costarricense
cough la tos, **8.1**
to have a cough tener tos, **8.1**
to **cough** tener tos, **8.1**
counter el mostrador, **11.1**
country el país, **11.2**
foreign country el país extranjero, **11.2**
course el curso, **2.1**
elective course el curso opcional
required course el curso obligatorio
court la cancha, **2.1**
basketball court la cancha de básquetbol, **7.2**
indoor court la cancha cubierta, **9.1**
outdoor court la cancha al aire libre, **9.1**
tennis court la cancha de tenis, **9.1**
courtesy la cortesía, **BV**
cousin el/la primo(a), **6.1**
to **cover** cubrir
to **create** crear
credit card la tarjeta de crédito, **14.1**
Creole el/la criollo(a)
crew la tripulación, **11.2**

Cuban cubano(a)
Cuban American cubanoamericano(a)
to **cultivate** cultivar
cultural cultural
cup la taza, **14.1**
World Cup la Copa mundial
curtain (stage) el telón, **10.2**
custom la costumbre
customer el/la cliente, **5.1**
customs la aduana, **11.2**
to **cut** cortar, **14.1**

D

dad el papá
to **dance** bailar, **4.2**
dark (haired) moreno(a), **1.1**
data los datos
date la fecha, **BV**
What is today's date? ¿Cuál es la fecha de hoy?, **BV**
to **date** datar
daughter la hija, **6.1**
day el día, **BV**
day before yesterday anteayer
deaf person el/la sordo(a)
death la muerte
December diciembre, **BV**
to **decide** decidir
to **declare** declarar
to **defeat** derrotar
degree (temperature) el grado, **9.2**
delay: with a delay con una demora, **11.1;** con retraso, **13.2**
delicious delicioso(a), rico, **14.2;** sabroso(a)
to **delight** encantar
to **deliver** entregar
deluxe de lujo
departure la salida, **11.1**
arrival and departure screen la pantalla de llegadas y salidas, **11.1**
departure board el tablero de salidas, **13.1**
departure gate la puerta de salida, la sala de salida, **11.1**
departure hour la hora de salida
descendant el/la descendiente
design el diseño
designer el/la diseñador(a)
dessert el postre, **5.1**
destination el destino, **11.1**
diagnosis la diagnosis, **8.2**
dialog el diálogo
diamond el diamante
to **die** morir (ue, u)
difference la diferencia
different diferente
difficult duro(a), difícil, **2.1**
to **dig** excavar
dining car el coche-comedor, el coche-cafetería, **13.2**
dining room el comedor, **6.2**
dinner la cena, **5.2**
to have dinner cenar
direct directo(a), **11**
director el/la director(a)
discipline la asignatura, la disciplina, **2.1**
to **discover** descubrir
to **discuss** discutir
to **disembark** desembarcar, **11.2**
dish el plato, **14.1**
disk: compact disk el disco compacto, **4.2**
diskette el disquete, **3.1**
to **dive** bucear, **9.1**
to **divide** dividir
diving el buceo, **9.1**
divorced: to get divorced divorciarse
doctor el/la médico(a), **8.2**
doctor's office la consulta del médico, el consultorio, **8.2**
to **do** hacer, **11**
to do well (on an exam) salir bien (en un examen)
dog el perro, **6.1**
domestic doméstico(a), **2.1**
Dominican dominicano(a), **2.1**
Dominican Republic la República Dominicana
donkey el asno
door la puerta
dose la dosis, **8.2**
dot: on the dot en punto, **4.1**
doubles dobles, **9.1**
doubt la duda
doughnut (a type of) el churro
dozen la docena
drawing el dibujo
dream el sueño
dreamed of imaginado(a)
dress el vestido
to **dribble (basketball)** driblar, **7.2**
drink (beverage) el refresco, **5.1;** la bebida
to **drink** beber, **5.1**
to drink water (milk, coffee) tomar agua (leche, café), **14.1**
druggist el/la farmacéutico(a), **8.2**
drugstore la farmacia, **8.2**
dubbed doblado(a), **10.1**
during durante

E

e-mail el correo electrónico
each cada, **1.2**
early temprano, **12.1**
to **earn** ganar
easel el caballete
east el este
easy fácil, **2.1**
to **eat** comer, **5.1**
to eat breakfast desayunarse, tomar el desayuno, **12.1**
economical económico(a), **12.2**
economics: home economics la economía doméstica, **2.1**
economy la economía
Ecuadorean ecuatoriano(a), **2.1**
education: physical education la educación física, **2.2**
egg el huevo, **5.2**
eggplant la berenjena, **14.2**
eight ocho, **BV**
eight hundred ochocientos(as), **3.2**

eighteen dieciocho, **BV**
eighth octavo(a), **6.2**
eighty ochenta, **2.1**
electronic mail (e-mail) el correo electrónico
elegant elegante
element el elemento
elevator el ascensor, **6.2**
eleven once, **BV**
else: Anything else? ¿Algo más?, **5.2**
No, nothing else. No, nada más, **5.2**
emotion la emoción
emphasis el énfasis
to **emphasize** dar énfasis, enfatizar
employee el/la empleado(a), el/la dependiente(a), **3.1**
enamored: to become enamored of (to fall for) flechar
enchilada la enchilada, **BV**
end el fin, **BV**
at the end of a fines de
enemy el/la enemigo(a)
energy la energía, **8**
English el inglés, **2.2**
to **enjoy** gozar
to enjoy oneself divertirse (ie, i), **12.2**
enough bastante, **1.1**
to **enter** entrar, **4.1**
entire entero(a)
episode el episodio
epoch la época
equation la ecuación
equipment el equipo, **7.1**
to **erase** borrar, **3.1**
eraser la goma de borrar, **3.1**
errant: knight errant el caballero andante
especially especialmente, particularmente, sobre todo
essentially esencialmente
to **establish** fundar
esteemed estimado(a)
ethnic étnico(a)
Europe la Europa
evening la noche
evening gown el traje de gala
Good evening. Buenas noches., **BV**
in the evening por la noche
everyone todos, **2.2;** todo el mundo
everything todos(as)
exactly exactamente, **11**
to **exaggerate** exagerar, **11**
exam el examen, **4.2**
to **examine** examinar, **8.2**
example: for example por ejemplo
to **excavate** excavar
excavation la excavación
excellent excelente
Excuse (me). Perdón.
exhibition (art) la exposición (de arte), **10.1**
to **exist** existir
expedition la expedición
expensive caro(a), **3.2**
expert el/la experto(a), **9.2**
to **explain** explicar, **4.2**
explosion la explosión
expression la expresión
means of expression el modo de expresión
extraordinary extraordinario(a)
extreme extremo(a)
eye el ojo

F

face la cara, **12.1**
faithful fiel
to **fall asleep** dormirse (ue, u), **12.1**
false falso(a)
fame la fama
family la familia, **6.1**
family (related to) familiar
famous famoso(a), **1.2**
fan (sports) el/la aficionado(a)
fantastic fantástico(a), **1.2**
fare la tarifa
fast rápido(a)
as fast as possible a toda prisa
fat gordo(a), **1.2**
father el padre, **6.1**
father-in-law el suegro
favorite favorito(a)
fear el miedo, el terror
February febrero, **BV**
fever la fiebre, **8.1**
to have a fever tener fiebre, **8.1**
few pocos(as), **2.1**
a few unos(as)
fiancé(e) el/la novio(a)
field el campo
baseball field el campo de béisbol, **7.2**
soccer field el campo de fútbol, **7.1**
fifteen quince, **BV**
fifteen-year-old (girl) la quinceañera
fifth quinto(a), **6.2**
fifty cincuenta, **2.1**
to **fight** luchar
figurative figurativo(a)
film la película, **6.2;** el film, **10.1**
finally por fin
to **find** hallar; encontrar (ue)
fine bien, **BV;** Conforme., **14.2**
fine-looking gallardo(a)
finger el dedo
first primero(a), **BV**
fish el pescado, **5.2**
five cinco, **BV**
five hundred quinientos(as) **3.2**
flight el vuelo, **11.1**
flight attendant el/la asistente de vuelo, **11.2**
flight number el número del vuelo, **11.1**
floor la planta, el piso, **6.2**
ground floor la planta baja, **6.2**
flower la flor
flu la gripe, **8.1**
to **fly** volar (ue)
folder la carpeta, **3.1**
folk healer el/la curandero(a)
to **follow** seguir (i, i)
following siguiente
fond of aficionado(a)
food la comida, **5.2;** el alimento, el comestible, **14.2**
foolish tonto(a)
foot el pie, **7.1**

on foot a pie, 4.1
for por, para
for example por ejemplo
foreign extranjero(a), 11.2
fork el tenedor, 14.1
to form formar
forty cuarenta, 2.1
to found fundar
four cuatro, BV
four hundred cuatrocientos(as), 3.2
fourteen catorce, BV
fourth cuarto(a), 6.2
frank franco(a)
free libre, 5.1
French el francés, 2.2
French fries las papas fritas, 5.1
fresh fresco(a)
Friday el viernes, BV
fried frito(a), 5.1
friend el/la amigo(a), el/la compañero(a), 1.1
frightful espantoso
from de, BV
front: in front of delante de, 10.1
frozen congelado(a), helado(a), 5.1
frozen foods los productos congelados, 5.2
fruit la fruta, 5.2
to fry freír (i, i), 14.1
full (train, bus, etc.) completo(a)
funny cómico(a); gracioso(a), 1.1
furious furioso(a)
furniture los muebles
fury la furia
future el futuro

G

gallant gallardo(a)
game el partido, 7.1; el juego, 7.2
baseball game el juego de béisbol, 7.2
garage el garaje, 6.2
garden el jardín, 6.2
garlic el ajo, 14.2
gate: departure gate la puerta de salida, 11.1
generally generalmente
generous generoso(a), 1.2
gentleman el señor, BV
geography la geografía, 2.2
geometry la geometría, 2.2
German el alemán, 2.1
to get a good (bad) grade sacar una nota buena (mala), 4.2
to get dressed vestirse (i, i); ponerse la ropa, 12.1
to get off (bus, train, etc.) bajar(se) (del bus, tren, etc.), 13.2
to get on abordar; subir, 13.1
to get on (horse) montar (caballo)
to get on board (bus, train, etc.) subir (al bus, tren, etc.), 13.1
to get up levantarse, 12.1
giant el gigante
gift el regalo, 6.1
girl la muchacha, 1.1
to give dar, 4.2; regalar (gift)
to give (throw) a party dar una fiesta, 4.2
to give up renunciar
glass (drinking) el vaso, 12.1
glove el guante, 7.2
to go ir, 4.1
to go by bicycle ir en bicicleta, 12.2
to go by car ir en coche
to go back volver (ue)
to go down bajar
to go home volver a casa
to go shopping ir de compras, 5.2
to go through pasar por, 11.1
to go to bed acostarse (ue), 12.1
to go up subir, 6.2
to go (walk) around andar
goal el gol, 7.1; la portería, 7.1
to score a goal meter un gol, 7.1
goalie el/la portero(a), 7.1
goalkeeper el/la portero(a), 7.1
godfather el padrino
godmother la madrina
godparents los padrinos
gold el oro
good bueno(a); buen
Good afternoon. Buenas tardes., BV
Good evening. Buenas noches., BV
Good morning. Buenos días., BV
good-bye! ¡adiós!, ¡chao!, BV
good-looking guapo(a), bonito(a), lindo(a), 1.1
Gosh! ¡Dios mío!, 11
gossip: piece of gossip el chisme
grade la nota, 4.2
grammar la gramática
grandchildren los nietos, 6.1
granddaughter, la nieta, 6.1
grandfather el abuelo, 6.1
grandmother la abuela, 6.1
grandparents los abuelos, 6.1
grandson el nieto, 6.1
gray gris, 3.2
great gran(de)
great event el buen suceso
greater mayor
green verde, 3.2
green bean la judía verde, 5.2
greeting el saludo, BV
ground el suelo
group el grupo
to guard guardar, 7.1
Guatemalan guatemalteco(a)
to guess adivinar
guitar la guitarra
gulf el golfo
gymnasium el gimnasio

H

hair el pelo, 12.1
half medio(a), 5.2
half an hour media hora, 14
second half el segundo tiempo, 7.1
ham el jamón, 5.1
hamburger la hamburguesa, 5.1
hand la mano, 7.1
to shake hands dar la mano

handsome guapo(a), **1.1**
to **hang** colgar (ue)
to **happen** pasar
What happened (to you)? ¿Qué te pasó?
happy contento(a), **8.1**
hard duro(a), **2.1**
hardworking ambicioso(a), **1.1**
hat el sombrero, la gorra, **3.2**
to **have** tener (ie), **6.1**
to have chills tener escalofríos, **8.1**
to have a cold tener catarro, estar resfriado(a), **8.1**
to have a drink (snack) tomar un refresco (una merienda), **4.2**
to have a fever tener fiebre, **8.1**
to have a headache tener dolor de cabeza, **8.1**
to have a sore throat tener dolor de garganta, **8.1**
to have a stomachache tener dolor de estómago, **8.1**
to have to tener que
They're having a good time. Lo están pasando muy bien., **12.2**
he él, **1.1**
head la cabeza, **7.1**
headache el dolor de cabeza, **8.1**
health la salud, **8.1**
to **hear** oír
heart el corazón
heartthrob el galán
Hello! ¡Hola!, **BV**; ¡Diga! (answering the telephone—Spain), **14.2**
to **help** ayudar, **13.1**
her su, **6.1**; la *(pron.)*
here aquí
Here is (are)... Aquí tiene...
heritage la ascendencia
hero el héroe
Hi! ¡Hola!, **BV**
to **hide** esconder
high alto(a), **1.1**
high school el colegio, la escuela secundaria, la escuela superior, **1.1**
hike: to take a hike dar una caminata, **12.2**
him lo
his su, **6.1**
historical histórico(a)
history la historia, **2.1**
to **hit (tennis)** golpear, **9.1**; **(baseball)** batear, **7.2**
hole el agujero
home la casa, **6.2**
at home en casa
country home la casa de campo
home economics la economía doméstica, **2.2**
home plate (baseball) el platillo, **7.2**
home run el jonrón, **7.2**
homeless desamparado(a)
homeless children los niños desamparados
honest honesto(a), **1.2**
honor el honor
horrible horrible
hospital el hospital, **8.2**
hot: It's hot. Hace calor., **9.1**
hotel (inexpensive) el hostal, **12.2**
hour la hora
per hour por hora
house la casa, **6.2**
apartment house la casa de apartamentos (departamentos), **6.2**
private house la casa privada (particular), **6.2**
how? ¿como?, **1.1**
How absurd! ¡Qué absurdo!
How are you? ¿Qué tal?, **BV**; ¿Cómo estás?, **8.1**
How many? ¿Cuántos(as)?, **2.1**
How much? ¿Cuánto?, **3.1**
How much does it cost? ¿Cuánto es?, ¿Cuánto cuesta?, **3.1**
How old is (are)... ¿Cuántos años tiene(n)... ?, **6.1**
human humano(a)
human being el ser humano
humble humilde
hungry: to be hungry tener hambre, **14.1**
to **hurt** doler (ue), **8.2**
My... hurt(s) me Me duele(n)..., **8.2**
husband el marido, el esposo, **6.1**

I

I yo, **1.2**
ice cream el helado, **5.1**
chocolate (vanilla) ice cream el helado de chocolate (de vainilla), **5.1**
iced tea el té helado, **5.1**
idea la idea
ideal ideal, **1.2**
idealist el/la idealista
if si
illusion la ilusión
imagined imaginado(a)
immediately enseguida, inmediatamente, **5.1**
immense inmenso(a)
to **imply that** dar a entender
important importante
impossible imposible
in en
in front of delante de
Inca el/la inca
to **include** incluir, **5.1**
included incluido(a), **5.1**
Is the tip included? ¿Está incluido el servicio?, **5.1**
incredible increíble
independence la independencia
Indian indio(a)
to **indicate** indicar, **11.1**
indicator el indicador, **7.1**
indigenous indígena
individual individual, **7.2**
individual sport el deporte individual, **7.2**
inexpensive barato(a), **3.2**
influence la influencia
to **inform** informar, **13.2**
information la información

inhabitant el/la habitante
injection la inyección, 8.2
inheritance la herencia
inning la entrada, 7.2
insane loco(a)
to inspect inspeccionar, 11.2
to inspect (check) the ticket revisar el boleto, 11.1
inspection: passport inspection el control de pasaportes, 11.2
inspection: security inspection el control de seguridad, 11.1
instant el instante
instruction la instrucción
instrument el instrumento
integral íntegro(a)
intelligent inteligente, 2.1
interest el interés
to interest interesar
interesting interesante, 2.1
intermediate intermedio(a)
international internacional
interpretation la interpretación
interview la entrevista, 4.1
invitation la invitación
to invite invitar (a), 6.1
island la isla
it la *(f.)*; lo *(m.)*
Italian italiano(a)

J

jacket la chaqueta, el saco, 3.2
jai alai la pelota vasca
January enero, BV
jingle el retintín
July julio, BV
to jump saltar
to jump up sobresaltar
June junio, BV

K

keyboard el teclado
to kick tirar (con el pie), 7.1
to kick the ball tirar el balón, 7.2
kilogram el kilo, 5.2
king el rey
kitchen la cocina, 6.2
knapsack la mochila, 3.1
knee la rodilla, 7.1
knife el cuchillo, 14.1
knight el caballero
knight errant el caballero andante
knight's attendant el escudero
to know saber, 11.2; conocer, 11.1
to know how saber, 11.2

L

laboratory el laboratorio, 2.1
lady la dama
lady-in-waiting la dama
lake el lago
lamb el cordero, 14.2
lance la lanza
to land aterrizar, 11.2
landscape el paisaje
language la lengua, 2.2
large grande
last último(a)
last night anoche, 9.2
last week la semana pasada, 9.2
last weekend el fin de semana pasado
last year el año pasado, 9.2
late tarde; con una demora, 11.1; con retraso, 13.2
later luego, BV
See you later! ¡Hasta luego!, BV
Latin el latín, 2.2
Latin latino(a)
Latin America Latinoamérica
Latin American latinoamericano(a)
lazy perezoso(a), 1.1
league la liga
Major Leagues las Grandes Ligas
to learn aprender, 5.1
to leave salir
to leave late salir tarde, 11.1
to leave on time salir a tiempo, 11.1
to leave something behind dejar, 14.1
lecture la conferencia
left izquierdo(a), 7.1
leg la pierna, 7.1
lemonade la limonada, BV
to lend prestar, 4.2
lesson la lección, 4.2
to let dejar; permitir, 11.1
let's see a ver
Will you please let me see your passport? Mepermite ver su pasaporte, por favor?, 11.1
letter la carta, 6.2; (of the alphabet) la letra, 11.1
lettuce la lechuga, 5.2
liberator el/la libertador(a)
life la vida
school life la vida escolar
to lift levantar
light la luz
to light encender (ie)
like el gusto
to like gustar
Lima: from Lima (Peru) limeño(a)
line (of people) la cola, la fila, 10.1
linen el lienzo
to listen (to) escuchar, 4.2
listen! ¡oye!, 1.1
literal literal
literary literario(a)
literature la literatura, 2.1
little: a little poco(a)
to live vivir, 5.2
live vivo(a)
living viviente
living creature el ser viviente
living room la sala, 6.2
lobster la langosta, 14.2
local local, 13.2
long largo(a), 3.2
Look! ¡Mira!
to look at mirar, 3.1
to look at oneself mirarse, 12.1
to look for buscar, 3.1
to lose perder (ie), 7.1
lotion: suntan lotion la loción bronceadora, 9.1
lotto el loto
lover el/la enamorado(a)
low bajo(a), 4.2
to lower bajar
luggage el equipaje, 11.1

carry-on luggage el equipaje de mano, **11.1**
luggage claim ticket el talón, **11.1**
lunch el almuerzo, **5.2**
luxurious lujoso(a)

M

ma'am la señora, **BV**
made hecho(a)
Madrid (native of) madrileño(a)
magazine la revista, **6.2**
magnificent magnífico(a)
mail el correo
e-mail (electronic mail) el correo electrónico
main principal
mainly principalmente
Major Leagues las Grandes Ligas
majority la mayor parte, la mayoría
to **make** hacer
to make a basket (basketball) encestar, **7.2**
to make the bed hacer la cama, **13**
makeup el maquillaje, **12.1**
to put one's makeup on maquillarse, ponerse el maquillaje, **12.1**
male el varón
man el hombre, el señor
manner la manera, el modo
many muchos(as), **2.1**
map el mapa
March marzo, **BV**
marker el marcador, **3.1**
market el mercado, **5.2**
marmalade la mermelada, **5.2**
marriage el matrimonio
married: to be married estar casado(a)
marvelous maravilloso(a)
mass la masa
master el/la maestro(a)
material el material, **3.1**
mathematics las matemáticas, **2.2**
matter: What's the matter (with you)? ¿Qué te pasa?
May mayo, **BV**
Maya el/la maya
me mí, **5.1;** me, **8**
meal la comida, **5.2**
meaning el significado, el sentido
means el medio, el modo
by no means de ninguna manera, **1.1**
means of expression el modo de expresión
meat la carne, **5.2**
medal la medalla
medical office la consulta del médico, el consultorio, **8.2**
medicine (drug) el medicamento, **8.2**; **(discipline, field),** la medicina, **8.2**
medium el medio
melancholic melancólico(a)
member el miembro, **4.2**
menu el menú, **5.1**
mestizo el/la mestizo(a)
Mexican mexicano(a), **1.1**
Mexican American mexicanoamericano(a)
microbe el microbio, **2.1**
microscope el microscopio, **2.1**
microscopic microscópico(a)
middle: middle school la escuela intermedia
midnight la medianoche
mile la milla
milk la leche
million el millón
mineral water el agua mineral, **12.2**
minute el minuto
mirror el espejo, **12.1**
to **miss the bus** perder el autobús (la guagua, el camión), **10.1**
Miss señorita, **BV**
mixed mixto(a)
mixture la mezcla
model el modelo
modem el módem
modern moderno(a)
mom la mamá
moment el momento
Monday el lunes, **BV**
money el dinero, **14.1**
monitor el monitor
monster el monstruo
month el mes, **BV**
monument el monumento
mood el humor, **8.1**
to be in a bad mood estar de mal humor, **8.1**
to be in a good mood estar de buen humor, **8.1**
moon la luna
more más
moreover además
morning la mañana
Good morning. Buenos días., **BV**
in the morning por la mañana
this morning esta mañana
mother la madre, **6.1**
motive el motivo
to **mount (horse)** montar (caballo)
mountain la montaña
mountain range la sierra
mouse el ratón
to **move** mover (ue)
movie la película, **6.2;** el film, **10.1**
movie theater el cine, **10.1**
Mr. el señor, **BV**
Mrs. la señora, **BV**
Ms. la señorita, la señora, **BV**
much mucho, **3.2**
mulatto el/la mulato(a)
multiplication la multiplicación
to **multiply** multiplicar
mural el mural, **10.2**
muralist el/la muralista
museum el museo, **10.1**
music la música, **2.2**
my mi, **6.1**

N

name el nombre
My name is. . . . Me llamo… , **12.1**
napkin la servilleta, **14.1**
national nacional

nationality la nacionalidad, **1.2**
what nationality? ¿de qué nacionalidad?
native indígena
natural: natural resources los recursos naturales
natural sciences las ciencias naturales
near cerca de, **6.2**
necessary necesario(a)
neck el cuello
necktie la corbata, **3.2**
to **need** necesitar, **3.1**
neighbor el/la vecino(a)
nephew el sobrino, **6.1**
nervous nervioso(a), **8.1**
net la red
to go over the net pasar por encima de la red, **9.1**
to surf the Net navegar por la red
nettle la ortiga
never jamás, never
new nuevo(a)
news las noticias, **6.2**
newspaper el periódico, **6.2**
newsstand el quiosco, **13.1**
next próximo(a), **13.2**
nice simpático(a), **1.2**
Nice to meet you. Mucho gusto.
niece la sobrina, **6.1**
night la noche
at night por la noche
Good night. Buenas noches., **BV**
last night anoche, **9.2**
nine nueve, **BV**
nine hundred novecientos(as), **3.2**
nineteen diecinueve, **BV**
ninety noventa, **2.1**
ninth noveno(a), **6.2**
no no, **BV**
by no means de ninguna manera, **1.1**
no one nadie
noble noble
nobody nadie
none ninguno(a), **1.1**
noon el mediodía
north el norte
North America la América del Norte
North American norteamericano(a)
northwest noroeste, **8**
no-smoking section la sección de no fumar, **11.1**
not at all de ninguna manera
notable notable
note: to take notes tomar apuntes, **4.2**
to **note** apuntar
notebook el cuaderno, el bloc, **3.1**
nothing nada, **5.2**
Nothing else. Nada más., **5.2**
novel la novela
novelist el/la novelista
November noviembre, **BV**
now ahora, **4.2**
now and then de vez en cuando
nowadays hoy día
number el número, **1.2**
flight number el número del vuelo, **11.1**
seat number el número del asiento, **11.1**
nuptial nupcial

O

object el objeto
obligatory obligatorio(a), **2.1**
observation la observación
to **observe** observar
observer el/la observador(a)
obstacle el obstáculo
occupied (taken) ocupado(a), **5.1**
ocean el océano
o'clock: It's (two) o'clock. Son las (dos).
October octubre, **BV**
of de, **BV**
of course! ¡claro!
official oficial
oil el aceite, **14.2**
OK! ¡vale!
old anciano(a), antiguo(a), viejo(a), **6.1**
olive: olive oil el aceite de oliva
on en
on board a bordo de, **11.2**
on the contrary al contrario
on the dot en punto, **4.1**
on time a tiempo, **11.1**
on top of encima de; sobre, **9.1**
once and for all definitivamente, **11**
one uno, **BV**
one hundred cien(to), **2.1**
one thousand mil, **3.2**
one-way: one-way ticket el billete sencillo, **13.1**
only sólo, solamente
to **open** abrir, **8.2**
to open one's suitcases abrir las maletas, **11.2**
opening: opening of school la apertura de clases
opera la ópera, **2.1**
opinion: What's your opinion? ¿Qué opinas?
operator el/la operador(a)
optional opcional
orally oralmente
orange (color) anaranjado(a), **3.2**
orange (fruit) la naranja, **5.2**
orange juice el jugo de naranja, **12.1**
order la orden, **5.1**
organism el organismo
origin el origen
original: in its original language version en versión original, **10.1**
orphanage el orfanato
Otavalo (of or from) otavaleño(a)
other otro(a), **2.2**
our nuestro(a)
outdoor al aire libre
outfielder el/la jardinero(a), **7.2**
outskirts los alrededores
over por encima de
to **owe** deber

P

to **pack one's suitcase** hacer la maleta, **11.2**
package el paquete, **5.2**
page la página
Web page la página Web
pain el dolor, **8.1**
I have a pain in . . . Tengo dolor de... , **8.2**
to **paint** pintar
painter el/la pintor(a)
painting el cuadro, la pintura, **2.1**
pair el par, **3.2**
pair of tennis shoes el par de tenis, **3.2**
Panamanian panameño(a), **2.1**
pants el pantalón, **3.2**
paper el papel, **3.1**
sheet of paper la hoja de papel, **3.1**
parents los padres, **6.1**
park el parque
parka el anorak, **9.2**
part la parte
party la fiesta, **4.2**
to give (throw) a party dar una fiesta, **4.2**
pass (permission) el pase
to **pass** pasar, **7.2**
passenger el/la pasajero(a), **11.1**
passport el pasaporte, **11.1**
passport inspection el control de pasaportes, **11.2**
past pasado(a)
patient el/la enfermo(a), **8.1**
to **pay** pagar, **3.1**
to pay attention prestar atención, **4.2;** hacer caso
pea el guisante, **5.2**
peaceful tranquilo(a)
pen la pluma; **(ballpoint)** el bolígrafo, **3.1**
pencil el lápiz, **3.1**
peninsula la península
penny el centavo
people la gente
pepper la pimienta, **14.1**
percent por ciento
performance la función, la representación, **10.2**
to put on a performance dar una representación, **10.2**
to **permit** permitir, **11.1**
person la persona, **1.2**
Peruvian peruano(a)
peso el peso, **BV**
petition la petición
pharmacist el/la farmacéutico(a), **8.2**
pharmacy la farmacia, **8.2**
photo la foto
photograph la fotografía
phrase la frase
physical education la educación física, **2.2**
physics la física, **2.2**
piano el piano
to **pick up** recoger
to pick up (claim) the luggage recoger el equipaje, **11.2**
picture el cuadro, **10.2**
pig (pork) el cerdo, **14.2**
pill la pastilla, la píldora, la tableta, **8.2**
pilot el/la piloto, **11.2**
pink rosado(a), **3.2**
piping (embroidery) el cordoncillo
pitcher el/la lanzador(a), el/la pícher, **7.2**
pizza la pizza, **BV**
place el lugar, el sitio
to **place** colocar, meter, **7.1**
to place one's suitcase poner la maleta, **11.2**
plane el avión, **11.1**
plate el plato, **14.1**
home plate el platillo, **7.2**
plateau la mesa
platform (railroad) el andén, **13.1**
play la obra teatral, **10.2**
to **play** jugar (ue), **7.1**
player el/la jugador(a), **7.1**
baseball player el/la jugador(a) de béisbol, **7.2**
playwright el/la dramaturgo(a)
plaza la plaza
pleasant agradable
please por favor, **BV**
P.M. de la tarde, de la noche
pocket el bolsillo
pocketbook la bolsa, **13.1**
poem el poema
poet el poeta
poetry la poesía
point (score) el tanto, el punto, **7.1**
cardinal points los puntos cardinales
to score a point marcar un tanto, **7.1**
pole: ski pole el bastón, **9.2**
pool la alberca, la piscina, **9.1**
political político(a)
poncho el poncho
poor pobre
poor boy (girl) (/)el/la pobre
popular popular, **2.1**
popularity la popularidad
pork el cerdo, **14.2**
porter el/la maletero(a), el mozo, **13.1**
portrait el retrato
possibility la posibilidad
possible posible
potato la papa, **5.1**
mashed potatoes el puré de papas
to **practice** practicar
pre-Columbian precolombino(a)
to **prefer** preferir (ie, i)
to **prepare** preparar, **4.2**
to **prescribe** recetar, **8.2**
prescription la receta, **8.2**
to **present** presentar
pretty hermoso(a), lindo(a), bonito(a), bello(a), **1.1**
price el precio
priest el sacerdote
primary primario(a)
princess la princesa
principal principal
printer la impresora
private particular, privado(a), **6.2**
private house la casa particular (privada), **6.2**
prize el premio
Nobel Prize el Premio Nóbel
problem el problema

to **process** procesar
procession la procesión
to **proclaim** proclamar
produced producido(a)
product el producto, **2.1**
professor el/la profesor(a), **2.1**
program (TV) la emisión, **6.2**
sports program la emisión deportiva, **6.2**
to **project** proyectar, **10.1**
promise la promesa
protoplasm el protoplasma
public público(a)
to **publish** publicar
Puerto Rican puertorriqueño(a)
to **pull out** arrancar
puppy el perrito
purchase la compra, **3.1**
pure puro(a)
to **put** poner, **11.1**
to put on clothes ponerse la ropa, **12.1**
to put on a performance dar una representación, **10.2**
to put on makeup ponerse el maquillaje, maquillarse, **12.1**

Q

quarrel la disputa
quarter: a quarter to menos cuarto
a quarter past y cuarto
queen la reina
question la pregunta
to ask a question preguntar
quetzal el quetzal
quickly rápido
quite bastante, **1.1**

R

racquet la raqueta, **9.1**
railroad el ferrocarril
railway platform el andén, **13.1**
railroad station la estación de ferrocarril, **13.1**
railroad track la vía, **13.1**
to **rain: It's raining.** Llueve., **9.1**
rate la tarifa
rather bastante, **1.1**
razor la navaja, **12.1**
to **read** leer, **5.1**
reading la lectura
ready listo(a)
realist el/la realista
realistic realista
really realmente
rear (in the) atrás
reasonable razonable
to **rebound** rebotar
to **receive** recibir, **5.1**
to receive a good (bad) grade recibir una nota buena (mala), **4.2**
recently recientemente; recién
rectangle el rectángulo
red rojo(a), **3.2**
reduced reducido(a)
to **reflect** reflexionar, reflejar
reflection el reflejo
refreshment el refresco, **5.1**
region la región
regular regular, **2.2**
relative el/la pariente, **6.1**
religious religioso(a)
to **remain** quedar, **7.1**
to **remember** acordarse (ue) de, **3.2**
to **renounce** renunciar
to **rent** alquilar, rentar, **10.1**
to **repeat** repetir (i, i)
to **replace** reemplazar
report el reportaje
to **represent** representar
republic la república
Dominican Republic la República Dominicana
to **request** pedir (i, i), **14.1**
required: required course el curso obligatorio, **2.1**
reservation la reservación
to **reserve** reservar, **14.2**
reserved reservado(a), **13.2**
resident el/la residente
resort: seaside resort el balneario, **9.1**
resource el recurso
natural resources los recursos naturales
rest lo demás
restaurant el restaurante, **14.1**
to **return** volver (ue), **7.1**;
(something) devolver (ue), **7.2**
rice el arroz, **5.2**
rich rico(a); con mucha plata
right derecho(a), **7.1**
right away enseguida, **5.1**
river el río
to **roll** rodar
roll (bread) el pan dulce, **5.1**
roll of toilet paper el rollo de papel higiénico, **12.2**
romantic romántico(a)
room la sala, el salón, el cuarto, la pieza, **4.1**
bathroom el cuarto de baño, **6.2**
classroom la sala (el salón) de clase, **4.1**
dining room el comedor, **6.2**
living room la sala, **6.2**
waiting room la sala de espera, **13.1**
rose la rosa
round-trip ticket el billete de ida y vuelta, **13.1**
routine la rutina, **12.1**
row (of seats) la fila, **10.1**
royal real
rubber la goma, **3.1**
ruin la ruina
rumor el rumor
to **run** correr, **7.2**
rural rural

S

to **sacrifice** sacrificar
sad triste
sail (of a mill) el aspa
sailboard la plancha de vela, **9.1**
saint el santo
salad la ensalada, **5.1**
salesperson el/la dependiente(a), el/la empleado(a), **3.1**
salt la sal, **14.1**
same mismo(a), **2.1**
sand la arena, **9.1**

sandal el huarache, el alparagata
sandwich el bocadillo, **5.1**, el sándwich, **BV**
sash la faja
Saturday el sábado, **BV**
saucer el platillo, **14.1**
to **save** salvar
to **say** decir
scale la báscula, **11.1**
scene la escena
schedule el horario, **13.1**
school schedule el horario escolar
school la escuela, el colegio, **1.1**
elementary school la escuela primaria
high school el colegio, la escuela secundaria, la escuela superior
middle school la escuela intermedia
school (pertaining to) escolar
school bus el bus escolar, **4.1**
school life la vida escolar, **4.1**
school schedule el horario escolar
school supplies los materiales escolares, **3.1**
science la ciencia, **2.2**
natural sciences las ciencias naturales
social sciences las ciencias sociales
scientific científico(a)
scientist el/la científico(a)
score el tanto, **7.1**
to **score: to score a goal** meter un gol, **7.1**
to score a point marcar un tanto, **7.1**
scoreboard el tablero indicador, **7.1**
screen la pantalla, **10.1**
sculptor el/la escultor(a), **10.2**
sculpture la escultura
sea el mar, **9.1**
Caribbean Sea el mar Caribe
search: in search of en busca de
season la estación, **BV**
seasoning el condimento, **14.1**
seat (theater) la butaca, **10.1; (airplane, train, etc.)** el asiento, **11.1;** la plaza, **13.2**
seat number el número del asiento, **11.1**
second segundo(a), **6.2**
second half el segundo tiempo, **7.1**
secondary secundario(a), **1.1**
secret secreto(a)
security: security control el control de seguridad, **11.1**
to **see** ver, **5.1**
See you later! ¡Hasta luego!, **BV**
See you soon! ¡Hasta mañana!, **BV**
See you tomorrow! ¡Hasta mañana!, **BV**
to see a film ver una película, **10.2**
to **select** seleccionar
selection la selección
to **sell** vender, **5.2;** despachar, **8.2**
to **send** transmitir, enviar
sentence la frase
September septiembre, **BV**
series la serie
World Series la Serie mundial
serious serio(a), **1.1**
to **serve** servir (i, i), **14.1**
service (tip) el servicio, **5.1**
set (theater) el escenario, **10.2**
to **set the table** poner la mesa, **14.1**
seven siete, **BV**
seven hundred setecientos(as), **3.2**
seventeen diecisiete, **BV**
seventh séptimo(a), **6.2**
seventy setenta, **2.1**
several varios(as)
to **sew** coser
sewing la costura
to **shake hands** dar la mano
shampoo el champú, **12.2**
sharp en punto, **4.1**
to **shave** afeitarse, **12.1**
shaving cream la crema de afeitar, **12.1**
shawl el poncho
she ella, **1.1**
sheet: sheet of paper la hoja de papel, **3.1**
shellfish el marisco, **5.2**
sherbet el sorbete
to **shine** brillar, **9.1**
shirt la camisa, **3.2**
shoe el zapato, **3.2**
shoe size el número, **3.2**
shoe store la zapatería
to **shop** ir de compras, **5.2**
short (person) bajo(a), **1.1; (length)** corto(a), **3.2**
short story la historieta
shorts el pantalón corto, **3.2**
shot (injection) la inyección, **8.2**
show la sesión, **10.1;** el espectáculo, **10.2**
to see a show ver un espectáculo, **10.2**
shower: to take a shower tomar una ducha, **12.1**
shrimp el camarón, **14.2**
shy tímido(a), **1.2**
sick enfermo(a), **8.1**
sick person el/la enfermo(a), **8.1**
side el lado; *(adj.)* lateral, **13.2**
sierra la sierra
to **sigh** suspirar
similar parecido(a), similar
simple sencillo(a); simple
since como; desde, **1.2**
sincere sincero(a), **1.2**
to **sing** cantar, **4.2**
single soltero(a)
single-celled monocelular
singles (tennis) singles, **9.1**
sir el señor, **BV**
sister la hermana, **6.1**
to **sit down** sentarse (ie), **12.1**
six seis, **BV**
six hundred seiscientos(as), **3.2**
sixteen dieciséis, **BV**
sixth sexto(a), **6.2**
sixty sesenta, **2.1**

size (clothes) el tamaño, la talla; **(shoes)** el número, **3.2**
What size do you take? ¿Qué talla (número) usa Ud.?, ¿Qué número usa (calza) Ud.?, **3.2**
ski el esquí, **9.2**
water-ski el esquí acuático, **9.1**
to **ski** esquiar, **9.1**
ski lift el telesquí, **9.2**
ski pole el bastón, **9.2**
ski resort la estación de esquí, **9.2**
ski slope la pista, **9.2**
skier el/la esquiador(a), **9.2**
skiing el esquí, **9.2**
skirt la falda, **3.2**
sky el cielo, **9.1**
to **sleep** dormir (ue, u)
sleeping bag el saco de dormir, **12.2**
sleeping car el coche-cama, **13.2**
small pequeño(a), **2.1**
smile: little smile la sonrisita
smoking (no-smoking) section la sección de (no) fumar, **13.1**
snack la merienda, **4.2**
to have (eat) a snack tomar una merienda, **4.2**
sneakers los tenis, **3.2**
to **sneeze** estornudar, **8.1**
snow la nieve, **9.2**
to **snow** nevar (ie), **9.2**
so tan
so much tanto(a)
soap el jabón, **12.2**
bar of soap la barra (la pastilla) de jabón, **12.2**
soccer el fútbol, **2.1**
soccer field el campo de fútbol, **7.1**
social sciences las ciencias sociales
society la sociedad
sociology la sociología
socks los calcetines, **3.2**
solution la solución
to **solve** resolver (ue)
some algunos(as), **4.1**
something algo, **5.2**
sometimes a veces, **7.1**
son el hijo, **6.1**
soon pronto, **BV;** dentro de poco
See you soon! ¡Hasta pronto!, **BV**
sorbet el sorbete
sore throat el dolor de garganta, **8.1**
soup la sopa, **5.1**
south el sur
South America la América del Sur
South American sudamericano(a)
southwest el sudoeste
Spanish español(a)
Spanish American hispanoamericano(a)
Spanish speaker el/la hispanohablante
Spanish (language) el español, **2.2**
Spanish-speaking hispanohablante
to **speak** hablar, **3.1**
special especial
specialty la especialidad
spectator el/la espectador(a), **7.1**
to **spend: to spend the weekend** pasar el fin de semana, **9.1**
spoon (tablespoon) la cuchara, **14.1; (teaspoon)** la cucharita, **14.1**
sport el deporte, **7.2**
individual sport el deporte individual
team sport el deporte de equipo
sports (related to) deportivo(a), **6.2**
sports program (TV) la emisión deportiva, **6.2**
spouse el/la esposo(a), **6.1**
spring la primavera, **BV**
square la plaza
squire el escudero
stadium el estadio, **7.1**
stage el escenario, la escena, **10.2**
to come (go) on stage entrar en escena, **10.2**
stairway la escalera, **6.2**
standing de pie
star la estrella
state el estado
station la estación, **13.1**
subway station la estación de metro, **10.1**
train station la estación de ferrocarril, **13.1**
stationery: stationery store la papelería, **3.1**
statue la estatua, **2.1**
to **stay in bed** guardar cama, **8.1**
steak el biftec, **5.2**
stomach el estómago, **8.1**
stomachache el dolor de estómago, **8.1**
stop la parada, **13.1**
to **stop** parar, bloquear, **7.1**
store la tienda, **3.2**
clothing store la tienda de ropa, **3.2**
department store la tienda de departamentos
stationery store la papelería, **3.1**
to **store** almacenar
story: little story la historieta
strategy la estrategia
stream el arroyo
street la calle, **6.2**
strong fuerte
structure la estructura
student el/la alumno(a), **1.1;** el/la estudiante
student I.D. card la tarjeta de identidad estudiantil
study el estudio
to **study** estudiar, **4.1**
stupendous estupendo(a)
style el estilo
subject la asignatura, la disciplina, **2.2**
subtitle el subtítulo, **10.1**
The movie has subtitles. El film lleva subtítulos., **10.1**
to **subtract** restar
suburb el suburbio, la colonia
subway el metro, **10.1**

subway station la estación de metro, **10.1**
such tal
suckling pig el lechón, **14.2**
to **suffer** sufrir
suit el traje, **3.2**
bathing uit el traje de baño, el bañador, **9.1**
suitcase la maleta, **11.1**
to pack one's suitcase hacer la maleta, **11.2**
summer el verano, **BV**
sun el sol, **9.1**
to **sunbathe** tomar el sol, **9.1**
sunblock la crema protectora, **9.1**
Sunday el domingo, **BV**
sunglasses los anteojos de sol, las gafas de sol, **9.1**
sunny: It's sunny. Hace (Hay) sol., **9.1**
suntan lotion la crema protectora, la loción bronceadora, **9.1**
superior superior
supermarket el supermercado, **5.2**
supplies: school supplies los materiales escolares, **3.1**
to **surf** practicar la tabla hawaiana, **9.1**
to surf the Net navegar por la red
surfboard la tabla hawaiana, **9.1**
surfing el surfing, **9.1**
sweet roll el pan dulce, **5.1**
sweetheart el/la enamorado(a)
to **swim** nadar, **9.1**
swimsuit el bañador, el traje de baño, **9.1**
swimming la natación, **9.1**
underwater swimming el buceo, **9.1**
swimming pool la alberca, la piscina, **9.1**
symptom el síntoma, **8.2**

T

T-shirt el T-shirt, la camiseta, **3.2**
table la mesa, **5.1**
to set the table poner la mesa, **14.1**
tablecloth el mantel, **14.1**
tablespoon la cuchara, **14.1**
tablet la tableta, **8.2**
taco el taco, **BV**
Taino taíno(a)
to **take** tomar, **4.1**
to take a bath bañarse, **12.1**
to take a flight tomar un vuelo, **11.1**
to take a hike dar una caminata, **12.2**
to take a nap echar (tomar) una siesta
to take a shower tomar una ducha, **12.1**
to take a trip hacer un viaje, **11.2**
to take notes tomar apuntes, **4.2**
to take off (airplane) despegar, **11.2**
to take photos tomar fotos
to take (clothing size) usar, **3.2**
to take (shoe size) calzar, **3.2**
to take time tardar
taken ocupado(a), **5.1**
to **talk** hablar, conversar, **3.1**
tall alto(a), **1.1**
tamale el tamal, **BV**
taxi el taxi, **10.2**
tea el té, **5.1**
iced tea el té helado, **5.1**
to **teach** enseñar, **4.1**
teacher el/la maestro(a), el/la profesor(a), **2.1**
team el equipo, **7.1**
team sport el deporte de equipo, **7.2**
teaspoon la cucharita, **14.1**
technology la tecnología
teeth los dientes, **12.2**
telephone el teléfono
to speak on the telephone hablar por teléfono
telephone (related to) telefónico(a)
television la televisión, **6.2**
to **tell** decir
temperature la temperatura, **9.2**
ten diez, **BV**
to **tend to** soler (ue)
tender tierno(a)
tennis el tenis, **2.1**
tennis court la cancha de tenis, **9.1**
tennis game el juego de tenis, **9.1**
tennis player el/la tenista, **9.1**
tennis shoes los tenis, **3.2**
pair of tennis shoes el par de tenis, **3.2**
tenth décimo(a), **6.2**
term el término
terminal la terminal
terrace la terraza
terrible terrible
terror el terror
test el examen, **4.2**
to give a test dar un examen, **4.2**
thank you gracias, **BV**
that aquel; eso, **4.1**
at that time en aquel entonces
that's right (true)! ¡verdad!
the el, la, **1.1**
theater el teatro, **10.2**
theatrical teatral, **10.2**
their sus, **6.1**
them las *(f. pl.)*; los *(m. pl.)*
theme el tema
then luego, **BV**; entonces, **2.1**
there allí
there is/are hay, **BV**
they ellos(as), **2.1**
thin flaco(a), **1.2**; delgado(a)
thing la cosa
to **think** pensar (ie), opinar
to think so creer
third tercer(o), **6.2**
thirsty: to be thirsty tener sed, **14.1**
thirteen trece, **BV**
thirty treinta, **BV**
thirty-one treinta y uno, **2.1**
this este (esta)
thistle el cardo
thought el pensamiento
thousand mil, **3.2**
three tres, **BV**

three hundred trescientos(as), **3.2**
throat la garganta, **8.1**
to have a sore throat tener dolor de garganta, **8.1**
to **throw** lanzar, **7.1;** tirar, **7.2**
Thursday el jueves, **BV**
ticket el boleto, la entrada, **7.2;** el ticket, **9.2;** el billete, **11.1**
one-way ticket el billete sencillo, **13.1**
round-trip ticket el billete de ida y vuelta, **13.1**
ticket window la ventanilla, la boletería, **9.2;** la taquilla, **10.1**
tie la corbata, **3.2**
tied (score) empatado(a), **7.1**
The score is tied. El tanto queda empatado., **7.1**
time el tiempo; la vez; la hora
at times a veces
at what time? ¿a qué hora?
on time a tiempo
one more time une vez más, **12**
timid tímido(a), **1.2**
tiny diminuto(a)
tip el servicio, **5.1;** la propina, **14.1**
Is the tip included? ¿Está incluido el servicio?
to leave a tip dejar una propina, **14.1**
tired cansado(a), **8.1**
to a; con destino a, **11.1**
toast el pan tostado, **5.2**
toasted tostado(a), **5.2**
today hoy, **BV**
together junto(a), **5.1**
toilet paper el papel higiénico, **12.2**
to **tolerate** consentir (ie, i)
tomato el tomate, **5.2**
tomorrow el mañana, **BV**
See you tomorrow! ¡Hasta mañana!, **BV**
tonight esta noche, **9.2**
too también, **1.2**
too much demasiado
tooth el diente, **12.1**
toothbrush el cepillo de dientes, **12.2**
toothpaste la pasta dentrífica, **12.2**
tube of toothpaste el tubo de pasta dentífrica, **12.1**
tortilla la tortilla, **5.1**
to **touch** tocar
touch el contacto
tour la gira, **12.2**
tourist el/la turista
toward hacia
towel: beach towel la toalla playera, **9.1**
town el pueblo
toy el juguete
track la vía, **13.1**
tradition la tradición
traffic el tráfico
trail (ski) la pista, **9.2**
train el tren, **13.1**
local train el tren local, **13.2**
nonstop train el tren directo, **13.2**
train car el coche, el vagón, **13.1**
train station la estación de ferrocarril, **13.1**
to **transfer** transbordar, **13.2**
to **transmit** transmitir
triangle el triángulo
to **travel** viajar
to travel by air viajar en avión, **11.1**
tree el árbol
trip el viaje, **11.1**
to take a trip hacer un viaje, **11.1**
triumphant triunfante
trousers el pantalón, **3.2**
trousseau el ajuar de novia
true verdadero(a)
true value el valor real
trunk (of a car) el/la maletero(a), **11.1**
truth la verdad
to **try** tratar
tube el tubo, **12.2**
Tuesday el martes, **BV**
tuna el atún, **5.2**
to **turn around** revolver (ue)
twelve doce, **BV**
twenty veinte, **BV**
twenty-one veintiuno, **BV**
two dos, **BV**
two hundred doscientos(as), **3.2**
type el tipo
typical típico(a)

U

ugly feo(a), **1.1**
uncle el tío, **6.1**
aunt(s) and uncle(s) los tíos, **6.1**
under bajo, debajo (de)
undershirt la camiseta, **3.2**
to **understand** comprender, **5.1**
unit la unidad
uniform el uniforme
United States los Estados Unidos
university la universidad
university (related to) universitario(a)
until hasta, **BV**
urban urbano(a)
us nos
to **use** usar, **3.2**
usually generalmente

V

vacation la vacación
vanilla ***(adj.)*** de vainilla, **5.1**
vanilla ice cream el helado de vainilla, **5.1**
various varios(as)
to **vary** variar
veal la ternera, **14.2**
vegetable el vegetal, **5.2;** la legumbre
vegetarian el/la vegetariano(a)
Venezuelan venezolano(a)
version: in (its) original version en versión original, **10.1**
very muy, **BV**
very well muy bien, **BV**
vest el chaleco
victorious victorioso(a)
video el video, **4.2**

509

video store la tienda de videos, **10.1**
view la vista, **BV**
vinegar el vinagre, **14.2**
violin el violín, **2.1**
visible visible
vital vital
voice la voz
volleyball el voleibol, **2.1**
volume (book) el tomo
vowel la vocal

W

to **wait (for)** esperar, **11.1**
waiter el camarero, el mesero, **5.1**
waiting room la sala de espera, **13.1**
waitress la camarera, la mesera, **5.1**
to **wake up** despertarse, **12.1**
to **walk** andar (around, through)
wall la pared; **(of a jai alai court)** el frontón
to **want** querer (ie), desear, **3.2**
war la guerra
to **wash oneself** lavarse, **12.1**
to wash one's face (hands, etc.) lavarse la cara (las manos, etc.), **12.1**
to **watch** mirar, ver, **3.1**
water el agua *(f.)*, **9.1**
watercolor la acuarela
waterskiing el esquí acuático, **9.1**
to go waterskiing esquiar en el agua, **9.1**
wave la ola, **9.1**
way la manera, el modo, **1.1**
we nosotros(as), **2.1**
weapon el arma *(f.)*
to **wear** llevar, usar; **(shoe size)** calzar, **3.2**
weather el tiempo, **9.1**
The weather is bad. Hace mal tiempo., **9.1**
The weather is nice. Hace buen tiempo., **9.1**
Wednesday el miércoles, **BV**
week la semana, **BV**
last week la semana pasada, **9.2**
weekend el fin de semana, **BV**
last weekend el fin de semana pasado
to **weigh** pesar
to **welcome** dar la bienvenida, **11.2**
well bien; pues, **BV**
very well muy bien, **BV**
west el oeste
what? ¿qué?, ¿cuál?, ¿cuáles?, ¿cómo?, **1.1**
What is he (she, it) like? ¿Cómo es?, **1.1**
What is it? ¿Qué es?, **1.1**
What is today's date? ¿Cuál es la fecha de hoy?, **BV**
What time is it? ¿Qué hora es?
when cuando
for when ¿para cuándo?, **14.2**
when? ¿cuándo?
where donde, adonde, **1.2**
where? ¿dónde?, ¿adónde?
¿Where is he (she, it) from? ¿De dónde es?, **1.1**
which? ¿cuál?, ¿cuáles?, **BV**
while el rato
while mientras
white blanco(a), **3.2**
who? ¿quién?, **1.1;** quiénes, **2.1**
Who is it (he, she)? ¿Quién es?, **1.1**
whole entero(a)
why? ¿por qué?
wife la esposa, la mujer, **6.1**
to **win** ganar, **7.1**
windmill el molino de viento
to **windsurf** practicar la plancha de vela, **9.1**
winter el invierno, **BV**
wise sabio(a)
to **wish** querer (ie), desear, **3.2**
with con
within dentro de
woman la dama
wool la lana
word la palabra
work el trabajo; la obra
work of art la obra de arte
to **work** trabajar, **3.2**
world el mundo
world (related to) mundial
World Cup la Copa mundial
World Series la Serie mundial
worldwide mundial
to **wrap** envolver (ue)
wrap el poncho
to **write** escribir, **5.1**
writing pad el bloc, **3.1**

Y

year el año, **BV**
last year el año pasado, **9.2**
this year este año, **9.2**
to be . . . years old tener... años, cumplir... años, **6.1**
yellow amarillo(a), **3.2**
yesterday ayer, **9.2**
the day before yesterday anteayer
yesterday afternoon ayer por la tarde, **9.2**
yesterday morning ayer por la mañana, **9.2**
yogurt el yogur, **5.2**
you tú *(sing. fam.)*, Ud. *(sing. form.)*; Uds. *(pl.)*; te *(fam. pron.)*, le *(pron.)*
You're welcome. De nada., No hay de qué., **BV**
young joven, **6.1**
as a young person de joven
young person el/la joven, **8.1**
your tu(s), su(s)
youth hostel el albergue juvenil (para jóvenes), **12.2**

Z

zero cero, **BV**
zone la zona

Índice gramatical

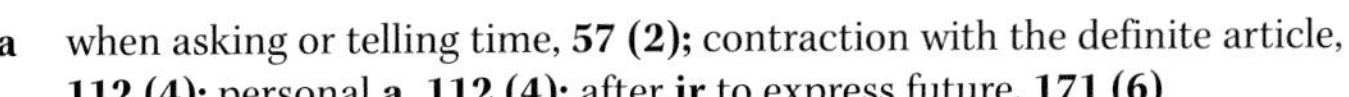

511

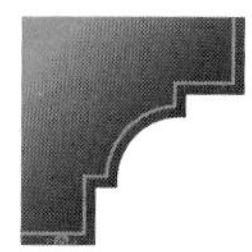

Credits

Photographs
Aitchison, Stewart/DDB Stock Photo: 212T. Arruza, Tony/Bruce Coleman Inc.: 54T, 258BM. Art Resource (Prado Museum): 181, 183T. Aubry, Daniel/Odyssey/Chicago: 371T. Augustin, Byron/ DDB Stock Photo: 447M. Barrow, Scott: 315, 321. Bean, Tom/Tony Stone Images: 107. Benn, Oliver/Tony Stone Images: 88T, 313B. Bibikow, Walter/FPG International: 278B. Borchi, Massimo/ Atlantide/Bruce Coleman Inc.: 10TL, 370T. Boyer, Dale E./Photo Researchers Inc.: 83(#2). Bruce Coleman Inc.: 32B, 33T. Brunskill, Clive/Allsport: 193. Bruty, Simon/Allsport USA: 209. Bryant, Dave/DDB Stock Photo: 305. Bryant, Doug/DDB Stock Photo: 309TR, 458. Burnett, Mark C./Stock Boston: 118T. Cannon, David/Allsport: 190TL. Carrasco, Ricardo: 34L. Carrillo, Jose/ PhotoEdit: 180. Carton, J.C./Bruce Coleman Inc.: 35T, 335. Cassidy, Anthony/ Tony Stone Images: 460-461. Castro, Harold/ FPG International: 281T. Chaplow, Michelle: 3TL&M, 5T, 16B, 41, 43R, 75, 79M, 86L, 87L, 98T, 99T, 100T&M, 102, 104T, 111TR, 123 , 126T, 146, 148, 149, 152, 155, 166, 172T, 178T, 203, 206, 208B, 230T, 233, 261B, 268T, 288, 290, 297T, 304T, 318, 322, 325T, 330, 342, 354, 361, 363, 380TR, 384, 401BR, 427, R7, R20R. Chaplow, Michelle/Andalucia Slide Library: 424R, 435. Cinti, Roberto R./Bruce Coleman Inc.: 441T. Clyde, G./FPG International: 87R. Cohen, Stuart/Comstock: R31. Contreras Chacel, Jorge/ International Stock: 307M, 431B. Corbis-Bettman: 30T. Corsetti, Marco/FPG International: 264L, 282. Courau, J.P./DDB Stock Photo: 445. Cozzi, Guido/Atlantide/Bruce Coleman Inc.: 34R, 154R, 356T, 368T. Culver Pictures, Inc.: 292BR. Curtis, John/DDB Stock Photo: 264R. Daemrich, Robert E./Tony Stone Images: 258TR. Dalda Fotographia: 187B. Dekovic, Gene: 307T. Delgado, Luis: 3BL, 4, 13, 23B, 24TR, 28, 32T, 36T, 42, 44T, 61L, 74, 76, 77TR, 78, 79T, 81T, 91, 112, 116T&M, 120T, 121, 140T&M, 143, 162B, 169, 189, 196B, 198, 199T, 218, 246, 247, 248, 258L 260T, 267, 271, 274, 302, 304B, 306T, 316, 327, 334B, 358, 364, 366, 368B, 372L, 373B, 379, 380, 382, 386, 388, 394, 396, 401B, 401M, 401MR, 407, 410, 411, 414, 424T, 432, R3, R15B. Derke/O'Hara/Tony Stone Images: 280L. Donnezan, Herve/Photo Researchers Inc.: 151. Driendl, Jerry/FPG International: 61R. EFE Reportajes: 381. Ehlers, Chad/Tony Stone Images: 9M. Elmer, Carlos/FPG International: R26. Esbin-Anderson/The Image Works: 185B. Fenton, Cheryl: 12B, 40L, 70B, 77B, 77ML, 78, 90, 96B, 132B, 157B, 158B, 188B, 226B, 256B, 286B, 314B, 350B, 359, 377B, 378B, 406B, 441R, 450, 456. Fischer, Curt: 14L, 18, 19, 20, 22, 24TL, 35T, 43L, 44B, 46, 47, 48, 60, 72, 77MR, 79T, 88B, 90, 99B, 103, 113, 138M, 150R, 153, 161, 170B, 190R, 194, 195TL, 195BR, 205, 228, 229, 231, 232B, 250, 251B, 251T, 262ML, 262R, 336, 352, 353, 356B, 357, 359, 401TL, 408, 412, 422B, 424M, 426, R1. Fisher, Ken/Tony Stone Images: R15T. Franken, Owen/Stock Boston: 372R. Frazier, David: 82, R25. Frazier, David R./Photo Researchers Inc.: 202B. Freeman, M./Bruce Coleman Inc.: 399. Frerck, Robert/Odyssey/Chicago: 5B, 35B, 49, 63R, 69B, 71, 83(#3), 151R, 212B, 243, 251M, 253, 280R, 285B, 287, 295, 299, 307B, 309B, 312B, 337, 368M, 370BR, 371B, 398BL, 452, R12, R14B, R21, R22, R23R. Frerck, Robert/ Tony Stone Images: 21B, 255B. Frerck, Robert/Woodfin Camp & Assoc.: 30B, 31, 281L, R5, R13, R17. Fried, Robert/DDB Stock Photo: 27TR, 59. Fried, Robert/Robert Fried Photography: xiT, 7, 51, 83(#5), 88MC, 167L&BR, 186M, 211T, 213B, 240L, 258TM, 277L, 297B, 319, 369, 387R, 392T, 397T, 397B, 398MR, 398TL, 425B, 453T. Fried, Robert/Stock Boston: xiiT, 398ML. Fried, Robert/ Tom Stack & Assoc.: 27TL, 64ML. Fuller, Timothy: 1, 3BR, 14R, 16T, 21T, 24B, 27B, 58, 73, 83(#1), 84, 100B, 101B, 139TL, 139TR, 140B, 176, 227, 230ML, 234, 236T, 259, 413, 422T, 434, R19, R20L. Courtesy of Dr. Antonio Gassett: 249R. Gillham, K./Photo 20-20: 370BL. Ginn, Robert/PhotoEdit: 64B. Gottschalk, Manfred/ Tom Stack & Assoc.: 62R. Graham, Ken/Tony Stone Images: xiv. Grande, J.L.G./Tourist Office of Spain: 268B. Grantpix/Stock Boston: 154L. Grebliunas, Paul/Tony Stone Images: 451. Gridley, Peter/FPG International: 261T. Heaton, Dallas & John /WestLight: 111BR, 175, 291. Hersch, H. Huntly/DDB Stock Photo: 64MR. Hollenbeck, Cliff/International Stock: 2B, 125B, 213T. House of El Greco, Toledo, Spain: 183B, 301T, 390. Ikeda/ International Stock: 387L. Image Club Graphics: 90, 195MR, 197T. Jacques & Natasha Gilman Collection: 182T. Jangoux, Jacques/Tony Stone Images: 332R. Karp, Ken: 2T, 3TR, 9T, 17L, 23T, 29, 45, 54B, 55, 77TL, 79B, 81B, 85, 108T, 114, 134, 162T, 163, 178B, 202T, 232T, 236B, 239B, 241, 244, 270, 293B, 343, 362, 365, 374, 417T, 419T, 420, R4T, R11T, R14T, R30. Kerstitch, Alex/Bruce Coleman Inc.: 120BL. Leah, David/Allsport: 192. Leah, David/ Allsport Mexico: 196T, 210B, 217B. Lloyd, Harvey/The Stock Market: 119T. Macia, Rafael/Photo Researchers, Inc.: 334T. Manske, Thaine/The Stock Market: R8. Markewitz, Scott/ FPG International: 279R. Marriott, Paul/Empics Ltd.: 208T. Mason, Douglas/Woodfin Camp & Assoc.: 141. Mays, Buddy/ International Stock: 278T. Maze, Stephanie/Woodfin Camp & Assoc.: 262TL. McCutcheon, Shaw/Bruce Coleman Inc.: 88ML. McIntyre, Loren/Woodfin Camp & Assoc.: 88MR. McIntyre, Will & Deni/Photo Researchers Inc.: 329. McVey, Ken/ International Stock: 160. Melloan, Cathlyn/Tony Stone Images: 293M. Menzel, Peter: 150L, 447T, R9. Messerschmidt, Joachim/ FPG International: 326. Courtesy of Mexicana Airlines: 341B. Miyazaki, Yoichiro/FPG International: 391. Morgan Cain & Associates: 126B, 138T, 144, 204B, 355, 402, 417B, R6. Morgan, Warren/WestLight: 170T. Muller, Kal/Woodfin Camp & Assoc.: 220. Murphy-Larronde, Suzanne/DDB Stock Photo: 64TR, 83(#4), 309M. Murphy-Larronde, Suzanne/FPG International: R11M. The Museum of Modern Art, New York. Photograph ©1996 The Museum of Modern Art, New York. National Palace, Patio Coridor, Mexico City: 65. National Palace, Mexico City: 423. O'Keefe, Timothy/Bruce Coleman Inc.: 277B. Organization of American States: 33B. Courtesy Oscar de la Renta: 89T. Pcholkin, Vladimir/ FPG International: 260M, 300. Pensinger, Doug/Allsport: 210T. Peterson, Chip & Rosa Maria : 453BR, 457. Philadelphia Museum of Art, A. E. Gallatin Collection: 105. PhotoDisc, Inc.: 86R. Photoworks/P. Lang/DDB Stock Photo: 344. Prado Museum, Madrid, Spain: 301. Raga, Jose Fuste/The Stock Market: 93, 108B. Randklev, James/Tony Stone Images: 62L. Rivademar, D./ Odyssey/Chicago: 332L. Rondeau, Pascal/Allsport UK Ltd.: 258BR. Rosendo, Luis/FPG International: 116B, 116M, 117. Sacks, David/FPG International: 173. St./© 1999 Estate of Pablo

Picasso/Artists Rights Society (ARS), New York: 31. Sapieha, Nicolas/Art Resource: 63L. Savage, Chuck/The Stock Market: 64TM. Schafer, Kevin/Tony Stone Images: R16. Schmitt, Conrad J.: 119B. Sewell, Michael Evan: 120BR. Simson, David/Stock Boston: 10BL, 10BR. Sitton, Hugh/Tony Stone Images: 276R. Smestad, Mark: 6T, 17R, 36B, 97, 101T, 110, 167M. Stack, Tom & Therisa/Tom Stack & Assoc.: 16M, 104B, 211M. Superstock: 257. Szymanski, Chuck/International Stock: 405B. Taylor, Pam/Bruce Coleman Inc.: 453BL. Telegraph Color Library/FPG International: 133, 179B, 397M. Travelpix/FPG International: 276L. Turner, John Terence/FPG International: 279L. UPI/Corbis-Bettmann: 119M. Vautier, Mireille/Woodfin Camp & Assoc.: 281M. Venegas, Martin/Allsport Mexico: 201. Vidler, Steve/Leo de Wys Inc.: 37. Viesti, Joe/Viesti Associates, Inc.: 118B, 351. Von Tumpling-Manning, Caroline/FPG International: 277TR. Wallick, Phillip/International Stock: 258MR. Welsch, Ulrike: 10TR, 309TL, 312T. Welsch, Ulrike/Photo Researchers Inc.: 167TR. Wheeler, Nik: 159. Whitby, Ron/FPG International: 249L. Wolfe, Bernard P./Photo Researchers Inc.: 373T. Young, Tess & David/Tom Stack & Assoc.: 444. Young-Wolff, David/Photo Edit: 9B, 11B, 64TL. Zuckerman, Jim/WestLight: 333.

Illustration

Barrow, Ann: 182B. Broad, David: 29, 59, 85B, 115, 147, 177B, 207, 245, 275, 303, 331, 367, 395, 421B. Gregory, Lane: 25, 52, 76, 106, 109, 122, 137, 185T. Harden, Laurie: 102, 103. Jaekel, Susan: 75, 92, 115, 136, 138, 139, 184T, 414T, 416. Lacamara, Carlos: 7, 56, 57, 174, 211R, 260, 271T, 273, 294, 301B, 308, 365, 396BR, R10, R28, R33. Lazor-Behr, Beverly: 26, 53, 228. LeMonnier, Joe: 14, 30, 32, 34, 39, 42, 55, 383. Magovern, Peg: 408, 409. Maxey, Betty: 190, 191, 194T, 194MR, 194B, 195ML. McCreary, Jane: 15, 37, 93, 163, 234T, 235, 238, 339, 358, 375, 419B, 429B. Merrilees, Rebecca: 135. Miller, Lyle: 19, 440, 442, 443, 448, 449, 454, 455. Moore, Stephen: 193B, 200, 354, 360. Ordaz, Frank: 237T, 300T, 362. Sauk, Ed: 113. Schofield, Den: 14, 43, 98, 381, 384, 385, 403. Simison, D.J.: 17, 20, 45, 51, 73, 92, 105, 135, 160, 161, 164, 165, 233, 269, 292, 293, 316M, 317, 320, 321, R2, R18. Strebel, Carol: 352, 353, 374T, 380, 381. Thewlis, Diana: 169, 221, 252T, 288, 289, 310. Treatner, Meryl: 263, 357. Yu, Qin-Zhong: 191, 195TR.

Vista credits

Ecuador - Now
1 - Cotopaxi volcano: ©Eduardo Gill/Black Star/PNI. 2 - City of Guayaquil: Matteo Torri/Imago Latin Stock. 3 - Oil excavation: ©Tayacan/Panos Pictures. 4 - Handmade rugs: Robert Frerck/Woodfin Camp & Associates. 5 - Shrimp packing: Matteo Torri/Imago Latin Stock. 6 - Sea lions: ©David Fritts/AllStock/PNI. 7 - Banana farm: Matteo Torri/Imago Latin Stock.
Ecuador - Then
1 - Harvesting barley: ©Jeremy Horner/Panos Pictures.
2 - Woman at market: Robert Frerck/Odyssey Productions/Chicago. 3 - Rain forest: ©Wolfgang Kaehler. 4 - New Cathedral: Suzanne L. Murphy/DDB Stock Photo. 5 - Independence Plaza: Patricia Sydney Straub/DDB Stock Photo. 6 - Marine iguanas: Kevin Schafer, Martha Hill/AllStock/PNI. 7 - Making Panama hats: ©Jeremy Horner/Panos Pictures.
Mexico - Now
1 - Alhóndiga: David Alan Harvey. 2 - Maya girl: Danny Lehman/©Corbis. 3 - Stock exchange: Poulides/Thatcher/Tony Stone Images. 4 - Picking grapefruit: Kal Muller/Woodfin Camp & Associates. 5 - Television assembly: Mark Segal/Tony Stone Images. 6 - Oil platform crew: Stuart Franklin. 7 - Reforma Monument: Peter Menzel/Stock, Boston/PNI.
Mexico - Then
1 - Uxmal ruins: Bill Ross/Woodfin Camp & Associates. 2 - Olmec statue: ©Mireille Vautier/Woodfin Camp & Associates. 3 - Tzotzil Indian market: ©Robert Frerck/Woodfin Camp & Associates.
4 - Blue skies: David Alan Harvey. 5 - Singers: David Alan Harvey.
6 - Cane chair weaver: Kevin Schafer/Tony Stone Images.
7 - Fishermen: Robert Frerck/Tony Stone Images.
España - Now
1 - Guggenheim: Photo by David Heald. 2 - Málaga: ©Robert Frerck/Woodfin Camp & Associates. 3 - Paseo del Prado: ©Kim Newton/Woodfin Camp & Associates. 4 - Fishing boats: ©Richard During/AllStock/PNI. 5 - Sagrada Familia: Adina Tovy/DDB Stock Photo. 6 - Art conservation lab: Louis Mazzatenta. 7 - Basque shepherd: Joanna B. Pinneo.
España - Then
1 - Plaza Mayor: Oliver Benn/Tony Stone Images. 2 - Hillside town: Robert Frerck/Woodfin Camp & Associates.
3 - Celebration: Tor Eigeland. 4 - Moorish arches: Jon Bradley/Tony Stone Images. 5 - 14th-century castle: Patrick Ward/©Corbis. 6 - Spanish riding school: Robert Frerck/Woodfin Camp & Associates.
Puerto Rico - Now
1 - Tropical vegetation: ©Tom Bean 1992. 2 - Radio telescope: ©Dan McCoy/Rainbow/PNI. 3 - Laguna del Condado: ©Len Kaufman/Black Star/PNI. 4 - Ponce Museum: Joan Iaconetti.
5 - Pineapple harvest: Robert Frerck/Odyssey Production/Chicago. 6 - Athletic competitor: Stephanie Maze. 7 - Cathedral: Macduff Everton.
Puerto Rico - Then
1 - La Princessa Promenade: Stuart Westmorland/Tony Stone Images. 2 - Plaza de Armas: ©Wolfgang Kaehler. 3 - Residential area: Robert W. Madden. 4 - Traditional folk dance: Suzanne Murphy-Larronde/DDB Stock Photo. 5 - Coqui frog: ©Kevin Schafer. 6 - Fruit stand: Robert Frerck/Odyssey Productions/Chicago. 7 - Three Kings parade: Suzanne Murphy-Larronde/DDB Stock Photo.

Maps

Eureka Cartography, Berkeley, CA.

Special thanks to Debbie Costello, Barbara Luck and Alisa Peres for loan of the chapter opener objects from their collections.